EMPLOYMENT DISCRIMINATION LAW

CASES AND NOTES

■ ■ ■

By

Mack A. Player

Professor of Law
Dean Emeritus
School of Law
Santa Clara University

Martin H. Malin

Professor of Law
Director, Institute for Law & Workplace
Chicago–Kent College of Law
Illinois Institute of Technology

AMERICAN CASEBOOK SERIES®

WEST®

A Thomson Reuters business

Mat #41063124

© 2012 Thomson Reuters
    610 Opperman Drive
    St. Paul, MN 55123
    1–800–313–9378
Printed in the United States of America

ISBN: 978–0–314–26789–4

To and for my spouse, Jeanne M.L. Player. But also to Hugo and Audrey Player, my grandchildren, who might enjoy seeing their names in print.

MAP

To and for Joyce Willenborg, my wife and best friend, and our children Martha and Catherine.

MHM

FOREWORD

GOALS AND PURPOSES

These are *teaching* materials, not a reference source. The goal is to provide only that which can be taught and absorbed in a single three unit semester course. We leave to others the task of compiling all of relevant cases, noting minor distinctions, and referencing the rich secondary scholarly commentary. To the end of "teachability" many principal cases have been heavily edited, with concurring and dissenting opinions much reduced if not eliminated. The reader will note, too, that we have attempted to be Spartan in our notes; avoiding string citations and including a minimal number of those oft-annoying "questions without answers." We did not deem it necessary to provide a reference to every statement or include specific page citations to references. As a "bottom line" we have attempted to make the materials as uncluttered and digestible as possible in a surprisingly deep and complex subject. Our goal is that students using these materials will have contemplated what is essential, avoiding the dangerous temptation of directing attention to so much flora that they risk getting lost in the underbrush.

ORGANIZATION

PART I— "PROLOGUE" is brief. We have not included any significant "history," or the oft-seen philosophical musings. We simply wanted to introduce the parameters of the course, note the common law "default," and summarize the roles of the Equal Employment Opportunity Commission.

PART II—BASIC PRINCIPLES, as the heading suggests, covers the six universal principles that all students in the field should master, each principle having its own chapter: (1) Coverage & scope, (2) Classes protected by the statutes, (3) Defenses and justifications for use of protected classifications; (4) "Terms and Conditions of Employment" that define the scope of the statutes, (5) The concept of "Discrimination," and finally, (6) The meaning of the statutory term "Because of."

PART III–PROVING VIOLATIONS addresses the rules that govern the proof of the elements covered in PART II, in particular the methods of (1) proving motive, and (2) establishing liability based on the adverse impact of "neutral" devices upon one of the protected classes. We have reserved until mid-course these "practical" and often complex problems believing, based on experience, that covering what needs to be proved (PART II) should precede analysis of how those elements are proved. The Part concludes with the difficult to categorize issues of retaliation and compensation distinctions.

PART IV is dedicated to enforcement, that includes (1) Procedures (which are quite complex) and (2) Remedies.

STATUTORY MATERIALS

There is not in this publication, nor in a collateral supplement, a full reproduction of statutory materials. Some segments are reproduced as an integrated element of the materials, and there are relevant excerpts quoted in the cases and produced in the notes. It is not that we think that having a ready access to the full statutes is unimportant. But we believe a more efficient access method is for the student to refer to these materials electronically, reproducing them as they wish. Below are the core statutory materials that should be accessed and reproduced for daily classroom use:

1. **Title VII of the Civil Rights Act of 1964.**

   42 U.S.C. s 2000(e), www.eeoc.gov/laws/statutes/title vii

2. **Age Discrimination in Employment Act of 1967.**

   29 U.S.C. s 621, www.eeoc.gov/laws/statutes/adea

3. **Americans With Disabilities Act of 1991 as amended in 2009.**

   42 U.S.C s 12101–12102, 12111–12213, www.eeoc.gov/laws/statutes/ada

AN APOLOGY

Covering topics of race, sex, national origin, and religion are fraught with dangers of unintended offense. Aware of this risk we have, nevertheless, left the words in decisions as reported. In our notes we have attempted to use terms that refer to peoples as they appear at this time to prefer. One possible exception; we have avoided use of the term "African–American" in the belief that in the context of "race" discrimination, the term is potentially confusing. If we have used identifications which offend we apologize.

Unavoidably, the materials include curses and defamatory terms that might immediately shock. But these are the words used and are part of the factual underpinning of the cases themselves. Again, we reproduced what is found in the cases. In our notes we avoided euphemisms such as "N——," or "the N word." Among professionals avoidance of words that would actually be expressed in the work place seemed unnecessary and potentially confusing. For example, a white supervisor is unlikely to shout at his black co-worker, "N word." For any discomfort caused by reading insulting or demeaning terms we apologize, as no insult is intended.

ON EDITING

In editing materials our prime directive was "readability." Nonetheless, we followed relatively conventional rules. Where we deleted portions of original materials, we indicated the deletion with asterisks rather than ellipses simply because asterisks are easier to see. However, where the original contained ellipses within its quotation of other material we retain the ellipses. Without notations we edited out citations that were not central to the opinion, eliminated largely superfluous subsequent histories such as "certiorari denied," and removed non-critical footnotes. Where footnotes were included, we retained their original numbering.

ACKNOWLEDGEMENTS

Dean Player deeply appreciates the invaluable contributions of his spouse, Jeanne M.L. Player whose years of practical experience in the field allowed her to provide innumerable insights and serve as a substantive guide, sounding-board and proof reader. Without her assistance and support this work would not have been completed. Abigail King, Dean Player's administrative assistant, deserves kudos for her patience as much as for her many technical skills. Thanks also to Santa Clara University for providing time and space.

Professor Malin acknowledges the very valuable technical, clerical, and administrative of his administrative assistant, Sharon Wyatt–Jordan. He also acknowledges the financial support from the Marshall–Ewell Research Fund at IIT Chicago–Kent College of Law.

The authors thank the Employee Rights & Employment Policy Journal for granting permission to reproduce "Discrimination Remedies: The Shape of Lawsuits, the Shape of the Law:" Proceedings of the 2008 Annual Meeting of the Association of American Law Schools Sections on Employment Discrimination law and Remedies, 12 Employee Rights & Employment Policy journal 297 (2008).

Summary of Contents

TABLE OF CONTENTS

TABLE OF CASES

The principal cases are in bold type. Cases cited or discussed in the text are in roman type. References are to pages. Cases cited in principal cases and within other quoted materials are not included.

EMPLOYMENT DISCRIMINATION LAW
CASES AND NOTES

PART 1

PROLOGUE

■ ■ ■

A. THE SUBJECT

In 2010 nearly 100,000 formal charges of work place discrimination were filed with the Equal Employment Opportunity Commission (EEOC), the primary, but not the sole, federal agency charged with policing invidious work place discrimination. These new filings were in addition to the over 86,000 pending, unresolved charges. Each term the Supreme Court typically resolves three or more cases in the area. Bottom line: employment discrimination is one of the most active and dynamic areas of American public law.

"Employment discrimination" occupies a wide but ill defined region between "civil rights law" and "labor law." The subject has an historical and ideological "civil rights" connection in that it promises individuals a right to be free from invidious, class-based discrimination in the work place. The core statutory protection, "Title VII" is but one title of the comprehensive Civil Rights Act of 1964,[1] a statute that guaranteed protections against discrimination in various aspects of life such as housing and public accommodations. Nonetheless, discrimination in the work place deals with the employment relationship, or "labor law," which has been regulated for generations by evolving common law principles, and since the early 20th Century by federal labor relations statutes.[2]

Surrounding both labor law and work place discrimination law is a miscellany of statutes that grant a range of protections to workers: minimum wage and premium pay for overtime work,[3] regulation of pensions and similar benefits programs,[4] occupational health and safety,[5] obligations on employers to notify workers in advance of plant closing or

---

1. 42 U.S.C.§ 2000e.

2. Labor relations law is governed by two statutes, the National Labor Relations Act, 29 U.S.C. § 157, and the Railway Labor Act, 45 U.S.C. § 151.

3. Fair Labor Standards Act, 29 U.S.C. § 201.

4. Employee Retirement and Income and Security Act of 1974 (ERISA), 29 U.S.C. § 1000, and COBRA 29 U.S.C § 1161.

5. OSHA, 29 U.S.C. § 651.

1

mass lay off,[6] and restrictions on employers administering or utilizing polygraphs.[7]

At their junctures these broad categories overlap and contribute to each other. The complete practitioner of employment law needs to be knowledgeable in all these areas. Yet, practicalities of teaching and learning require that each must be considered and studied separately.

B. "EMPLOYMENT DISCRIMINATION"— THE COURSE

1. CORE: THE BIG THREE

Employment discrimination law at the federal level does not involve a single comprehensive code. Would that it did! Rather, federal employment discrimination involves no less than nine distinct statutory schemes. It is generally accepted, however, that the core of federal employment discrimination law is found in the three distinct but closely related statutes administered by the federal Equal Employment Opportunity Commission (EEOC):

    a. Title VII of the Civil Rights Act of 1964 ("Title VII"), which prohibits work place discrimination because of race, color, national origin, sex, and religion.[8]

    b. The Age Discrimination in Employment Act (ADEA) which prohibits work place discrimination because of "age."[9]

    c. The Americans With Disabilities Act (ADA) whose broad prohibitions in many contexts proscribe discrimination against "qualified individuals" on the basis of mental or physical disability.[10] Title I of this comprehensive statute reaches non-federal employment.

2. SIX "SATELLITES"

Six important statutes surround the "core three" and must be touched upon in any study of work place discrimination:

    a. The Civil Rights Act of 1868[11] *(or "§ 1981")*, proscribes race discrimination in the making and enforcing of all contracts. Employment is considered such a "contract."

    b. The Equal Pay Act of 1963 (EPA) requires employers to provide male and female workers with equal rates of pay for work that is

---

  6. WARN Act, 29 U.S.C. § 2101.

  7. Employee Polygraph Protection Act, 29 U.S.C. § 2001.

  8. 42 U.S.C. § 2000e.

  9. 29 U.S.C. § 623.

  10. 42 U.S.C. § 1201. Protection against disabilities discrimination in the workplace has become so expansive that demands of time and space require this topic to be given less than full treatment. The consequence of this growth of disabilities law broadly is the creation of a distinct, separate subject.

  11. 42 U.S.C. § 1981.

"equal."[12] The EPA was an amendment to the Fair Labor Standards Act (which since the 1930s has established federal minimum wage and overtime standards).

c. The Family and Medical Leave Act[13] *(FMLA)* imposes on large employers an obligation to provide unpaid leave for eligible employees based on the medical needs of the employee or of close family members or following birth or adoption of a child. While the FMLA is a broad worker's rights statute, it often is invoked in claims involving pregnancy, age, and disability discrimination.

d. The Immigration Reform and Control Act of 1986[14] sets national immigration policy, but in doing so duplicates Title VII in its prohibition of "national origin" discrimination. Significantly, it adds a prohibition not found in the core statutes, by proscribing some forms of discrimination on the basis of citizenship.

e. The Genetic Information and Non–Disclosure Act of 2008 (GINA), 42 U.S.C.A. 2000ff) prohibits inquiries into, and employer reliance upon, medical and physical conditions that might disclose genetic information. It is thus a significant, but relatively narrow, supplement to the Americans With Disabilities Act.

f. The Uniformed Services Employment and Reemployment Act of 1994 (USERRA):[15] (1) prohibits discrimination against persons because of their uniformed military service, (2) requires reemployment without loss of seniority and other benefits of persons who have completed their military service, and (3) prohibits the discharge of reemployed service members except for cause for one year after reemployment. Because USERRA creates a distinct class of persons protected against work place discrimination in terms similar to the core statutes, completeness requires its inclusion in a study of work place discrimination.

3. IMPORTANT BUT EXCLUDED

As noted above, there remains a large area of the law that a complete employment law practitioner should master. Each can have an impact on the core of employment discrimination law, and will be noted herein in passing, but for practical reasons these protections must be studied elsewhere.

a. Labor-management relations: Two major statutes prohibit employers from discriminating against workers who engage in forming labor organizations or engage in other "concerted activities" for "their mutual aid and protection. The latter protection is important when employees allege that they have been retaliated against because of their opposition to

---

12. 29 U.S.C. § 206(d).

13. 29 U.S.C. § 2601.

14. 8 U.S.C. § 102.

15. 38 U.S.C. § 4311.

an employer's perceived discrimination. The two labor relations statutes also establish a structure for a collective relationship between employers and employee representatives, and the use of economic weapons such as strikes, boycotts, and lockouts.[16]

b. The Constitution: As it affects only "state action," the Constitution plays a minor role regulating *private* employment law. Nonetheless the Constitution plays a major role in protecting **government** employees: state and federal, against all forms of invidious treatment, including, but not limited to, those protections granted by employment discrimination statutes. Nevertheless, aside from occasional references, this important area of discrimination must be left to the study of constitutional law.

c. Civil rights: There are many "civil rights" statutes which prohibit a wide range of discrimination (*e.g.,* housing, education, federal fund recipients, as well as employment). These statutes often provide work place protections which largely parallel those provided by the "core three."[17]

4. STATE FAIR EMPLOYMENT LAW

Federal employment discriminations statutes do not pre-empt state laws that provide protection **parallel to, or greater than,** *protection provided by federal law.* **California Fed. Sav. & Loan Ass'n v. Guerra,** 479 U.S. 272, 107 S.Ct. 683, 93 L.Ed.2d 613 (1987). State law, thus, can be an important component of employment discrimination law. For example, some state statutes add classes of protection not found in the federal statutes, such as prohibiting discrimination because of marital status and sexual orientation. They may prohibit age or disability discrimination not proscribed by federal law. State statutes may provide more expansive coverage, reaching smaller employers. States may have more efficient administrative mechanisms and may allow different remedies for successful plaintiffs. State courts occasionally give more expansive substantive interpretations to state statutory provisions than federal courts have given to similar language in the federal statutes. Evidentiary burdens of presentation and persuasion may differ in state and federal courts. For the most part, however, state statutes largely mirror federal statutes, and state courts have tended to be guided by federal precedents. While there will be occasional references herein to possible differences in state and federal law, the focus of this work is *federal law.*

C. THE HISTORY

Western industrial democracies today have accepted with little ongoing public debate that work place discrimination on the basis of race, sex,

---

16. National Labor Relations Act (NLRA), 29 U.S.C. §§ 157 and 158(a)1 and (3); Railway Labor Act, 45 U.S.C. § 151.

17. *See, e.g.,* Title VI of the Civil Rights Act of 1964, 42 U.S.C. § 2000d, and Title IX of the Education Amendments, 20 U.S.C. § 1681.

national origin, and religion is inappropriate.[18] Only the rare voice challenges the legitimacy of governments prohibiting private employers from engaging in such invidious discrimination.[19] This current widespread acceptance of fair employment practice law is relatively recent. In the mid–20th Century fewer than 50% of Americans believed that blacks should be given employment opportunity equal to whites.[20] Civil rights legislation of the 1960s was vigorously opposed by a significant portion of the populace and their political representatives. This opposition to fair employment practices was fueled not only by prejudices and stereotypes but also by a strong strain of *laissez faire* libertarianism that has produced perhaps the most unregulated, untaxed capitalism among economically mature nations.

Title VII of the 1964 Civil Rights Act was seen as a "revolutionary" step. The federal government was now telling employers that they could not use prescribed criteria in selecting, compensating, and dismissing their workers. This sweeping governmental limitation on employer autonomy represented a major shift in American political and legal thought. No longer was it a question of the legitimacy of government interference with employer decision-making, but the extent such governmental intrusion was appropriate. With the conceptual barrier of unrestrained employer autonomy broken by Title VII, additional legislation protecting workers followed.

With Title VII of the 1964 Civil Rights as a model, Congress enacted the Age Discrimination in Employment Act in 1968 (ADEA), while lifting some language found in the Equal Pay Act of 1963 (EPA). The ADEA was followed by the Rehabilitation Act of 1973, which prohibited federal agencies and employers with federal government funding or contracts from discrimination against individuals with disabilities. The Rehabilitation Act served as a forerunner of the Americans With Disabilities Act of 1990 which extended this protection broadly to most employers. The Reconstruction Era Civil Rights Act (42 U.S.C. § 1981) was broadly construed by the Supreme Court to reach purely private discrimination in the formation and termination of the employment contract.[21] All of these statutes have been extensively amended, often in response to narrow, restrictive interpretations by the Court.

D. THE EQUAL EMPLOYMENT OPPORTUNITY COMMISSION (EEOC)

Enforcement of rights created by the core statutes depends on the initiative of the victims of workplace discrimination. Victims must initiate the

---

18. See, Article 13, *Treaty of Amsterdam,* that sets policies for the member states of the European Union.

19. See, Epstein, *The Forbidden Grounds, The Case Against Employment Discrimination Laws* (Harvard U. Press. 1992).

20. Burstein, *Discrimination, Jobs, and Politics: The Struggle for Equal Employment Opportunity in the United States Since the New Deal* (Univ. Chicago Press, 1985).

21. Johnson v. Railway Express Agency, 421 U.S. 454, 95 S.Ct. 1716, 44 L.Ed.2d 295 (1975) (Title VII did not implicitly overrule or modify the protections of the 1866 statute. Remedies under each statute may be pursued independently).

process by filing charges of discrimination, "exhaust" administrative processes of the Equal Employment Opportunity Commission, and, in the vast majority of cases, initiate private suits against the offending entity.

To understand the materials which follow, one needs to have a general, preliminary understanding of the critical roles of the Equal Employment Opportunity Commission (EEOC).

The EEOC is the federal agency created by Title VII of the Civil Rights Act of 1964 to interpret and enforce that statute. That authority has been expanded to include the Age Discrimination in Employment Act, the Americans With Disabilities Act, and the Equal Pay Act. The EEOC is a five member, presidentially appointed commission whose members serve five year fixed terms. The Commission itself establishes broad policies, promulgates regulations, and publishes interpretative guidance. It is empowered to file charges of discrimination against covered entities, and ultimately file law suits based on the charges. An Office of General Counsel of the EEOC is authorized to direct the Commission's litigation efforts. Regional offices of the EEOC are located in major cities throughout the United States. The EEOC has six functions:

1. Intake and Investigation: Individuals seeking legal redress *must* file a written charge with the EEOC before initiating litigation. The vast majority of charges are filed by individuals. Regional offices of the EEOC receive such charges and notify the party charged with discrimination. The EEOC is directed to investigate the charge, and is granted broad pre-litigation subpoena power to secure disclosure of relevant information. *See, e.g.*, **University of Penn. v. EEOC,** 493 U.S. 182, 110 S.Ct. 577, 107 L.Ed.2d 571 (1990) (as part of its investigation the EEOC may subpoena internal memoranda of a university tenure committee. Such does not violate any common law privilege nor is such information protected by the First Amendment).

2. Conciliation: If the investigation of the charge discloses reasonable cause to believe a violation has occurred, the EEOC is directed to undertake conciliation and attempt an informal resolution. If informal resolution attempts fail, the EEOC is directed to notify the charging party of the failure. The charging party is then free to file a law suit against the charged entity in a state or a federal district court.

3. Resolution: After the charge is filed and its conciliation efforts have failed, the EEOC has very limited adjudicatory responsibilities. Unlike many federal enforcement agencies, such as the National Labor Relations Board or the Federal Trade Commission, the EEOC in private sector cases *does not* conduct formal administrative or adversarial hearings to resolve complaints, subject to the limited judicial review provided by the Administrative Procedure Act. In *all* cases involving private employers, and most cases involving employees of state or local governments,[22] formal enforcement is through a judicial action, usually filed by the individual charging party. The subsequent judicial proceeding is a trial *de novo*, independent from any fact finding the EEOC may have undertaken as part of its investigation and conciliation efforts. Since 1991, on all claims requesting damages, there is a right to trial by jury.

4. Litigation: While most enforcement suits are brought by private parties, after notice from the EEOC that conciliation efforts have failed, the EEOC, Office of General Counsel, is authorized to file suit in the name of the Commission. The EEOC is not authorized to file suit until conciliation efforts have been undertaken and have failed.

Suit by the EEOC General Counsel will pre-empt future private suits by the charging party. Given its limited resources the EEOC typically files suit only where there is a perceived pattern of discrimination or to litigate a particularly important legal issue. The EEOC may intervene in suits previously filed by private parties and file "friend of court" briefs on key legal issues.

5. Interpretation and Guidance: The EEOC has some authority, particularly under the ADA, to promulgate formal interpretive regulations. It also has the authority, frequently exercised, to issue less formal interpretive guidelines and policy statements. These guidelines assist employers, advise employees, and, as the cases which follow will demonstrate, are accorded varying degrees of deference by the courts. By regulation the EEOC requires employers to prominently display notices informing employees of their rights and remedies under the federal statutes.

6. Record Gathering and Keeping: Through regulations the EEOC requires covered employers to maintain employment records and file statistical reports with the Commission.

E. COMMON LAW TRADITION

A first step in studying employment discrimination is to become aware of the common law of the particular state. State common law is important for two reasons: (1) *Default*: where **statutes** (federal or state) provide the employee with **no relief,** the state's common law principles will be the default position that regulates the employee/employer relationship, and (2) *Supplement:* even where statutes provide a source for relief, state common law may provide additional and supplemental remedies.

---

22. There are two situations in which the EEOC is assigned an adjudicatory role. The first is on claims made by *federal employees*. Federal employees may *elect* to have the employing agency decision heard and resolved by the EEOC, in which case a formal hearing is conducted before an EEOC administrative judge. Decisions of administrative judges *against the federal agency*, confirmed by the Commission if an appeal is taken, may be enforced against the employing federal agency by the EEOC without judicial intervention. The second is where charges are made by high level state employees. Such claims are heard in a formal adjudication before the EEOC which makes a "final" determination subject to limited judicial review.

WAGENSELLER v. SCOTTSDALE MEMORIAL HOSPITAL

Supreme Court of Arizona, 1985
147 Ariz. 370, 710 P.2d 1025

FELDMAN, JUSTICE.

Catherine Sue Wagenseller petitioned this court to review a decision of the court of appeals affirming in part the trial court's judgment in favor of Scottsdale Memorial Hospital and certain Hospital employees (defendants). The trial court had dismissed all causes of action on defendants' motion for summary judgment. The court of appeals affirmed in part and remanded, ruling that the only cause of action available to plaintiff was the claim against her supervisor. We granted review to consider the law of this state with regard to the employment-at-will doctrine. The issues we address are:

1. Is an employer's right to terminate an at-will employee limited by any rules which, if breached, give rise to a cause of action for wrongful termination?

2. If "public policy" or some other doctrine does form the basis for such an action, how is it determined?

3. Did the trial court err, when it determined as a matter of law that the terms of Scottsdale Memorial Hospital's personnel policy manual were not part of the employment contract?

4. Do employment contracts contain an implied covenant of "good faith and fair dealing," and, if so, what is the nature of the covenant?

* * *

FACTUAL BACKGROUND

Catherine Wagenseller began her employment at Scottsdale Memorial Hospital as a staff nurse in March 1975, having been personally recruited by the manager of the emergency department * * *. Wagenseller was an "at-will" employee—one hired without specific contractual term. Smith was her supervisor. In August 1978, Wagenseller was assigned to the position of ambulance charge nurse, and approximately one year later was promoted to the position of paramedic coordinator, a newly approved management position in the emergency department. Three months later, on November 1, 1979, Wagenseller was terminated.

* * *. For more than four years, Smith and Wagenseller maintained a friendly, professional, working relationship. In May 1979, they joined a group consisting largely of personnel from other hospitals for an eight-day camping and rafting trip down the Colorado River. * * * Wagenseller states that this [trip] included public urination, defecation and bathing, heavy drinking, and "grouping up" with other rafters. Wagenseller did not participate in any of these activities. She also refused to join in the group's staging of a parody of the song "Moon River," which allegedly concluded with members of the group "mooning" the audience. Smith and others allegedly performed the "Moon River" skit twice at the Hospital following the group's return from the river, but Wagenseller declined to participate there as well.

Wagenseller contends that her refusal to engage in these activities caused her relationship with Smith to deteriorate and was the proximate cause of her termination. She claims that following the river trip Smith began harassing her, using abusive language and embarrassing her in the company of other staff. Other emergency department staff reported a similar marked change in Smith's behavior toward Wagenseller after the trip, although Smith denied it.

Up to the time of the river trip, Wagenseller had received consistently favorable job performance evaluations. Two months before the trip, Smith completed an annual evaluation report in which she rated Wagenseller's performance as "exceed[ing] results expected," the second highest of five possible ratings. In August and October 1979, Wagenseller met first with Smith and then with Smith's successor, Jeannie Steindorff, to discuss some problems regarding her duties as paramedic coordinator and her attitude toward the job. On November 1, 1979, following an exit interview at which Wagenseller was asked to resign and refused, she was terminated.

* * * Wagenseller brought suit against the Hospital, its personnel administrators, and her supervisor, Kay Smith.

Wagenseller, an "at-will" employee, contends that she was fired for reasons which contravene public policy and without legitimate cause related to job performance. She claims that her termination was wrongful, and that damages are recoverable under both tort and contract theories. The Hospital argues that an "at-will" employee may be fired for cause, without cause, or for "bad" cause. We hold that in the absence of contractual provision such an employee may be fired for good cause or for no cause, but not for "bad" cause.

THE EMPLOYMENT–AT–WILL DOCTRINE

History

As early as 1562, the English common law presumed that an employment contract containing an annual salary provision or computation was for a one-year term. Originally designed for the protection of seasonal farm workers, the English rule expanded over the years to protect factory workers as well. Workers were well protected under this rule, for the one-year presumption was not easy to overcome. English courts held an employer liable for breaching the employment contract if he terminated an employee at any time during the year without "reasonable cause to do so. To uphold an employer's discharge of an employee without a showing of "good cause," the courts required a clear expression of a contrary intent as evidenced either on the face of the contract or by a clearly defined custom of the industry.

In the early nineteenth century, American courts borrowed the English rule. The legal rationale embodied in the rule was consistent with the nature of the predominant master-servant employment relationship at the time because it reflected the master's duty to make provision for the general well-being of his servants. In addition, the master was under a duty to employ the servant for a term, either a specified or implied time of service, and could not terminate him strictly at will. The late nineteenth century, however, brought the Industrial Revolution; with it came the decline of the master-servant relationship and the rise of the more impersonal employer-employee relationship. In apparent response to the economic changes sweeping the country, American courts abandoned the English rule and adopted the employment-at-will doctrine. This new doctrine gave the employer freedom to terminate an at-will employee for any reason, good or bad.

The at-will rule has been traced to an 1877 treatise by H.G. Wood, in which he wrote:

> With us the rule is inflexible, that a general or indefinite hiring is *prima facie* a hiring at will, and if the servant seeks to make it out a yearly hiring, the burden is upon him to establish it by proof.... [I]t is an indefinite hiring and is determinable at the will of either party.... *H.G. Wood, Law of Master and Servant* § 134 at 273 (1877).

As commentators and courts later would point out, none of the four cases cited by Wood actually supported the rule. Wood's rule also ran directly counter to another American treatise that stated the one-year presumption as the rule that some courts continued to follow.

However unsound its foundation, Wood's at-will doctrine was adopted by the New York courts * * * and soon became the generally accepted American rule. In 1932, this court first adopted the rule for Arizona: "The general rule in regard to contracts for personal services, ... where no time limit is provided, is that they are terminable at pleasure by either party, or at most upon reasonable notice." Thus, an employer was free to fire an employee hired for an indefinite term "for good cause, for no cause, or even for cause morally wrong, without being thereby guilty of legal wrong." *Dover Copper Minimg Co. v. Doenges*, 40 Ariz. 349, 357, 12 P.2d 288, 290–92 (1932).

Present–Day Status of the At–Will Rule

In recent years there has been apparent dissatisfaction with the absolutist formulation of the common law at-will rule. The Illinois Supreme Court is representative of courts that have acknowledged a need for a less mechanical application of the rule:

> With the rise of large corporations conducting specialized operations and employing relatively immobile workers who often have no other place to market their skills, recognition that the employer and em-

ployee do not stand on equal footing is realistic. In addition, unchecked employer power, like unchecked employee power, has been seen to present a distinct threat to the public policy carefully considered and adopted by society as a whole. As a result, it is now recognized that a proper balance must be maintained among the employer's interest in operating a business efficiently and profitably, the employee's interest in earning a livelihood, and society's interest in seeing its public policies carried out. *Palmateer v. International Harvester Co.,* 85 Ill.2d 124, 129, 52 Ill.Dec. 13, 15, 421 N.E.2d 876, 878 (1981).

Today, courts in three-fifths of the states have recognized some form of a cause of action for wrongful discharge.

The trend has been to modify the at-will rule by creating exceptions to its operation. Three general exceptions have developed. * * * Wagenseller raises all three doctrines.

THE PUBLIC POLICY EXCEPTION

The public policy exception to the at-will doctrine began with a narrow rule permitting employees to sue their employers when a statute expressly prohibited their discharge. This formulation was then expanded to include any discharge in violation of a statutory expression of public policy. *See Petermann v. Teamsters Local 396,* 174 Cal.App.2d 184, 344 P.2d 25 (1959) (discharge for refusal to commit perjury). Courts later allowed a cause of action for violation of public policy, even in the absence of a specific statutory prohibition. *See Nees v. Hocks,* 272 Or. 210, 536 P.2d 512 (1975) (discharge for being absent from work to serve on jury duty). The New Hampshire Supreme Court announced perhaps the most expansive rule when it held an employer liable for discharging an employee who refused to go out with her foreman. The court concluded that termination "motivated by bad faith or malice or based on retaliation is not [in] the best interest of the economic system or the public good and constitutes a breach of the employment contract." *Monge v. Beebe Rubber Co.,* 114 N.H. 130, 133, 316 A.2d 549, 551 (1974). Although no other court has gone this far, a majority of the states have now either recognized a cause of action based on the public policy exception or have indicated their willingness to consider it, given appropriate facts. The key to an employee's claim in all of these cases is the proper definition of a public policy that has been violated by the employer's actions.

Before deciding whether to adopt the public policy exception, we first consider what kind of discharge would violate the rule. The majority of courts require, as a threshold showing, a "clear mandate" of public policy. The leading case recognizing a public policy exception to the at-will doctrine is *Palmateer v. International Harvester Co., supra,* which holds that an employee stated a cause of action for wrongful discharge when he claimed he was fired for supplying information to police investigating alleged criminal violations by a co-employee. Addressing the issue of what constitutes "clearly mandated public policy," the court stated:

There is no precise definition of the term. In general, it can be said that public policy concerns what is right and just and what affects the citizens of the State collectively. It is to be found in the State's constitution and statutes and, when they are silent, in its judicial decisions. Although there is no precise line of demarcation dividing matters that are the subject of public policies from matters purely personal, a survey of cases in other States involving retaliatory discharges shows that a matter must strike at the heart of a citizen's social rights, duties, and responsibilities before the tort will be allowed.

Other courts have allowed a cause of action where an employee was fired for refusing to violate a specific statute. *E.g., Petermann v. Teamsters Local 396, supra* (declined to commit perjury before a legislative committee); *Tameny v. Atlantic Richfield Co.,* 164 Cal.Rptr. 839, 164 Cal.Rptr. 839, 610 P.2d 1330 (1980) (would not engage in price-fixing); *Sheets v. Teddy's Frosted Foods,* 179 Conn. 471, 427 A.2d 385 (1980) (insisted that employer comply with state Food, Drug, and Cosmetic Act); *Trombetta v. Detroit, Toledo & Ironton Railroad Co.,* 81 Mich.App. 489, 265 N.W.2d 385 (1978) (refused to alter state-mandated pollution control reports); *O'Sullivan v. Mallon,* 160 N.J.Super. 416, 390 A.2d 149 (1978) (would not perform medical procedure for which she was not licensed); *Harless v. First National Bank,* 162 W.Va. 116, 246 S.E.2d 270 (1978) (would not violate consumer protection law). Failure to perform an act which would violate provisions of the Oregon state constitution formed the basis for a cause of action in *Delaney v. Taco Time International,* 297 Or. 10, 681 P.2d 114 (1984) (declined to sign a false and arguably tortious statement regarding a co-employee). Similarly, courts have found terminations improper where to do otherwise would have impinged on the employee's exercise of statutory rights or duties. *E.g., Glenn v. Clearman's Golden Cock Inn,* 192 Cal.App.2d 793, 13 Cal.Rptr. 769 (1961) (right to join a union); *Midgett v. Sackett–Chicago,* 105 Ill.2d 143, 85 Ill.Dec. 475, 473 N.E.2d 1280 (1984) (filing of a workers' compensation claim by a union member protected by a collective bargaining agreement); *Frampton v. Central Indiana Gas Co.,* 260 Ind. 249, 297 N.E.2d 425 (1973) (filing of a workers' compensation claim); *Nees v. Hocks, supra* (requesting not to be excused from jury duty). A division of our court of appeals recently adopted the public policy exception, ruling that the discharge of an at-will employee who refused to conceal a violation of Arizona's theft statute was contrary to public policy. *Vermillion v. AAA Pro Moving & Storage* 146 Ariz. 215 at 216, 704 P.2d 1360 at 1361. (App.1985). * * *.

It is difficult to justify this court's further adherence to a rule which permits an employer to fire someone for "cause morally wrong." So far as we can tell, no court faced with a termination that violated a "clear mandate of public policy" has refused to adopt the public policy exception. Certainly, a court would be hard-pressed to find a rationale to hold that an employer could with impunity fire an employee who refused to commit perjury. Why should the law imply an agreement which would give the employer such power? It may be argued, of course, that our economic system functions best if employers are given wide latitude in dealing with employees. We assume that it is in the public interest that employers continue to have that freedom. We also believe, however, that the interests of the economic system will be fully served if employers may fire for good cause or without cause. The interests of society as a whole will be promoted if employers are forbidden to fire for cause which is "morally wrong."

We therefore adopt the public policy exception to the at-will termination rule. We hold that an employer may fire for good cause or for no cause. He may not fire for bad cause-that which violates public policy. * * *

We turn then to the questions of where "public policy" may be found and how it may be recognized and articulated. As the expressions of our founders and those we have elected to our legislature, our state's constitution and statutes embody the public conscience of the people of this state. It is thus in furtherance of their interests to hold that an employer may not with impunity violate the dictates of public policy found in the provisions of our statutory and constitutional law.

We do not believe, however, that expressions of public policy are contained only in the statutory and constitutional law, nor do we believe that all statements made in either a statute or the constitution are expressions of public policy. Turning first to the identification of other sources, we note our agreement with the following:

> Public policy is usually defined by the political branches of government. Something "against public policy" is something that the Legislature has forbidden. But the Legislature is not the only source of such policy. In common-law jurisdictions the courts too have been sources of law, always subject to legislative correction, and with progressively less freedom as legislation occupies a given field. It is the courts, to give one example that originated the whole doctrine that certain kinds of businesses-common carriers and innkeepers-must serve the public without discrimination or preference. In this sense, then, courts make law, and they have done so for years. *Lucas v. Brown & Root,* 736 F.2d 1202, 1205 (8th Cir.1984).

Other state courts have similarly recognized judicial decisions as a source of public policy. * * * Thus, we will look to the pronouncements of our founders, our legislature, and our courts to discern the public policy of this state.

All such pronouncements, however, will not provide the basis for a claim of wrongful discharge. Only those which have a singularly *public* purpose will have such force. * * *

Where the interest involved is merely private or proprietary, the exception does not apply. In *Pierce v. Ortho Pharmaceutical Corp.,* [84 N.J. 58, 417 A.2d 505 (1980)] for instance, the court held that the plaintiff did not have a cause of action for wrongful discharge based on her refusal to do certain research, where she had failed to articulate a clear public policy that had been violated. Citing the personal nature of Dr. Pierce's opposition, the court stated:

> Chaos would result if a single doctor engaged in research were allowed to determine, according to his or her individual conscience, whether a project should continue. An employee does not have a right to continued employment when he or she refuses to conduct research simply because it would contravene his or her personal morals. * * * 84 N.J. at 75, 417 A.2d at 514.

Although an employee facing such a quandary may refuse to do the work believed to violate her moral philosophy, she may not also claim a right to continued employment. The Oregon Supreme Court announced a similar limitation when it refused to recognize a cause of action for the discharge of an employee who claimed he was wrongfully terminated for exercising his statutory right as a stockholder to examine the books of his corporate employer. *Campbell v. Ford Industries,* 274 Or. 243, 546 P.2d 141 (1976). The court based its determination on its finding that the right claimed was "not one of public policy, but the private and proprietary interest of stockholders, as owners of the corporation."

However, some legal principles, whether statutory or decisional, have a discernible, comprehensive public purpose. A state's criminal code provides clear examples of such statutes. Thus, courts in other jurisdictions have consistently recognized a cause of action for a discharge in violation of a criminal statute. In a seminal case involving the public policy exception, *Petermann v. International Brotherhood of Teamsters Local 396,* 174 Cal.App.2d 184, 344 P.2d 25 (1959), the California Court of Appeals upheld an employee's right to refuse to commit perjury, stating:

> The public policy of this state as reflected in the Penal Code ... would be seriously impaired if it were to be held that one could be discharged by reason of his refusal to commit perjury. To hold that one's continued employment could be made contingent upon his commission of a felonious act at the instance of his employer would be to encourage criminal conduct upon the part of both the employee and employer and would serve to contaminate the honest administration of public affairs. This is patently contrary to the public welfare.

Although we do not limit our recognition of the public policy exception to cases involving a violation of a criminal statute, we do believe that our duty will seldom be clearer than when such a violation is involved. We agree with the Illinois Supreme Court that "[t]here is no public policy more basic, nothing more implicit in the concept of ordered liberty, than the enforcement of a State's criminal code."

In the case before us, Wagenseller refused to participate in activities which arguably would have violated our indecent exposure statute, A.R.S. § 13–1402. She claims that she was fired because of this refusal. The statute provides:

Indecent exposure; classifications:

A. A person commits indecent exposure if he or she exposes his or her genitals or anus or she exposes the areola or nipple of her breast or breasts and another person is present, and the defendant is reckless about whether such other person, as a reasonable person, would be offended or alarmed by the act.

B. Indecent exposure is a class 1 misdemeanor. Indecent exposure to a person under the age of fifteen years is a class 6 felony.

While this statute may not embody a policy which "strikes at the heart of a citizen's social right, duties and responsibilities" as clearly and forcefully as a statute prohibiting perjury, we believe that it was enacted to preserve and protect the commonly recognized sense of public privacy and decency. The statute does, therefore, recognize bodily privacy as a "citizen's social right." We disagree with the court of appeals' conclusion that a minor violation of the statute would not violate public policy. The nature of the act, and not its magnitude, is the issue. The legislature has already concluded that acts fitting the statutory description contravene the public policy of this state. We thus uphold this state's public policy by holding that termination for refusal to commit an act which might violate A.R.S. § 13–1402 may provide the basis of a claim for wrongful discharge. The relevant inquiry here is not whether the alleged "mooning" incidents were either felonies or misdemeanors or constituted purely technical violations of the statute, but whether they contravened the important public policy interests embodied in the law. The law enacted by the legislature establishes a clear policy that public exposure of one's anus or genitals is contrary to public standards of morality. We are compelled to conclude that termination of employment for refusal to participate in public exposure of one's buttocks[5] is a termination contrary to the policy of this state, even if, for instance, the employer might have grounds to believe that all of the onlookers were voyeurs and would not be offended. In this situation, there might be no crime, but there would be a violation of public policy to compel the employee to do an act ordinarily proscribed by the law.

* * *

Thus, in an at-will hiring we continue to recognize the presumption or to imply the covenant of termination at the pleasure of either party, whether with or without cause. Firing for bad cause-one against public policy articulated by constitutional, statutory, or decisional law-is not a right inherent in the at-will contract, or in any other contract, even if expressly

---

5. We have little expertise in the techniques of mooning. We cannot say as a matter of law, therefore, whether mooning would always violate the statute by revealing the mooner's anus or genitalia. That question could only be determined, we suppose, by an examination of the facts of each case. We deem such an inquiry unseemly and unnecessary in a civil case. Compelled exposure of the bare buttocks, on pain of termination of employment, is a sufficient violation of the *policy* embodied in the statute to support the action, even if there would have been no technical violation of the statute.

provided. Such a termination violates rights guaranteed to the employee by law and is tortious.

THE "PERSONNEL POLICY MANUAL" EXCEPTION

* * * * [I]n addition to relying on the public policy analysis to restrict the operation of the terminable-at-will rule, courts have turned to the employment contract itself, finding in it implied terms that limit the employer's right of discharge. Two types of implied contract terms have been recognized by the courts: implied-in-law terms and implied-in-fact terms. An implied-in-law term arises from a duty imposed by law where the contract itself is silent; it is imposed even though the parties may not have intended it, and it binds the parties to a legally enforceable duty, just as if they had so contracted explicitly. * * *

An implied-in-fact contract term, on the other hand, is one that is inferred from the statements or conduct of the parties. It is not a promise defined by the law, but one made by the parties, though not expressly. Courts have found such terms in an employer's policy statements regarding such things as job security and employee disciplinary procedures, holding that by the conduct of the parties these statements may become part of the contract, supplementing the verbalized at-will agreement, and thus limiting the employer's absolute right to discharge an at-will employee. Arizona is among the jurisdictions that have recognized the implied-in-fact contract term as an exception to the at-will rule. * * * In *Leikvold v. Valley View Community* Hospital, [141 Ariz. 544, 688 P.2d 170 (1984)], this court held that a personnel manual can become part of an employment contract and remanded the cause for a jury determination as to whether the particular manual given to Leikvold had become part of her employment contract * * *.

* * * In October 1978, Scottsdale Memorial Hospital established a four-step disciplinary procedure to achieve the Hospital's stated policy of "provid[ing] fair and consistent discipline as required to assist with the improvement of employees' behavior or performance." Subject to 32 listed exceptions, prior to being terminated a Hospital employee must be given a verbal warning, a written performance warning, a letter of formal reprimand, and a notice of dismissal. The manual further qualifies the mandatory procedure by providing that the 32 exceptions "are not inclusive and are only guidelines." In appealing her dismissal, Wagenseller cited violations of this procedure, but the trial court ruled as a matter of law that the manual had not become part of the employment contract between Wagenseller and the Hospital. The court of appeals held that the Hospital's failure to follow the four-step disciplinary procedure did not violate Wagenseller's contract rights because she failed to prove her reliance on the procedure as a part of her employment contract. We disagree with both of these rulings.

Whether any particular personnel manual modifies any particular employment-at-will relationship and becomes part of the particular employment contract is a *question of fact*. Evidence relevant to this factual decision includes the language used in the personnel manual as well as the employer's course of conduct and oral representations regarding it.

Thus, * * * [the] entry of summary judgment was inappropriate "[b]ecause a material question-whether the policies manual was incorporated into and became part of the terms of the employment contract-remain[ed] in dispute." The court may determine as a matter of law the proper construction of contract terms which are "clear and unambiguous." Here, the court of appeals ruled, in effect, that the Hospital had adequately disclaimed any liability for failing to follow the procedure it had established. It found this disclaimer in the final item in the Hospital's list of exceptions to its disciplinary procedure: "These major and minor infractions are not inclusive and are only guidelines." The court concluded that the effect of this "clear" and "conspicuous" provision was "to create, by its terms, no rights at all."

We do not believe this document, read in its entirety, has the clarity that the court of appeals attributed to its individual portions. One reading the document might well infer that the Hospital had established a procedure that would generally apply in disciplinary actions taken against employees. * * *

THE "GOOD FAITH AND FAIR DEALING" EXCEPTION

We turn next to a consideration of implied-in-law contract terms which may limit an employer's right to discharge an at-will employee. Wagenseller claims that discharge without good cause breaches the implied-in-law covenant of good faith and fair dealing contained in every contract. *See* Restatement (Second) of Contracts § 205; 5 *S. Williston, The Law of Contracts* § 670 at 159 (3d ed. 1961). In the context of this case, she argues that discharge without good cause violates the covenant of good faith and is, therefore, wrongful. The covenant requires that neither party do anything that will injure the right of the other to receive the benefits of their agreement. The duty not to act in bad faith or deal unfairly thus becomes a part of the contract, and, as with any other element of the contract, the remedy for its breach generally is on the contract itself. In certain circumstances, breach of contract, including breach of the covenant of good faith and fair dealing, may provide the basis for a tort claim.

The question whether a duty to terminate only for good cause should be implied into all employment-at-will contracts has received much attention in the case law and other literature. Courts have generally rejected the invitation to imply such a duty in employment contracts, voicing the concern that to do so would place undue restrictions on management and would infringe the employer's "legitimate exercise of management discretion." We think this concern is appropriate.
* * *

Were we to adopt such a rule, we fear that we would tread perilously close to abolishing completely the at-will doctrine and establishing by judicial fiat the benefits which employees can and should get *only* through collective bargaining agreements or tenure provisions. While we do not reject the propriety of such a rule, we are not persuaded that it should be the result of judicial decision. * * *

We do, however, recognize an implied covenant of good faith and fair dealing in the employment-at-will contract, although that covenant does not create a duty for the employer to terminate the employee only for good cause. * * * The covenant does protect an employee from a discharge based on an employer's desire to avoid the payment of benefits already earned by the employee, such as the sales commissions * * * but not the tenure required to earn the pension and retirement benefits * * *. Thus, plaintiff here has a right to receive the benefits that were a part of her employment agreement with defendant Hospital. To the extent, however, that the benefits represent a claim for prospective employment, her claim must fail. * * *

NOTES

1. *Whistleblower Statutes:* Federal law, 5 U.S.C. (various), 103 Stat. 16, protects *federal employees* who expose government violations of the law, gross waste of funds, or actions that present specific public health or safety concerns. Many states have similar protection for their public employees. A few states, including California, have broad whistleblower statutes that prohibit retaliation by *private employers* against employees who report violations of the law. *See, Cal.Lab.Code s 1102.5.* Scope and protections vary widely. *See* Callahan & Dworkin, *The State of State Whistleblower* Protection, 38 Am.Bus. L.J. 99 (2000); Malin, *Protecting the Whistleblower from Retaliatory Discharge*, 16 U.Mich.J.L.Ref. 277 (1983).

2. *Other torts:* Employer treatment of an employee may also give rise to traditional common law torts, such as assault, battery, invasion of privacy, intentional infliction of emotional harm, and defamation *See e.g., Bodewig v. K–Mart, Inc.,* 635 P.2d 657 (Ore. 1981); *Zinda v. Louisiana Pacific Corp.,* 440 N.W.2d 548 (Wis. 1989), *Aker v. New York & Co.,* 364 F.Supp.2d 661 (N.D. Ohio 2005).

3. While most states now recognize the concept of "wrongful discharge," state interpretations of the extent of "public policy" protection against discharge vary widely. Some, like the principal case, give a relatively broad interpretation to the principal. Others narrowly limit protection.

4. The Restatement of Employment Law, Sec. 402 (Tentative Draft, May 2009), proposes subjecting employers to common law tort liability for disciplining employees who acts both reasonably and in good faith by: (1) refusing to commit an act that the employee believes violates: (a) the law, (b) an established code of professional conduct, or (c) an occupational code that protects a public interest; (2) performing a public duty that the employee believes is imposed by law; (3) filing charges or claiming benefits allowed by law; (4) refusing to waive a non-waivable right or refusing to agree to a condition of employment that would violate public policy; (5) reporting or inquiring about conduct that the employee believes would violate the law; (6) engaging in activity that furthers a public policy that is "substantial."

Part 2

Basic Principles

■ ■ ■

CHAPTER 1

COVERAGE AND SCOPE

■ ■ ■

Title VII of the Civil Rights Act of 1964, the Age Discrimination in Employment Act of 1967 and the Americans With Disabilities Act of 1990, as well as important, but secondary statutory protections apply only to "employers;" not to all employers, only those of a minimum size as measured by the number of their "employees." In addition, the statutes only proscribe action the "employer" takes against "employees" or applicants for "employment."

A. "EMPLOYER"

CLACKAMAS GASTROENTEROLOGY ASSOC. v. WELLS

Supreme Court of the United States, 2003
538 U.S. 440, 123 S.Ct. 1673, 155 L.Ed.2d 615

JUSTICE STEVENS delivered the opinion of the Court.

The Americans with Disabilities Act of 1990 (ADA or Act) 42 U.S.C. § 12101 *et seq.,* like other federal antidiscrimination legislation,[1] is inapplicable to very small businesses. Under the ADA an "employer" is not covered unless its workforce includes "15 or more employees for each working day in each of 20 or more calendar weeks in the current or preceding calendar year." § 12111(5). The question in this case is whether four physicians actively engaged in medical practice as shareholders and directors of a professional corporation should be counted as "employees."

* * * Relying on an "economic realities" test adopted by the Seventh Circuit in *EEOC v. Dowd & Dowd, Ltd.,* 736 F.2d 1177, 1178 (1984), the

---

1. See, *e.g.,* 29 U.S.C. § 630(b) (setting forth a 20–employee threshold for coverage under the Age Discrimination in Employment Act of 1967 (ADEA)); 42 U.S.C. § 2000e(b) (establishing a 15–employee threshold for coverage under Title VII of the Civil Rights Act of 1964).Petitioner, Clackamas Gastroenterology Associates, P. C., is a medical clinic in Oregon. It employed respondent, Deborah Anne Wells, as a bookkeeper from 1986 until 1997. After her termination, she brought this action against the clinic alleging unlawful discrimination on the basis of disability under Title I of the ADA. Petitioner denied that it was covered by the Act and moved for summary judgment, asserting that it did not have 15 or more employees for the 20 weeks required by the statute. It is undisputed that the accuracy of that assertion depends on whether the four physician-shareholders who own the professional corporation and constitute its board of directors are counted as employees.

District Court concluded that the four doctors were "more analogous to partners in a partnership than to shareholders in a general corporation" and therefore were "not employees for purposes of the federal antidiscrimination laws."

A divided panel of the Court of Appeals for the Ninth Circuit reversed. * * * [T]he majority held that the use of any corporation, including a professional corporation, " 'precludes any examination designed to determine whether the entity is in fact a partnership.' " It saw "no reason to permit a professional corporation to secure the 'best of both possible worlds' by allowing it both to assert its corporate status in order to reap the tax and civil liability advantages and to argue that it is like a partnership in order to avoid liability for unlawful employment discrimination." * * *

II

* * * The definition of the term in the ADA simply states that an "employee" is "an individual employed by an employer." That surely qualifies as a mere "nominal definition" that is "completely circular and explains nothing." In [*Nationwide Mut. Ins. Co. v. Darden*, 503 U.S. 318, 322, 112 S.Ct. 1344, 117 L.Ed.2d 581 (1992), we explained that " 'when Congress has used the term "employee" without defining it, we have concluded that Congress intended to describe the conventional master-servant relationship as understood by common-law agency doctrine.'

* * *

[T]he common law's definition of the master-servant relationship does provide helpful guidance. At common law the relevant factors defining the master-servant relationship focus on the master's control over the servant. The general definition of the term servant in the Restatement (Second) of Agency s 2(2) (1958), for example, refers to a person whose work is "controlled or is subject to the right to control by the master." ("A servant is a person employed to perform services in the affairs of another and who with respect to the physical conduct in the performance of the services is subject to the other's control or right to control"). In addition, the Restatement's more specific definition of the term servant lists factors to be considered when distinguishing between servants and independent contractors, the first of which is "the extent of control" that one may exercise over the details of the work of the other. We think that the common-law element of control is the principal guidepost that should be followed in this case.

This is the position that is advocated by the Equal Employment Opportunity Commission (EEOC), the agency that has special enforcement responsibilities under the ADA and other federal statutes containing similar threshold issues for determining coverage. It argues that a court should examine "whether shareholder-directors operate independently and manage the business or instead are subject to the firm's control." According to the EEOC's view, "[i]f the shareholder-directors operate independently and manage the business, they are proprietors and not employees; if they are subject to the firm's control, they are employees."

Specific EEOC guidelines discuss both the broad question of who is an "employee" and the narrower question of when partners, officers, members of boards of directors, and major shareholders qualify as employees. With respect to the broad question, the guidelines list 16 factors * * * that may be relevant to "whether the employer controls the means and manner of the worker's work performance."[8] The guidelines list six factors to be considered in answering the narrower question, which they frame as "whether the individual acts independently and participates in managing the organization, or whether the individual is subject to the organization's control."

We are persuaded by the EEOC's focus on the common-law touchstone of control, and specifically by its submission that each of the following six factors is relevant to the inquiry whether a shareholder-director is an employee:

> "Whether the organization can hire or fire the individual or set the rules and regulations of the individual's work
>
> "Whether and, if so, to what extent the organization supervises the individual's work
>
> "Whether the individual reports to someone higher in the organization
>
> "Whether and, if so, to what extent the individual is able to influence the organization
>
> "Whether the parties intended that the individual be an employee, as expressed in written agreements or contracts
>
> "Whether the individual shares in the profits, losses, and liabilities of the organization." EEOC Compliance Manual 605:0009.[10]

As the EEOC's standard reflects, an employer is the person, or group of persons, who owns and manages the enterprise. The employer can hire and fire employees, can assign tasks to employees and supervise their performance, and can decide how the profits and losses of the business are to be distributed. The mere fact that a person has a particular title—such as partner, director, or vice president—should not necessarily be used to determine whether he or she is an employee or a proprietor. Nor should the mere existence of a document styled "employment agreement" lead inexorably to the conclusion that either party is an employee. * * * Rather, as was true in applying common law rules to the independent-contractor-versus-employee issue * * * the answer to whether a share-

---

8. For example, the EEOC considers whether the work requires a high level of skill or expertise, whether the employer furnishes the tools, materials and equipment, and whether the employer has the right to control when, where, and how the worker performs the job.

10. The EEOC asserts that these six factors need not necessarily be treated as "exhaustive." The answer to whether a shareholder-director is an employee or an employer cannot be decided in every case by a " 'shorthand formula or magic phrase.' "

holder-director is an employee depends on " 'all of the incidents of the relationship . . . with no one factor being decisive.' "

* * *

Accordingly, * * * we reverse the judgment of the Court of Appeals and remand the case to that court for further proceedings consistent with this opinion.

JUSTICE GINSBURG, with whom JUSTICE BREYER joins, dissenting.

In 1996, Clackamas had 4 physician-shareholders and at least 14 other employees for 28 full weeks; in 1997, it had 4 physician-shareholders and at least 14 other employees for 37 full weeks. (to be covered by the Act, an employer must have the requisite number of employees "for each working day in each of 20 or more calendar weeks in the current or preceding calendar year"). Beyond question, the corporation would have been covered by the ADA had one of the physician-shareholders sold his stake in the business and become a "mere" employee. Yet such a change in ownership arrangements would not alter the magnitude of Clackamas' operation: In both circumstances, the corporation would have had at least 18 people on site doing the everyday work of the clinic for the requisite number of weeks.

The Equal Employment Opportunity Commission's approach, which the Court endorses, it is true, "excludes from protection those who are most able to control the firm's practices and who, as a consequence, are least vulnerable to the discriminatory treatment prohibited by the Act." As this dispute demonstrates, however, the determination whether the physician-shareholders are employees of Clackamas affects not only whether they may sue under the ADA, but also—and of far greater practical import—whether employees like bookkeeper Deborah Anne Wells are covered by the Act. Because the character of the relationship between Clackamas and the doctors supplies no justification for withholding from clerical worker Wells federal protection against discrimination in the workplace, I would affirm the judgment of the Court of Appeals.

NOTES

1. *Jurisdictional?* Lack of coverage does not deprive a court of subject matter jurisdiction. Therefore, failure of a defendant to raise lack of coverage in a timely fashion waives any objection thereto. ***Arbaugh v. Y & H Corp.***, 546 U.S. 500, 126 S.Ct. 1235, 163 L.Ed.2d 1097 (2006).

2. *Exclusions:* Title VII specifically *excludes* certain entities from the definition of "employer."

a. *Membership clubs:* Bona fide, tax exempt membership clubs established and maintained for defined social or recreational purposes or which promote a common literary, scientific, or political objective. The club also must maintain meaningful conditions that limit or screen membership. 42 U.S.C. § 2000e(b).

b. *Indian tribes:* 42 U.S.C. § 2000e–(b). "Indian tribe" includes the federally recognized quasi-sovereign political units of Native Americans as well as distinct corporations owned and controlled by sovereign tribes. *Pink v. Modoc Indian Health Project, Inc.,* 157 F.3d 1185 (9th Cir.1998); *Dille v. Council of Energy Resource Tribes,* 801 F.2d 373 (10th Cir. 1986).

c. *Military:* The relationship between the military and uniformed military personnel, including service in the National Guard, is not one of "employment." *Helm v. California,* 722 F.2d 507 (9th Cir. 1983). However, the statutes do cover civilian workers in "military departments." *See, Meister v. Texas Adj. Gen. Dep't.,* 233 F.3d 332 (5th Cir. 2000).

3. *Counting "Employees:"* To be an "employer" the entity must have the requisite number of "employees" (15 under Title VII and the ADA, and 20 under the ADEA) for "each working day for twenty or more calendar weeks in the current or previous calendar year." The requisite twenty weeks in a calendar year need not be consecutive weeks. "Each working day" during the calendar week is determined by the employer's payroll for the week. Thus, to be counted all that is required is that the "employee" be on the payroll for that week. The number of days or hours the employee may work during that week is not material. ***Walters v. Metropolitan Educ. Enter.,*** 519 U.S. 202, 117 S.Ct. 660, 136 L.Ed.2d 644 (1997).

4. *Governments: State and local governments* are within the definition of "employer".

The definition of "employer" specifically excludes the *federal government.* However, federal executive departments are covered by a distinct section of the core statutes. *See, e.g.,* 42 U.S.C. § 2000e–16. The substantive outcomes for federal employees will parallel that of non-federal employees. However, enforcement procedures, time limits for filing charges and suits, and remedies all differ dramatically from those applied to non-federal employees.

Foreign governments operating in the United States are neither excluded from nor included in the statutory definition of "employer." Nonetheless, when functioning in a sovereign capacity, such as an embassy or consulate, foreign government actions are not subject to United States employment laws. ***McCulloch v. Sociedad Nacional de Marineros de Honduras,*** 372 U.S. 10, 83 S.Ct. 671, 9 L.Ed.2d 547 (1963). Commercial or proprietary enterprises, even where wholly owned and controlled by a foreign government, are subject to the employment discrimination statutes. *Wickes v. Olympic Airways,* 745 F.2d 363 (6th Cir. 1984).[22]

---

22. Foreign employers, government or private, are subject to treaties between the governments of the United States and the "guest nation" that not only permit companies of the guest nation to do business in the United States, but commonly allow companies of guest nations discretion to hire certain employees (usually executives, experts, and professionals) "of their choice." Such treaties, (of "friendship, commerce, and navigation," or FCN), generally do not apply to corporations incorporated in the United States regardless of underlying ownership. ***Sumitomo Shoji America, Inc. v. Avagliano***, 457 U.S. 176, 102 S.Ct. 2374, 72 L.Ed.2d 765 (1982). Such treaties also tend to be limited to their precise terms. Thus, in *MacNamara v. Korean Air Lines,* 863 F.2d 1135 (3d Cir. 1988), a treaty with the Republic of Korea allowing Korean companies to select executives "of their choice" was construed to authorize only a preference for Korean nationals. It did not authorize the Korean corporation doing business in the U.S. to engage in broad race or sex discrimination.

5. *Extra–Territoriality:* The statutes specifically reach actions of American companies and their foreign subsidiaries with respect to the employment of American citizens in a foreign country, subject to one significant proviso. It will not be unlawful for an employer to take any action involving an employee working in a foreign country where compliance with the U.S. statutes would cause the employer to violate the laws of the country where the work is taking place. The statutes do not apply to *aliens* employed outside the United States. 42 U.S.C. § 2000e–1. Thus, a United States firm recruiting and hiring Mexicans in Mexico for work to be performed in the United States, will not have those hiring practices subject to review under the statutes. *Reyes–Gaona v. North Carolina Growers Ass'n*, 250 F.3d 861 (4th Cir. 2001).

6. *Individuals and decision-makers:* Although the statutes define "employer" to include "any agent of such a person" the weight of authority holds that individual employees, including supervisors responsible for the discriminatory action, cannot be personally liable for statutory violations. *Fantini v. Salem State College,* 557 F.3d 22 (1st Cir. 2009). States, however, may impose individual liability for violations of state law.

B. "EMPLOYMENT"

1. THE STANDARD: "RIGHT OF CONTROL" OR "ECONOMIC DEPENDENCE"?

Action by a covered "employer" must affect a "term or condition of *employment*" of an "*employee*" or "applicant for *employment.*" Treatment of individuals who do not hold an "employment" relationship with a covered "employer" is beyond the scope of the core employment discrimination statutes.

Most lower courts use the definition of "employee" applied to determine whether an employer is of the size necessary for coverage (*Clackamas Gastroenterology Assoc. v. Wells, supra page 20)* to determine also whether discrimination by the covered "employer" is "employment." Most courts have rejected analyzing "employment" in terms of the economic dependence of the worker on the "employer," and deny protection to workers who do not satisfy the common law standards of "employee" discussed in *Clackamas, supra.* Illustrations:

Alberty–Velez v. Corporacion de Puerto Rico Para La Difusion Publica, 361 F.3d 1 (1st Cir. 2004), applied the common law "right of control" standard to hold that a television personality being paid for developing and presenting community interest stories was not in an employment relationship with the covered "employer" but was working for the "employer" as an independent contractor.

Alexander v. Rush North Shore Medical Center, 101 F.3d 487 (7th Cir. 1996), held that a physician who held a "staff" position at defendant hospital where he was required to be "on call" at the hospital at specified times was an independent contractor, and not an employee of the hospital.

Lerohl v. Friends of Minn. Sinfonia, 322 F.3d 486 (8th Cir. 2003), ruled that a musician who played in a symphony orchestra and received much of his income for his performing with the symphony was an unprotected independent contractor even though the employer determined what music would be played, when and where it would be rehearsed and performed, with the conductor directing the plaintiff on precisely how the music should be played.

Consider:

1. *Hishon v. King and Spalding,* 467 U.S. 69, 104 S.Ct. 2229, 81 L.Ed.2d 59 (1984), involved denial of an associate in a large law firm promotion to an equity partner. In narrow reasoning, the Court held that the associate's denial was of a "term or condition" of her current "employment" when she was denied the promotion from that "employment" for discriminatory reasons.

2. *Price Waterhouse v. Hopkins,* 490 U.S. 228, 109 S.Ct. 1775, 104 L.Ed.2d 268 (1989), made the sweeping statement in a footnote: "[D]ecisions pertaining to advancement to partnership are, of course, subject to challenge under Title VII."

2. INDIRECT PROTECTION: PAST AND FUTURE "EMPLOYEES"

a. *Robinson v. Shell Oil Co.,* 519 U.S. 337, 117 S.Ct. 843, 136 L.Ed.2d 808 (1997), held that the term "employee" covers a former employee to the extent that defendant—a covered "employer"—interfered with the former employee's *securing employment elsewhere* by providing poor references in retaliation for the "employee" having filed discrimination charges against the defendant, the former "employer."

b. *Association of Mexican–American Educators v. California,* 231 F.3d 572 (9th Cir. 2000)(en banc), held that as state certification was effectively required for employment as a public school teacher, the act of denying a teaching certificate was an "employment" action subject to Title VII scrutiny. California, an "employer," by its action in denying a certificate was impairing the ability of individuals to secure "employment" at other employers.

c. *Woodard v. Virginia Bd. of Bar Examiners,* 598 F.2d 1345 (4th Cir. 1979), is contrary, holding that failure of an applicant to be admitted to practice law was not an "employment" action for which the state bar examiners could be liable under Title VII.

3. THE RECONSTRUCTION ERA CIVIL RIGHTS ACT

Unlike the three core statutes, 42 U.S.C. § 1981 does not require an employer/employee relationship, but applies to *all "contracts."* Not only is there no requirement of an "employment" relationship there is no minimum number of "employees" required for coverage. Thus, denial, termination, or discrimination in "independent," as well as employment "contracts," because of" race violate this statute.

4. STUDENTS AND (OTHER) PRISONERS

Individuals who have a relationship with an "employer" that is predominately educational or penal in nature are not "employees" of that "employer." *Vanskike v. Peters,* 974 F.2d 806 (7th Cir. 1992) (Fair Labor Standards Act). However, if the services performed are not a part of the educational or rehabilitation process, and distinct compensation is paid for the work, the individual could be considered an "employee." *Baker v. McNeil Island Corrections Center,* 859 F.2d 124 (9th Cir. 1988).

5. TEMPORARY, "LEASED," "SHARED," AND SEASONAL WORKERS

Many employers engage "temporary" or "seasonal" workers to meet their staffing needs. Often this is accomplished by the client, or leasing firm, contracting with a staffing agency which supplies the requested workers. The staffing firm may be more than a simple referral service or "employment agency." Rather the staffing firm may pre-select workers, provide or manage benefits of the worker being assigned to a job at the client firm. The employer where the work is actually performed—the client firm—directs the day-to-day job performance. If performance of the worker is deemed unsatisfactory, the worker is referred back to the staffing firm, who makes an independent decision as to whether the worker will be referred for future jobs. When the temporary job ends, the worker returns for future referrals to other employers. As the work is temporary, courts may mischaracterize the worker as an independent contractor. However, when they perform work, side-by-side, with other employees, the temporary worker should be considered an employee of the client firm. *Vizcaino v. Microsoft,* 120 F.3d 1006 (9th Cir. 1997). Under some circumstances, the worker can *also* been an employee of the staffing firm, depending on factors such as control and compensation arrangements, making the firms "joint employers" of the worker, and thus jointly liable for any discriminatory actions. *Redd v. Summers,* 232 F.3d 933 (D.C.Cir. 2000).

C. "LABOR ORGANIZATIONS" AND "EMPLOYMENT AGENCIES"

1. **Labor Organizations** with the defined number of "employees" will be an "employer" in their employment relations, subject to the obligations imposed on "employers."

In the capacity as a "labor organization" three kinds of union discrimination are proscribed: (1) excluding or expelling from union membership, or otherwise discriminating in the *internal affairs* of the union; (2) *referrals* for employment or segregating or classifying in a way that tends *to deprive individuals of employment opportunities*; and (3) causing or attempting to *cause employer discrimination* that would violate the acts. 42 U.S.C. § 2000e–2(c).

Coverage of a "labor organization" is more complex than that for "employers." Broadly stated, however, a labor organization is one that "exists for the purpose of dealing with employers concerning terms and conditions of employment" and, wholly apart from the number of its employees, has 15 or more *members*. 42 U.S.C. §§ 2000e–(d) and (e). In addition to 15 *members*, the organization must seek to represent employees of a defined "employer" (as defined above).

2. Employment Agencies: Employment agencies with the requisite number of employees, will be an "employer" in their employment relations with their own workers.

Regardless of the number of employees, however, an "employment agency" will be covered in its referral services if it regularly undertakes, with or without compensation, "to procure employees for *an employer*." Procuring "employees" for an "employer" must be the primary purpose of the entity and meet a "common sense" conception of the term. *See, e.g., Greenfield v. Field Enterprises, Inc.,* 4 FEP Cases 548 (N.D.Ill. 1972) (newspaper printing "help wanted" advertisements of employers does not make the newspaper a covered employment agency.); *Kaplowitz v. University of Chicago,* 387 F.Supp. 42 (N.D. Ill. 1974) (university, apart from its career service/placement department, is not an employment agency).

An entity covered as an "employment agency" may not discriminate in its referrals, engage in its own discriminatory "classifications," or honor discriminatory requests from employers. 42 U.S.C. § 2000e–2(b).

CHAPTER 2

PROTECTED CLASSES

■ ■ ■

A. RACE AND COLOR

McDONALD v. SANTA FE TRAIL TRANSPORTATION CO.

Supreme Court of the United States, 1976
427 U.S. 273, 96 S.Ct. 2574, 49 L.Ed.2d 493

JUSTICE MARSHALL delivered the opinion of the Court.

I

* * * On September 26, 1970, petitioners, both white, and Charles Jackson, a Negro employee of Santa Fe, were jointly and severally charged with misappropriating 60 one-gallon cans of antifreeze which was part of a shipment Santa Fe was carrying for one of its customers. Six days later, petitioners were fired by Santa Fe, while Jackson was retained. * * *

[T]he District Court * * * concluded, * * * that "the dismissal of white employees charged with misappropriating company property while not dismissing a similarly charged Negro employee does not raise a claim upon which Title VII relief may be granted."

The Court of Appeals affirmed [on different grounds] * * *. We reverse.

II

Title VII of the Civil Rights Act of 1964 prohibits the discharge of "any individual" because of "such individual's race," § 703(a)(1). Its terms are not limited to discrimination against members of any particular race. Thus, although we were not there confronted with racial discrimination against whites, we described the Act in *Griggs v. Duke Power Co.* as prohibiting "[d]iscriminatory preference for *any* [racial] group, *minority* or *majority.*" Similarly the EEOC, whose interpretations are entitled to great deference, has consistently interpreted Title VII to proscribe racial discrimination in private employment against whites on the same terms as racial discrimination against nonwhites, holding that to proceed otherwise would "constitute a derogation of the Commission's Congressional mandate to eliminate all practices which operate to disadvantage the employment opportunities of any group protected by Title VII, including Caucasians." EEOC Decision No. 74B31.

This conclusion is in accord with uncontradicted legislative history to the effect that Title VII was intended to "cover white men and white women and all Americans," 110 Cong.Rec. 2578 (1964) (remarks of Rep. Celler), and create an "obligation not to discriminate against whites. We therefore hold today that Title VII prohibits racial discrimination against the white petitioners in this case upon the same standards as would be applicable were they Negroes and Jackson white.[1]

* * *

At this stage of the litigation the claim against Local 988 must go with the claim against Santa Fe, for in substance the complaint alleges that the union shirked its duty properly to represent McDonald, and instead "acquiesced and/or joined in" Santa Fe's alleged racial discrimination against him. Local 988 argues that as a matter of law it should not be subject to liability under Title VII in a situation, such as this, where some but not all culpable employees are ultimately discharged on account of joint misconduct, because in representing all the affected employees in their relations with the employer, the union may necessarily have to compromise by securing retention of only some. We reject the argument. The same reasons which prohibit an employer from discriminating on the basis of race among the culpable employees apply equally to the union; and whatever factors the mechanisms of compromise may legitimately take into account in mitigating discipline of some employees, under Title VII race may not be among them.

Thus, we conclude that the District Court erred in dismissing both petitioners' Title VII claims against Santa Fe, and petitioner McDonald's Title VII claim against Local 988.

III

Title 42 U.S.C. § 1981 provides in pertinent part: "All persons within the jurisdiction of the United States shall have the same right in every State and Territory to make and enforce contracts * * * as is enjoyed by white citizens. * * *." We have previously held, where discrimination against Negroes was in question, that § 1981 affords a federal remedy against

---

1. Local 988 explicitly concedes that it makes no difference that petitioners are white and Jackson Negro, rather than the other way around. Santa Fe, while conceding that "across-the-board discrimination in favor of minorities could never be condoned consistent with Title VII," contends nevertheless that "such discrimination * * * in isolated cases which cannot reasonably be said to burden whites as a class unduly," such as is alleged here, "may be acceptable." We cannot agree. There is no exception in the terms of the Act for isolated cases; on the contrary, "Title VII tolerates no racial discrimination, subtle or otherwise." McDonnell Douglas Corp. v. Green.

Santa Fe disclaims that the actions challenged here were any part of an affirmative action program, and we emphasize that we do not consider here the permissibility of such a program, whether judicially required or otherwise prompted.

discrimination in private employment on the basis of race, and respondents do not contend otherwise. The question here is whether § 1981 prohibits racial discrimination in private employment against whites as well as nonwhites.

While neither of the courts below elaborated its reasons for not applying § 1981 to racial discrimination against white persons, respondents suggest two lines of argument to support that judgment. First, they argue that by operation of the phrase "as is enjoyed by white citizens," § 1981 unambiguously limits itself to the protection of nonwhite persons against racial discrimination. Second, they contend that such a reading is consistent with the legislative history of the provision, which derives its operative language from § 1 of the Civil Rights Act of 1866. The 1866 statute, they assert, was concerned predominantly with assuring specified civil rights to the former Negro slaves freed by virtue of the Thirteenth Amendment, and not at all with protecting the corresponding civil rights of white persons.

We find neither argument persuasive. Rather, our examination of the language and history of § 1981 convinces us that § 1981 is applicable to racial discrimination in private employment against white persons.

First, we cannot accept the view that the terms of § 1981 exclude its application to racial discrimination against white persons. On the contrary, the statute explicitly applies to "*all* persons" (emphasis added), including white persons. While a mechanical reading of the phrase "as is enjoyed by white citizens" would seem to lend support to respondents' reading of the statute, we have previously described this phrase simply as emphasizing "the racial character of the rights being protected." In any event, whatever ambiguity there may be in the language of § 1981 is clarified by an examination of the legislative history of § 1981's language as it was originally forged in the Civil Rights Act of 1866. * * *

* * * Unlikely as it might have appeared in 1866 that white citizens would encounter substantial racial discrimination of the sort proscribed under the Act, the statutory structure and legislative history persuade us that the 39th Congress was intent upon establishing in the federal law a broader principle than would have been necessary simply to meet the particular and immediate plight of the newly freed Negro slaves. And while the statutory language has been somewhat streamlined in reenactment and codification, there is no indication that § 1981 is intended to provide any less than the Congress enacted in 1866 regarding racial discrimination against white persons. Thus, we conclude that the District Court erred in dismissing petitioners' claims under § 1981 on the ground that the protections of that provision are unavailable to white persons.

The judgment of the Court of Appeals for the Fifth Circuit is reversed, and the case is remanded for further proceedings consistent with this opinion.

ROGERS v. AMERICAN AIRLINES

United States District Court, Southern District of New York, 1981
527 F.Supp. 229

SOFAER, DISTRICT JUDGE.

Plaintiff is a black woman who seeks $10,000 damages, injunctive, and declaratory relief against enforcement of a grooming policy of the defendant American Airlines that prohibits employees in certain employment categories from wearing an all-braided hairstyle. Plaintiff has been an American Airlines employee for approximately eleven years, and has been an airport operations agent for over one year. Her duties involve extensive passenger contact, including greeting passengers, issuing boarding passes, and checking luggage. She alleges that the policy violates her rights under the Thirteenth Amendment of the United States Constitution, under Title VII of the Civil Rights Act, and under 42 U.S.C. § 1981 (1976), in that it discriminates against her as a woman, and more specifically as a black woman. She claims that denial of the right to wear her hair in the "corn row" style intrudes upon her rights and discriminates against her. Plaintiff has exhausted her administrative remedies and has been issued a right to sue letter by the Equal Employment Opportunity Commission ("EEOC").

Defendants move to dismiss plaintiff's claims. * * *

* * * Plaintiff's assertion that the policy has practical effect only with respect to women is not supported by any factual allegations. Many men have hair longer than many women. Some men have hair long enough to wear in braids if they choose to do so. * * *.

The considerations with respect to plaintiff's race discrimination claim would clearly be the same, except for plaintiff's assertion that the "corn row" style has a special significance for black women. She contends that it "has been, historically, a fashion and style adopted by Black American women, reflective of cultural, historical essence of the Black women in American society." "The style was 'popularized' so to speak, within the larger society, when [the actress] Cicely Tyson adopted the same for an appearance on nationally viewed Academy Awards presentation several years ago.... It was and is analogous to the public statement by the late Malcolm X regarding the Afro hair style.... At the bottom line, the completely braided hair style, sometimes referred to as corn rows, has been and continues to be part of the cultural and historical essence of Black American women." "There can be little doubt that, if American adopted a policy which foreclosed Black women/all women from wearing hair styled as an 'Afro/bush,' that policy would have very pointedly racial dynamics and consequences reflecting a vestige of slavery unwilling to die (that is, a master mandate that one wear hair divorced from one's historical and cultural perspective and otherwise consistent with the 'white master' dominated society and preference thereof)."

Plaintiff is entitled to a presumption that her arguments, largely repeated in her affidavit, are true. But the grooming policy applies equally to members of all races, and plaintiff does not allege that an all-braided hair style is worn exclusively or even predominantly by black people. Moreover, it is proper to note that defendants have alleged without contravention that plaintiff first appeared at work in the all-braided hairstyle on or about September 25, 1980, soon after the style had been popularized by a white actress in the film "10." Plaintiff may be correct that an employer's policy prohibiting the "Afro/bush" style might offend Title VII and section 1981. But if so, this chiefly would be because banning a natural hairstyle would implicate the policies underlying the prohibition of discrimination on the basis of immutable characteristics. In any event, an all-braided hairstyle is a different matter. It is not the product of natural hair growth but of artifice. An all-braided hair style is an "easily changed characteristic," and, even if socioculturally associated with a particular race or nationality, is not an impermissible basis for distinctions in the application of employment practices by an employer. * * *

Although the Act may shield "employees' psychological as well as economic fringes" from employer abuse, *see Rogers v. EEOC*, 454 F.2d 234, 238 (5th Cir. 1971) (optical clinic's practice of segregating patients on the basis of national origin may create a "discriminatory atmosphere" in violation of minority employees' rights), plaintiff's allegations do not amount to charging American with "a practice of creating a working environment heavily charged with ethnic or racial discrimination," or one "so heavily polluted with discrimination as to destroy completely the emotional and psychological stability of minority group workers...." * * * Moreover, the airline did not require plaintiff to restyle her hair. It suggested that she could wear her hair as she liked while off duty, and permitted her to pull her hair into a bun and wrap a hairpiece around the bun during working hours.

This action is dismissed * * *.

NOTES

1. *Native Americans*: Discrimination favoring or harming indigenous Americans (Eskimos, Native Hawaiians, American "Indians") is "race discrimination." *Weahkee v. Perry,* 587 F.2d 1256 (D.C.Cir.1978). However, § 703(i) of Title VII provides: "Nothing contained in this title shall apply to *any business or enterprise on or near an Indian reservation* with respect to any publicly announced employment practice of such business or enterprise under which a preferential treatment is given to any individual because he is an Indian living on or near a reservation." 42 U.S.C. § 2000e–2(i). Moreover, as § 701(b) of Title VII excludes Indian tribes from the definition of "employer" employment practices of tribes are not subject to the statutory proscriptions. *EEOC v. Fond du Lac Heavy Equipment & Const. Co.,* 986 F.2d 246 (8th Cir.1993).

2. *"Color"*: Title VII reaches not only "race" but also discrimination because of "color." Presumably, it would proscribe discrimination by an

African–American supervisor, who does not discriminate against blacks generally, or against whites, but favors persons of African heritage with dark skin over persons of African heritage with light skin. *Walker v. Secretary of Treasury, IRS,* 713 F.Supp. 403 (N.D.Ga.1989).

PARR v. WOODMEN OF THE WORLD LIFE INSURANCE CO.

United States Court of Appeals, Eleventh Circuit, 1986
791 F.2d 888

HATCHETT, CIRCUIT JUDGE:

Appellant, Don L. Parr, a white man married to a black woman, seeks reversal of the judgment of the district court dismissing his complaint against Woodmen of the World Life Insurance Company (Woodmen), in which he alleged that the company discriminated against him "because of race" in violation of Title VII of the Civil Rights Act of 1964, and 42 U.S.C. § 1981. Finding that Parr's complaint set forth sufficient allegations to state a claim under both statutes, we reverse.

Background

In late May or early June of 1982, Parr applied for a position as an insurance salesman with Woodmen. He had experience as an insurance salesman and was well-qualified for the position. The Woodmen manager who interviewed Parr told him that he would probably be hired, but that he would have to return for a second interview. The manager also told Parr that Woodmen did not employ or sell insurance to black people. Parr told the employment service which had set up his interview of the manager's remarks and informed the employment service that he was married to a black woman. A representative of the employment service told Woodmen of Parr's interracial marriage, whereupon Woodmen's manager informed the employment service that he would advise against hiring Parr. Parr was not hired.

A. *Section 1981 Claim*

* * *

Parr's issue, whether a claim of discrimination based upon an interracial marriage is cognizable under section 1981, is not a novel one. This court's predecessor addressed the precise issue in *Faraca v. Clements,* 506 F.2d 956 (5th Cir.1975). Faraca, a white man married to a black woman, brought a section 1981 action against the director of the Georgia Mental Retardation Center. The director had refused to hire Faraca because of his interracial marriage. The former Fifth Circuit, holding that section 1981 proscribed such conduct, upheld the judgment of the district court awarding Faraca compensatory damages. *Faraca* is binding on this court.

Other circuits that have considered the issue agree with the former Fifth Circuit that a claim of discrimination due to an interracial relationship is cognizable under section 1981.

In light of this precedent, Woodmen only contends that we should not recognize a claim of discrimination based on an interracial marriage or association under section 1981 because such a claim should not be recognized under Title VII. This contention is without merit. We hold that section 1981 prohibits discrimination based upon an interracial marriage or association, and that the district court erred in dismissing Parr's complaint which alleged such discrimination.

B.   The Title VII Claim

Title VII prohibits racially discriminatory employment practices. The statute has been held to prohibit discrimination against white as well as black persons. *McDonald v. Santa Fe Trail Transportation Company,* 427 U.S. 273, 96 S.Ct. 2574, 49 L.Ed.2d 493 (1976).

In dismissing Parr's action, the district court simply stated that "[t]he alleged discrimination complained of is not proscribed by Title VII." Woodmen contends that the district court's holding is correct because Parr did not allege that he was discriminated against because of *his* race. Parr contends that the district court erred because Title VII is to be broadly construed, and a party need not specifically allege that he was discriminated against because of *his* race, but only show that adverse actions taken against him involved racial considerations.

* * * In *Ripp v. Dobbs Houses, Inc.,* 366 F.Supp. 205 (N.D.Ala.1973), a white male who was discharged because of his association with black employees brought an action against his employer pursuant to Title VII. Stressing that Title VII prohibits discrimination against an individual because of "such individual's race," the court dismissed the complaint because "plaintiff makes no complaint that he has suffered any detriment on account of *his* race." * * *

In *Whitney v. Greater New York Corporation of Seventh Day Adventists,* 401 F.Supp. 1363 (S.D.N.Y.1975), where a white woman claimed that she was discharged in violation of Title VII because she maintained a social relationship with a black man, the court expressly rejected the *Ripp* analysis, stating:

> Manifestly, if Whitney was discharged because, as alleged, the defendant disapproved of a social relationship between a white woman and a black man, the plaintiff's race was as much a factor in the decision to fire her as that of her friend. Specifying as she does that she was discharged because she, a white woman, associated with a black, her complaint falls within the statutory language that she was "[d]ischarged * * * because of [her] race."

* * *

We * * * find *Whitney's* logic irrefutable. Where a plaintiff claims discrimination based upon an interracial marriage or association, he alleges, by definition, that he has been discriminated against because of *his* race. It makes no difference whether the plaintiff specifically alleged in his complaint that he has been discriminated against because of *his* race. As this court's predecessor stated in *Culpepper v. Reynolds Metals Co.*, 421 F.2d 888, 891 (5th Cir.1970):

> Title VII of the 1964 Civil Rights Act provides us with a clear mandate from Congress that no longer will the United States tolerate this form of discrimination. It is, therefore, the duty of the courts to make sure that the Act works, and the intent of Congress is not hampered by a combination of a strict construction of the statute in a *battle with semantics.*

* * * Woodmen argues that unlike the plaintiffs in *Whitney* * * * Parr cannot claim that *but for* his race being different from his wife's, he would have been hired. In other words, Woodmen contends that Parr cannot state a claim based upon discrimination due to an interracial relationship because he also claimed that Woodmen discriminated against blacks. Woodmen argues that if Parr's allegations are true, had Parr been black, he still would not have been hired. Consequently, in Woodmen's view, Parr's race was of no significance in the hiring decision, and thus his claim should not be cognizable. Woodmen's contentions are not persuasive. Had Parr been black, he would not have been hired, but that is a lawsuit for another day. Parr alleged that he was discriminated against because of his interracial marriage. Title VII proscribes race-conscious discriminatory practices. It would be folly for this court to hold that a plaintiff cannot state a claim under Title VII for discrimination based on an interracial marriage because, had the plaintiff been a member of the spouse's race, the plaintiff would still not have been hired.

Finally, while we have noted that section 1981 and Title VII are not coextensive in coverage, this court has held that when the two statutes are used as parallel bases of relief, their legal elements are identical. Thus, it would be inconsistent to hold that Parr could state a claim of discrimination based upon an interracial marriage pursuant to section 1981, but not Title VII.

Accordingly, we reverse and remand.

NOTES

1. *Marriage only?* The reasoning of the principal case is not limited to marriage or family relationships, but has been applied to a white employee who was harassed because of her perceived friendly relationships to black employees. *Barrett v. Whirlpool Corp.*, 556 F.3d 502 (6th Cir. 2009).

2. *Favoritism for friends and neighbors:*

a. **Roberts v. Gadsden Mem. Hosp.,** 835 F.2d 793 (11th Cir. 1988), involved a white supervisor who routinely filled vacancies with his "drinking buddies" who all were white. The court held that such "good old boy" methods of hiring in a social environment where races were not socially integrated necessarily amounted to race discrimination.

b. **Bonilla v. Oakland Scavenger Co.,** 697 F.2d 1297 (9th Cir. 1982), held that when all the shareholders of the corporate employer were white family members and their friends, granting special benefits to employees of the employer who were shareholders was race discrimination.

B. "NATIONAL ORIGIN"

1. GENERALLY: TITLE VII: CITIZENSHIP AND ALIENAGE

ESPINOZA v. FARAH MANUFACTURING CO.

Supreme Court of the United States, 1973
414 U.S. 86, 94 S.Ct. 334, 38 L.Ed.2d 287

JUSTICE MARSHALL delivered the opinion of the Court.

This case involves interpretation of the phrase "national origin" in Tit. VII of the Civil Rights Act of 1964. Petitioner Cecilia Espinoza is a lawfully admitted resident alien who was born in and remains a citizen of Mexico. She resides in San Antonio, Texas, with her husband, Rudolfo Espinoza, a United States citizen. In July 1969, Mrs. Espinoza sought employment as a seamstress at the San Antonio division of respondent Farah Manufacturing Co. Her employment application was rejected on the basis of a longstanding company policy against the employment of aliens. After exhausting their administrative remedies with the Equal Employment Opportunity Commission, petitioners commenced this suit in the District Court alleging that respondent had discriminated against Mrs. Espinoza because of her "national origin" in violation of § 703 of Tit. VII. The District Court granted petitioners' motion for summary judgment, holding that a refusal to hire because of lack of citizenship constitutes discrimination on the basis of "national origin." The Court of Appeals reversed, concluding that the statutory phrase "national origin" did not embrace citizenship. We granted the writ to resolve this question of statutory construction, and now affirm.

Section 703 makes it "an unlawful employment practice for an employer to fail or refuse to hire * * * any individual * * * because of such individual's race, color, religion, sex, or national origin." Certainly the plain language of the statute supports the result reached by the Court of Appeals. The term "national origin" on its face refers to the country where a person was born, or, more broadly, the country from which his or her ancestors came.

The statute's legislative history, though quite meager in this respect, fully supports this construction. The only direct definition given the phrase "national origin" is the following remark made on the floor of the House of Representatives by Congressman Roosevelt, Chairman of the House Subcommittee which reported the bill: "It means the country from which you or your forebears came. * * * You may come from Poland, Czechoslovakia, England, France, or any other country." 110 Cong. Rec. 2549 (1964). We also note that an earlier version of § 703 had referred to discrimination because of "race, color, religion, national origin, or *ances-*

try." The deletion of the word "ancestry" from the final version was not intended as a material change, *see* H.R.Rep. No. 914, 88th Cong., 1st Sess. 87 (1963), suggesting that the terms "national origin" and "ancestry" were considered synonymous.

There are other compelling reasons to believe that Congress did not intend the term "national origin" to embrace citizenship requirements. Since 1914, the Federal Government itself, through Civil Service Commission regulations, has engaged in what amounts to discrimination against aliens by denying them the right to enter competitive examination for federal employment. But it has never been suggested that the citizenship requirement for federal employment constitutes discrimination because of national origin, even though since 1943, various Executive Orders have expressly prohibited discrimination on the basis of national origin in Federal Government employment.

Moreover, § 701(b) of Tit. VII, in language closely paralleling § 703, makes it "the policy of the United States to insure equal employment opportunities for Federal employees without discrimination because of * * * national origin * * *." The legislative history of that section reveals no mention of any intent on Congress' part to reverse the longstanding practice of requiring federal employees to be United States citizens. To the contrary, there is every indication that no such reversal was intended. Congress itself has on several occasions since 1964 enacted statutes barring aliens from federal employment. The Treasury, Postal Service, and General Government Appropriation Act, 1973, for example, provides that "no part of any appropriation contained in this or any other Act shall be used to pay the compensation of any officer or employee of the Government of the United States * * * unless such person (1) is a citizen of the United States."

To interpret the term "national origin" to embrace citizenship requirements would require us to conclude that Congress itself has repeatedly flouted its own declaration of policy. This Court cannot lightly find such a breach of faith. So far as federal employment is concerned, we think it plain that Congress has assumed that the ban on national-origin discrimination in § 701(b) did not affect the historical practice of requiring citizenship as a condition of employment. And there is no reason to believe Congress intended the term "national origin" in § 703 to have any broader scope.

* * *

The District Court drew primary support for its holding from an interpretative guideline issued by the Equal Employment Opportunity Commission which provides:

"Because discrimination on the basis of citizenship has the effect of discriminating on the basis of national origin, a lawfully immigrated alien who is domiciled or residing in this country may not be discriminated against on the basis of his citizenship * * *." 29 CFR § 1606.1(d) (1972).

Like the Court of Appeals, we have no occasion here to question the general validity of this guideline insofar as it can be read as an expression of the Commission's belief that there may be many situations where discrimination on the basis of citizenship would have the effect of discriminating on the basis of national origin. In some instances, for example, a citizenship requirement might be but one part of a wider scheme of unlawful national-origin discrimination. In other cases, an employer might use a citizenship test as a pretext to disguise what is in fact national-origin discrimination. Certainly Tit. VII prohibits discrimination on the basis of citizenship whenever it has the purpose or effect of discriminating on the basis of national origin. "The Act proscribes not only overt discrimination but also practices that are fair in form, but discriminatory in operation." *Griggs v. Duke Power Co.*, 401 U.S. 424, 431, 91 S.Ct. 849, 853, 28 L.Ed.2d 158 (1971).

It is equally clear, however, that these principles lend no support to petitioners in this case. There is no indication in the record that Farah's policy against employment of aliens had the purpose or effect of discriminating against persons of Mexican national origin.[2] It is conceded that Farah accepts employees of Mexican origin, provided the individual concerned has become an American citizen. Indeed, the District Court found that persons of Mexican ancestry make up more than 96% of the employees at the company's San Antonio division, and 97% of those doing the work for which Mrs. Espinoza applied. While statistics such as these do not automatically shield an employer from a charge of unlawful discrimination, the plain fact of the matter is that Farah does not discriminate against persons of Mexican national origin with respect to employment in the job Mrs. Espinoza sought. She was denied employment, not because of the country of her origin, but because she had not yet achieved United States citizenship. In fact, the record shows that the worker hired in place of Mrs. Espinoza was a citizen with a Spanish surname.

The Commission's guideline may have significance for a wide range of situations, but not for a case such as this where its very premise "that discrimination on the basis of citizenship has the effect of discrimination on the basis of national origin" is not borne out.[3] It is also significant to

---

2. There is no suggestion, for example, that the company refused to hire aliens of Mexican or Spanish-speaking background while hiring those of other national origins. Respondent's president informed the EEOC's Regional Director investigating the charge that once in its history the company had made a single exception to its policy against hiring aliens, but the nationality of the individual concerned is not revealed in the record. While the company asks job applicants whether they are United States citizens, it makes no inquiry as to their national origin.

3. It is suggested that a refusal to hire an alien always disadvantages that person because of the country of his birth. A person born in the United States, the argument goes, automatically obtains citizenship at birth, while those born elsewhere can acquire citizenship only through a long and sometimes difficult process. The answer to this argument is that it is not the employer who places the burdens of naturalization on those born outside the country, but Congress itself, through laws enacted pursuant to its constitutional power "[t]o establish an uniform Rule of Naturalization." U.S. Const., Art. 1, 8, cl. 4.

Petitioners' reliance on Phillips v. Martin Marietta Corp., 400 U.S. 542, 91 S.Ct. 496, 27 L.Ed.2d 613 (1971), is misplaced for similar reasons. In Phillips we held it unlawful under 703 to have "one hiring policy for women and another for men * * *." Farah, however, does not have a

note that the Commission itself once held a different view as to the meaning of the phrase "national origin." When first confronted with the question, the Commission, through its General Counsel, said: " 'National origin' refers to the country from which the individual or his forebears came * * *, not to whether or not he is a United States citizen * * *." The Commission's more recent interpretation of the statute in the guideline relied on by the District Court is no doubt entitled to great deference, but that deference must have limits where, as here, application of the guideline would be inconsistent with an obvious congressional intent not to reach the employment practice in question. Courts need not defer to an administrative construction of a statute where there are "compelling indications that it is wrong."

Finally, petitioners seek to draw support from the fact that Tit. VII protects all individuals from unlawful discrimination, whether or not they are citizens of the United States. We agree that aliens are protected from discrimination under the Act. That result may be derived not only from the use of the term "any individual" in § 703, but also as a negative inference from the exemption in § 702, which provides that Tit. VII "shall not apply to an employer with respect to the employment of aliens outside any State * * *." Title VII was clearly intended to apply with respect to the employment of aliens inside any State.

The question posed in the present case, however, is not whether aliens are protected from illegal discrimination under the Act, but what kinds of discrimination the Act makes illegal. Certainly it would be unlawful for an employer to discriminate against aliens because of race, color, religion, sex, or national origin for example, by hiring aliens of Anglo–Saxon background but refusing to hire those of Mexican or Spanish ancestry. Aliens are protected from illegal discrimination under the Act, but nothing in the Act makes it illegal to discriminate on the basis of citizenship or alienage.

We agree with the Court of Appeals that neither the language of the Act, nor its history, nor the specific facts of this case indicate that respondent has engaged in unlawful discrimination because of national origin.[5]

Affirmed.

JUSTICE DOUGLAS, dissenting.

It is odd that the Court which holds that a State may not bar an alien from the practice of law or deny employment to aliens can read a federal

different policy for the foreign born than for those born in the United States. It requires of all that they be citizens of the United States.

5. Petitioners argue that respondent's policy of discriminating against aliens is prohibited by 42 U.S.C.A. 1981, which provides: "All persons within the jurisdiction of the United States shall have the same right in every State and Territory to make and enforce contracts, to sue, be parties, give evidence, and to the full and equal benefit of all laws and proceedings for the security of persons and property as is enjoyed by white citizens * * *." This issue was neither raised before the courts below nor presented in the petition for a writ of certiorari. Accordingly we express no views thereon.

statute that prohibits discrimination in employment on account of "national origin" so as to permit discrimination against aliens.

Alienage results from one condition only: being born outside the United States. Those born within the country are citizens from birth. It could not be more clear that Farah's policy of excluding aliens is *de facto* a policy of preferring those who were born in this country. Therefore the construction placed upon the "national origin" provision is inconsistent with the construction this Court has placed upon the same Act's protections for persons denied employment on account of race or sex. * * *

The construction placed upon the statute in the majority opinion is an extraordinary departure from prior cases, and it is opposed by the Equal Employment Opportunity Commission, the agency provided by law with the responsibility of enforcing the Act's protections. The Commission takes the only permissible position: that discrimination on the basis of alienage *always* has the effect of discrimination on the basis of national origin. Refusing to hire an individual because he is an alien "is discrimination based on birth outside the United States and is thus discrimination based on national origin in violation of Title VII." * * * The Commission's interpretation of the statute is entitled to great weight.

* * *

Mrs. Espinoza is a permanent resident alien, married to an American citizen, and her children will be native-born American citizens. But that first generation has the greatest adjustments to make to their new country. Their unfamiliarity with America makes them the most vulnerable to exploitation and discriminatory treatment. * * *

The majority decides today that in passing sweeping legislation guaranteeing equal job opportunities, the Congress intended to help only the immigrant's children, excluding [the immigrant]. I cannot impute that niggardly an intent to Congress.

NOTES

1. *Hyphenated Americans:* Title VII prohibits discrimination against or in favor of Americans based on their family origins, such as Italian–Americans, Irish–Americans, Slavic–Americans, etc. *Berke v. Ohio Dep't of Public Welfare,* 628 F.2d 980 (6th Cir.1980). Discrimination against *persons* with Hispanic surnames is national origin discrimination, and may also be a form of race or color discrimination. *Manzanares v. Safeway Stores, Inc.,* 593 F.2d 968, 971 (10th Cir.1979).

2. *Origins without a nation:* "National origin" has not been construed literally to be limited to existing nation states. "National origin" includes distinct regional or ethnic origins which may not constitute recognized nations, such as Palestine or Armenia. *Pejic v. Hughes Helicopters,* 840 F.2d 667 (9th Cir.1988). Discrimination against a person because they are Roma ("Gypsy") or who are Cajuns (French speaking Americans whose ancestors immigrated to Louisiana two hundred years ago from Acadia, now the

Canadian province of Nova Scotia), is "national origin" discrimination. *Roach v. Dresser,* 494 F.Supp. 215 (W.D.La. 1980).

Puerto Rico is a Commonwealth of the United States. Puerto Ricans are Americans who may immigrate freely to the mainland and travel on U.S. passports. Puerto Rico is not recognized internationally as an independent nation. Yet discrimination on the basis of Puerto Rican origins is "national origin." Accordingly, a compensation system whereby those working in Puerto Rico were paid less than employees working on the U.S. mainland was national origin discrimination. *Earnhardt v. Commonwealth of Puerto Rico,* 744 F.2d 1 (1st Cir.1984). *Cf. Ramos v. Baxter Health Care Corp., Inc.,* 360 F.3d 53 (1st Cir. 2004).

2. LANGUAGE

***Hernandez v. New York,* 500 U.S. 352, 371, 111 S.Ct. 1859, 1872–73, 114 L.Ed.2d 395 (1991):** "It may well be, for certain ethnic groups, and in some communities, that proficiency in a particular language, like skin color, should be treated as a surrogate for race under an equal protection analysis."

The position of the EEOC is:

"The primary language of an individual is often an essential national origin characteristic. Census data utilizes the language spoken in the household as a primary determinate in classifying the national origin of family members." 29 C.F.R. § 1606.7.

RODRIGUEZ v. FEDEX FREIGHT EAST, INC.

United States Court of Appeals, Sixth Circuit, 2007
487 F.3d 1001

Moore, Circuit Judge.

Plaintiff–Appellant Jose Antonio Rodriguez ("Rodriguez") sued his former employer, Defendant–Appellee FedEx Freight East, Inc. ("FedEx"), in a Michigan state court, alleging that FedEx discriminated and retaliated against him on the basis of his race, in violation of Michigan's Elliott–Larsen Civil Rights Act. Citing the parties' diversity of citizenship, FedEx removed the suit to the United States District Court for the Eastern District of Michigan. * * * [T]he district court[dismissed plaintiff's claim].

I. BACKGROUND

Rodriguez began working * * * as a truck driver in 1999, under the supervision of Regional Human Resource Manager Rodney Adkinson ("Adkinson"). * * *

In June 2002, Rodriguez told Adkinson that he (Rodriguez) was interested in becoming a FedEx supervisor. Adkinson recommended that Rodriguez take FedEx's Leadership Apprentice Course ("LAC"), and Rodriguez subsequently enrolled in that program. While Rodriguez was taking LAC classes, three supervisory positions became vacant. According to then-Customer Service Manager Jon McKibbon ("McKibbon"), Rodriguez applied and was twice interviewed for at least one of those positions. McKibbon found Rodriguez to be qualified for the position and claims that he would have hired Rodriguez but for Adkinson's stated concern that Rodriguez's accent and speech pattern would adversely impact Rodriguez's ability to rise through the company ranks. Former FedEx Manager Dale Williams ("Williams") similarly avers that, when he asked Adkinson why Rodriguez had not been selected for promotion, Adkinson replied with disparaging remarks concerning Rodriguez's "language" and "how he speaks" and stated that Rodriguez was difficult to understand. * * *

* * *

III. ANALYSIS

* * *

B. Rodriguez's Discrimination Claims

1. Failure to Promote

"Cases brought pursuant to [Michigan state law] are analyzed under the same evidentiary framework used in Title VII cases." "Intentional discrimination can be proven by direct and circumstantial evidence." "In discrimination cases, direct evidence is that evidence which, if believed, requires the conclusion that unlawful discrimination was at least a motivating factor in the employer's actions." "Consistent with this definition, direct evidence of discrimination does not require a factfinder to draw any inferences in order to conclude that the challenged employment action was motivated at least in part by prejudice against members of the protected group." "In direct evidence cases, once a plaintiff shows that the prohibited classification played a motivating part in the employment decision, the burden of both production and persuasion shifts to the employer to prove that it would have terminated the employee even if it had not been motivated by impermissible discrimination." *Nguyen v. City of Cleveland,* 229 F.3d 559, 563 (6th Cir.2000).

* * *

Our precedents, though admittedly not perfectly clear concerning this issue, suggest that the evidence is direct. In *Ang v. Procter & Gamble Co.,* 932 F.2d 540 (6th Cir.1991), we stated that "accent and national origin are inextricably intertwined." We also noted that "[t]he [Equal Employment Opportunity Commission ("EEOC")] recognizes linguistic discrimination as national origin discrimination" and that our earlier opinion in *Berke v. Ohio Dep't of Pub. Welfare,* 628 F.2d 980, 981 (6th Cir.1980), "also recognized that discrimination based on manner of speaking can be national origin discrimination." * * *

* * * *See Akouri v. Florida Dep't of Transp.*, 408 F.3d 1338, 1347–48 (11th Cir.2005) (holding that a supervisor's statement that the plaintiff had not been promoted because his fellow employees "are all white and they are not going to take orders from you, especially if you have an accent" constituted direct evidence, "because the statement relates directly to the [employer's] decision . . . and blatantly states that the reason [that the plaintiff] was passed over for the promotion was his ethnicity"); *Ghosh v. Getto*, 146 Fed.Appx. 840, 846 (7th Cir.2005) (rejecting the plaintiff's argument that a co-worker's statement that "people are biased and prejudiced against you if you're not white, if you speak with an accent" constituted direct evidence only because the statement did "not belie a prejudicial mind set on the part of the decision maker, but rather observations of how *third parties* might be prejudiced."

The question, then, is whether FedEx has borne its burden by demonstrating that it would have refused to promote Rodriguez even absent a discriminatory motive. FedEx argues that Rodriguez's failure to complete the LAC, combined with FedEx's claimed policy against promoting drivers directly into supervisory positions, satisfy that burden. Because it is for the district court to make this determination, applying the appropriate standard, in the first instance, we vacate the grant of summary judgment in favor of FedEx on Rodriguez's failure-to-promote claim and remand that claim for further proceedings.

* * *

NOTES

1. *Is or merely evidence of?* *Rodriguez* held that the employer's statement was "direct evidence" of race or national origin discrimination. The court concluded: "The question, then, is whether FedEx has borne its burden by demonstrating that it would have refused to promote Rodriguez even absent a discriminatory motive."

Section 703(m) provides:

"An unlawful employment practice is established when the complaining party demonstrates that race, color, religion, sex, or national origin was <u>*a*</u> motivating factor for any employment practice, even though other factors also motivated the practice."

Fragante v. City & County of Honolulu, 888 F.2d 591 (9th Cir. 1989):

"The record conclusively shows that [plaintiff] Fragante was not selected because of the deleterious effect his Filipino accent had upon his ability to communicate orally, not merely because he had such an accent. This is a critical distinction. Employers may lawfully base an employment decision upon an individual's accent when—but only when—it interferes with job performance." * * *

"There is nothing improper about an employer making such an *honest* assessment of a candidate for a job when oral communication skills pertain to a BFOQ * * *. Employers are permitted to base their non-selection on requirements such as the oral ability to communicate effectively in English, if the requirement is 'reasonably necessary to the normal operation of that particular business or enterprise.' 42 U.S.C. § 2000e2(e)(1)."

Is the court saying that discrimination based on accent is not facial national origin discrimination? Or that it is, and as such, can be a legitimate *only* if the employer can establish that the absence of a strong accent is a bona fide occupational qualification (BFOQ)? *See, Chapter 3 infra, for discussion of the BFOQ defense.*

2. *Accent vs. fluency*: A distinction must be made between fluency in English, and fluency that is accompanied by an identifiable accent. Discriminating against one because of her inability to speak and understand a language, even if national origin discrimination, is justified easily under the bona fide occupational qualification defense. Employees must be sufficiently fluent to be able to understand instructions and communicate with their supervisors. By contrast,the accent of a fluent person can also be tied to the nation or region from where that person originates, and may approach it being an "immutable characteristic" of national origins. One may become fluent with study, but sheding an accent that betrays non-U.S. origins is extremely difficult. As opposed to fluency, however, and with possible exception of actors or announcers, it is much more difficult for an employer to show that the absence of a native accent is reasonably necessary for successful job performance.

3. RECONSTRUCTION ERA CIVIL RIGHTS ACT (42 U.S.C. § 1981): ETHNICITY AS "RACE"

SAINT FRANCIS COLLEGE v. AL–KHAZRAJI

Supreme Court of the United States, 1987
481 U.S. 604, 107 S.Ct. 2022, 95 L.Ed.2d 582

JUSTICE WHITE delivered the opinion of the Court.

Respondent, a citizen of the United States born in Iraq, was an associate professor at St. Francis College, one of the petitioners here. In January 1978, he applied for tenure; the Board of Trustees denied his request on February 23, 1978. * * * He worked his last day at the college on May 26, 1979. In June 1979, he filed complaints with the Pennsylvania Human Relations Commission and the Equal Employment Opportunities Commission. The state agency dismissed his claim and the EEOC issued a right-to-sue letter on August 6, 1980.

On October 30, 1980, respondent filed a *pro se* complaint in the District Court alleging a violation of Title VII of the Civil Rights Act of 1964 and claiming discrimination based on national origin, religion, and/or race. Amended complaints were filed, adding claims under 42 U.S.C. §§ 1981, 1983, 1985(3), 1986, and state law. * * * Even if racial discrimination was deemed to have been alleged, the District Court ruled that s 1981 does not reach claims of discrimination based on Arabian ancestry.

* * *

Reaching the merits, the Court of Appeals held that respondent had alleged discrimination based on race and that although under current racial classifications Arabs are Caucasians, respondent could maintain his § 1981 claim. * * *

We granted certiorari, limited to * * * the question whether a person of Arabian ancestry was protected from racial discrimination under § 1981, and now affirm the judgment of the Court of Appeals. * * *

II

Section 1981 provides:

> "All persons within the jurisdiction of the United States shall have the same right in every State and Territory to make and enforce contracts, to sue, be parties, give evidence, and to the full and equal benefit of all laws and proceedings for the security of persons and property as is enjoyed by white citizens, and shall be subject to like punishment, pains, penalties, taxes, licenses, and exactions of every kind, and to no other."

Although § 1981 does not itself use the word "race," the Court has construed the section to forbid all "racial" discrimination in the making of private as well as public contracts. *Runyon v. McCrary,* 427 U.S. 160, 96 S.Ct. 2586, 2593, 49 L.Ed.2d 415 (1976). The petitioner college, although a private institution, was therefore subject to this statutory command. There is no disagreement among the parties on these propositions. The issue is whether respondent has alleged *racial* discrimination within the meaning of § 1981.

Petitioners contend that respondent is a Caucasian and cannot allege the kind of discrimination § 1981 forbids. Concededly, *McDonald v. Santa Fe Trail Transportation Co.,* 427 U.S. 273, 96 S.Ct. 2574, 49 L.Ed.2d 493 (1976), held that white persons could maintain a § 1981 suit; but that suit involved alleged discrimination against a white person in favor of a black, and petitioner submits that the section does not encompass claims of discrimination by one Caucasian against another. We are quite sure that the Court of Appeals properly rejected this position.

Petitioner's submission rests on the assumption that all those who might be deemed Caucasians today were thought to be of the same race when § 1981 became law in the 19th century; and it may be that a variety of ethnic groups, including Arabs, are now considered to be within the Caucasian race.[10] The understanding of "race" in the 19th century,

---

10. There is a common popular understanding that there are three major human races Caucasoid, Mongoloid, and Negroid. Many modern biologists and anthropologists, however, criticize racial classifications as arbitrary and of little use in understanding the variability of human beings. It is said that genetically homogeneous populations do not exist and traits are not discontinuous between populations; therefore, a population can only be described in terms of relative frequencies of various traits. Clear-cut categories do not exist. The particular traits which have generally been chosen to characterize races have been criticized as having little biological significance. It has been found that differences between individuals of the same race are often

however, was different. Plainly, all those who might be deemed Caucasian today were not thought to be of the same race at the time § 1981 became law.

In the middle years of the 19th century, dictionaries commonly referred to race as a "continued series of descendants from a parent who is called the *stock,*" N. Webster, An American Dictionary of the English Language 666 (New York 1830), "[t]he lineage of a family," 2 N. Webster, A Dictionary of the English Language 411 (New Haven 1841), or "descendants of a common ancestor," J. Donald, Chambers' Etymological Dictionary of the English Language 415 (London 1871). The 1887 edition of Webster's expanded the definition somewhat: "The descendants of a common ancestor; a family, tribe, people or nation, believed or presumed to belong to the same stock." It was not until the 20th century that dictionaries began referring to the Caucasian, Mongolian, and Negro races, 8 The Century Dictionary and Cyclopedia 4926 (1911), or to race as involving divisions of mankind based upon different physical characteristics. Webster's Collegiate Dictionary 794 (3d ed. 1916). Even so, modern dictionaries still include among the definitions of race "a family, tribe, people, or nation belonging to the same stock." Webster's Third New International Dictionary 1870 (1971); Webster's Ninth New Collegiate Dictionary 969 (1986).

Encyclopedias of the 19th century also described race in terms of ethnic groups, which is a narrower concept of race than petitioners urge. Encyclopedia Americana in 1858, for example, referred to various races such as Finns, Gypsies, Basques, and Hebrews. The 1863 version of the New American Cyclopaedia divided the Arabs into a number of subsidiary races, represented the Hebrews as of the Semitic race, and identified numerous other groups as constituting races, including Swedes, Norwegians, Germans, Greeks, Finns, Italians, Spanish, Mongolians, Russians, and the like. The Ninth edition of the Encyclopedia Britannica also referred to Arabs, Jews, and other ethnic groups such as Germans, Hungarians, and Greeks, as separate races.

These dictionary and encyclopedic sources are somewhat diverse, but it is clear that they do not support the claim that for the purposes of § 1981, Arabs, Englishmen, Germans, and certain other ethnic groups are to be considered a single race. We would expect the legislative history of § 1981, which the Court held in *Runyon v. McCrary* had its source in the Civil Rights Act of 1866, as well as the Voting Rights Act of 1870, to reflect this common understanding, which it surely does. The debates are replete with references to the Scandinavian races, Latin, Spanish, and Anglo–Saxon races, Jews, and Mexicans. Gypsies were referred to as a race. Likewise, the Germans:

> "Who will say that Ohio can pass a law enacting that no man of the German race * * * shall ever own any property in Ohio, or shall ever

greater than the differences between the "average" individuals of different races. These observations and others have led some, but not all, scientists to conclude that racial classifications are for the most part sociopolitical, rather than biological, in nature.

make a contract in Ohio, or ever inherit property in Ohio, or ever come into Ohio to live, or even to work? If Ohio may pass such a law, and exclude a German citizen * * * because he is of the German nationality or race, then may every other State do so."

There was a reference to the Caucasian race, but it appears to have been referring to people of European ancestry.

The history of the 1870 Act reflects similar understanding of what groups Congress intended to protect from intentional discrimination. It is clear, for example, that the civil rights sections of the 1870 Act provided protection for immigrant groups such as the Chinese. This view was expressed in the Senate. In the House, Representative Bingham, as declaring "that the States shall not hereafter discriminate against the immigrant from China and in favor of the immigrant from Prussia, nor against the immigrant from France and in favor of the immigrant from Ireland."

Based on the history of § 1981, we have little trouble in concluding that Congress intended to protect from discrimination identifiable classes of persons who are subjected to intentional discrimination solely because of their ancestry or ethnic characteristics. Such discrimination is racial discrimination that Congress intended § 1981 to forbid, whether or not it would be classified as racial in terms of modern scientific theory.[11] The Court of Appeals was thus quite right in holding that § 1981, "at a minimum," reaches discrimination against an individual "because he or she is genetically part of an ethnically and physiognomically distinctive subgrouping of *homo sapiens*." It is clear from our holding, however, that a distinctive physiognomy is not essential to qualify for § 1981 protection. If respondent on remand can prove that he was subjected to intentional discrimination based on the fact that he was born an Arab, rather than solely on the place or nation of his origin, or his religion, he will have made out a case under § 1981.

The judgment of the Court of Appeals is accordingly affirmed. * * *

NOTES

1. *Jews:* In the companion case of **Shaare Tefila Congregation v. Cobb.**, 481 U.S. 615, 107 S.Ct. 2019, 95 L.Ed.2d 594 (1987), the Court of Appeals had held that discrimination against Jews was not race discrimination, as required by the 1866 Act (42 U.S.C. § 1982). The Supreme Court reversed, holding:

> As *St. Francis* makes clear, the question before us is not whether Jews are considered to be a separate race by today's standards, but whether at the time § 1982 was adopted, Jews constituted a group of people that

---

11. We note that under prior cases, discrimination by States on the basis of ancestry violates the Equal Protection Clause of the Fourteenth Amendment. *Hernandez v. Texas,* 347 U.S. 475, 479, 74 S.Ct. 667, 671, 98 L.Ed. 866 (1954); *Oyama v. California,* 332 U.S. 633, 646, 68 S.Ct. 269, 275, 92 L.Ed. 249 (1948); *Hirabayashi v. United States,* 320 U.S. 81, 100, 63 S.Ct. 1375, 1385, 87 L.Ed. 1774 (1943).

Congress intended to protect. It is evident from the legislative history of the section reviewed in *St. Francis College*, a review that we need not repeat here, that Jews and Arabs were among the peoples then considered to be distinct races and hence within the protection of the statute. Jews are not foreclosed from stating a cause of action against other members of what today is considered to be part of the Caucasian race.

2. *Muslims?* Had plaintiff alleged that he had been discriminated against, not because he was Iraqi (or perhaps Arab) but because he was Muslim, would this state a 1981 claim? How does this differ from discrimination because one is Jewish? It could lie in the distinction between Jews as a distinct identity as "people" who share common historical roots, language (Hebrew) and sense of a unique ethnic place in Palestine, to be distinguished from the religion that they generally share, Judaism. Thus, a person could be ethnically Jewish yet not follow the religion of Judaism. Conversely, a person of Western European stock who converted to Judaism might not be considered ethnically as "Jewish."

3. *"Make and Enforce:" A broader coverage:* Responding to narrow Supreme Court interpretations of the "make and enforce" provisions of the original statute, The Civil Rights Act of 1991 amended the statute to state:

> [T]he term [in the statute] "make and enforce" contracts includes the making, performance, modification and termination of contracts, and the enjoyment of all benefits, privileges, terms, and conditions of the contractual relationship.

In addition the 1991 amendments specifically provide that § 1981 rights "are protected against impairment by non-governmental discrimination and impairment under color of State law." 42 U.S.C. § 1981(c).

4. CITIZENS AND "INTENDING CITIZENS"

THE IMMIGRATION REFORM AND CONTROL ACT OF 1986

8 U.S.C.A. § 1324B

(a) Prohibition of discrimination based on national origin or citizenship status

(1) General rule

It is an unfair immigration-related employment practice for a person or other entity to discriminate against any individual (other than an unauthorized alien, as defined in section 1324a(h)(3) of this section) with respect to the hiring, or recruitment or referral for a fee, of the individual for employment or the discharging of the individual from employment:

(A) because of such individual's national origin, or

(B) in the case of a protected individual (as defined in paragraph (3)), because of such individual's citizenship status.

(2) Exceptions

Paragraph (1) shall not apply to—

(A) a person or other entity that employs three or fewer employees,

(B) a person's or entity's discrimination because of an individual's national origin if the discrimination with respect to that person or entity and that individual is covered under section 2000e-(2) of Title 42, or

(C) discrimination because of citizenship status which is otherwise required in order to comply with law, regulation, or executive order, or required by Federal, State, or local government contract, or which the Attorney General determines to be essential for an employer to do business with an agency or department of the Federal, State, or local government.

(3) Definition of protected individual

As used in paragraph (1), the term "protected individual" means an individual who—

(A) is a citizen or national of the United States, or

(B) is an alien who is lawfully admitted for permanent residence, is granted the status of an alien lawfully admitted for temporary residence under section 1160(a), 1161(a), or 1255a(a)(1) of this title, is admitted as a refugee under section 1157 of this title, or is granted asylum under section 1158 of this title; but does not include:

(i) an alien who fails to apply for naturalization within six months of the date the alien first becomes eligible (by virtue of period of lawful permanent residence) to apply for naturalization * * * and

(ii) an alien who has applied on a timely basis, but has not been naturalized as a citizen within 2 years after the date of the application, unless the alien can establish that the alien is actively pursuing naturalization, except that time consumed in the Service's processing the application shall not be counted toward the 2–year period.

(4) Additional exception providing right to prefer equally qualified citizens

Notwithstanding any other provision of this section, it is not an unfair immigration-related employment practice for a person or other entity to prefer to hire, recruit, or refer an individual who is a citizen or national of the United States over another individual who is an alien if the two individuals are equally qualified.

(5) Prohibition of intimidation or retaliation * * *

(6) Treatment of certain documentary practices as employment practices

For purposes of paragraph (1), a person's or other entity's request, for purposes of satisfying the requirements of section 1324a(b) of this title, for more or different documents than are required under such section or refusing to honor documents tendered that on their face reasonably appear to be genuine shall be treated as an unfair immigration-related employment practice relating to the hiring of individuals.

NOTES

1. *Procedures*: The procedures to enforce the Immigration Act differ markedly from those provided by Title VII. Within 180 days of the discriminatory act the aggrieved party must file a written charge with the *Special Counsel,* an office within the *United States Department of Justice.* The EEOC is **NOT** involved. The Special Counsel is authorized to initiate hearings against the charged party before an administrative law judge. If the Special Counsel takes no action, it must so notify the charging party, and the charging party is free to file a charge before the administrative law judge. Judicial review is to the United States Courts of Appeals, and is limited to a review of the administrative determination. Petitions for review must be filed within 60 days of the final order of the Administrative Law Judge. 8 U.S.C. §§ 1324b(b)–(i).

2. *Undocumented aliens*: Under the Act, 8 U.S.C. § 1324a, an employer cannot legally employ or retain in employment an undocumented worker. That is, discrimination against undocumented aliens is *required* by the IRCA. Moreover, the Act expressly excludes undocumented aliens from protection against citizenship or national origin discrimination.

C. SEX

1. GENERALLY

UNITED AUTO WORKERS v. JOHNSON CONTROLS, INC.

Supreme Court of the United States, 1991
499 U.S. 187, 111 S.Ct. 1196, 113 L.Ed.2d 158

JUSTICE BLACKMUN delivered the opinion of the Court.

In this case we are concerned with an employer's gender-based fetal-protection policy. May an employer exclude a fertile female employee from certain jobs because of its concern for the health of the fetus the woman might conceive?

I

Respondent Johnson Controls, Inc., manufactures batteries. In the manufacturing process, the element lead is a primary ingredient. Occupational exposure to lead entails health risks, including the risk of harm to any fetus carried by a female employee.

* * *

[I]n 1982, Johnson Controls shifted from a policy of warning to a policy of exclusion. * * *

> "... [I]t is [Johnson Controls'] policy that women who are pregnant or who are capable of bearing children will not be placed into jobs

involving lead exposure or which could expose them to lead through the exercise of job bidding, bumping, transfer or promotion rights."

The policy defined "women ... capable of bearing children" as "[a]ll women except those whose inability to bear children is medically documented." It further stated that an unacceptable work station was one where, "over the past year," an employee had recorded a blood lead level of more than 30 micrograms per deciliter or the work site had yielded an air sample containing a lead level in excess of 30 micrograms per cubic meter.

* * *

[The District Court concluded, among other things, that defendant's policy was not facial discrimination "because of sex" but had only an indirect effect on women. The Court of Appeals affirmed.]

The bias in Johnson Controls' policy is obvious. Fertile men, but not fertile women, are given a choice as to whether they wish to risk their reproductive health for a particular job. Section 703(a) of the Civil Rights Act of 1964 prohibits sex-based classifications in terms and conditions of employment, in hiring and discharging decisions, and in other employment decisions that adversely affect an employee's status. Respondent's fetal-protection policy explicitly discriminates against women on the basis of their sex. The policy excludes women with childbearing capacity from lead-exposed jobs and so creates a facial classification based on gender. Respondent assumes as much in its brief before this Court.

Nevertheless, the Court of Appeals assumed, as did the two appellate courts that already had confronted the issue, that sex-specific fetal-protection policies do not involve facial discrimination. These courts analyzed the policies as though they were facially neutral, and had only a discriminatory effect upon the employment opportunities of women. * * * That assumption, however, was incorrect.

First, Johnson Controls' policy classifies on the basis of gender and childbearing capacity, rather than fertility alone. Respondent does not seek to protect the unconceived children of all its employees. Despite evidence in the record about the debilitating effect of lead exposure on the male reproductive system, Johnson Controls is concerned only with the harms that may befall the unborn offspring of its female employees. * * * This Court faced a conceptually similar situation in *Phillips v. Martin Marietta Corp.*, 400 U.S. 542, 91 S.Ct. 496, 27 L.Ed.2d 613 (1971), and found sex discrimination because the policy established "one hiring policy for women and another for men-each having pre-school-age children." Johnson Controls' policy is facially discriminatory because it requires only a female employee to produce proof that she is not capable of reproducing.

Our conclusion is bolstered by the Pregnancy Discrimination Act (PDA) in which Congress explicitly provided that, for purposes of Title VII, discrimination " 'on the basis of sex' " includes discrimination "because of or on the basis of pregnancy, childbirth, or related medical conditions." "The

Pregnancy Discrimination Act has now made clear that, for all Title VII purposes, discrimination based on a woman's pregnancy is, on its face, discrimination because of her sex." In its use of the words "capable of bearing children" in the 1982 policy statement as the criterion for exclusion, Johnson Controls explicitly classifies on the basis of potential for pregnancy. Under the PDA, such a classification must be regarded, for Title VII purposes, in the same light as explicit sex discrimination. Respondent has chosen to treat all its female employees as potentially pregnant; that choice evinces discrimination on the basis of sex.

We concluded above that Johnson Controls' policy is not neutral because it does not apply to the reproductive capacity of the company's male employees in the same way as it applies to that of the females. Moreover, the absence of a malevolent motive does not convert a facially discriminatory policy into a neutral policy with a discriminatory effect. Whether an employment practice involves disparate treatment through explicit facial discrimination does not depend on why the employer discriminates but rather on the explicit terms of the discrimination. In *Martin Marietta, supra,* the motives underlying the employers' express exclusion of women did not alter the intentionally discriminatory character of the policy. Nor did the arguably benign motives lead to consideration of a business necessity defense. The question in that case was whether the discrimination in question could be justified under § 703(e) as a BFOQ. The beneficence of an employer's purpose does not undermine the conclusion that an explicit gender-based policy is sex discrimination under § 703(a) and thus may be defended only as a BFOQ. * * *

[The BFOQ defense segment of the Court's opinion is reproduced, *infra, page 195.*]

ONCALE v. SUNDOWNER OFFSHORE SERVICES, INC.

Supreme Court of the United States, 1998
523 U.S. 75, 118 S.Ct. 998, 140 L.Ed.2d 201

JUSTICE SCALIA delivered the opinion of the Court

* * *

* * * In late October 1991, Oncale was working for respondent Sundowner Offshore Services on a Chevron U.S.A., Inc., oil platform in the Gulf of Mexico. He was employed as a roustabout on an eight-man crew. * * * On several occasions, Oncale was forcibly subjected to sex-related, humiliating actions against him by [three men on the crew] in the presence of the rest of the crew. [These men] also physically assaulted Oncale in a sexual manner, and [one man] threatened him with rape. * * *

[T]he district court held that "Mr. Oncale has no cause of action under Title VII for harassment by male co-workers." The Fifth Circuit affirmed] * * *

Title VII's prohibition of discrimination "because of . . . sex" protects men as well as women, and in the related context of racial discrimination in the workplace we have rejected any conclusive presumption that an employer will not discriminate against members of his own race. In *Johnson v. Transportation Agency, Santa Clara Cty.*, 480 U.S. 616, 107 S.Ct. 1442, 94 L.Ed.2d 615 (1987), a male employee claimed that his employer discriminated against him because of his sex when it preferred a female employee for promotion. Although we ultimately rejected the claim on other grounds [the presence of a valid affirmative action program to remedy a conspicuous imbalance of female employees], we did not consider it significant that the supervisor who made that decision was also a man. If our precedents leave any doubt on the question, we hold today that nothing in Title VII necessarily bars a claim of discrimination "because of . . . sex" merely because the plaintiff and the defendant (or the person charged with acting on behalf of the defendant) are of the same sex.

Courts have had little difficulty with that principle in cases like Johnson, where an employee claims to have been passed over for a job or promotion. But when the issue arises in the context of a "hostile environment" sexual harassment claim, the state and federal courts have taken a bewildering variety of stances. * * *

We see no justification in the statutory language or our precedents for a categorical rule excluding same-sex harassment claims from the coverage of Title VII. As some courts have observed, male-on-male sexual harassment in the workplace was assuredly not the principal evil Congress was concerned with when it enacted Title VII. But statutory prohibitions often go beyond the principal evil to cover reasonably comparable evils, and it is ultimately the provisions of our laws rather than the principal concerns of our legislators by which we are governed. Title VII prohibits discriminat[ion] . . . because of . . . sex in the "terms" or "conditions" of employment. Our holding that this includes sexual harassment must extend to sexual harassment of any kind that meets the statutory requirements. * * *

NOTE

Harris v. Forklift Systems, Inc., 510 U.S. 17, 114 S.Ct. 367, 126 L.Ed.2d 295 (1993), held that unwelcomed advances as well as overtly hostile treatment can be actionable sex discrimination even though no tangible job benefit has been denied the employee. The treatment, however, must be sufficiently severe to adversely affect a "term or condition" of employment. The adverse treatment will be "because of sex" where one sex is treated differently than the other. ***UAW v. Johnson Controls, Inc.,*** *supra*. However, even in the absence of differential treatment, the sexual nature of the conduct toward a victim may be seen as "sex." *Cherry v. Shaw Coastal, Inc.*, 668 F.3d 182 (5th Cir. 2012). Thus, as suggested by ***Oncale***, treating one man differently than other men can be "because of sex" if the hostile treatment is overtly sexual in nature. *Rene v. MGM Grand Hotel, Inc.*, 305 F.3d 1061 (9th Cir.2002) (en banc). Harassment and related issues will be covered in Chapter 4.

2. "SEX" OR "SOCIAL RELATIONSHIP?"

Meritor Savings Bank v. Vinson, 477 U.S. 57, 106 S.Ct. 2399, 91 L.Ed.2d 49 (1986), rejected the argument that denying tangible job benefits (e.g., hiring, retention, promotion, compensation) to a female worker because she refused to have a romantic or sexual relationship with her supervisor was discrimination based on a "social relationship," outside the protection of Title VII. The denial of tangible benefits because the employee rejected a sexual relationship was based, at least in part, on the worker's female sex.

MILLER v. DEPARTMENT OF CORRECTIONS

Supreme Court of California, 2005
36 Cal.4th 446, 30 Cal.Rptr.3d 797, 115 P.3d 77

GEORGE, C.J.

Plaintiffs, two former employees at the Valley State Prison for Women [(VSPW)], claim that the warden of the prison at which they were employed accorded unwarranted favorable treatment to numerous female employees with whom the warden was having sexual affairs, and that such conduct constituted sexual harassment in violation of the California Fair Employment and Housing Act (FEHA). (Gov.Code, § 12900 et seq.) The trial court granted summary judgment in favor of defendants, concluding that the conduct in question did not support a claim of sexual harassment, and the Court of Appeal affirmed. We must determine whether, in light of the evidence presented in support of and in opposition to the summary judgment motion, the lower courts properly found that plaintiffs failed to present a prima facie case of sexual harassment under the FEHA.

* * *

B

The FEHA expressly prohibits sexual harassment in the workplace. It is an unlawful employment practice "[f]or an employer ... because of ... sex ... to harass an employee...." (Gov.Code, § 12940, subd. (j)(1).) The FEHA also provides that "[sexual] [h]arassment of an employee ... by an employee, other than an agent or supervisor, shall be unlawful if the entity, or its agents or supervisors, knows or should have known of this conduct and fails to take immediate and appropriate corrective action." For the purposes of the relevant provisions of the FEHA, " 'harassment' because of sex includes sexual harassment, gender harassment, and harassment based on pregnancy, childbirth, or related medical conditions."

* * *

Our courts frequently turn to federal authorities interpreting Title VII of the Civil Rights Act of 1964. Although the FEHA explicitly prohibits

sexual harassment of employees, while Title VII does not, the two enact-
ments share the common goal of preventing discrimination in the workplace. Federal courts agree with guidelines established by the Equal
Employment Opportunity Commission (EEOC), the agency charged with
administering Title VII, in viewing sexual harassment as constituting
sexual discrimination in violation of Title VII. In language comparable to
that found in the FEHA and in FEHC regulations, federal regulatory
guidelines define sexual harassment as including unwelcome sexual advances, requests for sexual favors, and other verbal or physical conduct of
a sexual nature that has the "purpose or effect of unreasonably interfering with an individual's work performance or creating an intimidating,
hostile, or offensive working environment." (29 C.F.R. § 1604.11(a)(3).)

* * *

[T]he EEOC discusses sexual favoritism that is more than isolated and
that is based upon consensual affairs: "If favoritism based upon the
granting of sexual favors is widespread in a workplace, both male and
female colleagues who do not welcome this conduct can establish a hostile
work environment in violation of Title VII regardless of whether any
objectionable conduct is directed at them and regardless of whether those
who were granted favorable treatment willingly bestowed the sexual
favors. In these circumstances, a message is implicitly conveyed that the
managers view women as 'sexual playthings,' thereby creating an atmosphere that is demeaning to women. Both men and women who find this
offensive can establish a violation if the conduct is 'sufficiently severe or
pervasive "to alter the conditions of [their] employment and create an
abusive working environment."' An analogy can be made to a situation in
which supervisors in an office regularly make racial, ethnic or sexual
jokes. Even if the targets of the humor 'play along' and in no way display
that they object, co-workers of any race, national origin or sex can claim
that this conduct, which communicates a bias against protected class
members, creates a hostile work environment for them.

In addition, according to the EEOC, "[m]anagers who engage in widespread sexual favoritism may also communicate a message that the way
for women to get ahead in the workplace is by engaging in sexual conduct
or that sexual solicitations are a prerequisite to their fair treatment . . .]
This can form the basis of an implicit 'quid pro quo' harassment claim for
female employees, as well as a hostile environment claim for both women
and men who find this offensive."

* * *

C

Over a period of several years, Warden Kuykendall engaged concurrently
in sexual affairs with three subordinate employees, Bibb, Patrick, and
Brown. There was evidence these affairs began in 1991 and continued
until 1998. The affairs occurred first while Kuykendall and the women
worked at CCWF [Central California Women's Facility], then continued

when these individuals all transferred to VSPW. Kuykendall served in a management capacity at both institutions and served as warden at VSPW. When Kuykendall transferred from CCWF to VSPW, there was evidence he caused his sexual partners to be transferred to the new institution to join him. There was evidence Kuykendall promised and granted unwarranted and unfair employment benefits to the three women. One of the unfair employment benefits granted to Brown evidently was the power to abuse other employees who complained concerning the affairs. When plaintiffs complained, they suffered retaliation (and they believed two other employees were similarly targeted). Kuykendall refused to intervene and himself retaliated by withdrawing previously granted accommodations for Miller's disability after she cooperated with the internal affairs investigation.

Further, there was evidence that advancement for women at VSPW was based upon sexual favors, not merit. For example,[Warden] Kuykendall pressured Miller and other employees on the personnel selection committee to agree to transfer Bibb [a current paramour of Warden Kuykendall] to VSPW and promote her to the position of correctional counselor, despite the conclusion of the committee that she was not eligible or qualified. Committee members were told to set aside their professional judgment because Kuykendall wanted them to "make it happen."

In addition, on two occasions [Warden] Kuykendall promoted Brown [another subordinate with whom Kuykendall was having an affair] to facility captain positions in preference to [Plaintiff] Miller, although Miller was more qualified. Brown enjoyed an unprecedented pace of promotion to the managerial position of associate warden, causing outraged employees to ask such questions as, "What do I have to do, 'F' my way to the top?" Even Brown acknowledged that affairs between supervisors and subordinates were common in the Department and were widely viewed as a method of advancement. Indeed, Brown made it known to Miller that the facility captain promotion belonged to her because of her intimate relationship with Kuykendall, announcing that if she were not awarded the promotion she would "take him [Kuykendall] down" because she "knew every scar on his body."

There also was evidence that Kuykendall promoted Bibb from clerical to correctional staff duties despite her lack of qualifications, and at the same time refused to permit Mackey [another of Kuykendall's romantic favorites] to secure the on-the-job training that would have enabled her to make a similar advance. On the basis of her knowledge of Kuykendall's sexual affairs, Mackey believed the reason he denied her this opportunity was that she was not his sexual partner.

The evidence suggested Kuykendall viewed female employees as "sexual playthings" and that his ensuing conduct conveyed this demeaning message in a manner that had an effect on the work force as a whole. Various employees, including plaintiffs, observed Kuykendall and Bibb fondling one another on at least three occasions at work-related social gatherings.

One employee reported that Kuykendall had placed his arm around her and another female employee during one such social event, adding that Kuykendall had engaged in unwelcome fondling of her as well. Bibb and Brown bragged to other employees, including plaintiffs, of their power to extort benefits from Kuykendall. Jealous scenes between the sexual partners occurred in the presence of Miller and other employees. Several employees informed the internal affairs investigator that persons who were engaged in sexual affairs with Kuykendall received special benefits. When Miller last complained to Kuykendall, he told her that Brown was manipulative, adding he was "finished" with Brown and should have chosen Miller—a comment Miller reasonably took to mean that he should have chosen Miller for a sexual affair.

There was evidence Kuykendall's sexual favoritism not only blocked the way to merit-based advancement for plaintiffs, but also caused them to be subjected to harassment at the hands of Brown, whose behavior Kuykendall refused or failed to control even after it escalated to physical assault. * * *

Considering all the circumstances "from the perspective of a reasonable person in the plaintiff's position" and noting that the present case is before us on appeal after a grant of summary judgment, we conclude that the foregoing evidence created at least a triable issue of fact on the question whether Kuykendall's conduct constituted sexual favoritism widespread enough to constitute a hostile work environment in which the "message [was] implicitly conveyed that the managers view women as 'sexual playthings' " or that "the way for women to get ahead in the workplace is by engaging in sexual conduct" thereby "creating an atmosphere that is demeaning to women." * * *

D

* * * California law (like the EEOC policy statement quoted above) provides that plaintiffs may establish the existence of a hostile work environment even when they themselves have not been sexually propositioned. Further, as the EEOC policy statement points out, even widespread favoritism based upon *consensual* sexual affairs may imbue the workplace with an atmosphere that is demeaning to women because a message is conveyed that managers view women as "sexual playthings" or that the way required to secure advancement is to engage in sexual conduct with managers. In focusing upon the question whether the sexual favoritism was coercive, the Court of Appeal overlooked the principle that even in the absence of coercive behavior, certain conduct creates a work atmosphere so demeaning to women that it constitutes an actionable hostile work environment.
* * *

Defendants attempt to counter plaintiffs' claims by referring to a number of the cases holding that isolated preferential treatment of a sexual partner, *standing alone,* does not constitute sexual discrimination. * * *

In such instances, the discrimination is said to turn merely on personal preference, and male and female nonfavored employees are equally disadvantaged. Although we do not dispute the principle stated by these cases, we believe the Court of Appeal and defendants err in equating the present case with those cases. Whether or not Kuykendall was motivated by personal preference or by discriminatory intent, a hostile work environment was shown to have been created by widespread favoritism. As discussed, plaintiffs in the present case alleged far more than that a supervisor engaged in an isolated workplace sexual affair and accorded special benefits to a sexual partner. They proffered evidence demonstrating the effect of widespread favoritism on the work environment, namely the creation of an atmosphere that was demeaning to women. Further, as the EEOC policy statement observes, an atmosphere that is sufficiently demeaning to women may be actionable by both men and women.

* * *

Certainly, the presence of mere office gossip is insufficient to establish the existence of widespread sexual favoritism, but the evidence of such favoritism in the present case includes admissions by the participants concerning the nature of the relationships, boasting by the favored women, eyewitness accounts of incidents of public fondling, repeated promotion despite lack of qualifications, and Kuykendall's admission he could not control Brown because of his sexual relationship with her-a matter confirmed by the Department's internal affairs report. Indeed, it is ironic that, according to defendants, a jury should not be permitted to consider evidence of widespread sexual favoritism that the Department itself found convincing.

Finally, defendants warn that plaintiffs' position, if adopted, would inject the courts into relationships that are private and consensual and that occur within a major locus of individual social life for both men and women-the workplace. According to defendants, social policy favors rather than disfavors such relationships, and the issue of personal privacy should give courts pause before allowing claims such as those advanced by plaintiffs to proceed. Defendants urge it is safer to treat sexual favoritism as merely a matter of personal preference, and to recall that the FEHA is not intended to regulate sexual relationships in the workplace, nor to establish a civility code governing that venue.

We do not believe that defendants' concerns about regulating personal relationships are well founded, because it is not the relationship, but its effect on the workplace, that is relevant under the applicable legal standard. * * *

NOTES

1. ***Ackel v. National Communications***, 339 F.3d 376 (5th Cir. 2003): "[While Plaintiff] does not allege that she was ever harassed by [her supervisor] Hardesty, she nevertheless contends that she should survive summary judgment on her sexual harassment claim because she was

removed as Thibodeaux's assistant as a result of Hardesty's favoritism for Gross and then was terminated for complaining about that favoritism. As we noted in *Green v. Administrators of the Tulane Educational Fund*, 284 F.3d 642, 656 n. 6 (5th Cir. 2002), however, "courts have held that when an employer discriminates in favor of a paramour, such an action is not sex-based discrimination, as the favoritism, while unfair, disadvantages both sexes alike for reasons other than gender." Here, any discrimination suffered by Myers with respect to her transfer was based not on her gender but instead on the fact that she happened to occupy a position in which Hardesty allegedly wished to place Gross. Similarly, the fact that Myers may have been terminated for complaining about favorable treatment received by Gross is unrelated to Myers' gender. Accordingly, Myers cannot state a claim for sexual harassment under Title VII."

What if the plaintiff in *Akel* had been a man? Could it not be argued that he was removed from a job, at least in part, because he was not female, and that the favoritism for Gross, was, at least in part, because Gross was female. *King v. Palmer*, 778 F.2d 878 (D.C.Cir. 1985), indicated that this would be "sex" discrimination.

2. *Consensual relationships and their termination:* Courts, reluctant to enter the thicket of office romances, have tended to hold that the worker who loses her position upon the supervisor ending the consensual romantic relationship has no claim of sex discrimination. Perhaps this is a visceral feeling that having received an employment benefit because of her willingness to have sex, she lacks standing to complain about the loss of the benefit when the sexual relationship ended. *Mosher v. Dollar Tree Stores*, 240 F.3d 662 (7th Cir. 2001). Nonetheless, *Holly D. v. California Institute of Technology*, 339 F.3d 1158 (9th Cir. 2003), indicated that a claim would be stated if the supervisor indicated to the subordinate employee that maintaining job benefits was conditioned upon her *continuing* a sexual relationship that was consensual when initiated. Moreover, if the supervisor wants to resume a relationship that has cooled, but the employee refuses, and is subjected to retaliation or continuing badgering to resume the affair, this may constitute actionable sex discrimination. *See, Llampallas v. Mini–Circuits Lab, Inc.*, 163 F.3d 1236 (11th Cir. 1998).

3. STEREOTYPING

PRICE WATERHOUSE v. HOPKINS

Supreme Court of the United States, 1989
490 U.S. 228, 109 S.Ct. 1775, 104 L.Ed.2d 268

JUSTICE BRENNAN announced the judgment of the Court and delivered an opinion in which JUSTICE MARSHALL, JUSTICE BLACKMUN and JUSTICE STEVENS join.

Ann Hopkins was a senior manager in an office of Price Waterhouse when she was proposed for partnership in 1982. She was neither offered nor denied admission to the partnership; instead, her candidacy was held for reconsideration the following year. When the partners in her office later refused to repropose her for partnership, she sued Price Waterhouse under Title VII of the Civil Rights Act of 1964, charging that the firm had discriminated against her on the basis of sex in its decisions regarding partnership. Judge Gesell in the Federal District Court for the District of Columbia ruled in her favor on the question of liability, and the Court of Appeals for the District of Columbia Circuit affirmed. We granted certiorari * * *.

I

At Price Waterhouse, a nationwide professional accounting partnership, a senior manager becomes a candidate for partnership when the partners in her local office submit her name as a candidate. All of the other partners in the firm are then invited to submit written comments on each candidate—either on a "long" or a "short" form, depending on the partner's degree of exposure to the candidate. Not every partner in the firm submits comments on every candidate. After reviewing the comments and interviewing the partners who submitted them, the firm's Admissions Committee makes a recommendation to the Policy Board. This recommendation will be either that the firm accept the candidate for partnership, put her application on "hold," or deny her the promotion outright. The Policy Board then decides whether to submit the candidate's name to the entire partnership for a vote, to "hold" her candidacy, or to reject her. The recommendation of the Admissions Committee, and the decision of the Policy Board, are not controlled by fixed guidelines: a certain number of positive comments from partners will not guarantee a candidate's admission to the partnership, nor will a specific quantity of negative comments necessarily defeat her application. Price Waterhouse places no limit on the number of persons whom it will admit to the partnership in any given year.

Ann Hopkins had worked at Price Waterhouse's Office of Government Services in Washington, D.C., for five years when the partners in that office proposed her as a candidate for partnership. Of the 662 partners at the firm at that time, 7 were women. Of the 88 persons proposed for partnership that year, only 1—Hopkins—was a woman. Forty-seven of these candidates were admitted to the partnership, 21 were rejected, and 20—including Hopkins—were "held" for reconsideration the following year. Thirteen of the 32 partners who had submitted comments on Hopkins supported her bid for partnership. Three partners recommended that her candidacy be placed on hold, eight stated that they did not have an informed opinion about her, and eight recommended that she be denied partnership.[12]

* * *

Judge Gesell * * * conclude[d] that Hopkins "had no difficulty dealing with clients and her clients appear to have been very pleased with her

---

12. Decisions pertaining to advancement to partnership are, of course, subject to challenge under Title VII. *Hishon v. King & Spalding*, 467 U.S. 69, 104 S.Ct. 2229, 81 L.Ed.2d 59 (1984).

work" and that she "was generally viewed as a highly competent project leader who worked long hours, pushed vigorously to meet deadlines and demanded much from the multidisciplinary staffs with which she worked."

On too many occasions, however, Hopkins' aggressiveness apparently spilled over into abrasiveness. Staff members seem to have borne the brunt of Hopkins' brusqueness. Long before her bid for partnership, partners evaluating her work had counseled her to improve her relations with staff members. Although later evaluations indicate an improvement, Hopkins' perceived shortcomings in this important area eventually doomed her bid for partnership. Virtually all of the partners' negative remarks about Hopkins—even those of partners supporting her—had to do with her "interpersonal skills." Both "[s]upporters and opponents of her candidacy," stressed Judge Gesell, "indicated that she was sometimes overly aggressive, unduly harsh, difficult to work with and impatient with staff."

There were clear signs, though, that some of the partners reacted negatively to Hopkins' personality because she was a woman. One partner described her as "macho"; another suggested that she "overcompensated for being a woman"; a third advised her to take "a course at charm school". Several partners criticized her use of profanity; in response, one partner suggested that those partners objected to her swearing only "because it's a lady using foul language." Another supporter explained that Hopkins "ha[d] matured from a tough-talking somewhat masculine hard-nosed mgr to an authoritative, formidable, but much more appealing lady candidate." But it was the man who, as Judge Gesell found, bore responsibility for explaining to Hopkins the reasons for the Policy Board's decision to place her candidacy on hold who delivered the *coup de grace:* in order to improve her chances for partnership, Thomas Beyer advised, Hopkins should "walk more femininely, talk more femininely, dress more femininely, wear make-up, have her hair styled, and wear jewelry."

Dr. Susan Fiske, a social psychologist and Associate Professor of Psychology at Carnegie–Mellon University, testified at trial that the partnership selection process at Price Waterhouse was likely influenced by sex stereotyping. Her testimony focused not only on the overtly sex-based comments of partners but also on gender-neutral remarks, made by partners who knew Hopkins only slightly, that were intensely critical of her. One partner, for example, baldly stated that Hopkins was "universally disliked" by staff and another described her as "consistently annoying and irritating;" yet these were people who had had very little contact with Hopkins. According to Fiske, Hopkins' uniqueness (as the only woman in the pool of candidates) and the subjectivity of the evaluations made it likely that sharply critical remarks such as these were the product of sex stereotyping—although Fiske admitted that she could not say with certainty whether any particular comment was the result of stereotyping. Fiske based her opinion on a review of the submitted comments, explaining that it was commonly accepted practice for social psychologists to reach this kind of conclusion without having met any of the people involved in the decisionmaking process.

In previous years, other female candidates for partnership also had been evaluated in sex-based terms. As a general matter, Judge Gesell concluded, "[c]andidates were viewed favorably if partners believed they maintained their femin[in]ity while becoming effective professional managers"; in this environment, "[t]o be identified as a 'women's lib[b]er' was regarded as [a] negative comment." In fact, the judge found that in previous years "[o]ne partner repeatedly commented that he could not consider any woman seriously as a partnership candidate and believed that women were not even capable of functioning as senior managers—yet the firm took no action to discourage his comments and recorded his vote in the overall summary of the evaluations."

Judge Gesell found that Price Waterhouse legitimately emphasized interpersonal skills in its partnership decisions, and also found that the firm had not fabricated its complaints about Hopkins' interpersonal skills as a pretext for discrimination. Moreover, he concluded, the firm did not give decisive emphasis to such traits only because Hopkins was a woman; although there were male candidates who lacked these skills but who were admitted to partnership, the judge found that these candidates possessed other, positive traits that Hopkins lacked.

The judge went on to decide, however, that some of the partners' remarks about Hopkins stemmed from an impermissibly cabined view of the proper behavior of women, and that Price Waterhouse had done nothing to disavow reliance on such comments. He held that Price Waterhouse had unlawfully discriminated against Hopkins on the basis of sex by consciously giving credence and effect to partners' comments that resulted from sex stereotyping. Noting that Price Waterhouse could avoid equitable relief by proving by clear and convincing evidence that it would have placed Hopkins' candidacy on hold even absent this discrimination, the judge decided that the firm had not carried this heavy burden. The Court of Appeals affirmed the District Court's ultimate conclusion * * *

* * *

[The Court's extensive discussion of causation and respective burdens of proof upon plaintiff presenting evidence of defendant's proscribed motivation is omitted.]

C

In saying that gender played a motivating part in an employment decision, we mean that, if we asked the employer at the moment of the decision what its reasons were and if we received a truthful response, one of those reasons would be that the applicant or employee was a woman. In the specific context of sex stereotyping, an employer who acts on the basis of a belief that a woman cannot be aggressive, or that she must not be, has acted on the basis of gender.

Although the parties do not overtly dispute this last proposition, the placement by Price Waterhouse of "sex stereotyping" in quotation marks throughout its brief seems to us an insinuation either that such stereotyping was not present in this case or that it lacks legal relevance. We reject both possibilities. As to the existence of sex stereotyping in this case, we are not inclined to quarrel with the District Court's conclusion that a number of the partners' comments showed sex stereotyping at work. As for the legal relevance of sex stereotyping, we are beyond the day when an employer could evaluate employees by assuming or insisting that they matched the stereotype associated with their group, for " '[i]n forbidding employers to discriminate against individuals because of their sex, Congress intended to strike at the entire spectrum of disparate treatment of men and women resulting from sex stereotypes.' " An employer who objects to aggressiveness in women but whose positions require this trait places women in an intolerable and impermissible catch 22: out of a job if they behave aggressively and out of a job if they do not. Title VII lifts women out of this bind.

Remarks at work that are based on sex stereotypes do not inevitably prove that gender played a part in a particular employment decision. The plaintiff must show that the employer actually relied on her gender in making its decision. In making this showing, stereotyped remarks can certainly be *evidence* that gender played a part. In any event, the stereotyping in this case did not simply consist of stray remarks. On the contrary, Hopkins proved that Price Waterhouse invited partners to submit comments; that some of the comments stemmed from sex stereotypes; that an important part of the Policy Board's decision on Hopkins was an assessment of the submitted comments; and that Price Waterhouse in no way disclaimed reliance on the sex-linked evaluations. This is not, as Price Waterhouse suggests, "discrimination in the air"; rather, it is, as Hopkins puts it, "discrimination brought to ground and visited upon" an employee. By focusing on Hopkins' specific proof, however, we do not suggest a limitation on the possible ways of proving that stereotyping played a motivating role in an employment decision, and we refrain from deciding here which specific facts, "standing alone," would or would not establish a plaintiff's case, since such a decision is unnecessary in this case. * * *

The District Court found that sex stereotyping "was permitted to play a part" in the evaluation of Hopkins as a candidate for partnership. Price Waterhouse disputes both that stereotyping occurred and that it played any part in the decision to place Hopkins' candidacy on hold. In the firm's view, in other words, the District Court's factual conclusions are clearly erroneous. We do not agree.

In finding that some of the partners' comments reflected sex stereotyping, the District Court relied in part on Dr. Fiske's expert testimony. * * *

Indeed, we are tempted to say that Dr. Fiske's expert testimony was merely icing on Hopkins' cake. It takes no special training to discern sex stereotyping in a description of an aggressive female employee as requiring "a course at charm school." Nor, turning to Thomas Beyer's memorable advice to Hopkins, does it require expertise in psychology to know that, if an employee's flawed "interpersonal skills" can be corrected by a soft-hued suit or a new shade of lipstick, perhaps it is the employee's sex and not her interpersonal skills that has drawn the criticism.

Price Waterhouse also charges that Hopkins produced no evidence that sex stereotyping played a role in the decision to place her candidacy on hold. As we have stressed, however, Hopkins showed that the partnership solicited evaluations from all of the firm's partners; that it generally relied very heavily on such evaluations in making its decision; that some of the partners' comments were the product of stereotyping; and that the firm in no way disclaimed reliance on those particular comments, either in Hopkins' case or in the past. Certainly a plausible—and, one might say, inevitable—conclusion to draw from this set of circumstances is that the Policy Board in making its decision did in fact take into account all of the partners' comments, including the comments that were motivated by stereotypical notions about women's proper deportment.

* * *

Nor is the finding that sex stereotyping played a part in the Policy Board's decision undermined by the fact that many of the suspect comments were made by supporters rather than detractors of Hopkins. A negative comment, even when made in the context of a generally favorable review, nevertheless may influence the decisionmaker to think less highly of the candidate; the Policy Board, in fact, did not simply tally the "yeses" and "noes" regarding a candidate, but carefully reviewed the content of the submitted comments. The additional suggestion that the comments were made by "persons outside the decisionmaking chain"—and therefore could not have harmed Hopkins—simply ignores the critical role that partners' comments played in the Policy Board's partnership decisions.

* * *

[JUSTICE WHITE and JUSTICE O'CONNOR, concurred in the judgment. They did not contest the portion of the Court's analysis of sexual stereotyping. Concurring in the judgment JUSTICE O'CONNOR noted:]

* * *

[S]tray remarks in the workplace, while perhaps probative of sexual harassment, cannot justify requiring the employer to prove that its hiring or promotion decisions were based on legitimate criteria. Nor can statements by nondecisionmakers, or statements by decisionmakers unrelated to the decisional process itself, suffice to satisfy the plaintiff's burden in this regard. In addition, in my view testimony such as Dr. Fiske's in this case, standing alone, would not justify shifting the burden of persuasion to the employer. Race and gender always "play a role" in an employment decision in the benign sense that these are human characteristics of which decisionmakers are aware and about which they may comment in a perfectly neutral and nondiscriminatory fashion. For example, in the context of this case, a mere reference to "a lady candidate" might show that gender "played a role" in the decision, but by no means could support a rational fact finder's inference that the decision was made "because of" sex. What is required is what Ann Hopkins showed here: direct evidence that decisionmakers placed substantial negative reliance on an illegitimate criterion in reaching their decision.

[The dissenting opinion of JUSTICE KENNEDY, joined by JUSTICE SCALIA, is omitted.]

* * *

NOTES

The principal case can be interpreted in three ways:

(1) "Evidence of:" The expressed views of Ms. Hopkin's perceived masculinity was merely evidence of pervasive sex discrimination at Price Waterhouse.

(2) "Burden upon:" The perceptions that female partners in the accounting firm should not be "too masculine" placed a burden on women, a "Catch 22," that partners need to be aggressive, but women should not be.

(3) "Is:" When the employer requires the female sex to conform to its gender perceptions of feminity, this is *per se* "sex" discrimination.

JESPERSEN v. HARRAH'S OPERATING COMPANY, INC.

United States Court of Appeals, Ninth Circuit, 2006
444 F.3d 1104

SCHROEDER, CHIEF JUDGE

We took this sex discrimination case en banc in order to reaffirm our circuit law concerning appearance and grooming standards * * *

The plaintiff, Darlene Jespersen, was terminated from her position as a bartender at the sports bar in Harrah's Reno casino not long after Harrah's began to enforce its comprehensive uniform, appearance and grooming standards for all bartenders. The standards required all bartenders, men and women, to wear the same uniform of black pants and white shirts, a bow tie, and comfortable black shoes. The standards also included grooming requirements that differed to some extent for men and women, requiring women to wear some facial makeup and not permitting men to wear any. Jespersen refused to comply with the makeup requirement and was effectively terminated for that reason.

The district court granted summary judgment to Harrah's on the ground that the appearance and grooming policies imposed equal burdens on both men and women bartenders because, while women were required to use makeup and men were forbidden to wear makeup, women were allowed to have long hair and men were required to have their hair cut to a length above the collar. The district court also held that the policy could not run afoul of Title VII because it did not discriminate against Jespersen on the basis of the "immutable characteristics" of her sex. * * * The district court granted summary judgment to Harrah's on all claims.

The three-judge panel affirmed, but on somewhat different grounds. The panel majority held that Jespersen, on this record, failed to show that the appearance policy imposed a greater burden on women than on men. It pointed to the lack of any affidavit in this record to support a claim that the burdens of the policy fell unequally on men and women. Accordingly, the panel did not agree with the district court that grooming policies could never discriminate as a matter of law. * * *

We agree with the district court and the panel majority that on this record, Jespersen has failed to present evidence sufficient to survive summary judgment on her claim that the policy imposes an unequal burden on women. * * *

I.　BACKGROUND

Plaintiff Darlene Jespersen worked successfully as a bartender at Harrah's for twenty years and compiled what by all accounts was an exemplary record. During Jespersen's entire tenure with Harrah's, the company maintained a policy encouraging female beverage servers to wear makeup. The parties agree, however, that the policy was not enforced until 2000. In February 2000, Harrah's implemented a "Beverage Department Image Transformation" program at twenty Harrah's locations, including its casino in Reno. Part of the program consisted of new grooming and appearance standards, called the "Personal Best" program. The program contained certain appearance standards that applied equally to both sexes, including a standard uniform of black pants, white shirt, black vest, and black bow tie. Jespersen has never objected to any of these policies. The program also contained some sex-differentiated appearance requirements as to hair, nails, and makeup.

In April 2000, Harrah's amended that policy to require that women wear makeup. Jespersen's only objection here is to the makeup requirement. The amended policy provided in relevant part:

> All Beverage Service Personnel, in addition to being friendly, polite, courteous and responsive to our customer's needs, must possess the ability to physically perform the essential factors of the job as set forth in the standard job descriptions. They must be well groomed, appealing to the eye, be firm and body toned, and be comfortable with maintaining this look while wearing the specified uniform. Additional factors to be considered include, but are not limited to, hair styles, overall body contour, and degree of comfort the employee projects while wearing the uniform.

* * *

Beverage Bartenders and Barbacks will adhere to these additional guidelines:

- Overall Guidelines (applied equally to male/ female):

- Appearance: Must maintain Personal Best image portrayed at time of hire.

- Jewelry, if issued, must be worn. Otherwise, tasteful and simple jewelry is permitted; no large chokers, chains or bracelets.

- No faddish hairstyles or unnatural colors are permitted.

  - Males:

- Hair must not extend below top of shirt collar. Ponytails are prohibited.

- Hands and fingernails must be clean and nails neatly trimmed at all times. No colored polish is permitted.

- Eye and facial makeup is not permitted.

- Shoes will be solid black leather or leather type with rubber (non skid) soles.

  - Females:

- Hair must be teased, curled, or styled every day you work. Hair must be worn down at all times, no exceptions.

- Stockings are to be of nude or natural color consistent with employee's skin tone. No runs.

- Nail polish can be clear, white, pink or red color only. No exotic nail art or length.

- Shoes will be solid black leather or leather type with rubber (non skid) soles.

- Make up (face powder, blush and mascara) must be worn and applied neatly in complimentary colors. Lip color must be worn at all times.

Jespersen did not wear makeup on or off the job, and in her deposition stated that wearing it would conflict with her self-image. It is not disputed that she found the makeup requirement offensive, and felt so uncomfortable wearing makeup that she found it interfered with her ability to perform as a bartender. Unwilling to wear the makeup, and not qualifying for any open positions at the casino with a similar compensation scale, Jespersen left her employment with Harrah's.

* * *

Harrah's moved for summary judgment, supporting its motion with documents giving the history and purpose of the appearance and grooming policies. Harrah's argued that the policy created similar standards for both men and women, and that where the standards differentiated on the basis of sex, as with the face and hair standards, any burdens imposed fell equally on both male and female bartenders.

In her deposition testimony, attached as a response to the motion for summary judgment, Jespersen described the personal indignity she felt as a result of attempting to comply with the makeup policy. Jespersen testified that when she wore the makeup she "felt very degraded and very demeaned." In addition, Jespersen testified that "it prohibited [her] from doing [her] job" because "[i]t affected [her] self-dignity ... [and] took away [her] credibility as an individual and as a person." Jespersen made no cross-motion for summary judgment, taking the position that the case should go to the jury. Her response to Harrah's motion for summary judgment relied solely on her own deposition testimony regarding her subjective reaction to the makeup policy, and on favorable customer feedback and employer evaluation forms regarding her work.

The record therefore does not contain any affidavit or other evidence to establish that complying with the "Personal Best" standards caused burdens to fall unequally on men or women, and there is no evidence to suggest Harrah's motivation was to stereotype the women bartenders. Jespersen relied solely on evidence that she had been a good bartender, and that she had personal objections to complying with the policy, in order to support her argument that Harrah's " 'sells' and exploits its women employees." Jespersen contended that as a matter of law she had made a prima facie showing of gender discrimination, sufficient to survive summary judgment on both of her claims.

* * *

III.   SEX STEREOTYPING

In *Price Waterhouse* the plaintiff, Ann Hopkins, was denied partnership in the national accounting firm of Price Waterhouse because some of the partners found her to be too aggressive. While some partners praised Hopkins's " 'strong character, independence and integrity[,]' " others commented that she needed to take " 'a course at charm school[.]' " The Supreme Court determined that once a plaintiff has established that gender played "a motivating part in an employment decision, the defendant may avoid a finding of liability only by proving by a preponderance of the evidence that it would have made the same decision even if it had not taken the plaintiff's gender into account."

Consequently, in establishing that "gender played a motivating part in an employment decision," a plaintiff in a Title VII case may introduce evidence that the employment decision was made in part because of a sex stereotype. According to the Court, this is because "we are beyond the day when an employer could evaluate employees by assuming or insisting that they matched the stereotype associated with their group, for 'in forbidding employers to discriminate against individuals because of their sex, Congress intended to strike at the entire spectrum of disparate treatment of men and women resulting from sex stereotypes.' It was therefore impermissible for Hopkins's employer to place her in an untenable Catch–22: she needed to be aggressive and masculine to excel at her job, but was denied partnership for doing so because of her employer's gender stereotype. Instead, Hopkins was advised to " 'walk more femininely, talk more femininely, dress more femininely, wear make up, have her hair styled, and wear jewelry.' "

The stereotyping in Price Waterhouse interfered with Hopkins' ability to perform her work; the advice that she should take "a course at charm school" was intended to discourage her use of the forceful and aggressive techniques that made her successful in the first place. Impermissible sex stereotyping was clear because the very traits that she was asked to hide were the same traits considered praiseworthy in men.

Harrah's "Personal Best" policy is very different. The policy does not single out Jespersen. It applies to all of the bartenders, male and female. It requires all of the bartenders to wear exactly the same uniforms while interacting with the public in the context of the entertainment industry. It is for the most part unisex, from the black tie to the non-skid shoes. There is no evidence in this record to indicate that the policy was adopted to make women bartenders conform to a commonly-accepted stereotypical image of what women should wear. The record contains nothing to suggest the grooming standards would objectively inhibit a woman's ability to do the job. The only evidence in the record to support the stereotyping claim is Jespersen's own subjective reaction to the makeup requirement.

Judge Pregerson's dissent improperly divides the grooming policy into separate categories of hair, hands, and face, and then focuses exclusively on the makeup requirement to conclude that the policy constitutes sex stereotyping. This parsing, however, conflicts with established grooming standards analysis. The requirements must be viewed in the context of the overall policy. The dissent's conclusion that the unequal burdens analysis allows impermissible sex stereotyping to persist if imposed equally on both sexes is wrong because it ignores the protections of *Price Waterhouse* our decision preserves. If a grooming standard imposed on either sex amounts to impermissible stereotyping, something this record does not establish, a plaintiff of either sex may challenge that requirement under *Price Waterhouse*.

We respect Jespersen's resolve to be true to herself and to the image that she wishes to project to the world. We cannot agree, however, that her objection to the makeup requirement, without more, can give rise to a claim of sex stereotyping under Title VII. If we were to do so, we would come perilously close to holding that every grooming, apparel, or appearance requirement that an individual finds personally offensive, or in conflict with his or her own self-image, can create a triable issue of sex discrimination.

This is not a case where the dress or appearance requirement is intended to be sexually provocative, and tending to stereotype women as sex objects. In [*EEOC v.*] *Sage Realty*, 507 F.Supp. 599 (S.D.N.Y.1981, the plaintiff was a lobby attendant in a hotel that employed only female lobby attendants and required a mandatory uniform. The uniform was an octagon designed with an opening for the attendant's head, to be worn as a poncho, with snaps at the wrists and a tack on each side of the poncho, which was otherwise open. The attendants wore blue dancer pants as part of the uniform but were prohibited from wearing a shirt, blouse, or skirt under the outfit. There, the plaintiff was required to wear a uniform that was "short and revealing on both sides [such that her] thighs and portions of her buttocks were exposed." Jespersen, in contrast, was asked only to wear a unisex uniform that covered her entire body and was designed for men and women. The "Personal Best" policy does not, on its face, indicate any discriminatory or sexually stereotypical intent on the part of Harrah's.

* * * Nor is this a case of sexual harassment. Following *Price Waterhouse*, our court has held that sexual harassment of an employee because of that employee's failure to conform to commonly-accepted gender stereotypes is sex discrimination in violation of Title VII. In *Nichols [v. Azteca Restaurant Enterprises, Inc.*, 256 F.3d 864 (9th Cir. 2001)], a male waiter was systematically abused for failing to act "as a man should act," for walking and carrying his tray "like a woman," and was derided for not having sexual intercourse with a female waitress who was his friend. Applying *Price Waterhouse*, our court concluded that this harassment was actionable discrimination because of the plaintiff's sex. In *Rene [v. MGM Grand Hotel, Inc.*, 305 F.3d 1061 (9th Cir. 2002)], the homosexual plaintiff stated a Title VII sex stereotyping claim because he endured assaults "of a sexual nature" when Rene's co-workers forced him to look at homosexual pornography, gave him sexually-oriented "joke" gifts Nichols and Rene are not grooming standards cases, but provide the framework for this court's analysis of when sex stereotyping rises to the level of sex discrimination for Title VII purposes. Unlike the situation in both Rene and Nichols, Harrah's actions have not condoned or subjected Jespersen to any form of alleged harassment. It is not alleged that the "Personal Best" policy created a hostile work environment.

Nor is there evidence in this record that Harrah's treated Jespersen any differently than it treated any other bartender, male or female, who did not comply with the written grooming standards applicable to all bartenders. Jespersen's claim here materially differs from Hopkins' claim in Price Waterhouse because Harrah's grooming standards do not require Jespersen to conform to a stereotypical image that would objectively impede her ability to perform her job requirements as a bartender.

We emphasize that we do not preclude, as a matter of law, a claim of sex-stereotyping on the basis of dress or appearance codes. Others may well be filed, and any bases for such claims refined as law in this area evolves. This record, however, is devoid of any basis for permitting this particular claim to go forward, as it is limited to the subjective reaction of a single employee, and there is no evidence of a stereotypical motivation on the part of the employer. This case is essentially a challenge to one small part of what is an overall apparel, appearance, and grooming policy that applies largely the same requirements to both men and women. As we said in Nichols, in commenting on grooming standards, the touch-stone is reasonableness. A makeup requirement must be seen in the context of the overall standards imposed on employees in a given workplace.

PREGERSON, CIRCUIT JUDGE, with whom JUDGES KOZINSKI, GRABER, and W. FLETCHER join, dissenting:

The majority contends that it is bound to reject Jespersen's sex stereotyping claim because she presented too little evidence-only her "own subjective reaction to the makeup requirement." I disagree. Jespersen's evidence showed that Harrah's fired her because she did not comply with a grooming policy that imposed a facial uniform (full makeup) on only female bartenders. Harrah's stringent "Personal Best" policy required female beverage servers to wear foundation, blush, mascara, and lip color, and to ensure that lip color was on at all times. Jespersen and her female colleagues were required to meet with professional image consultants who in turn created a facial template for each woman. Jespersen was required not simply to wear makeup; in addition, the consultants dictated where and how the makeup had to be applied.

Quite simply, her termination for failing to comply with a grooming policy that imposed a facial uniform on only female bartenders is discrimination "because of" sex. Such discrimination is clearly and unambiguously impermissible under Title VII, which requires that "gender must be *irrelevant* to employment decisions." *Price Waterhouse v. Hopkins,* 490 U.S. 228, 240, 109 S.Ct. 1775, 104 L.Ed.2d 268 (1989).[2]

Notwithstanding Jespersen's failure to present additional evidence, little is required to make out a sex-stereotyping-as distinct from an undue burden-claim in this situation. In *Price Waterhouse,* the Supreme Court held that an employer may not condition employment on an employee's conformance to a sex stereotype associated with their gender. As the majority recognizes, *Price Waterhouse* allows a Title VII plaintiff to "introduce evidence that the employment decision was made in part because of a sex stereotype." It is not entirely clear exactly what this evidence must be, but nothing in *Price Waterhouse* suggests that a certain type or quantity of evidence is required to prove a prima facie case of discrimination.

Moreover, *Price Waterhouse* recognizes that gender discrimination may manifest itself in stereotypical notions as to how women should dress and *present themselves, not only as to how they should behave. Hopkins, the Price* Waterhouse plaintiff, offered individualized evidence, describing

---

2. Title VII identifies only one circumstance in which employers may take gender into account in making an employment decision—namely, "when gender is a 'bona fide occupational qualification [(BFOQ)] reasonably necessary to the normal operation of th[e] particular business or enterprise.' " *Dothard v. Rawlinson,* 433 U.S. 321, 334, 97 S.Ct. 2720, 53 L.Ed.2d 786 (1977) (recognizing that the BFOQ was meant to be an extremely narrow exception to the general prohibition of discrimination on the basis of sex). Harrah's has not attempted to defend the "Personal Best" makeup requirement as a BFOQ. In fact, there is little doubt that the "Personal Best" policy is not a business necessity, as Harrah's quietly disposed of this policy after Jespersen filed this suit. Regardless, although a BFOQ is a defense that an employer may raise, it does not preclude the employee from demonstrating the elements of a prima facie case of discrimination and presenting her case to a jury.

events in which she was subjected to discriminatory remarks. However, the Court did not state that such evidence was required. * * *

The fact that Harrah's required female bartenders to conform to a sex stereotype by wearing full makeup while working is not in dispute, and the policy is described at length in the majority opinion. This policy did not, as the majority suggests, impose a "grooming, apparel, or appearance requirement that an individual finds personally offensive," but rather one that treated Jespersen differently from male bartenders "because of" her sex. I believe that the fact that Harrah's designed and promoted a policy that required women to conform to a sex stereotype by wearing full makeup is sufficient "direct evidence" of discrimination.

The majority contends that Harrah's "Personal Best" appearance policy is very different from the policy at issue in *Price Waterhouse* in that it applies to both men and women. I disagree. As the majority concedes, "Harrah's 'Personal Best' policy contains sex-differentiated requirements regarding each employee's hair, hands, and face." The fact that a policy contains sex-differentiated requirements that affect people of both genders cannot excuse a particular requirement from scrutiny. By refusing to consider the makeup requirement separately, and instead stressing that the policy contained some gender-neutral requirements, such as color of clothing, as well as a variety of gender-differentiated requirements for "hair, hands, and face," the majority's approach would permit otherwise impermissible gender stereotypes to be neutralized by the presence of a stereotype or burden that affects people of the opposite gender, or by some separate non-discriminatory requirement that applies to both men and women. By this logic, it might well have been permissible in *Frank v. United Airlines, Inc.,* 216 F.3d 845 (9th Cir.2000), to require women, but not men, to meet a medium body frame standard *if* that requirement were imposed as part of a "physical appearance" policy that also required men, but not women, to achieve a certain degree of upper body muscle definition. But the fact that employees of both genders are subjected to gender-specific requirements does not necessarily mean that particular requirements are not motivated by gender stereotyping.

Because I believe that we should be careful not to insulate appearance requirements by viewing them in broad categories, such as "hair, hands, and face," I would consider the makeup requirement on its own terms. Viewed in isolation—or, at the very least, as part of a narrower category of requirements affecting employees' faces—the makeup or facial uniform requirement becomes closely analogous to the uniform policy held to constitute impermissible sex stereotyping in *Carroll v. Talman Federal Savings & Loan Ass'n of Chicago,* 604 F.2d 1028, 1029 (7th Cir.1979). In *Carroll,* the defendant bank required women to wear employer-issued uniforms, but permitted men to wear business attire of their own choosing. The Seventh Circuit found this rule discriminatory because it suggested to the public that the uniformed women held a "lesser professional status" and that women could not be trusted to choose appropriate business attire.

Just as the bank in *Carroll* deemed female employees incapable of achieving a professional appearance without assigned uniforms, Harrah's regarded women as unable to achieve a neat, attractive, and professional appearance without the facial uniform designed by a consultant and required by Harrah's. The inescapable message is that women's undoctored faces compare unfavorably to men's, not because of a physical difference between men's and women's faces, but because of a cultural assumption—and gender-based stereotype—that women's faces are incomplete, unattractive, or unprofessional without full makeup. We need not denounce all makeup as inherently offensive, just as there was no need to denounce all uniforms as inherently offensive in *Carroll,* to conclude that *requiring* female bartenders to wear full makeup is an impermissible sex stereotype and is evidence of discrimination because of sex. Therefore, I strongly disagree with the majority's conclusion that there "is no evidence in this record to indicate that the policy was adopted to make women bartenders conform to a commonly-accepted stereotypical image of what women should wear."

I believe that Jespersen articulated a classic case of *Price Waterhouse* discrimination and presented undisputed, material facts sufficient to avoid summary judgment. Accordingly, Jespersen should be allowed to present her case to a jury. Therefore, I respectfully dissent.

[Plaintiff's also argued that because men and women were treated differently under defendant's grooming code, that difference in treatment was discrimination. The court held that it was not, for reasons reproduced *infra at page 258.*]

NOTES

1. *Distinguishing Price Waterhouse from Jesperson:* The *Price Waterhouse* stereotyping went to a characteristic that could be considered "immutable," Ms. Hopkins' personality (or more accurately her gender characteristics). The stereotyping that Ms. Jesperson found objectionable was not an "immutable" aspect of her character. Rather, the employer's rule went to a manner of dress and appearance that the employer preferred and that was within Ms. Jesperson's ability to alter. Reconsider *Rogers v. American Airlines, supra, p. 32,* where physical characteristic of hair that was a an immutable characteristic of race (Afro bush) could be "race," but mere styling of hair, even though associated with one race, was not immutable, and thus was not considered "race." Note, too, that Ms. Jesperson was not faced with the "catch 22" confronting Ms. Hopkins.

With those possible distinctions in mind, consider in *Nichols v. Azteca Restaurant Enterprises, Inc.,* 256 F.3d 864, 874–75 (9th Cir.2001), in which the Ninth Circuit had previously held that harassment "based upon the perception that [the male plaintiff] was effeminate" is discrimination because of sex. It relied upon on the stereotype concept established in *Price Waterhouse v. Hopkins, supra.*

2. ***Lewis v. Heartland Inns of America, LLC*** 591 F.3d 1033 (8th Cir. 2010), involved the dismissal of a hotel admission desk clerk because she had

a "tomboyish," "Ellen DeGeneres kind of look," rather than a "pretty" and "Midwestern girl" appearance preferred by the employer. This was held to be impermissible sex stereotyping.

4. GENDER, ORIENTATION, AND IDENTITY

DeSANTIS v. PACIFIC TELEPHONE & TELEGRAPH CO.

United States Court of Appeals, Ninth Circuit, 1979
608 F.2d 327

CHOY, CIRCUIT JUDGE.

Male and female homosexuals brought three separate federal district court actions claiming that their employers or former employers discriminated against them in employment decisions because of their homosexuality. They alleged that such discrimination violated Title VII of the Civil Rights Act of 1964 * * *. The district courts dismissed the complaints as failing to state claims * * *. Plaintiffs below appealed. * * * We affirm.

* * *

II. Title VII Claim

Appellants argue first that the district courts erred in holding that Title VII does not prohibit discrimination on the basis of sexual preference. They claim that in prohibiting certain employment discrimination on the basis of "sex," Congress meant to include discrimination on the basis of sexual orientation. They add that in a trial they could establish that discrimination against homosexuals disproportionately affects men and that this disproportionate impact and correlation between discrimination on the basis of sexual preference and discrimination on the basis of "sex" requires that sexual preference be considered a subcategory of the "sex" category of Title VII.

    A. Congressional Intent in Prohibiting "Sex" Discrimination

* * *

Giving the statute its plain meaning, this court concludes that Congress had only the traditional notions of "sex" in mind. Later legislative activity makes this narrow definition even more evident. Several bills have been introduced to *amend* the Civil Rights Act to prohibit discrimination against "sexual preference." None have [sic] been enacted into law.

Congress has not shown any intent other than to restrict the term "sex" to its traditional meaning. Therefore, this court will not expand Title VII's application in the absence of Congressional mandate. The manifest purpose of Title VII's prohibition against sex discrimination in employment is to ensure that men and women are treated equally, absent a bona fide relationship between the qualifications for the job and the person's sex.

We conclude that Title VII's prohibition of "sex" discrimination applies only to discrimination on the basis of gender and should not be judicially extended to include sexual preference such as homosexuality.

B. Disproportionate Impact

Appellants argue that recent decisions dealing with disproportionate impact require that discrimination against homosexuals fall within the purview of Title VII. They contend that these recent decisions, like *Griggs v. Duke Power Co.*, 401 U.S. 424, 91 S.Ct. 849, 28 L.Ed.2d 158 (1971), establish that any employment criterion that affects one sex more than the other violates Title VII. * * * They claim that in a trial they could prove that discrimination against homosexuals disproportionately affects men both because of the greater incidence of homosexuality in the male population and because of the greater likelihood of an employer's discovering male homosexuals compared to female homosexuals.

Assuming that appellants can otherwise satisfy the requirement of *Griggs,* we do not believe that *Griggs* can be applied to extend Title VII protection to homosexuals. * * * Appellants now ask us to employ the disproportionate impact decisions as an artifice to "bootstrap" Title VII protection for homosexuals under the guise of protecting men generally.

This we are not free to do. Adoption of this bootstrap device would frustrate congressional objectives * * * not effectuate congressional goals * * *. It would achieve by judicial "construction" what Congress did not do and has consistently refused to do on many occasions. * * *

C. Differences in Employment Criteria

Appellants next contend that recent decisions have held that an employer generally may not use different employment criteria for men and women. They claim that if a male employee prefers males as sexual partners, he will be treated differently from a female who prefers male partners. They conclude that the employer thus uses different employment criteria for men and women and violates the Supreme Court's warning in *Phillips v. Martin Marietta Corp.*, 400 U.S. 542, 91 S.Ct. 496, 27 L.Ed.2d 613 (1971):

> The Court of Appeals therefore erred in reading this section as permitting one hiring policy for women and another for men. * * *

We must again reject appellants' efforts to "bootstrap" Title VII protection for homosexuals. While we do not express approval of an employment policy that differentiates according to sexual preference, we note that whether dealing with men or women the employer is using the same criterion: it will not hire or promote a person who prefers sexual partners of the same sex. Thus this policy does not involve different decisional criteria for the sexes.

D. Interference With Association

Appellants argue that the EEOC has held that discrimination against an employee because of the race of the employee's friends may constitute discrimination based on race in violation of Title VII. They contend that analogously discrimination because of the sex of the employees' sexual partner should constitute discrimination based on sex.

Appellants, however, have not alleged that appellees have policies of discriminating against employees because of the gender of their friends. That is, they do not claim that the appellees will terminate anyone with a male (or female) friend. They claim instead that the appellees discriminate against employees who have a certain type of relationship, i.e., homosexual relationship with certain friends. As noted earlier, that relationship is not protected by Title VII. Thus, assuming that it would violate Title VII for an employer to discriminate against employees because of the gender of their friends, appellants' claims do not fall within this purported rule.

* * *

SNEED, CIRCUIT JUDGE (Concurring and dissenting): I concur in the majority's opinion save subpart B of Part II thereof.

* * *

My point of difference with the majority is merely that the male appellants * * * are not using that case "as an artifice to 'bootstrap' Title VII protection for homosexuals under the guise of protecting men generally." Their claim, if established properly, would in fact protect males generally. I would permit them to try to make their case and not dismiss it on the pleadings.

NOTES

1. *Orientation is different from "Sex:"* The "bootstraps" discussion of *DeSantis* was rejected, in *Nichols v. Azteca Restaurant Enterprises,* 256 F.3d 864 (9th Cir. 2001). Nonetheless, courts continue to adhere to *DeSantis'* basic holding that under Title VII "sex" refers to the strict physical distinction between males and females, and as such does not prohibit discrimination based on sexual orientation or practices. *Etsitty v. Utah Transit Auth.,* 502 F.3d 1215 (10th Cir. 2007).

2. *Federal Service and the military:* A Presidential Executive Order prohibits "sexual orientation" discrimination in the federal service. E.O. 13,160 (2000). This order is not enforced through EEOC proceedings. E.O. 13,160 does not apply to the uniformed military services. Since the 1990s, the military applied to its uniformed personnel a "don't ask, don't tell" policy. The services would not inquire into the sexual orientation of service men and women. However, personnel were subject to discharge from the military if they disclosed their non-heterosexual orientation. This policy was reversed by legislation in December 2010.

3. *Sexual Orientation as a "Disability?"* The Americans With Disabilities Act expressly *excludes* homosexuality and bisexuality from the definition of disability along with a further exclusion of "certain conditions" of "transvestism, transsexualism, pedophilia, exhibitinism, voyeurism, gender identity disorders not resulting from physical impairments, or other sexual behavior disorders." 42 U.S.C. §§ 12211(a) and (b). Neither disability nor gay/lesbian rights advocates have asserted that gender orientation or identity should be considered a "disability."

4. *Sex–Plus:* If an employer refused to hire gay men but was indifferent as to the sexual orientation of women, this could be a form of traditional sex discrimination discussed in *United Auto Workers v. Johnson Controls, supra, page* 51 in that the employer is applying one standard for males and a different, more lenient, standard for females.

5. *Reverse Discrimination:* As long as *DeSantis'* holds sway, is it safe to assume that it is permissible under Title VII for an employer to *prefer* homosexuals over straight persons?

SMITH v. CITY OF SALEM, OHIO

United States Court of Appeals for the Sixth Circuit, 2004
378 F.3d 566

COLE, CIRCUIT JUDGE

Plaintiff–Appellant Jimmie L. Smith appeals from a judgment of the United States District Court for the Northern District of Ohio dismissing his claims against his employer, Defendant–Appellant City of Salem, Ohio, and various City officials * * * Smith, who considers himself a transsexual and has been diagnosed with Gender Identity Disorder, alleged that Defendants discriminated against him in his employment on the basis of sex. He asserted claims pursuant to Title VII of the Civil Rights Act of 1964. The district court dismissed those claims * * *

For the following reasons, we reverse the judgment of the district court and remand the case for further proceedings consistent with this opinion.

I. BACKGROUND

The following facts are drawn from Smith's complaint. Smith is—and has been, at all times relevant to this action—employed by the city of Salem, Ohio, as a lieutenant in the Salem Fire Department (the "Fire Department"). Prior to the events surrounding this action, Smith worked for the Fire Department for seven years without any negative incidents. Smith—biologically and by birth a male—is a transsexual and has been diagnosed with Gender Identity Disorder ("GID"), which the American Psychiatric Association characterizes as a disjunction between an individual's sexual organs and sexual identity. American Psychiatric Association, Diagnostic and Statistical Manual of Mental Disorders 576–582 (4th ed.2000). After being diagnosed with GID, Smith began "expressing a more feminine appearance on a full-time basis"—including at work—in accordance with international medical protocols for treating GID. Soon thereafter, Smith's co-workers began questioning him about his appearance and commenting that his appearance and mannerisms were not "masculine enough." As a result, Smith notified his immediate supervisor, Defendant Thomas Eastek, about his GID diagnosis and treatment. He also informed Eastek of the likelihood that his treatment would eventually include complete physical transformation from male to female. Smith had approached Eastek in order to answer any questions Eastek might have concerning his appearance and manner and so that Eastek could address Smith's co-workers' comments and inquiries. Smith specifically asked Eastek, and Eastek promised, not to divulge the substance of their conversation to any of his superiors, particularly to Defendant Walter Greenamyer, Chief of the Fire Department. In short order, however, Eastek told Greenamyer about Smith's behavior and his GID.

Greenamyer then met with Defendant C. Brooke Zellers, the Law Director for the City of Salem, with the intention of using Smith's transsexualism and its manifestations as a basis for terminating his employment. * * *

During [a city commission] meeting, Greenamyer, DeJane, and Zellers agreed to arrange for the Salem Civil Service Commission to require Smith to undergo three separate psychological evaluations with physicians of the City's choosing. They hoped that Smith would either resign or refuse to comply. If he refused to comply, Defendants reasoned, they could terminate Smith's employment on the ground of insubordination.

* * * [A few days later] Greenamyer suspended Smith for one twenty-four hour shift, based on his alleged infraction of a City and/or Fire Department policy.

      * * *

1. Sex Stereotyping

* * *

In his complaint, Smith asserts Title VII claims of retaliation and employment discrimination "because of . . . sex." The district court dismissed Smith's Title VII claims on the ground that he failed to state a claim for sex stereotyping pursuant to *Price Waterhouse v. Hopkins*, 490 U.S. 228, 109 S.Ct. 1775, 104 L.Ed.2d 268 (1989). The district court implied that Smith's claim was disingenuous, stating that he merely "invokes the term-of-art created by *Price Waterhouse*, that is, 'sex-stereotyping,' " as an end run around his "real" claim, which, the district court stated, was "based upon his transsexuality." The district court then held that "Title VII does not prohibit discrimination based on an individual's transsexualism."

Relying on *Price Waterhouse*—which held that Title VII's prohibition of discrimination "because of . . . sex" bars gender discrimination, including discrimination based on sex stereotypes—Smith contends on appeal that he was a victim of discrimination "because of . . . sex" both because of his gender non-conforming conduct and, more generally, because of his identification as a transsexual. We find both bases of discrimination actionable pursuant to Title VII.

We first address whether Smith has stated a claim for relief, pursuant to *Price Waterhouse's* prohibition of sex stereotyping, based on his gender non-conforming behavior and appearance. In *Price Waterhouse*, the plaintiff, a female senior manager in an accounting firm, was denied partnership in the firm, in part, because she was considered "macho." She was advised that she could improve her chances for partnership if she were to take "a course at charm school," "walk more femininely, talk more femininely, dress more femininely, wear make-up, have her hair styled, and wear jewelry." Six members of the Court agreed that such comments bespoke gender discrimination, holding that Title VII barred not just discrimination because Hopkins was a woman, but also sex stereotyping— that is, discrimination because she failed to *act* like a woman. As Judge Posner has pointed out, the term "gender" is one "borrowed from grammar to designate the sexes as viewed as social rather than biological classes." Richard A. Posner, Sex and Reason, 24–25 (1992). The Supreme Court made clear that in the context of Title VII, discrimination because of "sex" includes gender discrimination: "In the context of sex stereotyping, an employer who acts on the basis of a belief that a woman cannot be aggressive, or that she must not be, has acted on the basis of gender." The Court emphasized that "we are beyond the day when an employer could evaluate employees by assuming or insisting that they matched the stereotype associated with their group."

Smith contends that the same theory of sex stereotyping applies here. His complaint sets forth the conduct and mannerisms which, he alleges, did not conform with his employers' and co-workers' sex stereotypes of how a man should look and behave. Smith's complaint states that, after being diagnosed with GID, he began to express a more feminine appearance and manner on a regular basis, including at work. The complaint states that his co-workers began commenting on his appearance and mannerisms as not being masculine enough; and that his supervisors at the Fire Department and other municipal agents knew about this allegedly unmasculine conduct and appearance. The complaint then describes a high-level meeting among Smith's supervisors and other municipal officials regarding his employment. Defendants allegedly schemed to compel Smith's resignation by forcing him to undergo multiple psychological evaluations of his gender non-conforming behavior. The complaint makes clear that these meetings took place soon after Smith assumed a more feminine appearance and manner and after his conversation about this with Eastek. In addition, the complaint alleges that Smith was suspended for twenty-four hours for allegedly violating an unenacted municipal policy, and that the suspension was ordered in retaliation for his pursuing legal remedies after he had been informed about Defendants' plan to intimidate him into resigning. In short, Smith claims that the discrimination he experienced was based on his failure to conform to sex stereotypes by expressing less masculine, and more feminine mannerisms and appearance.

Having alleged that his failure to conform to sex stereotypes concerning how a man should look and behave was the driving force behind Defendants' actions, Smith has sufficiently pleaded claims of sex stereotyping and gender discrimination.

In so holding, we find that the district court erred in relying on a series of pre-*Price Waterhouse* cases from other federal appellate courts holding that transsexuals, as a class, are not entitled to Title VII protection because "Congress had a narrow view of sex in mind" and "never considered nor intended that [Title VII] apply to anything other than the traditional concept of sex." *Ulane v. Eastern Airlines, Inc.,* 742 F.2d 1081, 1085, 1086 (7th Cir.1984); *see also Holloway v. Arthur Andersen & Co.,* 566 F.2d 659, 661–63 (9th Cir.1977) (refusing to extend protection of Title VII to transsexuals because discrimination against transsexuals is based on "gender" rather than "sex"). It is true that, in the past, federal appellate courts regarded Title VII as barring discrimination based only on "sex" (referring to an individual's anatomical and biological characteristics), but not on "gender" (referring to socially-constructed norms associated with a person's sex). *See, e.g., Ulane,* 742 F.2d at 1084 (construing "sex" in Title VII narrowly to mean only anatomical sex rather than gender); *Sommers v. Budget Mktg., Inc.,* 667 F.2d 748, 750 (8th Cir.1982) (holding that transsexuals are not protected by Title VII because the "plain meaning" must be ascribed to the term "sex" in the absence of clear congressional intent to do otherwise); *Holloway,* 566 F.2d at 661–63 (refusing to extend protection of Title VII to transsexuals because discrimination against transsexualism is based on "gender" rather than "sex;" and "sex" should be given its traditional definition based on the anatomical characteristics dividing "organisms" and "living beings" into male and female). In this earlier jurisprudence, male-to-female transsexuals (who were the plaintiffs in *Ulane, Sommers,* and *Holloway*)—as biological males whose outward behavior and emotional identity did not conform to socially-prescribed expectations of masculinity—were denied Title VII protection by courts because they were considered victims of "gender" rather than "sex" discrimination.

However, the approach in *Holloway, Sommers,* and *Ulane*—and by the district court in this case—has been eviscerated by *Price Waterhouse.* By holding that Title VII protected a woman who failed to conform to social expectations concerning how a woman should look and behave, the Supreme Court established that Title VII's reference to "sex" encompasses both the biological differences between men and women, and gender discrimination, that is, discrimination based on a failure to conform to stereotypical gender norms. *Rene v. MGM Grand Hotel, Inc.,* 305 F.3d 1061, 1068 (9th Cir.2002) (en banc) (Pregerson, J., concurring) (noting that the Ninth Circuit had previously found that "same-sex gender stereotyping of the sort suffered by Rene—i.e. gender stereotyping of a male gay employee by his male co-workers" constituted actionable harassment under Title VII and concluding that "[t]he repeated testimony that his co-workers treated Rene, in a variety of ways, 'like a woman' constitutes ample evidence of gender stereotyping"); *Bibby v. Philadelphia Coca Cola Bottling Co.,* 260 F.3d 257, 262–63 (3d Cir.2001) (stating that a plaintiff may be able to prove a claim of sex discrimination by showing that the "harasser's conduct was motivated by a belief that the victim did not conform to the stereotypes of his or her gender"); *Nichols v. Azteca Rest. Enters., Inc.,* 256 F.3d 864, 874–75 (9th Cir.2001) (holding that harassment "based upon the perception that [the plaintiff] is effeminate" is discrimination because of sex, in violation of Title VII), *Doe v. Belleville,*

119 F.3d 563, 580–81 (7th Cir.1997) (holding that "Title VII does not permit an employee to be treated adversely because his or her appearance or conduct does not conform to stereotypical gender roles" and explaining that "a man who is harassed because his voice is soft, his physique is slight, his hair long, or because in some other respect he exhibits his masculinity in a way that does not meet his coworkers' idea of how men are to appear and behave, is harassed 'because of his sex' '').

After *Price Waterhouse,* an employer who discriminates against women because, for instance, they do not wear dresses or makeup, is engaging in sex discrimination because the discrimination would not occur but for the victim's sex. It follows that employers who discriminate against men because they *do* wear dresses and makeup, or otherwise act femininely, are also engaging in sex discrimination, because the discrimination would not occur but for the victim's sex. *See, e.g., Nichols,* 256 F.3d 864 (Title VII sex discrimination and hostile work environment claim upheld where plaintiff's male co-workers and supervisors repeatedly referred to him as "she" and "her" and where co-workers mocked him for walking and carrying his serving tray "like a woman"); *Higgins v. New Balance Athletic Shoe, Inc.,* 194 F.3d 252, 261 n. 4 (1st Cir.1999) ("[J]ust as a woman can ground an action on a claim that men discriminated against her because she did not meet stereotyped expectations of femininity, a man can ground a claim on evidence that other men discriminated against him because he did not meet stereotypical expectations of masculinity.")

Yet some courts have held that this latter form of discrimination is of a different and somehow more permissible kind. For instance, the man who acts in ways typically associated with women is not described as engaging in the same activity as a woman who acts in ways typically associated with women, but is instead described as engaging in the different activity of being a transsexual (or in some instances, a homosexual or transvestite). Discrimination against the transsexual is then found not to be discrimination "because of . . . sex," but rather, discrimination against the plaintiff's unprotected status or mode of self-identification. In other words, these courts superimpose classifications such as "transsexual" on a plaintiff, and then legitimize discrimination based on the plaintiff's gender non-conformity by formalizing the non-conformity into an ostensibly unprotected classification. Such was the case here: despite the fact that Smith alleges that Defendants' discrimination was motivated by his appearance and mannerisms, which Defendants felt were inappropriate for a male, the district court expressly declined to discuss the applicability of *Price Waterhouse.* The district court therefore gave insufficient consideration to Smith's well-pleaded claims concerning his contra-gender behavior, but rather accounted for that behavior only insofar as it confirmed for the court Smith's status as a transsexual, which the district court held precluded Smith from Title VII protection.

Such analyses cannot be reconciled with *Price Waterhouse,* which does not make Title VII protection against sex stereotyping conditional or provide any reason to exclude Title VII coverage for non sex-stereotypical behavior simply because the person is a transsexual. As such, discrimination against a plaintiff who is a transsexual—and therefore fails to act like and/or identify with the gender norms associated with his or her sex—is no different from the discrimination directed against Ann Hopkins in *Price Waterhouse,* who, in sex-stereotypical terms, did not act like a woman. Sex stereotyping based on a person's gender non-conforming behavior is impermissible discrimination, irrespective of the cause of that behavior; a label, such as "transsexual," is not fatal to a sex discrimination claim where the victim has suffered discrimination because of his or her gender non-conformity. Accordingly, we hold that Smith has stated a claim for relief pursuant to Title VII's prohibition of sex discrimination.

Even if Smith had alleged discrimination based only on his self-identification as a transsexual—as opposed to his specific appearance and behavior—this claim too is actionable pursuant to Title VII. By definition, transsexuals are individuals who fail to conform to stereotypes about how those assigned a particular sex at birth should act, dress, and self-identify. *Ergo,* identification as a transsexual is the statement or admission that one wishes to be the opposite sex or does not relate to one's birth sex. Such an admission—for instance the admission by a man that he self-identifies as a woman and/or that he wishes to be a woman—itself violates the prevalent sex stereotype that a man should perceive himself as a man. Discrimination based on transsexualism is rooted in the insistence that sex (organs) and gender (social classification of a person as belonging to one sex or the other) coincide. This is the very essence of sex stereotyping. Accordingly, to the extent that Smith also alleges discrimination based solely on his identification as a transsexual, he has alleged a claim of sex stereotyping pursuant to Title VII. As noted above, Smith's birth sex is male and this is the basis for his protected class status under Title VII even under this formulation of his claim.

Finally, we note that, in its opinion, the district court repeatedly places the term "sex stereotyping" in quotation marks and refers to it as a "term of art" used by Smith to disingenuously plead discrimination because of transsexualism. Similarly, Defendants refer to sex stereotyping as "the *Price Waterhouse* loophole." These characterizations are almost identical to the treatment that *Price Waterhouse* itself gave sex stereotyping in its briefs to the U.S. Supreme Court. As we do now, the Supreme Court noted the practice with disfavor, stating:

> In the specific context of sex stereotyping, an employer who acts on the basis of a belief that a woman cannot be aggressive, or that she must not be, has acted on the basis of gender. Although the parties do not overtly dispute this last proposition, the placement by Price Waterhouse of "sex stereotyping" in quotation marks throughout its brief seems to us an insinuation either that such stereotyping was not present in this case or that it lacks legal relevance. We reject both possibilities.

* * *

NOTES

1. *Transsexual as "sex:"* The court avoided addressing whether discrimination because of one's transsexualism is "sex." Unlike orientation, plaintiff was changing sexual reproductive organs which could be considered "sex." *Schroer v. Billington,* 577 F.Supp.2d 293 (D.D.C. 2008); *Glenn v. Brumby,* 663 F.3d 1312 (11th Cir. 2011) ("sex" within the analysis of the 14th Amendment.)

2. The analysis of the principal case, which is in accord with the weight of authority, presents a problem that requires artful pleading. Assume, an employee who exhibits "masculine" gender characteristics that are consistent with his male sex, is discriminated against when the employer discovers that the employee's sexual orientation is homosexual. Such discrimination is not "sex" discrimination in violation of Title VII. *Hamm v. Weyauwega Milk Products, Inc.,* 332 F.3d 1058 (7th Cir. 2003); *Dawson v. Bumble & Bumble,* 398 F.3d 211 (2d Cir. 2005); *Anderson v. Napolitano,* 93 EPD ¶ 43,825 (S.D. Fla, 2010).

3. *State Law*: While Congress continues to fail to enact proposed legislation protecting sexual orientation, as of 2009 twenty one states and more than 100 municipalities, including most major cities, prohibit such discrimination.

4. *"Don't ask":* Employer inquiries about sexuality or administering psychological tests that may disclose sexual orientation may violate the individual's right of privacy under state law. *Soroka v. Dayton Hudson Corp.,* 18 Cal.App.4th 1200 (1991).

5. PREGNANCY AND CHILDBIRTH

a. Non–Discrimination: Clause 1 of the PDA

The Pregnancy Discrimination Act of 1978 amended Title VII by inserting a new section, 701(k):

> The terms "because of sex" or "on the basis of sex" include, but are not limited to, because of or on the basis of pregnancy, childbirth, or related medical conditions; and women affected by pregnancy, childbirth, or related medical conditions shall be treated the same for all employment-related purposes, including receipt of benefits under fringe benefit programs, as other persons not so affected but similar in their ability or inability to work. * * * 42 U.S.C. § 2000e–(k)

NOTE

Structurally the PDA did not make "pregnancy, childbirth, and related medical conditions" protected classes within section 703 of Title VII, but placed the protection in the definition section of the statute. Note the two clauses in this "definition." First, is an unambiguous statement that pregnancy, childbirth, and related medical conditions *are* "sex," suggesting that any distinction based on pregnancy or childbirth is *per se* sex discrimination. However, this broad definition of sex is followed by a second conjunctive clause that requires employers to accord treatment for pregnancy, childbirth, and related medical conditions "the same for all employment-related purposes," as it treats "other persons not so affected." This purpose of this second clause was to overturn the holding and reasoning of *General Electric Co. v. Gilbert,* 429 U.S. 125, 97 S.Ct. 401, 50 L.Ed.2d 343 (1976), which had held that the general prohibition against sex discrimination in § 703(a) did not require employers who had health benefit plans to include pregnancy, childbirth, and related medical conditions in those plans.

However, the positive requirement language in this second clause left open the possibility of a negative implication that the second clause modifies the first by declaring that even where the employer makes distinctions based on pregnancy, childbirth, or related conditions, this action will not violate § 701(k) if it treats pregnancy-related conditions the same as it treats other medical conditions. **NEWPORT NEWS SHIPBUILDING AND DRY DOCK CO. V. E.E.O.C.**, 462 U.S. 669, 103 S.Ct. 2622, 77 L.Ed.2d (1983), footnote 14 stated: "The meaning of the first clause is not limited by the specific language in the second clause, which explains application of the general principle to women employee." Consider this in light of the cases which follow.

HALL v. NALCO COMPANY

United States Court of Appeals, Seventh Circuit, 2008
534 F.3d 644

SYKES, CIRCUIT JUDGE.

Cheryl Hall maintains she was fired by Nalco Company for taking time off from work to undergo in vitro fertilization after being diagnosed with infertility. She filed this suit under Title VII of the Civil Rights Act of 1964, as amended by the Pregnancy Discrimination Act ("PDA"), alleging her termination constituted discrimination on the basis of sex. Without reaching the merits of her claim, the district court granted summary judgment for Nalco on the ground that Hall could not prove sex discrimination because infertility is a gender-neutral condition.

We reverse. The focus of any Title VII sex-discrimination claim is whether the employer treated the employee differently because of the employee's sex. The PDA amended Title VII to provide that discrimination "because of" sex includes discrimination "because of or on the basis of pregnancy, childbirth, or related medical conditions." 42 U.S.C. § 2000e(k). Although infertility affects both men and women, Hall claims she was terminated for undergoing a medical procedure—a particular form of surgical impregnation—performed only on women on account of their childbearing capacity. Because adverse employment actions taken on account of childbearing capacity affect only women, Hall has stated a cognizable sex-discrimination claim under the language of the PDA.

Whether allegations of the type Hall has made state a claim for relief under Title VII is an issue of first impression in this circuit; we are also unaware that any other circuit has addressed the precise question presented here. Title VII makes it unlawful for an employer to discharge or otherwise discriminate against an employee in the terms and conditions of employment "because of such individual's . . . sex." In 1978 the Pregnancy Discrimination Act [PDA], amended Title VII to include the following definitional provision [The court here recites the above section 701(k)] * * *

The PDA was enacted to overrule the Supreme Court's decision in *General Electric Co. v. Gilbert,* 429 U.S. 125, 97 S.Ct. 401, 50 L.Ed.2d 343 (1976), which had held that excluding pregnancy from a list of nonoccupational disabilities covered by an employer's disability benefits plan did not amount to discrimination on the basis of sex.

The PDA created no new rights or remedies, but clarified the scope of Title VII by recognizing certain inherently gender-specific characteristics that may not form the basis for disparate treatment of employees. "[T]he simple test" in any Title VII sex-discrimination claim is whether the employer action in question treats an employee "in a manner which but for that person's sex would be different." The enactment of the PDA did not change this basic approach. The PDA "made clear that, for all Title VII purposes, discrimination based on a woman's pregnancy is, on its face, discrimination because of her sex." The same is true for disparate treatment based on childbirth and medical conditions related to pregnancy or childbirth.

The district court concluded that Hall's allegations do not state a Title VII claim because infertility is a gender-neutral condition entitled to no protection under the language of the PDA. In reaching this conclusion, the court relied primarily on two cases from other circuits holding that the PDA does not require employer insurance policies to cover infertility treatment so long as both male and female treatments are excluded. *See Saks v. Franklin Covey Co.,* 316 F.3d 337, 345 (2d Cir.2003) ("Because reproductive capacity is common to both men and women, we do not read the PDA as introducing a completely new classification of prohibited discrimination based solely on reproductive capacity."); *Krauel v. Iowa Methodist Med. Ctr.,* 95 F.3d 674, 680 (8th Cir.1996) ("[B]ecause the policy of denying insurance benefits for treatment of fertility problems applies to both female and male workers and thus is gender-neutral," it does not violate the PDA.).

Both *Saks* and *Krauel* distinguished the Supreme Court's decision in *International Union v. Johnson Controls, Inc.,* 499 U.S. 187, 111 S.Ct. 1196, 113 L.Ed.2d 158 (1991), * * *. Implicit in this holding is that classifications based on "fertility alone"—and by like implication, infertility alone-are not prohibited by the PDA, which reaches only gender-specific classifications. As the Second Circuit noted in *Saks,* this conclusion is necessary to reconcile the PDA with Title VII because "[i]ncluding infertility within the PDA's protection as a 'related medical condition[ ]' would result in the anomaly of defining a class that simultaneously includes equal numbers of both sexes and yet is somehow vulnerable to sex discrimination."

The district court's emphasis on this issue of "infertility alone" is therefore misplaced in the factual context of this case. As *Johnson Controls* illustrates, even where (in)fertility is at issue, the employer conduct complained of must actually *be gender neutral* to pass muster. The employer policy in *Johnson Controls* ran afoul of this mandate because its justification was the effect of lead exposure on fertility—an effect implicating both women and men—yet it barred only fertile women from employment. The Court concluded that the policy did not classify based on the gender-neutral characteristic of fertility alone, but rather on the gender-specific characteristic of childbearing capacity, or "potential for pregnancy," and was therefore invalid under the PDA.

Nalco's conduct, viewed in the light most favorable to Hall, suffers from the same defect as the policy in *Johnson Controls*. Employees terminated for taking time off to undergo IVF—just like those terminated for taking time off to give birth or receive other pregnancy-related care—will always be women. This is necessarily so; IVF is one of several assisted reproductive technologies that involves a surgical impregnation procedure Thus, contrary to the district court's conclusion, Hall was terminated not for the gender-neutral condition of infertility, but rather for the gender-specific quality of childbearing capacity.

* * *

It is clear that it is "sex" discrimination to discharge or refuse to hire a woman because she is pregnant, recently gave birth, or because the employer fears that she may become pregnant. Discharging her because of medical complications associated with pregnancy, such as a miscarriage, or because of her own medical complications following the birth likewise is proscribed sex discrimination.

STOUT v. BAXTER HEALTHCARE CORP.

United States Court of Appeals, Fifth Circuit, 2002
282 F.3d 856

GARWOOD, CIRCUIT JUDGE:

In this putative class action Plaintiff–Appellant Wilma Stout (Stout) sued Defendant–Appellee Baxter Healthcare Corp. (Baxter) pursuant to Title VII of the Civil Rights Act of 1964, as amended by the Pregnancy Discrimination Act of 1978 (PDA).[1] Stout appeals a summary judgment in favor of Baxter and the denial of her cross motion for summary judgment. Finding no error, we affirm.

Stout was hired by Baxter as a material handler in May of 1998. Pursuant to Baxter's standard policy, Stout was a probationary employee for the

---

1. Stout is only asserting a claim under the PDA; the Family and Medical Leave Act (FMLA), 29 U.S.C. §§ 2601–2654, is not at issue in this case. The FLMA does not apply to employees, such as Stout, who have been employed less than twelve months or who have worked less than 1,250 hours during the previous twelve months.

first ninety days of her employment. During this probationary period, Baxter evaluates new hires' job skills and performance. Probationary employees are subject to a strict attendance policy: anyone who misses more than three days during the period is terminated. Baxter does not provide vacation time or medical leave for probationary employees.

Stout, who was pregnant during the probationary period, received positive performance reviews and maintained a perfect attendance record during her first two months. But, beginning on August 14, 1998, Stout was absent for more than three days of work after she experienced early labor and suffered a miscarriage that rendered her medically unable to work for over two weeks. Stout notified her supervisor of her condition immediately, and provided a medical excuse a week later, but Baxter terminated Stout on August 21 because her absenteeism was clearly in excess of that permitted during the probationary period.

After receiving a right-to-sue letter from the Equal Employment Opportunity Commission (EEOC), Stout sued Baxter claiming pregnancy discrimination under the PDA and alleging that she was fired "because of" her pregnancy * * *

Title VII of the Civil Rights Act prohibits an employer from "discriminat[ing] against any individual with respect to . . . compensation, terms, conditions, or privileges of employment, because of such individual's . . . sex. . . ." The PDA amended Title VII by explicitly including discrimination based on pregnancy and related medical conditions within the definition of sex discrimination. * * *

Stout's claim of disparate treatment has no merit. She argues that she was fired "because of" her pregnancy. But, to the contrary, *all* of the evidence in the record indicates that she "was fired because of her absenteeism, not because of her pregnancy." There is no evidence she would have been treated differently if her absences had been due to some reason unrelated to pregnancy or if she had been absent the same amount but not pregnant. Baxter's policy does not in any way mention or focus on pregnancy, childbirth or any related medical condition. So far as here relevant, it merely limits the permissible absenteeism, on any basis, of all probationary employees. Although Baxter's policy results in the dismissal of any pregnant or post-partum employee who misses more than three days of work during the probationary period, it equally requires the termination of any non-pregnant employee who misses more than three days. There is no evidence in the record that Stout was treated any differently than any other employee who failed to comply with Baxter's probationary attendance policy. Such a policy does not violate the PDA: "[T]he [PDA] does not protect a pregnant employee from being discharged for being absent from work even if her absence is due to pregnancy or to complications of pregnancy, unless the absences of nonpregnant employees are overlooked." The district court properly granted Baxter's summary judgment motion with respect to her disparate treatment claim.

NOTES

1. ***NASHVILLE GAS CO. v. SATTY,*** 434 U.S. 136, 98 S.Ct. 347, 54 L.Ed.2d 356 (1977), which pre-dated the PDA, held that an employer rule causing employees to lose accumulated seniority while on pregnancy leave imposed a unique burden on women, and such *burdens* constitute sex discrimination, even if other reasons requiring leave result in a similar loss of seniority. Thus, pregnancy was being treated the same as other conditions similarly affecting the ability to work, but because pregnancy was a *burden* suffered only by women, such a disadvantage imposed only on women was "sex" discrimination.

2. *Accommodation or reassignment:* A pregnant woman does not seek leave, but based on medical advice seeks reassignment to less strenuous duties that require little standing or lifting. If the employer regularly assigns light duty for other medical conditions, to refuse such accommodation for the employee's pregnancy would be sex discrimination. *Ensley–Gaines v. Runyon,* 100 F.3d 1220 (6th Cir. 1996). However, if the employer has no such practice the PDA may not demand such an accommodation for pregnancy. *Walsh v. National Computer Systems,* 332 F.3d 1150 (8th Cir. 2003). *Serendnyj v. Beverly Healthcare, LLC,* 656 F.3d 540 (7th Cir. 2011), went even further. The employer had accommodated persons who had defined "disabilities" under the Americans With Disabilities Act or who suffered from work related medical conditions by assigning them light work, but refused to make a similar light-work reassignment for a pregnant employee. Held: absent a practice of reassigning light work for *non-disabling and non-work related* medical conditions, the employer had not engaged in sex discrimination. Reconsider *Nashville Gas Co. v. Satty, supra,* note 1.

3. ***Family and Medical Leave Act (FMLA)*** 29 U.S.C. §§ 2601 *et seq.* The FMLA requires the grant of up to 12 weeks per year of *unpaid* leave to workers for the purpose of: a) birth, care, or adoption of a child, b) serious health condition of the employee, or c) to care for a seriously ill spouse, child or parent of the employee. The FMLA is covered in more detail, *infra* page 108.

b. Abortions

DOE v. C.A.R.S PROTECTION PLUS, INC.

United States Court of Appeals, Third Circuit, 2008
527 F.3d 358

NYGAARD, CIRCUIT JUDGE.

Jane Doe sued her former employer, C.A.R.S. Protection Plus, Inc. (CARS), alleging employment discrimination based on gender, in violation of Title VII of the Civil Rights Act. The District Court granted the employer's motion for summary judgment, finding that Doe had failed to establish a *prima facie* case of discrimination. We will reverse.

* * *

I.

A.

CARS does business in several states insuring used cars. CARS hired Jane Doe as a graphic artist in June 1999. * * * Fred Kohl, Vice–President and part-owner of the company, was Doe's supervisor. In May of 2000, Doe learned that she was pregnant. When she told Kohl she was pregnant, she asked Kohl about making up any time missed for doctor's appointments. Kohl told Doe they would "play it by ear."

* * *

On Wednesday, August 9th, Doe learned that her baby had severe deformities and her physician recommended that her pregnancy be terminated. That afternoon, Doe's husband again telephoned Kohl and told him that Doe would not be at work the next day. Kohl approved the absence and asked that Doe's husband call him the following day.

Doe had an additional doctor's appointment on Thursday, August 10th. Doe's husband testified that he called CARS again on that Thursday. * * * [H]e spoke with Kohl and told him that the pregnancy would be terminated the following day. Doe's husband requested that she be permitted to take one week of vacation the following week. According to Doe's husband's testimony, Kohl approved the request for a one-week vacation. Her pregnancy was terminated on Friday, August 11, 2000. Neither Doe nor her husband called Kohl over the weekend of August 12th.

A funeral was arranged for Doe's baby on Wednesday, August 16th. Kohl gave Leona Dunnett (the baby's aunt) permission to take one hour off work to attend the funeral. * * * After the funeral * * * Doe called Kohl who told her that she had been discharged.

* * *

We note at the outset that Doe does not assert a typical pregnancy discrimination claim. She does not claim, for example, that she was discriminated against because she was pregnant or that she had been fired while on maternity leave. Instead, she argues that she was discharged because she underwent a surgical abortion. Whether the protections generally afforded pregnant women under the PDA also extend to women who have elected to terminate their pregnancies is a question of first impression in this Circuit.

II.

A.

* * * [In] *Curay–Cramer v. Ursuline Acad. of Wilmington, Delaware*, 450 F.3d 130 (3d Cir.2006), the Appellant argued that Title VII's opposition clause protects any employee who has had an abortion, who contemplates having an abortion, or who supports the rights of women who do so. Although we did not directly address the question in that case, we pointed to a decision of the Court of Appeals for the Sixth Circuit with approval:

We note that the Sixth Circuit Court of Appeals has held that "an employer may not discriminate against a woman employee because 'she has exercised her right to have an abortion.'" *Turic v. Holland Hospitality, Inc.,* 85 F.3d 1211, 1214 (6th Cir.1996). Extending that principle, the Sixth Circuit further held that an employer "cannot take adverse employment action against a female employee for merely thinking about what she has a right to do. * * *

* * * The EEOC guidelines interpreting this section, to which we give a high degree of deference * * * expressly state that an abortion is covered by Title VII:

> The basic principle of the [PDA] is that women affected by pregnancy and related conditions must be treated the same as other applicants and employees on the basis of their ability or inability to work. A woman is therefore protected against such practices as being fired ... merely because she is pregnant or has had an abortion.

Appendix 29 C.F.R. pt. 1604 App. (1986). Similarly, the legislative history of section 2000e(k) provides the following guidance:

> Because [the PDA] applies to all situations in which women are "affected by pregnancy, childbirth, and related medical conditions," its basic language covers women who chose to terminate their pregnancies. Thus, no employer may, for example, fire or refuse to hire a woman simply because she has exercised her right to have an abortion.

Clearly, the plain language of the statute, together with the legislative history and the EEOC guidelines, support a conclusion that an employer may not discriminate against a woman employee because she has exercised her right to have an abortion. We now hold that the term "related medical conditions" includes an abortion.

B

* * *

Neither party disputes that Doe has met her burden on the first three elements of a *prima facie* pregnancy discrimination case: 1) she is or was pregnant and that her employer knew she was pregnant; 2) she was qualified for her job; and, 3) she suffered an adverse employment decision. It is the fourth element that is in dispute, namely whether there is some nexus between her pregnancy and her employment termination that would permit a fact-finder to infer unlawful discrimination.

The evidence most often used to establish this nexus is that of disparate treatment, whereby a plaintiff shows that she was treated less favorably than similarly situated employees who are not in plaintiff's protected class. Although we have held that "the PDA does not require that employers treat pregnant employees better than other temporarily disabled employees" [T]he PDA does require that employers treat pregnant employees no worse. Comparing Doe to other non-pregnant workers who were temporarily disabled, we conclude that Doe has provided sufficient evidence to satisfy the fourth element of the *prima facie* case and has thus raised an inference of discrimination sufficient to defeat summary judgment.

3.

Our factual analysis starts with CARS' somewhat less than compassionate leave policies. A memorandum authored by Kohl reveals that CARS employees were given no personal or sick leave. After one year on the job, employees were given five days' paid vacation. After five years' employment, they were given ten days. Any time taken off during a work day was to be deducted from the employee's vacation time or be unpaid.

* * * The record shows that different CARS employees were treated differently. Mike King, for example, suffered a heart attack while he was employed by CARS and testified that, although he or his wife did call to tell Kohl he was still in the hospital, they did not do so daily, and that he was paid during his absence. King missed two and a half days of work due to his heart attack. Babich also testified that King's wife called in once to tell the office how he was doing, but that no one called every day.

Another employee, Bruce Boynton, left work in the middle of the day and admitted himself into a psychiatric hospital. Kohl called Boynton while he was in the hospital and told him to report back to work or be fired. On another occasion, Boynton went to the emergency room after work. He called Kohl the next morning and called at least once more during the three days he missed for a hernia and back problem.

The testimony of Alivia Babich, Kohl's secretary, confirms this disparate treatment. Babich testified that for every employee, CARS had a "separate set of rules" and that there was no uniformly enforced rule concerning the use of vacation or sick time. She specifically indicated that there was no rule at CARS which required an employee who was sick to call the company every day to report that they would miss work due to illness. Babich also testified that when CARS employee Michael King suffered a heart attack, neither King nor his wife called-in every day. Further, Babich testified that at least two other employees who missed work due to illness were not required to telephone the company every day. This testimony indicates that although other employees were not expected to call the office every day, Doe's employment was terminated for precisely this reason. This testimony alone satisfies Doe's burden of establishing that other employees who were similarly situated were treated differently than her. * * *

Finally, Doe argues that her discharge only three working days after having an abortion raises an inference of discrimination because the temporal proximity between her abortion and the adverse employment action is "unusually suggestive." We have held temporal proximity sufficient to create an inference of causality to defeat summary judgment. * * *

Here, Doe was fired on the day her baby was buried, just three working days after she notified Kohl that she would have to undergo an abortion. Because the District Court found Doe's discharge to coincide with her failure to "make further phone calls to Kohl as he had asked her to do," it reasoned that the timing was not unusually suggestive of discrimination. The temporal proximity, however, is sufficient here to meet Doe's minimal *prima facie* case burden as to the causal connection element. *See e.g. Fasold v. Justice,* 409 F.3d 178, 189–90 (3d Cir.2005) (discussing a period less than one month and noting that "a short period of time" may provide the evidentiary basis of an inference of retaliation).

Summary judgment is to be used sparingly in employment discrimination cases, especially where, as here, we are viewing the case at first glance. Mindful that the plaintiff's burden at this first stage is not particularly onerous, we conclude that Doe has established a *prima facie* case.

* * *

NOTES

1. *Rationale: The Two Clauses of the PDA:* The court seemed to require a showing that the employer treated plaintiff's absence because of an abortion differently from other medical conditions. Should not an adverse action based upon an abortion be facial sex discrimination, under the first clause of the PDA without regard to whether plaintiff received dissimilar treatment?

2. *Public Policy:* As long as a woman has a constitutionally protected right of privacy that guarantees to her a right to secure an abortion, would not the employer's dismissal for exercising that right contravene public policy, and thus could be a wrongful discharge under state tort law?

c. Benefits for Pregnancy: Clause 2 of the PDA

NEWPORT NEWS SHIPBUILDING AND DRY DOCK COMPANY v. EQUAL EMPLOYMENT OPPORTUNITY COMMISSION

Supreme Court of the United States, 1983
462 U.S. 669, 103 S.Ct. 2622, 77 L.Ed.2d 89

JUSTICE STEVENS delivered the opinion of the Court.

In 1978 Congress decided to overrule our decision in *General Electric Co. v. Gilbert,* 429 U.S. 125, 97 S.Ct. 401, 50 L.Ed.2d 343 (1976), by amending Title VII of the Civil Rights Act of 1964 "to prohibit sex discrimination on the basis of pregnancy." On the effective date of the act, petitioner amended its health insurance plan to provide its female employees with hospitalization benefits for pregnancy-related conditions to the same extent as for other medical conditions. The plan continued, however, to provide less favorable pregnancy benefits for spouses of male employees. The question presented is whether the amended plan complies with the amended statute.

Petitioner's plan provides hospitalization and medical-surgical coverage for a defined category of employees and a defined category of dependents. Dependents covered by the plan include employees' spouses, unmarried children between 14 days and 19 years of age, and some older dependent children. Prior to April 29, 1979, the scope of the plan's coverage for eligible dependents was identical to its coverage for employees. All covered males, whether employees or dependents, were treated alike for purposes of hospitalization coverage. All covered females, whether employees or dependents, also were treated alike. Moreover, with one relevant exception, the coverage for males and females was identical. The exception was a limitation on hospital coverage for pregnancy that did not apply to any other hospital confinement.

After the plan was amended in 1979, it provided the same hospitalization coverage for male and female employees themselves for all medical conditions, but it differentiated between female employees and spouses of male employees in its provision of pregnancy-related benefits. In a booklet describing the plan, petitioner explained the amendment that gave rise to this litigation in this way:

"B. Effective April 29, 1979, maternity benefits for female employees will be paid the same as any other hospital confinement as described in question 16. This applies only to deliveries beginning on April 29, 1979 and thereafter.

"C. Maternity benefits for the wife of a male employee will continue to be paid as described in part 'A' of this question."

In turn, Part A stated, "The Basic Plan pays up to $500 of the hospital charges and 100% of reasonable and customary for delivery and anesthesiologist charges." As the Court of Appeals observed, "To the extent that the hospital charges in connection with an uncomplicated delivery may exceed $500, therefore, a male employee receives less complete coverage of spousal disabilities than does a female employee."

* * *

Ultimately the question we must decide is whether petitioner has discriminated against its male employees with respect to their compensation, terms, conditions, or privileges of employment because of their sex within the meaning of § 703(a)(1) of Title VII. Although the Pregnancy Discrimination Act has clarified the meaning of certain terms in this section, neither that Act nor the underlying statute contains a definition of the word "discriminate." In order to decide whether petitioner's plan discriminates against male employees because of *their* sex, we must therefore go beyond the bare statutory language. Accordingly, we shall consider whether Congress, by enacting the Pregnancy Discrimination Act, not only overturned the specific holding in *General Electric v. Gilbert, supra,* but also rejected the test of discrimination employed by the Court in that case. We believe it did. Under the proper test petitioner's plan is unlawful, because the protection it affords to married male employees is less comprehensive than the protection it affords to married female employees.

I

At issue in *General Electric v. Gilbert* was the legality of a disability plan that provided the company's employees with weekly compensation during periods of disability resulting from nonoccupational causes. Because the plan excluded disabilities arising from pregnancy, the District Court and the Court of Appeals concluded that it discriminated against female employees because of their sex. This Court reversed.

After noting that Title VII does not define the term "discrimination," the Court applied an analysis derived from cases construing the Equal Protection Clause of the Fourteenth Amendment to the Constitution. The *Gilbert* opinion quoted at length from a footnote in *Geduldig v. Aiello,* 417 U.S. 484, 94 S.Ct. 2485, 41 L.Ed.2d 256 (1974), a case which had upheld the constitutionality of excluding pregnancy coverage under California's disability insurance plan.[12] "Since it is a finding of sex-based discrimination that must trigger, in a case such as this, the finding of an unlawful employment practice under § 703(a)(1)," the Court added, "*Geduldig* is precisely in point in its holding that an exclusion of pregnancy from a disability-benefits plan providing general coverage is not a gender-based discrimination at all."

The principal emphasis in the text of the *Geduldig* opinion, unlike the quoted footnote, was on the reasonableness of the State's cost justifications for the classification in its insurance program.

* * * When Congress amended Title VII in 1978, it unambiguously expressed its disapproval of both the holding and the reasoning of the Court in the *Gilbert* decision. It incorporated a new subsection in the "definitions" applicable "[f]or the purposes of this subchapter." The first clause of the Act states, quite simply: "The terms 'because of sex' or 'on the basis of sex' include, but are not limited to, because of or on the basis of pregnancy, childbirth, or related medical conditions."[14] The House Report stated, "It is the Committee's view that the dissenting Justices correctly interpreted the Act." Similarly, the Senate Report quoted passages from the two dissenting opinions, stating that they "correctly

---

12. " 'While it is true that only women can become pregnant, it does not follow that every legislative classification concerning pregnancy is a sex-based classification like those considered in *Reed* [*v. Reed, 404 U.S. 71 (1971)*]" Normal pregnancy is an objectively identifiable physical condition with unique characteristics. Absent a showing that distinctions involving pregnancy are mere pretexts designed to effect an invidious discrimination against the members of one sex or the other, lawmakers are constitutionally free to include or exclude pregnancy from the coverage of legislation such as this on any reasonable basis, just as with respect to any other physical condition.

   " 'The lack of identity between the excluded disability and gender as such under this insurance program becomes clear upon the most cursory analysis. The program divides potential recipients into two groups-pregnant women and nonpregnant persons. While the first group is exclusively female, the second includes members of both sexes.' "

14. The meaning of the first clause is not limited by the specific language in the second clause, which explains the application of the general principle to women employees.

express both the principle and the meaning of title VII." Proponents of the bill repeatedly emphasized that the Supreme Court had erroneously interpreted Congressional intent and that amending legislation was necessary to reestablish the principles of Title VII law as they had been understood prior to the *Gilbert* decision. Many of them expressly agreed with the views of the dissenting Justices

As petitioner argues, congressional discussion focused on the needs of female members of the work force rather than spouses of male employees. This does not create a "negative inference" limiting the scope of the act to the specific problem that motivated its enactment. Congress apparently assumed that existing plans that included benefits for dependents typically provided no less pregnancy-related coverage for the wives of male employees than they did for female employees. When the question of differential coverage for dependents was addressed in the Senate Report, the Committee indicated that it should be resolved "on the basis of existing title VII principles." The legislative context makes it clear that Congress was not thereby referring to the view of Title VII reflected in this Court's *Gilbert* opinion. Proponents of the legislation stressed throughout the debates that Congress had always intended to protect *all* individuals from sex discrimination in employment-including but not limited to pregnant women workers. Against this background we review the terms of the amended statute to decide whether petitioner has unlawfully discriminated against its male employees.

II

Section 703(a) makes it an unlawful employment practice for an employer to "discriminate against any individual with respect to his compensation, terms, conditions, or privileges of employment, because of such individual's race, color, religion, sex, or national origin. . . ." Health insurance and other fringe benefits are "compensation, terms, conditions, or privileges of employment." Male as well as female employees are protected against discrimination. Thus, if a private employer were to provide complete health insurance coverage for the dependents of its female employees, and no coverage at all for the dependents of its male employees, it would violate Title VII.[22] Such a practice would not pass the simple test of Title VII discrimination that we enunciated in *Los Angeles Department of Water & Power v. Manhart,* 435 U.S. 702, 711, 98 S.Ct. 1370, 1377, 55 L.Ed.2d 657 (1978), for it would treat a male employee with dependents "in a manner which but for that person's sex would be different." The same result would be reached even if the magnitude of the discrimination were smaller. For example, a plan that provided complete hospitalization coverage for the spouses of female employees but did not cover spouses of male

---

22. Consistently since 1970 the EEOC has considered it unlawful under Title VII for an employer to provide different insurance coverage for spouses of male and female employees. See Guidelines On Discrimination Because of Sex, 29 CFR 1604.9(d);

Similarly, in our Equal Protection Clause cases we have repeatedly held that, if the spouses of female employees receive less favorable treatment in the provision of benefits, the practice discriminates not only against the spouses but also against the female employees on the basis of sex. *Frontiero v. Richardson,* 411 U.S. 677, 688, 93 S.Ct. 1764, 1771, 36 L.Ed.2d 583 (1973)

employees when they had broken bones would violate Title VII by discriminating against male employees.

Petitioner's practice is just as unlawful. Its plan provides limited pregnancy-related benefits for employees' wives, and affords more extensive coverage for employees' spouses for all other medical conditions requiring hospitalization. Thus the husbands of female employees receive a specified level of hospitalization coverage for all conditions; the wives of male employees receive such coverage except for pregnancy-related conditions. [24] Although *Gilbert* concluded that an otherwise inclusive plan that singled out pregnancy-related benefits for exclusion was nondiscriminatory on its face, because only women can become pregnant, Congress has unequivocally rejected that reasoning. The 1978 Act makes clear that it is discriminatory to treat pregnancy-related conditions less favorably than other medical conditions. Thus petitioner's plan unlawfully gives married male employees a benefit package for their dependents that is less inclusive than the dependency coverage provided to married female employees.

There is no merit to petitioner's argument that the prohibitions of Title VII do not extend to discrimination against pregnant spouses because the statute applies only to discrimination in employment. A two-step analysis demonstrates the fallacy in this contention. The Pregnancy Discrimination Act has now made clear that, for all Title VII purposes, discrimination based on a woman's pregnancy is, on its face, discrimination because of her sex. And since the sex of the spouse is always the opposite of the sex of the employee, it follows inexorably that discrimination against female spouses in the provision of fringe benefits is also discrimination against male employees.[25] By making clear that an employer could not discriminate on the basis of an employee's pregnancy, Congress did not erase the original prohibition against discrimination on the basis of an employee's sex.

In short, Congress' rejection of the premises of *General Electric v. Gilbert* forecloses any claim that an insurance program excluding pregnancy coverage for female beneficiaries and providing complete coverage to similarly situated male beneficiaries does not discriminate on the basis of sex. Petitioner's plan is the mirror image of the plan at issue in *Gilbert*. The pregnancy limitation in this case violates Title VII by discriminating against male employees.[26]

---

24. This policy is analogous to the exclusion of broken bones for the wives of male employees, except that both employees' wives and employees' husbands may suffer broken bones, but only employees' wives can become pregnant.

25. See n. 22, *supra*. This reasoning does not require that a medical insurance plan treat the pregnancies of employees' wives the same as the pregnancies of female employees. For example, as the EEOC recognizes. An employer might provide full coverage for employees and no coverage at all for dependents. Similarly, a disability plan covering employees' children may exclude or limit maternity benefits. Although the distinction between pregnancy and other conditions is, according to the 1978 Act, discrimination "on the basis of sex," the exclusion affects male and female *employees* equally since both may have pregnant dependent daughters. The EEOC's guidelines permit differential treatment of the pregnancies of dependents who are not spouses.

26. Because the 1978 Act expressly states that exclusion of pregnancy coverage is gender-based discrimination on its face, it eliminates any need to consider the average monetary value of the plan's coverage to male and female employees.

The judgment of the Court of Appeals is *Affirmed*.

JUSTICE REHNQUIST, with whom JUSTICE POWELL joins, dissenting.

* * *

In a case presenting a relatively simple question of statutory construction, the Court pays virtually no attention to the language of the Pregnancy Discrimination Act or the legislative history pertaining to that language.

* * *

It is undisputed that in § 703(a)(1) the word "individual" refers to an employee or applicant for employment. As modified by the first clause of the definitional provision of the Pregnancy Discrimination Act, the proscription in § 703(a)(1) is for discrimination "against any individual . . . *because of such individual's . . . pregnancy,* childbirth, or related medical conditions." This can only be read as referring to the pregnancy of an *employee*.

That this result was not inadvertent on the part of Congress is made very evident by the second clause of the Act, language that the Court essentially ignores in its opinion. When Congress in this clause further explained the proscription it was creating by saying that "women affected by pregnancy . . . shall be treated the same . . . as other persons not so affected but *similar in their ability or inability to work*" it could only have been referring to *female employees*. * * *

The Court concedes that this is a correct reading of the second clause. Then in an apparent effort to escape the impact of this provision, the Court asserts that "[t]he meaning of the first clause is not limited by the specific language in the second clause." I do not disagree. But this conclusion does not help the Court, for as explained above, when the definitional provision of the first clause is inserted in § 703(a)(1), it says the very same thing: the proscription added to Title VII applies only to female employees.

The plain language of the Pregnancy Discrimination Act leaves little room for the Court's conclusion that the Act was intended to extend beyond female employees. The Court concedes that "congressional discussion focused on the needs of female members of the work force rather than spouses of male employees." In fact, the singular focus of discussion on the problems of the *pregnant worker* is striking.

* * *

NOTES

1. In light of the Court's footnote 14 consider again the question of whether facial discrimination because of pregnancy is permissible even when

---

The cost of providing complete health insurance coverage for the dependents of male employees, including pregnant wives, might exceed the cost of providing such coverage for the dependents of female employees. But although that type of cost differential may properly be analyzed in passing on the constitutionality of a State's health insurance plan, see *Geduldig v. Aiello, supra,* no such justification is recognized under Title VII once discrimination has been shown. 29 CFR § 1604.9(e) (1982) ("It shall not be a defense under Title VII to a charge of sex discrimination in benefits that the cost of such benefits is greater with respect to one sex than the other.")

the employer treats pregnancy and childbirth the same as other medical conditions.

2. *Abortion:* Review *Doe v. C.A.R.S. Protection Plus, supra p.* 89. A proviso in § 701(k) states:

> This subsection shall not require an employer to pay for health insurance benefits for abortion, except where the life of the mother would be endangered if the fetus were carried to term, or except where medical complications have arisen from an abortion: Provided nothing herein shall preclude an employer from providing abortion benefits or otherwise affect bargaining agreements in regard to abortion.

3. *Contraception:*

> Contraception is a means by which a woman controls her ability to become pregnant. The PDA's prohibition on discrimination against women based on their ability to become pregnant thus necessarily includes a prohibition on discrimination related to a woman's use of contraceptives. * * * Respondents could not discharge an employee from her job because she uses contraceptives. So, too, Respondents may not discriminate in their health insurance plan by denying benefits for prescription contraceptives when they provide benefits for comparable drugs and devices.

EEOC Decision Dec. 14, 2000. www.eeoc.gov/policy/docs/decision-contraception. 2 EP Guide Para 6878. *Accord, Erickson v. Bartell Drug Co.,* 141 F.Supp.2d 1266 (W.D.Wash 2001).

In reaching its conclusion the EEOC noted, not only that a woman's regulation of her reproduction is a major preventive care health benefit to women, but that contraceptives are widely prescribed for treatment of numerous serious non-pregnancy related medical conditions that exclusively affect women. Moreover, studies have shown that women typically spend about 70% more out-of-pocket for their health care costs than do men (about $300 more), and that prescription contraceptives constitute the largest single factor of that disproportionate cost. *Catholic Charities of Sacramento v. Superior Court,* 109 Cal.Rptr.2d 176 (2001) *aff'd,* 85 P.3d 67 (2004). Thus, exclusion of contraceptives from prescription coverage imposes a health risk burden on women not suffered by men, and in the alternative, imposes on women employees a significant disproportionate economic burden.

Nonetheless, *In re Union Pacific R.R.,* 479 F.3d 936 (8th Cir. 2007), relying primarily on the fact that the employer's drug prescription plan excluded contraception coverage for both men and women (conveniently ignoring that males do not need prescriptions to secure contraceptives) held in a 2–1 decision that exclusion of contraceptive coverage did not violate the PDA.

Would a plan that broadly covered surgical procedures such as removal of the gall bladder, appendix, and prostate, but excluded hysterectomies, violate the PDA? If such sex-specific exclusion violates the PDA, would the plan be in compliance with the PDA simply because it also excluded visectomies? *In re*

Union Pacific R.R., supra, suggests that the PDA is not being violated by such "equal" treatment. *But see,* Law, *Sex Discrimination & Insurance,* 73 Wash. L.Rev. 363 (1998).

About half the states, including California, expressly require inclusion of contraception in all health care plans. *E.g.,* Cal.Health & Safety Code, Sec. 1367.25; Ins.Code, Sec. 10123.196. This mandate is not seen as violating the First Amendment when applied to religious charities, hospitals, and schools. *Catholic Charities of Sacramento v. Superior Court,* 109 Cal.Rptr.2d 176 (2001) *aff'd,* 85 P.3d 67 (2004).

6. MARRIAGE, MARITAL STATUS, CHILDREN, AND CHILDCARE

a. Generally, "Sex–Plus" Classifications

***Phillips v. Martin Marietta Corp.*, 400 U.S. 542, 91 S.Ct. 496, 27 L.Ed.2d 613 (1971),** involved an employer who refused to employ *women* who had pre-school aged children. The court of appeals held that this practice did not violate Title VII in that it involved a practice not proscribed by Title VII, having young children. That it was applicable to women, but not men, was not determinative, in that sex "plus" a neutral, or lawful, factor was deemed not sex discrimination. In effect, Title VII was read to require discrimination *solely* because of sex. The Supreme Court, per curiam, reversed, stating:

> The Civil Rights Act of 1964 requires that persons of like qualifications be given employment opportunities irrespective of their sex. The Court of Appeals therefore erred in reading this section as permitting one hiring policy for women and another for men—each having pre-school-aged children.

In ***Fleming v. Ayers & Assoc.*,** 948 F.2d 993 (6th Cir.1991), the employer refused to hire plaintiff due to high insurance costs associated with her child's illness at birth. The court assumed that discriminating against an *individual* because the individual had a child was not proscribed sex discrimination. The court went on to find that "related medical conditions" in § 701(k) refers to medical conditions of the pregnant employee, not to the child that she delivered. As there was no evidence that male employees with sick children were treated differently, discriminating against a woman because of her sick child did not violate Title VII.

b. Marriage, Non–Marriage

Approximately one half of the states, including California, prohibit discrimination because of one's marital or family status. Title VII has no similar protection. The prohibition against "sex" discrimination does not include marriage or marital status. Thus, requiring all employees to be single (or married), or refusing to employ *persons* who have been divorced would not be discrimination because of "sex." *Little v. Wuerl,* 929

F.2d.944 (3d Cir. 1991). However, if such rules are applied to one sex only, barring married women, but not married men, the rule would be discrimination against women because of their "sex." *Sprogis v. United Airlines,* 444 F.2d 1194 (7th Cir. 1971).

Employers may refuse to employ individuals who are married *to each other.* A "no spouse" rule enforced equally against both sexes is not facial sex discrimination. *EEOC v. Rath Packing Co.,* 787 F.2d 318 (8th Cir. 1986). Similarly, an employer may impose a non-fraternization policy that prohibits employees from having social relationships with each other. If enforced equally against both sexes, it is a permissible neutral rule. *See e.g, Duchon v. Cajon Co.,* 791 F.2d 43 (6th Cir. 1986).

c. Nepotism

Thomas v. Washington County School Bd.*,* 915 F.2d 922 (4th Cir. 1990), held that *preference* for a spouse of current employee stated no Title VII claim. "Nepotism is not *per se* violative of Title VII." Accord: *Platner v. Cash & Thomas Contractors, Inc.* 908 F.2d 902 (11th Cir. 1990).

d. Unwed Pregnancy

As "sex" is defined to include "pregnancy" it would seem that Title VII proscribes discrimination against a woman who is pregnant *and* unmarried. This would appear to be a form of "sex-plus" discrimination proscribed in *Phillips v. Martin Marietta, supra. Cline v. Catholic Diocese of Toledo,* 206 F.3d 651 (6th Cir. 2000). It has been argued that such discrimination is based on the individual's "immoral" conduct not upon her sex. However, as this immorality rule would be applied only to, and would impose a burden only upon, women it would still seem to be a form of sex discrimination. *See,* ***Nashville Gas Co. v. Satty,*** 434 U.S. 136, 98 S.Ct. 347, 54 L.Ed.2d 356 (1977).

e. Childcare Responsibilities

CHADWICK v. WELLPOINT, INC.

United States Court of Appeals, First Circuit, 2009
561 F.3d 38

STAHL, CIRCUIT JUDGE.

Laurie Chadwick brought a claim of sex discrimination under Title VII, against WellPoint, Inc. and Anthem Health Plans of Maine, Inc. (collectively, "WellPoint"), after she was denied a promotion. She alleged that her employer failed to promote her because of a sex-based stereotype that women who are mothers, particularly of young children, neglect their jobs in favor of their presumed childcare responsibilities. Having carefully reviewed the record, we are convinced that the district court erred in granting summary judgment in favor of WellPoint and therefore reverse and remand for further proceedings. * * *

I. Background

* * *

Chadwick was a long-time employee of WellPoint, an insurance company, in its Maine office. She was hired by WellPoint in 1997, and was promoted in 1999 to the position of "Recovery Specialist II," which involved the pursuit of overpayment claims and claims for reimbursement from third parties. In 2006, encouraged by her supervisor, she applied for a promotion to a management position entitled "Recovery Specialist Lead" or "Team Lead." In this position, the successful candidate would be responsible for the recovery function for the region encompassing Maine, New Hampshire, and Connecticut. Because Chadwick was already performing several of the responsibilities of the Team Lead position and based on her supervisor's comments, Chadwick believed she was the frontrunner for the position. In addition, on her most recent performance evaluation in 2005, she had received excellent reviews, scoring a 4.40 out of a possible 5.00 points.

There were two finalists for the Team Lead position, Chadwick and another in-house candidate, Donna Ouelette. While Chadwick had held the Recovery Specialist II position for seven years, Ouelette had only been promoted to that position about a year earlier. In addition, Ouelette had scored lower than Chadwick, though satisfactorily, on her most recent performance review, receiving a 3.84 out of a possible 5.0 points.

Three managers interviewed the two finalists: Linda Brink, who had previously supervised and worked closely with Chadwick; Dawn Leno, the Director of Recovery; and Nanci Miller, Chadwick's immediate supervisor. Nanci Miller was the ultimate decisionmaker for the promotion but she considered input from Brink and Leno in reaching her decision. Based on her own perceptions and those of Brink and Leno, Miller graded Ouelette's interview performance higher than Chadwick's. Miller subsequently offered the promotion to Ouelette over Chadwick.

At the time of the promotion decision, Chadwick was the mother of an eleven-year-old son and six-year-old triplets in kindergarten. There is no allegation, insinuation, or for that matter evidence that Chadwick's work performance was negatively impacted by any childcare responsibilities she may have had. Indeed, Miller, the decisionmaker, did not know that Chadwick was the mother of young triplets until shortly before the promotion decision was made. Apparently, Chadwick's husband, the primary caretaker for the children, stayed home with them during the day while Chadwick worked. He also worked off-hour shifts, presumably nights and weekends, when Chadwick was at home with the children. During the same period, Chadwick was also taking one course a semester at the University of Southern Maine.

Chadwick alleges that WellPoint denied her the promotion based on the sex-based stereotype that mothers, particularly those with young children, neglect their work duties in favor of their presumed childcare obligations.

To support this claim, Chadwick points to the fact that she was significantly more qualified for the promotion than was Ouelette, and also highlights three statements made by management around the time of the promotion decision.

First, on May 9, 2006, two months before the decision was reached, Miller, the decisionmaker, found out that Chadwick had three six-year-old children (in addition to an eleven-year-old son). Miller sent an email to Chadwick stating, "Oh my—I did not know you had triplets. Bless you!"

Second, during Chadwick's interview with Brink, her former supervisor, she was asked how she would respond if an associate did not complete a project on time. Unhappy with Chadwick's answer, Brink replied, "Laurie, you are a mother [.] [W]ould you let your kids off the hook that easy if they made a mess in [their] room[?] [W]ould you clean it or hold them accountable?"

Third, and most important, when Miller informed Chadwick that she did not get the promotion, Miller explained:

> It was nothing you did or didn't do. It was just that you're going to school, you have the kids and you just have a lot on your plate right now.

In the same conversation, Miller said that, "if [the three interviewers] were in your position, they would feel overwhelmed." Finally, Miller also told Chadwick that, "there would be something better down the road," and that Chadwick would look back and say "it's a good thing that that opportunity didn't work out because I'm happier with this down the road."

* * *

Procedurally, WellPoint moved for summary judgment following discovery. * * * The district court concluded that Chadwick's claim could not proceed to a jury because "[n]othing in Miller's words show[ed] that" Chadwick was not promoted because of her sex, nor was there a "general atmosphere" of sex-based assumptions in the workplace. Chadwick now appeals.

II.   Discussion

* * *

a.   Legal Background

Title VII of the Civil Rights Act of 1964 prohibits discrimination based on sex. Notably, the Act does not prohibit discrimination based on caregiving responsibility. Chadwick's claim can be characterized as a "sex plus" claim. This denomination refers to the situation where "an employer classifies employees on the basis of sex *plus* another characteristic." The terminology may be a bit misleading, however, because the "plus" does not mean that more than simple sex discrimination must be alleged; rather, it describes the case where "not all members of a disfavored class are discriminated against." In other words, "[i]n such cases the employer does not discriminate against the class of men or women as a whole but rather treats differently a subclass of men or women." Here, Chadwick alleges that the subclass being discriminated against based on sex is women with children, particularly young children. Ultimately, regardless of the label given to the claim, the simple question posed by sex discrimination suits is whether the employer took an adverse employment action *at least in part* because of an employee's sex.

The type of discrimination Chadwick alleges involves stereotyping based on sex. The Supreme Court identified sex-based stereotyping as an impermissible form of discrimination in *Price Waterhouse v. Hopkins,* * * * The Supreme Court held that such remarks were evidence of sex-based stereotyping, which in turn suggested that sex discrimination was the cause of the failure to promote. The Court pointedly said, "[W]e are beyond the day when an employer could evaluate employees by assuming or insisting that they matched the stereotype associated with their group."

The Supreme Court and several circuits, including this one, have had occasion to confirm that the assumption that a woman will perform her job less well due to her presumed family obligations is a form of sex-stereotyping and that adverse job actions on that basis constitute sex discrimination. *See Nevada Dep't of Human Res. v. Hibbs,* 538 U.S. 721, 730, 123 S.Ct. 1972, 155 L.Ed.2d 953 (2003); Back, 365 F.3d at 120 (identifying sex-stereotyping where employer stated that a woman could not "be a good mother" and work long hours, and that a woman "would not show the same level of commitment . . . because [she] had little ones at home").

* * *

In the simplest terms, * * * unlawful sex discrimination occurs when an employer takes an adverse job action on the assumption that a woman, because she is a woman, will neglect her job responsibilities in favor of her presumed childcare responsibilities. It is undoubtedly true that if the work performance of a woman (or a man, for that matter) actually suffers due to childcare responsibilities (or due to any other personal obligation or interest), an employer is free to respond accordingly, at least without incurring liability under Title VII. However, an employer is not free to assume that a woman, because she is a woman, will necessarily be a poor worker because of family responsibilities. The essence of Title VII in this context is that women have the right to prove their mettle in the work arena without the burden of stereotypes regarding whether they can fulfill their responsibilities.

b. Chadwick's Claim

We turn now to the specific facts of Chadwick's claim, mindful that we are judging merely the claim's viability under summary judgment, rather than as to ultimate liability.* * *

* * * Given the common stereotype about the job performance of women with children and given the surrounding circumstantial evidence presented by Chadwick, we believe that a reasonable jury could find that Well-Point would not have denied a promotion to a similarly qualified man because he had "too much on his plate" and would be "overwhelmed" by the new job, given "the kids" and his schooling. * * *

NOTE

1. *Sex–Plus or Stereotyping?* The principal case returns to the problem of defining "stereotype." At first glance the case seems to be a simple application of *UAW v. Johnson Controls, supra p.* 51 (refusal to hire women who were fertile). Plaintiff was not hired because she had triplets. The problem was that, unlike *Johnson Controls,* WellPoint had no clear rule excluding females, but not males, who had pre-school children. The "stereotype" relied upon by the court differs from the one identified in *Price Waterhouse v. Hopkins, supra p.* 60. In *Price Waterhouse* the female plaintiff was denied a promotion because she failed to meet a gender *image* of being appropriately feminine. The "stereotype" relied upon by WellPoint was based on an *assumption* that women would be hindered in their job by having young triplets at home. The court appeared to rely on a "stereotype" concept to assume that a similarly situated father of triplets would not have been burdened by this fact. The "stereotype" relied upon resembles the *assumption* that a woman subjected to a demand for sexual favors in return for job benefits would not have been so treated had she been a man. *See, Meritor Savings Bank FSB v. Vinson,* 477 U.S. 57, 106 S.Ct. 2399, 91 L.Ed.2d 49 (1986).

SCHAFER v. BOARD OF PUBLIC EDUCATION, PITTSBURGH

United States Court of Appeals, Third Circuit, 1990
903 F.2d 243

HIGGINBOTHAM, CHIEF JUDGE.

This is a sex discrimination case under Title VII of the Civil Rights Act of 1964. Gerald Schafer (Schafer or employee), claims that he was impermissibly denied a one-year childrearing leave which was available to female employees, at their option, under the collective bargaining agreement between appellees, the Board of Public Education of the School District of Pittsburgh, Pennsylvania (the Board), and the Pittsburgh Federation of Teachers, Local 400, American Federation of Teachers, AFL–CIO (the Federation or union). Schafer also alleges that as a result of the denial of the leave, he was forced to resign from his position as a teacher.

* * *

I.

Schafer, a male, was employed as a teacher by the Board, from August 1978 until December 14, 1981. In late August or early September of 1981, Schafer requested an unpaid leave of absence for the 1981–1982 school year for the purpose of childrearing. Schafer requested the leave from Charles Allebrand, the Board's Assistant Personnel Director for Special Education, pursuant to Article 31, § 3(c) of the collective bargaining agreement between the Board and the Federation.[1] Allebrand advised Schafer that he had never known a male to be granted such a leave, although females were routinely granted them. Allebrand suggested that Schafer apply for a ninety-day unpaid emergency leave, but he also provided Schafer with an application for the one-year leave. Schafer claims that he informed Allebrand that if he did not receive the one year leave and could not find appropriate child care, he would be forced to resign.

Schafer was granted the three-month unpaid emergency leave to expire on December 14, 1981. He also applied for unpaid childrearing leave from the expiration of the three-month emergency leave to the end of the school year. On November 20, 1981, the Board informed Schafer that his application for childrearing leave was denied. Schafer alleges that he was unable to obtain appropriate child care. On November 30, 1981, he submitted a letter of resignation to be effective on December 14, 1981. In his letter of resignation, Schafer stated that he was forced to resign because he was refused leave to care for his son.

* * *

On August 9, 1989, appellees filed a joint motion for summary judgment, alleging that the leave policy was a permissible accommodation to females * * * The district court granted the motion on September 15, 1989, interpreting the leave in question as one of *maternity* and not childrearing and concluding that [*California Fed. Sav. & Loan Ass'n v. Guerra,* [479

---

1. Article 31, "Leaves of Absence Provisions" of the Collective Bargaining Agreement between Pittsburgh Board of Education and Pittsburgh Federation of Teachers provides in pertinent part:

Maternity leave and maternity-related provisions:

. . .

b. All female teachers shall be entitled to maternity leave, regardless of length of service.

c. The right of female teachers to use sick leave instead of the maternity leave provisions of Subsection 3b shall continue to apply to the actual time of the disability due to childbirth and the period of recovery immediately thereafter. If this provision for the use of accumulated sick leave at the time of childbirth and any period of disability immediately preceding or following that time (or unpaid leave if the employee has exhausted all of her sick leave days) is used, the maternity leave entitlement continues not to be applicable to the involved female employee. However, leaves without Board pay for personal reasons relating to childbearing or childrearing, if they commence immediately following such sick leave absence (either paid or unpaid) due to childbirth and the period of recovery immediately thereafter, shall be available to female teachers and other female personnel. Such leaves shall not exceed one (1) year in length from the date of their inception, but may be of shorter duration as requested by the female applicant. This sick leave provision is applicable to all female personnel. No medical examination may be required by the School Board for at least six (6) weeks after the birth of the child; however, the period of absence under sick leave provisions may only be for any period of disability.

d. Persons on maternity leave are covered under Section 5 and Section 6 of this Article. Maternity leave is limited to a maximum of one (1) year, but may be of shorter duration. . . .

U.S. 272, 107 S.Ct. 683, 93 L.Ed.2d 613 (1987)] permitted this favorable treatment to pregnant females. * * *

II

Appellees' Motion for Summary Judgment

They [the employers] argue that the PDA, as interpreted by the Supreme Court in *Guerra,* permits favorable treatment of pregnant females. This court has not heretofore considered whether, under *Guerra,* an employer may provide up to one year childrearing leave to females after giving birth, without a showing of disability, but may deny childrearing leave to males who are fathers of newborn infants.

In *Guerra,* a pregnant worker's employer, joined by a trade association of employers and another organization representing businesses in California, brought suit seeking a declaration that a California statute requiring employers to provide leave and reinstatement to employees disabled by pregnancy was preempted by Title VII. The majority in *Guerra* held that Title VII, as amended by the PDA, does not preempt a state statute mandating limited favorable treatment of pregnant employees. A narrower majority held that limited preferential treatment of pregnant employees for the period of actual physical disability would not violate Title VII.

We agree with the district court's conclusion that the leave at issue in the collective bargaining agreement is not a fringe benefit as characterized by the appellant. The relevant portions of Article 31 pertain to maternity benefits and other portions relate to childrearing benefits. We disagree with the district court's holding that *Guerra* allows preferential treatment to employees who have recently given birth to a child without a simultaneous showing of a continuing disability related to either the pregnancy or to the delivery of the child.

In *Guerra,* the Court emphasized the limited nature of the benefits at issue and noted that the statute would allow benefits to "cover only the period of *actual physical disability* on account of pregnancy." *Guerra* permits favorable leave treatment when the disability is related to pregnancy. The inquiry here is whether, under *Guerra,* a leave for up to one year for childrearing is related to the conditions of pregnancy, childbirth or related medical conditions. Article 31, § 3(c) allows a pregnant teacher two options: (1) a period of sick leave combined with an unpaid leave for childbearing or childrearing for a maximum of one year, or (2) maternity leave not exceeding one year. There is no requirement under Article 31, § 3(c) that the female be disabled in order to obtain the unpaid leave for up to one year (for either childrearing or childbearing). The essential facts in *Guerra* are dissimilar to the present situation, where the childrearing leave is made available to females only, without a showing of a disability related to pregnancy or childbearing.

There is no evidence in the record that suggests that the normal maternity disability due to "pregnancy, childbirth, or related medical conditions" extends to one year. We hold as a matter of law that Article 31, § 3(c) of the collective bargaining agreement contravenes Title VII and is thus per se void for any leave granted beyond the period of actual physical disability on account of pregnancy, childbirth or related medical conditions. Accordingly, we will reverse the district court's grant of the appellees' motion for summary judgment * * *

NOTES

1. ***California Fed. Sav. & Loan Ass'n v. Guerra,*** 479 U.S. 272, 107 S.Ct. 683, 93 L.Ed.2d 613 (1987), discussed in the principal case, held that state law which required employers to provide protections for pregnancy and childbirth beyond what was required by federal law was not pre-empted under the Supremacy Clause of the Constitution (Art.VI, cl.2). Presumably, employers who voluntarily provide additional *pregnancy* benefits do not violate Title VII when they do not provide male workers equivalent leave or benefits. However, when the benefits granted to women are for *childcare,* a different situation is presented.

2. Would an employer violate Title VII if it granted benefits only to "the primary provider of childcare?" Consider also the Family and Medical Leave Act. *See,* Malin, *Fathers and Parental Leave,* 72 Tex.L.Rev. 1047 (1994); Selmi, *Family Leave and the Gender Wage Gap,* 78 N.C.L.Rev. 707 (2000), and Selmi, *The Work Family Conflict: An Essay on Employers, Men and Responsibility,* 4 U.St.Thomas L.J. 573 (2007).

FAMILY AND MEDICAL LEAVE ACT OF 1993 (FMLA)
29 U.S.C. § 2601 et seq.

[A]n eligible employee shall be entitled to a total of 12 workweeks of leave during any 12–month period for one or more of the following:

(A) Because of the birth of a son or daughter of the employee and in order to care for such son or daughter.

(B) Because of the placement of a son or daughter with the employee for adoption or foster care.

(C) In order to care for the spouse, or a son, daughter, or parent, of the employee, if such spouse, son, daughter or parent has a serious health condition.

(D) Because of a serious health condition that makes the employee unable to perform the functions of the position of such employee.

(2) Expiration of Entitlement. The entitlement to leave under subparagraphs (A) and (B) of paragraph (1) for a birth or placement of a son or daughter shall expire at the end of the 12–month period beginning on the date of such birth or placement.

 * * *

"[L]eave granted * * * may consist of unpaid leave."

29 U.S.C. §§ 2612(a) and (c)

* * *(1) [A]ny eligible employee who takes leave under [this statute] for the intended purpose of the leave shall be entitled, on return from such leave.

(A) to be restored by the employer to the position of employment held by the employee when the leave commenced; or

(B) to be restored to an equivalent position with equivalent employment benefits, pay, and other terms and conditions of employment.

(2) Loss of Benefits. The taking of leave under [this tile] shall not result in the loss of any employment benefit accrued prior to the date on which the leave commenced.

(3) Limitations: Nothing in this section shall be construed to entitle any restored employee to

(A) the accrual of any seniority or employment benefits during any period of leave; or

(B) any right, benefit, or position of employment other than any right, benefit, or position to which the employee would have been entitled had the employee not taken the leave.

29 U.S.C. § 2614(a)

* * *

(1) Exercise of Rights: It shall be unlawful for any employer to interfere with, restrain, or deny the exercise of or the attempt to exercise, any right provided under this title.

(2) Discrimination: It shall be unlawful for any employer to discharge or in any other manner discriminate against any individual for opposing any practice made unlawful by this title.

* * *

NOTES

1. The Act provides that while on leave granted by the Act, the employer shall maintain the employee on any "group health plan" generally provided employees, with the proviso that the employer may recover the costs of such health plan coverage if the employee fails to return to work for reasons other than the continuation of the health condition that entitled the employee to the leave or conditions beyond the control of the employee. 29 U.S.C. § 2416(c).

2. *Reinstatement:* An employer may deny reinstatement to an employee seeking to return from FMLA authorized leave only by carrying the burden of proving "reasonable cause" for denying the employee full reinstatement. Employees need not prove they are "qualified" for reinstatement. *Sanders v. City of Newport,* 657 F.3d 772 (9th Cir. 2011).

3. *Coverage and Eligibility:* To be covered by the FMLA an "employer" must have at least **50** employees. To be "eligible" for FMLA leave the employee must have been employed for the previous *12–month period and during that period worked at least 1,250 hours.* Eligibility requirements are strictly construed. *Pirant v. United States Postal Service,* 542 F.3d 202 (7th Cir. 2008).

4. *Notice:* The statute provides that when "practicable," an "eligible" employee shall provide the employer 30 days notice upon learning of the need for leave. 29 U.S.C. § 2612(e). Department of Labor Regulations state, however, that, "It is expected that the employee will give notice to the employer within no more than one or two working days of learning of the *need for leave,* except in extraordinary circumstances where such notice is not feasible." 29 C.F.R. § 825.303(a). Even if leave would otherwise be authorized, employees who absent themselves without giving such notice may be terminated. *Brown v. Automotive Comp. Holdings, LLC,* 622 F.3d 685 (7th Cir. 2010).

This notice requirement does not demand a formal invoking of the statute. *Tate v. Farmland Indus., Inc.,* 268 F.3d 989 (10th Cir. 2001). However, a telephone call merely informing the employer of a family member's funeral or that the employee was not "feeling well" would not constitute a leave request. *de la Rama v. Illinois Dep't of Human Serv.,* 541 F.3d 681 (7th Cir. 2008); *Scobey v. Nucor Steel–Ark.,* 580 F.3d 781 (8th Cir. 2009).

5. *Seriousness of the medical condition:* To be eligible for leave to care for a child, the child's illness must result in the child being absent from school for at least three days. The limited authority indicates that the FMLA does not require employers to grant eligible employees leave to care for short term, routine, non-incapacitating conditions of family members like the flu, a strained ankle, physical examinations, or routine dental work. *Ducharme v. Cape Indus. Inc.,* 2002 WL 31545980 (E.D.Mich.2002). Nonetheless, to be "serious" the condition need not be totally incapacitating nor chronic. *Navarro v. Pfizer Corp.,* 261 F.3d 90 (1st Cir. 2001) (plaintiff's adult pregnant daughter's hypertension which precluded caring for other children was sufficiently "serious").

6. *Supporting medical certificate:* Upon receiving the employee's notice and request for medical leave, the employer may require the employee to provide a certificate of incapacity issued by a health care provider. 29 U.S.C.§ 2613(a). The employer's request for a medical certificate must be written, detailing the employee's obligations, and the consequences flowing from the employee's failure. 29 C.F.R. § 825.301(b)(1)(ii). The employee has 15 days after receiving demand for a medical certificate to supply the employer with the requested medical certificate. The employer may not terminate the employee until the employee has been absent for more than fifteen days without providing the requested certification. However, unless the employer makes an appropriate written demand for a certificate of incapacity, the employee may not be dismissed for failing to provide a certificate. *Branham v. Gannett Satellite Inf. Network,* 619 F.3d 563 (6th Cir. 2010).

7. *Length of Leave—Employer Plans:* Employers may provide leave longer than the 12 weeks accorded by the FMLA. However, the employer may

consider such leave as being concurrent with, rather than cumulative to, FMLA required leave. ***Ragsdale v. Wolverine World Wide, Inc.,*** 535 U.S. 81, 122 S.Ct. 1155, 152 L.Ed.2d 167 (2002). When eligible spouses are employed by the same employer each would seem to be entitled to take their authorized leave independent of each other and thus consecutively, but the employer may limit their aggregate leave to 12 weeks for the couple, except for leave for the employee's own serious health condition. 29 U.S.C. § 2612(f).

8. *Intermittent leave or reduced schedules:* Where leave is sought for the birth or adoption of a child the FMLA does not require the granting of intermittent or reduced work schedules. However, to care for a serious health condition of the employee or of a spouse, child or parent, leave may be taken intermittently or on a reduced leave schedule "when medically necessary." 29 U.S.C. § 2612(b). *See, Arban v. West Pub. Corp.,* 345 F.3d 390 (6th Cir. 2003).

9. *Pregnancy:* Implementing regulations indicate that normal pregnancy—be distinguished from childbirth—is not per se a "serious health condition" requiring the grant of leave. 29 C.F.R. s 825.114(a)(2)(i). However, at the point her pregnancy renders the woman unable to work or to perform essential functions of her particular job she will considered as having a "serious health condition." 29 U.S.C. s 2612(a)(1)(D). At this point the pregnant employee may claim complete, reduced, or intermittent leave as is necessary for her medical condition. *Whitaker v. Bosch Braking Systems Div.,* 180 F.Supp.2d 922 (W.D. Mich. 2001)(employee experiencing a "normal" pregnancy and could work standing 8 hours a day, must be allowed a "leave" for all hours beyond 8 per day when standing for more than that period would threaten her health)

10. *Paid or Unpaid?* FMLA required leave is *unpaid.* Employers may, and some do, provide for paid leave. A few states, including California, require the grant of leave under terms similar to the FMLA, and, in addition, provide compensation for all or part of that leave paid through a worker's compensation style funding program.

D.   RELIGION AND RELIGIOUS PRACTICES

1.   "RELIGION" DEFINED

a.   The Constitution

The First Amendment to Constitution guarantees to individuals the "free exercise," and prohibits government "establishment of" "religion."[40] In addressing its free exercise, "religion" has been defined to "include moral or ethical beliefs as to what is right or wrong which are sincerely held with the strength of traditional religious views." ***United States v. Seeger,*** 380 U.S. 163, 85 S.Ct. 850, 13 L.Ed.2d 733 (1965). "Sincerely held beliefs" need not be espoused by any traditional religion, nor will the belief system be deprived of being "religion" merely because it

---

40. These provisions apply only to governmental action and not to private employers. However, as to governmental employees, the constitutional protections will parallel the protections of Title VII.

is inconsistent with the doctrines of the individual's professed religion. *Thomas v. Review Board of Indiana,* 450 U.S. 707, 101 S.Ct. 1425, 67 L.Ed.2d 624 (1981). But the Court has distinguished "religion" from "purely secular views" that are not protected by the First Amendment. *Frazee v. Illinois Dep't of Employment Security,* 489 U.S. 829, 109 S.Ct. 1514, 103 L.Ed.2d 914 (1989). Moreover, the state may regulate conduct through neutral laws of general applicability even if the proscribed conduct is required by one's religion. Thus, without infringing the First Amendment a state may deny unemployment benefits to an individual discharged from his job for smoking peyote—a "class B felony"—even though the individual's use of the drug was "religiously inspired." *Employment Division, Dep't of Human Resources of Oregon v. Smith,* 494 U.S. 872, 110 S.Ct. 1595, 108 L.Ed.2d 876 (1990).

b. Title VII: Generally

Title VII prohibits discrimination against individuals because of their "religion." "Religion" is defined to include "all aspects of religious observance and practice, as well as belief." 42 U.S.C. § 2000e–(j). This lack of statutory clarity does not often cause difficulty. Discrimination against an individual because he/she does, or does not, follow the teaching or traditions of established faiths, such as Roman Catholic, Protestant, Hindu, Judaism, Islam, Buddhist, or Latter Day Saints is clearly within the language and purposes of Title VII. "Religion" includes subdivisions, synods, and schisms of broader religions, such as "Reform," "Orthodox," "Sunni," "Eastern," etc.

c. The EEOC's Inclusive View

In interpreting Title VII's protection for "religion" the EEOC has embraced the broad interpretation used by the Supreme Court in addressing the First Amendment:

> [R]eligious practices include moral or ethical beliefs as to what is right and wrong that are sincerely held with the strength of traditional religious views. * * * The fact that no religious group espouses such beliefs or the fact that the religious group to which the individual professes to belong may not accept such belief will not determine whether the belief is a religious belief of [the individual]. 29 C.F.R. § 1605.1.

This definition would include the unorthodox such as Wicca ("witchcraft"), *Van Koten v. Family Health Management, Inc.,* 134 F.3d 375 (7th Cir. 1998), and Native American spirituality. *See Brown v. Woodland Joint Unified Sch. Dist.,* 27 F.3d 1373 (9th Cir. 1994) (not a Title VII case). As it is with constitutional litigation, so it is under Title VII; it is difficult to distinguish protected "sincerely held moral and ethical beliefs" from unprotected, "purely secular beliefs." For example, *Peterson v. Wilmur Communications, Inc.,* 205 F.Supp. 2d 1014 (E.D.Wis.2002), found that a group which denied the Holocaust, advocated driving Jews from their "control over the nation," promulgated a doctrine of white supremacy, and stated that blacks were "savages" who should be "shipped back to Africa" was a protected "religion." However, *Bellamy v. Mason's Stores, Inc.,* 368 F.Supp. 1025 (E.D.Va. 1973), *aff'd* 508 F.2d 504 (4th Cir. 1974), held, notwithstanding the organization's considerable "pomp and ceremony" that included use of the Bible, burning crosses, and the "sincerely held belief" that their God decreed the separation of the races, the Ku Klux Klan was a political organization, and thus not a protected "religion. Consider the "Nation of Islam" (aka "Black Muslims") whose rhetoric may contain considerable amount of political advocacy for economic justice and protests that may include verbal attacks on whites and Jews. *Ali v. Southeast Neighborhood House,* 519 F.Supp. 489 (D.D.C. 1981).

(i) *Abortion and Free Choice:* In the EEOC's broad view, an individual's opposition to abortion is a protected religious belief. *EEOC v. University of Detroit,* 701 F.Supp. 1326 (E.D.Mich. 1988); *Wilson v. United States West Communications,* 58 F.3d 1337 (8th Cir. 1995). If *opposing* abortion on ethical and religious grounds is a protected "religious belief," can it be assumed that an equally strong belief in a woman's right to chose to have an abortion also is a "religious" belief? Or is that belief an unprotected "political" position?

(ii) *War:* Opposition to all war on ethical grounds would probably be considered "religious," even if the individual was not a formal member of a religious group that espoused pacificsm. *United States v. Seeger, supra.* What if that opposition is a strongly held individual belief that this *particular war* is both bad policy for the nation as well unethical (*e.g.,* the U.S. invasion of Iraq)?

(iii) *Same Sex Marriage:* As much of the opposition to same sex marriage is asserted on religious grounds, discrimination against those individuals because of this particular belief could be deemed "religious." Conversely, there are those who assert the ethical right of homosexuals to marry, relying heavily, though not exclusively, on political or constitutional grounds. This assertion may, or may not, have a religious foundation. Is it "religious?" *Shahar v. Bowers,* 114 F.3d 1097 (11th Cir. 1997)(en banc).

d.   A More Restrictive Approach

Some courts have adopted a multi-part standard that looks beyond an individual's sincerely held ethical belief on a particular topic and balances a number of objective factors, no one of which is controlling:

(i) *The nature of the ideas:* Are the beliefs espoused by any recognized religion? If not, are the beliefs widely shared? One's purely personal view suggests that the belief or practice is not "religious." *Brown v. Pena,* 441 F.Supp. 1382 (S.D.Fla. 1977) *aff'd* 589 F.2d 1113 (5th Cir. 1979)(individual belief in the ethical benefits of eating pet food not "religious."). Objecting to a bawdy work place atmosphere is unlikely to be protected "religion." *Rivera v. Puerto Rico Aqueduct & Sewers Auth.,* 331 F.3d 183 (1st Cir. 2003).

(ii) The belief an element of comprehensive belief system. For one's ethical views on a subject to be "religion," they should be an element of a broader ethical code. Beliefs that address a single or limited number of questions, such as homosexuality, abortion, or diet, tend to be outside the meaning of "religious" even if the view is widely held and a religious group may have advanced similar beliefs. *Friedman v. Southern Cal. Permanente Medical Group,* 102 Cal.App.4th 39, 125 Cal.Rptr.2d 663 (2002).

(iii) Formality and structure: The ideas comprising a religion normally would have some roots in an organization that has formal external signs that may be analogized to accepted religions, such as services, meeting places, observation of holidays, publications or efforts at promulgation, rituals or ceremonial functions, a clergy, finances, and a structure or organization. The absence of any such features suggests that ideas are more political than religious.

(iv) A supreme being? One earmark of religions is that they make reference to an extra-human ordering of human behavior that is similar to a "god" found in traditional religions. The presence of such a reference in one's beliefs suggests they are "religious." Absence suggests that the beliefs are "political." *See, Malnak v. Yogi,* 592 F.2d 197 (3d Cir. 1979); *Alvarado v. City of San Jose,* 94 F.3d 1223 (9th Cir. 1996).

e. No Religion: The Atheist

Discrimination against atheists or deists based on their lack of religious beliefs or their acceptance of a "god" is discrimination because of "religion." *Reed v. Great Lakes Companies, Inc.,* 330 F.3d 931 (7th Cir. 2003). Thus, requiring a non-believer to participate in employer conducted prayer services is proscribed religious discrimination. *EEOC v. Townley Engineering & Mfg. Co.,* 859 F.2d 610 (9th Cir. 1988).

2. "RELIGIOUS OBSERVANCES AND PRACTICES"

a. Defined

The statutory definition of "religion" includes "religious observance and practice." Observing Sabbath and holy days, attending church conventions, and teaching Bible study classes are "religious observances and practices," as are following the dress or grooming standard dictates of one's faith, such as head or face coverings, facial hair, and the display of symbols of faith, such as crosses or Stars of David. Thus, had Ms. Jesperson in *Jesperson v. Harrah's Operating Co., supra, p. 66* objected to wearing makeup on grounds that it was prohibited by her religious beliefs, her refusal would have been entitled to protection.

As the practice imposed by the sincere belief must be "religious," as opposed to secular, a problem is presented similar to that of defining what constitutes a religious belief. Attending a religious synod is a "religious practice" that would require a reasonable accommodation. Attending a picnic or sporting event has been held to be a secular event that need not be accommodated even if sponsored by a church. *Wessling v. Kroger Co.*, 554 F.Supp. 548 (E.D.Mich. 1982). Displaying a picture of a religious leader or quotations from a scripture would be a religious practice requiring accommodation, while display of a Confederate battle flag is a secular practice that requires no accommodation. *Storey v. Burns Int'l Security Servs.*, 390 F.3d 760 (3d Cir. 2004).

b. Triggering an Obligation to Accommodate

1. Bona fide belief: The employee must establish the belief to be "sincerely held," as opposed a "conversion of convenience" asserted to avoid the employer's work rules. *Jones v. TEK Industries, Inc.*, 319 F.3d 355 (8th Cir. 2003).

2. Notice and request: Even when sincere the employee may not simply follow the religious practice, without first giving the employer an opportunity to make or suggest accommodations. *Goldmeier v. Allstate Ins. Co.*, 337 F.3d 629 (6th Cir. 2003).

c. The Employer's Obligation to Accommodate

The employer can justify discrimination based the employee's religious observances or practices only if the employer:

is unable to reasonably accommodate to an employee's religious observance or practice without undue hardship on the conduct of the employer's business. 42 U.S.C.C. § 2000(e)(j).

ANSONIA BOARD OF EDUCATION v. PHILBROOK

Supreme Court of the United States, 1986
479 U.S. 60, 107 S.Ct. 367, 93 L.Ed.2d 305

CHIEF JUSTICE REHNQUIST delivered the opinion of the Court.

Petitioner Ansonia Board of Education has employed respondent Ronald Philbrook since 1962 to teach high school business and typing classes in Ansonia, Connecticut. In 1968, Philbrook was baptized into the Worldwide Church of God. The tenets of the church require members to refrain from secular employment during designated holy days, a practice that has caused respondent to miss approximately six schooldays each year. We are asked to determine whether the employer's efforts to adjust respondent's work schedule in light of his beliefs fulfill its obligation under § 701(j) of the Civil Rights Act of 1964 to "reasonably accommodate to an employee's ... religious observance or practice without undue hardship on the conduct of the employer's business." [1]

---

1. The reasonable accommodation duty was incorporated into the statute, somewhat awkwardly, in the definition of religion. Title VII's central provisions make it an unlawful employment practice for an employer "to fail or refuse to hire or to discharge any individual, or otherwise to discriminate against any individual with respect to his compensation, terms, conditions, or privileges of employment, because of such individual's ... religion ...," or "to

Since the 1967–1968 school year, the school board's collective-bargaining agreements with the Ansonia Federation of Teachers have granted to each teacher 18 days of leave per year for illness, cumulative to 150 and later to 180 days. Accumulated leave may be used for purposes other than illness as specified in the agreement. A teacher may accordingly use five days' leave for a death in the immediate family, one day for attendance at a wedding, three days per year for attendance as an official delegate to a national veteran's organization, and the like. With the exception of the agreement covering the 1967–1968 school year, each contract has specifically provided three days' annual leave for observance of mandatory religious holidays, as defined in the contract. Unlike other categories for which leave is permitted, absences for religious holidays are not charged against the teacher's annual or accumulated leave.

The school board has also agreed that teachers may use up to three days of accumulated leave each school year for "necessary personal business." Recent contracts limited permissible personal leave to those uses not otherwise specified in the contract. This limitation dictated, for example, that an employee who wanted more than three leave days to attend the convention of a national veterans organization could not use personal leave to gain extra days for that purpose. Likewise, an employee already absent three days for mandatory religious observances could not later use personal leave for "[a]ny religious activity," or "[a]ny religious observance." Since the 1978–1979 school year, teachers have been allowed to take one of the three personal days without prior approval; use of the remaining two days requires advance approval by the school principal.

The limitations on the use of personal business leave spawned this litigation. Until the 1976–1977 year, Philbrook observed mandatory holy days by using the three days granted in the contract and then taking unauthorized leave. His pay was reduced accordingly. In 1976, however, respondent stopped taking unauthorized leave for religious reasons, and began scheduling required hospital visits on church holy days. He also worked on several holy days. Dissatisfied with this arrangement, Philbrook repeatedly asked the school board to adopt one of two alternatives. His preferred alternative would allow use of personal business leave for religious observance, effectively giving him three additional days of paid leave for that purpose. Short of this arrangement, respondent suggested that he pay the cost of a substitute and receive full pay for additional days off for religious observances.[3] Petitioner has consistently rejected both proposals.

---

limit, segregate, or classify his employees ... in any way which would deprive or tend to deprive any individual of employment opportunities or otherwise adversely affect his status as an employee, because of such individual's ... religion...." Section 701(j), 42 U.S.C. § 2000e(j), was added in 1972 to illuminate the meaning of religious discrimination under the statute. It provides that "[t]he term 'religion' includes all aspects of religious observance and practice, as well as belief, unless an employer demonstrates that he is unable to reasonably accommodate to an employee's or prospective employee's religious observance or practice without undue hardship on the conduct of the employer's business."

3. The suggested accommodation would reduce the financial costs to Philbrook of unauthorized absences. In 1984, for example, a substitute cost $30 per day, and respondent's loss in pay from an unauthorized absence was over $130.

* * *

[T]he District Court concluded that Philbrook had failed to prove a case of religious discrimination because he had not been placed by the school board in a position of violating his religion or losing his job.

The Court of Appeals for the Second Circuit reversed and remanded * * * for further proceedings. It held that a prima facie case of discrimination is established when an employee shows that

" '(1) he or she has a bona fide religious belief that conflicts with an employment requirement; (2) he or she informed the employer of this belief; (3) he or she was disciplined for failure to comply with the conflicting employment requirement.' "

Philbrook established his case, the court held, by showing that he had a sincere religious belief that conflicted with the employer's attendance requirements, that the employer was aware of the belief, and that he suffered a detriment—namely, a loss of pay—from the conflict. The court then assumed that the employer's leave policy constituted a reasonable accommodation to Philbrook's belief. It held, however, that "[w]here the employer and the employee each propose a reasonable accommodation, Title VII requires the employer to accept the proposal the employee prefers unless that accommodation causes undue hardship on the employer's conduct of his business." The Court of Appeals remanded for consideration of the hardship that would result from Philbrook's suggestions.

We granted certiorari to * * * address whether the Court of Appeals erred in finding that Philbrook established a prima facie case of religious discrimination and in opining that an employer must accept the employee's preferred accommodation absent proof of undue hardship. We find little support in the statute for the approach adopted by the Court of Appeals, but we agree that the ultimate issue of reasonable accommodation cannot be resolved without further factual inquiry. We accordingly affirm the judgment of the Court of Appeals remanding the case to the District Court for additional findings.

As we noted in our only previous consideration of § 701(j), its language was added to the 1972 amendments on the floor of the Senate with little discussion. *Trans World Airlines, Inc. v. Hardison,* 432 U.S. 63, 74, n. 9, 97 S.Ct. 2264, 2271, n. 9, 53 L.Ed.2d 113 (1977). In *Hardison,* we determined that an accommodation causes "undue hardship" whenever that accommodation results in "more than a *de minimis* cost" to the employer. Hardison had been discharged because his religious beliefs would not allow him to work on Saturdays and claimed that this action violated the employer's duty to effect a reasonable accommodation of his beliefs. Because we concluded that each of the suggested accommodations would impose on the employer an undue hardship, we had no occasion to consider the bounds of a prima facie case in the religious accommodation context or whether an employer is required to choose from available accommodations the alternative preferred by the employee. The employer in *Hardison* simply argued that all conceivable accommodations would result in undue hardship, and we agreed.

* * *

We may * * * proceed to the question whether the employer's proposed accommodation of respondent's religious practices comports with the statutory mandate of § 701(j).

[T]he Court of Appeals assumed that the employer had offered a reasonable accommodation of Philbrook's religious beliefs. This alone, however, was insufficient in that court's view to allow resolution of the dispute. The court observed that the duty to accommodate "cannot be defined without reference to undue hardship." It accordingly determined that the accommodation obligation includes a duty to accept "the proposal the employee prefers unless that accommodation causes undue hardship on the employer's conduct of his business." * * *

We find no basis in either the statute or its legislative history for requiring an employer to choose any particular reasonable accommodation. By its very terms the statute directs that any reasonable accommodation by the employer is sufficient to meet its accommodation obligation. The employer violates the statute unless it "demonstrates that [it] is unable to reasonably accommodate . . . an employee's . . . religious observance or practice without undue hardship on the conduct of the employer's business." Thus, where the employer has already reasonably accommodated the employee's religious needs, the statutory inquiry is at an end. The employer need not further show that each of the employee's alternative accommodations would result in undue hardship. As *Hardison* illustrates, the extent of undue hardship on the employer's business is at issue only where the employer claims that it is unable to offer any reasonable accommodation without such hardship. Once the Court of Appeals assumed that the school board had offered to Philbrook a reasonable alternative, it erred by requiring the Board to nonetheless demonstrate the hardship of Philbrook's alternatives.

The legislative history of § 701(j), * * * is of little help in defining the employer's accommodation obligation. To the extent it provides any indication of congressional intent, however, we think that the history supports our conclusion. Senator Randolph, the sponsor of the amendment that became § 701(j), expressed his hope that accommodation would be made with "flexibility" and "a desire to achieve an adjustment." Consistent with these goals, courts have noted that "bilateral cooperation is appropriate in the search for an acceptable reconciliation of the needs of the employee's religion and the exigencies of the employer's business." Under the approach articulated by the Court of Appeals, however, the employee is given every incentive to hold out for the most beneficial accommodation, despite the fact that an employer offers a reasonable resolution of the conflict. This approach, we think, conflicts with both the language of the statute and the views that led to its enactment. We accordingly hold that an employer has met its obligation under § 701(j) when it demonstrates that it has offered a reasonable accommodation to the employee.[6]

The remaining issue in the case is whether the school board's leave policy constitutes a reasonable accommodation of Philbrook's religious beliefs. * * * We think that there are insufficient factual findings as to the manner in which the collective-bargaining agreements have been interpreted in order for us to make that judgment initially. We think that the school board policy in this case, requiring respondent to take unpaid leave for holy day observance that exceeded the amount allowed by the collective-bargaining agreement, would generally be a reasonable one. In enacting § 701(j), Congress was understandably motivated by a desire to assure the individual additional opportunity to observe religious practices, but it did not impose a duty on the employer to accommodate at all costs. The provision of unpaid leave eliminates the conflict between employment requirements and religious practices by allowing the individual to observe fully religious holy days and requires him only to give up compensation for a day that he did not in fact work. Generally speaking, "[t]he direct effect of [unpaid leave] is merely a loss of income for the period the employee is not at work; such an exclusion has no direct effect upon either employment opportunities or job status." *Nashville Gas Co. v. Satty,* 434 U.S. 136, 145, 98 S.Ct. 347, 353, 54 L.Ed.2d 356 (1977).

But unpaid leave is not a reasonable accommodation when paid leave is provided for all purposes *except* religious ones. A provision for paid leave "that is part and parcel of the employment relationship may not be doled out in a discriminatory fashion, even if the employer would be free ... not to provide the benefit at all." Such an arrangement would display a discrimination against religious practices that is the antithesis of reasonableness. Whether the policy here violates this teaching turns on factual inquiry into past and present administration of the personal business leave provisions of the collective-bargaining agreement. The school board contends that the necessary personal business category in the agreement, like other leave provisions, defines a limited purpose leave. Philbrook, on the other hand, asserts that the necessary personal leave category is not so limited, operating as an open-ended leave provision that may be used for a wide range of secular purposes in addition to those specifically provided for in the contract, but not for similar religious purposes. We do not think that the record is sufficiently clear on this point for us to make the necessary factual findings, and we therefore affirm the judgment of the Court of Appeals remanding the case to the District Court. The latter court on remand should make the necessary findings as to past and

---

6. The Court of Appeals found support for its decision in the EEOC's guidelines on religious discrimination. Specifically, the guidelines provide that "when there is more than one means of accommodation which would not cause undue hardship, the employer ... must offer the alternative which least disadvantages the individual with respect to his or her employment opportunities." 29 CFR § 1605.2(c)(2)(ii) (1986). * * * To the extent that the guideline, like the approach of the Court of Appeals, requires the employer to accept any alternative favored by the employee short of undue hardship, we find the guideline simply inconsistent with the plain meaning of the statute. * * *

existing practice in the administration of the collective-bargaining agreements.

JUSTICE MARSHALL, concurring in part and dissenting in part.

I agree with the Court's conclusion that, if the school board provides paid leave "for all purposes *except* religious ones," its accommodation of Philbrook's religious needs would be unreasonable and thus violate Title VII. * * *

The Court's analysis in *Trans World Airlines, Inc. v. Hardison,* 432 U.S. 63, 97 S.Ct. 2264, 53 L.Ed.2d 113 (1977), is difficult to reconcile with its holding today. In *Hardison,* the Court held that the employer's chosen work schedule was a reasonable accommodation but nonetheless went on to consider and reject each of the alternative suggested accommodations. The course followed in *Hardison* should have been adopted here as well. "Once it is determined that the duty to accommodate sometimes requires that an employee be exempted from an otherwise valid work requirement, the only remaining question is ...: Did [the employer] prove that *it exhausted all reasonable accommodations,* and that the *only remaining alternatives would have caused undue hardship* on [the employer's] business?"

* * *

NOTES

TRANS WORLD AIRLINES, INC. v. HARDISON, **432 U.S. 63, 97 S.Ct. 2264, 53 L.Ed.2d 113 (1977),** discussed in the principal case, involved an employee whose religious beliefs prohibited him from working on Saturday, his Sabbath. His lack of seniority under a collective bargaining agreement between employer and union resulted in his being assigned to the Saturday shift. The union was unwilling to waive the contractual seniority provisions to force an unwilling senior employee into the Saturday shift. The employer refused to offer premium pay to induce a co-worker to trade shifts with the plaintiff. The Court noted that the employer had reduced its work force on the weekends to a "bare minimum," had sought, unsuccessfully, to find alternative assignments and to secure a voluntary "job swap" that would not have required plaintiff to work on Saturday. The Court then held, that "to require TWA to bear more than de minimis cost in order to give Hardison Saturdays off is an undue hardship." The Court then observed that "the seniority system represents a neutral way of minimizing the number of occasions when an employee must work on a day that he would prefer to have off." Accordingly, reasonable accommodation did not require setting aside a neutral system, such as seniority, for allocating shift assignments, nor impose on employers even relatively small economic costs.

UNITED STATES AIRWAYS v. BARNETT, **535 U.S. 391, 122 S.Ct. 1516, 152 L.Ed.2d 589 (2002),** in interpreting the Americans With Disabilities Act, held that "reasonable accommodation" does not require an employer to disregard even unilaterally imposed non-contractual seniority systems that are regularly followed.

Determination of whether accommodation is "reasonable" depends on the analysis of the unique situation of the particular employer and the job the employee performs. Generalizations are impossible. A few illustrations:

1. *Schedule adjustments:* Minor adjustments that impose no major imposition on co-workers, such as allowing a worker to leave work a few minutes early in order to observe his Sabbath are often deemed "reasonable." *See, EEOC v. Ilona of Hungary, Inc.,* 108 F.3d 1679 (7th Cir. 1997). However, allowing a postal route carrier to be off every Saturday is not reasonable in that it would impose a hardship on co-workers who would be forced into Saturday work. *Harrell v. Donahue,* 638 F.3d 975 (8th Cir. 2011).

2. *Grooming rules:* Allowing head coverings or display of modest religious symbols, in most jobs, would be a reasonable accommodation to the employer's grooming requirements. Where religious practice impairs efficiency or places the employee or others in danger, relaxation of the rule usually imposes an "undue hardship." *Bhatia v. Chevron U.S.A., Inc.,* 734 F.2d 1382 (9th Cir. 1984) (facial hair would interfere with firefighter's use of a gas mask). Female Muslim prison guards who desire to cover their hair, forehead, neck, shoulders and chest with a khimar need not be accommodated as such clothing presents issues of prison security. *EEOC v. The GEO Group,* 616 F.3d 265 (3d Cir. 2010). Even when the modification imposes no safety risk, when a particular uniform is imposed for purposes of identification or general esprit, modifications may not be reasonable. For example, allowing visible body piercings on a greeter at a retail store would not be a reasonable accommodation. *Cloutier v. Costco Wholesale Corp.,* 390 F.3d 126 (1st Cir. 2004).

Reconsider, *Jesperson v. Harrah's Operating Co., supra, page 66,* with Ms. Jesperson asserting her religious beliefs as a reason for refusing to wear facial make up. Would it be a reasonable accommodation to require Harrah to waive its rule. (Re-read the history of Harrah's rule.)

3. *Job duties*: A job may require an employee to perform some duties that offend his religious beliefs, such as a pharmacist dispensing contraceptives or a police officer assigned to guard an abortion clinic. Even where the requested relief from the duty does not conflict with seniority and imposes no significant burden on co-workers, some courts have held that accommodation obligations do not allow employees to determine which customers they will serve. Others see occasional adjustments as a reasonable accommodation. Compare, *Stormans, Inc. v. Selecky,* 524 F.Supp.2d 1245 (W.D.Wash. 2007) *rev'd* 586 F.3d 1109 (9th Cir. 2009) with *Rodriguez v. City of Chicago,* 156 F.3d 771 (7th Cir. 1998).

4. *Religious displays:* Permitting a Christmas wreath or Jewish menorah or allowing employees to have Bibles or Korans on their semi-private work stations may be a reasonable accommodations to the worker's religion. When an employee posted on the wall of his office, a work of "art" depicting a religious theme in violation of a sweeping rule against religious depictions in the work place, the employer should have explored accommodation of the employee's practice. *Dixon v. Hallmark Companies,* 627 F.3d 849 (11th Cir. 2010).

5. *Proselytizing:* Denying employees the right to discuss religion at the workplace during non-working periods in a way that employees are allowed to

discuss sports or politics is probably proscribed religious discrimination. However, accommodation obligations do not extend to allowing active proselytizing of co-workers, offering overtly religious greetings to customers, or displaying ethical expressions that may trigger undue workplace disputes. *See,* e.g., *Wilson v. United States West Communications,* 58 F.3d 1337 (8th Cir. 1995).

3.   RELIGIONS DISCRIMINATING BECAUSE OF RELIGION

a.   Generally: Section 702(a) of Title VII Provides

This title shall not apply to an employer * * * to a religious corporation, association, educational institution, or society with respect to the employment of individuals of a particular religion to perform work connected with the carrying on by such corporation, association, educational institution, or society of its activities.

Prior to 1972 courts made distinctions between secular and religious activities of the religious organization. Amendments in that year made it clear that the exemption allowing religious organizations to discriminate on the basis of religion applied to all of the activities of the religious organization, *secular as well as religious.* Thus, in the operation of a secular activity such as a gymnasium, the religious organization was permitted to hire only members of that religion. **Corporation of Presiding Bishop v. Amos,** 483 U.S. 327, 107 S.Ct. 2862, 97 L.Ed.2d 273 (1987)(at least so long as the secular business had some relationship to the religious organization, the statutory exemption for secular activities of the religion did not unconstitutionally "establish" religion).

b.   "Religious" Organization

An employer that operates a traditional for-profit business, such as the manufacture of mining equipment, does not qualify as an exempt "religious corporation" simply because its proprietors are religious persons and use their secular business to re-enforce their religious values. *EEOC v. Townley Engineering & Mfg. Co.,* 859 F.2d 610 (9th Cir. 1988). However, a divided court in *Spencer v. World Vision, Inc.,* 633 F.3d 723 (9th Cir. 2011), held that a "Christian humanitarian" organization was a "religious organization" even though it was not affiliated with any organized church or religious order. The per curiam opinion listed four necessary elements to qualify for the exemption: (1) organization for a religious purpose, (2) primarily engaged in carrying out that purpose, (3) consistently holds itself out to the public as promoting that purpose, and (4) refrains from any significant commercial enterprise, such as engaging in exchanges of goods or services. Concurring judges emphasized the need for the organization to have tax exempt status. *LeBoon v. Lancaster Jewish Community Center, Ass'n.,* 503 F.3d 217 (3d Cir. 2007), indicated, however, that the exemption would be available only to organizations that were owned or significantly controlled by an established religious order.

Educational institutions claiming the religious entity exemption will be evaluated for the institution's religious activities, religious focus of the curriculum, religious affiliation of the students and faculty, as well as the history and stated mission of the institution. Merely because a school was founded by a religious order, at one time had a close religious affiliation, and maintains some religious orientation does not insure that institution has not evolved into a secular institution, and thus no longer is able to claim the exemption. *EEOC v. Kamehameha Schools*, 990 F.2d 458 (9th Cir. 1993).

c. Only Religious Discrimination

A religious organization employer may discriminate on the basis of the individual's religious faith or church membership, but also for non-compliance with the religious doctrines of the religious organization employer. *See, Little v. Wuerl*, 929 F.2d 944 (3d Cir. 1991)(remarriage after divorce) and *Curay–Cramer v. Ursuline Academy of Wilmington*, 450 F.3d 130 (3d Cir. 2006) (public support of the right of women to secure an abortion).

d. Ministerial Exception

As to non-religious discrimination (e.g., race, sex, age, national origin disabilities), religious organizations may claim an implicit "ministerial exception." This implied exemption, mandated by the First Amendment, immunizes the religion against having to defend charges of discrimination in the selection, pay, and retention of "ministers" or persons "important to the spiritual and pastoral mission of the church." *Hosanna–Tabor Evangelical Lutheran Church and School v. E.E.O.C.*, ___ U.S. ___, 132 S.Ct. 694 (2012). *See* Chapter 3B, *infra*, for discussion.

E. AGE

GENERAL DYNAMICS LAND SYSTEMS, INC. v. CLINE

Supreme Court of the United States, 2004
540 U.S. 581, 124 S.Ct. 1236, 157 L.Ed.2d 1094

JUSTICE SOUTER delivered the opinion of the Court.

The Age Discrimination in Employment Act of 1967 forbids discriminatory preference for the young over the old. The question in this case is whether it also prohibits favoring the old over the young. We hold it does not.

I

In 1997, a collective-bargaining agreement between petitioner General Dynamics and the United Auto Workers eliminated the company's obligation to provide health benefits to subsequently retired employees, except as to then-current workers at least 50 years old. Respondents (collectively, Cline) were then at least 40 and thus protected by the Act, but under 50 and so without promise of the benefits. All of them objected to the new terms, although some had retired before the change in order to get the prior advantage, some retired afterwards with no benefit, and some worked on, knowing the new contract would give them no health coverage when they were through.

Before the Equal Employment Opportunity Commission (EEOC or Commission) they claimed that the agreement violated the ADEA, because it "discriminate[d against them] ... with respect to ... compensation, terms, conditions, or privileges of employment, because of [their] age," § 623(a)(1). The EEOC agreed, and invited General Dynamics and the union to settle informally with Cline.

When they failed, Cline brought this action against General Dynamics, combining claims under the ADEA and state law. The District Court called the federal claim one of "reverse age discrimination," upon which, it observed, no court had ever granted relief under the ADEA. It dismissed in reliance on the Seventh Circuit's opinion in *Hamilton v. Caterpillar, Inc.*, 966 F.2d 1226 (1992), that "the ADEA 'does not protect ... the younger *against* the older,'"

A divided panel of the Sixth Circuit reversed, with the majority reasoning that the prohibition of § 623(a)(1), covering discrimination against "any individual ... because of such individual's age," is so clear on its face that if Congress had meant to limit its coverage to protect only the older worker against the younger, it would have said so. The court acknowledged the conflict of its ruling with earlier cases, but it criticized the cases going the other way for paying too much attention to the "hortatory, generalized language" of the congressional findings incorporated in the ADEA. The Sixth Circuit drew support for its view from the position taken by the EEOC in an interpretive regulation.[1]

* * * We granted certiorari to resolve the conflict among the Circuits, and now reverse.

II

The common ground in this case is the generalization that the ADEA's prohibition covers "discriminat[ion] ... because of [an] individual's age," 29 U.S.C. § 623(a)(1), that helps the younger by hurting the older. In the abstract, the phrase is open to an argument for a broader construction, since reference to "age" carries no express modifier and the word could be read to look two ways. This more expansive possible understanding does not, however, square with the natural reading of the whole provision prohibiting discrimination, and in fact Congress's interpretive clues speak almost unanimously to an understanding of discrimination as directed against workers who are older than the ones getting treated better.

---

1. 29 CFR § 1625.2(a) (2003) ("[I]f two people apply for the same position, and one is 42 and the other 52, the employer may not lawfully turn down either one on the basis of age, but must make such decision on the basis of some other factor"). We discuss this regulation at greater length.

Congress chose not to include age within discrimination forbidden by Title VII of the Civil Rights Act of 1964, being aware that there were legitimate reasons as well as invidious ones for making employment decisions on age. Instead it called for a study of the issue by the Secretary of Labor, who concluded that age discrimination was a serious problem, but one different in kind from discrimination on account of race.[2] The Secretary spoke of disadvantage to older individuals from arbitrary and stereotypical employment distinctions (including then-common policies of age ceilings on hiring), but he examined the problem in light of rational considerations of increased pension cost and, in some cases, legitimate concerns about an older person's ability to do the job. When the Secretary ultimately took the position that arbitrary discrimination against older workers was widespread and persistent enough to call for a federal legislative remedy, he placed his recommendation against the background of common experience that the potential cost of employing someone rises with age, so that the older an employee is, the greater the inducement to prefer a younger substitute. The report contains no suggestion that reactions to age level off at some point, and it was devoid of any indication that the Secretary had noticed unfair advantages accruing to older employees at the expense of their juniors.

Congress then asked for a specific proposal, which the Secretary provided in January 1967. Extensive House and Senate hearings ensued.

The testimony at both hearings dwelled on unjustified assumptions about the effect of age on ability to work. * * * The hearings specifically addressed higher pension and benefit costs as heavier drags on hiring workers the older they got. * * * The record thus reflects the common facts that an individual's chances to find and keep a job get worse over time; as between any two people, the younger is in the stronger position, the older more apt to be tagged with demeaning stereotype. Not surprisingly, from the voluminous records of the hearings, we have found (and Cline has cited) nothing suggesting that any workers were registering complaints about discrimination in favor of their seniors.

Nor is there any such suggestion in the introductory provisions of the ADEA, which begins with statements of purpose and findings that mirror the Wirtz Report and the committee transcripts. The findings stress the impediments suffered by "older workers ... in their efforts to retain ... and especially to regain employment," "the [burdens] of arbitrary age limits regardless of potential for job performance,"; the costs of "otherwise desirable practices [that] may work to the disadvantage of older persons," and "the incidence of unemployment, especially long-term unemployment[, which] is, relative to the younger ages, high among older

---

2. That report found that "[e]mployment discrimination because of race is identified ... with ... feelings about people entirely unrelated to their ability to do the job. There is *no* significant discrimination of this kind so far as older workers are concerned. The most closely related kind of discrimination in the non-employment of older workers involves their rejection because of assumptions about the effect of age on their ability to do a job *when there is in fact no basis for these assumptions.*" Report of the Secretary of Labor, The Older American Worker: Age Discrimination in Employment 2 (June 1965) (hereinafter Wirtz Report).

workers," The statutory objects were "to promote employment of older persons based on their ability rather than age; to prohibit arbitrary age discrimination in employment; [and] to help employers and workers find ways of meeting problems arising from the impact of age on employment."

In sum, except on one point, all the findings and statements of objectives are either cast in terms of the effects of age as intensifying over time, or are couched in terms that refer to "older" workers, explicitly or implicitly relative to "younger" ones. The single subject on which the statute speaks less specifically is that of "arbitrary limits" or "arbitrary age discrimination." But these are unmistakable references to the Wirtz Report's finding that "[a]lmost three out of every five employers covered by [a] 1965 survey have in effect age limitations (most frequently between 45 and 55) on new hires which they apply without consideration of an applicant's other qualifications." The ADEA's ban on "arbitrary limits" thus applies to age caps that exclude older applicants, necessarily to the advantage of younger ones.

Such is the setting of the ADEA's core substantive provision, § 4 (as amended, 29 U.S.C. § 623), prohibiting employers and certain others from "discriminat[ion] ... because of [an] individual's age," whenever (as originally enacted) the individual is "at least forty years of age but less than sixty-five years of age".[4] The prefatory provisions and their legislative history make a case that we think is beyond reasonable doubt, that the ADEA was concerned to protect a relatively old worker from discrimination that works to the advantage of the relatively young.

Nor is it remarkable that the record is devoid of any evidence that younger workers were suffering at the expense of their elders, let alone that a social problem required a federal statute to place a younger worker in parity with an older one. Common experience is to the contrary, and the testimony, reports, and congressional findings simply confirm that Congress used the phrase "discriminat[ion] ... because of [an] individual's age" the same way that ordinary people in common usage might speak of age discrimination any day of the week. One commonplace conception of American society in recent decades is its character as a "youth culture," and in a world where younger is better, talk about discrimination because of age is naturally understood to refer to discrimination against the older.

This same, idiomatic sense of the statutory phrase is confirmed by the statute's restriction of the protected class to those 40 and above. If Congress had been worrying about protecting the younger against the older, it would not likely have ignored everyone under 40. The youthful deficiencies of inexperience and unsteadiness invite stereotypical and discriminatory thinking about those a lot younger than 40, and prejudice suffered by a 40–year–old is not typically owing to youth, as 40–year–olds

---

4. In 1978, Congress changed the upper age limit to 70 years, and then struck it entirely in 1986. The President transferred authority over the ADEA from the Department of Labor to the EEOC in 1978. Congress has also made other changes, including extending the ADEA to government employees (state, local, and federal), and adding § 633a), and clarifying that it extends, with certain exceptions, to employee benefits.

sadly tend to find out. The enemy of 40 is 30, not 50. Even so, the 40–year threshold was adopted over the objection that some discrimination against older people begins at an even younger age; female flight attendants were not fired at 32 because they were too young, Thus, the 40–year threshold makes sense as identifying a class requiring protection against preference for their juniors, not as defining a class that might be threatened by favoritism toward seniors.

* * *

III

Cline and *amicus* EEOC proffer three rejoinders in favor of their competing view that the prohibition works both ways. First, they say (as does Justice THOMAS, *post*) that the statute's meaning is plain when the word "age" receives its natural and ordinary meaning and the statute is read as a whole giving "age" the same meaning throughout. And even if the text does not plainly mean what they say it means, they argue that the soundness of their version is shown by a colloquy on the floor of the Senate involving Senator Yarborough, a sponsor of the bill that became the ADEA. Finally, they fall back to the position (fortified by Justice SCALIA's dissent) that we should defer to the EEOC's reading of the statute. On each point, however, we think the argument falls short of unsettling our view of the natural meaning of the phrase speaking of discrimination, read in light of the statute's manifest purpose.

A

The first response to our reading is the dictionary argument that "age" means the length of a person's life, with the phrase "because of such individual's age" stating a simple test of causation: "discriminat[ion] ... because of [an] individual's age" is treatment that would not have occurred if the individual's span of years had been longer or shorter. The case for this reading calls attention to the other instances of "age" in the ADEA that are not limited to old age, such as 29 U.S.C. § 623(f), which gives an employer a defense to charges of age discrimination when "age is a bona fide occupational qualification." Cline and the EEOC argue that if "age" meant old age, § 623(f) would then provide a defense (old age is a bona fide qualification) only for an employer's action that on our reading would never clash with the statute (because preferring the older is not forbidden).

The argument rests on two mistakes. First, it assumes that the word "age" has the same meaning wherever the ADEA uses it. But this is not so, and Cline simply misemploys the "presumption that identical words used in different parts of the same act are intended to have the same meaning." Cline forgets that "the presumption is not rigid and readily yields whenever there is such variation in the connection in which the words are used as reasonably to warrant the conclusion that they were employed in different parts of the act with different intent." The presumption of uniform usage thus relents when a word used has several commonly understood meanings among which a speaker can alternate in the course of an ordinary conversation, without being confused or getting confusing.

"Age" is that kind of word. As JUSTICE THOMAS agrees, the word "age" standing alone can be readily understood either as pointing to any number of years lived, or as common shorthand for the longer span and concurrent aches that make youth look good. Which alternative was probably intended is a matter of context; we understand the different choices of meaning that lie behind a sentence like "Age can be shown by a driver's license," and the statement, "Age has left him a shut-in." So it is easy to understand that Congress chose different meanings at different places in the ADEA, as the different settings readily show. Hence the second flaw in Cline's argument for uniform usage: it ignores the cardinal rule that "[s]tatutory language must be read in context [since] a phrase 'gathers meaning from the words around it.'" The point here is that we are not asking an abstract question about the meaning of "age"; we are seeking the meaning of the whole phrase "discriminate ... because of such individual's age," where it occurs in the ADEA, 29 U.S.C. § 623(a)(1). As we have said, social history emphatically reveals an understanding of age discrimination as aimed against the old, and the statutory reference to age discrimination in this idiomatic sense is confirmed by legislative history. For the very reason that reference to context shows that "age" means "old age" when teamed with "discrimination," the provision of an affirmative defense when age is a bona fide occupational qualification readily shows that "age" as a qualification means comparative youth. As context tells us that "age" means one thing in § 623(a)(1) and another in § 623(f), so it also tells us that the presumption of uniformity cannot sensibly operate here.

The comparisons Justice THOMAS urges to *McDonald v. Santa Fe Trail Transp. Co.,* and *Oncale v. Sundowner Offshore Services, Inc.,* serve to clarify our position. Both cases involved Title VII of the Civil Rights Act of 1964, and its prohibition on employment discrimination "because of [an] individual's *race* ... [or] *sex*," The term "age" employed by the ADEA is not, however, comparable to the terms "race" or "sex" employed by Title VII. "Race" and "sex" are general terms that in every day usage require modifiers to indicate any relatively narrow application. We do not commonly understand "race" to refer only to the black race, or "sex" to refer only to the female. But the prohibition of age discrimination is readily read more narrowly than analogous provisions dealing with race and sex. That narrower reading is the more natural one in the textual setting, and it makes perfect sense because of Congress's demonstrated concern with distinctions that hurt older people.

B

The second objection has more substance than the first, but still not enough. The record of congressional action reports a colloquy on the Senate floor between two of the legislators most active in pushing for the

ADEA, Senators Javits and Yarborough. Senator Javits began the exchange by raising a concern mentioned by Senator Dominick, that "the bill might not forbid discrimination between two persons each of whom would be between the ages of 40 and 65." Senator Javits then gave his own view that, "if two individuals ages 52 and 42 apply for the same job, and the employer selected the man aged 42 solely ... because he is younger than the man 52, then he will have violated the act," and asked Senator Yarborough for his opinion. Senator Yarborough answered that "[t]he law prohibits age being a factor in the decision to hire, as to one age over the other, whichever way [the] decision went."

Although in the past we have given weight to Senator Yarborough's views on the construction of the ADEA because he was a sponsor, his side of this exchange is not enough to unsettle our reading of the statute. * * * What matters is that the Senator's remark, "whichever way [the] decision went," is the only item in all the 1967 hearings, reports, and debates going against the grain of the common understanding of age discrimination. Even from a sponsor, a single outlying statement cannot stand against a tide of context and history, not to mention 30 years of judicial interpretation producing no apparent legislative qualms.

C

The third objection relies on a reading consistent with the Yarborough comment, adopted by the agency now charged with enforcing the statute, as set out at 29 CFR § 1625.2(a) (2003). * * *

The parties contest the degree of weight owed to the EEOC's reading, with General Dynamics urging us that *Skidmore v. Swift & Co.*, 323 U.S. 134, 65 S.Ct. 161, 89 L.Ed. 124 (1944), sets the limit, while Cline and the EEOC say that § 1625.2(a) deserves greater deference under *Chevron U.S.A. Inc. v. Natural Resources Defense Council, Inc.*, 467 U.S. 837, 104 S.Ct. 2778, 81 L.Ed.2d 694 (1984). * * * [W]e neither defer nor settle on any degree of deference because the [EEOC interpretation] is clearly wrong.

* * * Here, regular interpretive method leaves no serious question, not even about purely textual ambiguity in the ADEA. The word "age" takes on a definite meaning from being in the phrase "discriminat[ion] ... because of such individual's age," occurring as that phrase does in a statute structured and manifestly intended to protect the older from arbitrary favor for the younger.

IV

We see the text, structure, purpose, and history of the ADEA, along with its relationship to other federal statutes, as showing that the statute does not mean to stop an employer from favoring an older employee over a younger one. The judgment of the Court of Appeals is *Reversed.*

JUSTICE SCALIA, dissenting.

* * * The question in this case is whether, in the absence of an affirmative defense, the ADEA prohibits an employer from favoring older over younger workers when both are protected by the Act, *i.e.,* are 40 years of age or older.

The Equal Employment Opportunity Commission (EEOC) has answered this question in the affirmative. In 1981, the agency adopted a regulation which states, in pertinent part:

> "It is unlawful in situations where this Act applies, for an employer to discriminate in hiring or in any other way by giving preference because of age between individuals 40 and over. Thus, if two people apply for the same position, and one is 42 and the other 52, the employer may not lawfully turn down either one on the basis of age, but must make such decision on the basis of some other factor." 29 C.F.R. § 1625.2(a) (2003).

This regulation represents the interpretation of the agency tasked by Congress with enforcing the ADEA.

The Court brushes aside the EEOC's interpretation as "clearly wrong." I cannot agree with the contention upon which that rejection rests: that "regular interpretive method leaves no serious question, not even about purely textual ambiguity in the ADEA." It is evident, for the reasons given in Part II of Justice THOMAS's dissenting opinion, that the Court's interpretive method is anything but "regular." And for the reasons given in Part I of that opinion, the EEOC's interpretation is neither foreclosed by the statute nor unreasonable.

* * * I would defer to the agency's authoritative conclusion. I respectfully dissent.

JUSTICE THOMAS, with whom JUSTICE KENNEDY joins, dissenting.

This should have been an easy case. The plain language of 29 U.S.C. § 623(a)(1) mandates a particular outcome: that the respondents are able to sue for discrimination against them in favor of older workers. The agency charged with enforcing the statute has adopted a regulation and issued an opinion as an adjudicator, both of which adopt this natural interpretation of the provision. And the only portion of legislative history relevant to the question before us is consistent with this outcome. Despite the fact that these traditional tools of statutory interpretation lead inexorably to the conclusion that respondents can state a claim for discrimination against the relatively young, the Court, apparently disappointed by this result, today adopts a different interpretation. In doing so, the Court, of necessity, creates a new tool of statutory interpretation, and then proceeds to give this newly created "social history" analysis dispositive weight. Because I cannot agree with the Court's new approach to interpreting antidiscrimination statutes, I respectfully dissent. * * *

NOTE

1. *State law? Ace Electrical Contractors, Inc. v. IBEW, Local 292,* 414 F.3d 896 (8th Cir. 2005), involved a policy whereby in all units with more than four employees, at least one of every five workers would be over age fifty. During an economic contraction, this policy resulted in the layoff of younger workers based on their age. A divided court held this to be age discrimination under a *state statute* similar in wording to the ADEA.

HAZEN PAPER COMPANY v. BIGGINS

Supreme Court of the United States, 1993
507 U.S. 604, 113 S.Ct. 1701, 123 L.Ed.2d 338

JUSTICE O'CONNOR delivered the opinion of the Court.

* * *

I

Petitioner Hazen Paper Company manufactures coated, laminated, and printed paper and paperboard. The company is owned and operated by two cousins, petitioners Robert Hazen and Thomas N. Hazen. The Hazens hired respondent Walter F. Biggins as their technical director in 1977. They fired him in 1986, when he was 62 years old.

Respondent brought suit against petitioners in the United States District Court for the District of Massachusetts, alleging a violation of the ADEA. * * * The case was tried before a jury, which rendered a verdict for respondent on his ADEA claim and also found violations of the Employee Retirement Income Security Act of 1974 (ERISA), 29 U.S.C. § 1140, and state law. * * *

The United States Court of Appeals for the First Circuit affirmed judgment for respondent on both the ADEA and ERISA counts * * *

In affirming the judgments of liability, the Court of Appeals relied heavily on the evidence that petitioners had fired respondent in order to prevent his pension benefits from vesting. That evidence, as construed most favorably to respondent by the court, showed that the Hazen Paper pension plan had a 10–year vesting period and that respondent would have reached the 10–year mark had he worked "a few more weeks" after being fired. There was also testimony that petitioners had offered to retain respondent as a consultant to Hazen Paper, in which capacity he would not have been entitled to receive pension benefits. The Court of Appeals found this evidence of pension interference to be sufficient for ERISA liability, and also gave it considerable emphasis in upholding ADEA liability. After summarizing all the testimony tending to show age discrimination, the court stated:

"Based on the foregoing evidence, the jury could reasonably have found that Thomas Hazen decided to fire [respondent] before his pension rights vested and used the confidentiality agreement [that petitioners had asked respondent to sign] as a means to that end. The jury could also have reasonably found that age was inextricably intertwined with the decision to fire [respondent]. If it were not for [respondent's] age, sixty-two, his pension rights would not have been within a hairbreadth of vesting. [Respondent] was fifty-two years old when he was hired; his pension rights vested in ten years."

* * *

We granted certiorari. * * * [D]oes an employer's interference with the vesting of pension benefits violate the ADEA?

II

A

* * *

As we explained in *EEOC v. Wyoming,* 460 U.S. 226, 103 S.Ct. 1054, 75 L.Ed.2d 18 (1983), Congress' promulgation of the ADEA was prompted by its concern that older workers were being deprived of employment on the basis of inaccurate and stigmatizing stereotypes.

"Although age discrimination rarely was based on the sort of animus motivating some other forms of discrimination, it was based in large part on stereotypes unsupported by objective fact.... Moreover, the available empirical evidence demonstrated that arbitrary age lines were in fact generally unfounded and that, as an overall matter, the performance of older workers was at least as good as that of younger workers." *Id.* at 231, 103 S.Ct., at 1057–1058.

Thus the ADEA commands that "employers are to evaluate [older] employees ... on their merits and not their age." Employers cannot rely on age as a proxy for an employee's remaining characteristics, such as productivity, but must instead focus on those factors directly.

When the employer's decision *is* wholly motivated by factors other than age, the problem of inaccurate and stigmatizing stereotypes disappears. This is true even if the motivating factor is correlated with age, as pension status typically is. Pension plans typically provide that an employee's accrued benefits will become nonforfeitable, or "vested," once the employee completes a certain number of years of service with the employer. On average, an older employee has had more years in the work force than a younger employee, and thus may well have accumulated more years of service with a particular employer. Yet an employee's age is analytically distinct from his years of service. An employee who is younger than 40, and therefore outside the class of older workers as defined by the ADEA may have worked for a particular employer his entire career, while an older worker may have been newly hired. Because age and years of service are analytically distinct, an employer can take account of one while ignoring the other, and thus it is incorrect to say that a decision based on years of service is necessarily "age based."

The instant case is illustrative. Under the Hazen Paper pension plan, as construed by the Court of Appeals, an employee's pension benefits vest after the employee completes 10 years of service with the company. Perhaps it is true that older employees of Hazen Paper are more likely to be "close to vesting" than younger employees. Yet a decision by the company to fire an older employee solely because he has nine-plus years of service and therefore is "close to vesting" would not constitute discriminatory treatment on the basis of age. The prohibited stereotype ("Older employees are likely to be ___") would not have figured in this decision, and the attendant stigma would not ensue. The decision would not be the result of an inaccurate and denigrating generalization about age, but would rather represent an *accurate* judgment about the employee-that he indeed is "close to vesting."

We do not mean to suggest that an employer *lawfully* could fire an employee in order to prevent his pension benefits from vesting. Such conduct is actionable under § 510 of ERISA, as the Court of Appeals rightly found in affirming judgment for respondent under that statute. But it would not, without more, violate the ADEA. That law requires the employer to ignore an employee's age (absent a statutory exemption or defense); it does not specify further characteristics that an employer must also ignore. Although some language in our prior decisions might be read to mean that an employer violates the ADEA whenever its reason for firing an employee is improper in any respect, * * * this reading is obviously incorrect. For example, it cannot be true that an employer who fires an older black worker because the worker is black thereby violates the ADEA. The employee's race is an improper reason, but it is improper under Title VII, not the ADEA.

We do not preclude the possibility that an employer who targets employees with a particular pension status on the assumption that these employees are likely to be older thereby engages in age discrimination. Pension status may be a proxy for age, not in the sense that the ADEA makes the two factors equivalent, but in the sense that the employer may suppose a correlation between the two factors and act accordingly. Nor do we rule out the possibility of dual liability under ERISA and the ADEA where the decision to fire the employee was motivated both by the employee's age and by his pension status. Finally, we do not consider the special case where an employee is about to vest in pension benefits as a result of his *age*, rather than years of service, and the employer fires the employee in order to prevent vesting. That case is not presented here. Our holding is simply that an employer does not violate the ADEA just by interfering with an older employee's pension benefits that would have vested by virtue of the employee's years of service.

* * *

NOTES

1. *Apply **Hazen Paper** to the following:*

a. Employer grants larger pay raises to employees with less than five years of service than to employees with more than five years of service. ***Smith v. City of Jackson,*** 544 U.S. 228, 125 S.Ct. 1536, 161 L.Ed.2d 410 (2005).

b. A higher paid worker (who is also older) is dismissed and replaced with a newly hired worker who is younger and who is paid a lower salary. The employer's reason for replacing the older worker was economic; it was attempting to cut cost by replacing high paid workers with lower wage workers. *Anderson v. Baxter Healthcare Corp.,* 13 F.3d 1120 (7th Cir. 1994).

c. Newly hired workers are paid salaries higher than that of incumbent workers for work that is identical. *Davidson v. Board of Governors, State Colleges & Universities,* 920 F.2d 441 (7th Cir. 1990).

d. In determining order of lay off the employer utilizes "reverse seniority." That is, the most senior workers are laid off before junior workers. Thus, a person with 10 years seniority will be laid off, while one with 1 year of seniority will be retained. *Allen v. Highlands Hosp. Corp.* 545 F.3d 387 (6th Cir. 2008).

e. Younger workers (those not eligible for "normal" retirement) but who retired because they have a job related disability are provided a bonus that is not given to disabled employees who are also eligible for "normal" retirement benefits. "Normal" retirement benefits are accorded to employees who have worked at least 20 years, or have reached age of 55 and have no less than 5 years of service. ***Kentucky Retirement Systems v. EEOC,*** 554 U.S. 135, 128 S.Ct. 2361, 171 L.Ed.2d 322 (2008).

2. *Mandatory Retirement:* Some nations which broadly proscribe age discrimination for workers below a certain age (e.g., 65), either permit, or in some cases require, involuntary retirement of workers reaching a certain age. In 1986 the ADEA was amended to eliminate such an upper age limit on protection. Thus, with few exceptions, mandated retirement based on age violates the ADEA.

At one time the Court held that the provisos in the ADEA permitting employers to observe bona fide retirement programs to impose retirement ages that were integrated into the program. That interpretation was specifically overruled by the 1986 amendments which provide:

1) No "seniority system shall require or permit the involuntary retirement of any individual * * * because of the age of such individual and

2) "No such employee benefit plan or voluntary early retirement incentive plan shall excuse the failure to hire any individual, and no such employee benefit plan shall require or permit the involuntary retirement of any individual * * * because of the age of such individual. 29 U.S.C. § 623(f)(2)(A) and (B).

3. *Exceptions* where involuntary retirement is permitted:

a. *Bona fide executives* who have been in the position for no less than two years, who have reached age 65, and are covered by the employer's nonforfeitable benefit program that provides no less than $44,000 per year from the employer provided program. 29 U.S.C. § 631(c).

b. *Public Safety Workers:* State and local public safety workers, such as police officers and firefighters, may be subjected to maximum hiring ages and to mandatory retirement where the employer provides regular individualized evaluations of fitness that would allow older workers to remain qualified. The system, however, must be regularly applied. If exceptions are regularly granted the minimum hiring and mandatory retirement ages cannot be invoked. See, *Davis v. Indiana State Police,* 541 F.3d 760 (7th Cir. 2008).

c. *Age as a BFOQ:* In a limited number of high risk jobs such as pilots and bus drivers, the employer may be able to establish on a case-by-case basis that workers in the excluded age group present an unacceptable risk of harm to third parties that cannot be reduced to acceptable levels through individualized evaluations of fitness, and on this basis the employer may assert that a younger age is a bona fide occupational qualification. The BFOQ defense will be discussed *infra* Chapter 3A.

d. *Federal Regulations* applicable to such high risk jobs as airline pilots and air traffic controllers may override the general age discrimination provisions of the ADEA. See, ***Johnson v. City Council of Baltimore,*** 472 U.S. 353, 105 S.Ct. 2717, 86 L.Ed.2d 286 (1985), which implicitly sanctioned such federal regulations by holding that state governments could not "borrow" the federal regulations making them a BFOQ for similar state occupations.

F. DISABILITIES AND IMPAIRMENTS

1. THE AMERICANS WITH DISABILITIES ACT: INTRODUCTION

EQUAL EMPLOYMENT OPPORTUNITY COMMISSION (EEOC) INTERPRETIVE GUIDANCE ON TITLE I OF THE AMERICANS WITH DISABILITIES ACT

Appendix to Code of Federal Regulations Part 1630 (April 2011)

The Americans with Disabilities Act (ADA) is a landmark piece of civil rights legislation signed into law on July 26, 1990, and amended effective January 1, 2009. 42 U.S.C. 12101 *et seq.* In passing the ADA, Congress recognized that "discrimination against individuals with disabilities continues to be a serious and pervasive social problem" and that the "continuing existence of unfair and unnecessary discrimination and prejudice denies people with disabilities the opportunity to compete on an equal basis and to pursue those opportunities for which our free society is justifiably famous, and costs the United States billions of dollars in unnecessary expenses resulting from dependency and nonproductivity." * * * The ADA prohibits discrimination in a wide range of areas, including employment, public services, and public accommodations.

Title I of the ADA prohibits disability-based discrimination in employment. The Equal Employment Opportunity Commission * * * is responsible for enforcement of title I (and parts of title V) of the ADA. * * * Under title I of the ADA, covered entities may not discriminate against qualified individuals on the basis of disability in regard to job application procedures, the hiring, advancement or discharge of employees, employee compensation, job training, or other terms, conditions, and privileges of employment. 42 U.S.C. 12112(a). * * * As with other civil rights laws, individuals seeking protection under these anti-discrimination provisions of the ADA generally must allege and prove that they are members of the "protected class."[1] Under the ADA, this typically means they have to show that they meet the statutory definition of "disability." * * *

In the original ADA, Congress defined "disability" as (1) a physical or mental impairment that substantially limits one or more major life activities of an individual; (2) a record of such an impairment; or (3) being regarded as having such an impairment. Congress patterned these three parts of the definition of disability—the "actual," "record of," and "regarded as" prongs—after the definition of "handicap" found in the Rehabilitation Act of 1973. By doing so, Congress intended that the relevant case law developed under the Rehabilitation Act would be generally applicable to the term "disability" as used in the ADA. * * * [The ADA did not repeal the Rehabilitation Act of 1973. Indeed the ADA directed in 29 U.S.C. §§ 791(g), 793(g) and 794(d) "The standards used to determine * * * whether a complaint alleging employment discrimination under this section shall be the standards applied under title I of the Americans with Disabilities Act." Moreover, the Rehabilitation Act is the sole source of relief for federal employees. Ed.]

The holdings of several Supreme Court cases sharply narrowed the broad scope of protection Congress originally intended under the ADA, thus eliminating protection for many individuals whom Congress intended to protect. For example, in *Sutton* v. *United Air Lines, Inc.,* 527 U.S. 471 (1999), the Court ruled that whether an impairment substantially limits a major life activity is to be determined with reference to the ameliorative effects of mitigating measures. In *Sutton,* the Court also adopted a restrictive reading of the meaning of being "regarded as" disabled under the ADA's definition of disability. Subsequently, in *Toyota Motor Mfg., Ky., Inc.* v. *Williams,* 534 U.S. 184 (2002), the Court held that the terms "substantially" and "major" in the definition of disability "need to be interpreted strictly to create a demanding standard for qualifying as disabled" under the ADA, and that to be substantially limited in perform-

---

1. Claims of improper disability-related inquiries or medical examinations, improper disclosure of confidential medical information, or retaliation may be brought by any applicant or employee, not just individuals with disabilities. *See,* e.g., *Cossette* v. *Minnesota Power & Light,* 188 F.3d 964, 969–70 (8th Cir. 1999); *Fredenburg* v. *Contra Costa County Dep't of Health Servs.,* 172 F.3d 1176, 1182 (9th Cir. 1999); *Griffin* v. *Steeltek, Inc.,* 160 F.3d 591, 594 (10th Cir. 1998). Likewise, a nondisabled applicant or employee may challenge an employment action that is based on the disability of an individual with whom the applicant or employee is known to have a relationship or association. *See* 42 U.S.C. 12112(b)(4).

ing a major life activity under the ADA, "an individual must have an impairment that prevents or severely restricts the individual from doing activities that are of central importance to most people's daily lives."

As a result of these Supreme Court decisions, lower courts ruled in numerous cases that individuals with a range of substantially limiting impairments were not individuals with disabilities, and thus not protected by the ADA. Congress concluded that these rulings imposed a greater degree of limitation and expressed a higher standard than it had originally intended, and * * * unduly precluded many individuals from being covered under the ADA.

Consequently, Congress amended the ADA with the Americans with Disabilities Act Amendments Act of 2008 (ADAAA). The ADAAA * * * became effective on January 1, 2009. [T]he primary purpose of the ADAAA is to make it easier for people with disabilities to obtain protection under the ADA. * * * [T]he ADAA's rules of construction require that the definition of "disability" "shall be construed in favor of broad coverage of individuals under the ADA, to the maximum extent permitted by the terms of the ADA." 42 U.S.C. § 12102(4)(A).

---

2. NON–DISCRIMINATION—IMPAIRMENTS

One of the most significant changes made by the ADAAA was to sever conceptually "impairment" from "disability." The original Act, 42 U.S.C. § 12102, defined "disability" with respect to an individual to mean:

(A) a physical or mental impairment that substantially limits one or more major life activities of such individual;

(B) a record of such an impairment; or

(C) being regarded as having such an impairment.

The ADAAA added at the end of subparagraph (C) the phrase: *"as described in paragraph 3."* Critical "paragraph 3" provides:

(A) An individual meets the requirement of 'being regarded as having such an impairment' if the individual establishes that he or she has been subjected to an action prohibited under this chapter because of an actual or perceived physical or mental impairment *whether or not the impairment limits or is perceived to limit a major life activity.*

EEOC INTERPRETIVE GUIDANCE: APPENDIX

Section 1630.2(*l*): "Regarded as Substantially Limited in a Major Life Activity"

Coverage under the "regarded as" prong of the definition of disability should not be difficult to establish. Under the third prong of the definition of disability, an individual is "regarded as having such an impairment" if the individual is subjected to an action prohibited by the ADA because of an actual or perceived impairment that is not "transitory and minor."

This third prong of the definition of disability was originally intended to express Congress's understanding that "unfounded concerns, mistaken beliefs, fears, myths, or prejudice about disabilities are often just as disabling as actual impairments, and [its] corresponding desire to prohibit discrimination founded on such perceptions." In passing the original ADA, Congress relied extensively on the reasoning of *School Board of Nassau County* v. *Arline,* 480 U.S. at 282–83 [construing the Rehabilitation Act] "that the negative reactions of others are just as disabling as the actual impact of an impairment." The ADAAA reiterates Congress's reliance on the broad views enunciated in that decision * * *.

* * * [T]o qualify for coverage under the "regarded as" prong, an individual is not subject to any functional test. The concepts of "major life activities" and "substantial limitation" simply are not relevant in evaluating whether an individual is "regarded as having such an impairment."

To illustrate how straightforward application of the "regarded as" prong is, if an employer refused to hire an applicant because of skin graft scars, the employer has regarded the applicant as an individual with a disability. Similarly, if an employer terminates an employee because he has cancer, the employer has regarded the employee as an individual with a disability.

* * * Whether a covered entity can ultimately establish a defense to liability is an inquiry separate from, and follows after, a determination that an individual was regarded as having a disability. Thus, for example, an employer who terminates an employee with angina from a manufacturing job that requires the employee to work around machinery, believing that the employee will pose a safety risk to himself or others if he were suddenly to lose consciousness, has regarded the individual as disabled. Whether the employer has a defense (e.g., that the employee posed a direct threat to himself or coworkers) is a separate inquiry.

As prescribed in the ADA Amendments Act, the regulations provide an exception to coverage under the "regarded as" prong where the impairment on which a prohibited action is based is both transitory (having an actual or expected duration of six months or less) and minor. The regulations make clear (at § 1630.2(l)(2) and § 1630.15(f)) that this exception is a defense to a claim of discrimination. * * * [A]s an exception to the general rule for broad coverage under the "regarded as" prong, this limitation on coverage should be construed narrowly. * * *

An individual covered only under the "regarded as" prong is not entitled to reasonable accommodation. 42 U.S.C. § 12201(h). Thus, in cases where reasonable accommodation is not at issue, the third prong provides a more straightforward framework for analyzing whether discrimination occurred. As Congress observed in enacting the ADAAA: "[W]e expect [the first] prong of the definition to be used only by people who are affirmatively seeking reasonable accommodations or modifications. Any individual who has been discriminated against because of an impairment—short of being granted a reasonable accommodation or modification—should be bringing a claim under the third prong of the definition which will require no showing with regard to the severity of his or her impairment."

NOTES

1. *Disability Discrimination is Different!* The Supreme Court has noted, that unlike race or sex discrimination, which "frequently bears no relationship to ability to perform or contribute to society," individuals with disabilities "as a group are indeed different from others not sharing their misfortune." The ADA mandate to make reasonable accommodations to persons with disabilities upsets "entirely reasonable [goals] to conserve scarce financial resources by hiring employees who are able to use existing facilities" and can adjust to the employer's work place structures and assignments." *City of Cleburne v. Cleburne,* **473 U.S. 432, 105 S.Ct. 3249, 87 L.Ed.2d 313 (1985).** Protecting persons with disabilities thus was seen by the Court as more of a social welfare initiative than a civil rights protection, which resulted in a conclusion that the constitutional authority to enact the ADA came, not from the Fourteenth Amendment, but by Congress's power to regulate interstate commerce. As such, the ability of *private individuals to secure monetary relief* against state governments was limited by the Eleventh Amendment. *Board of Trustees, University of Alabama v. Garrett,* **531 U.S. 356, 121 S.Ct. 955, 148 L.Ed.2d 866 (2001).**[23]

a. "Physical or Mental Impairment"

All three subparagraphs, or prongs—A and B and C—of 42 U.S.C. § 12102 depend upon a definition of "physical or mental impairment." A plaintiff proceeding under the third prong—(C)—must (1) be perceived as having an *"impairment,"* (2) can, *without accommodations,* perform *"essential"* job duties, and (3) demonstrate that they were discriminated against by the covered entity "because of" their real or perceived impairment. The ADA precludes claims by individuals *without* a disability based upon favorable treatment received by persons who have a real or perceived impairment. 42 U.S.C. § 12201(g).

EEOC INTERPRETIVE GUIDANCE: APPENDIX

Section 1630.2(h)

It is important to distinguish between conditions that are impairments and physical, psychological, environmental, cultural, and economic characteristics that are not impairments. The definition of the term "impairment" does not include physical characteristics such as eye color, hair color, left-handedness, or height, weight, or muscle tone that are within

---

23. See, Cox, *Crossroads and Signposts, The ADA Amendment Act of 2008,* 85 Ind.L.J. 187 (2010).

"normal" range and are not the result of a physiological disorder. The definition, likewise, does not include characteristic predisposition to illness or disease. Other conditions, such as pregnancy, that are not the result of a physiological disorder are also not impairments. However, a pregnancy-related impairment that substantially limits a major life activity is a disability under the first prong of the definition. Alternatively, a pregnancy-related impairment may constitute a "record of" a substantially limiting impairment," or may be covered under the "regarded as" prong if it is the basis for a prohibited employment action and is not "transitory and minor."

The definition of an impairment also does not include common personality traits such as poor judgment or a quick temper where these are not symptoms of a mental or psychological disorder. Environmental, cultural, or economic disadvantages such as poverty, lack of education, or a prison record are not impairments. Advanced age, in and of itself, is also not an impairment. However, various medical conditions commonly associated with age, such as hearing loss, osteoporosis, or arthritis would constitute impairments within the meaning of this part.[24]

COOK v. STATE OF RHODE ISLAND, DEPT. OF MENTAL HEALTH

United States Court of Appeals, First Circuit, 1993.
10 F.3d 17

SELYA, CIRCUIT JUDGE

I. Background

At the times material hereto, defendant-appellant Department of Mental Health, Retardation, and Hospitals (MHRH), * * * operated the Ladd Center as a residential facility for retarded persons. Plaintiff-appellee Bonnie Cook worked at Ladd as an institutional attendant for the mentally retarded (IABMR) from 1978 to 1980, and again from 1981 to 1986. Both times she departed voluntarily, leaving behind a spotless work record. The defendant concedes that Cook's past performance met its legitimate expectations.

In 1988, when plaintiff reapplied for the identical position, she stood 5'2" tall and weighed over 320 pounds. During the routine pre-hire physical, a

---

24. The ADA also prohibits discrimination against a qualified, *but not disabled individual* because of the known disability of an individual with whom the non disabled individual is known to have a relationship or association. 42 U.S.C. § 12112(B)(4). This provision has interpreted to apply to adverse personnel actions based on: *(1). "Expense:"* The employer dismisses the employee because the disability of the employee's spouse or children covered by the employer's benefit plan would impose direct or indirect costs on the employer. *Dewitt v. Proctor Hospital,* 517 F.3d 944 (7th Cir. 2008). *(2) Association:* The employee is dismissed because his homosexual companion is infected with HIV or AIDS and the employer fears that the employee may become infected. *Larimer v. International Business Machines, Corp.,* 370 F.3d 698 (7th Cir. 2004). And *(3) Distraction:* The employer fears that the employee caring for the family member or close friend with the disability would interfere with the employee be distracted or be forced to miss work. *Den Hartog v. Wassatch Academy,* 129 F.3d 1076 (10th Cir. 1997).

nurse employed by MHRH concluded that plaintiff was morbidly obese but found no limitations that impinged upon her ability to do the job. Notwithstanding that plaintiff passed the physical examination, MHRH balked. It claimed that Cook's morbid obesity compromised her ability to evacuate patients in case of an emergency and put her at greater risk of developing serious ailments (a "fact" that MHRH's hierarch speculated would promote absenteeism and increase the likelihood of workers' compensation claims). Consequently, MHRH refused to hire plaintiff for a vacant IABMR position.

Cook did not go quietly into this dark night. Invoking section 504, [of the Rehabilitation Act] she sued MHRH in federal district court. MHRH moved to dismiss the complaint, averring that morbid obesity can never constitute a handicap within the meaning of the Rehabilitation Act. * * *

In due season, the parties tried the case to a jury. At the close of the evidence, appellant moved for judgment as a matter of law. The court reserved decision, and submitted the case on special interrogatories (to which appellant interposed no objections). The jury answered the interrogatories favorably to plaintiff and, by means of the accompanying general verdict, awarded her $100,000 in compensatory damages. The district court denied appellant's motions for judgment as a matter of law and for a new trial, entered judgment on the verdict, and granted equitable relief to the plaintiff. * * *[7]

III. Analysis

* * *

A

The plaintiff proceeded below on a perceived disability theory, positing that she was fully able although MHRH regarded her as physically impaired. * * *

On one hand, the jury could plausibly have found that plaintiff had a physical impairment; after all, she admittedly suffered from morbid obesity, and she presented expert testimony that morbid obesity is a physiological disorder involving a dysfunction of both the metabolic system and the neurological appetite-suppressing signal system, capable of causing adverse effects within the musculoskeletal, respiratory, and cardiovascular systems. On the second hand, the jury could have found that plaintiff, although not handicapped, was treated by MHRH as if she had a physical impairment. Indeed, MHRH's stated reasons for its refusal to hire "its concern that Cook's limited mobility impeded her ability to evacuate patients in case of an emergency, and its fear that her condition augured a

---

7. The medical profession considers a person morbidly obese if she weighs either more than twice her optimal weight or more than 100 pounds over her optimal weight. While Cook had been corpulent during her prior tours of duty, she had not then attained a state of morbid obesity. The jury found, inter alia, that plaintiff, apart from her handicap or perceived handicap, was qualified to perform the duties of the IA–MR position; and that the defendant did not reasonably believe plaintiff lacked such qualifications.

heightened risk of heart disease, thereby increasing the likelihood of workers' compensation claims" show conclusively that MHRH treated plaintiff's obesity as if it actually affected her musculoskeletal and cardio-vascular systems.

B

Appellant counterattacks on two fronts. Neither foray succeeds.

1. Mutability. MHRH baldly asserts that "mutable" conditions are not the sort of impairments that can find safe harbor in the lee of section 504. It executes this assertion by claiming that morbid obesity is a mutable condition and that, therefore, one who suffers from it is not handicapped within the meaning of the federal law because she can simply lose weight and rid herself of any concomitant disability. This suggestion is as insubstantial as a pitchman's promise.

We think it is important to recognize that appellant has no legitimate complaint about the trial court's choice among the possible variations on the applicable legal theme. The district judge sang appellant's song, instructing the jury, at appellant's urging, that a "condition or disorder is not an impairment unless it ... constitutes an immutable condition that the person affected is powerless to control. Thus, appellant's mutability complaint is necessarily addressed to the facts. As such, it is belied by the record.

In deciding this issue, the jury had before it credible evidence that metabolic dysfunction, which leads to weight gain in the morbidly obese, lingers even after weight loss. Given this evidence, the jury reasonably could have found that, though people afflicted with morbid obesity can treat the manifestations of metabolic dysfunction by fasting or perennial undereating, the physical impairment itself "a dysfunctional metabolism" is permanent.

There is, moreover, another dissonant chord in appellant's paean to mutability. Even if immutability were normally a prerequisite to finding a covered impairment, as the district court's charge suggested, the logic of a perceived disability case, as embodied in the regulations, would nonetheless defeat the doctrine's application. So long as the prospective employer responds to a perceived disability in a way that makes clear that the employer regards the condition as immutable, no more is exigible. * * *

2. Voluntariness. Appellant's second assault regains no ground. MHRH asseverates that, because morbid obesity is caused, or at least exacerbated, by voluntary conduct, it cannot constitute an impairment falling within the ambit of section 504. But, this asseveration rests on a legally faulty premise. The Rehabilitation Act contains no language suggesting that its protection is linked to how an individual became impaired, or whether an individual contributed to his or her impairment. On the contrary, the Act indisputably applies to numerous conditions that may be caused or exacer-bated by voluntary conduct, such as alcoholism, AIDS, diabetes, cancer

resulting from cigarette smoking, heart disease resulting from excesses of various types, and the like. * * *

* * *

MHRH has not offered a hint of any non-weight-related reason for rejecting plaintiff's application. Rather, it has consistently conceded that it gave plaintiff the cold shoulder because Dr. O'Brien denied her medical clearance. The record is pellucid that Dr. O'Brien's refusal had three foci, each of which related directly to plaintiff's obesity. On this record, there was considerable room for a jury to find that appellant declined to hire Cook "due solely to" her perceived handicap.

NOTES

1. *Compare*: *Cassista v. Community Foods Inc.*, 5 Cal.4th 1050, 22 Cal.Rptr.2d 287, 856 P.2d 1143 (1993), where plaintiff, five feet, four inches tall, and weighing three hundred and five pounds, was unable to demonstrate that her obesity was a result of a psychological condition affecting one or more of her body systems, and consequently did not suffer from an "impairment."

2. *"Physical impairment:"* Chronic "bad back," "tennis elbow," migraine headaches, even erectile dysfunction have been held to be "impairments." *Arrieta–Colon v. Wal–Mart, Inc.*, 434 F.3d 75 (1st Cir. 2006).

3. *"Mental impairment"* is any medically recognized "mental or psychological disorder such as intellectual disability, organic brain syndrome, or mental illness." 29 CFR § 1603.3(h)(2) (2011). Included would be bi-polar conditions, learning disabilities, dyslexia, and attention deficit disorders. *See, Doebele v. Sprint/United Management*, 342 F.3d 1117 (10th Cir. 2003).

4. *Exclusions from "Impairment"*

a. *Sexual Orientation and "Disorders:"* "[H]omosexuality and bisexuality are not impairments and as such are not disabilities under this Act." 42 U.S.C. § 12211(a) "[T]he term "disability shall not include: transvestism, transsexualism, pedophilia, exhibitionism, voyeurism, gender identity disorders not resulting from physical impairments, or other sexual behavior disorders; 42 U.S.C. § 12211(b)(1).

b. *Social disorders*: Compulsive gambling, kleptomania, pyromania, and psychoactive substance use disorders resulting from current illegal use of drugs are excluded from the definition of "disability." 42 U.S.C. §§ 12211(b)(2) and (3).

---

b. "Transitory and Minor"

The ADAAA provides:

(B) ["Being regarded as having such an impairment'] shall not apply to impairments that are transitory and minor. Transitory impairments are those with an actual or expected duration of 6 months or less.

The 2011 Interpretative Regulations *"Appendix, Section 1630.15(f)* provide:

> It may be a defense to a charge of discrimination where coverage would be shown solely under the "regarded as" prong of the definition of disability that the impairment is (in the case of an actual impairment) or would be (in the case of a perceived impairment) both transitory and minor. * * * Section 1630.15(f)(2) [of the Regulations] explains that the determination of "transitory and minor" is made objectively. For example, an individual who is denied a promotion because he has a minor back injury would be "regarded as" an individual with a disability if the back impairment lasted or was expected to last more than six months. Although minor, the impairment is not transitory. * * *
>
> The relevant inquiry is whether the actual or perceived impairment on which the employer's action was based is objectively "transitory and minor," not whether the employer claims it subjectively believed the impairment was transitory and minor. For example, an employer who terminates an employee whom it believes has bipolar disorder cannot take advantage of this exception by asserting that it believed the employee's impairment was transitory and minor, since bipolar disorder is not objectively transitory and minor. At the same time, an employer that terminated an employee with an objectively "transitory and minor" hand wound, mistakenly believing it to be symptomatic of HIV infection, will nevertheless have "regarded" the employee as an individual with a disability, since the covered entity took a prohibited employment action based on a perceived impairment (HIV infection) that is not "transitory and minor."

Thus, it would seem, if the impairment in fact substantially limits a major life activity, such as the ability to walk, breathe, or care for one's self the "impairment" could not be considered "minor." Accordingly, broken limbs, heart attacks, and corrective surgery may be sufficiently serious to be "impairments" even if the condition lasts less than six months. *See, Katz v. City Metal Co.*, 87 F.3d 26 (1st Cir. 1996).

c. "Qualified"

(1) Generally: Section 102, of the ADA requires the plaintiff with an impairment to be a *"qualified individual."* An individual is "qualified" if he/she possess the requisite skill, experience and educational requirements for the position **and** can perform *essential functions* of such position. 42

U.S.C. § 12111(8) Section 501(h), 42 U.S.C. § 12201, inserted by the ADAAA states: Since "a covered entity under title I [*i.e.* an "employer"] need not provide a reasonable accommodation * * * to an individual who meets the definition of disability * * * solely upon [being regarded as having such an impairment]," an individual with a perceived "impairment" will be protected against discrimination, only if the individual actually can perform *"essential"* job functions without an accommodation.

(2) *Qualification standards:* An individual is not "qualified" if he or she lacks the skill or an educational credential necessary to perform the job. For example, if the job involves driving a commercial vehicle, the individual is not "qualified" if he or she cannot secure the necessary drivers licenses, even if the inability to secure the license was the result of the impairment. An individual who lacks a uniformly required educational credential, such as a high school diploma, is not qualified even though a mental illness precluded securing the credential. ***Albertson's Inc. v. Kirkingburg***, 527 U.S. 555, 119 S.Ct. 2162, 144 L.Ed.2d 518 (1999). *Johnson v. Board of Trustees*, 666 F.3d 561 (9th Cir. 2011) (individual who could not secure required certificate because of bipolar disorder is not "qualified.") While the employer has no obligation to explore alternatives to the qualification standard, such "qualification standards" may not be used if the individual can demonstrate that they:

> screen out or tend to screen out an individual with a disability or a class of individuals with disabilities unless the standard, test, or selection criteria, as used by the covered entity is shown to be job-related for the position in question and is consistent with business necessity.

42 U.S.C. § 12112(b)(6)

(3) *"Essential" vs. Non–Essential Functions*

SKERSKI v. TIME WARNER CABLE COMPANY

United States Court of Appeals, Third Circuit, 2001
257 F.3d 273

SLOVITER, CIRCUIT JUDGE.

Appellant Larry S. Skerski filed suit in the United States District Court for the Western District of Pennsylvania against his former employer Time Warner Cable Co., alleging discrimination on the basis of a disability in violation of the Americans with Disabilities Act ("ADA"). The District Court granted Time Warner's motion for summary judgment and Skerski appeals.

I

At all times relevant to this action, appellee Time Warner operated a television cable franchise in the Coraopolis/Moon Township area of Western Pennsylvania. Time Warner's predecessor, New Channels, hired Skerski in 1982 to upgrade cable converters in customers' homes. Several months later, Skerski was trained and began working as a cable service technician to install and disconnect cable television service for customers. As part of his job as an installer technician, Skerski serviced cable wires at aerial cable plants (hereafter referred to as "overhead work") and underground plants (hereafter referred to as "underground work"). Performing the overhead work required Skerski to climb ladders, poles, and towers, and work at heights. In his deposition testimony, Skerski first asserted that "there was more underground [work] than over head [work]," but he later agreed that approximately 50% of his job required climbing. The written description of Skerski's job prepared by New Channels included "repetitive . . . pole climbing . . . and ladder climbing" among the "Physical Tasks."

In May 1993, more than 10 years after he began working as an installer technician at New Channels, Skerski began experiencing dizziness, nausea, and irregular heartbeats while working at heights. In June 1993, Skerski was examined by Dr. Stephen G. Brodsky and was diagnosed as having a panic and anxiety disorder associated with premature ventricular contractions of the heart. Dr. Brodsky referred Skerski to Dr. Stuart L. Steinberg, a psychologist, for his panic condition. Dr. Steinberg recommended that Skerski cease climbing ladders and poles, and otherwise working at heights.

Upon learning of Dr. Steinberg's diagnosis, Skerski's supervisor at New Channels, David Kane, modified Skerski's schedule so as to permit him to continue working as an installer technician. Thus, New Channels limited Skerski's assignments to underground work. The assignments were distributed each day at Kane's direction. Skerski continued to perform under this "modified arrangement," after New Channels was acquired by Time Warner in March 1995, and until January 1997.

Under Time Warner, Skerski's job effectively remained the same. Time Warner's written description of Skerski's position listed the nine essential functions as:

1. Conducts CLI testing and repairs, checks amplifier levels in the feeder system for signal quality, and handles routine plant maintenance.

2. Performs FSM calibration and repairs system problems (i.e., power supplies, active and passive devices and cable).

3. Responds to and completes subscriber technical service calls. Repairs include, but are not limited to: drop wiring, matching xformers, converter replacement, and TV fine tuning.

4. Repairs and replaces strand, lashing, pole line transfers and general construction.

5. Installs new trunk, feeder cables, and associated hardware.

6. Installs and maintains subscriber control and distribution system for multi-subscriber systems.

7. Maintains and stocks necessary materials and tools for company vehicle.

8. Records data on system equipment and operation/services and accurately completes all paperwork as assigned.

9. Recognizes, practices, and enforces safety rules and procedures when performing technical tasks.

Each essential function described aspects of that function. One of the four aspects under the fourth essential function was "[m]ay climb poles to perform line transfers." The position description also included "climbing" within the "Special Skills, Knowledges and Abilities" section. As in the New Channels' description, the "Physical Requirements" section included "[c]limbing on ladders, telephone poles, and/or towers."

* * * Hanning * * * [plaintiff's] immediate supervisor, [i]n October 1996 gave [plaintiff] Skerski a below-standard performance review because of his inability to climb. Time Warner concedes that otherwise "Skerski's performance was superior." However, at that time Hanning told Skerski that Time Warner could not permit him to continue working on his modified no-climbing schedule. According to Skerski, this was the first time since the onset of his panic and anxiety disorder in 1993 that anyone at either New Channels or Time Warner had demanded that he climb. * * *

At the end of January 1997, Skerski accepted the warehouse position but stated in his deposition that he did so "only under duress," as Time Warner "[was] threatening [him] with termination."
* * *

Skerski commenced this civil action under the Americans with Disabilities Act in February 1998, seeking to recover money damages from Time Warner and reinstatement to his "modified duty status" as an installer technician. * * *

II

* * *

The [trial] court determined that as a matter of law Skerski is not a "qualified individual" under the ADA, and therefore held that he had failed to set forth a *prima facie* case of discrimination that could survive Time Warner's motion for summary judgment.

Under the ADA, a "qualified individual" is one "who, with or without reasonable accommodation, can perform the essential functions of the employment position that such individual holds or desires." 42 U.S.C. § 12111(8). To satisfy this requirement, a plaintiff must first demonstrate that s/he "satisfies the requisite skill, experience, education and other job-related requirements of the employment position that such individual holds or desires." Second, a plaintiff must establish that s/he, "with or without reasonable accommodation, can perform the essential functions of the position held or sought." There is no dispute as to the first part of this analysis as Time Warner readily concedes that Skerski was an experienced installer technician. Rather, the issues in the instant case revolve around the latter question.

* * * First, we must determine whether Skerski can perform the essential functions of his job *without* accommodation. If this is the case, we will consider him a "qualified individual," * * * If we determine that genuine issues of material fact exist as to whether Skerski is a "qualified individual" under the ADA, we must reverse the District Court's grant of summary judgment to Time Warner and remand the case for trial.

A.

Climbing as an "Essential Function"

Skerski first argues that the District Court erred in determining that climbing is an essential function of his job as an installer technician as a matter of law. He contends that, at the very least, there is a genuine issue of material fact as to whether climbing is essential which should be reserved for a jury.

We look first to the relevant agency regulations to determine whether climbing is an essential function of Skerski's job as an installer technician. A job's "essential functions" are defined in 29 C.F.R. § 1630.2(n)(1) as those that are "fundamental," not "marginal." The regulations list several factors for consideration in distinguishing the fundamental job functions from the marginal job functions, including: (1) whether the performance of the function is "the reason the position exists;" (2) whether there are a "limited number of employees available among whom the performance of that job function can be distributed;" and (3) whether the function is "highly specialized so that the incumbent in the position is hired for his or her expertise." 29 C.F.R. § 1630.2(n)(2). The regulations further set forth a non-exhaustive list of seven examples of evidence that are designed to assist a court in identifying the "essential functions" of a job. They include:

(i) The employer's judgment as to which functions are essential;

(ii) Written job descriptions prepared before advertising or interviewing applicants for the job;

(iii) The amount of time spent on the job per forming the function;

(iv) The consequences of not requiring the incumbent to perform the function;

(v) The terms of a collective bargaining agreement;

(vi) The work experience of past incumbents in the jobs; and/or

(vii) The current work experience of incumbents in similar jobs.

29 C.F.R. § 1630.2(n)(3).

As is apparent, "[w]hether a particular function is essential is a factual determination that must be made on a case by case basis." EEOC Interpretive Guidance on Title I of the Americans with Disabilities Act, 29 C.F.R. pt. 1630, App. 1630.2(n) (2000). It follows that none of the factors nor any of the evidentiary examples alone are necessarily dispositive.

In granting summary judgment, the District Court stated that "reasonable jurors could only find that climbing is an essential element of the installer technician position." Referring to the regulations, the District Court found significant that Time Warner's own judgment and the written job descriptions issued by both Time Warner and New Channels suggested that climbing was an essential job requirement, and that Skerski himself admitted in his deposition that as an installer technician he spent a considerable portion of his time climbing. The court further dismissed Skerski's reliance on evidence that another co-worker spent most of his time working on underground work, explaining that "Skerski does not ... introduce any evidence suggesting that this co-worker *never* climbs."

Looking to the three factors included in § 1630.2(n)(2), it is evident that two are not present in this case as installer technicians are not hired solely to climb or even because of their climbing expertise. On the other hand, the other factor supports the District Court's conclusion that climbing is an essential function of the job of installer technician. There is evidence to suggest that Time Warner employs a limited number of installer technicians in Skerski's work area—only 7 or 8, according to Skerski—and that this small number hampers Time Warner's ability to allow certain technicians to avoid climbing. The significance of this factor is pointed out in the Interpretive Guidance to § 1630.2(n), which explains, "if an employer has a relatively small number of available employees for the volume of work to be performed, it may be necessary that each employee perform a multitude of different functions. Therefore, the performance of those functions by each employee becomes more critical and the options for reorganizing the work become more limited."

But this is only one of the three factors. Moreover, consideration of the seven evidentiary examples included in § 1630.2(n)(3) suggests caution against any premature determination on essential functions as at least some of them lean in Skerski's favor. Of course, as required by § 1630.2(n)(3)(i), we owe some deference to Time Warner and its own judgment that climbing is essential to the installer technician position. And the written job descriptions, as the District Court noted, "clearly identify climbing as a job requirement." However, describing climbing as a requirement is not necessarily the same as denominating climbing as an essential function. In fact, the job descriptions prepared by both New Channels and Time Warner list various duties and responsibilities under the heading "Essential Functions," but neither identifies climbing as "essential." Instead, New Channels includes climbing under the heading "Physical Tasks," and Time Warner includes climbing under "Special Skills []" and "Physical Requirements." Although "may climb poles" is listed as an aspect of one of Time Warner's essential functions, the failure of both job descriptions to list "climbing" under the heading "Essential Functions" suggests one could view climbing as a useful skill or method to perform the essential functions of the job but that it is not itself an essential function of the installer technician position.

The distinction was made by Representative Fish when he introduced amendments to the bill that became the ADA relating to the definition of a "qualified individual" and the reasonable accommodation requirement and which were incorporated into the ADA. In his comments, he stated:

> [T]he essential function requirement focuses on the desired result rather than the means of accomplishing it. For example, in one case under the Rehabilitation Act, the employer required each employee to be able to perform the job with both arms. *Prewitt v. U.S. Postal Service,* 662 F.2d 292 (5th Cir.1981). The plaintiff was unable to do this because his disability resulted in limited mobility in his left arm. The court found that the essential function of the job was the ability to lift and carry mail which the employee had proven that he could do, not the ability to use both arms. Moreover, the court found that the employer was required to adapt the work environment to determine whether the employee with the disability could perform the essential requirements of the job with reasonable adaptations.

* * *

Among the facts and circumstances relevant to each case is, of course, the employee's actual experience as well as that of other employees. It is undisputed that from the time Skerski began as an installer technician in 1982 until the time he was diagnosed with his panic disorder in 1993, a significant portion of his job responsibilities required climbing. There is a basis to find that Skerski spent approximately 50% of his time before his 1993 diagnosis performing work that required climbing. However, for the three and a half years after his diagnosis in which he continued to work as an installer technician, Skerski performed virtually no overhead work at all. He only did so when he was "trying to see if [he] could do it." As we noted above, Time Warner conceded that Skerski continuously received high ratings for his performance during this time. Skerski testified at his deposition that there always was enough underground work to do, that he always worked 40 hour weeks and even worked enough to earn a couple thousand dollars per year in overtime, and that he had never experienced problems at work because of his panic disorder until Hanning became his supervisor in the fall of 1996.

For further support, Skerski points to the experience of one of his co-workers, Bill Bajnowski, who allegedly worked almost exclusively on underground assignments. We are unable to give that experience much weight because Bajnowski, unlike Skerski, was never put on "modified" duty, and Skerski admitted that no other installer technicians had ever been restricted from overhead work like he was.

Skerski argues that his own experience exemplifies that no negative consequences resulted from his failure to perform the climbing function of his job, which is another of the illustrations listed in the regulations. However, there is support in the record for Time Warner's contention that Skerski's inability to climb caused it considerable administrative difficulties. Approximately 75%, or 170 miles, of Time Warner's cable system in the relevant area consists of overhead aerial cable, which requires installer technicians to climb to service the cables. Hanning testified that Skerski's inability to climb "made the routing process extremely cumbersome," because the assignment process had to be done by hand instead of computer. He also claimed that Skerski's inability to climb necessitated the hiring of outside contract labor to meet demand, and that Skerski was not always as busy as he should have been due to his restricted work schedule. In an affidavit, Michael Flynn, Time Warner's technical operations manager in Skerski's area since January 1998, stated that the need to climb on a particular assignment may not be determined until the technician actually arrives at the location of the service call and it is therefore often difficult to predict whether overhead or underground work will be needed on a given day.

But Time Warner's evidence does not stand undisputed. Skerski testified that he always knew in advance whether an assignment would require climbing, and that his former supervisors Kane and Gruseck each had doled out assignments by hand without difficulty. Moreover, at oral argument before us, Time Warner's counsel acknowledged that he knows of no instance in which Skerski went out on assignment, only to have to return because the assignment required climbing. And Skerski claimed in his letter of November 24, 1996 that his "fellow employees, both field and office, have expressed their support in the companies [sic] accommodation with my current position."

* * *

In light of the conflicting deposition testimonies offered by Skerski and Hanning, it is unclear what effect Skerksi's inability to climb had on the servicing of Time Warner's cable system in the Coraopolis area.

We do not suggest that the District Court here had no basis for its conclusion that climbing is an essential function of Skerski's position as installer technician or even that, if we were the triers of fact, we would not so hold. But upon reviewing the three factors listed in 29 C.F.R. § 1630.2(n)(2) and the seven evidentiary examples provided by 29 C.F.R. § 1630.2(n)(3), it is apparent that a genuine issue of material fact exists as to whether climbing is an essential function of the job of installer technician at Time Warner. Although the employer's judgment and the written job descriptions may warrant some deference, Skerski has put forth considerable evidence that contradicts Time Warner's assertions, particularly the uncontradicted fact that following his 1993 diagnosis he worked for more than three years as an installer technician for Time Warner without ever having to perform over head work. Moreover, certain evidence suggests that during these three-plus years Skerski received repeated commendations for his work and never received any complaints from supervisors or co-workers, that is until Hanning became his immediate supervisor in the fall of 1996.

Skerski's situation is not dissimilar from that of Deane, a nurse who was unable to do heavy lifting without assistance. The hospital for which she worked contended that lifting was an essential function of her position, and that because she was unable to lift she was not a "qualified individual" under the ADA. Deane conceded that lifting was part of a nurse's duties but claimed that the heavy lifting she was restricted from doing was not an essential function of a nurse. In light of the evidence produced by both, this court *en banc* found that there was a genuine issue of material fact that must be decided by a jury. *See Deane [v. Pocono Med. Ctr.],* 142 F.3d [138,] 148 [3d Cir. 1998]. We therefore conclude that the District Court incorrectly decided that "reasonable jurors could only find that climbing is an essential element of the installer technician *position.*" Because a genuine issue of material fact exists as to whether climbing is an essential function, and therefore whether Skerksi is a "qualified individual" under the ADA, this case must be remanded for trial.

NOTES

1. As the critical determination of whether a particular job function that plaintiff cannot perform is "essential" is a question of fact (*Miller v. Illinois Dep't of Transp.,* 643 F.3d 190 (7th Cir. 2011)), and elements will vary with the content of each job, outcomes are difficult to predict and generalizations impossible. *Kellogg v. Energy Safety Services, Inc.,* 544 F.3d 1121 (10th Cir. 2008). For example, the ability to drive a motor vehicle may be "essential" to one job, such as package delivery service, and not essential for an office manager who is expected to drive to make bank deposits. *Lovejoy v. NOCO Motor Fuel, Inc.,* 263 F.3d 208 (2d Cir. 2001). Lifting may be essential for a nurse in a particular institution, (*Deane v. Pocono Med. Ctr.,* 142 F.3d 138 (3d Cir. 1998 (en banc)), but not for a airport gate attendant. *Summerville v. Trans World Airlines, Inc.,* 219 F.3d 855 (8th Cir. 2000). Stooping was essential for a housekeeping supervisor, (*Alexander v. Northland Inn,* 321 F.3d 723 (8th Cir. 2003)), but not for the manager of an auto dealership. *Pals v. Schepel Buick & GMC Truck, Inc.,* 220 F.3d 495 (7th Cir. 2000). Even indistinguishable facts may produce different jury verdicts at different times. *See e.g., Kuehl v. Wal–Mart Stores, Inc.,* 909 F.Supp. 794 (D.Colo. 1995) and *EEOC v. Wal-Mart Stores, Inc.,* 477 F.3d 561 (8th Cir. 2007).

2. *Burdens:* The court must determine which party is responsible for establishing that plaintiff is "qualified." This is important, not only to guide the court in making summary judgment decisions, but also because the jury must be instructed on where to place the risk of non-persuasion. *Hamlin v. Charter Township of Flint,* 165 F.3d 426 (6th Cir. 1999), placed this burden on the defendant to prove that plaintiff *cannot* perform an essential job duty. Placing the ultimate risk burden on defendant was justified on the grounds that other provisions of the ADA prohibit an employer from using qualifica-

tion standards to deny employment "unless the standard . . . is shown to be job-related for the position in question and is consistent with business necessity." 42 U.S.C. § 12112(b)(6). Placing the burden of persuasion on the defendant is also consistent with the direction of the 2008 Amendments that courts should construe the statutory language generously in favor of coverage.

Fenny v. Dakota, Minnesota, & Eastern R. Co., 327 F.3d 707 (8th Cir. 2003), provided a modified, shifting burdens approach. That court placed an initial burden on the employer to present some evidence of the "essential" nature of the functions that the disabled plaintiff is unable to perform. If the employer presents credible evidence that the functions plaintiff cannot perform are "essential," the burden shifts back to the plaintiff to persuade the fact finder that, in fact, the functions plaintiff cannot perform are not essential.

Congress gave little guidance, indicating only that burdens on this issue would be those developed under the earlier Rehabilitation Act. Unfortunately, decisions under the Rehabilitation Act reflect a similar division. *Compare, Pushkin v. University of Colo.*, 658 F.2d 1372, 1387 (10th Cir. 1981), *with Doe v. New York Univ.*, 666 F.2d 761, 766 (2d Cir. 1981).

d. Defenses

(1) Transitory and Minor: As noted above, discrimination based on an impairment that is both "transitory" (meaning having a duration of six months or less) AND minor (meaning not impairing a "major life activity) does not violate the ADA. It is the employer who must prove that the impairment is both transitory and minor.

(2) Direct threat to health or safety: The ADA provides that " 'qualification standards' may include a requirement that an individual shall not pose a direct threat to the health or safety of *other individuals* in the workplace." 42 U.S.C. § 12113(b). "Direct threat" is explained in the statute only to mean "significant risk to health or safety of *others* * * *." This has been further refined by EEOC regulations:

> The determination that an individual poses a 'direct threat' shall be based on an individual's present ability to safely perform the essential functions of the job. This assessment shall be based on reasonable medical judgment that relies on the most current medical knowledge or on the best available objective evidence. In determining whether an individual would pose a direct threat, the factors to be considered include:
>
> (1) The duration of the risk
>
> (2) The nature and severity of the potential harm
>
> (3) The likelihood that the potential harm will occur; and
>
> (4) The imminence of the potential harm.

29 C.F.R. § 1630.2(r).

BRAGDON v. ABBOTT

Supreme Court of the United States, 1998
524 U.S. 624, 118 S.Ct. 2196, 141 L.Ed.2d 540

JUSTICE KENNEDY delivered the opinion of the Court.

[Plaintiff was infected by the HIV virus. Defendant was a dentist who refused to provide treatment to plaintiff based on his good faith fear that plaintiff's virus might be transmitted] * * * We granted certiorari to review, first, whether HIV infection is a disability under the ADA when the infection has not yet progressed to the so-called symptomatic phase; and, second, whether the Court of Appeals, in affirming a grant of summary judgment, cited sufficient material in the record to determine, as a matter of law, that respondent's infection with HIV posed no direct threat to the health and safety of her treating dentist.

* * *

I

The District Court ruled in favor of the plaintiffs, holding that respondent's HIV infection satisfied the ADA's definition of disability. The court held further that petitioner raised no genuine issue of material fact as to whether respondent's HIV infection would have posed a direct threat to the health or safety of others during the course of a dental treatment.

The Court of Appeals affirmed. * * *

II

* * *

The first step in the inquiry * * * requires us to determine whether respondent's condition constituted a physical impairment. * * *

The disease follows a predictable and, as of today, an unalterable course. Once a person is infected with HIV, the virus invades different cells in the blood and in body tissues. * * *

The initial stage of HIV infection is known as acute or primary HIV infection. In a typical case, this stage lasts three months. The virus concentrates in the blood. The assault on the immune system is immediate. The victim suffers from a sudden and serious decline in the number of white blood cells. * * *

After the symptoms associated with the initial stage subside, the disease enters what is referred to sometimes as its asymptomatic phase. The term is a misnomer, in some respects, for clinical features persist throughout, including lymphadenopathy, dermatological disorders, oral lesions, and bacterial infections. * * *

In light of the immediacy with which the virus begins to damage the infected person's white blood cells and the severity of the disease, we hold it is an impairment from the moment of infection. * * *

III

Notwithstanding the protection given respondent by the ADA's definition of disability, [defendant] could have refused to treat her if her infectious condition "pose[d] a direct threat to the health or safety of others." The ADA defines a direct threat to be "a significant risk to the health or safety of others that cannot be eliminated by a modification of policies, practices, or procedures or by the provision of auxiliary aids or services." * * *

The ADA's direct threat provision stems from the recognition in School Bd. of Nassau Cty. v. Arline, 480 U.S. 273, 287, 107 S.Ct. 1123, 1130–1131, 94 L.Ed.2d 307 (1987), of the importance of prohibiting discrimination against individuals with disabilities while protecting others from significant health and safety risks, resulting, for instance, from a contagious disease. * * *

The existence, or nonexistence, of a significant risk must be determined from the standpoint of the [defendant] * * * and the risk assessment must be based on medical or other objective evidence. As a health care professional, petitioner had the duty to assess the risk of infection based on the objective, scientific information available to him and others in his profession. His belief that a significant risk existed, even if maintained in good faith, would not relieve him from liability. To use the words of the question presented, petitioner receives no special deference simply because he is a health care professional. It is true that Arline reserved "the question whether courts should also defer to the reasonable medical judgments of private physicians on which an employer has relied." At most, this statement reserved the possibility that employers could consult with individual physicians as objective third-party experts. It did not suggest that an individual physician's state of mind could excuse discrimination without regard to the objective reasonableness of his actions.

Our conclusion that courts should assess the objective reasonableness of the views of health care professionals without deferring to their individual judgments does not answer the implicit assumption in the question presented, whether petitioner's actions were reasonable in light of the available medical evidence. In assessing the reasonableness of petitioner's actions, the views of public health authorities, such as the U.S. Public Health Service, CDC, and the National Institutes of Health, are of special weight and authority. The views of these organizations are not conclusive, however. A health care professional who disagrees with the prevailing medical consensus may refute it by citing a credible scientific basis for deviating from the accepted norm.

We have reviewed so much of the record as necessary to illustrate the application of the rule to the facts of this case. For the most part, the Court of Appeals followed the proper standard in evaluating the petitioner's position and conducted a thorough review of the evidence.* * *

We conclude the proper course is to give the Court of Appeals the opportunity to determine whether our analysis of some of the studies cited by the parties would change its conclusion that petitioner presented neither objective evidence nor a triable issue of fact on the question of risk. In remanding the case, we do not foreclose the possibility that the Court of Appeals may reach the same conclusion it did earlier. A remand will permit a full exploration of the issue through the adversary process.

The determination of the Court of Appeals that respondent's HIV infection was a disability under the ADA is affirmed. The judgment is vacated, and the case is remanded for further proceedings consistent with this opinion.

JUSTICE STEVENS, with whom JUSTICE BREYER joins, concurring.

The Court's opinion demonstrates that respondent's HIV infection easily falls within the statute's definition of "disability." Moreover, the Court's discussion in Part III of the relevant evidence has persuaded me that the judgment of the Court of Appeals should be affirmed. I do not believe [defendant] has sustained his burden of adducing evidence sufficient to raise a triable issue of fact on the significance of the risk posed by treating respondent in his office. * * * Because I am in agreement with the legal analysis in JUSTICE KENNEDY'S opinion, in order to provide a judgment supported by a majority, I join that opinion even though I would prefer an outright affirmance.

CHIEF JUSTICE REHNQUIST, with whom JUSTICE SCALIA and JUSTICE THOMAS join, and with whom JUSTICE O'CONNOR joins as to Part II, concurring in the judgment in part and dissenting in part.

* * *

II

* * * The Court vacates * * * remands the case to the lower court, presumably so that it may "determine whether our analysis of some of the studies cited by the parties would change its conclusion that petitioner presented neither objective evidence nor a triable issue of fact on the question of risk." I agree that the judgment should be vacated, although I am not sure I understand the Court's cryptic direction to the lower court.

"[D]irect threat" is defined as a "significant risk to the health or safety of others that cannot be eliminated by a modification of policies, practices, or procedures or by the provision of auxiliary aides or services." This statutory definition of a direct threat consists of two parts. First, a court must ask whether treating the infected patient without precautionary techniques would pose a "significant risk to the health or safety of others." Whether a particular risk is significant depends on:

> " "(a) the nature of the risk (how the disease is transmitted), (b) the duration of the risk (how long is the carrier infectious), (c) the severity of the risk (what is the potential harm to third parties) and (d) the probabilities the disease will be transmitted and will cause varying degrees of harm.' " *School Bd. of Nassau Cty. v. Arline*, 480 U.S. 273, 288, 107 S.Ct. 1123, 1131, 94 L.Ed.2d 307 (1987).

Even if a significant risk exists, a health practitioner will still be required to treat the infected patient if "a modification of policies, practices, or procedures" (in this case, universal precautions) will "eliminat[e]" the risk.

* * * I disagree with the Court, however, that "[i]n assessing the reasonableness of petitioner's actions, the views of public health authorities ... are of special weight and authority." Those views are, of course, entitled to a presumption of validity when the actions of those authorities themselves are challenged in court, and even in disputes between private parties where Congress has committed that dispute to adjudication by a public health authority. But in litigation between private parties originating in the federal courts, I am aware of no provision of law or judicial practice that would require or permit courts to give some scientific views more credence than others simply because they have been endorsed by a politically appointed public health authority (such as the Surgeon General). In litigation of this latter sort, which is what we face here, the credentials of the scientists employed by the public health authority, and the soundness of their studies, must stand on their own. * * *

Applying these principles here, it is clear to me that [defendant] petitioner has presented more than enough evidence to avoid summary judgment on the "direct threat" question. * * * At a minimum, petitioner's evidence was sufficient to create a triable issue on this question, and summary judgment was accordingly not appropriate.

NOTES

1. **CHEVRON USA v. ECHAZABAL, 536 U.S. 73, 122 S.Ct. 2045, 153 L.Ed.2d 82 (2002).** The ADA literally allows as a defense a direct threat to the "health or safety of *others.*" Nonetheless, plaintiff could be denied a job because of *his* hepatitis if the objective weight of medical evidence established toxicities in the work place posed a direct threat to the plaintiff's *own health,* even though his condition posed no threat to the health or safety of others.

2. *Burden:* The EEOC and some courts hold that proof of the "direct threat" is a defense that must be established by the defendant. *Nunes v. Wal-Mart Stores,* 164 F.3d 1243 (9th Cir. 1999). *Moses v. American Nonwovens, Inc.,* 97 F.3d 446 (11th Cir. 1996), indicated, however, that absence of a "direct threat" to the health of safety of others was necessary for plaintiff to establish that he is "qualified".

3. *Good faith:* The good faith of the defendant, even relying on an evaluation of professionals will not carry defendant's burden where defendant's expert opinion is not in accord with prevailing professional authority. *Echazabal v. Chevron, USA, Inc.,* 336 F.3d 1023 (9th Cir. 2003) (on remand from *Chevron U.S.A. v. Echazabal, supra*).

4. *Balancing:* Where there is a remote chance that plaintiff's disease is communicable through casual contact, it is unlikely that the disease presents a "direct threat" to the safety of others when infection, if contacted, presents little threat of serious harm to those who contact it. However, when the

consequences and extent of harm are severe or life endangering, even a relatively small possibility of contagion can be considered a "direct threat." *Compare, Harris v. Thigpen,* 941 F.2d 1495 (11th Cir. 1991), with *Mauro v. Borgess Medical Center,* 137 F.3d 398 (6th Cir.1998).

5. *Collateral claims of disability:* **CLEVELAND v. POLICY MANAGEMENT SYSTEMS CORP., 526 U.S. 795, 119 S.Ct. 1597, 143 L.Ed.2d 966 (1999).** The Social Security Disability Insurance Program (SSDI) provides benefits to persons unable to perform previous work or engage in substantial gainful employment because of a "disability." An employer asserted that an individual's claim of total disability under SSDI estops the individual from claiming that he or she can perform "essential job functions" and thus is "qualified" for employment under the ADA. The Court held that as the factual and legal basis for the SSDI claim are often different from the ADA standards, an SSDI claim of disability did not automatically preclude an assertion that the individual is "qualified" to hold the job under the ADA. Nonetheless, an individual may have the burden of explaining prior assertions of "total disability" such as establishing rehabilitation since the time the SSDI claim was made.

---

3. "IMPAIRMENTS" THAT MUST BE ACCOMMODATED

a. Introduction and Review

42 U.S.C. § 12112(a) provides that unlawful discrimination includes not making reasonable accommodation to the known physical or mental limitations of an otherwise qualified individual with a disability unless, the covered entity can demonstrate that the accommodation would impose an undue hardship on the operation of the business of the covered entity.

As noted above, the 2008 Amendments make the critical distinction between "impairments" that may not be the basis for discrimination (but need not be accommodated), and impairments that "substantially limit a major life activity." The latter are "disabilities" which require reasonable accommodations that do not impose on employers an undue hardship.

"Disability" is defined in the ADA as "a physical or mental impairment that substantially limits one or more major life activities." Three elements must be examined: (1) is the condition an "impairment," (which has been examined above); (2) does the impairment affect a "major life activity;" and finally (3) does the impairment "substantially limit" that "major life activity."

The 2008 Amendments to the ADA (ADAAA) did not change this original definition. However, as noted above, the statute now directs that the determination of whether an individual has a disability "shall be construed in favor of broad coverage to the maximum extent permitted by the terms of the [ADA]." Accordingly, authority prior to 2009 must be reviewed in light of the broader, more inclusive interpretative standards required by the ADAAA.

b. "Major Life Activities"

Toyota Mfg. Inc. v. Williams, supra, held that to be a "major life activity" the impairment must affect activities "that are of central importance to daily life." That an individual's physical inability to lift her arms beyond shoulder level might severely restrict in her ability to perform many daily household tasks would not render that person "disabled" (and thus not entitled to an accommodation). The ADAAA specifically rejected this demanding interpretation.

EEOC INTERPRETATIVE REGULATIONS (2011)

Section 1630.2(i)
APPENDIX

Congress anticipated that protection under the ADA would now extend to a wider range of cases, in part as a result of the expansion of the category of major life activities. For purposes of clarity, the Amendments Act provides an illustrative list of major life activities, including caring for oneself, performing manual tasks, seeing, hearing, eating, sleeping, walking, standing, lifting, bending, speaking, breathing, learning, reading, concentrating, thinking, communicating, and working. The ADA Amendments expressly made this statutory list of examples of major life activities non-exhaustive, and the regulations include sitting, reaching, and interacting with others as additional examples. * * *

The ADA as amended also explicitly defines "major life activities" to include the operation of "major bodily functions." * * *

The [EEOC 2011] regulations include all of those major bodily functions identified in the ADA Amendments Act's non-exhaustive list of examples and add a number of others that are consistent with the body systems listed in the regulations' definition of "impairment" (at § 1630.2(h)) * * * Thus, special sense organs, skin, genitourinary, cardiovascular, hemic, lymphatic, and musculoskeletal functions are major bodily functions not included in the statutory list of examples but included in § 1630.2(i)(1)(ii). * * * The regulations also provide that the operation of a major bodily function may include the operation of an individual organ within a body system. This would include, for example, the operation of the kidney, liver, pancreas, or other organs.

The link between particular impairments and various major bodily functions should not be difficult to identify. Because impairments, by definition, affect the functioning of body systems, they will generally affect major bodily functions. For example, cancer affects an individual's normal cell growth; diabetes affects the operation of the pancreas and also the function of the endocrine system; and Human Immunodeficiency Virus

(HIV) infection affects the immune system. Likewise, sickle cell disease affects the functions of the hemic system, lymphedema affects lymphatic functions, and rheumatoid arthritis affects musculoskeletal functions.

* * * [T]he courts [have] struggled to analyze whether the impact of HIV infection substantially limits various major life activities of a five-year-old child, * * * [that] an individual with cirrhosis of the liver caused by Hepatitis B is not disabled because liver function—unlike eating, working, or reproducing—'is not integral to one's daily existence;' and [a case] * * * in which the court concluded that the plaintiff's stage three breast cancer did not substantially limit her ability to care for herself, sleep, or concentrate. * * * [E]ach of these cases could establish a [substantial limitation] on major bodily functions that would qualify them for protection under the ADA.

* * * As a result of the ADA Amendments Act's rejection of the holding in *Toyota Motor Mfg., Ky., Inc.* v. *Williams,* 534 U.S. 184 (2002), whether an activity is a "major life activity" is not determined by reference to whether it is of "central importance to daily life." Indeed, this holding was at odds with the earlier Supreme Court decision of *Bragdon* v. *Abbott,* 524 U.S. 624 (1998), which held that a major life activity (in that case, reproduction) does not have to have a "public, economic or daily aspect."

Accordingly, the regulations provide that in determining other examples of major life activities, the term "major" shall not be interpreted strictly to create a demanding standard for disability.

* * * Thus, for example, lifting is a major life activity regardless of whether an individual who claims to be substantially limited in lifting actually performs activities of central importance to daily life that require lifting. Similarly, the Commission anticipates that the major life activity of performing manual tasks (which was at issue in *Toyota*) could have many different manifestations, such as performing tasks involving fine motor coordination, or performing tasks involving grasping, hand strength, or pressure. Such tasks need not constitute activities of central importance to most people's daily lives, nor must an individual show that he or she is substantially limited in performing all manual tasks.

* * * The ADAAA explicitly states that an impairment need only substantially limit one major life activity to be considered a disability under the ADA. ADAAA Section 4(a); 42 U.S.C. 12102(4)(C). "This responds to and corrects those courts that have required individuals to show that an impairment substantially limits more than one life activity." In addition, this rule of construction is "intended to clarify that the ability to perform one or more particular tasks within a broad category of activities does not preclude coverage under the ADA." To the extent cases pre-dating the applicability of the 2008 Amendments Act reasoned otherwise, they are contrary to the law as amended. (citing *Holt* v. *Grand Lake Mental Health Ctr., Inc.,* 443 F. 3d 762 (10th Cir. 2006) (holding an individual with cerebral palsy who could not independently perform certain specified

manual tasks was not substantially limited in her ability to perform a "broad range" of manual tasks)).

For example, an individual with diabetes is substantially limited in endocrine function and thus an individual with a disability * * *. He need not also show that he is substantially limited in eating * * * An individual whose normal cell growth is substantially limited due to lung cancer need not also show that she is substantially limited in breathing or respiratory function. And an individual with HIV infection is substantially limited in the function of the immune system, and therefore is an individual with a disability without regard to whether his or her HIV infection substantially limits him or her in reproduction.

In addition, an individual whose impairment substantially limits a major life activity need not additionally demonstrate a resulting limitation in the ability to perform activities of central importance to daily life in order to be considered an individual with a disability under § 1630.2(g)(1)(i) or § 1630.2(g)(1)(ii), as cases relying on the Supreme Court's decision in *Toyota Motor Mfg., Ky., Inc.* v. *Williams,* 534 U.S. 184 (2002), had held prior to the ADA Amendments Act.

Thus, for example, someone with an impairment resulting in a 20–pound lifting restriction that lasts or is expected to last for several months is substantially limited in the major life activity of lifting, and need not also show that he is unable to perform activities of daily living that require lifting in order to be considered substantially limited in lifting.

---

c. "Substantially Limited"

"RULES OF CONSTRUCTION" EEOC REGULATIONS (2011)

1630.(j)(1)(i):

APPENDIX

[N]ot every individual with a physical or mental impairment is covered by the first prong of the definition of disability in the ADA. * * * [A]n individual must establish that an impairment substantially limits a major life activity. That has not changed—nor will the necessity of making this determination on an individual basis. However, what the ADAAA changed is the standard required for making this determination.

* * * It is clear in the text and legislative history of the ADAAA that Congress concluded the courts had incorrectly construed "substantially limits," * * *. Congress extensively deliberated over whether a new term other than "substantially limits" should be adopted to denote the appropriate functional limitation necessary under the first and second prongs of the definition of disability. Ultimately, Congress affirmatively opted to

retain this term in the Amendments Act, rather than replace it. * * * Instead, Congress determined "a better way * * * to express [its] disapproval of *Sutton* and *Toyota* * * * is to retain the words 'substantially limits,' but clarify that it is not meant to be a demanding standard." * * *

As Congress noted in the legislative history of the ADAAA, "[t]o be clear, the purposes section conveys our intent to clarify not only that 'substantially limits' should be measured by a lower standard than that used in *Toyota,* but also that the definition of disability should not be unduly used as a tool for excluding individuals from the ADA's protections." Put most succinctly, "substantially limits" "is not meant to be a demanding standard."

> Section 1630.2(j)(1)(ii) states: "An impairment is a disability within the meaning of this section if it substantially limits the ability of an individual to perform a major life activity as compared to most people in the general population. An impairment need not prevent, or significantly or severely restrict, the individual from performing a major life activity in order to be considered substantially limiting. Nonetheless, not every impairment will constitute a 'disability' within the meaning of this section."

2) "Condition, Manner, or Duration:" EEOC Regulations, Appendix, Section 1630.2(j)(4):

The regulations provide that facts such as the "condition, manner, or duration" of an individual's performance of a major life activity may be useful in determining whether an impairment results in a substantial limitation. * * *

* * * [T]he condition or manner under which a major life activity can be performed may refer to the way an individual performs a major life activity. Thus, the condition or manner under which a person with an amputated hand performs manual tasks will likely be more cumbersome than the way that someone with two hands would perform the same tasks.

Condition or manner may also describe how performance of a major life activity affects the individual with an impairment. For example, an individual whose impairment causes pain or fatigue that most people would not experience when performing that major life activity may be substantially limited. Thus, the condition or manner under which someone with coronary artery disease performs the major life activity of walking would be substantially limiting if the individual experiences shortness of breath and fatigue when walking distances that most people could walk without experiencing such effects. * * *

"Duration" refers to the length of time an individual can perform a major life activity or the length of time it takes an individual to perform a major life activity, as compared to most people in the general population. For example, a person whose back or leg impairment precludes him or her from standing for more than two hours without significant pain would be substantially limited in standing, since most people can stand for more than two hours without significant pain. However, a person who can walk for ten miles continuously is not substantially limited in walking merely because on the eleventh mile, he or she begins to experience pain because most people would not be able to walk eleven miles without experiencing some discomfort. * * *

Condition, manner, or duration may also suggest the amount of time or effort an individual has to expend when performing a major life activity because of the effects of an impairment, even if the individual is able to achieve the same or similar result as someone without the impairment. For this reason, the regulations include language which says that the outcome an individual with a disability is able to achieve is not determinative of whether he or she is substantially limited in a major life activity.

Thus, someone with a learning disability may achieve a high level of academic success, but may nevertheless be substantially limited in the major life activity of learning because of the additional time or effort he or she must spend to read, write, or learn compared to most people in the general population. As Congress emphasized in passing the Amendments Act, "[w]hen considering the condition, manner, or duration in which an individual with a specific learning disability performs a major life activity, it is critical to reject the assumption that an individual who has performed well academically cannot be substantially limited in activities such as learning, reading, writing, thinking, or speaking." * * *

Finally, "condition, manner, or duration" are not intended to be used as a rigid three-part standard that must be met to establish a substantial limitation. * * * Rather, in referring to "condition, manner, *or* duration," the regulations make clear that these are merely the types of facts that may be considered in appropriate cases. * * *

Section 1630.2(j)(1)(ix) [of the EEOC Regulations] states: "The six-month 'transitory' part of the 'transitory and minor' exception to 'regarded as' coverage in § 1630.2(*l*) does not apply to the definition of 'disability' under § 1630.2(g)(1)(i) or § 1630.2(g)(1)(ii). * * *

The regulations include a clear statement that the definition of an impairment as transitory, that is, "lasting or expected to last for six months or less," only applies to the "regarded as" (third) prong of the definition of "disability" as part of the "transitory and minor" defense to "regarded as" coverage. It does not apply to the first or second prong of the definition of disability.

* * * At the same time, "[t]he duration of an impairment is one factor that is relevant in determining whether the impairment substantially limits a major life activity. Impairments that last only for a short period of time are typically not covered, although they may be covered if sufficiently severe."

———————

d. Mitigating Measures

Rejecting the Court's decision in *Sutton v. United Airlines,* 527 U.S. 471, 119 S.Ct. 2139, 144 L.Ed.2d 450 (1999), the ADAAA and implementing EEOC regulations state specifically:

"The determination of whether an impairment substantially limits a major life activity shall be made without regard to the ameliorative effects of mitigating measures. However, the ameliorative effects of ordinary eyeglasses or contact lenses shall be considered in determining whether an impairment substantially limits a major life activity."

* * * This provision in the ADAAA and the EEOC's regulations "is intended to eliminate the catch–22 that exist[ed] * * * where individuals who are subjected to discrimination on the basis of their disabilities [we]re frequently unable to invoke the ADA's protections because they [we]re not considered people with disabilities when the effects of their medication, medical supplies, behavioral adaptations, or other interventions [we]re considered." To the extent cases pre-dating the 2008 Amendments Act reasoned otherwise, they are contrary to the law as amended.

An individual who, because of the use of a mitigating measure, has experienced no limitations, or only minor limitations, related to the impairment may still be an individual with a disability, where there is evidence that in the absence of an effective mitigating measure the individual's impairment would be substantially limiting. For example, someone who began taking medication for hypertension before experiencing substantial limitations related to the impairment would still be an individual with a disability if, without the medication, he or she would now be substantially limited in functions of the cardiovascular or circulatory system.

* * * The Amendments Act provides an "illustrative but non-comprehensive list of the types of mitigating measures that are not to be considered." * * * Since it would be impossible to guarantee comprehensiveness in a finite list, the list of examples of mitigating measures provided in the ADA and the regulations is non-exhaustive. * * *

The determination of whether or not an individual's impairment substantially limits a major life activity is unaffected by whether the individual chooses to forgo mitigating measures. For individuals who do not use a mitigating measure (including for example medication or reasonable accommodation that could alleviate the effects of an impairment), the availability of such measures has no bearing on whether the impairment substantially limits a major life activity. * * *

The ADA Amendments Act and the regulations state that "ordinary eyeglasses or contact lenses" *shall* be considered in determining whether someone has a disability. This is an exception to the rule that the ameliorative effects of mitigating measures are not to be taken into account." Nevertheless, as discussed in greater detail below at

§ 1630.10(b), if an applicant or employee is faced with a qualification standard that requires uncorrected vision (as the plaintiffs in the *Sutton* case were), and the applicant or employee who is adversely affected by the standard brings a challenge under the ADA, an employer will be required to demonstrate that the qualification standard is job related and consistent with business necessity.* * *

e. Episodic or in Remission

The ADAAA and Section 1630.2(j)(1)(vii) of the 2011 EEOC Regulations states: "An impairment that is episodic or in remission is a disability if it would substantially limit a major life activity when active." The Appendix explains:

> * * * "This provision is intended to reject the reasoning of court decisions concluding that certain individuals with certain conditions— such as epilepsy or post traumatic stress disorder—were not protected by the ADA because their conditions were episodic or intermittent." The legislative history provides: "This * * * rule of construction thus rejects the reasoning of the courts in cases like *Todd* v. *Academy Corp.* [57 F. Supp. 2d 448, 453 (S.D. Tex. 1999)] where the court found that the plaintiff's epilepsy, which resulted in short seizures during which the plaintiff was unable to speak and experienced tremors, was not sufficiently limiting, at least in part because those seizures occurred episodically. It similarly rejects the results reached in cases [such as *Pimental* v. *Dartmouth–Hitchock Clinic,* 236 F. Supp. 2d 177, 182–83 (D.N.H. 2002)] where the courts have discounted the impact of an impairment [such as cancer] that may be in remission as too short-lived to be substantially limiting. * * * Other examples of impairments that may be episodic include, but are not limited to, hypertension, diabetes, asthma, major depressive disorder, bipolar disorder, and schizophrenia. The fact that the periods during which an episodic impairment is active and substantially limits a major life activity may be brief or occur infrequently is no longer relevant to determining whether the impairment substantially limits a major life activity. For example, a person with post-traumatic stress disorder who experiences intermittent flashbacks to traumatic events is substantially limited in brain function and thinking.

4. "ACCOMMODATIONS:" "REASONABLE" AND NOT IMPOSING AN "UNDUE HARDSHIP"

A person with a disability as defined in the so-called "A and B prongs," and who possesses required credentials to perform the job cannot be discriminated against because of the disability. If the person cannot perform job duties deemed "essential" *without* an accommodation, the question becomes whether the the person could perform those essential duties *with* an accommodation. If the person with the disability could perform the essential duties with an accommodation for that disability, the next question is whether the accommodation required is "reasonable". If the accommodation is "reasonable" the individual with the disability is "qualified," and the ADA makes it proscribed discrimination for the employer to refuse to make such an accommodation, unless to do so would impose on this employer an "undue hardship." Note how the "reasonable accommodation/undue hardship" language of the ADA largely mirrors that found in Title VII's requirement that employers accommodate religious observances and practices. Consider the different outcomes notwithstanding the nearly identical statutory language.

U.S. AIRWAYS, INC. v. BARNETT

Supreme Court of the United States, 2002
535 U.S. 391, 122 S.Ct. 1516, 152 L.Ed.2d 589

JUSTICE BREYER delivered the opinion of the Court.

The Americans with Disabilities Act of 1990 (ADA or Act), prohibits an employer from discriminating against an "individual with a disability" who, with "reasonable accommodation," can perform the essential functions of the job. This case, arising in the context of summary judgment, asks us how the Act resolves a potential conflict between: (1) the interests of a disabled worker who seeks assignment to a particular position as a "reasonable accommodation," and (2) the interests of other workers with superior rights to bid for the job under an employer's seniority system. In such a case, does the accommodation demand trump the seniority system?

In our view, the seniority system will prevail in the run of cases. As we interpret the statute, to show that a requested accommodation conflicts with the rules of a seniority system is ordinarily to show that the accommodation is not "reasonable." Hence such a showing will entitle an employer/defendant to summary judgment on the question-unless there is more. The plaintiff remains free to present evidence of special circumstances that make "reasonable" a seniority rule exception in the particular case. And such a showing will defeat the employer's demand for summary judgment.

I

In 1990, Robert Barnett, the plaintiff and respondent here, injured his back while working in a cargo-handling position at petitioner U.S. Airways, Inc. He invoked seniority rights and transferred to a less physically demanding mailroom position. Under U.S. Airways' seniority system, that position, like others, periodically became open to seniority-based employee bidding. In 1992, Barnett learned that at least two employees senior to him intended to bid for the mailroom job. He asked U.S. Airways to accommodate his disability-imposed limitations by making an exception that would allow him to remain in the mailroom. After permitting Barnett to continue his mailroom work for five months while it considered the matter, U.S. Airways eventually decided not to make an exception. And Barnett lost his job.

Barnett then brought this ADA suit claiming, among other things, that he was an "individual with a disability" capable of performing the essential functions of the mailroom job, that the mailroom job amounted to a "reasonable accommodation" of his disability, and that U.S. Airways, in refusing to assign him the job, unlawfully discriminated against him. US Airways moved for summary judgment. It supported its motion with appropriate affidavits, contending that its "well-established" seniority system granted other employees the right to obtain the mailroom position.

The District Court found that the undisputed facts about seniority warranted summary judgment in U.S. Airways' favor. The Act says that an employer who fails to make "reasonable accommodations to the known physical or mental limitations of an [employee] with a disability" discriminates "*unless*" the employer "can demonstrate that the accommodation would impose an *undue hardship* on the operation of [its] business." 42 U.S.C. § 12112(b)(5)(A). The court said:

> "[T]he uncontroverted evidence shows that the USAir seniority system has been in place for 'decades' and governs over 14,000 USAir Agents. Moreover, seniority policies such as the one at issue in this case are common to the airline industry. Given this context, it seems clear that the USAir employees were justified in relying upon the policy. As such, any significant alteration of that policy would result in undue hardship to both the company and its non-disabled employees."

An en banc panel of the United States Court of Appeals for the Ninth Circuit reversed. It said that the presence of a seniority system is merely "a factor in the undue hardship analysis." And it held that "[a] case-by-case fact intensive analysis is required to determine whether any particular reassignment would constitute an undue hardship to the employer."

US Airways petitioned for certiorari, asking us to decide whether

> "the [ADA] requires an employer to reassign a disabled employee to a position as a 'reasonable accommodation' even though another employee is entitled to hold the position under the employer's bona fide and established seniority system."

We agreed to answer U.S. Airways' question.

II

In answering the question presented, we must consider the following statutory provisions. First, the ADA says that an employer may not "discriminate against a qualified individual with a disability." 42 U.S.C. § 12112(a). Second, the ADA says that a "qualified" individual includes "an individual with a disability who, *with* or without *reasonable accommodation,* can perform the essential functions of" the relevant "employment position." § 12111(8). Third, the ADA says that "discrimination" includes an employer's "*not making reasonable accommodations* to the known physical or mental limitations of an otherwise qualified ... employee, *unless* [the employer] can demonstrate that the accommodation would

impose an *undue hardship* on the operation of [its] business."
§ 12112(b)(5)(A). Fourth, the ADA says that the term " 'reasonable accommodation' may include ... reassignment to a vacant position."
§ 12111(9)(B).

The parties interpret this statutory language as applied to seniority
systems in radically different ways. In U.S. Airways' view, the fact that an
accommodation would violate the rules of a seniority system always shows
that the accommodation is not a "reasonable" one. In Barnett's polar
opposite view, a seniority system violation never shows that an accommodation sought is not a "reasonable" one. Barnett concedes that a violation
of seniority rules might help to show that the accommodation will work
"undue" employer "hardship," but that is a matter for an employer to
demonstrate case by case. We shall initially consider the parties' main
legal arguments in support of these conflicting positions.

A

US Airways' claim that a seniority system virtually always trumps a
conflicting accommodation demand rests primarily upon its view of how
the Act treats workplace "preferences." Insofar as a requested accommodation violates a disability-neutral workplace rule, such as a seniority rule,
it grants the employee with a disability treatment that other workers
could not receive. Yet the Act, U.S. Airways says, seeks only "equal"
treatment for those with disabilities. It does not, it contends, require an
employer to grant preferential treatment. Cf. H.R.Rep. No. 101–485,
U.S.Code Cong. & Admin.News 1990, pp. 303, 348–349; (employer has no
"obligation to prefer *applicants* with disabilities over other *applicants*").
Hence it does not require the employer to grant a request that, in
violating a disability-neutral rule, would provide a preference.

While linguistically logical, this argument fails to recognize what the Act
specifies, namely, that preferences will sometimes prove necessary to
achieve the Act's basic equal opportunity goal. The Act requires preferences in the form of "reasonable accommodations" that are needed for
those with disabilities to obtain the *same* workplace opportunities that
those without disabilities automatically enjoy. By definition any special
"accommodation" requires the employer to treat an employee with a
disability differently, *i.e.,* preferentially. And the fact that the difference in
treatment violates an employer's disability-neutral rule cannot by itself
place the accommodation beyond the Act's potential reach.

Were that not so, the "reasonable accommodation" provision could not
accomplish its intended objective. Neutral office assignment rules would
automatically prevent the accommodation of an employee whose disability-
imposed limitations require him to work on the ground floor. Neutral
"break-from-work" rules would automatically prevent the accommodation
of an individual who needs additional breaks from work, perhaps to permit
medical visits. Neutral furniture budget rules would automatically prevent
the accommodation of an individual who needs a different kind of chair or
desk. Many employers will have neutral rules governing the kinds of

actions most needed to reasonably accommodate a worker with a disability. See 42 U.S.C. § 12111(9)(b) (setting forth examples such as "job restructuring," "part-time or modified work schedules," "acquisition or modification of equipment or devices," "and other similar accommodations"). Yet Congress, while providing such examples, said nothing suggesting that the presence of such neutral rules would create an automatic exemption. Nor have the lower courts made any such suggestion. Cf. *Garcia–Ayala v. Lederle Parenterals, Inc.*, 212 F.3d 638, 648 (C.A.1 2000) (requiring leave beyond that allowed under the company's own leave policy); *Hendricks–Robinson v. Excel Corp.*, 154 F.3d 685, 699 (C.A.7 1998) (requiring exception to employer's neutral "physical fitness" job requirement).

In sum, the nature of the "reasonable accommodation" requirement, the statutory examples, and the Act's silence about the exempting effect of neutral rules together convince us that the Act does not create any such automatic exemption. The simple fact that an accommodation would provide a "preference"—in the sense that it would permit the worker with a disability to violate a rule that others must obey—cannot, *in and of itself,* automatically show that the accommodation is not "reasonable." As a result, we reject the position taken by U.S. Airways * * *.

US Airways also points to the ADA provisions stating that a " 'reasonable accommodation' may include ... reassignment to a *vacant* position." § 12111(9)(B). And it claims that the fact that an established seniority system would assign that position to another worker automatically and always means that the position is not a "vacant" one. Nothing in the Act, however, suggests that Congress intended the word "vacant" to have a specialized meaning. And in ordinary English, a seniority system can give employees seniority rights allowing them to bid for a "vacant" position. The position in this case was held, at the time of suit, by Barnett, not by some other worker; and that position, under the U.S. Airways seniority system, became an "open" one. Moreover, U.S. Airways has said that it "reserves the right to change any and all" portions of the seniority system at will. Consequently, we cannot agree with U.S. Airways about the position's vacancy; nor do we agree that the Act would automatically deny Barnett's accommodation request for that reason.

B

Barnett argues that the statutory words "reasonable accommodation" mean only "effective accommodation," authorizing a court to consider the requested accommodation's ability to meet an individual's disability-related needs, and nothing more. On this view, a seniority rule violation, having nothing to do with the accommodation's effectiveness, has nothing to do with its "reasonableness." It might, at most, help to prove an "undue hardship on the operation of the business." But, he adds, that is a matter that the statute requires the employer to demonstrate, case by case.

In support of this interpretation Barnett points to Equal Employment Opportunity Commission (EEOC) regulations stating that "reasonable accommodation means.... [m]odifications or adjustments ... that *enable* a qualified individual with a disability to perform the essential functions of [a] position." 29 CFR § 1630(*o*)(ii) (2001). Barnett adds that any other view would make the words "reasonable accommodation" and "undue hardship" virtual mirror images—creating redundancy in the statute. And he says that any such other view would create a practical burden of proof dilemma.

The practical burden of proof dilemma arises, Barnett argues, because the statute imposes the burden of demonstrating an "undue hardship" upon the employer, while the burden of proving "reasonable accommodation" remains with the plaintiff, here the employee. This allocation seems sensible in that an employer can more frequently and easily prove the presence of business hardship than an employee can prove its absence. But suppose that an employee must counter a claim of "seniority rule violation" in order to prove that an "accommodation" request is "reasonable." Would that not force the employee to prove what is in effect an absence, *i.e.,* an absence of hardship, despite the statute's insistence that the employer "demonstrate" hardship's presence?

These arguments do not persuade us that Barnett's legal interpretation of "reasonable" is correct. For one thing, in ordinary English the word "reasonable" does not mean "effective." It is the word "accommodation," not the word "reasonable," that conveys the need for effectiveness. An *ineffective* "modification" or "adjustment" will not *accommodate* a disabled individual's limitations. Nor does an ordinary English meaning of the term "reasonable accommodation" make of it a simple, redundant mirror image of the term "undue hardship." The statute refers to an "undue hardship on the operation of the business." Yet a demand for an effective accommodation could prove unreasonable because of its impact, not on business operations, but on fellow employees—say, because it will lead to dismissals, relocations, or modification of employee benefits to which an employer, looking at the matter from the perspective of the business itself, may be relatively indifferent.

Neither does the statute's primary purpose require Barnett's special reading. The statute seeks to diminish or to eliminate the stereotypical thought processes, the thoughtless actions, and the hostile reactions that far too often bar those with disabilities from participating fully in the Nation's life, including the workplace. These objectives demand unprejudiced thought and reasonable responsive reaction on the part of employers and fellow workers alike. They will sometimes require affirmative conduct to promote entry of disabled people into the work force. They do not, however, demand action beyond the realm of the reasonable.

Neither has Congress indicated in the statute, or elsewhere, that the word "reasonable" means no more than "effective." The EEOC regulations do say that reasonable accommodations "enable" a person with a disability to perform the essential functions of a task. But that phrasing simply emphasizes the statutory provision's basic objective. The regulations do not say that "enable" and "reasonable" mean the same thing. And as discussed below, no court of appeals has so read them. Finally, an ordinary language interpretation of the word "reasonable" does not create the "burden of proof" dilemma to which Barnett points. Many of the lower courts, while rejecting both U.S. Airways' and Barnett's more absolute views, have reconciled the phrases "reasonable accommodation" and "undue hardship" in a practical way.

They have held that a plaintiff/employee (to defeat a defendant/employer's motion for summary judgment) need only show that an "accommodation" seems reasonable on its face, *i.e.,* ordinarily or in the run of cases.

Once the plaintiff has made this showing, the defendant/employer then must show special (typically case-specific) circumstances that demonstrate undue hardship in the particular circumstances.

Not every court has used the same language, but their results are functionally similar. In our opinion, that practical view of the statute, applied consistently with ordinary summary judgment principles, avoids Barnett's burden of proof dilemma, while reconciling the two statutory phrases ("reasonable accommodation" and "undue hardship").

III

The question in the present case focuses on the relationship between seniority systems and the plaintiff's need to show that an "accommodation" seems reasonable on its face, *i.e.,* ordinarily or in the run of cases. We must assume that the plaintiff, an employee, is an "individual with a disability." He has requested assignment to a mailroom position as a "reasonable accommodation." We also assume that normally such a request would be reasonable within the meaning of the statute, were it not for one circumstance, namely, that the assignment would violate the rules of a seniority system. See § 12111(9) ("reasonable accommodation" may include "reassignment to a vacant position"). Does that circumstance mean that the proposed accommodation is not a "reasonable" one?

In our view, the answer to this question ordinarily is "yes." The statute does not require proof on a case-by-case basis that a seniority system should prevail. That is because it would not be reasonable in the run of cases that the assignment in question trump the rules of a seniority system. To the contrary, it will ordinarily be unreasonable for the assignment to prevail.

A

Several factors support our conclusion that a proposed accommodation will not be reasonable in the run of cases. Analogous case law supports this conclusion, for it has recognized the importance of seniority to employee-management relations. This Court has held that, in the context of a Title VII religious discrimination case, an employer need not adapt to an employee's special worship schedule as a "reasonable accommodation" where doing so would conflict with the seniority rights of other employees. *Trans World Airlines, Inc. v. Hardison,* 432 U.S. 63, 79–80, 97 S.Ct. 2264, 53 L.Ed.2d 113 (1977). The lower courts have unanimously found that collectively bargained seniority trumps the need for reasonable accommodation in the context of the linguistically similar Rehabilitation Act. And several Circuits, though differing in their reasoning, have reached a similar conclusion in the context of seniority and the ADA. All these cases discuss *collectively bargained* seniority systems, not systems (like the present system) which are unilaterally imposed by management. But the relevant seniority system advantages, and related difficulties that result from violations of seniority rules, are not limited to collectively bargained systems.

For one thing, the typical seniority system provides important employee benefits by creating, and fulfilling, employee expectations of fair, uniform treatment. These benefits include "job security and an opportunity for steady and predictable advancement based on objective standards." They include "an element of due process," limiting "unfairness in personnel decisions." And they consequently encourage employees to invest in the employing company, accepting "less than their value to the firm early in their careers" in return for greater benefits in later years.

Most important for present purposes, to require the typical employer to show more than the existence of a seniority system might well undermine the employees' expectations of consistent, uniform treatment—expectations upon which the seniority system's benefits depend. That is because such a rule would substitute a complex case-specific "accommodation" decision made by management for the more uniform, impersonal operation of seniority rules. Such management decisionmaking, with its inevitable discretionary elements, would involve a matter of the greatest importance to employees, namely, layoffs; it would take place outside, as well as inside, the confines of a court case; and it might well take place fairly often. We can find nothing in the statute that suggests Congress intended to undermine seniority systems in this way. And we consequently conclude that the employer's showing of violation of the rules of a seniority system is by itself ordinarily sufficient.

B

The plaintiff (here the employee) nonetheless remains free to show that special circumstances warrant a finding that, despite the presence of a seniority system (which the ADA may not trump in the run of cases), the requested "accommodation" is "reasonable" on the particular facts. That is because special circumstances might alter the important expectations described above. The plaintiff might show, for example, that the employer, having retained the right to change the seniority system unilaterally, exercises that right fairly frequently, reducing employee expectations that the system will be followed—to the point where one more departure, needed to accommodate an individual with a disability, will not likely make a difference. The plaintiff might show that the system already contains exceptions such that, in the circumstances, one further exception is unlikely to matter. We do not mean these examples to exhaust the kinds of showings that a plaintiff might make. But we do mean to say that the plaintiff must bear the burden of showing special circumstances that make an exception from the seniority system reasonable in the particular case. And to do so, the plaintiff must explain why, in the particular case, an exception to the employer's seniority policy can constitute a "reasonable accommodation" even though in the ordinary case it cannot.

IV

In its question presented, U.S. Airways asked us whether the ADA requires an employer to assign a disabled employee to a particular position even though another employee is entitled to that position under the employer's "established seniority system." We answer that *ordinarily* the ADA does not require that assignment. Hence, a showing that the assignment would violate the rules of a seniority system warrants summary judgment for the employer—unless there is more. The plaintiff must present evidence of that "more," namely, special circumstances surrounding the particular case that demonstrate the assignment is nonetheless reasonable.

Because the lower courts took a different view of the matter, and because neither party has had an opportunity to seek summary judgment in accordance with the principles we set forth here, we vacate the Court of Appeals' judgment and remand the case for further proceedings consistent with this opinion.

* * *

JUSTICE O'CONNOR, concurring.

I agree with portions of the opinion of the Court, but I find problematic the Court's test for determining whether the fact that a job reassignment violates a seniority system makes the reassignment an unreasonable accommodation under the Americans with Disabilities Act of 1990. Although a seniority system plays an important role in the workplace, * * * I would prefer to say that the effect of a seniority system on the reasonableness of a reassignment as an accommodation for purposes of the ADA depends on whether the seniority system is legally enforceable. * * *

The ADA specifically lists "reassignment to a vacant position" as one example of a "reasonable accommodation." 42 U.S.C. § 12111(9)(B) (1994 ed.). In deciding whether an otherwise reasonable accommodation involving a reassignment is unreasonable because it would require an exception to a seniority system, I think the relevant issue is whether the seniority system prevents the position in question from being vacant. * * * [W]hen an employee ceases working in a workplace with a legally enforceable seniority system, the employee's former position does not become vacant if the seniority system entitles another employee to it. Instead, the employee entitled to the position under the seniority system immediately becomes the new "possessor" of that position. In a workplace with an unenforceable seniority policy, however, an employee expecting assignment to a position under the seniority policy would not have any type of contractual right to the position and so could not be said to be its "possessor." The position therefore would become vacant.

* * * Indeed, the legislative history of the Act confirms that Congress did not intend reasonable accommodation to require bumping other employees.

Petitioner's Personnel Policy Guide for Agents, which contains its seniority policy, specifically states that it is "*not* intended to be a contract (express or implied) or otherwise to create legally enforceable obligations," and that petitioner "reserves the right to change any and all of the stated policies and procedures in [the] Guide at any time, without advanc[e] notice." Lodging of Respondent 2 (emphasis in original). Petitioner conceded at oral argument that its seniority policy does not give employees any legally enforceable rights. Tr. of Oral Arg. 16. Because the policy did not give any other employee a right to the position respondent sought, the position could be said to have been vacant when it became open for bidding, making the requested accommodation reasonable.

* * *

JUSTICE SCALIA, with whom JUSTICE THOMAS joins, dissenting.

* * *

The Court begins its analysis by describing the ADA as declaring that an employer may not " 'discriminate against a qualified individual with a disability.' " In fact the Act says more: an employer may not "discriminate against a qualified individual with a disability *because of the disability* of such individual." It further provides that discrimination includes "not making reasonable accommodations *to the known physical or mental limitations* of an otherwise qualified individual with a disability. § 12112(b)(5)(A)

Read together, these provisions order employers to modify or remove (within reason) policies and practices that burden a disabled person "because of [his] disability." In other words, the ADA eliminates workplace barriers only if a disability prevents an employee from overcoming them-those barriers that would not be barriers *but for* the employee's disability. These include, for example, work stations that cannot accept the employee's wheelchair, or an assembly-line practice that requires long periods of standing. But they do not include rules and practices that bear no more heavily upon the disabled employee than upon others-even though an exemption from such a rule or practice might in a sense "make up for" the employee's disability. It is not a required accommodation, for example, to pay a disabled employee more than others at his grade level— even if that increment is earmarked for massage or physical therapy that would enable the employee to work with as little physical discomfort as his co-workers. * * *

So also with exemption from a seniority system, which burdens the disabled and the nondisabled alike. In particular cases, seniority rules may have a harsher effect upon the disabled employee than upon his co-workers. If the disabled employee is physically capable of performing only one task in the workplace, seniority rules may be, for him, the difference between employment and unemployment. But that does not make the seniority system a disability-related obstacle, any more than harsher impact upon the more needy disabled employee renders the salary system a disability-related obstacle. When one departs from this understanding, the ADA's accommodation provision becomes a standardless grab bag-leaving it to the courts to decide which workplace preferences (higher salary, longer vacations, reassignment to positions to which others are entitled) can be deemed "reasonable" to "make up for" the particular employee's disability.

* * * The ADA already prohibits employers from discriminating against the disabled with respect to "hiring, advancement, or discharge . . . and other terms, conditions, and privileges of employment." § 12112(a). Surely, the argument goes, a disabled employee must be given preference over a nondisabled employee when a vacant position appears.

This argument seems to me quite mistaken. The right to be given a vacant position so long as there are no obstacles to that appointment (including another candidate who is better qualified, if "best qualified" is the workplace rule) is of considerable value. If an employee is hired to fill a position but fails miserably, he will typically be fired. Few employers will search their organization charts for vacancies to which the low-performing employee might be suited. The ADA, however, prohibits an employer from firing a person whose disability is the cause of his poor performance without first seeking to place him in a vacant job where the disability will not affect performance. Such reassignment is an accommodation *to the disability* because it removes an obstacle (the inability to perform the functions of the assigned job) arising solely from the disability. * * *

Although, as I have said, the uncertainty cast upon bona fide seniority systems is the least of the ill consequences produced by today's decision, a few words on that subject are nonetheless in order. Since, under the Court's interpretation of the ADA, *all* workplace rules are eligible to be used as vehicles of accommodation, the one means of saving seniority systems is a judicial finding that accommodation through the suspension of *those* workplace rules would be unreasonable. The Court is unwilling, however, to make that finding categorically, with respect to all seniority systems. Instead, it creates (and "creates" is the appropriate word) a *rebuttable presumption* that exceptions to seniority rules are not "reasonable" under the ADA, but leaves it free for the disabled employee to show that *under the "special circumstances" of his case,* an exception would be "reasonable." The employee would be entitled to an exception, for example, if he showed that "one more departure" from the seniority rules "will not likely make a difference."

I have no idea what this means. When is it possible for a departure from seniority rules to "not likely make a difference"? * * *

JUSTICE SOUTER, with whom JUSTICE GINSBURG joins, dissenting.

"[R]eassignment to a vacant position," is one way an employer may "reasonabl[y] accommodat[e]" disabled employees under the Americans with Disabilities Act of 1990 (ADA). The Court today holds that a request for reassignment will nonetheless most likely be unreasonable when it would violate the terms of a seniority system imposed by an employer. Although I concur in the Court's appreciation of the value and importance of seniority systems, I do not believe my hand is free to accept the majority's result and therefore respectfully dissent.

Nothing in the ADA insulates seniority rules from the "reasonable accommodation" requirement, in marked contrast to Title VII of the Civil Rights Act of 1964 and the Age Discrimination in Employment Act of 1967, each of which has an explicit protection for seniority. Because Congress modeled several of the ADA's provisions on Title VII, its failure to replicate Title VII's exemption for seniority systems leaves the statute ambiguous, albeit with more than a hint that seniority rules do not inevitably carry the day.

In any event, the statute's legislative history resolves the ambiguity. The Committee Reports from both the House of Representatives and the Senate explain that seniority protections contained in a collective-bargaining agreement should not amount to more than "a factor" when it comes to deciding whether some accommodation at odds with the seniority rules is "reasonable" nevertheless. * * *

This legislative history also specifically rules out the majority's reliance on *Trans World Airlines, Inc. v. Hardison*, 432 U.S. 63, 97 S.Ct. 2264, 53 L.Ed.2d 113 (1977), a case involving a request for a religious accommodation under Title VII that would have broken the seniority rules of a collective-bargaining agreement. We held that such an accommodation would not be "reasonable," and said that our conclusion was "supported" by Title VII's explicit exemption for seniority systems. The committees of both Houses of Congress dealing with the ADA were aware of this case and expressed a choice against treating it as authority under the ADA, with its lack of any provision for maintaining seniority rules.

Because a unilaterally imposed seniority system enjoys no special protection under the ADA, a consideration of facts peculiar to this very case is needed to gauge whether Barnett has carried the burden of showing his proposed accommodation to be a "reasonable" one despite the policy in force at U.S. Airways. The majority describes this as a burden to show the accommodation is "plausible" or "feasible," and I believe Barnett has met it.

* * * There was no evidence in the District Court of any unmanageable ripple effects from Barnett's request, or showing that he would have

overstepped an inordinate number of seniority levels by remaining where he was.

In fact, it is hard to see the seniority scheme here as any match for Barnett's ADA requests, since U.S. Airways apparently took pains to ensure that its seniority rules raised no great expectations. In its policy statement, U.S. Airways said that "[t]he Agent Personnel Policy Guide is *not* intended to be a contract" and that "USAir reserves the right to change any and all of the stated policies and procedures in this Guide at any time, without advanced notice." While I will skip any state-by-state analysis of the legal treatment of employee handbooks (a source of many lawyers' fees) it is safe to say that the contract law of a number of jurisdictions would treat this disclaimer as fatal to any claim an employee might make to enforce the seniority policy over an employer's contrary decision.

With U.S. Airways itself insisting that its seniority system was noncontractual and modifiable at will, there is no reason to think that Barnett's accommodation would have resulted in anything more than minimal disruption to U.S. Airways's operations, if that. Barnett has shown his requested accommodation to be "reasonable," and the burden ought to shift to U.S. Airways if it wishes to claim that, in spite of surface appearances, violation of the seniority scheme would have worked an undue hardship. I would therefore affirm the Ninth Circuit.

VANDE ZANDE v. WISCONSIN DEP'T OF ADMINISTRATION

United States Court of Appeals, Seventh Circuit, 1995
44 F.3d 538

POSNER, CHIEF JUDGE.

* * *

The * * * problematic case is that of an individual who has a vocationally relevant disability-an impairment such as blindness or paralysis that limits a major human capability, such as seeing or walking. In the common case in which such an impairment interferes with the individual's ability to perform up to the standards of the workplace, or increases the cost of employing him, hiring and firing decisions based on the impairment are not "discriminatory" in a sense closely analogous to employment discrimination on racial grounds. The draftsmen of the Act knew this. But they were unwilling to confine the concept of disability discrimination to cases in which the disability is irrelevant to the performance of the disabled person's job. Instead, they defined "discrimination" to include an employer's "not making reasonable accommodations to the known physical or mental limitations of an otherwise qualified individual with a disability who is an applicant or employee, unless ... [the employer] can demonstrate that the accommodation would impose an undue hardship on the operation of the . . . [employer's] business.''

The term "reasonable accommodations" is not a legal novelty, even if we ignore its use (arguably with a different meaning, however, in the provision of Title VII forbidding religious discrimination in employment. It is one of a number of provisions in the employment subchapter that were borrowed from regulations issued by the Equal Employment Opportunity Commission in implementation of the Rehabilitation Act of 1973, 29 U.S.C. §§ 701 *et seq.* Indeed, to a great extent the employment provisions of the new Act merely generalize to the economy as a whole the duties, including that of reasonable accommodation, that the regulations under the Rehabilitation Act imposed on federal agencies and federal contractors. We can therefore look to the decisions interpreting those regulations for clues to the meaning of the same terms in the new law.

It is plain enough what "accommodation" means. The employer must be willing to consider making changes in its ordinary work rules, facilities, terms, and conditions in order to enable a disabled individual to work. The difficult term is "reasonable." The plaintiff in our case, a paraplegic, argues in effect that the term just means apt or efficacious. An accommodation is reasonable, she believes, when it is tailored to the particular individual's disability. A ramp or lift is thus a reasonable accommodation for a person who like this plaintiff is confined to a wheelchair. Considerations of cost do not enter into the term as the plaintiff would have us construe it. Cost is, she argues, the domain of "undue hardship" (another term borrowed from the regulations under the Rehabilitation Act-a safe harbor for an employer that can show that it would go broke or suffer other excruciating financial distress were it compelled to make a reasonable accommodation in the sense of one effective in enabling the disabled person to overcome the vocational effects of the disability.

These are questionable interpretations both of "reasonable" and of "undue hardship." To "accommodate" a disability is to make some change that will enable the disabled person to work. An unrelated, inefficacious change would not be an accommodation of the disability at all. So "reasonable" may be intended to qualify (in the sense of weaken) "accommodation," in just the same way that if one requires a "reasonable effort" of someone this means less than the maximum possible effort, or in law that the duty of "reasonable care," the cornerstone of the law of negligence, requires something less than the maximum possible care. It is understood in that law that in deciding what care is reasonable the court considers the cost of increased care. (This is explicit in Judge Learned Hand's famous formula for negligence. Similar reasoning could be used to flesh out the meaning of the word "reasonable" in the term "reasonable accommodations." It would not follow that the costs and benefits of altering a workplace to enable a disabled person to work would always have to be quantified, or even that an accommodation would have to be deemed unreasonable if the cost exceeded the benefit however slightly. But, at the very least, the cost could not be disproportionate to the benefit.

Even if an employer is so large or wealthy—or, like the principal defendant in this case, is a state, which can raise taxes in order to finance any accommodations that it must make to disabled employees—that it may not be able to plead "undue *hardship*," it would not be required to expend enormous sums in order to bring about a trivial improvement in the life of a disabled employee. If the nation's employers have potentially unlimited financial obligations to 43 million disabled persons, the Americans with Disabilities Act will have imposed an indirect tax potentially greater than the national debt. We do not find an intention to bring about such a radical result in either the language of the Act or its history. The preamble actually "markets" the Act as a cost saver, pointing to "billions of dollars in unnecessary expenses resulting from dependency and nonproductivity." The savings will be illusory if employers are required to expend many more billions in accommodation than will be saved by enabling disabled people to work.

The concept of reasonable accommodation is at the heart of this case. The plaintiff sought a number of accommodations to her paraplegia that were turned down. The principal defendant as we have said is a state, which does not argue that the plaintiff's proposals were rejected because accepting them would have imposed undue hardship on the state or because they would not have done her any good. The district judge nevertheless granted summary judgment for the defendants on the ground that the evidence obtained in discovery, construed as favorably to the plaintiff as the record permitted, showed that they had gone as far to accommodate the plaintiff's demands as reasonableness, in a sense distinct from either aptness or hardship-a sense based, rather, on considerations of cost and proportionality-required. On this analysis, the function of the "undue hardship" safe harbor, like the "failing company" defense to antitrust liability, is to excuse compliance by a firm that is financially distressed, even though the cost of the accommodation to the firm might be less than the benefit to disabled employees.

This interpretation of "undue hardship" is not inevitable-in fact probably is incorrect. It is a defined term in the Americans with Disabilities Act, and the definition is "an action requiring significant difficulty or expense." The financial condition of the employer is only one consideration in determining whether an accommodation otherwise reasonable would impose an undue hardship. The legislative history equates "undue hardship" to "unduly costly." These are terms of relation. We must ask, "undue" in relation to what? Presumably (given the statutory definition and the legislative history) in relation to the benefits of the accommodation to the disabled worker as well as to the employer's resources.

So it seems that costs enter at two points in the analysis of claims to an accommodation to a disability. The employee must show that the accommodation is reasonable in the sense both of efficacious and of proportional to costs. Even if this prima facie showing is made, the employer has an opportunity to prove that upon more careful consideration the costs are excessive in relation either to the benefits of the accommodation or to the employer's financial survival or health. In a classic negligence case, the idiosyncrasies of the particular employer are irrelevant. Having above-average costs, or being in a precarious financial situation, is not a defense to negligence. One interpretation of "undue hardship" is that it permits an employer to escape liability if he can carry the burden of proving that a disability accommodation reasonable for a normal employer would break him.

Lori Vande Zande, aged 35, is paralyzed from the waist down as a result of a tumor of the spinal cord. Her paralysis makes her prone to develop pressure ulcers, treatment of which often requires that she stay at home for several weeks. The defendants and the amici curiae argue that there is no duty of reasonable accommodation of pressure ulcers because they do not fit the statutory definition of a disability. * * * But an intermittent impairment that is a characteristic manifestation of an admitted disability is, we believe, a part of the underlying disability and hence a condition that the employer must reasonably accommodate. * * * * We hold that Vande Zande's pressure ulcers are a part of her disability, and therefore a part of what the State of Wisconsin had a duty to accommodate-reasonably.

Vande Zande worked for the housing division of the state's department of administration for three years, beginning in January 1990. The housing division supervises the state's public housing programs. Her job was that of a program assistant, and involved preparing public information materials, planning meetings, interpreting regulations, typing, mailing, filing, and copying. In short, her tasks were of a clerical, secretarial, and administrative-assistant character. In order to enable her to do this work, the defendants, as she acknowledges, "made numerous accommodations relating to the plaintiff's disability." As examples, in her words, "they paid the landlord to have bathrooms modified and to have a step ramped; they bought special adjustable furniture for the plaintiff; they ordered and paid for one-half of the cost of a cot that the plaintiff needed for daily personal care at work; they sometimes adjusted the plaintiff's schedule to perform backup telephone duties to accommodate the plaintiff's medical appointments; they made changes to the plans for a locker room in the new state office building; * * *

But she complains that the defendants did not go far enough in two principal respects. One concerns a period of eight weeks when a bout of pressure ulcers forced her to stay home. She wanted to work full time at home and believed that she would be able to do so if the division would provide her with a desktop computer at home (though she already had a laptop). Her supervisor refused, and told her that he probably would have only 15 to 20 hours of work for her to do at home per week and that she would have to make up the difference between that and a full work week out of her sick leave or vacation leave. In the event, she was able to work all but 16.5 hours in the eight-week period. She took 16.5 hours of sick leave to make up the difference. As a result, she incurred no loss of income, but did lose sick leave that she could have carried forward indefinitely. * * *

She argues that a jury might have found that a reasonable accommodation required the housing division either to give her the desktop computer or to excuse her from having to dig into her sick leave to get paid for the hours in which, in the absence of the computer, she was unable to do her work at home. No jury, however, could in our view be permitted to stretch the concept of "reasonable accommodation" so far. Most jobs in organizations public or private involve team work under supervision rather than solitary unsupervised work, and team work under supervision generally cannot be performed at home without a substantial reduction in the quality of the employee's performance. This will no doubt change as communications technology advances, but is the situation today. Generally, therefore, an employer is not required to accommodate a disability by allowing the disabled worker to work, by himself, without supervision, at home. This is the majority view. * * * The District of Columbia Circuit disagrees. *Langon v. Dept. of Health & Human Services,* 959 F.2d 1053, 1060–61 (D.C.Cir.1992); *Carr v. Reno,* 23 F.3d 525, 530 (D.C.Cir.1994). But we think the majority view is correct. An employer is not required to allow disabled workers to work at home, where their productivity inevitably would be greatly reduced. * * * No doubt to this as to any generalization about so complex and varied an activity as employment there are exceptions, * * * but it would take a very extraordinary case for the employee to be able to create a triable issue of the employer's failure to allow the employee to work at home.

And if the employer, because it is a government agency and therefore is not under intense competitive pressure to minimize its labor costs or maximize the value of its output, or for some other reason, bends over backwards to accommodate a disabled worker—goes further than the law requires—by allowing the worker to work at home, it must not be punished for its generosity by being deemed to have conceded the reasonableness of so far-reaching an accommodation. That would hurt rather than help disabled workers. Wisconsin's housing division was not required by the Americans with Disabilities Act to allow Vande Zande to work at home; even more clearly it was not required to install a computer in her home so that she could avoid using up 16.5 hours of sick leave.

* * *

Her second complaint has to do with the kitchenettes in the housing division's building, which are for the use of employees during lunch and coffee breaks. Both the sink and the counter in each of the kitchenettes were 36 inches high, which is too high for a person in a wheelchair. The building was under construction, and the kitchenettes not yet built, when the plaintiff complained about this feature of the design. But the defendants refused to alter the design to lower the sink and counter to 34 inches, the height convenient for a person in a wheelchair. Construction of the building had begun before the effective date of the Americans with

Disabilities Act, and Vande Zande does not argue that the failure to include 34–inch sinks and counters in the design of the building violated the Act. She could not argue that; the Act is not retroactive. But she argues that once she brought the problem to the attention of her supervisors, they were obliged to lower the sink and counter, at least on the floor on which her office was located but possibly on the other floors in the building as well, since she might be moved to another floor. All that the defendants were willing to do was to install a shelf 34 inches high in the kitchenette area on Vande Zande's floor. That took care of the counter problem. As for the sink, the defendants took the position that since the plumbing was already in place it would be too costly to lower the sink and that the plaintiff could use the bathroom sink, which is 34 inches high.

Apparently it would have cost only about $150 to lower the sink on Vande Zande's floor; to lower it on all the floors might have cost as much as $2,000, though possibly less. Given the proximity of the bathroom sink, Vande Zande can hardly complain that the inaccessibility of the kitchenette sink interfered with her ability to work or with her physical comfort. Her argument rather is that forcing her to use the bathroom sink for activities (such as washing out her coffee cup) for which the other employees could use the kitchenette sink stigmatized her as different and inferior; she seeks an award of compensatory damages for the resulting emotional distress. We may assume without having to decide that emotional as well as physical barriers to the integration of disabled persons into the workforce are relevant in determining the reasonableness of an accommodation. But we do not think an employer has a duty to expend even modest amounts of money to bring about an absolute identity in working conditions between disabled and nondisabled workers. The creation of such a duty would be the inevitable consequence of deeming a failure to achieve identical conditions "stigmatizing." That is merely an epithet. We conclude that access to a particular sink, when access to an equivalent sink, conveniently located, is provided, is not a legal duty of an employer. The duty of reasonable accommodation is satisfied when the employer does what is necessary to enable the disabled worker to work in reasonable comfort.

* * * AFFIRMED.

NOTES

1. *Reassignment: U.S. Airways v. Barnett, supra,* broadly endorses the position that in the absence of a seniority system directing otherwise, reassignment of plaintiff to the light duty "mailroom" normally would be a "reasonable accommodation." Some authority had held that reasonable accommodation requires re-assignment of a qualified disabled employee to a vacant position *even though other employees bidding for the position have superior qualifications. Smith v. Midland Brake, Inc.,* 180 F.3d 1154 (10th Cir. 1999)(en banc). Others have held that reasonable accommodation requires only that the disabled employee be accorded a *right to apply* for the

vacancy and be considered for it. Requiring an employer to give a minimally qualified disabled employee preference in filling a vacancy over a clearly better qualified non-disabled worker is not a "reasonable accommodation." *Huber v. Wal–Mart Stores, Inc.,* 486 F.3d 480 (8th Cir. 2007).

2. *Equipment Modification:* **SKERSKI v. TIME WARNER CABLE COMPANY,** 257 F.3d 273 (3d Cir. 2001). The facts are reproduced, *supra, page* 145. In part A, the court concluded that a factual issue was presented as to whether climbing for an installer was an "essential" function of the job. The court continued:

> Skerski argues that even if climbing is an essential function, there is a genuine issue of material fact whether he can, with a "reasonable accommodation," perform the job as an installer technician, and that summary judgment was therefore improper.

> * * * According to the ADA, a "reasonable accommodation" includes:

>> job restructuring, part-time or modified work schedules, reassignment to a vacant position, acquisition or modification of equipment or devices, appropriate adjustment or modifications of examinations, training materials or policies, the provision of qualified readers or interpreters, and other similar accommodations for individuals with disabilities. 42 U.S.C. § 12111(9)(B).

> The relevant regulations define reasonable accommodations as "[m]odifications or adjustments to the work environment, or to the manner or circumstances under which the position held or desired is customarily performed, that enable a qualified individual with a disability to perform the essential functions of that position." 29 C.F.R. § 1630.2(*o*) (1)(ii).

> In *Walton v. Mental Health Ass'n of Southeastern Pa.,* 168 F.3d 661 (3d Cir.1999), this court established that, "[o]n the issue of reasonable accommodation, the plaintiff bears only the burden of identifying an accommodation, the costs of which, facially, do not clearly exceed its benefits." Summary judgment may be granted for a defendant only "in cases in which the plaintiff's proposal is either *clearly ineffective* or *outlandishly costly.*"

> If the plaintiff satisfies his or her burden, the defendant then has the burden to demonstrate that the proposed accommodation creates an "undue hardship" for it. The ADA defines "undue hardship" as "an action requiring significant difficulty or expense, when considered in light of [a series of factors]." 42 U.S.C. § 12111(10)(A). Among the factors to be considered are "the effect on expenses and resources, or the impact otherwise of such accommodation upon the operation of the facility." 42 U.S.C. § 12111(10)(B).

> . . .

> Skerski contends that Time Warner should have permitted him to use a bucket truck to work at heights as an installer technician, which would have enabled him to avoid climbing. Skerski testified in his deposition that, in response to Hanning's demand in the fall of 1996 that he resume the climbing functions of his installer technician position, he offered to use a bucket truck instead, and that this bucket truck would enable him

to perform all of the required overhead work. Although Time Warner rejected this proposition, Skerski further testified that it was his understanding that Time Warner had a bucket truck available for use at the time. Time Warner does not contest Skerski's claim * * *.

[W]e find present here a genuine issue of material fact as to whether providing Skerksi with a bucket truck would have been a reasonable accommodation. * * *

3. *Assistants, readers, etc.: In **Borkowski v. Valley Central School Dist.,*** 63 F.3d 131 (2d Cir. 1995), a disability prohibited an elementary school librarian/teacher from standing, which disability inhibited her ability to maintain classroom discipline. Her requested accommodation was for a classroom assistant who would assist her in maintaining discipline. The request was denied, and plaintiff was dismissed. The trial court granted summary judgment to the employer, holding as a matter of law reasonable accommodation did not require hiring another person to do a duty for the disabled individual. The Court of Appeals reversed. The court distinguished between an accommodation that would have another person perform duties that *eliminate* an essential function of the job—which need not be accommodated—from an accommodation that "permits the individual with a disability to perform that essential function."

> The accommodation suggested by Ms. Borkowski appears, at first blush, to resemble more closely one that would eliminate an essential function of a library teacher * * * than one that would permit Ms. Borkowski to perform that function. Yet, viewing the record * * * in the light most favorable to Ms. Borkowski, we cannot say that no reasonable jury could conclude otherwise.

The court then noted that Ms. Borkowski had been provided an aide for her library duties, as well as the implementing guidelines that contemplated use of assistants as possible reasonable accommodations, making such an accommodation for Ms. Borkowski "at least facially reasonable." The court concluded:

> It may be that the School District can show that the benefits an aide would give are too small in relation to the cost of an aide. It may be also that the District can demonstrate that in this and other districts provision of an aide would impact school budgets sufficiently to be an unreasonable or undue burden. * * * But in the absence of evidence regarding school district budgets, the cost of providing an aide of this sort, or any like kind of information, we are unable to conclude that unreasonableness or undue hardship has been established * * *.

EEOC v. UPS Supply Chain Solutions, 620 F.3d 1103 (9th Cir. 2010), held that the reasonableness of the accommodation is an issue of fact. In this case a deaf employee who was required to attend weekly staff meetings, sought to have an American Sign Language (ASL) interpreter provided at the meetings to enable him to fully participate. The court held that the jury could find that merely providing plaintiff with pre-and post-meeting written notes was not a reasonable accommodation, and that an ASL interpreter at the meetings was a "reasonable" accommodation that should have been provided.

(The court did not address whether such an accommodation would constitute an "undue hardship.")

4. *Personal items:* EEOC guidance distinguishes between on-site, "job related" modifications or assistance, such as sound amplifiers, large type print, and voice recognition technology, that may be "reasonable," from "personal items" that an employee would use in their personal daily life activity such as wheel chairs, medication, prosthesis, hearing aids, eye glasses, or home health care assistance, which would be unreasonable. 29 C.F.R. § 1630 (2008) App. § 1630.9.

5. *Job modifications:* An accommodation is not reasonable if it would fundamentally alter the nature of the job duties the disabled individual has performed or alter the nature of the employer's business organization. 29 C.F.R. § 1630.2(n). For example, while an employer may be required to allow a transfer to an existing light duty job vacancy, (See, *U.S.Airways, supra, page* 166) it need not *create* such a light duty job classification. The employer need not slow production schedules or realign key job duties by assigning all light tasks to the disabled worker and reassigning heavy duty tasks to other employees. *Milton v. Scrivner, Inc.,* 53 F.3d 1118 (10th Cir. 1995).

6. *Leaves of absence:* As *Vande Zande* held an employee who consistently is unable to report to work cannot perform essential job duties. Moreover, courts consistently hold that allowing the employee to do extensive work at home is not a reasonable accommodation. *E.g., Spangler v. Federal Home Loan Bank,* 278 F.3d 847 (8th Cir. 2002). However, modern electronic communications might cause this premise to be revisited. *See,* EEOC *Enforcement Compliance Manual, Vol.II, No.915.002*

While the ADA's list of possible reasonable accommodation does not include the grant of medical leaves, the weight of authority does recognize, however, that unpaid leaves of absence often are a reasonable accommodation even where substitute workers must be employed. *Humphrey v. Memorial Hospitals Ass'n,* 239 F.3d 1128 (9th Cir. 2001). For example, *Garcia–Ayala v. Lederle Parenterals, Inc.,* 212 F.3d 638 (1st Cir. 2000), held that a medical leave to treat cancer that exceeded one year may be a required reasonable accommodation.

Verizon Communications had a "no fault attendance plan" that resulted in disciplining employees who accumulated a designated number of "chargeable absences." Verizon allegedly failed to adjust its plan to accommodate workers whose absences were the result of disabilities. The EEOC filed a nation-wide suit challenging the policy. The parties entered into a consent decree (D.Md.) in which Verizon agreed to modify its practice and pay $20 million in settlement of the claim. (CCH.Labor Law Reports, July, 20, 2011).

7. *The 2008 Amendments* to the ADA did not redefine the duty of employers to make reasonable accommodations to known disabilities of qualified individuals. However, the prime directive was to give the statute an expansive interpretation suggests that courts should be expansive in requiring accommodation of disabilities. Pre–2009 authority should be evaluated in that light.

Review The Family and Medical Leave Act (29 U.S.C. § 2601 *et seq.* That statute requires "eligible employees" of covered employers to be provided up to 12 weeks of unpaid leave during any 12 month period in order to treat "serious health conditions." The seriousness of the health condition for which leave must be granted need only render the employee unable to perform essential job duties. Accordingly to be entitled to leave under the FMLA the condition need not reach the level of being a "disability" as defined by the ADA. 29 C.F.R. § 825.115

5. "RECORD OF"

EEOC REGULATIONS (2011) APPENDIX

Section 1630.2(k)

The second prong of the definition of "disability" provides that an individual with a record of an impairment that substantially limits a major life activity is an individual with a disability. The intent of this provision, in part, is to ensure that people are not discriminated against because of a history of disability. For example, the "record of" provision would protect an individual who was treated for cancer ten years ago but who is now deemed to be free of cancer, from discrimination based on that prior medical history. This provision also ensures that individuals are not discriminated against because they have been misclassified as disabled. * * *

This part of the definition is satisfied where evidence establishes that an individual has had a substantially limiting impairment. The impairment indicated in the record must be an impairment that would substantially limit one or more of the individual's major life activities. There are many types of records that could potentially contain this information, including but not limited to, education, medical, or employment records.

* * * The terms "substantially limits" and "major life activity" under this second prong of the definition of "disability" are to be construed in accordance with the same principles applicable under the "actual disability" prong, as set forth in § 1630.2(j).

* * * Thus, an individual who has cancer that is currently in remission is an individual with a disability under the "actual disability" prong because he has an impairment that would substantially limit normal cell growth when active. He is also covered by the "record of" prong based on his history of having had an impairment that substantially limited normal cell growth.

Finally, this section of the EEOC's regulations makes it clear that an individual with a record of a disability is entitled to a reasonable accommodation currently needed for limitations resulting from or relating to the past substantially limiting impairment. * * *

6. ALCOHOL AND DRUG USE

Alcoholism and drug addictions are impairments under the ADA. *Bailey v. Georgia–Pacific Corp.*, 306 F.3d 1162, 1167 (1st Cir. 2002). "Impairment" requires the individual to be suffering from medically recognized *addiction,* to be distinguished from simple use or misuse of alcohol or drugs. Refusal to hire or dismissing a non-addicted individual merely because he has "a drinking problem" or "can't hold his liquor" is not discrimination on the basis of a medically recognized *impairment. Kozisek v. County of Seward,* 539 F.3d 930 (8th Cir. 2008). Since the 2008 Amendments the addiction need not, however, affect major life activities. Thus, discrimination because of *perceived* addiction is proscribed even if any internal bodily functions have not been significantly impaired or manifested any adverse affect on the addict's activities.

Discrimination based on one's participation in a alcohol or drug rehabilitation programs is expressly prohibited, provided that plaintiff is no longer "engaging in such use." 42 U.S.C. § 12114(b) One is considered "no longer engaging in such use" only when they have been "drug free for a significant period of time." *Zenor v. El Paso Healthcare System, Ltd.*, 176 F.3d 847 (5th Cir. 1999) (addict in a rehabilitation program and drug free for 5 weeks can still be considered "currently using" illegal drugs, and thus not protected).

Protection of addicts is subject to the following critical provisos:

Moreover, 42 U.S.C. § 12114:

(a) [T]he term "qualified individual with a disability" shall not include any employee or applicant who is currently engaging in the illegal use of drugs, when the covered entity acts on the basis of such use.

* * *

(c) A covered entity—

(1) may prohibit the illegal use of drugs and the use of alcohol at the workplace by all employees;

(2) may require that employees shall not be under the influence of alcohol or be engaging in the illegal use of drugs at the workplace;

(3) may require that employees behave in conformance with the requirements established under the Drug–Free Workplace Act of 1988 (41 U.S.C. 701 et seq.);

(4) may hold an employee who engages in the illegal use of drugs or who is an alcoholic to the same qualification standards for employment or job performance and behavior that such entity holds other

employees, even if any unsatisfactory performance or behavior is related to the drug use or alcoholism of such employee; and

(5) may, with respect to Federal regulations regarding alcohol and the illegal use of drugs, require * * * that—

(A) employees comply with the standards established in such regulations of the Department of Defense * * *of the Nuclear Regulatory Commission, [and] such regulations of the Department of Transportation, * * *

Finally, subsection d provides that a test to determine the illegal use of drugs shall not be considered a medical examination, and that "Nothing in this title shall be construed to encourage, prohibit, or authorize the conducting of drug testing for the illegal use of drugs by job applicants or employees or making employment decisions based on such test results."

NOTES

1. *Job qualifications and standards:* A person addicted to drugs or alcohol must have necessary qualifications, such as driver's licenses, to perform essential job duties, and must be able to comply with generally applicable attendance and performance standards. Addiction is no defense to inability to secure necessary credentials or reliably perform essential job duties. *Despears v. Milwaukee County,* 63 F.3d 635 (7th Cir. 1995)(alcoholism resulted in convictions for driving under the influence, which ultimately caused plaintiff to lose his driver's license. Plaintiff was lawfully discharged for lacking the necessary driver's license.)

2. *Testing:* An employer is free to test applicants and employees for illegal drugs and may fire or refuse to employ individuals who fail such drug tests because of that individual's "current use of illegal drugs" even if the use had no adverse effect on the employee's job performance. *Lopez v. Pacific Maritime Ass'n,* 657 F.3d 762 (9th Cir. 2011).

Alcoholics are given somewhat more protection. Unless the addiction to alcohol (1) adversely affects the employee's job performance, (2) the employee is intoxicated while on the premises in violation of employer rules, or (3) the alcohol is consumed or brought onto the premises contrary to the employer's rules, the mere fact that the *alcoholic* has currently imbibed alcohol away from the work place is no basis for discrimination against an alcoholic.

3. *"Currently using:"*

"Current illegal use of drugs means that the illegal use of drugs was recent enough to justify an employer's reasonable belief that a person's drug use is current or that continuing use is a real and ongoing problem." 143 Con. Rec. H. 103–01 (1997).

One is considered "currently using" illegal drugs even though the individual is not at the moment engaging in such use. *Shafer v. Preston Memorial Hospital,* 107 F.3d 274 (4th Cir. 1997). "The [current use] provision is not intended to be limited to persons who use drugs on the day of, or within a matter of days or weeks before the employment action in question." H.R.Rep. No. 101–596, p. 64 (1990).

4. *"Direct Threat"*: An employer may assert that addiction presents a "direct threat to health or safety of others, a defense discussed, *supra*. In *Altman v. New York City Health Hospitals, Corp.,* 903 F.Supp. 503 (S.D.N.Y. 1995), *aff'd,* 100 F.3d 1054 (2d Cir. 1996), the chief of medicine at a hospital had treated patients while he was intoxicated. He completed a rehabilitation program, and had been alcohol free for three months. Based on a perceived danger of relapse and the danger this would pose to patients should the physician suffer a relapse, the hospital was justified in its refusal to reinstate the physician.

5. *Family and Medical Leave Act,* 29 U.S.C. § 2601 (FMLA): Department of Labor regulations provide that alcohol and drug abuse can be a "serious health condition" under the FMLA for which an employee must be allowed leave in order to receive "inpatient medical care" or "continuing treatment by a health care provider" for their "condition." 29 C.F.R. §§ 825.114 and 119. Unlike the ADA, the FMLA does not require the alcohol or drug abuse to have reached the level of medical addiction. However, the FMLA does not authorize a worker to take simply take leave because the condition prevents her from reporting to work, nor does it override an employer's rules regarding sobriety at the workplace. *Ames v. Home Depot, USA,* 629 F.3d 665 (7th Cir. 2011).

7. "INTERACTIVE PROCESS"

The individual seeking an accommodation must identify the nature of the disability and the accommodation that would allow the individual to perform essential job duties. EEOC regulations require that when an apparently reasonable accommodation is suggested, the employer who does not make the requested accommodation must engage in an informal "interactive process" that explores with the disabled individual the reasonableness of the request and alternatives that might meet the individual's needs with less hardship on the employer. 29 C.F.R. § 1630.2(*o*)(3). Refusal of the employee to undertake this "problem solving" approach by insisting that his proposed accommodation be implemented may prevent a challenge to the reasonableness of the employer's proposed accommodation.

It is unclear what consequences, if any, flow from an employer's failure to engage fully in the process. Neither the ADA nor implementing EEOC directives suggest liability based on employer failures to engage in the process. Nonetheless, rejection of employee-suggested accommodations without re-engaging the individual in a problem solving dialogue may preclude grant of summary judgment to the employer (*Taylor v. Phoenixville School Dist.,* 184 F.3d 296 (3d Cir. 1999)) or may create a presumption that the individual's suggested accommodation is reasonable. *Shapiro v. Township of Lakewood,* 292 F.3d 356 (3d Cir. 2002). Fully engaging in the interactive process will allow employers to avoid damages in the event they are ultimately held liable for failure to make a reasonable accommodation. See, 42 U.S.C. § 1981A(a)(3).

California law specifically requires employers to engage in the interactive process. Cal.Gov't Code, § 12940(n). Unlike the ADA, failure to so engage constitutes a distinct violation of the state statute. It is unclear whether liability will be established solely on the basis of the employer's failure to engage in the process. *Scotch v. Art Institute of California,* 173 Cal. App.4th 968, 93 Cal.Rptr.3d 338 (2009) (No liability for failure to undertake the process where reasonable accommodation could not have been made). Contrast: *Gelfo v. Lockheed Martin Corp.,* 140 Cal.App.4th 34, 43 Cal.Rptr.3d 874 (2006) (Duty is to engage in interactive process even where the individual had no disability).

8. MEDICAL EXAMINATIONS AND INQUIRIES

THE AMERICANS WITH DISABILITIES ACT OF 1990

29 U.S.C.A. § 12112(d)

* * *

(2) Pre-employment.—

(A) Prohibited examination or inquiry.—Except as provided in paragraph (3), a covered entity shall not conduct a medical examination or make inquiries of a job applicant as to whether such applicant is an individual with a disability or as to the nature or severity of such disability.

(B) Acceptable inquiry.—A covered entity may make pre-employment inquiries into the ability of an applicant to perform job-related functions.

(3) Employment entrance examination.—A covered entity may require a medical examination after an offer of employment has been made to a job applicant and prior to the commencement of the employment duties of such applicant, and may condition an offer of employment on the results of such examination, if—

(A) all entering employees are subjected to such an examination regardless of disability;

(B) information obtained regarding the medical condition or history of the applicant is collected and maintained on separate forms and in separate medical files and is treated as a confidential medical record, except that—

(i) supervisors and managers may be informed regarding necessary restrictions on the work or duties of the employee and necessary accommodations;

(ii) first aid and safety personnel may be informed, when appropriate, if the disability might require emergency treatment; and

(iii) government officials investigating compliance with this chapter shall be provided relevant information on request; and (C) the results of such examination are used only in accordance with this subchapter.

(4) Examination and inquiry.—

(A) Prohibited examinations and inquiries.—A covered entity shall not require a medical examination and shall not make inquiries of an employee as to whether such employee is an individual with a disability or as to the nature or severity of the disability, unless such examination or inquiry is shown to be job related and consistent with business necessity.

(B) Acceptable examinations and inquiries.—A covered entity may conduct voluntary medical examinations, including voluntary medical histories, which are part of an employee health program available to employees at that work site. A covered entity may make inquiries into the ability of an employee to perform job-related functions.

(C) Requirement.—Information obtained under subparagraph (B) regarding the medical condition or history of any employee are subject to the requirements of subparagraphs (B) and (C) of paragraph (3).* * *

GENETIC INFORMATION NON-DISCLOSURE ACT OF 2008

SEC. 202.　EMPLOYER PRACTICES.

* * * (b) Acquisition of Genetic Information.—It shall be an unlawful employment practice for an employer to request, require, or purchase genetic information with respect to an employee or a family member of the employee except—

(1) where an employer inadvertently requests or requires family medical history of the employee or family member of the employee;

(2) where—

(A) health or genetic services are offered by the employer, including such services offered as part of a wellness program;

(B) the employee provides prior, knowing, voluntary, and written authorization;

(C) only the employee (or family member if the family member is receiving genetic services) and the licensed health care professional or board certified genetic counselor involved in providing such services receive individually identifiable information concerning the results of such services; and

(D) any individually identifiable genetic information provided under subparagraph (C) in connection with the services provided under subparagraph (A) is only available for purposes of such services and shall not be disclosed to the employer except in aggregate terms that do not disclose the identity of specific employees;

(3) where an employer requests or requires family medical history from the employee to comply with the certification provisions of section 103 of the Family and Medical Leave Act of 1993 (29 U.S.C. 2613) or such requirements under State family and medical leave laws;

(4) where an employer purchases documents that are commercially and publicly available (including newspapers, magazines, periodicals, and books, but not including medical databases or court records) that include family medical history;

(5) where the information involved is to be used for genetic monitoring of the biological effects of toxic substances in the workplace, but only if—

(A) the employer provides written notice of the genetic monitoring to the employee;

(B) (i) the employee provides prior, knowing, voluntary, and written authorization; or (ii) the genetic monitoring is required by Federal or State law;

(C) the employee is informed of individual monitoring results;

(D) the monitoring is in compliance with—

(i) any Federal genetic monitoring regulations, * * *or

(ii) State genetic monitoring regulations, in the case of a State that is implementing genetic monitoring regulations under the authority of the Occupational Safety and Health Act of 1970 (29 U.S.C. 651 et seq.); and

(E) the employer, excluding any licensed health care professional or board certified genetic counselor that is involved in the genetic monitoring program, receives the results of the monitoring only in aggregate terms that do not disclose the identity of specific employees; or

(6) where the employer conducts DNA analysis for law enforcement purposes as a forensic laboratory or for purposes of human remains identification, and requests or requires genetic information of such employer's employees, but only to the extent that such genetic information is used for analysis of DNA identification markers for quality control to detect sample contamination.

(c) Preservation of Protections.—In the case of information to which any of paragraphs (1) through (6) of subsection (b) applies, such information may not be used in violation of paragraph (1) or (2) of subsection (a) or treated or disclosed in a manner that violates section 206.

NOTES

1. The above restrictions and prohibitions protect applicants and employees regardless of whether these individuals suffer from an impairment or disability.

2. Requiring that an employee produce a note from a physician justifying a request for receiving sick leave is not a proscribed inquiry. *Lee v. City of Columbus,* 636 F.3d 245 (6th Cir. 2011).

3. EEOC regulations implementing GINA are found at 29 C.F.R. Part 1635 (Nov. 2010).

G. MILITARY SERVICE

THE UNIFORMED SERVICES EMPLOYMENT AND REEMPLOYMENT ACT OF 1994 (USERRA)

38 U.S.C.

Section 4311(a): A person who is a member of * * * performs * * * has performed * * * or has an obligation to perform service in a uniformed [military] service shall not be denied employment, re-employment, retention in employment promotion, or any other benefit of employment by an employer on the basis of that [military] service.

Section 4312(a) [subject to some qualifications] any person whose absence from a position of employment is necessitated by reason of service in the uniformed services shall be entitled to the reemployment rights and benefits * * *

Section 4313(a)(1): a person entitled to reemployment under section 4312 upon completion of service in the uniformed services shall be promptly reemployed * * *.

Section 4316(a): a person who is rereemployed under this chapter is entitled to the seniority and other benefits determined by seniority that the person had at the date of the commencement of the service * * * plus the additional rights and benefits that such person would have attained if that person remained continuously employed.

* * *

(c) person who is reemployed by an employer under this chapter shall not be discharged from such employment except for cause, (1) within one year after the date of such reemployment if the person's period of service before reemployment was more than 180 days, * * *.

NOTES

1. USERRA language prohibiting only denial of a "benefit of employ-ment" requires plaintiff to prove that the employer's treatment caused her "significant harm." ***Lisdahl v. Mayo Foundation,*** 633 F.3d 712 (8th Cir. 2011). It is doubtful that liability can be based solely upon the employer creating a hostile environment that does not affect a tangible "benefit." ***Carder v. Continental Airlines***, 636 F.3d 172 (5th Cir. 2011).

2. Section 712 of Title VII (42 U.S.C. § 2000e–11) provides: "Nothing contained in this chapter shall be construed to repeal or modify any Federal State, territorial, or local law creating special rights or preferences for veterans."

CHAPTER 3

DEFENSES AND JUSTIFICATIONS: PERMISSIBLE USE OF PROTECTED CLASSIFICATIONS

■ ■ ■

A. THE BONA FIDE OCCUPATIONAL QUALIFICATION

UNITED AUTO WORKERS v. JOHNSON CONTROLS, INC.

Supreme Court of the United States, 1991
499 U.S. 187, 111 S.Ct. 1196, 113 L.Ed.2d 158

JUSTICE BLACKMUN delivered the opinion of the Court.

* * *

In this case we are concerned with an employer's gender-based fetal-protection policy. May an employer exclude a fertile female employee from certain jobs because of its concern for the health of the fetus the woman might conceive?

I

Respondent Johnson Controls, Inc., manufactures batteries. In the manufacturing process, the element lead is a primary ingredient. Occupational exposure to lead entails health risks, including the risk of harm to any fetus carried by a female employee.

* * *

[I]n 1982, Johnson Controls shifted from a policy of warning to a policy of exclusion. * * *

> "... [I]t is [Johnson Controls'] policy that women who are pregnant or who are capable of bearing children will not be placed into jobs involving lead exposure or which could expose them to lead through the exercise of job bidding, bumping, transfer or promotion rights."

The policy defined "women ... capable of bearing children" as "[a]ll women except those whose inability to bear children is medically documented." It further stated that an unacceptable work station was one where, "over the past year," an employee had recorded a blood lead level of more than 30 micrograms per deciliter or the work site had yielded an air sample containing a lead level in excess of 30 micrograms per cubic meter.

II

* * *

The District Court granted summary judgment for defendant-respondent Johnson Controls. Applying a three-part business necessity defense derived from fetal-protection cases in the Courts of Appeals for the Fourth and Eleventh Circuits, the District Court concluded that while "there is a disagreement among the experts regarding the effect of lead on the fetus," the hazard to the fetus through exposure to lead was established by "a considerable body of opinion"; that although "[e]xpert opinion has been provided which holds that lead also affects the reproductive abilities of men and women ... [and] that these effects are as great as the effects of exposure of the fetus ... a great body of experts are of the opinion that the fetus is more vulnerable to levels of lead that would not affect adults"; and that [plaintiffs] had "failed to establish that there is an acceptable alternative policy which would protect the fetus." The court stated that, in view of this disposition of the business necessity defense, it did not "have to undertake a bona fide occupational qualification's [sic] (BFOQ) analysis."

[In the segment of the opinion reproduced *supra at page* 51. The Court concluded that defendant's policy was facial discrimination "because of sex."]

The Court of Appeals for the Seventh Circuit, sitting en banc, affirmed the summary judgment by a 7-to-4 vote. * * * With its ruling, the Seventh Circuit became the first Court of Appeals to hold that a fetal-protection policy directed exclusively at women could qualify as a BFOQ. * * *

IV

Under § 703(e)(1) of Title VII, an employer may discriminate on the basis of "religion, sex, or national origin in those certain instances where religion, sex, or national origin is a bona fide occupational qualification reasonably necessary to the normal operation of that particular business or enterprise." 42 U.S.C. § 2000e–2(e)(1). We therefore turn to the question whether Johnson Controls' fetal-protection policy is one of those "certain instances" that come within the BFOQ exception.

The BFOQ defense is written narrowly, and this Court has read it narrowly We have read the BFOQ language of § 4(f) of the Age Discrimination in Employment Act of 1967 (ADEA), 29 U.S.C. § 623(f)(1), which tracks the BFOQ provision in Title VII, just as narrowly. Our emphasis on the restrictive scope of the BFOQ defense is grounded on both the language and the legislative history of § 703.

The wording of the BFOQ defense contains several terms of restriction that indicate that the exception reaches only special situations. The statute thus limits the situations in which discrimination is permissible to "certain instances" where sex discrimination is "reasonably necessary" to the "normal operation" of the "particular" business. Each one of these terms—certain, normal, particular—prevents the use of general subjective standards and favors an objective, verifiable requirement. But the most telling term is "occupational"; this indicates that these objective, verifiable requirements must concern job-related skills and aptitudes.

JUSTICE WHITE defines "occupational" as meaning related to a job. According to him, any discriminatory requirement imposed by an employer is "job-related" simply because the employer has chosen to make the requirement a condition of employment. In effect, he argues that sterility may be an occupational qualification for women because Johnson Controls has chosen to require it. This reading of "occupational" renders the word mere surplusage. "Qualification" by itself would encompass an employer's idiosyncratic requirements. By modifying "qualification" with "occupational," Congress narrowed the term to qualifications that affect an employee's ability to do the job.

Johnson Controls argues that its fetal-protection policy falls within the so-called safety exception to the BFOQ. Our cases have stressed that discrimination on the basis of sex because of safety concerns is allowed only in narrow circumstances. In *Dothard v. Rawlinson,* this Court indicated that danger to a woman herself does not justify discrimination. We there allowed the employer to hire only male guards in contact areas of maximum-security male penitentiaries only because more was at stake than the "individual woman's decision to weigh and accept the risks of employment." We found sex to be a BFOQ inasmuch as the employment of a female guard would create real risks of safety to others if violence broke out because the guard was a woman. Sex discrimination was tolerated because sex was related to the guard's ability to do the job-maintaining prison security. We also required in *Dothard* a high correlation between sex and ability to perform job functions and refused to allow employers to use sex as a proxy for strength although it might be a fairly accurate one.

Similarly, some courts have approved airlines' layoffs of pregnant flight attendants at different points during the first five months of pregnancy on the ground that the employer's policy was necessary to ensure the safety of passengers. In two of these cases, the courts pointedly indicated that fetal, as opposed to passenger, safety was best left to the mother.

We considered safety to third parties in *Western Airlines, Inc. v. Criswell, supra,* in the context of the ADEA. We focused upon "the nature of the flight engineer's tasks," and the "actual capabilities of persons over age 60" in relation to those tasks. Our safety concerns were not independent of the individual's ability to perform the assigned tasks, but rather involved the possibility that, because of age-connected debility, a flight engineer might not properly assist the pilot, and might thereby cause a safety emergency. Furthermore, although we considered the safety of third parties in *Dothard* and *Criswell,* those third parties were indispensable to the particular business at issue. In *Dothard,* the third parties were the inmates; in *Criswell,* the third parties were the passengers on the plane. We stressed that in order to qualify as a BFOQ, a job qualification must relate to the " 'essence,' " or to the "central mission of the employer's business."

JUSTICE WHITE ignores the "essence of the business" test and so concludes that "protecting fetal safety while carrying out the duties of battery manufacturing is as much a legitimate concern as is safety to third parties in guarding prisons (*Dothard*) or flying airplanes (*Criswell*)." By limiting his discussion to cost and safety concerns and rejecting the "essence of the business" test that our case law has established, he seeks to expand what is now the narrow BFOQ defense. Third-party safety considerations properly entered into the BFOQ analysis in *Dothard* and *Criswell* because they went to the core of the employee's job performance. Moreover, that performance involved the central purpose of the enterprise. Justice WHITE attempts to transform this case into one of customer safety. The unconceived fetuses of Johnson Controls' female employees, however, are neither customers nor third parties whose safety is essential to the business of battery manufacturing. No one can disregard the possibility of injury to future children; the BFOQ, however, is not so broad that it transforms this deep social concern into an essential aspect of battery making.

Our case law, therefore, makes clear that the safety exception is limited to instances in which sex or pregnancy actually interferes with the employee's ability to perform the job. This approach is consistent with the language of the BFOQ provision itself, for it suggests that permissible distinctions based on sex must relate to ability to perform the duties of the job. Johnson Controls suggests, however, that we expand the exception to allow fetal-protection policies that mandate particular standards for pregnant or fertile women. We decline to do so. Such an expansion contradicts not only the language of the BFOQ and the narrowness of its exception, but also the plain language and history of the PDA.

The PDA's amendment to Title VII contains a BFOQ standard of its own: Unless pregnant employees differ from others "in their ability or inability to work," they must be "treated the same" as other employees "for all employment-related purposes." This language clearly sets forth Congress' remedy for discrimination on the basis of pregnancy and potential pregnancy. Women who are either pregnant or potentially pregnant must be treated like others "similar in their ability ... to work. In other words, women as capable of doing their jobs as their male counterparts may not be forced to choose between having a child and having a job.

* * *

The legislative history confirms what the language of the PDA compels. Both the House and Senate Reports accompanying the legislation indicate that this statutory standard was chosen to protect female workers from being treated differently from other employees simply because of their capacity to bear children.

* * *

This history counsels against expanding the BFOQ to allow fetal-protection policies. The Senate Report * * * states that employers may not require a pregnant woman to stop working at any time during her pregnancy unless she is unable to do her work. Employment late in pregnancy often imposes risks on the unborn child, but Congress indicated that the employer may take into account only the woman's ability to get her job done. With the PDA, Congress made clear that the decision to become pregnant or to work while being either pregnant or capable of becoming pregnant was reserved for each individual woman to make for herself.

* * * We reiterate our holdings in *Criswell* and *Dothard* that an employer must direct its concerns about a woman's ability to perform her job safely and efficiently to those aspects of the woman's job-related activities that fall within the "essence" of the particular business.[4]

Nor can concerns about the welfare of the next generation be considered a part of the "essence" of Johnson Controls' business. Judge Easterbrook in this case pertinently observed: "It is word play to say that 'the job' at Johnson [Controls] is to make batteries without risk to fetuses in the same way 'the job' at Western Air Lines is to fly planes without crashing."

Johnson Controls argues that it must exclude all fertile women because it is impossible to tell which women will become pregnant while working with lead. This argument is somewhat academic in light of our conclusion that the company may not exclude fertile women at all; it perhaps is worth noting, however, that Johnson Controls has shown no "factual basis for believing that all or substantially all women would be unable to perform safely and efficiently the duties of the job involved." Even on this sparse record, it is apparent that Johnson Controls is concerned about only a small minority of women. Of the eight pregnancies reported among

---

4. * * * We have never addressed privacy-based sex discrimination and shall not do so here because the sex-based discrimination at issue today does not involve the privacy interests of Johnson Controls' customers. Nothing in our discussion of the "essence of the business test," however, suggests that sex could not constitute a BFOQ when privacy interests are implicated. See, e.g., Backus v. Baptist Medical Center, 510 F.Supp. 1191 (ED Ark.1981) (essence of obstetrics nurse's business is to provide sensitive care for patient's intimate and private concerns), vacated as moot. We have no difficulty concluding that Johnson Controls cannot establish a BFOQ. Fertile women, as far as appears in the record, participate in the manufacture of batteries as efficiently as anyone else. Johnson Controls' professed moral and ethical concerns about the welfare of the next generation do not suffice to establish a BFOQ of female sterility. Decisions about the welfare of future children must be left to the parents who conceive, bear, support, and raise them rather than to the employers who hire those parents. Congress has mandated this choice through Title VII, as amended by the PDA. Johnson Controls has attempted to exclude women because of their reproductive capacity. Title VII and the PDA simply do not allow a woman's dismissal because of her failure to submit to sterilization.

the female employees, it has not been shown that any of the babies have birth defects or other abnormalities. The record does not reveal the birth rate for Johnson Controls' female workers, but national statistics show that approximately nine percent of all fertile women become pregnant each year. Johnson Controls' fear of prenatal injury, no matter how sincere, does not begin to show that substantially all of its fertile women employees are incapable of doing their jobs.

VI

A word about tort liability and the increased cost of fertile women in the workplace is perhaps necessary. One of the dissenting judges in this case expressed concern about an employer's tort liability and concluded that liability for a potential injury to a fetus is a social cost that Title VII does not require a company to ignore. It is correct to say that Title VII does not prevent the employer from having a conscience. The statute, however, does prevent sex-specific fetal-protection policies. These two aspects of Title VII do not conflict.

More than 40 States currently recognize a right to recover for a prenatal injury based either on negligence or on wrongful death. According to Johnson Controls, however, the company complies with the lead standard developed by OSHA and warns its female employees about the damaging effects of lead. It is worth noting that OSHA gave the problem of lead lengthy consideration and concluded that "there is no basis whatsoever for the claim that women of childbearing age should be excluded from the workplace in order to protect the fetus or the course of pregnancy." Instead, OSHA established a series of mandatory protections which, taken together, "should effectively minimize any risk to the fetus and newborn child." Without negligence, it would be difficult for a court to find liability on the part of the employer. If, under general tort principles, Title VII bans sex-specific fetal-protection policies, the employer fully informs the woman of the risk, and the employer has not acted negligently, the basis for holding an employer liable seems remote at best.

* * *

If state tort law furthers discrimination in the workplace and prevents employers from hiring women who are capable of manufacturing the product as efficiently as men, then it will impede the accomplishment of Congress' goals in enacting Title VII. Because Johnson Controls has not argued that it faces any costs from tort liability, not to mention crippling ones, the pre-emption question is not before us. We therefore say no more than that the concurrence's speculation appears unfounded as well as premature.

The tort-liability argument reduces to two equally unpersuasive propositions. First, Johnson Controls attempts to solve the problem of reproductive health hazards by resorting to an exclusionary policy. Title VII plainly forbids illegal sex discrimination as a method of diverting attention from an employer's obligation to police the workplace. Second, the specter of an award of damages reflects a fear that hiring fertile women will cost more. The extra cost of employing members of one sex, however, does not provide an affirmative Title VII defense for a discriminatory refusal to hire members of that gender. Indeed, in passing the PDA, Congress considered at length the considerable cost of providing equal treatment of pregnancy and related conditions, but made the "decision to forbid special treatment of pregnancy despite the social costs associated therewith."

We, of course, are not presented with, nor do we decide, a case in which costs would be so prohibitive as to threaten the survival of the employer's business. We merely reiterate our prior holdings that the incremental cost of hiring women cannot justify discriminating against them.

* * *

The judgment of the Court of Appeals is reversed, and the case is remanded for further proceedings consistent with this opinion.

[The opinion of JUSTICE WHITE, joined by CHIEF JUSTICE REHNQUIST and JUSTICE KENNEDY, concurring in part and concurring in the judgment, and the opinion of JUSTICE SCALIA concurring in the judgment are omitted.]

WESTERN AIR LINES v. CRISWELL

Supreme Court of the United States, 1985
472 U.S. 400, 105 S.Ct. 2743, 86 L.Ed.2d 321

JUSTICE STEVENS delivered the opinion of the Court.

The petitioner, Western Air Lines, Inc., requires that its flight engineers retire at age 60. Although the Age Discrimination in Employment Act of 1967 (ADEA), generally prohibits mandatory retirement, * * * the Act provides an exception "where age is a bona fide occupational qualification [BFOQ] reasonably necessary to the normal operation of the particular business." A jury concluded that Western's mandatory retirement rule did not qualify as a BFOQ even though it purportedly was adopted for safety reasons. The question here is whether the jury was properly instructed on the elements of the BFOQ defense.[2]

I

In its commercial airline operations, * * * aircraft require three crew members in the cockpit: a captain, a first officer, and a flight engineer. "The 'captain' is the pilot and controls the aircraft. He is responsible for

---

2. In *Trans World Airlines, Inc. v. Thurston*, 469 U.S. 111, 105 S.Ct. 613, 83 L.Ed.2d 523 (1985), decided earlier this Term, TWA allowed flight engineers to continue working past age 60, and allowed pilots to downbid to flight engineer positions provided that they were able to find an open position prior to their 60th birthdays. Pilots who were displaced for any reason besides the Federal Aviation Administration's age–60 rule, however, were permitted to "bump" less senior persons occupying flight engineer positions without waiting for vacancies to occur. We held that this transfer policy discriminated among pilots on the basis of age, and violated the ADEA. Since TWA did not impose an under–age–60 qualification for flight engineers, however, it had no occasion to rely on the same BFOQ theory presented here by Western.

all phases of its operation. The 'first officer' is the copilot and assists the captain. The 'flight engineer' usually monitors a side-facing instrument panel. He does not operate the flight controls unless the captain and the first officer become incapacitated."

A regulation of the Federal Aviation Administration (FAA) prohibits any person from serving as a pilot or first officer on a commercial flight "if that person has reached his 60th birthday." 14 CFR § 121.383(c) (1985). The FAA has justified the retention of mandatory retirement for pilots on the theory that "incapacitating medical events" and "adverse psychological, emotional, and physical changes" occur as a consequence of aging. "The inability to detect or predict with precision an individual's risk of sudden or subtle incapacitation, in the face of known age-related risks, counsels against relaxation of the rule."

At the same time, the FAA has refused to establish a mandatory retirement age for flight engineers. "While a flight engineer has important duties which contribute to the safe operation of the airplane, he or she may not assume the responsibilities of the pilot in command." Moreover, available statistics establish that flight engineers have rarely been a contributing cause or factor in commercial aircraft "accidents" or "incidents."

In 1978, respondents Criswell and Starley were captains operating DC–10 * * * [aircraft for] Western. Both men celebrated their 60th birthdays in July 1978. Under the collective-bargaining agreement in effect between Western and the union, cockpit crew members could obtain open positions by bidding in order of seniority. In order to avoid mandatory retirement under the FAA's under–age–60 rule for pilots, Criswell and Starley applied for reassignment as flight engineers. Western denied both requests, ostensibly on the ground that both employees were members of the company's retirement plan which required all crew members to retire at age 60. For the same reason, respondent Ron, a career flight engineer, was also retired in 1978 after his 60th birthday.

* * * As originally enacted in 1967, the Act provided an exception to its general proscription of age discrimination for any actions undertaken "to observe the terms of a ... bona fide employee benefit plan such as a retirement, pension, or insurance plan, which is not a subterfuge to evade the purposes of this Act." In April 1978, however, Congress amended the statute to prohibit employee benefit plans from requiring the involuntary retirement of any employee because of age.

Criswell, Starley, and Ron brought this action against Western contending that the under–age–60 qualification for the position of flight engineer violated the ADEA. In the District Court, Western defended, in part, on the theory that the age–60 rule is a BFOQ "reasonably necessary" to the safe operation of the airline. * * *

As the District Court summarized, the evidence at trial established that the flight engineer's "normal duties are less critical to the safety of flight than those of a pilot." The flight engineer, however, does have critical functions in emergency situations and, of course, might cause considerable disruption in the event of his own medical emergency.

The actual capabilities of persons over age 60, and the ability to detect disease or a precipitous decline in their faculties, were the subject of conflicting medical testimony. Western's expert witness, a former FAA Deputy Federal Air Surgeon, was especially concerned about the possibility of a "cardiovascular event" such as a heart attack. He testified that "with advancing age the likelihood of onset of disease increases and that in persons over age 60 it could not be predicted whether and when such diseases would occur."

The plaintiffs' experts, on the other hand, testified that physiological deterioration is caused by disease, not aging, and that "it was feasible to determine on the basis of individual medical examinations whether flight deck crew members, including those over age 60, were physically qualified to continue to fly." These conclusions were corroborated by the nonmedical evidence:

> "The record also reveals that both the FAA and the airlines have been able to deal with the health problems of pilots on an individualized basis. Pilots who have been grounded because of alcoholism or cardiovascular disease have been recertified by the FAA and allowed to resume flying. Pilots who were unable to pass the necessary examination to maintain their FAA first class medical certificates, but who continued to qualify for second class medical certificates were allowed to 'down-grade' from pilot to [flight engineer]. There is nothing in the record to indicate that these flight deck crew members are physically better able to perform their duties than flight engineers over age 60 who have not experienced such events or that they are less likely to become incapacitated.".

Moreover, several large commercial airlines have flight engineers over age 60 "flying the line" without any reduction in their safety record.

The jury was instructed that the "BFOQ defense is available only if it is reasonably necessary to the normal operation or essence of defendant's business." The jury was informed that "the essence of Western's business is the safe transportation of their passengers." The jury was also instructed:

"One method by which defendant Western may establish a BFOQ in this case is to prove:

> "(1) That in 1978, when these plaintiffs were retired, it was highly impractical for Western to deal with each second officer over age 60 on an individualized basis to determine his particular ability to perform his job safely; and

> "(2) That some second officers over age 60 possess traits of a physiological, psychological or other nature which preclude safe and efficient job performance that cannot be ascertained by means other than knowing their age.

"In evaluating the practicability to defendant Western of dealing with second officers over age 60 on an individualized basis, with respect to the medical testimony, you should consider the state of the medical art as it existed in July 1978."

The jury rendered a verdict for the plaintiffs, and awarded damages.

* * * [T]he Court of Appeals rejected Western's contention that the instruction on the BFOQ defense was insufficiently deferential to the airline's legitimate concern for the safety of its passengers. We granted certiorari to consider the merits of this question.

II

* * *

Shortly after the passage of the Act, the Secretary of Labor, who was at that time charged with its enforcement, adopted regulations declaring that the BFOQ exception to the ADEA has only "limited scope and application" and "must be construed narrowly." The Equal Employment Opportunity Commission (EEOC) adopted the same narrow construction of the BFOQ exception after it was assigned authority for enforcing the statute. The restrictive language of the statute and the consistent interpretation of the administrative agencies charged with enforcing the statute convince us that, like its Title VII counterpart, the BFOQ exception "was in fact meant to be an extremely narrow exception to the general prohibition" of age discrimination contained in the ADEA.

III

In *Usery v. Tamiami Trail Tours, Inc.*, 531 F.2d 224 (1976), the Court of Appeals for the Fifth Circuit was called upon to evaluate the merits of a BFOQ defense to a claim of age discrimination. Tamiami Trail Tours, Inc., had a policy of refusing to hire persons over–age–40 as intercity bus drivers. At trial, the bus company introduced testimony supporting its theory that the hiring policy was a BFOQ based upon safety considerations-the need to employ persons who have a low risk of accidents. In evaluating this contention, the Court of Appeals drew on its Title VII precedents, and concluded that two inquiries were relevant.

First, the court recognized that some job qualifications may be so peripheral to the central mission of the employer's business that *no* age discrimination can be "reasonably *necessary* to the normal operation of the particular business."[18] The bus company justified the age qualification for

---

18. *Diaz v. Pan American World Airways, Inc.*, 442 F.2d 385 (CA5 1971), provided authority for this proposition. In *Diaz* the court had rejected Pan American's claim that a female-only qualification for the position of in-flight cabin attendant was a BFOQ under Title VII. The District Court had upheld the qualification as a BFOQ finding that the airline's passengers preferred the "pleasant environment" and the "cosmetic effect" provided by female attendants, and that most men were unable to perform effectively the "non-mechanical functions" of the job. The Court of Appeals rejected the BFOQ defense concluding that these considerations "are tangential to the essence of the business involved."

"[T]he job qualifications which the employer invokes to justify his discrimination must be *reasonably necessary* to the essence of his business-here, the *safe* transportation of bus passengers

hiring its drivers on safety considerations, but the court concluded that this claim was to be evaluated under an objective standard.

This inquiry "adjusts to the safety factor" by ensuring that the employer's restrictive job qualifications are "reasonably necessary" to further the overriding interest in public safety. In *Tamiami,* the court noted that no one had seriously challenged the bus company's safety justification for hiring drivers with a low risk of having accidents.

Second, the court recognized that the ADEA requires that age qualifications be something more than "convenient" or "reasonable"; they must be "reasonably necessary . . . to the particular business," and this is only so when the employer is compelled to rely on age as a proxy for the safety-related job qualifications validated in the first inquiry.[19] This showing could be made in two ways. The employer could establish that it " 'had reasonable cause to believe, that is, a factual basis for believing, that all or substantially all [persons over the age qualifications] would be unable to perform safely and efficiently the duties of the job involved.' " In *Tamiami,* the employer did not seek to justify its hiring qualification under this standard.

Alternatively, the employer could establish that age was a legitimate proxy for the safety-related job qualifications by proving that it is " 'impossible or highly impractical' " to deal with the older employees on an individualized basis. "One method by which the employer can carry this burden is to establish that some members of the discriminated-against class possess a trait precluding safe and efficient job performance that cannot be ascertained by means other than knowledge of the applicant's membership in the class." In *Tamiami,* the medical evidence on this point was conflicting, but the District Court had found that individual examinations could not determine which individuals over the age of 40 would be unable to operate the buses safely. The Court of Appeals found that this finding of fact was not "clearly erroneous," and affirmed the District Court's judgment for the bus company on the BFOQ defense.

* * *

Considering the narrow language of the BFOQ exception, the parallel treatment of such questions under Title VII, and the uniform application of the standard by the federal courts, the EEOC, and Congress, we conclude that this two-part inquiry properly identifies the relevant consid-

---

from one point to another. The greater the safety factor, measured by the likelihood of harm and the probable severity of that harm in case of an accident, the more stringent may be the job qualifications designed to insure safe driving."

19. *Weeks v. Southern Bell Telephone & Telegraph Co.,* 408 F.2d 228 (CA5 1969), provided authority for this proposition. In *Weeks* the court rejected Southern Bell's claim that a male-only qualification for the position of switchman was a BFOQ under Title VII. Southern Bell argued, and the District Court had found, that the job was "strenuous," but the court observed that that "finding is extremely vague." The court rejected the BFOQ defense concluding that "using these class stereotypes denies desirable positions to a great many women perfectly capable of performing the duties involved." Moreover, the employer had made no showing that it was "impossible or highly impractical to deal with women on an individualized basis."

erations for resolving a BFOQ defense to an age-based qualification purportedly justified by considerations of safety. * * *

IV

* * *

Reasonably Necessary Job Qualifications

Western relied on two different kinds of job qualifications to justify its mandatory retirement policy. First, it argued that flight engineers should have a low risk of incapacitation or psychological and physiological deterioration. At this vague level of analysis respondents have not seriously disputed—nor could they—that the qualification of good health for a vital crew member is reasonably necessary to the essence of the airline's operations. Instead, they have argued that age is not a necessary proxy for that qualification.

On a more specific level, Western argues that flight engineers must meet the same stringent qualifications as pilots, and that it was therefore quite logical to extend to flight engineers the FAA's age–60 retirement rule for pilots. Although the FAA's rule for pilots, adopted for safety reasons, is relevant evidence in the airline's BFOQ defense, it is not to be accorded conclusive weight. * * * In this case, the evidence clearly established that the FAA, Western, and other airlines all recognized that the qualifications for a flight engineer were less rigorous than those required for a pilot.

In the absence of persuasive evidence supporting its position, Western nevertheless argues that the jury should have been instructed to defer to "Western's selection of job qualifications for the position of [flight engineer] that are reasonable in light of the safety risks." This proposal is plainly at odds with Congress' decision, in adopting the ADEA, to subject such management decisions to a test of objective justification in a court of law. The BFOQ standard adopted in the statute is one of "reasonable necessity," not reasonableness.

In adopting that standard, Congress did not ignore the public interest in safety. That interest is adequately reflected in instructions that track the language of the statute. When an employer establishes that a job qualification has been carefully formulated to respond to documented concerns for public safety, it will not be overly burdensome to persuade a trier of fact that the qualification is "reasonably necessary" to safe operation of the business. The uncertainty implicit in the concept of managing safety risks always makes it "reasonably necessary" to err on the side of caution in a close case. The employer cannot be expected to establish the risk of an airline accident "to a certainty, for certainty would require running the risk until a tragic accident would prove that the judgment was sound." When the employer's argument has a credible basis in the record, it is difficult to believe that a jury of laypersons—many of whom no doubt have flown or could expect to fly on commercial air carriers—would not defer in a close case to the airline's judgment. Since the instructions in this case would not have prevented the airline from raising this contention to the jury in closing argument, we are satisfied that the verdict is a consequence of a defect in Western's proof rather than a defect in the trial court's instructions.

* * *

Age as a Proxy for Job Qualifications

Western contended below that the ADEA only requires that the employer establish "a rational basis in fact" for believing that identification of those persons lacking suitable qualifications cannot occur on an individualized basis. This "rational basis in fact" standard would have been tantamount to an instruction to return a verdict in the defendant's favor. Because that standard conveys a meaning that is significantly different from that conveyed by the statutory phrase "reasonably necessary," it was correctly rejected by the trial court.

* * * Congress expressly decided that problems involving age discrimination in employment should be resolved on a "case-by-case basis" * * *.

The "rational basis" standard is also inconsistent with the preference for individual evaluation expressed in the language and legislative history of the ADEA. * * *

The judgment of the Court of Appeals is *Affirmed.*

NOTES

1. Federal flight aviation regulations noted in the principal case set the ages of pilots and flight controllers and provide a defense to claims under the ADEA, avoiding in such cases any BFOQ issue. *Starr v. FAA,* 589 F.2d 307 (7th Cir. 1978). In 1996 ADEA amendments permit state and local governments to set hiring and retirement ages for public safety officers, including those who have law enforcement and fire fighting duties by establishing regular evaluations of fitness.

2. The Americans With Disabilities Act has no bona fide occupational qualification defense. However, to be protected against discrimination based on an impairment, the ADA requires that the individual be "qualified" to perform essential job duties. "The term 'qualification standards' may include a requirement that an individual shall not pose a direct threat to the health or safety of other individuals in the workplace." 29 U.S.C.A. 12113(b). See p. 153 *infra.*

HENRY v. MILWAUKEE COUNTY

United States Court of Appeals, Seventh Circuit, 2008
539 F.3d 573

RIPPLE, CIRCUIT JUDGE.

In 1997, Milwaukee County's Juvenile Detention Center instituted a policy that required each unit of the facility to be staffed at all times by at least one officer of the same sex as the detainees housed on that unit. Because there were far more male units than female units at the facility, this policy had the effect of reducing the number of shifts available for female officers. Ersol Henry and Terri Lewis, both female officers at the facility, brought this action * * * alleging sex discrimination and retaliation in violation of Title VII, * * *

I

BACKGROUND

A

At the time relevant to this appeal, Ersol Henry and Terri Lewis were employed as Juvenile Corrections Officers ("JCOs") at the Milwaukee County Juvenile Detention Center ("JDC"). The JDC, part of the Wisconsin State Juvenile Justice System, is a detention facility designed to house temporarily juveniles awaiting juvenile court proceedings.

* * *

Most juveniles at the JDC are detained there for only a short period of time. The average length of stay is ten days, although for those juveniles awaiting their initial court appearances, the average stay is approximately three weeks. Juveniles often are detained for as little as one day. Occasionally, a juvenile may be detained there for as long as one year.

* * * A new, non-linear juvenile detention facility was completed in April 1996. The new JDC contains common rooms, classrooms and recreation rooms where the juveniles spend the majority of their daytime hours. At night, however, the juveniles are confined to their living areas, which are assigned based on their sex, age and classification.

The living areas at the new facility are organized into seven single-sex "pods." Each can accommodate between 11 and 22 juveniles of the same sex.[1] Each pod consists of a number of individual cells, a control center desk from which the staff can monitor the cells and communicate with the pod via intercom, and a common area or "day room" with tables, chairs and a television. The individual cells each contain a bed, a toilet, a desk and a small storage area. The entire cell, including the toilet, is visible from the outside through a window in the cell door.

The juveniles are monitored at all times by JCOs. During the first (morning) and second (evening) shifts, two JCOs are assigned to supervise each pod. During the third (night) shift, when the juveniles are locked inside their cells and generally are asleep, only one JCO is assigned to monitor each pod. In addition to the JCOs assigned to pods, the JDC also has a male and a female "runner" on duty at all times. The runner is a JCO who is responsible for performing the intake procedures for newly-admitted juveniles, including any necessary pat-downs and supervision of

---

1. One pod at the JDC was reserved for females. The other six pods housed male juveniles.

showering during the night hours.[2] Another staff member monitors the central control center at all times.

The advent of the new facility provided an opportunity * * * to shift the JDC's method of supervision from an indirect model to a direct model and to encourage JCOs to have greater interaction with the juveniles they monitored. Accordingly, in 1997 * * * a new role model/mentoring program [was instituted] at the JDC. The staff, including the JCOs, received basic training in mentoring, role modeling and child development in order to equip them to interact more effectively with the juveniles. * * * [F]urtherance of this program required that a staff member of the same sex be available on each pod at all times throughout the day and night to mentor the juveniles.[3]

Prior to the move to the new facility, JCOs had been assigned to shifts without regard to the sex of the officer. [The] * * * new policy, however, required that each pod be staffed at all times by at least one JCO of the same sex as the juveniles housed on the pod. During the day shifts, when two JCOs staffed each pod, one of the two JCOs could be of the opposite sex; however, during the night shifts, when only one JCO staffed each pod, the sole JCO on duty had to be of the same sex as the juveniles in the pod. Because the JDC housed far more male juveniles than female juveniles,[4] [the]. * * * same-sex role model mentoring policy afforded male JCOs more opportunities for work than those available to female JCOs. The night shift was particularly problematic. It was perceived as the easiest shift; those officers assigned to it received premium pay; and it afforded the most opportunities for overtime.

During the time of their employment as JCOs, Ms. Henry and Ms. Lewis primarily worked one of the day shifts. Prior to 1997, however, they each had earned a substantial amount of additional income from voluntary overtime, predominantly by working the night shift. According to a collective bargaining agreement, voluntary overtime at the JDC traditionally had been apportioned according to seniority. Employees with the most seniority could "put in" for overtime, and they would receive the first opportunities to work their preferred shifts. Ms. Lewis and Ms. Henry were relatively senior employees, and they often were able to work overtime at the old JDC.

After * * * the same-sex pod policy [was instituted], however, far fewer women were allowed to work the third shift because there were far fewer female pods than male pods at the facility. As a result of the same-sex role model/mentoring program, most of the available night shifts with premi-

---

2. Other than these newly-admitted juveniles, all regular showering takes place on the second shift.

3. Although the juveniles generally are confined to their cells at night, cell occupants can, and occasionally do, talk with JCOs through their doors. Staff members are permitted to speak with the juveniles through their doors at night; however, they are not permitted to enter the individual cells at night except in an emergency. If they do enter the cells at night, an alarm will sound.

4. The ratio of male detainees to female detainees at the JDC was between 4:1 and 6:1 during the relevant time period. Six of the pods at the new JDC were reserved for males; one was reserved for females.

um pay were reserved for male employees. Female officers like Ms. Henry and Ms. Lewis no longer were able to get the same number of overtime hours as they previously had received. Instead, male employees with less seniority were allowed to work these shifts. Consequently, Ms. Henry and Ms. Lewis received significantly less compensation than they had received prior to the institution of the same-sex role model/mentoring program.

B

* * *

After a three-day bench trial, the district court concluded that the same-sex staffing policy on the third shift was a BFOQ. It found that "[t]he essence of the JDC's business is to ensure and promote the care, rehabilitation, safety and security of the juveniles entrusted to its care." * * * [I]t then concluded that "same gender role modeling furthers the twin goals of rehabilitation and security in the juvenile detention setting," and that "[s]ame gender shift assignments serve to protect the privacy interests of the juvenile detainees." Finally, relying on general studies that heterosexual assaults are statistically more likely than homosexual assaults, the court found that "[s]ame gender shift assignments also serve the goals of risk management and security." In the district court's view, the "alternative to protecting against this risk ... is to hire an additional staff member for each pod on third shift at an approximate cost of $750,000 per year." Accordingly, it found that gender was a BFOQ for JCOs working the third shift; therefore, the sex-based shift assignments did not violate the anti-discrimination provisions of Title VII.

* * *

Ms. Henry and Ms. Lewis timely appealed.

II

DISCUSSION

A

The Supreme Court has cautioned that the BFOQ defense is written narrowly and is to be read narrowly. It has made clear that the defense is "meant to be an extremely narrow exception to the general prohibition of discrimination on the basis of sex," * * * that "discrimination based on sex is valid only when the *essence* of the business operation would be undermined."

Employers bear the burden of establishing the affirmative defense that a particular qualification is a BFOQ. *Everson v. Mich. Dep't of Corr.*, 391 F.3d 737, 748 (6th Cir.2004). Employers also bear the burden of proving that they could not rearrange job responsibilities or otherwise eliminate the clash between the business necessities and the employment opportunities of female officers. *Torres v. Wis. Dept. of Health & Social Servs.*, 838 F.2d 944, 953 n. 6 (7th Cir.1988) (reheard and reversed on other grounds in *Torres*, 859 F.2d 1523).

B

Before the district court, Milwaukee County relied on a series of cases from this and other circuits that examined whether sex could be a BFOQ for officers in adult female correctional facilities. In each of these cases, the court held that the goals of security, safety, privacy and rehabilitation could, in some circumstances, justify sex-based assignments in female prisons. Milwaukee County submits that, like the sex-specific shift assignments in adult female correctional facilities, the sex-specific assignments at issue here should be upheld because they are necessary to protect the juveniles' safety and privacy and to further the facility's rehabilitative goals.

In *Torres,* we determined that the unique circumstances of the female prison at issue required prison administrators to "innovate and experiment." In the course of our decision, we noted that, because prison administrators in general face unusually difficult challenges in dealing with the "perplexing sociological problems of how best to achieve the goals of the penal function in the criminal justice system: to punish justly, to deter future crime, and to return imprisoned persons to society with an improved chance of being useful, law-abiding citizens," prison administrators' decisions must receive some degree of deference. Accordingly, although the decisions of prison officials are not accorded as much deference in Title VII cases as they are in constitutional cases, their decisions "are entitled to substantial weight *when they are the product of a reasoned decision-making process,* based on available information and experience." Milwaukee County contends that, like in *Torres,* the administrators of the JDC were entitled to substantial deference in their decision to implement a sex-specific policy regarding shift assignments. In its view, the goals and circumstances of the juvenile detention context, when compared to the female corrections context, are equally complex and challenging.

We agree that the administrators of juvenile detention facilities, like the administrators of female correctional facilities, are entitled to substantial deference when fashioning policies to further the goals of the facility. We do not agree, however, that the discretion accorded to these individuals in either context is effectively unlimited. A defendant ultimately must introduce sufficient evidence to prove that the administrator's judgment-that a particular sex classification is reasonably necessary to the normal operation of the institution-is "the product of a reasoned decision-making process, based on available information and experience."

The district court concluded that the JDC's policy of assigning shifts according to an employee's sex was based on its administrator's reasonable belief that the policy would "promote" the goals of rehabilitation, security and privacy. All of these functions are, as the district court concluded, essential to the mission of the JDC. However, Title VII's standard is not satisfied simply because a policy *promotes* an essential function of an institution. Although sex-based assignments might be *helpful* in pursuing these goals, in order to satisfy the anti-discrimination strictures of Title VII, Milwaukee County must show that the contested sex classifications are *"reasonably necessary."*

We must conclude that Milwaukee County's contention that sex-based assignments are *reasonably necessary* to achieve these goals, at least on the third shift, is not supported by the record before us. The employer, Milwaukee County, has the burden to demonstrate that it could not rearrange job responsibilities to eliminate or minimize the conflict between the inmates' privacy, security and rehabilitation interests and the employees' rights under Title VII. Although reducing the number of opposite-sex staff on the pods may *help* to promote security, efficient risk management and privacy, Milwaukee County has failed to establish that its policy was *reasonably necessary* for these goals. We address each proffered justification in turn.

The evidence in the record does not support the conclusion that the juveniles' safety or security, or the institution's ability to manage risk effectively, was at all in jeopardy because of the presence of opposite-sex JCOs on the third shift. The district court correctly asserted that heterosexual assaults and misconduct are statistically more likely than homosexual attacks. The record establishes, however, that there has not been a single instance of staff-on-inmate sexual assault at the JDC, on any shift, by either sex; nor has there been a significant problem with false accusations against the staff. Furthermore, other safety precautions, such as door alarms and the presence of supervisors, runners and video cameras, currently are working to prevent actual and alleged security breaches. Although Milwaukee County contends that a staff member may be able to circumvent the alarm system in order to enter a juvenile's cell at night, the record contains no evidence that this contingency has occurred or was likely to occur at the JDC.

More fundamentally, Milwaukee County offered no reasons why the numerous alternatives to same-sex staffing suggested by the plaintiffs at trial, such as improving the alarm system, installing additional cameras, leaving the doors open between the pods at night or increasing the frequency of supervisor patrols, would not have mitigated any concern. Notably, [the superintendent of the facility] testified at trial that he had not investigated the cost of any of these options. He did assert that adding an additional staff member on each of the pods during the third shift would have been prohibitively costly; however, he did not provide any data on this point, and such an augmentation in personnel certainly was not the only option available to minimize the already-minimal risk of staff-on-juvenile sexual assault. The BFOQ defense extends only to those policies that are "reasonably necessary to the normal operation" of the institution. It does not excuse investigation of and reliance upon alternatives that involve minor additional costs or inconveniences.

Milwaukee County's proffered privacy justification is even more difficult to justify on the record before us. The record affirmatively shows that the JDC allowed JCOs of the opposite sex to monitor the pods during both of the daytime shifts. It is undisputed that the vast majority of the time that the juveniles were unclothed occurred during these daytime shifts. Showering generally took place during the second shift, when members of the opposite sex were permitted to staff the pods. The only showering that occurred on the third shift was monitored by one of the runners who performed the intake procedures. The juveniles were provided with pajamas, which they were required to wear at night. They changed into this attire on the second shift, and they changed out of it on the first shift-again, while JCOs of the opposite sex were permitted to view them. Although Milwaukee County presented testimony that third-shift JCOs occasionally viewed juveniles using the toilet, masturbating or otherwise acting out sexually, it is undisputed that this situation occurred on the first and second shifts as well.

This situation is therefore very different from cases such as *Torres*, and *Everson* which involved the presence of male guards in the housing units of all-female prisons. In *Torres*, we held that the superintendent reasonably made a "professional judgment that giving women prisoners a living environment free from the presence of males in a position of authority was necessary to foster the goal of rehabilitation." In *Everson*, the court determined that, "given the endemic problem of sexual abuse in Michigan's female facilities" and other unique circumstances, the presence of male guards, at any time, in the housing units was a threat to "the security of the prison, the safety of inmates and the protection of the privacy rights of inmates," In *Everson* and *Torres*, prison officials permitted no officers of the opposite sex to guard the living units at any time because the specific needs of the institutions and the prisoners housed in those institutions reasonably required such a policy. The same-sex policy was aimed at a specific condition and was tailored to address that specific condition. The plans were quite clearly "the product of a reasoned decision-making process, based on available information and experience." Here, by contrast, we are faced with the fact that the JDC allowed JCOs of the opposite sex to guard the juveniles during those times when the privacy interests of the juveniles were most in jeopardy. Under these circumstances, we cannot say that, with respect to privacy concerns, the same-sex policy is the product of the same sort of comprehensive professional decision-making as exhibited in *Torres* and *Everson*. The inconsistencies in implementation cast a significant doubt on whether the policy is reasonably necessary to achieve the institution's goal of protecting the privacy interests of the juveniles. Therefore, on this factor as well, the record reveals a failure of proof on the part of Milwaukee County.

The County also contends that same-sex staffing on the third shift is necessary to further the JDC's mission of rehabilitation. Contrary to the submission of the plaintiffs, we have no doubt that the County is correct in stating that this goal is a very important goal of the institution.

The record contains substantial testimony from Mr. Wanta on this factor. He described the basis for his determination that a role model/mentoring policy was necessary to the JDC's rehabilitative efforts. He noted that, in formulating the policy, he had relied upon his own experience with juvenile corrections, information learned from his attendance at various seminars and committee meetings, his interviews with the juveniles and staff at the JDC, consultations with experts in the field and professional literature supporting such programs. Each of these sources suggested that the direct role modeling/mentoring form of supervision, rather than the indirect form of supervision, was the best available method of providing care and rehabilitation to juveniles in detention facilities. Mr. Wanta, in his professional judgment, concluded that institution of the direct role model/mentoring form of supervision was necessary to achieve the JDC's mission of rehabilitation. The foundation for his belief is well established in the record.

The conclusion that the effectiveness of these role model/mentoring programs requires the presence of at least one staff member of the same sex as the juveniles in each pod *at all times,* however, does not find the same strong foundation in the record. Mr. Wanta expressed his belief that same-sex role model/mentoring was more effective than cross-gender programs. He testified that, in formulating this view, he relied upon his own personal experiences, as well as literature on mentoring programs, which "indicate that gender mentoring improves the chances of child behavior changes being positive." He continued: "[A]ll the statistics and the research that I have seen indicates that a male mentoring a male, and a female mentoring a female, exponentially increases the chance of success than would cross-gender . . . mentoring."

* * *

We are well aware that the professionals who have the great responsibility for running penal institutions need to innovate and experiment if they are to succeed in resolving the crisis in this important area of governance. Indeed, we already have recognized that the inability to proffer solid empirical evidence in support of a particular policy certainly is not fatal to a BFOQ defense. Even if we defer to Mr. Wanta's judgment that a mentoring program is important to the success of juvenile institutions such as the one he manages, and even if we defer to his judgment with respect to the need for same-sex mentoring of juveniles in such an environment, we still must be satisfied in the present litigation that these professional judgments require a rigid rule that such a same-sex mentoring program reasonably necessitates the presence of a JCO of the same sex *at all times.* Milwaukee County had the responsibility to introduce sufficient evidence in the record to support the conclusion that such same-sex presence *at all times* was reasonably necessary to meet the institution's essential goals. Here, the record, although perhaps demonstrating the worth of a mentoring program and the usefulness of mentors of the same sex, does not present a sufficiently strong case with respect to the need for the presence of those mentors seven days a week and twenty-four hours a day.

At trial, Mr. Wanta explained how the JCOs were to act as role models and mentors at the JDC.

JCOs were not trained or expected to act as counselors; if any serious counseling was necessary, the JCOs were instructed to refer the juvenile to an on-site nurse trained in mental health. Instead, the JCOs carried out their role model/mentoring responsibilities by providing the juveniles with a constant model of proper behavior in their interactions with others.

Given this description of the role of JCOs in the mentoring program, we must conclude that the record does not respond to the question of why a JCO of the same sex is reasonably necessary during the night shift. According to the record, the opportunity for the JCO to interact with the juveniles on the third shift is very minimal. The third shift begins after the juveniles are locked down for the night, and the JCOs on third shift were instructed to encourage them to sleep. Although there was testimony at trial that staff occasionally spoke with juveniles through their doors at night, particularly when they were ill or acting out and it was necessary to calm them down, this interaction was kept to a minimum. There is no evidence that the JCOs ever spoke with the juveniles about confidential counseling matters at night. Indeed, because the other juveniles in the pod would have been able to hear any conversations that occurred, the JCOs testified at trial that they were encouraged to avoid these types of discussions on the third shift.

The County provided no reasons why opposite-sex JCOs were incapable of appropriately interacting with these juveniles to the extent necessary to provide a good behavioral role model on the third shift. Mr. Wanta's assertion that ''consistency'' in the same-sex mentoring program requires the presence of someone of the same sex within each pod at all times is simply not justified by the record. Furthermore, the County failed to provide evidence that the many non-discriminatory alternatives proffered by the plaintiffs would have been intolerable here. The plaintiffs questioned Mr. Wanta about numerous other possibilities for encouraging rehabilitation through the availability of same-sex staff, such as hiring more JCOs for the third shift, leaving the doors between pods open or increasing the frequency of supervisor rotations. They also noted that numerous other mechanisms to encourage rehabilitation already were in place at the facility, including educational programs, counselors, guest speakers, community mentors and other programs available to facilitate the JDC's mission. The County failed to explain why the presence of a same-sex JCO within each pod during the hours that the juveniles were sleeping was reasonably necessary to its rehabilitative efforts.

Accordingly, we must conclude that the County failed to meet its burden to prove that the sex-based classification at issue here was reasonably necessary for the rehabilitation, security or privacy functions of the JDC. Therefore, Milwaukee's BFOQ defense must fail. The JDC's third shift policy adversely affected the plaintiffs' employment. It is undisputed that overtime pay had been a significant and expected component of the plaintiffs' compensation prior to the institution of the sex-based policy. Not only did the majority of overtime work available occur on the third shift, but the third shift also offered a fifty cent per hour pay premium. Accordingly, the dramatic reduction in the opportunity for women to work on the third shift constituted an adverse employment action. See Lewis v. City of Chicago, 496 F.3d 645, 653–54 (7th Cir.2007) (holding that the denial of the opportunity for overtime pay, when that pay is a significant and recurring part of an employee's total earnings, can constitute an adverse employment action). Because the JDC's third-shift policy adversely affected the plaintiffs' employment opportunities, we must conclude that it is in violation of Title VII.

* * *

NOTES

1. *Customer preference:* **Diaz v. Pan American Airways**, 442 F.2d 385 (5th Cir. 1971), held that simply because male airline passengers may prefer female flight attendants did not justify refusing to hire male flight attendants. Such alleged customer preference for female workers did not go to the worker's ability to safely transport passengers. Any "soothing" effect female attendants might have on passengers was held not an "essential" element of the job.

2. *Marketing strategy:* **Wilson v. Southwest Airlines Co.**, 517 F.Supp. 292 (N.D.Tex. 1981), involved an airline that had adopted a "sexiness" marketing strategy designed to attract the male business traveler. Pursuant to that strategy, the airline refused to employ male flight attendants. Held: the female sex was not a BFOQ in that sex did not go to the "essence" of an airline's business of flying passengers.

3. *Authenticity or customer preference?* The legislative history of Title VII noted "authenticity" as an example of a BFOQ. For example, the female sex to model female clothing, or the male sex to play certain dramatic roles, or even allowing French to be a bona fide occupational qualification for food service personnel in a French restaurant, 29 C.F.R. § 1604.2 and 110 Cong. Rec. 7213. The so-called "Hooter's Defense" that relied upon the authenticity theme to justify hiring only young, attractive female wait persons in a restaurant/bar that relied upon a male-dominated clientele was expanded in *EEOC v. Joe's Stone Crab, Inc.*, 220 F.3d 1263 (11th Cir. 2000), to hold that a seafood restaurant attempting to create an "old world atmosphere" was justified in hiring only male waiters.

4. *Customs of foreign nations:* Employers may be confronted with "customers" from other nations who, based on their customs or traditions, resist dealing with females or persons of certain religions. This is but another form of "customer preference" that will not generally constitute a bona fide occupational qualification, particularly for business transacted in the United States. *Fernandez v. Wynn Oil Co.*, 653 F.2d 1273 (9th Cir. 1981). Occasionally, concern for the safety of the employee must be confronted. But as the principal cases hold, concern for the safety of the employee does not in itself justify denying persons of that class the employment opportunity. *Abrams v.*

Baylor College of Medicine, 805 F.2d 528 (5th Cir. 1986). Nonetheless, where the laws of the foreign nation would preclude such contact in that country or local "customs" would endanger the safety of the employee working there because of their sex or religion to the point that the employee would be unable to perform job duties, such foreign laws or "customs" can make sex or religion a bona fide occupational qualification. *Kern v. Dynalectron* Corp., 577 F.Supp. 1196 (N.D.Tex. 1983), *aff,* 746 F.2d 810 (5th Cir. 1984).

5. *Adjustments and Accommodations:* Consider an airline with a rule that removes from flight crew duties pilots, first officers, and cabin attendants upon their fourth month of pregnancy. First, would non-pregnancy be a BFOQ for such jobs? Yes! *See, Burwell v. Eastern Air Lines, Inc.,* 633 F.2d 361 (4th Cir. 1980). Second, if non-pregnancy is a BFOQ for the particular job, would a reasonable adjustment require the employer to reassign the pregnant employee to alternative ground duty positions, such as mechanic, desk agent, or a telephone service representative? No! Necessary adjustments do not require re-assignment of the worker to an entirely different job. *Levin v. Delta Air Lines,* 730 F.2d 994 (5th Cir. 1984).

6. *Race:* Title VII does *not* include "race" or "color" as a basis for a bona fide occupational qualification. This textual omission appears to have been conscious and based on an assumption that there are no circumstances where use of race is "necessary." *See, **Johnson v. California,*** 543 U.S. 499, 125 S.Ct. 1141, 160 L.Ed.2d 949 (2005) (segregation by race of prisoners in a penitentiary is not necessary and thus violates 14th Amendment). Thus, as the principal case notes, "privacy" concerns of patients in a nursing home who object to care-givers of a different sex may create a BFOQ, but objection by patients to black health care providers could not justify segregation of black workers. *Chaney v. Plainfield Healthcare Ctr.,* 612 F.3d 908 (7th Cir. 2010).

7. *Language:* Requiring workers to be able to speak English may be a form of national origin discrimination. Nonetheless, fluency in English will be "reasonably necessary" in most jobs to the level that workers can effectively communicate with English speaking supervisors, customers, and fellow workers. Similarly, discrimination based on one speaking with an understandable, but "foreign," accent is "national origin" discrimination. (*Rodreiguez, supra page 42*). *Fragante v. City & County of Honolulu,* 888 F.2d 591 (9th Cir. 1989). With the possible exception of radio or T.V. announcers, rarely is accentless speech "necessary" to perform essential job functions.

B.   RELIGIONS AND THE "MINISTERIAL EXCEPTION"

HOSANNA-TABOR EVANGELICAL LUTHERAN CHURCH AND SCHOOL v. E.E.O.C.

Supreme Court of the United States
—— U.S. 1783, 131 S.Ct. 1783, 179 L.Ed.2d 653 (2011)

CHIEF JUSTICE ROBERTS delivered the opinion of the Court.

Certain employment discrimination laws authorize employees who have been wrongfully terminated to sue their employers for reinstatement and damages. The question presented is whether the Establishment and Free Exercise Clauses of the First Amendment bar such an action when the employer is a religious group and the employee is one of the group's ministers.

I

A

Petitioner **Hosanna–Tabor** Evangelical Lutheran Church and School is a member congregation of the Lutheran Church–Missouri Synod, the second largest Lutheran denomination in America. **Hosanna–Tabor** operated a small school in Redford, Michigan, offering a "Christ-centered education" to students in kindergarten through eighth grade.

The Synod classifies teachers into two categories: "called" and "lay." "Called" teachers are regarded as having been called to their vocation by God through a congregation. To be eligible to receive a call from a congregation, a teacher must satisfy certain academic requirements. One way of doing so is by completing a "colloquy" program at a Lutheran college or university. The program requires candidates to take eight courses of theological study, obtain the endorsement of their local Synod district, and pass an oral examination by a faculty committee. A teacher who meets these requirements may be called by a congregation. Once called, a teacher receives the formal title "Minister of Religion, Commissioned." A commissioned minister serves for an open-ended term; at **Hosanna–Tabor**, a call could be rescinded only for cause and by a supermajority vote of the congregation.

"Lay" or "contract" teachers, by contrast, are not required to be trained by the Synod or even to be Lutheran. At **Hosanna–Tabor**, they were appointed by the school board, without a vote of the congregation, to one-year renewable terms. Although teachers at the school generally performed the same duties regardless of whether they were lay or called, lay teachers were hired only when called teachers were unavailable.

Respondent Cheryl Perich was first employed by **Hosanna–Tabor** as a lay teacher in 1999. After Perich completed her colloquy later that school year, **Hosanna–Tabor** asked her to become a called teacher. Perich accepted the call and received a "diploma of vocation" designating her a commissioned minister.

Perich taught kindergarten during her first four years at **Hosanna–Tabor** and fourth grade during the 2003–2004 school year. She taught math, language arts, social studies, science, gym, art, and music. She also taught a religion class four days a week, led the students in prayer and devotional exercises each day, and attended a weekly school-wide chapel service. Perich led the chapel service herself about twice a year.

Perich became ill in June 2004 with what was eventually diagnosed as narcolepsy. Symptoms included sudden and deep sleeps from which she could not be roused. Because of her illness, Perich began the 2004–2005 school year on disability leave. On January 27, 2005, however, Perich notified the school principal, Stacey Hoeft, that she would be able to report to work the following month. Hoeft responded that the school had already contracted with a lay teacher to fill Perich's position for the remainder of the school year. Hoeft also expressed concern that Perich was not yet ready to return to the classroom.

On January 30, **Hosanna–Tabor** held a meeting of its congregation at which school administrators stated that Perich was unlikely to be physically capable of returning to work that school year or the next. The congregation voted to offer Perich a "peaceful release" from her call, whereby the congregation would pay a portion of her health insurance premiums in exchange for her resignation as a called teacher. Perich refused to resign and produced a note from her doctor stating that she would be able to return to work on February 22. The school board urged Perich to reconsider, informing her that the school no longer had a position for her, but Perich stood by her decision not to resign.

On the morning of February 22—the first day she was medically cleared to return to work—Perich presented herself at the school. Hoeft asked her to leave but she would not do so until she obtained written documentation that she had reported to work. Later that afternoon, Hoeft called Perich at home and told her that she would likely be fired. Perich responded that she had spoken with an attorney and intended to assert her legal rights.

Following a school board meeting that evening, board chairman Scott Salo sent Perich a letter stating that **Hosanna–Tabor** was reviewing the process for rescinding her call in light of her "regrettable" actions. Salo subsequently followed up with a letter advising Perich that the congregation would consider whether to rescind her call at its next meeting. As grounds for termination, the letter cited Perich's "insubordination and disruptive behavior" on February 22, as well as the damage she had done to her "working relationship" with the school by "threatening to take legal action." The congregation voted to rescind Perich's call on April 10, and **Hosanna–Tabor** sent her a letter of termination the next day.

B

Perich filed a charge with the Equal Employment Opportunity Commission, alleging that her employment had been terminated in violation of the Americans with Disabilities Act. The ADA prohibits an employer from discriminating against a qualified individual on the basis of disability. § 12112(a). It also prohibits an employer from retaliating "against any individual because such individual has opposed any act or practice made unlawful by [the ADA] or because such individual made a charge, testified, assisted, or participated in any manner in an investigation, proceeding, or hearing under [the ADA]." § 12203(a).

The EEOC brought suit against **Hosanna–Tabor**, alleging that Perich had been fired in retaliation for threatening to file an ADA lawsuit. Perich intervened in the litigation, claiming unlawful retaliation under both the ADA and the Michigan Persons with Disabilities Civil Rights Act, Mich. Comp. Laws § 37.1602(a) (1979). The EEOC and Perich sought Perich's reinstatement to her former position (or frontpay in lieu thereof), along with backpay, compensatory and punitive damages, attorney's fees, and other injunctive relief.

* * * The District Court [held] that the suit was barred by the ministerial exception and granted summary judgment in **Hosanna–Tabor**'s favor. * * * The Court of Appeals for the Sixth Circuit vacated and remanded, directing the District Court to proceed to the merits of Perich's retaliation claims. The Court of Appeals recognized the existence of a ministerial exception barring certain employment discrimination claims against religious institutions—an exception "rooted in the First Amendment's guarantees of religious freedom." 597 F.3d 769, 777 (2010). The court concluded, however, that Perich did not qualify as a "minister" under the exception, noting in particular that her duties as a called teacher were identical to her duties as a lay teacher. * * * We granted certiorari.

II

The First Amendment provides, in part, that "Congress shall make no law respecting an establishment of religion, or prohibiting the free exercise thereof." We have said that these two Clauses "often exert conflicting pressures, and that there can be "internal tension ... between the Establishment Clause and the Free Exercise Clause," (plurality opinion). Not so here. Both Religion Clauses bar the government from interfering with the decision of a religious group to fire one of its ministers.

A

Controversy between church and state over religious offices is hardly new. * * * [The Court reviewed history from the Magna Carta (1215), through Tudor England, the Uniformity Act of 1662, and, finally, the American colonial experiences.]

It was against this background that the First Amendment was adopted. Familiar with life under the established Church of England, the founding generation sought to foreclose the possibility of a national church. * * * By forbidding the "establishment of religion" and guaranteeing the "free exercise thereof," the Religion Clauses ensured that the new Federal Government—unlike the English Crown—would have no role in filling ecclesiastical offices. The Establishment Clause prevents the Government from appointing ministers, and the Free Exercise Clause prevents it from interfering with the freedom of religious groups to select their own.

* * * [The Court discussed "two events involving President James Madison, 'the leading architect of the religion clauses of the First Amendment.' " In explaining President Madison's veto of an Act of Congress, Madison stated]:

"The bill enacts into, and establishes by law, sundry rules and proceedings relative purely to the organization and polity of the church incorporated, *and comprehending even the election and removal of the Minister of the same* ; so that no change could be made therein by the particular society, or by the general church of which it is a member, and whose authority it recognises."

* * *

C

Until today, we have not had occasion to consider whether this freedom of a religious organization to select its ministers is implicated by a suit alleging discrimination in employment. The Courts of Appeals, in contrast, have had extensive experience with this issue. Since the passage of Title VII of the Civil Rights Act of 1964, and other employment discrimination laws, the Courts of Appeals have uniformly recognized the existence of a "ministerial exception," grounded in the First Amendment, that precludes application of such legislation to claims concerning the employment relationship between a religious institution and its ministers.

We agree that there is such a ministerial exception. The members of a religious group put their faith in the hands of their ministers. Requiring a church to accept or retain an unwanted minister, or punishing a church for failing to do so, intrudes upon more than a mere employment decision. Such action interferes with the internal governance of the church, depriving the church of control over the selection of those who will personify its beliefs. By imposing an unwanted minister, the state infringes the Free Exercise Clause, which protects a religious group's right to shape its own faith and mission through its appointments. According the state the power to determine which individuals will minister to the faithful also violates the Establishment Clause, which prohibits government involvement in such ecclesiastical decisions.

The EEOC and Perich acknowledge that employment discrimination laws would be unconstitutional as applied to religious groups in certain circumstances. They grant, for example, that it would violate the First Amendment for courts to apply such laws to compel the ordination of women by the Catholic Church or by an Orthodox Jewish seminary. According to the EEOC and Perich, religious organizations could successfully defend against employment discrimination claims in those circumstances by invoking the constitutional right to freedom of association—a right "implicit" in the First Amendment. *Roberts v. United States Jaycees,* 468 U.S. 609, 622, 104 S.Ct. 3244, 82 L.Ed.2d 462 (1984). The EEOC and

Perich thus see no need—and no basis—for a special rule for ministers grounded in the Religion Clauses themselves.

We find this position untenable. The right to freedom of association is a right enjoyed by religious and secular groups alike. It follows under the EEOC's and Perich's view that the First Amendment analysis should be the same, whether the association in question is the Lutheran Church, a labor union, or a social club. That result is hard to square with the text of the First Amendment itself, which gives special solicitude to the rights of religious organizations. We cannot accept the remarkable view that the Religion Clauses have nothing to say about a religious organization's freedom to select its own ministers.

The EEOC and Perich also contend that our decision in *Employment Div., Dept. of Human Resources of Ore. v. Smith,* 494 U.S. 872, 110 S.Ct. 1595, 108 L.Ed.2d 876 (1990), precludes recognition of a ministerial exception. In *Smith,* two members of the Native American Church were denied state unemployment benefits after it was determined that they had been fired from their jobs for ingesting peyote, a crime under Oregon law. We held that this did not violate the Free Exercise Clause, even though the peyote had been ingested for sacramental purposes, because the "right of free exercise does not relieve an individual of the obligation to comply with a valid and neutral law of general applicability on the ground that the law proscribes (or prescribes) conduct that his religion prescribes (or proscribes)."

It is true that the ADA's prohibition on retaliation, like Oregon's prohibition on peyote use, is a valid and neutral law of general applicability. But a church's selection of its ministers is unlike an individual's ingestion of peyote. *Smith* involved government regulation of only outward physical acts. The present case, in contrast, concerns government interference with an internal church decision that affects the faith and mission of the church itself. (distinguishing the government's regulation of "physical acts" from its "lend[ing] its power to one or the other side in controversies over religious authority or dogma"). The contention that *Smith* forecloses recognition of a ministerial exception rooted in the Religion Clauses has no merit.

III

Having concluded that there is a ministerial exception grounded in the Religion Clauses of the First Amendment, we consider whether the exception applies in this case. We hold that it does.

Every Court of Appeals to have considered the question has concluded that the ministerial exception is not limited to the head of a religious congregation, and we agree. We are reluctant, however, to adopt a rigid formula for deciding when an employee qualifies as a minister. It is enough for us to conclude, in this our first case involving the ministerial exception, that the exception covers Perich, given all the circumstances of her employment.

To begin with, **Hosanna–Tabor** held Perich out as a minister, with a role distinct from that of most of its members. When **Hosanna–Tabor** extended her a call, it issued her a "diploma of vocation" according her the title "Minister of Religion, Commissioned." She was tasked with performing that office "according to the Word of God and the confessional standards of the Evangelical Lutheran Church as drawn from the Sacred Scriptures." The congregation prayed that God "bless [her] ministrations to the glory of His holy name, [and] the building of His church." In a supplement to the diploma, the congregation undertook to periodically review Perich's "skills of ministry" and "ministerial responsibilities," and to provide for her "continuing education as a professional person in the ministry of the Gospel."

Perich's title as a minister reflected a significant degree of religious training followed by a formal process of commissioning. To be eligible to become a commissioned minister, Perich had to complete eight college-level courses in subjects including biblical interpretation, church doctrine, and the ministry of the Lutheran teacher. She also had to obtain the endorsement of her local Synod district by submitting a petition that contained her academic transcripts, letters of recommendation, personal statement, and written answers to various ministry-related questions. Finally, she had to pass an oral examination by a faculty committee at a Lutheran college. It took Perich six years to fulfill these requirements. And when she eventually did, she was commissioned as a minister only upon election by the congregation, which recognized God's call to her to teach. At that point, her call could be rescinded only upon a supermajority vote of the congregation—a protection designed to allow her to "preach the Word of God boldly."

Perich held herself out as a minister of the Church by accepting the formal call to religious service, according to its terms. She did so in other ways as well. For example, she claimed a special housing allowance on her taxes that was available only to employees earning their compensation " 'in the exercise of the ministry.' " ("If you are not conducting activities 'in the exercise of the ministry,' you cannot take advantage of the parsonage or housing allowance exclusion" (quoting Lutheran Church–Missouri Synod Brochure on Whether the IRS Considers Employees as a Minister (2007)). In a form she submitted to the Synod following her termination, Perich again indicated that she regarded herself as a minister at **Hosanna–Tabor**, stating: "I feel that God is leading me to serve in the teaching ministry. . . . I am anxious to be in the teaching ministry again soon."

Perich's job duties reflected a role in conveying the Church's message and carrying out its mission. **Hosanna–Tabor** expressly charged her with "lead[ing] others toward Christian maturity" and "teach[ing] faithfully the Word of God, the Sacred Scriptures, in its truth and purity and as set forth in all the symbolical books of the Evangelical Lutheran Church." In fulfilling these responsibilities, Perich taught her students religion four days a week, and led them in prayer three times a day. Once a week, she took her students to a school-wide chapel service, and—about twice a year—she took her turn leading it, choosing the liturgy, selecting the hymns, and delivering a short message based on verses from the Bible. During her last year of teaching, Perich also led her fourth graders in a brief devotional exercise each morning. As a source of religious instruction, Perich performed an important role in transmitting the Lutheran faith to the next generation.

In light of these considerations—the formal title given Perich by the Church, the substance reflected in that title, her own use of that title, and the important religious functions she performed for the Church—we conclude that Perich was a minister covered by the ministerial exception.

In reaching a contrary conclusion, the Court of Appeals committed three errors. First, the Sixth Circuit failed to see any relevance in the fact that Perich was a commissioned minister. Although such a title, by itself, does not automatically ensure coverage, the fact that an employee has been ordained or commissioned as a minister is surely relevant, as is the fact that significant religious training and a recognized religious mission underlie the description of the employee's position. It was wrong for the Court of Appeals—and Perich, who has adopted the court's view—to say that an employee's title does not matter.

Second, the Sixth Circuit gave too much weight to the fact that lay teachers at the school performed the same religious duties as Perich. We express no view on whether someone with Perich's duties would be covered by the ministerial exception in the absence of the other considerations we have discussed. But though relevant, it cannot be dispositive that others not formally recognized as ministers by the church perform the same functions—particularly when, as here, they did so only because commissioned ministers were unavailable.

Third, the Sixth Circuit placed too much emphasis on Perich's performance of secular duties. It is true that her religious duties consumed only 45 minutes of each workday, and that the rest of her day was devoted to teaching secular subjects. The EEOC regards that as conclusive, contending that any ministerial exception "should be limited to those employees who perform exclusively religious functions." We cannot accept that view. Indeed, we are unsure whether any such employees exist. The heads of congregations themselves often have a mix of duties, including secular ones such as helping to manage the congregation's finances, supervising purely secular personnel, and overseeing the upkeep of facilities.

* * * The issue before us, however, is not one that can be resolved by a stopwatch. The amount of time an employee spends on particular activities is relevant in assessing that employee's status, but that factor cannot be considered in isolation, without regard to the nature of the religious functions performed and the other considerations discussed above.

Because Perich was a minister within the meaning of the exception, the First Amendment requires dismissal of this employment discrimination suit against her religious employer. The EEOC and Perich originally sought an order reinstating Perich to her former position as a called teacher. By requiring the Church to accept a minister it did not want, such an order would have plainly violated the Church's freedom under the Religion Clauses to select its own ministers.

Perich no longer seeks reinstatement, having abandoned that relief before this Court. But that is immaterial. Perich continues to seek frontpay in lieu of reinstatement, backpay, compensatory and punitive damages, and attorney's fees. An award of such relief would operate as a penalty on the Church for terminating an unwanted minister, and would be no less prohibited by the First Amendment than an order overturning the termination. Such relief would depend on a determination that **Hosanna–Tabor** was wrong to have relieved Perich of her position, and it is precisely such a ruling that is barred by the ministerial exception.

The EEOC and Perich suggest that **Hosanna–Tabor**'s asserted religious reason for firing Perich—that she violated the Synod's commitment to internal dispute resolution—was pretextual. That suggestion misses the point of the ministerial exception. The purpose of the exception is not to safeguard a church's decision to fire a minister only when it is made for a religious reason. The exception instead ensures that the authority to select and control who will minister to the faithful—a matter "strictly ecclesiastical,"—is the church's alone.

IV

The EEOC and Perich foresee a parade of horribles that will follow our recognition of a ministerial exception to employment discrimination suits. According to the EEOC and Perich, such an exception could protect religious organizations from liability for retaliating against employees for reporting criminal misconduct or for testifying before a grand jury or in a criminal trial. What is more, the EEOC contends, the logic of the exception would confer on religious employers "unfettered discretion" to violate employment laws by, for example, hiring children or aliens not authorized to work in the United States.

Hosanna–Tabor responds that the ministerial exception would not in any way bar criminal prosecutions for interfering with law enforcement investigations or other proceedings. Nor, according to the Church, would the exception bar government enforcement of general laws restricting eligibility for employment, because the exception applies only to suits by or on behalf of ministers themselves. * * *

The case before us is an employment discrimination suit brought on behalf of a minister, challenging her church's decision to fire her. Today we hold only that the ministerial exception bars such a suit. We express no view on whether the exception bars other types of suits, including actions by employees alleging breach of contract or tortious conduct by their religious employers. There will be time enough to address the applicability of the exception to other circumstances if and when they arise.

The interest of society in the enforcement of employment discrimination statutes is undoubtedly important. But so too is the interest of religious groups in choosing who will preach their beliefs, teach their faith, and carry out their mission. When a minister who has been fired sues her church alleging that her termination was discriminatory, the First Amendment has struck the balance for us. The church must be free to choose those who will guide it on its way.

The judgment of the Court of Appeals for the Sixth Circuit is reversed.

JUSTICE THOMAS, concurring.

* * *

JUSTICE ALITO, with whom JUSTICE KAGAN joins, concurring.

I join the Court's opinion, but I write separately to clarify my understanding of the significance of formal ordination and designation as a "minister" in determining whether an "employee" of a religious group falls within the so-called "ministerial" exception. The term "minister" is commonly used by many Protestant denominations to refer to members of their clergy, but the term is rarely if ever used in this way by Catholics, Jews, Muslims, Hindus, or Buddhists. In addition, the concept of ordination as understood by most Christian churches and by Judaism has no clear counterpart in some Christian denominations and some other religions. Because virtually every religion in the world is represented in the population of the United States, it would be a mistake if the term "minister" or the concept of ordination were viewed as central to the important issue of religious autonomy that is presented in cases like this one. Instead, courts should focus on the function performed by persons who work for religious bodies.

The First Amendment protects the freedom of religious groups to engage in certain key religious activities, including the conducting of worship services and other religious ceremonies and rituals, as well as the critical process of communicating the faith. Accordingly, religious groups must be free to choose the personnel who are essential to the performance of these functions.

The "ministerial" exception should be tailored to this purpose. It should apply to any "employee" who leads a religious organization, conducts worship services or important religious ceremonies or rituals, or serves as a messenger or teacher of its faith. If a religious group believes that the ability of such an employee to perform these key functions has been compromised, then the constitutional guarantee of religious freedom protects the group's right to remove the employee from his or her position.

I

* * * Religious autonomy means that religious authorities must be free to determine who is qualified to serve in positions of substantial religious importance. Different religions will have different views on exactly what qualifies as an important religious position, but it is nonetheless possible to identify a general category of "employees" whose functions are essential to the independence of practically all religious groups. These include those who serve in positions of leadership, those who perform important functions in worship services and in the performance of religious ceremonies and rituals, and those who are entrusted with teaching and conveying the tenets of the faith to the next generation.

Applying the protection of the First Amendment to roles of religious leadership, worship, ritual, and expression focuses on the objective functions that are important for the autonomy of any religious group, regardless of its beliefs. * * *

II

A

The Court's opinion today holds that the "ministerial" exception applies to Cheryl Perich (hereinafter respondent), who is regarded by the Lutheran Church–Missouri Synod as a commissioned minister. But while a ministerial title is undoubtedly relevant in applying the First Amendment rule at issue, such a title is neither necessary nor sufficient. As previously noted, most faiths do not employ the term "minister," and some eschew the concept of formal ordination. And at the opposite end of the spectrum, some faiths consider the ministry to consist of all or a very large percentage of their members. Perhaps this explains why, although every circuit to consider the issue has recognized the "ministerial" exception, no circuit has made ordination status or formal title determinative of the exception's applicability.

The Fourth Circuit was the first to use the term "ministerial exception," but in doing so it took pains to clarify that the label was a mere shorthand. See *Rayburn v. General Conference of Seventh–Day Adventists,* 772 F.2d 1164, 1168 (1985) (noting that the exception's applicability "does not depend upon ordination but upon the function of the position"). The Fourth Circuit traced the exception back to *McClure v. Salvation Army,* 460 F.2d 553 (C.A.5 1972), which invoked the Religion Clauses to bar a Title VII sex-discrimination suit brought by a woman who was described by the court as a Salvation Army "minister," although her actual title was "officer." See *McClure v. Salvation Army,* 323 F.Supp. 1100, 1101 (N.D.Ga.1971). A decade after *McClure,* the Fifth Circuit made clear that formal ordination was not necessary for the "ministerial" exception to apply. The court held that the members of the faculty at a Baptist seminary were covered by the exception because of their religious function in conveying church doctrine, even though some of them were not ordained ministers. See *EEOC v. Southwestern Baptist Theological Seminary*, 651 F.2d 277 (1981).

The functional consensus has held up over time, with the D.C. Circuit recognizing that "[t]he ministerial exception has not been limited to members of the clergy." *EEOC v. Catholic Univ.*, 83 F.3d 455, 461 (1996). The court in that case rejected a Title VII suit brought by a Catholic nun who claimed that the Catholic University of America had denied her tenure for a canon-law teaching position because of her gender. The court noted that "members of the Canon Law Faculty perform the vital function of instructing those who will in turn interpret, implement, and teach the law governing the Roman Catholic Church and the administration of its sacraments. Although Sister McDonough is not a priest, she is a member of a religious order who sought a tenured professorship in a field that is of fundamental importance to the spiritual mission of her Church."

The Ninth Circuit too has taken a functional approach, just recently reaffirming that "the ministerial exception encompasses more than a church's ordained ministers." *Alcazar v. Corp. of Catholic Archbishop of Seattle*, 627 F.3d 1288, 1291 (2010) (en banc); The Court's opinion today should not be read to upset this consensus.

B

The ministerial exception applies to respondent because, as the Court notes, she played a substantial role in "conveying the Church's message and carrying out its mission." She taught religion to her students four days a week and took them to chapel on the fifth day. She led them in daily devotional exercises, and led them in prayer three times a day. She also alternated with the other teachers in planning and leading worship services at the school chapel, choosing liturgies, hymns, and readings, and composing and delivering a message based on Scripture.

It makes no difference that respondent also taught secular subjects. While a purely secular teacher would not qualify for the "ministerial" exception, the constitutional protection of religious teachers is not somehow diminished when they take on secular functions in addition to their religious ones. What matters is that respondent played an important role as an instrument of her church's religious message and as a leader of its worship activities. Because of these important religious functions, **Hosanna–Tabor** had the right to decide for itself whether respondent was religiously qualified to remain in her office.

Hosanna–Tabor discharged respondent because she threatened to file suit against the church in a civil court. This threat contravened the Lutheran doctrine that disputes among Christians should be resolved internally without resort to the civil court system and all the legal wrangling it entails. In **Hosanna–Tabor**'s view, respondent's disregard for this doctrine compromised her religious function, disqualifying her from serving effectively as a voice for the church's faith. Respondent does not dispute that the Lutheran Church subscribes to a doctrine of internal dispute resolution, but she argues that this was a mere pretext for her firing, which was really done for nonreligious reasons.

For civil courts to engage in the pretext inquiry that respondent and the Solicitor General urge us to sanction would dangerously undermine the religious autonomy that lower court case law has now protected for nearly four decades. In order to probe the *real reason* for respondent's firing, a civil court—and perhaps a jury—would be required to make a judgment about church doctrine. The credibility of **Hosanna–Tabor**'s asserted reason for terminating respondent's employment could not be assessed without taking into account both the importance that the Lutheran Church attaches to the doctrine of internal dispute resolution and the degree to which that tenet compromised respondent's religious function. * * *

What matters in the present case is that **Hosanna–Tabor** believes that the religious function that respondent performed made it essential that she abide by the doctrine of internal dispute resolution; and the civil courts are in no position to second-guess that assessment. This conclusion rests not on respondent's ordination status or her formal title, but rather on her functional status as the type of employee that a church must be free to appoint or dismiss in order to exercise the religious liberty that the First Amendment guarantees.

NOTES

1. *"Minister?"* In light of the principal case could a religion announce that all of its employees are "ministers," and by prescribing a ritual of initiation at the time of employment avoid the statutory demands?

Conversely, consider situations, emphasized by the concurring opinion, where the employee is not recognized by the religion as being a "minister," but has significant duties related to the religious activities of the religious organization. For example, presumably a teacher of theology in a religious institution would be considered a "minister" even though not a member of the clergy. *EEOC v. Catholic University of America*, 83 F.3d 455 (D. C. Cir. 1996). By contrast, lay teachers of purely secular subjects (e.g., psychology or foreign language) in a largely secular, but religiously affiliated, academic institution, probably would not be subjected to the "ministerial exemption." *EEOC v. Mississippi College*, 626 F.2d 477 (5th Cir. 1980). Contrast:

a. *Skrzypczak v. Roman Catholic Diocese of Tulsa*, 611 F.3d 1238 (10th Cir. 2010), involved a plaintiff, a lay person, who served as the "Director of the Department of Religious Formation" for the Roman Catholic Diocese. As Director, plaintiff's principal responsibilities included, "[k]eep[ing] the Chancellor informed on the Department's activities, developing office goals, objectives, policies and programs; and overseeing their implementation; overseeing office staffing;" promoting "intra- and inter departmental collaboration and cooperation;" supervising "the Dioceasan Resources Libraries" and overseeing the budget in different offices. Plaintiff's duties also required her to "[s]upervise the Office of Religious Formation, Pastoral

Studies Institute and Office of Youth and Young Adult Ministry, overseeing office communications, publications, and reports." Finally, plaintiff taught or facilitated numerous religious studies courses at the Institute. Relying on the finding that plaintiff's duties were primarily administrative, rather than ministerial, the court rejected the church's claim that it was protected by a ministerial exemption. Does *Hosanna–Tabor* cast doubt on this holding?

b. ***Tomic v. Catholic Diocese of Peoria***, 442 F.3d 1036 (7th Cir. 2006). The employee was the "Music Director" for the church. Even though plaintiff was not "ordained," because music was integral part of the religious service, the court held that the person responsible for the music held a position important to the spiritual mission of the church. Accordingly, the church was able to assert the "ministerial exemption" to discrimination charges filed by this "director."

c. ***EEOC v. Pacific Press Pub. Ass'n***, 676 F.2d 1272 (9th Cir. 1982). Plaintiff served as an editorial secretary in a publishing house dedicated to printing and circulating the religious materials of the religion. The religion could not claim the ministerial exemption when charged with sex discrimination.

2. *Nature of the Discrimination Charged.*

a. Harassment: While the "ministerial exemption" may be asserted to defend charges of discrimination regarding hiring, dismissal, pay, and other tangible job benefits, the Ninth Circuit has held that the ministerial exemption had no application to charges of harassment. Because harassment itself is prohibited by church doctrine, the court found no intrusion into the "free exercise" of religion, and since federal discrimination law was consistent with church doctrine, it found no governmental "establishment" of religion through judicial enforcement of that law. ***Elvig v. Calvin Presbyterian Church***, 375 F.3d 951 (9th Cir. 2004). This decision appears not to recognize the obligation that the statutes impose on employers who are charged with not effectively remedying harassment by its supervisory employees, which in this case would be ministers of the religion. The required remedial response is to discipline, reassign, or perhaps even dismiss the harasser. *Infra, Chapter 4.* Unavoidably this would seem to inject courts into evaluating how a church assigns or disciplines members of its clergy charged with harassment. Other courts deem charges of harassment against ministerial employees are properly subject to the First Amendment restrictions on the full enforcement of the statute against the religious institution. *See, Kennedy v. St. Joseph's Ministries,* 657 F.3d 189 (4th Cir. 2011).

b. Failure to make reasonable accommodations: The principal case holds that the "ministerial exemption" is applicable to the Americans With Disabilities Act as applied to dismissal. Would the exemption immunize a church from having to make reasonable accommodations to a minister's physical or mental disabilities, such as making the pulpit wheelchair accessible? *See, Werft v. Desert S.W. Annual Conf. of the United Methodist Church,* 377 F.3d 1099 (9th Cir. 2004).

3. *Respecting Church Doctrines:* The concurring opinion in the principal case emphasized that the employee was allegedly disciplined because she

failed to follow church doctrine that prohibited its *ministers* from resorting to secular institutions to address internal church disputes. Consider a religious organization whose doctrine directs strict segregation of the sexes, and on this ground refuses to hire female employees for secular jobs because it would require contact with male co-workers, customers, or students (e.g. bus driver, teacher, or custodian). What of a religion that teaches inferiority of a particular race, for secular jobs, refuses to hire persons of that race?

The EEOC has held that failure to include contraceptives in employer-provided health care plans is sex discrimination in violation of the Pregnancy Discrimination Act amendment to Title VII. EEOC Decision Dec. 14, 2000. (www.eeoc.gov/policy/docs/decision contraception) 2 EP Guide, Para 6878. Imposing such an obligation as to ministers of a religious organization would seem to infringe the First Amendment, even if the church had no moral objections to such coverage. *McClure v. Salvation Army,* 460 F.2d 553 (5th Cir. 1972). However, as to its lay employees working in essentially secular functions of the religious order, such as hospitals, schools, or even charities, imposing an obligation on the religious organization to provide contraceptive coverage in health benefit plans has been upheld against constitutional challenges even when the mandate conflicted with church doctrine. *Catholic Charities of Sacramento v. Superior Court*, 90 Cal.App.4th 425, 109 Cal.Rptr. 2d 176 (2001) *aff'd*, 85 P.3d 67 (2004).

4. *Religious Organization?* Purely secular organizations that engage in commercial, profit-making activities cannot claim the implied "ministerial exemption" nor the statutory exemption of § 702(a) allowing religious organizations to discriminate on the basis of religion. *EEOC v.Townley Eng. & Mfg. Co.,* 859 F.2d 610 (9th Cir. 1988). Thus, a secular employer is unlikely to be able to claim a First Amendment right to engage in discrimination proscribed by law simply because the employer has personal religious objections to the application of the law or has religious beliefs that demand proscribed discrimination.

C. AFFIRMATIVE ACTION

TITLE VII: § 703(j)

Nothing contained in this title shall be interpreted to require any [covered entity] to grant preferential treatment to any individual or to any group because of race, color, religion, sex or national origin * * * on account of an imbalance which may exist with respect to the total number or percentage of persons of any race, color, religion, sex or national origin employed by any employer * * * in comparison with the total number or percentage of persons of such race, color, religion, sex, or national origin in any community, State, section, or other area, or in the available work force in any community, State section, or other area.

TITLE VII: § 703(i)

Nothing contained in this title shall apply to any business or enterprise on or near an Indian reservation with respect to any publically announced employment practice of such business or enterprise under which a preferential treatment is given to any individual because he is an Indian living on or near a reservation.

NOTES

1. *International Br'hd of Teamsters v. United States,* **431 U.S. 324, 97 S.Ct. 1843, 52 L.Ed.2d 396 (1977)**, reproduced *infra page 429.* To establish a "pattern of illegally motivated hiring practices" plaintiff relied heavily on the "inexorable zero" of minority truck drivers employed by the defendants compared to the number of minorities living in various metropolitan areas where defendants operated.

> Petitioners [defendant labor unions and employers] argue[d] that statistics, at least those comparing the racial composition of an employer's work force to the composition of the population at large should never be given decisive weight in a Title VII case because to do so would conflict with § 703(j) of the Act. * * * The argument fails in this case because the statistical evidence was not offered or used to support an erroneous theory that Title VII requires an employer's work force to be racially balanced. Statistics showing racial or ethnic imbalance are probative in a case such as this one only because such imbalance is often a telltale sign of purposeful discrimination; * * *. Evidence of long-lasting and gross disparity between the composition of a work force and that of the general population thus may be significant even though § 703(j) makes clear that Title VII imposes no requirement that a work force mirror the general population.

Teamsters, along with a companion case of *Hazelwood School Dist. v. United States,* **433 U.S. 299, 97 S.Ct. 2736, 53 L.Ed.2d 768 (1977)**, reproduced *infra, page* 434 established that illegal motivation can be established by statistical disparities. To avoid possible liability based on statistical imbalances employers were pressured to take affirmative steps to reduce existing disparities.

PRESIDENTIAL EXECUTIVE ORDER NUMBER 11246

30 FR 12319, 3 CFR 339 (1964–65 Comp.)

Section 201. The Secretary of Labor shall be responsible for the administration * * * of this Order. The Secretary shall adopt such rules and regulations and issue such orders as are deemed necessary and appropriate to achieves the purposes of * * * this Order.

Section 202. * * * [A]ll [federal] Government contracting agencies shall include in every Government contract hereafter entered into the following provisions: During the performance of this contract the contractor agrees as follows: (1) The contractor will not discriminate against any employee or applicant for employment because of race, color, religion, sex or national origin. The contractor will take affirmative action to ensure that applicants are employed, and that employees are treated during employment, without regard to their race, color, religion, sex, or national origin. Such action shall include, but not be limited to the following: employment; upgrading; demotion; transfer; recruitment or recruitment advertising; layoff or termination; rates of pay or other forms of compensation; and selection for training, including apprenticeships.

* * *

NOTES

1. *E.O. 11246* does not itself define the contracting employers' affirmative action obligations. Those obligations are defined by regulations issued by the Secretary of Labor. The order in its current form was issued by President Lyndon Johnson in 1965. The term "affirmative action" was originally found in the National Labor Relations Act of 1935 which authorized the National Labor Relations Board to order employers to reinstate actual victims of illegal treatment and to post notices assuring workers of their rights. "Affirmative action" took on much of its current meaning during the administration of President Richard Nixon in the early 1970s. Labor Department regulations for the first time required contracting employers, whether or not they had engaged in illegal discrimination, to take positive steps to increase the number and percentage of minority workers. As amended in 2000, Department of Labor regulations impose on contracting employers with 50 or more employees with contracts exceeding $50,000 an obligation to: (1) undertake a "utilization analysis" of their work force to determine whether there was an underrepresentation of minorities in discrete job categories. "When the percentage of minorities or women employed in a particular job group is less than would reasonably be expected given their availability percentage * * * [to establish] a percentage annual placement goal at least equal to the availability figure derived for women or minorities." 41 C.F.R. §§ 60–2.15(b) and 216(c). The regulations caution, however that "Placement goals serve as objectives or targets reasonably attainable by means of applying every good faith effort to make all aspects of the entire affirmative action program work." "Placement goals may not be rigid and inflexible quotas, which must be met, nor are they to be considered as either a ceiling or a floor for the employment of particular groups." Finally, "Placement goals do not provide the contractor with a justification to extend a preference to any individual, * * * or adversely affect an individual's employment status, on the basis of that person's race, color, religion, sex, or national origin." *Id.* §§ 21.6(e)(1) and (2).

2. *Enforcement of E.O. 11246* is through the Department of Labor, Office of Federal Contract Compliance Programs (OFCCP). Where contract compliance reviews disclose possible non-compliance with the employer's contractual commitment, the OFCCP may proceed with administrative enforcement including barring the offending employer from future government contracts or initiating judicial action to enforce the employer's contract obligations.

3. State and local governments have instituted similar affirmative action programs, some focusing on requiring contractors to subcontract certain percentage of the work to minority owned and controlled businesses.

4. Governmentally imposed affirmative action that relied upon race, national origin or sex was challenged by white males who were disadvantaged by the programs on two grounds: (1) such classifications, when imposed by governments, violate equal protection concepts of the Constitution, Amendments 5 and 14; and (2) that use of such classifications is a facial violation of Title VII. One avenue of the employer's defense to such suits, particularly against private employers under Title VII, could have been that the history and primary purpose of the statute was to protect racial minorities and women, not the white males complaining about the employer's affirmative action. That "defense" was rejected in *McDonald v. Santa Fe Trail Transp. Co.,* 427 U.S. 273, 96 S.Ct. 2574, 49 L.Ed.2d 493 (1976), reproduced p. 29 *supra.*

UNITED STEELWORKERS OF AMERICA v. WEBER

Supreme Court of the United States, 1979
443 U.S. 193, 99 S.Ct. 2721, 61 L.Ed.2d 480

JUSTICE BRENNAN delivered the opinion of the Court.

Challenged here is the legality of an affirmative action plan—collectively bargained by an employer and a union—that reserves for black employees 50% of the openings in an in-plant craft-training program until the percentage of black craft-workers in the plant is commensurate with the percentage of blacks in the local labor force. The question for decision is whether Congress, in Title VII of the Civil Rights Act of 1964 left employers and unions in the private sector free to take such race-conscious steps to eliminate manifest racial imbalances in traditionally segregated job categories. We hold that Title VII does not prohibit such race-conscious affirmative action plans.

I

In 1974, petitioner United Steelworkers of America (USWA) and petitioner Kaiser Aluminum & Chemical Corp. (Kaiser) entered into a master collective-bargaining agreement covering terms and conditions of employment at 15 Kaiser plants. The agreement contained, *inter alia,* an affirmative action plan designed to eliminate conspicuous racial imbalances in Kaiser's then almost exclusively white craft-work forces. Black craft-hiring goals were set for each Kaiser plant equal to the percentage of blacks in the respective local labor forces. To enable plants to meet these goals, on-the-job training programs were established to teach unskilled production workers—black and white—the skills necessary to become craft workers. The plan reserved for black employees 50% of the openings in these newly created in-plant training programs.

This case arose from the operation of the plan at Kaiser's plant in Gramercy, La. Until 1974, Kaiser hired as craft workers for that plant only persons who had had prior craft experience. Because blacks had long been excluded from craft unions,[1] few were able to present such creden-

---

1. Judicial findings of exclusion from crafts on racial grounds are so numerous as to make such exclusion a proper subject for judicial notice.

tials. As a consequence, prior to 1974 only 1.83% (5 out of 273) of the skilled craftworkers at the Gramercy plant were black, even though the work force in the Gramercy area was approximately 39% black.

Pursuant to the national agreement Kaiser altered its craft-hiring practice in the Gramercy plant. Rather than hiring already trained outsiders, Kaiser established a training program to train its production workers to fill craft openings. Selection of craft trainees was made on the basis of seniority, with the proviso that at least 50% of the new trainees were to be black until the percentage of black skilled craftworkers in the Gramercy plant approximated the percentage of blacks in the local labor force.

During 1974, the first year of the operation of the Kaiser–USWA affirmative action plan, 13 craft trainees were selected from Gramercy's production work force. Of these, seven were black and six white. The most senior black selected into the program had less seniority than several white production workers whose bids for admission were rejected. Thereafter one of those white production workers, respondent Brian Weber (hereafter respondent), instituted this class action in the United States District Court for the Eastern District of Louisiana.

The complaint alleged that the filling of craft trainee positions at the Gramercy plant pursuant to the affirmative action program had resulted in junior black employees' receiving training in preference to senior white employees, thus discriminating against respondent and other similarly situated white employees in violation of §§ 703(a) and of Title VII. The District Court held that the plan violated Title VII, entered a judgment in favor of the plaintiff class, and granted a permanent injunction prohibiting Kaiser and the USWA "from denying plaintiffs, Brian F. Weber and all other members of the class, access to on-the-job training programs on the basis of race." A divided panel of the Court of Appeals for the Fifth Circuit affirmed, holding that all employment preferences based upon race, including those preferences incidental to bona fide affirmative action plans, violated Title VII's prohibition against racial discrimination in employment. We granted certiorari. We reverse.

II

We emphasize at the outset the narrowness of our inquiry. Since the Kaiser–USWA plan does not involve state action, this case does not present an alleged violation of the Equal Protection Clause of the Fourteenth Amendment. Further, since the Kaiser–USWA plan was adopted voluntarily, we are not concerned with what Title VII requires or with what a court might order to remedy a past proved violation of the Act. The only question before us is the narrow statutory issue of whether Title VII *forbids* private employers and unions from voluntarily agreeing upon bona fide affirmative action plans that accord racial preferences in the manner and for the purpose provided in the Kaiser–USWA plan. That question was expressly left open in *McDonald v. Santa Fe Trail Transp. Co.*, 427 U.S. 273, 281 n. 8, 96 S.Ct. 2574, 2579, 49 L.Ed.2d 493 (1976), which held, in a case not involving affirmative action, that Title VII protects whites as well as blacks from certain forms of racial discrimination.

Respondent argues that Congress intended in Title VII to prohibit all race-conscious affirmative action plans. Respondent's argument rests upon a literal interpretation of §§ 703(a) and (d) of the Act. Those sections make it unlawful to "discriminate . . . because of . . . race" in hiring and in the selection of apprentices for training programs. Since, the argument runs, *McDonald v. Santa Fe Trail Transp. Co., supra,* settled that Title VII forbids discrimination against whites as well as blacks, and since the Kaiser–USWA affirmative action plan operates to discriminate against white employees solely because they are white, it follows that the Kaiser–USWA plan violates Title VII.

Respondent's argument is not without force. But it overlooks the significance of the fact that the Kaiser–USWA plan is an affirmative action plan voluntarily adopted by private parties to eliminate traditional patterns of racial segregation. In this context respondent's reliance upon a literal construction of §§ 703(a) and (d) and upon *McDonald* is misplaced. It is a "familiar rule that a thing may be within the letter of the statute and yet not within the statute, because not within its spirit nor within the intention of its makers." The prohibition against racial discrimination in §§ 703(a) and (d) of Title VII must therefore be read against the background of the legislative history of Title VII and the historical context from which the Act arose. Examination of those sources makes clear that an interpretation of the sections that forbade all race-conscious affirmative action would "bring about an end completely at variance with the purpose of the statute" and must be rejected.

Congress' primary concern in enacting the prohibition against racial discrimination in Title VII of the Civil Rights Act of 1964 was with "the plight of the Negro in our economy." Before 1964, blacks were largely relegated to "unskilled and semi-skilled jobs." Because of automation the number of such jobs was rapidly decreasing. As a consequence, "the relative position of the Negro worker [was] steadily worsening. In 1947 the nonwhite unemployment rate was only 64 percent higher than the white rate; in 1962 it was 124 percent higher." Congress considered this a serious social problem. * * *

Congress feared that the goals of the Civil Rights Act—the integration of blacks into the mainstream of American society—could not be achieved unless this trend were reversed. And Congress recognized that that would not be possible unless blacks were able to secure jobs "which have a future." As Senator Humphrey explained to the Senate:

> "What good does it do a Negro to be able to eat in a fine restaurant if he cannot afford to pay the bill? What good does it do him to be accepted in a hotel that is too expensive for his modest income? How can a Negro child be motivated to take full advantage of integrated educational facilities if he has no hope of getting a job where he can use that education?"

"Without a job, one cannot afford public convenience and accommodations. Income from employment may be necessary to further a man's education, or that of his children. If his children have no hope of getting a good job, what will motivate them to take advantage of educational opportunities?"

These remarks echoed President Kennedy's original message to Congress upon the introduction of the Civil Rights Act in 1963. * * *

Accordingly, it was clear to Congress that "[t]he crux of the problem [was] to open employment opportunities for Negroes in occupations which have been traditionally closed to them," and it was to this problem that Title VII's prohibition against racial discrimination in employment was primarily addressed.

It plainly appears from the House Report accompanying the Civil Rights Act that Congress did not intend wholly to prohibit private and voluntary affirmative action efforts as one method of solving this problem. The Report provides:

"No bill can or should lay claim to eliminating all of the causes and consequences of racial and other types of discrimination against minorities. There is reason to believe, however, that national leadership provided by the enactment of Federal legislation dealing with the most troublesome problems *will create an atmosphere conducive to voluntary or local resolution of other forms of discrimination.*"

Given this legislative history, we cannot agree with respondent that Congress intended to prohibit the private sector from taking effective steps to accomplish the goal that Congress designed Title VII to achieve. The very statutory words intended as a spur or catalyst to cause "employers and unions to self-examine and to self-evaluate their employment practices and to endeavor to eliminate, so far as possible, the last vestiges of an unfortunate and ignominious page in this country's history," cannot be interpreted as an absolute prohibition against all private, voluntary, race-conscious affirmative action efforts to hasten the elimination of such vestiges. It would be ironic indeed if a law triggered by a Nation's concern over centuries of racial injustice and intended to improve the lot of those who had "been excluded from the American dream for so long," constituted the first legislative prohibition of all voluntary, private, race-conscious efforts to abolish traditional patterns of racial segregation and hierarchy.

Our conclusion is further reinforced by examination of the language and legislative history of § 703(j) of Title VII. Opponents of Title VII raised two related arguments against the bill. First, they argued that the Act would be interpreted to *require* employers with racially imbalanced work forces to grant preferential treatment to racial minorities in order to integrate. Second, they argued that employers with racially imbalanced work forces would grant preferential treatment to racial minorities, even if not required to do so by the Act. Had Congress meant to prohibit all race-conscious affirmative action, as respondent urges, it easily could have answered both objections by providing that Title VII would not require or *permit* racially preferential integration efforts. But Congress did not choose such a course. Rather, Congress added § 703(j) which addresses only the first objection. The section provides that nothing contained in Title VII "shall be interpreted to *require* any employer ... to grant preferential treatment ... to any group because of the race ... of such ... group on account of" a *de facto* racial imbalance in the employer's work force. The section does *not* state that "nothing in Title VII shall be interpreted to *permit*" voluntary affirmative efforts to correct racial imbalances. The natural inference is that Congress chose not to forbid all voluntary race-conscious affirmative action.

The reasons for this choice are evident from the legislative record. Title VII could not have been enacted into law without substantial support from legislators in both Houses who traditionally resisted federal regulation of private business. Those legislators demanded as a price for their support that "management prerogatives, and union freedoms ... be left undisturbed to the greatest extent possible." Section 703(j) was proposed by Senator Dirksen to allay any fears that the Act might be interpreted in such a way as to upset this compromise. The section was designed to prevent § 703 of Title VII from being interpreted in such a way as to lead to undue "Federal Government interference with private businesses because of some Federal employee's ideas about racial balance or racial imbalance."[6] Clearly, a prohibition against all voluntary, race-conscious, affirmative action efforts would disserve these ends. Such a prohibition would augment the powers of the Federal Government and diminish traditional management prerogatives while at the same time impeding attainment of the ultimate statutory goals. In view of this legislative history and in view of Congress' desire to avoid undue federal regulation of private businesses, use of the word "require" rather than the phrase "require or permit" in § 703(j) fortifies the conclusion that Congress did not intend to limit traditional business freedom to such a degree as to prohibit all voluntary, race-conscious affirmative action.[7]

---

6. Title VI of the Civil Rights Act of 1964, considered in *University of California Regents v. Bakke*, 438 U.S. 265, 98 S.Ct. 2733, 57 L.Ed.2d 750 (1978), contains no provision comparable to § 703(j). This is because Title VI was an exercise of federal power over a matter in which the Federal Government was already directly involved: the prohibitions against race-based conduct contained in Title VI governed "program[s] or activit[ies] receiving Federal financial assistance."Congress was legislating to assure federal funds would not be used in an improper manner. Title VII, by contrast, was enacted pursuant to the commerce power to regulate purely private decisionmaking and was not intended to incorporate and particularize the commands of the Fifth and Fourteenth Amendments. Title VII and Title VI, therefore, cannot be read *in pari materia.*

7. Respondent argues that our construction of § 703 conflicts with various remarks in the legislative record. We do not agree. In Senator Humphrey's words, these comments were intended as assurances that Title VII would not allow establishment of systems "to *maintain* racial balance in employment." They were not addressed to temporary, voluntary, affirmative action measures undertaken to eliminate manifest racial imbalance in traditionally segregated job categories. Moreover, the comments referred to by respondent all preceded the adoption of § 703(j). After § 703(j) was adopted, congressional comments were all to the effect that employers would not be *required* to institute preferential quotas to avoid Title VII liability. There was no suggestion after the adoption of § 703(j) that wholly voluntary, race-conscious, affirmative action efforts would in themselves constitute a violation of Title VII. * * *

We therefore hold that Title VII's prohibition in §§ 703(a) and (d) against racial discrimination does not condemn all private, voluntary, race-conscious affirmative action plans.

III

We need not today define in detail the line of demarcation between permissible and impermissible affirmative action plans. It suffices to hold that the challenged Kaiser–USWA affirmative action plan falls on the permissible side of the line. The purposes of the plan mirror those of the statute. Both were designed to break down old patterns of racial segregation and hierarchy. Both were structured to "open employment opportunities for Negroes in occupations which have been traditionally closed to them."[8]

At the same time, the plan does not unnecessarily trammel the interests of the white employees. The plan does not require the discharge of white workers and their replacement with new black hirees. Nor does the plan create an absolute bar to the advancement of white employees; half of those trained in the program will be white. Moreover, the plan is a temporary measure; it is not intended to maintain racial balance, but simply to eliminate a manifest racial imbalance. Preferential selection of craft trainees at the Gramercy plant will end as soon as the percentage of black skilled craftworkers in the Gramercy plant approximates the percentage of blacks in the local labor force.

We conclude, therefore, that the adoption of the Kaiser–USWA plan for the Gramercy plant falls within the area of discretion left by Title VII to the private sector voluntarily to adopt affirmative action plans designed to eliminate conspicuous racial imbalance in traditionally segregated job categories.[9] Accordingly, the judgment of the Court of Appeals for the Fifth Circuit is

Reversed.

JUSTICE POWELL and JUSTICE STEVENS took no part in the consideration or decision of these cases.

JUSTICE BLACKMUN, concurring.

While I share some of the misgivings expressed in JUSTICE REHNQUIST'S dissent concerning the extent to which the legislative history of Title VII clearly supports the result the Court reaches today, I believe that additional considerations, practical and equitable, only partially perceived, if perceived at all, by the 88th Congress, support the conclusion reached by the Court today, and I therefore join its opinion as well as its judgment.

---

8. This is not to suggest that the freedom of an employer to undertake race-conscious affirmative action efforts depends on whether or not his effort is motivated by fear of liability under Title VII.

9. Our disposition makes unnecessary consideration of petitioners' argument that their plan was justified because they feared that black employees would bring suit under Title VII if they did not adopt an affirmative action plan. Nor need we consider petitioners' contention that their affirmative action plan represented an attempt to comply with Exec. Order No. 11246, 3 CFR 339.

I

In his dissent from the decision of the United States Court of Appeals for the Fifth Circuit, Judge Wisdom pointed out that this litigation arises from a practical problem in the administration of Title VII. The broad prohibition against discrimination places the employer and the union on what he accurately described as a "high tightrope without a net beneath them." If Title VII is read literally, on the one hand they face liability for past discrimination against blacks, and on the other they face liability to whites for any voluntary preferences adopted to mitigate the effects of prior discrimination against blacks.

In this litigation, Kaiser denies prior discrimination but concedes that its past hiring practices may be subject to question. Although the labor force in the Gramercy area was proximately 39% black, Kaiser's work force was less than 15% black, and its craftwork force was less than 2% black. Kaiser had made some effort to recruit black painters, carpenters, insulators, and other craftsmen, but it continued to insist that those hired have five years' prior industrial experience, a requirement that arguably was not sufficiently job related to justify under Title VII any discriminatory impact it may have had. * * * Yet when they did this, respondent Weber sued, alleging that Title VII prohibited the program because it discriminated against him as a white person and it was not supported by a prior judicial finding of discrimination against blacks.

Respondent Weber's reading of Title VII endorsed by the Court of Appeals, places voluntary compliance with Title VII in profound jeopardy. The only way for the employer and the union to keep their footing on the "tightrope" it creates would be to eschew all forms of voluntary affirmative action. Even a whisper of emphasis on minority recruiting would be forbidden. Because Congress intended to encourage private efforts to come into compliance with Title VII, Judge Wisdom [dissenting in the Court of Appeals] concluded that employers and unions who had committed "arguable violations" of Title VII should be free to make reasonable responses without fear of liability to whites. Preferential hiring along the lines of the Kaiser program is a reasonable response for the employer, whether or not a court, on these facts, could order the same step as a remedy. The company is able to avoid identifying victims of past discrimination, and so avoids claims for backpay that would inevitably follow a response limited to such victims. If past victims should be benefited by the program, however, the company mitigates its liability to those persons. Also, to the extent that Title VII liability is predicated on the "disparate effect" of an employer's past hiring practices, the program makes it less likely that such an effect could be demonstrated.

* * *

II

The Court, however, declines to consider the narrow "arguable violation" approach and adheres instead to an interpretation of Title VII that permits affirmative action by an employer whenever the job category in question is "traditionally segregated." The sources cited suggest that the Court considers a job category to be "traditionally segregated" when there has been a societal history of purposeful exclusion of blacks from the job category, resulting in a persistent disparity between the proportion of blacks in the labor force and the proportion of blacks among those who hold jobs within the category.

"Traditionally segregated job categories," where they exist, sweep far more broadly than the class of "arguable violations" of Title VII. The Court's expansive approach is somewhat disturbing for me because, as Justice REHNQUIST points out, the Congress that passed Title VII probably thought it was adopting a principle of nondiscrimination that would apply to blacks and whites alike. * * *

A closer look at the problem, however, reveals that in each of the principal ways in which the Court's "traditionally segregated job categories" approach expands on the "arguable violations" theory, still other considerations point in favor of the broad standard adopted by the Court, and make it possible for me to conclude that the Court's reading of the statute is an acceptable one. * * *

I also think it significant that, while the Court's opinion does not foreclose other forms of affirmative action, the Kaiser program it approves is a moderate one. The opinion notes that the program does not afford an absolute preference for blacks, and that it ends when the racial composition of Kaiser's craftwork force matches the racial composition of the local population. It thus operates as a temporary tool for remedying past discrimination without attempting to "maintain" a previously achieved balance. And if the Court has misperceived the political will, it has the assurance that because the question is statutory Congress may set a different course if it so chooses.

JUSTICE REHNQUIST, with whom CHIEF JUSTICE BURGER joins, dissenting.

* * *

Today's decision represents an equally dramatic and equally unremarked switch in this Court's interpretation of Title VII.

The operative sections of Title VII prohibit racial discrimination in employment *simpliciter*. Taken in its normal meaning and as understood by all Members of Congress who spoke to the issue during the legislative debates, this language prohibits a covered employer from considering race when making an employment decision, whether the race be black or white. Several years ago, however, a United States District Court held that "the dismissal of white employees charged with misappropriating company property while not dismissing a similarly charged Negro employee does not raise a claim upon which Title VII relief may be granted." *McDonald v. Santa Fe Trail Transp. Co.*, 427 U.S. 273, 278, 96 S.Ct. 2574, 2578, 49 L.Ed.2d 493 (1976). This Court unanimously reversed, concluding from the "uncontradicted legislative history" that "[T]itle VII prohibits racial discrimination against the white petitioners in this case upon the same standards as would be applicable were they Negroes...."

We have never wavered in our understanding that Title VII "prohibits *all* racial discrimination in employment, without exception for any group of particular employees." In *Griggs v. Duke Power Co.,* 401 U.S. 424, 431, 91 S.Ct. 849, 853, 28 L.Ed.2d 158 (1971), our first occasion to interpret Title VII, a unanimous Court observed that "[d]iscriminatory preference, for any group, minority or majority, is precisely and only what Congress has proscribed." And in our most recent discussion of the issue, we uttered words seemingly dispositive of this case: "It is clear beyond cavil that the obligation imposed by Title VII is to provide an equal opportunity for *each* applicant regardless of race, without regard to whether members of the applicant's race are already proportionately represented in the work force." *Furnco Construction Corp. v. Waters,* 438 U.S. 567, 579, 98 S.Ct. 2943, 2951, 57 L.Ed.2d 957 (1978).

Today, however, the Court behaves much like the Orwellian speaker * * * as if it had been handed a note indicating that Title VII would lead to a result unacceptable to the Court if interpreted here as it was in our prior decisions. Accordingly, without even a break in syntax, the Court rejects "a literal construction of § 703(a)" in favor of newly discovered "legislative history," which leads it to a conclusion directly contrary to that compelled by the "uncontradicted legislative history" unearthed in *McDonald* and our other prior decisions. Now we are told that the legislative history of Title VII shows that employers are free to discriminate on the basis of race: an employer may, in the Court's words, "trammel the interests of the white employees" in favor of black employees in order to eliminate "racial imbalance." * * *

There is perhaps no device more destructive to the notion of equality than the *numerous clausus*—the quota. Whether described as "benign discrimination" or "affirmative action," the racial quota is nonetheless a creator of castes, a two-edged sword that must demean one in order to prefer another. In passing Title VII, Congress outlawed *all* racial discrimination, recognizing that no discrimination based on race is benign, that no action disadvantaging a person because of his color is affirmative. With today's holding, the Court introduces into Title VII a tolerance for the very evil that the law was intended to eradicate, without offering even a clue as to what the limits on that tolerance may be. We are told simply that Kaiser's racially discriminatory admission quota "falls on the permissible side of the line." By going not merely *beyond*, but directly *against* Title VII's language and legislative history, the Court has sown the wind. Later courts will face the impossible task of reaping the whirlwind.

JOHNSON v. TRANSPORTATION AGENCY, SANTA CLARA COUNTY

Supreme Court of the United States, 1987
480 U.S. 616, 107 S.Ct. 1442, 94 L.Ed.2d 615

JUSTICE BRENNAN delivered the opinion of the Court.

Respondent, Transportation Agency of Santa Clara County, California, unilaterally promulgated an Affirmative Action Plan applicable, *inter alia,* to promotions of employees. In selecting applicants for the promotional position of road dispatcher, the Agency, pursuant to the Plan, passed over petitioner Paul Johnson, a male employee, and promoted a female employee applicant, Diane Joyce. The question for decision is whether in making the promotion the Agency impermissibly took into account the sex of the applicants in violation of Title VII of the Civil Rights Act of 1964. The District Court * * * held that respondent had violated Title VII. The Court of Appeals for the Ninth Circuit reversed. We granted certiorari. We affirm.[2]

I

A

In December 1978, the Santa Clara County Transit District Board of Supervisors adopted an Affirmative Action Plan (Plan) for the County Transportation Agency. The Plan * * * declared the County, because "mere prohibition of discriminatory practices is not enough to remedy the effects of past practices and to permit attainment of an equitable representation of minorities, women and handicapped persons." Relevant to this case, the Agency Plan provides that, in making promotions to positions within a traditionally segregated job classification in which women have been significantly underrepresented, the Agency is authorized to consider as one factor the sex of a qualified applicant.

In reviewing the composition of its work force, the Agency noted in its Plan that women were represented in numbers far less than their proportion of the County labor force in both the Agency as a whole and in five of seven job categories. Specifically, while women constituted 36.4% of the area labor market, they composed only 22.4% of Agency employees. Furthermore, women working at the Agency were concentrated largely in EEOC job categories traditionally held by women: women made up 76% of Office and Clerical Workers, but only 7.1% of Agency Officials and Administrators, 8.6% of Professionals, 9.7% of Technicians, and 22% of Service and Maintenance Workers. As for the job classification relevant to this case, none of the 238 Skilled Craft Worker positions was held by a

---

2. No constitutional issue was either raised or addressed in the litigation below. We therefore decide in this case only the issue of the prohibitory scope of Title VII. Of course, where the issue is properly raised, public employers must justify the adoption and implementation of a voluntary affirmative action plan under the Equal Protection Clause. See *Wygant v. Jackson Board of Education,* 476 U.S. 267, 106 S.Ct. 1842, 90 L.Ed.2d 260 (1986).

woman. The Plan noted that this underrepresentation of women in part reflected the fact that women had not traditionally been employed in these positions, and that they had not been strongly motivated to seek training or employment in them "because of the limited opportunities that have existed in the past for them to work in such classifications." The Plan also observed that, while the proportion of ethnic minorities in the Agency as a whole exceeded the proportion of such minorities in the County work force, a smaller percentage of minority employees held management, professional, and technical positions.[4]

The Agency stated that its Plan was intended to achieve "a statistically measurable yearly improvement in hiring, training and promotion of minorities and women throughout the Agency in all major job classifications where they are underrepresented." As a benchmark by which to evaluate progress, the Agency stated that its long-term goal was to attain a work force whose composition reflected the proportion of minorities and women in the area labor force. Thus, for the Skilled Craft category in which the road dispatcher position at issue here was classified, the Agency's aspiration was that eventually about 36% of the jobs would be occupied by women.

The Plan acknowledged that a number of factors might make it unrealistic to rely on the Agency's long-term goals in evaluating the Agency's progress in expanding job opportunities for minorities and women. Among the factors identified were low turnover rates in some classifications, the fact that some jobs involved heavy labor, the small number of positions within some job categories, the limited number of entry positions leading to the Technical and Skilled Craft classifications, and the limited number of minorities and women qualified for positions requiring specialized training and experience. As a result, the Plan counseled that short-range goals be established and annually adjusted to serve as the most realistic guide for actual employment decisions. Among the tasks identified as important in establishing such short-term goals was the acquisition of data "reflecting the ratio of minorities, women and handicapped persons who are working in the local area in major job classifications relating to those utilized by the County Administration," so as to determine the availability of members of such groups who "possess the desired qualifications or potential for placement." These data on qualified group members, along with predictions of position vacancies, were to serve as the basis for "realistic yearly employment goals for women, minorities and handicapped persons in each EEOC job category and major job classification."

The Agency's Plan thus set aside no specific number of positions for minorities or women, but authorized the consideration of ethnicity or sex as a factor when evaluating qualified candidates for jobs in which members of such groups were poorly represented. One such job was the road dispatcher position that is the subject of the dispute in this case.

---

4. While minorities constituted 19.7% of the County labor force, they represented 7.1% of the Agency's Officials and Administrators, 19% of its Professionals, and 16.9% of its Technicians.

B

On December 12, 1979, the Agency announced a vacancy for the promotional position of road dispatcher in the Agency's Roads Division. Dispatchers assign road crews, equipment, and materials, and maintain records pertaining to road maintenance jobs. The position requires at minimum four years of dispatch or road maintenance work experience for Santa Clara County. The EEOC job classification scheme designates a road dispatcher as a Skilled Craft Worker.

Twelve County employees applied for the promotion, including Joyce and Johnson. Joyce had worked for the County since 1970, serving as an account clerk until 1975. She had applied for a road dispatcher position in 1974, but was deemed ineligible because she had not served as a road maintenance worker. In 1975, Joyce transferred from a senior account clerk position to a road maintenance worker position, becoming the first woman to fill such a job. During her four years in that position, she occasionally worked out of class as a road dispatcher.

Petitioner Johnson began with the County in 1967 as a road yard clerk, after private employment that included working as a supervisor and dispatcher. He had also unsuccessfully applied for the road dispatcher opening in 1974. In 1977, his clerical position was downgraded, and he sought and received a transfer to the position of road maintenance worker. He also occasionally worked out of class as a dispatcher while performing that job.

Nine of the applicants, including Joyce and Johnson, were deemed qualified for the job, and were interviewed by a two-person board. Seven of the applicants scored above 70 on this interview, which meant that they were certified as eligible for selection by the appointing authority. The scores awarded ranged from 70 to 80. Johnson was tied for second with a score of 75, while Joyce ranked next with a score of 73. A second interview was conducted by three Agency supervisors, who ultimately recommended that Johnson be promoted. Prior to the second interview, Joyce had contacted the County's Affirmative Action Office because she feared that her application might not receive disinterested review. The Office in turn contacted the Agency's Affirmative Action Coordinator, whom the Agency's Plan makes responsible for, *inter alia,* keeping the Director informed of opportunities for the Agency to accomplish its objectives under the Plan. At the time, the Agency employed no women in any Skilled Craft position, and had never employed a woman as a road dispatcher. The Coordinator recommended to the Director of the Agency, James Graebner, that Joyce be promoted.

Graebner, authorized to choose any of the seven persons deemed eligible, thus had the benefit of suggestions by the second interview panel and by the Agency Coordinator in arriving at his decision. After deliberation, Graebner concluded that the promotion should be given to Joyce. As he testified: "I tried to look at the whole picture, the combination of her qualifications and Mr. Johnson's qualifications, their test scores, their expertise, their background, affirmative action matters, things like that. . . . I believe it was a combination of all those."

* * * The District Court found that Johnson was more qualified for the dispatcher position than Joyce, and that the sex of Joyce was the "*determining factor* in her selection." The court acknowledged that, since the Agency justified its decision on the basis of its Affirmative Action Plan, the criteria announced in *Steelworkers v. Weber,* 443 U.S. 193, 99 S.Ct. 2721, 61 L.Ed.2d 480 (1979), should be applied in evaluating the validity of the Plan. It then found the Agency's Plan invalid on the ground that the evidence did not satisfy *Weber's* criterion that the Plan be temporary. The Court of Appeals for the Ninth Circuit reversed, holding that the absence of an express termination date in the Plan was not dispositive, since the Plan repeatedly expressed its objective as the attainment, rather than the maintenance, of a work force mirroring the labor force in the County. The Court of Appeals added that the fact that the Plan established no fixed percentage of positions for minorities or women made it less essential that the Plan contain a relatively explicit deadline. The Court held further that the Agency's consideration of Joyce's sex in filling the road dispatcher position was lawful. The Agency Plan had been adopted, the court said, to address a conspicuous imbalance in the Agency's work force, and neither unnecessarily trammeled the rights of other employees, nor created an absolute bar to their advancement.

II

As a preliminary matter, we note that [plaintiff] bears the burden of establishing the invalidity of the Agency's Plan. Only last Term, in *Wygant v. Jackson Board of Education,* 476 U.S. 267, 277–278, 106 S.Ct. 1842, 1849, 90 L.Ed.2d 260 (1986), we held that "[t]he ultimate burden remains with the employees to demonstrate the unconstitutionality of an affirmative-action program," and we see no basis for a different rule regarding a plan's alleged violation of Title VII. This case also fits readily within the analytical framework set forth in *McDonnell Douglas Corp. v. Green,* 411 U.S. 792, 93 S.Ct. 1817, 36 L.Ed.2d 668 (1973). Once a plaintiff establishes a prima facie case that race or sex has been taken into account in an employer's employment decision, the burden shifts to the employer to articulate a nondiscriminatory rationale for its decision. The existence of an affirmative action plan provides such a rationale. If such a plan is articulated as the basis for the employer's decision, the burden shifts to the plaintiff to prove that the employer's justification is pretextual and the plan is invalid. As a practical matter, of course, an employer will generally seek to avoid a charge of pretext by presenting evidence in support of its plan. That does not mean, however, as petitioner suggests, that reliance on an affirmative action plan is to be treated as an affirmative defense requiring the employer to carry the burden of proving the validity of the plan. The burden of proving its invalidity remains on the plaintiff.

The assessment of the legality of the Agency Plan must be guided by our decision in *Weber, supra.*[6] [The Court here summarized the facts and holding in *Weber*]

We noted [in *Weber*] that the plan did not "unnecessarily trammel the interests of the white employees," since it did not require "the discharge of white workers and their replacement with new black *Weber* held that an employer seeking to justify the adoption of a plan need not point to its own prior discriminatory practices, nor even to evidence of an "arguable violation" on its part. Rather, it need point only to a "conspicuous . . . imbalance in traditionally segregated job categories." Our decision [in *Weber*] was grounded in the recognition that voluntary employer action can play a crucial role in furthering Title VII's purpose of eliminating the effects of discrimination in the workplace, and that Title VII should not be read to thwart such efforts.

In reviewing the employment decision at issue in this case, we must first examine whether that decision was made pursuant to a plan prompted by concerns similar to those of the employer in *Weber*. Next, we must determine whether the effect of the Plan on males and nonminorities is comparable to the effect of the Plan in that case.

The first issue is therefore whether consideration of the sex of applicants for Skilled Craft jobs was justified by the existence of a "manifest imbalance" that reflected underrepresentation of women in "traditionally segregated job categories." In determining whether an imbalance exists that would justify taking sex or race into account, a comparison of the percentage of minorities or women in the employer's work force with the percentage in the area labor market or general population is appropriate in analyzing jobs that require no special expertise, The requirement that the "manifest imbalance" relate to a "traditionally segregated job category" provides assurance both that sex or race will be taken into account in a manner consistent with Title VII's purpose of eliminating the effects of employment discrimination, and that the interests of those employees not benefiting from the plan will not be unduly infringed.

A manifest imbalance need not be such that it would support a prima facie case against the employer, * * * since we do not regard as identical the constraints of Title VII and the Federal Constitution on voluntarily adopted affirmative action plans. Application of the "prima facie" stan-

---

6. Justice SCALIA's dissent maintains that the obligations of a public employer under Title VII must be identical to its obligations under the Constitution, and that a public employer's adoption of an affirmative action plan therefore should be governed by *Wygant*. This rests on the following logic: Title VI embodies the same constraints as the Constitution; Title VI and Title VII have the same prohibitory scope; therefore, Title VII and the Constitution are coterminous for purposes of this case. The flaw is with the second step of the analysis, for it advances a proposition that we explicitly considered and rejected in *Weber*. As we noted in that case, Title VI was an exercise of federal power "over a matter in which the Federal Government was already directly involved," since Congress "was legislating to assure federal funds would not be used in an improper manner." "Title VII, by contrast, was enacted pursuant to the commerce power to regulate purely private decisionmaking and was not intended to incorporate and particularize the commands of the Fifth and Fourteenth Amendments. Title VII and Title VI, therefore, cannot be read *in pari materia*" * * *

dard in Title VII cases would be inconsistent with *Weber's* focus on statistical imbalance,[10] and could inappropriately create a significant disincentive for employers to adopt an affirmative action plan. A corporation concerned with maximizing return on investment, for instance, is hardly likely to adopt a plan if in order to do so it must compile evidence that could be used to subject it to a colorable Title VII suit.

* * *

As an initial matter, the Agency adopted as a benchmark for measuring progress in eliminating underrepresentation the long-term goal of a work force that mirrored in its major job classifications the percentage of women in the area labor market. * * * The Plan stressed that such goals "should not be construed as 'quotas' that must be met," but as reasonable aspirations in correcting the imbalance in the Agency's work force. These goals were to take into account factors such as "turnover, layoffs, lateral transfers, new job openings, retirements and availability of minorities, women and handicapped persons in the area work force who possess the desired qualifications or potential for placement." * * * From the outset, therefore, the Plan sought annually to develop even more refined measures of the underrepresentation in each job category that required attention.

* * *

The Agency's Plan emphatically did *not* authorize such blind hiring. It expressly directed that numerous factors be taken into account in making hiring decisions, including specifically the qualifications of female applicants for particular jobs. Thus, despite the fact that no precise short-term goal was yet in place for the Skilled Craft category in mid–1980, the Agency's management nevertheless had been clearly instructed that they were not to hire solely by reference to statistics. The fact that only the long-term goal had been established for this category posed no danger that personnel decisions would be made by reflexive adherence to a numerical standard.

---

10. The difference between the "manifest imbalance" and "prima facie" standards is illuminated by *Weber*. Had the Court in that case been concerned with past discrimination by the employer, it would have focused on discrimination in hiring skilled, not unskilled, workers, since only the scarcity of the former in Kaiser's work force would have made it vulnerable to a Title VII suit. In order to make out a prima facie case on such a claim, a plaintiff would be required to compare the percentage of black skilled workers in the Kaiser work force with the percentage of black skilled craft workers in the area labor market.

Weber obviously did not make such a comparison. Instead, it focused on the disparity between the percentage of black skilled craft workers in Kaiser's ranks and the percentage of blacks in the area labor force. Such an approach reflected a recognition that the proportion of black craft workers in the local labor force was likely as miniscule as the proportion in Kaiser's work force. The Court realized that the lack of imbalance between these figures would mean that employers in precisely those industries in which discrimination has been most effective would be precluded from adopting training programs to increase the percentage of qualified minorities. Thus, in cases such as *Weber,* where the employment decision at issue involves the selection of unskilled persons for a training program, the "manifest imbalance" standard permits comparison with the general labor force. By contrast, the "prima facie" standard would require comparison with the percentage of minorities or women qualified for the job for which the trainees are being trained, a standard that would have invalidated the plan in *Weber* itself.

Furthermore, in considering the candidates for the road dispatcher position in 1980, the Agency hardly needed to rely on a refined short-term goal to realize that it had a significant problem of underrepresentation that required attention. Given the obvious imbalance in the Skilled Craft category, and given the Agency's commitment to eliminating such imbalances, it was plainly not unreasonable for the Agency to determine that it was appropriate to consider as one factor the sex of Ms. Joyce in making its decision. The promotion of Joyce thus satisfies the first requirement enunciated in *Weber,* since it was undertaken to further an affirmative action plan designed to eliminate Agency work force imbalances in traditionally segregated job categories.

We next consider whether the Agency Plan unnecessarily trammeled the rights of male employees or created an absolute bar to their advancement. In contrast to the plan in *Weber,* which provided that 50% of the positions in the craft training program were exclusively for blacks, and to the consent decree upheld last Term in *Firefighters v. Cleveland,* 478 U.S. 501, 106 S.Ct. 3063, 92 L.Ed.2d 405 (1986), which required the promotion of specific numbers of minorities, the Plan sets aside no positions for women. The Plan expressly states that "[t]he 'goals' established for each Division should not be construed as 'quotas' that must be met." Rather, the Plan merely authorizes that consideration be given to affirmative action concerns when evaluating qualified applicants. As the Agency Director testified, the sex of Joyce was but one of numerous factors he took into account in arriving at his decision. The Plan thus resembles the "Harvard Plan" approvingly noted by Justice POWELL in *Regents of University of California v. Bakke,* 438 U.S. 265, 316–319, 98 S.Ct. 2733, 2761–2763, 57 L.Ed.2d 750 (1978), which considers race along with other criteria in determining admission to the college. As JUSTICE POWELL observed: "In such an admissions program, race or ethnic background may be deemed a 'plus' in a particular applicant's file, yet it does not insulate the individual from comparison with all other candidates for the available seats." Similarly, the Agency Plan requires women to compete with all other qualified applicants. *No* persons are automatically excluded from consideration; *all* are able to have their qualifications weighed against those of other applicants.

In addition, petitioner had no absolute entitlement to the road dispatcher position. Seven of the applicants were classified as qualified and eligible, and the Agency Director was authorized to promote any of the seven. Thus, denial of the promotion unsettled no legitimate, firmly rooted expectation on the part of petitioner. Furthermore, while petitioner in this case was denied a promotion, he retained his employment with the Agency, at the same salary and with the same seniority, and remained eligible for other promotions.

Finally, the Agency's Plan was intended to *attain* a balanced work force, not to maintain one. The Plan contains 10 references to the Agency's desire to "attain" such a balance, but no reference whatsoever to a goal of maintaining it. The Director testified that, while the "broader goal" of affirmative action, defined as "the desire to hire, to promote, to give opportunity and training on an equitable, non-discriminatory basis," is something that is "a permanent part" of "the Agency's operating philosophy," that broader goal "is divorced, if you will, from specific numbers or percentages."

The Agency acknowledged the difficulties that it would confront in remedying the imbalance in its work force, and it anticipated only gradual increases in the representation of minorities and women. It is thus unsurprising that the Plan contains no explicit end date, for the Agency's flexible, case-by-case approach was not expected to yield success in a brief period of time. Express assurance that a program is only temporary may be necessary if the program actually sets aside positions according to specific numbers. This is necessary both to minimize the effect of the program on other employees, and to ensure that the plan's goals "[are] not being used simply to achieve and maintain . . . balance, but rather as a benchmark against which" the employer may measure its progress in eliminating the underrepresentation of minorities and women. In this case, however, substantial evidence shows that the Agency has sought to take a moderate, gradual approach to eliminating the imbalance in its work force, one which establishes realistic guidance for employment decisions, and which visits minimal intrusion on the legitimate expectations of other employees. Given this fact, as well as the Agency's express commitment to "attain" a balanced work force, there is ample assurance that the Agency does not seek to use its Plan to maintain a permanent racial and sexual balance.

* * *

We therefore hold that the Agency appropriately took into account as one factor the sex of Diane Joyce in determining that she should be promoted to the road dispatcher position. The decision to do so was made pursuant to an affirmative action plan that represents a moderate, flexible, case-by-case approach to effecting a gradual improvement in the representation of minorities and women in the Agency's work force. Such a plan is fully consistent with Title VII, for it embodies the contribution that voluntary employer action can make in eliminating the vestiges of discrimination in the workplace. Accordingly, the judgment of the Court of Appeals is Affirmed.

[The concurring opinions of JUSTICE STEVENS and JUSTICE O'CONNOR and the dissenting opinions of JUSTICE WHITE and JUSTICE SCALIA, joined by CHIEF JUSTICE REHNQUIST and, in part, by JUSTICE WHITE, are omitted.]

NOTES

1. *Civil Rights Amendments of 1991:* Newly added § 703(m) provides:

[A]n unlawful employment practice is established when the complaining party demonstrates that race, color, religion, sex, or national origin was a motivating factor for any employment practice, even though other factors also motivated the practice.

This might suggest legislative overruling of the principal cases. However, § 116 of the amendments provided that "[n]othing in the amendments * * * shall affect court-ordered remedies, affirmative action, or conciliation agreements that are in accordance with the law." *Officers for Justice v. Civil Service Comm.,* 979 F.2d 721 (9th Cir. 1992), held, and the EEOC reconfirmed, that § 703(m) did not change affirmative action law as previously defined by the Court. 29 C.F.R. pt. 1608.

2. *Reasonable Means:* Reserving certain positions for persons of one race or sex is not reasonable, but resembles an inappropriate quota. Thus, when a black employee retires from a position, the plan cannot provide for filing that vacancy with a black person. *Hill v. Ross,* 183 F.3d 586 (7th Cir. 1999).

3. *Layoffs:* Note that the plans accepted in *Weber* and *Santa Clara County* were limited to hiring. Programs that provide for the *dismissal* of incumbent employees in order to hire additional women or minorities, or even using race or sex in determining layoffs occasioned by an economic adjustment, have been held to "unduly trammel" interests of white male employees. *Taxman v. Board of Edu. of Tp of Piscataway,* 91 F.3d 1547 (3d Cir. 1996).

4. *Tests:* Affirmative action generally envisions that employers will evaluate their selection devices for any adverse impact, and if the device produces a disproportionate impact on a protected class, the employer will utilize lesser discriminatory alternatives, or validate the job relatedness of that test by professional standards. However, the 1991 Amendments to Title VII provide:

> It shall be an unlawful employment practice for a respondent, in connection with the selection or referral of applicants or candidates for employment or promotions, to adjust the scores of, use different cutoff scores for, or otherwise alter the results of, employment related tests on the basis of race, color, religion, sex, or national origin. 42 U.S.C. § 703(*l*).

This proviso prohibiting racial "adjustment" would not facially apply if the employer simply disregarded the outcome of a selection device because of statistically disparate outcomes between the races. However,—

5. ***Ricci v. DeStefano,* 557 U.S. 557, 129 S.Ct. 2658, 174 L.Ed.2d 490 (2009),** *infra,* p. 331, held that a decision by an employer to ignore a test result because of its disproportionate barrier to hiring racial minorities was itself race discrimination that could not be justified by pursuit of a general affirmative action goal. The Court did allow, however, that a test having an adverse racial impact could be disregarded if there is a "strong basis in the evidence" for the employer to conclude that use of the test would impose on it Title VII liability. The Court indicated also that employers might evaluate a test for its racial impact *prior* to it being implemented. The evil the majority saw in disregarding results of a test already administered is that to do so frustrated legitimate expectations of the plaintiffs who were denied the benefit of the results.

6. *Wake of Ricci:* Note that the *Weber* Court rejected the argument that the threshold justification for use of racial considerations as part of an affirmative action plan required a prima facie showing of liability. Moreover, *Santa Clara County* confirms that the plaintiffs challenging the affirmative

action plan must carry the burden of proving failure to meet the *Weber* standards. As applied to setting aside a selection device based on its disproportionate effect, *Ricci* appears inconsistent with the *Weber* approach. As a threshold *Ricci* requires more than "a conspicuous imbalance," more than a *prima facie* showing of potential liability, but a "strong basis in the evidence" of its own liability to minority workers. *Ricci* implicitly also may have limited the application of the *Weber/Johnson* framework to existing forward looking "plans" implemented to remedy imbalances, and will not allow "affirmative action" to justify in-place systems that have in their application produced imbalance unless there is a "strong basis in evidence" that the existing system was illegal. *See,United States v. Brennan* 650 F.3d 65 (2d Cir. 2011).

7. *Constitutional Issues:* As a public employer Santa Clara County's plan was also subject to constitutional scrutiny. Note how the Court sidestepped that issue. Nonetheless, public employers and affirmative action regulations of the Department of Labor must be cognizant of constitutional constraints that differ from Title VII.

The first issue was whether "benign" use of race or sex to benefit, not harm, a "discrete and insular minority" was "suspect" and thus subject to "strict judicial scrutiny." Sharply divided Courts have concluded that all use of race was "suspect." However, the Court appeared to weaken somewhat the strictness of the scrutiny it would engage in. Strict scrutiny was not to be fatal in practice. ***Adarand Constructors, Inc. v. Pena,*** 515 U.S. 200, 115 S.Ct. 2097, 132 L.Ed.2d 158 (1995)

Generally stated in the employment context, remedying "identified" past discrimination against a protected class will be a "compelling governmental interest." However, remedying "societal discrimination" is probably insufficiently "compelling" to warrant the use of race in making hiring decisions. ***Wygant v. Jackson Board of Educ.,*** 476 U.S. 267, 106 S.Ct. 1842, 90 L.Ed.2d 260 (1986).

When confronted with "identified" underrepresentation, remedial responses that use race, national origin, or sex must be flexible, avoiding rigid numerical quotas. Using an applicant's race or sex as *one factor* among many that influence individual decisions will be reasonable. ***Grutter v. Bollinger,*** 539 U.S. 306, 123 S.Ct. 2325, 156 L.Ed.2d 304 (2003). The plan used in *Santa Clara County* thus appears consistent with the constitutional analysis of *Grutter v. Bollinger, supra.* However, setting a fixed 1–1 ratio, as was done in *Weber,* may not be the "narrowly tailored response" required by the Constitution. See, ***Gratz v. Bollinger,*** 539 U.S. 244, 123 S.Ct. 2411, 156 L.Ed.2d 257 (2003); ***Parents Involved v. Seattle School Dist. No. 1,*** 551 U.S. 701, 127 S.Ct. 2738, 168 L.Ed.2d 508 (2007).

CHAPTER 4

"TERMS, CONDITIONS, OR PRIVILEGES OF EMPLOYMENT"

■ ■ ■

A. GENERALLY

Differences in work place treatment are inevitable. Shifts, tasks and work stations must be assigned. Employees have disagreements with their supervisors. Harsh words may be exchanged. Regardless of any lurking invidious motive behind the employer's actions, the courts have resisted becoming "super personnel departments" that resolve routine work place distinctions and disagreements. The statutes "are not intended to reach every bigoted act or gesture that a worker might encounter in the work place." *Thompson v. Memorial Hosp. of Carbondale*, 625 F.3d 394 (7th Cir. 2010). Courts repeatedly recite the truism that the statutes do not impose a general code of civility or guarantee employees a fair minded or genial boss. *Lisdahl v. Mayo Foundation*, 633 F.3d 712 (8th Cir. 2011). Nonetheless, at some point, differences in treatment rise to the level of warranting judicial inquiry into the motivation for that treatment.

BURLINGTON NORTHERN & SANTA FE RAILWAY CO. v. WHITE

Supreme Court of the United States, 2006
548 U.S. 53, 126 S.Ct. 2405, 165 L.Ed.2d 345

JUSTICE BREYER delivered the opinion of the Court.

[This case involved Title VII's § 704's prohibition of *"discrimination"* against individuals for participating in proceedings or opposing practices made unlawful. The court of appeals had held that the *"terms or conditions of employment"* requirement of § 703 was implicit in the § 704 prohibition against retaliatory "discrimination," and that the reassignment and temporary suspension without loss of pay did not rise to the level of adversely affecting plaintiff's *"terms or conditions of employment."* The Supreme Court reversed. It first determined that: "Title VII's substantive provision and its anti-retaliation provision are not coterminous. * * * "We * * * reject the standards applied in the Courts of Appeals that have treated the anti-retaliation provision as forbidding the same conduct prohibited by the antidiscrimination provision and that have limited actionable retaliation to so-called "ultimate employment decisions." The Court then addressed whether the reassignment of the plaintiff violated the non-discrimination provisions of § 704.]

* * *

The anti-retaliation provision [of § 704] protects an individual not from all retaliation, but from retaliation that produces an injury or harm. * * * In our view, a plaintiff must show that a reasonable employee would have found the challenged action materially adverse, "which in this context means it well might have 'dissuaded a reasonable worker from making or supporting a charge of discrimination.' "

We speak of *material* adversity because we believe it is important to separate significant from trivial harms. Title VII, we have said, does not set forth "a general civility code for the American workplace." An employee's decision to report discriminatory behavior cannot immunize that employee from those petty slights or minor annoyances that often take place at work and that all employees experience. ("courts have held that personality conflicts at work that generate antipathy" and " 'snubbing' by supervisors and co-workers" are not actionable under § 704(a)). The anti-retaliation provision seeks to prevent employer interference with "unfettered access" to Title VII's remedial mechanism. It does so by prohibiting employer actions that are likely "to deter victims of discrimination from complaining to the EEOC," the courts, and their employers. And normally petty slights, minor annoyances, and simple lack of good manners will not create such deterrence.

We refer to reactions of a *reasonable* employee because we believe that the provision's standard for judging harm must be objective. An objective standard is judicially administrable. It avoids the uncertainties and unfair discrepancies that can plague a judicial effort to determine a plaintiff's unusual subjective feelings. We have emphasized the need for objective standards in other Title VII contexts, and those same concerns animate our decision here.

We phrase the standard in general terms because the significance of any given act of retaliation will often depend upon the particular circumstances. Context matters. "The real social impact of workplace behavior often depends on a constellation of surrounding circumstances, expectations, and relationships which are not fully captured by a simple recitation of the words used or the physical acts performed." A schedule change in an employee's work schedule may make little difference to many workers, but may matter enormously to a young mother with school-age children. A supervisor's refusal to invite an employee to lunch is normally trivial, a nonactionable petty slight. But to retaliate by excluding an employee from a weekly training lunch that contributes significantly to the employee's professional advancement might well deter a reasonable employee from complaining about discrimination. Hence, a legal standard that speaks in general terms rather than specific prohibited acts is preferable, for an "act that would be immaterial in some situations is material in others." * * *

Applying this standard to the facts of this case, we believe that there was a sufficient evidentiary basis to support the jury's verdict on White's retaliation claim. The jury found that two of Burlington's actions amounted to retaliation: the reassignment of White from forklift duty to standard track laborer tasks and the 37–day suspension without pay.

Burlington does not question the jury's determination that the motivation for these acts was retaliatory. But it does question the statutory significance of the harm these acts caused. The District Court instructed the jury to determine whether respondent "suffered a materially adverse change in the terms or conditions of her employment," and the Sixth Circuit upheld the jury's finding based on that same stringent interpretation of the anti-retaliation provision (the interpretation that limits § 704 to the same employment-related conduct forbidden by § 703). Our holding today makes clear that the jury was not required to find that the challenged actions were related to the terms or conditions of employment. And insofar as the jury also found that the actions were "materially adverse," its findings are adequately supported.

First, Burlington argues that a reassignment of duties cannot constitute retaliatory discrimination where, as here, both the former and present duties fall within the same job description. We do not see why that is so. Almost every job category involves some responsibilities and duties that are less desirable than others. Common sense suggests that one good way to discourage an employee such as White from bringing discrimination charges would be to insist that she spend more time performing the more arduous duties and less time performing those that are easier or more agreeable. That is presumably why the EEOC has consistently found "[r]etaliatory work assignments" to be a classic and "widely recognized" example of "forbidden retaliation."

To be sure, reassignment of job duties is not automatically actionable. Whether a particular reassignment is materially adverse depends upon the circumstances of the particular case, and "should be judged from the perspective of a reasonable person in the plaintiff's position, considering 'all the circumstances.'" But here, the jury had before it considerable evidence that the track laborer duties were "by all accounts more arduous and dirtier"; that the "forklift operator position required more qualifications, which is an indication of prestige"; and that "the forklift operator position was objectively considered a better job and the male employees resented White for occupying it." Based on this record, a jury could reasonably conclude that the reassignment of responsibilities would have been materially adverse to a reasonable employee.

Second, Burlington argues that the 37–day suspension without pay lacked statutory significance because Burlington ultimately reinstated White with backpay. Burlington says that "it defies reason to believe that Congress would have considered a rescinded investigatory suspension with full back pay" to be unlawful, particularly because Title VII, throughout much of its history, provided no relief in an equitable action for victims in White's position.

* * *

Neither do we find convincing any claim of insufficient evidence. White did receive backpay. But White and her family had to live for 37 days without income. They did not know during that time whether or when White could return to work. Many reasonable employees would find a month without a paycheck to be a serious hardship. And White described to the jury the physical and emotional hardship that 37 days of having "no income, no money" in fact caused. Indeed, she obtained medical treatment for her emotional distress. A reasonable employee facing the choice between retaining her job (and paycheck) and filing a discrimination complaint might well choose the former. That is to say, an indefinite suspension without pay could well act as a deterrent, even if the suspended employee eventually received backpay. Thus, the jury's conclusion that the 37–day suspension without pay was materially adverse was a reasonable one.

* * *

JUSTICE ALITO, concurring in the judgment.

* * * I would not adopt the majority's test but would hold that § 704(a) reaches only those discriminatory practices covered by § 703(a).

Applying this interpretation, I would affirm the decision of the Court of Appeals. The actions taken against respondent-her assignment to new and substantially less desirable duties and her suspension without pay-fall within the definition of an "adverse employment action."

* * * Here, as the Court of Appeals stated, "[i]n essence . . . the reassignment was a demotion." The "new position was by all accounts more arduous and 'dirtier,' and petitioner's sole stated rationale for the reassignment was that respondent's prior duties were better suited for someone with greater seniority. This was virtually an admission that respondent was demoted when those responsibilities were taken away from her.

I would hold that respondent's suspension without pay likewise satisfied the materially adverse employment action test. * * *

NOTES

1. **Meritor Savings Bank v. Vinson**, 477 U.S. 57, 106 S.Ct. 2399, 91 L.Ed.2d 49 (1986), held that the statutes are "not limited to economic or tangible discrimination * * * but strike at the entire spectrum of disparate treatment." The treatment need not cause physical or psychological injury nor adversely affect the worker's job performance. **Harris v. Forklift Systems,** 510 U.S. 17, 114 S.Ct. 367, 126 L.Ed.2d 295 (1993). *MeritorSavings* and *Harris* reflect an expansive reading of § 703. That reading appeared to be narrowed in **Oncale v. Sundowner Offshore Services, Inc.,** 523 U.S. 75,

118 S.Ct. 998, 140 L.Ed.2d 201 (1998): "Title VII * * * [cannot be expanded] into a general civility code: As we emphasized in *Meritor* and *Harris*, the statute does not reach genuine but innocuous differences in [treatment]. * * * [Title VII] forbids only behavior so objectively offensive as to alter the 'conditions of the victim's employment.' * * * [W]e have always regarded that requirement as crucial, and as sufficient to ensure that courts and juries do not mistake ordinary socializing in the workplace * * * for discriminatory 'conditions of employment.' * * * "

2. *Whether Differences in Treatment Are Minor or Significant:*

a. Work-place aesthetic differences, office locations, allocation of lunch and break times, or minor differences in the length of such breaks do not rise to being actionable "discrimination." Routine or temporary allocation of job duties within a worker's general job description rarely will be "discrimination" within the meaning of § 704, nor adversely affect a "term or condition of employment" triggering § 703 analysis. *Morales–Vallellanes v. Potter,* 605 F.3d 27 (1st Cir. 2010).

b. *"Lateral" transfers":* ***Stewart v. Ashcroft*, 352 F.3d 422 (D.C.Cir. 2003),** addressed a denial to plaintiff of a similar job with similar working conditions and identical tangible benefits:

"[W]e recognized that while generally lateral transfers, or the denial of them, could not be considered adverse employment actions, there are circumstances where they could be. * * * Just as withdrawing an employee's supervisory duties constitutes an adverse employment action, so too failing to select an employee for a position with substantially greater supervisory authority is an adverse employment action."

c. *Prestige:* ***Alvarado v. Texas Rangers***, 492 F.3d 605, 613 n.7 (5th Cir. 2007), held that transfers that caused only a "loss of subjective prestige," in the plaintiff's own mind cannot be an adverse action. However, transfers or loss of responsibilities resulting in the loss of *objective* standing or prestige as reasonably observed by third parties may constitute an adverse action, particularly in an action alleging § 704 retaliation.

d. *Evaluations:* Criticisms and less than satisfactory performance evaluations do not in themselves constitute actionable adverse employment actions. Nevertheless, written reprimands, or formal evaluations that have serious consequences, such as exposing the employee to removal, demotion, reassignment, or denial of pay increases can be considered adverse actions. ***Porter v. Shah,*** 606 F.3d 809 (D.C.Cir. 2010).

e. *Shifts:* ***CORNING GLASS WORKS v. BRENNAN,*** 417 U.S. 188, 94 S.Ct. 2223, 41 L.Ed.2d 1 (1974), held that under the Equal Pay Act, "working conditions" measures physical "surroundings" and differences in "hazards." The time of day work is performed is not a "working condition." However, as Title VII makes "reasonableness" and "context" critical, consider a single mother whose transfer to a night shift would, for her, make effective child care very difficult. *Watson v. CEVA Logistics U.S., Inc.*, 619 F.3d 936 (8th Cir. 2010).

f. *Re–Locations:* Reassignment to a different physical establishment that presents minimal inconvenience to the worker would not normally affect adversely a term of employment. However, if the assignment rendered commuting particularly burdensome or expensive to this particular employee, the reassignment might adversely affect this employee's "terms and conditions of employment." Compare: *Sanchez v. Denver Public Schools*, 164 F.3d 527 (10th Cir. 1998); *Wyatt v. City of Boston,* 35 F.3d 13 (1st Cir. 1994); and *Hoffman v. Rubin,* 193 F.3d 959 (8th Cir. 1999). As "discrimination" under § 704 requires only that the action of the employer "might have dissuaded a reasonable worker from making or supporting a charge of discrimination," a site location transfer could reasonably be seen has having such a chilling effect.

3. *Security Clearances:* Title VII, § 703(g) provides:

[I]t shall not be an unlawful employment practice for an employer to fail or refuse to hire . . . any individual, [or] for an employer to discharge any individual from any position, . . . if—

(1) the occupancy of such position, or access to the premises . . . is subject to any requirement imposed in the interest of the national security . . . ; and

(2) such individual has not fulfilled or has ceased to fulfill that requirement.

A government employee who held a position requiring a security clearance filed a charge of discrimination against his government employer. The employer initiated a security clearance investigation. Held: this was an adverse action under § 704 in that it could reasonably chill the filing of discrimination charges. **Rattigan v. Holder,** 643 F.3d 975 (D.C.Cir. 2011).

4. **The Uniformed Services Employment and Reemployment Act,** 38 U.S.C. § 4311(b), proscribes retaliation against persons for asserting rights under this Act. However, the proscriptive language differs from Title VII, prompting one court to require a military veteran alleging retaliation to establish that his treatment was sufficiently severe to constitute "significant harm." **Lisdahl v. Mayo Foundation**, 633 F.3d 712 (8th Cir. 2011).

B. WORK PLACE RULES

JESPERSEN v. HARRAH'S OPERATING COMPANY, INC.

United States Court of Appeals, Ninth Circuit, 2006
444 F.3d 1104

SCHROEDER, CHIEF JUDGE.

[The facts were reproduced *supra, page 66.* In Part I, there reproduced, the court held that sex based grooming requirements were not sex discrimination based on a sexual stereotype, but would be sex discrimination if the differences in fact burdened one sex.]

* * *

II.   UNEQUAL BURDENS

* * * Jespersen argues that the makeup requirement itself establishes a prima facie case of discriminatory intent and must be justified by Harrah's as a bona fide occupational qualification. Our settled law in this circuit, however, does not support Jespersen's position that a sex-based difference in appearance standards alone, without any further showing of disparate effects, creates a prima facie case.

In *Gerdom v. Cont'l Airlines, Inc.,* 692 F.2d 602 (9th Cir.1982), we considered the Continental Airlines policy that imposed strict weight restrictions on female flight attendants, and held it constituted a violation of Title VII. We did so because the airline imposed no weight restriction whatsoever on a class of male employees who performed the same or similar functions as the flight attendants. Indeed, the policy was touted by the airline as intended to "create the public image of an airline which offered passengers service by thin, attractive women, whom executives referred to as Continental's 'girls.'" In fact, Continental specifically argued that its policy was justified by its "desire to compete [with other airlines] by featuring attractive female cabin attendants[,]" a justification which this court recognized as "discriminatory on its face." The weight restriction was part of an overall program to create a sexual image for the airline.

In contrast, this case involves an appearance policy that applied to both male and female bartenders, and was aimed at creating a professional and very similar look for all of them. All bartenders wore the same uniform. The policy only differentiated as to grooming standards.

In *Frank v. United Airlines, Inc.,* 216 F.3d 845 (9th Cir. 2000), we dealt with a weight policy that applied different standards to men and women in a facially unequal way. The women were forced to meet the requirements of a medium body frame standard while men were required to meet only the more generous requirements of a large body frame standard. In that case, we recognized that "[a]n appearance standard that imposes different but essentially equal burdens on men and women is not disparate treatment." The United weight policy, however, did not impose equal burdens. On its face, the policy embodied a requirement that categorically " 'applie[d] less favorably to one gender[,]'" and the burdens imposed upon that gender were obvious from the policy itself."

This case stands in marked contrast, for here we deal with requirements that, on their face, are not more onerous for one gender than the other. Rather, Harrah's "Personal Best" policy contains sex-differentiated requirements regarding each employee's hair, hands, and face. While those individual requirements differ according to gender, none on its face places a greater burden on one gender than the other. Grooming standards that appropriately differentiate between the genders are not facially discriminatory.

We have long recognized that companies may differentiate between men and women in appearance and grooming policies, and so have other circuits. The material issue under our settled law is not whether the policies are different, but whether the policy imposed on the plaintiff creates an "unequal burden" for the plaintiff's gender.

Not every differentiation between the sexes in a grooming and appearance policy creates a "significantly greater burden of compliance[.] For example, in *Fountain [v. Safeway Stores, Inc.,* 555 F.2d 753, 755 (9th Cir.1977)], this court upheld Safeway's enforcement of its sex-differentiated appearance standard, including its requirement that male employees wear ties, because the company's actions in enforcing the regulations were not "overly burdensome to its employees. Similarly, as the Eighth Circuit has recognized, "[w]here, as here, such [grooming and appearance] policies are reasonable and are imposed in an evenhanded manner on all employees, slight differences in the appearance requirements for males and females have only a negligible effect on employment opportunities." Under established equal burdens analysis, when an employer's grooming and appearance policy does not unreasonably burden one gender more than the other, that policy will not violate Title VII.

Jespersen asks us to take judicial notice of the fact that it costs more money and takes more time for a woman to comply with the makeup requirement than it takes for a man to comply with the requirement that he keep his hair short, but these are not matters appropriate for judicial notice. Judicial notice is reserved for matters "generally known within the territorial jurisdiction of the trial court" or "capable of accurate and ready determination by resort to sources whose accuracy cannot reasonably be questioned." Fed.R.Evid. 201. The time and cost of makeup and haircuts is in neither category. The facts that Jespersen would have this court judicially notice are not subject to the requisite "high degree of indisputability" generally required for such judicial notice.

Our rules thus provide that a plaintiff may not cure her failure to present the trial court with facts sufficient to establish the validity of her claim by requesting that this court take judicial notice of such. Those rules apply here. Jespersen did not submit any documentation or any evidence of the relative cost and time required to comply with the grooming requirements by men and women. As a result, we would have to speculate about those issues in order to then guess whether the policy creates unequal burdens for women. This would not be appropriate.

Having failed to create a record establishing that the "Personal Best" policies are more burdensome for women than for men, Jespersen did not present any triable issue of fact. The district court correctly granted summary judgment on the record before it with respect to Jespersen's claim that the makeup policy created an unequal burden for women.

AFFIRMED.

KOZXINSKI, CIRCUIT JUDGE, with whom JUDGES GRABER and W. FLECTCHER join, dissenting:

* * * The majority is right that "[t]he [makeup] requirements must be viewed in the context of the overall policy." But I find it perfectly clear that Harrah's overall grooming policy is substantially more burdensome for women than for men. Every requirement that forces men to spend time or money on their appearance has a corresponding requirement that

is as, or more, burdensome for women: short hair v. "teased, curled, or styled" hair; clean trimmed nails v. nail length and color requirements; black leather shoes v. black leather shoes. The requirement that women spend time and money applying full facial makeup has no corresponding requirement for men, making the "overall policy" more burdensome for the former than for the latter. The only question is how much.

It is true that Jespersen failed to present evidence about what it costs to buy makeup and how long it takes to apply it. But is there any doubt that putting on makeup costs money and takes time? Harrah's policy requires women to apply face powder, blush, mascara and lipstick. You don't need an expert witness to figure out that such items don't grow on trees.

Nor is there any rational doubt that application of makeup is an intricate and painstaking process that requires considerable time and care. Even those of us who don't wear makeup know how long it can take from the hundreds of hours we've spent over the years frantically tapping our toes and pointing to our wrists. It's hard to imagine that a woman could "put on her face," as they say, in the time it would take a man to shave-certainly not if she were to do the careful and thorough job Harrah's expects. Makeup, moreover, must be applied and removed every day; the policy burdens men with no such daily ritual. While a man could jog to the casino, slip into his uniform, and get right to work, a woman must travel to work so as to avoid smearing her makeup, or arrive early to put on her makeup there.

It might have been tidier if Jespersen had introduced evidence as to the time and cost associated with complying with the makeup requirement, but I can understand her failure to do so, as these hardly seem like questions reasonably subject to dispute. We could-and should-take judicial notice of these incontrovertible facts.

Alternatively, Jespersen did introduce evidence that she finds it burdensome to *wear* makeup because doing so is inconsistent with her self-image and interferes with her job performance. * * * If you are used to wearing makeup-as most American women are-this may seem like no big deal. But those of us not used to wearing makeup would find a requirement that we do so highly intrusive. Imagine, for example, a rule that all judges wear face powder, blush, mascara and lipstick while on the bench. Like Jespersen, I would find such a regime burdensome and demeaning; it would interfere with my job performance. I suspect many of my colleagues would feel the same way.

* * * [Plaintiff] quit her job-a job she performed well for two decades-rather than put on the makeup. That is a choice her male colleagues were not forced to make. To me, this states a case of disparate burden, and I would let a jury decide whether an employer can force a woman to make this choice.

* * *

MALDONADO v. CITY OF ALTUS

United States Court of Appeals, Tenth Circuit, 2006
433 F.3d 1294

HARTZ, CIRCUIT JUDGE.

Plaintiffs are employees of the City of Altus, Oklahoma (City). They appeal the district court's grant of summary judgment dismissing all their claims against the City. * * * We reverse and remand with respect to Plaintiffs' claims against the City alleging disparate impact and disparate treatment under Title VII; intentional discrimination under § 1981; and violation of equal protection under 42 U.S.C. § 1983. * * *

I. BACKGROUND

A. Factual Background

Plaintiffs' claims stem from the City's promulgation of an English-only policy. Approximately 29 City employees are Hispanic, the only significant national-origin minority group affected by the policy. All Plaintiffs are Hispanic and bilingual, each speaking fluent English and Spanish.

In the spring of 2002 the City's Street Commissioner, Defendant Holmes Willis, received a complaint that because Street Department employees were speaking Spanish, other employees could not understand what was being said on the City radio. Willis informed the City's Human Resources Director, Candy Richardson, of the complaint, and she advised Willis that he could direct his employees to speak only English when using the radio for City business.

Plaintiffs claim that Willis instead told the Street Department employees that they could not speak Spanish at work at all and informed them that the City would soon implement an official English-only policy. * * *

In July 2002 the City promulgated the following official policy * * *:

> To insure effective communications among and between employees and various departments of the City, to prevent misunderstandings and to promote and enhance safe work practices, *all work related and business communications during the work day shall be conducted in the English language with the exception of those circumstances where it is necessary or prudent to communicate with a citizen,* business owner, organization or criminal suspect *in his or her native language due to the person or entity's limited English language skills.* The use of the English language during work hours and while engaged in City business includes face to face communication of work orders and directions as well as communications utilizing telephones, mobile telephones, cellular telephones, radios, computer or e-mail transmissions and all written forms of communications. * * * *This policy does not apply to strictly private communications between co-workers while they are on approved lunch hours or breaks or before or after work hours* while the employees are still on City property *if City property is*

not being used for the communication. Further, *this policy does not apply to strictly private communication between an employee and a family member* so long as the communications are limited in time and are not disruptive to the work environment. Employees are encouraged to be sensitive to the feelings of their fellow employees, including a possible feeling of exclusion if a co-worker cannot understand what is being said in his or her presence when a language other than English is being utilized.

Defendants state three primary reasons for adopting the policy:

> 1) workers and supervisors could not understand what was being said over the City's radios . . .; 2) non-Spanish speaking employees, both before and after the adoption of the Policy, informed management that they felt uncomfortable when their co-workers were speaking in front of them in a language they could not understand because they did not know if their co-workers were speaking about them; and 3) there were safety concerns with a non-common language being used around heavy equipment.

Although the district court observed "that there was no written record of any communication problems, morale problems or safety problems resulting from the use of languages other than English prior to implementation of the policy," it noted that Willis had testified that at least one employee complained about the use of Spanish by his co-workers before implementation of the policy and other non-Spanish speaking employees subsequently made similar complaints. Those city officials who were deposed could recount no incidents of safety problems caused by the use of a language other than English. * * *

The City has not disciplined anyone for violating the English-only policy.

Plaintiffs allege that the policy created a hostile environment for Hispanic employees, causing them "fear and uncertainty in their employment," and subjecting them to racial and ethnic taunting. They contend "that the English-only rule created a hostile environment because it pervasively-every hour of every work day-burdened, threatened and demeaned the [Plaintiffs] because of their Hispanic origin." Plaintiffs each stated in their affidavits:

> The English-only policy affects my work environment every day. It reminds me every day that I am second-class and subject to rules for my employment that the Anglo employees are not subject to. I feel that this rule is hanging over my head and can be used against me at any point when the City wants to have something to write me [up] for.

Evidence of ethnic taunting included Plaintiffs' affidavits stating that they had "personally been teased and made the subject of jokes directly because of the English-only policy[,]" and that they were "aware of other Hispanic co-workers being teased and made the subject of jokes because of the English-only policy." * * *

II. DISCUSSION

* * *

One might say that Plaintiffs have not been subjected to an unlawful employment practice because they are treated identically to non-Hispanics. They claim no discrimination with respect to their pay or benefits, their hours of work, or their job duties. And every employee, not just Hispanics, must abide by the English-only policy. But the Supreme Court has "repeatedly made clear that although Title VII mentions specific employment decisions with immediate consequences, the scope of the prohibition is not limited to economic or tangible discrimination, and that it covers more than terms and conditions in the narrow contractual sense." *Nat'l R.R. Passenger Corp. v. Morgan,* 536 U.S. 101, 115–16, 122 S.Ct. 2061, 153 L.Ed.2d 106 (2002). The conditions of work encompass the workplace atmosphere as well as the more tangible elements of the job. Title VII does not tolerate, for example, a racist or sexist work environment "that is sufficiently severe or pervasive to alter the conditions of the victim's employment and create an abusive working environment[.]" *Harris v. Forklift Sys., Inc.,* 510 U.S. 17, 21, 114 S.Ct. 367, 126 L.Ed.2d 295 (1993). * * * Plaintiffs allege that the City's English-only policy has created such an environment for Hispanic workers. Discrimination against Hispanics can be characterized as being based on either race or national origin.

To prevail on these claims, Plaintiffs need not show that the policy was created with discriminatory intent. * * *

The district court, relying principally on *Garcia v. Spun Steak Co.,* 998 F.2d 1480 (9th Cir.1993), concluded that Plaintiffs had "not shown that requiring them to use the English language in the workplace imposed significant, adverse effects on the terms, conditions or privileges of their employment, so as to create a prima facie case of disparate impact discrimination under Title VII." Even under *Spun Steak,* however, English-only policies are not always permissible; each case turns on its facts. Here, Plaintiffs have produced evidence that the English-only policy created a hostile atmosphere for Hispanics in their workplace. As previously set forth, all the Plaintiffs stated that they had experienced ethnic taunting as a result of the policy and that the policy made them feel like second-class citizens. * * *

Some of this evidence, as the district court pointed out, has diluted persuasive power because of the absence of specifics-who made what comment when and where. In a typical hostile-work-environment case, we might conclude that the evidence of co-worker taunting did not reach the threshold necessary for a Title VII claim.

There are, however, other considerations with respect to a *policy* that allegedly creates a hostile work environment. The policy itself, and not just the effect of the policy in evoking hostility by co-workers, may create or contribute to the hostility of the work environment. A policy requiring each employee to wear a badge noting his or her religion, for example, might well engender extreme discomfort in a reasonable employee who belongs to a minority religion, even if no co-worker utters a word on the matter. Here, the very fact that the City would forbid Hispanics from using their preferred language could reasonably be construed as an expression of hostility to Hispanics. At least that could be a reasonable inference if there was no apparent legitimate purpose for the restrictions. It would be unreasonable to take offense at a requirement that all pilots flying into an airport speak English in communications with the tower or between planes; but hostility would be a reasonable inference to draw from a requirement that an employee calling home during a work break speak only in English. The less the apparent justification for mandating English, the more reasonable it is to infer hostility toward employees whose ethnic group or nationality favors another language. For example, Plaintiffs presented evidence that the English-only policy extended beyond its written terms to include lunch hours, breaks, and even private telephone conversations, if non-Spanish-speaking co-workers were nearby. Absent a legitimate reason for such a restriction, the inference of hostility may be reasonable.

Our task in this appeal is not to determine whether Plaintiffs have established that they were subjected to a hostile work environment. Rather, in reviewing the grant of summary judgment to Defendants, we are to decide only whether a rational juror could find on this record that the impact of the English-only policy on Hispanic workers was "sufficiently severe or persuasive to alter the conditions of [their] employment and create an abusive working environment."

It is in this context that we consider the EEOC guideline on English-only workplace rules, 29 C.F.R. § 1606.7. Under the relevant provisions of the guideline: (1) an English-only rule that applies at all times is considered "a burdensome term and condition of employment," § 1606.7(a), presumptively constituting a Title VII violation; and (2) an English-only rule that applies only at certain times does not violate Title VII if the employer can justify the rule by showing business necessity, § 1606.7(b). The EEOC rationales for the guideline are: (1) English-only policies "may 'create an atmosphere of inferiority, isolation, and intimidation' that could make a 'discriminatory working environment,'" (2) "English-only rules adversely impact employees with limited or no English skills . . . by denying them a privilege enjoyed by native English speakers: the opportunity to speak at work," (3) "English-only rules create barriers to employment for employees with limited or no English skills," (4) "English-only rules prevent bilingual employees whose first language is not English from speaking in their most effective language," and (5) "the risk of discipline and termination for violating English-only rules falls disproportionately on bilingual employees as well as persons with limited English skills."

EEOC guidelines, "while not controlling upon the courts by reason of their authority, do constitute a body of experience and informed judgment to which courts and litigants may properly resort for guidance." In *Spun Steak* the Ninth Circuit rejected the English-only guideline outright because, in its view, nothing in the plain text or the legislative history of Title VII supported the guideline's presumption of a disparate impact. But we need not resolve the validity of that presumption. For our purposes, it is enough that the EEOC, based on its expertise and experience, has consistently concluded that an English-only policy, at least when no business need for the policy is shown, is likely in itself to "create an atmosphere of inferiority, isolation, and intimidation" that constitutes a "discriminatory working environment." § 1606.7(a). * * * We believe that these conclusions are entitled to respect, not as interpretations of the governing law, but as an indication of what a reasonable, informed person may think about the impact of an English-only work rule on minority employees, even if we might not draw the same inference. Assuming the reasonableness of the EEOC on the matter, we cannot say that on the record before us it would be unreasonable for a juror to agree that the City's English-only policy created a hostile work environment for its Hispanic employees. We are not suggesting that the guideline is evidence admissible at trial or should be incorporated in a jury instruction. What we are saying is only that a juror presented with the evidence presently on the record in this case would not be unreasonable in finding that a hostile work environment existed.

As an alternative ground for granting summary judgment on the disparate-impact claim, the district court held that Defendants "offered sufficient proof of business justification." It found "that city officials had received complaints that some employees could not understand what was being said on the City's radio frequency because other employees were speaking Spanish ... [and] that city officials received complaints from non-Spanish speaking employees who felt uncomfortable when their co-workers spoke Spanish in front of them." Based on these justifications, it concluded that "Defendants have met any burden they may have to demonstrate that the City's English-only policy was supported by an adequate business justification."

We disagree. One of Congress's stated purposes in passing the 1991 amendments to the Civil Rights Act was "to codify the concepts of 'business necessity' and 'job related' enunciated by the Supreme Court in *Griggs v. Duke Power Co.,* 401 U.S. 424, 91 S.Ct. 849, 28 L.Ed.2d 158 (1971), and in the other Supreme Court decisions prior to *Wards Cove Packing Co. v. Atonio,* 490 U.S. 642, 109 S.Ct. 2115, 104 L.Ed.2d 733 (1989)." Civil Rights Act of 1991, In *Griggs* the Supreme Court held that "Congress has placed on the employer the burden of showing that any given requirement must have a manifest relationship to the employment in question." The Court stressed that "[t]he touchstone is business necessity. If an employment practice which operates to [discriminate against a protected minority] cannot be shown to be related to job performance, the practice is prohibited."

Defendants' evidence of business necessity in this case is scant. As observed by the district court, "[T]here was no written record of any communication problems, morale problems or safety problems resulting from the use of languages other than English prior to implementation of the policy." And there was little undocumented evidence. Defendants cited only one example of an employee's complaining about the use of Spanish prior to implementation of the policy. Mr. Willis admitted that he had no knowledge of City business being disrupted or delayed because Spanish was used on the radio. In addition, "city officials who were deposed could give no specific examples of safety problems resulting from the use of languages other than English...." Moreover, Plaintiffs produced evidence that the policy encompassed lunch hours, breaks, and private phone conversations; and Defendants conceded that there would be no business reason for such a restriction.

On this record we are not able to affirm summary judgment based on a business necessity for the English-only policy. A reasonable person could find from this evidence that Defendants had failed to establish a business necessity for the English-only rule.

C. Disparate–Treatment

* * *

Plaintiffs contend that they were intentionally discriminated against by the creation of a hostile work environment. We have already held that there is sufficient evidence to support a finding of a hostile work environment. The issue remaining, therefore, is whether those who established the English-only policy did so with the intent to create a hostile work environment.

To begin with, the disparate impact of the English-only rule (creation of a hostile work environment) is in itself evidence of intent. As the Supreme Court stated in *International Brotherhood of Teamsters,* 431 U.S. at 335, 97 S.Ct. 1843 in a disparate-treatment case, "Proof of discriminatory motive ... can in some situations be inferred from the mere fact of differences in treatment."

Here, Plaintiffs can rely on more than just that inference. First, there is evidence that management realized that the English-only policy would likely lead to taunting of Hispanic employees: Street Commissioner Willis allegedly told two Hispanic employees about the policy in private because of concern that non-Hispanic employees would tease them if they learned of it. Also, a jury could find that there were no substantial work-related reasons for the policy (particularly if it believed Plaintiffs' evidence that the policy extended to nonwork periods), suggesting that the true reason was illegitimate. Further, the policy was adopted without prior consultation with Hispanic employees, or even prior disclosure to a consultant to the City who was conducting an investigation of alleged anti-Hispanic discrimination during the period when the English-only policy was under consideration. Finally, there is evidence that during a news interview the Mayor referred to the Spanish language as "garbage."

In our view, the record contains sufficient evidence of intent to create a hostile environment that the summary judgment on those claims must be set aside.

NOTES

1. *Uniform Rules:* The *Harrah's* rule made distinctions between protected classes. By contrast City of Altus' rule was uniform; it applied to all workers of all classes. How is uniform treatment of all workers "discrimination?" Consider applying a uniform rule for the sole purpose of burdening or disadvantaging a protected class, such as adopting a seniority rule to disadvantage women or a pen and paper test for the purpose of disadvantaging a minority group. The Court has long held that such purpose behind an ostensibly "neutral" rule is not neutral and thus is discriminatory. *Griggs v. Duke Power Co., infra page 318.*

In the principal cases, however, there was no apparent intent to disadvantage women or Hispanics. Here merges concepts of "discrimination," "terms or conditions of employment" and "because of."

2. *Background of the judges:* Much has been made recently of whether judges from different sex, ethnic, and racial backgrounds bring a different and useful perspective to judicial decision-making. The above two cases illustrate how that perspective may be significant.

C. INDIVIDUAL HARASSMENT

1. THE OBJECTIVE, "REASONABLE PERSON" STANDARD

Oncale v. Sundowner Offshore Services, Inc., 523 U.S. 75, 118 S.Ct. 998, 140 L.Ed.2d 201 (1998):

> "[T]he statute does not reach genuine but innocuous differences in the ways men and women routinely interact with members of the same and of the opposite sex. * * * [I]it forbids only behavior so objectively offensive as to alter the 'conditions' of the victim's employment. 'Conduct that is not severe or pervasive enough to create an objectively hostile or abusive work environment—an environment that a reasonable person would find hostile or abusive—is beyond Title VII purview. We have always regarded that requirement as crucial, and as sufficient to ensure that courts and juries do not mistake ordinary socializing in the workplace—such as male on male horseplay or intersexual flirtation—for discriminatory 'conditions of employment.'

> We have emphasized, moreover, that the objective severity of harassment should be judged from the perspective of a reasonable person in the plaintiff's position, considering 'all the circumstances' * * * That inquiry requires a careful consideration of the social context in which the particular behavior occurs and is experienced by its target. A

professional football player's working environment is not severely or pervasively abusive, for example if the coach smacks him on the buttocks as he heads onto the field—even if the same behavior would reasonably be experienced as abusive by the coach's secretary (male or female) back at the office. The real social impact of workplace behavior often depends on a constellation of surrounding circumstances, expectations, and relationships that cannot be captured by a simple recitation of the words used or the physical acts performed. Common sense and an appropriate sensitivity to social context, will enable courts and juries to distinguish between simple teasing or roughhousing among members of the same sex, and conduct which a reasonable person in the plaintiff's position would find severely hostile and abusive."

ELLISON v. BRADY, 924 F.2d 872 (9th Cir. 1991):

"[B]ecause women are disproportionately victims of rape and sexual assault, women have a stronger incentive to be concerned with sexual behavior. Women who are victims of mild forms of sexual harassment may understandably worry whether a harasser's conduct is merely a prelude to violent sexual assault. Men, who are rarely victims of sexual assault, may view sexual conduct in a vacuum without a full appreciation of the social setting or the underlying threat of violence that a woman may perceive. * * * [A] female plaintiff states a prima facie case of hostile environment sexual harassment when she alleges conduct which a reasonable woman would consider sufficiently severe or pervasive to alter the conditions of employment and create an abusive working environment. * * *

We note that the reasonable victim standard * * * classifies conduct as unlawful sexual harassment even when the harassers do not realize that their conduct creates a hostile working environment."

EQUAL EMPLOYMENT OPPORTUNITY COMMISSION v. NATIONAL EDUCATION ASSOCIATION, ALASKA

United States Court of Appeals, Ninth Circuit, 2005
422 F.3d 840

GOODWIN, CIRCUIT JUDGE.

This appeal presents the question whether harassing conduct directed at female employees may violate Title VII in the absence of direct evidence that the harassing conduct or the intent that produced it was because of sex. We hold that offensive conduct that is not facially sex-specific nonetheless may violate Title VII if there is sufficient circumstantial evidence of qualitative and quantitative differences in the harassment suffered by female and male employees.

The Equal Employment Opportunity Commission ("EEOC") brings this action against the National Education Association–Alaska ("NEA–Alaska") and the National Education Association ("NEA" or "NEA national") for violations of Title VII of the Civil Rights Act of 1964.

Three female employees filed EEOC charges against NEA–Alaska. * * * The district court granted summary judgment to both defendants, holding that a reasonable trier of fact could not find that the alleged harassment was "because of . . . sex" within the meaning of the statute. Plaintiffs timely appeal.

NEA–Alaska is a labor union that represents teachers and other public school employees. NEA–Alaska appointed Thomas Harvey Interim Assistant Executive Director in early 1998, and he began working in its Anchorage office. In August 1999, NEA–Alaska designated him Assistant Executive Director. He currently serves as Executive Director of NEA–Alaska. Carol Christopher was an employee designated as a "UniServ director" in the Anchorage office. In that capacity she helped local affiliates with organizing and training, from 1995 until she resigned in February 2000. Julie Bhend and Carmela Chamara were members of the Anchorage office's administrative support staff at all material times. Bhend began working for NEA–Alaska in 1993 and is still employed there; Chamara was employed by NEA–Alaska from 1997 until she resigned in August 2000. Both Christopher and Chamara have testified that their resignations were precipitated by Harvey's conduct, but only Christopher has claimed a constructive discharge.

The record reveals numerous episodes of Harvey shouting in a loud and hostile manner at female employees. The shouting was frequent, profane, and often public. The record shows little or no provocation for these episodes. * * *

Bhend and Chamara also testified to Harvey regularly "yelling" at them loudly and publicly for little or no reason.

Harvey's verbal conduct also had a hostile physical accompaniment. Christopher testified that Harvey regularly came up behind her silently as she was working, stood over her, and watched her for no apparent reason. Bhend testified that at an evaluation meeting where Harvey accused her of taking breaks with Christopher and another employee in order to talk behind his back, Harvey "lung[ed] across the table" at her and shook his fist at her. She also testified that on another occasion when she was comforting a local union president about an unrelated matter, Harvey came up behind her, grabbed her shoulders, and yelled "get back to your office." Chamara testified that in one instance, Harvey "pump[ed] his fist in [her] direction, trying to make a point, as was his custom. Stepping toward me to make the-make the point. I stepped back. I told him that he was being physically threatening." She went so far as to call the police and file a report on one occasion, on her therapist's advice that she document physical threats. The physical manifestation of Harvey's anger was also confirmed by other witnesses, including male employees. For example, Jeff Cloutier, another UniServ director, testified to Harvey's regular invasion of Christopher's and Bhend's "personal space."

Harvey's behavior clearly intimidated female employees. For example, Bhend testified that Harvey's behavior at her evaluation meeting put her in a "state of panic," and that she "felt that [she] was in jeopardy." She also testified that after that incident, she felt "physically threatened most of the time" on the job whenever Harvey was at the workplace. Indeed, Bhend went so far as to omit submission of a number of her overtime hours because she "was too scared of Mr. Harvey to turn them in to him." Like Bhend and Christopher, Chamara also testified that the impacts of the incidents with Harvey were not isolated, but created a general atmosphere of intimidation in the workplace that was "like working with a ticking time bomb because you're sitting by and you're waiting for your turn to be next." Jeff Cloutier testified, without prompting, to the "general fear of the women at our office."

The district court erred in its characterization of the boundaries of a cognizable Title VII sex-based hostile work environment claim, and summary judgment was inappropriate under the applicable law. The facts in the record, interpreted in the light most favorable to the plaintiffs, could lead a reasonable juror to conclude that Harvey's conduct, of which primarily women were the targets, was "because of . . . sex" within the meaning of the statute. The main factual question is whether Harvey's treatment of women differed sufficiently in quality and quantity from his treatment of men to support a claim of sex-based discrimination. Addressing that question, in this case, requires a clarification of what constitutes a legally significant difference in treatment of men and women.

The relevant content of the behavior in question includes repeated and severe instances of shouting, "screaming," foul language, invading employees' personal space (including one instance of grabbing a female employee from behind), and threatening physical gestures, all apparently following little or no provocation. Harvey's behavior was not, on its face, sex- or gender-related. No one testified that Harvey made sexual overtures or lewd comments, that he referred to women employees in gender-specific terms, or that he imposed gender-specific requirements upon women employees. The district court thought that these omissions in the evidence were fatal to the case.

However, there is no legal requirement that hostile acts be overtly sex- or gender-specific in content, whether marked by language, by sex or gender stereotypes, or by sexual overtures. While sex- or gender-specific content is one way to establish discriminatory harassment, it is not the only way: "direct comparative evidence about how the alleged harasser treated members of both sexes" is always an available evidentiary route. The ultimate question in either event is whether " 'members of one sex are exposed to disadvantageous terms or conditions of employment to which members of the other sex are not exposed.' "

The Supreme Court has held that "harassing conduct need not be motivated by sexual desire to support an inference of discrimination on the basis of sex." Moreover, plaintiffs do not need to prove that Harvey had a specific intent to discriminate against women or to target them "as women," as the district court put it, whether sexually or otherwise. "Title VII is not a fault-based tort scheme. Title VII is aimed at the consequences or effects of an employment practice and not at the . . . motivation of co-workers or employers." *Ellison v. Brady,* 924 F.2d 872, 880 (9th Cir.1991). There we held that conduct may be "unlawful sexual harassment even when harassers do not realize that their conduct creates a hostile working environment."

The district court erred in holding that the "because of . . . sex" element of the action requires that the behavior be either "of a sexual nature" or motivated by "sexual animus." The district court recognized that plaintiffs "presented substantial evidence that Harvey is rude, overbearing, obnoxious, loud, vulgar, and generally unpleasant" but nonetheless held that because "there is no evidence that any of the exchanges between Harvey and Plaintiffs were motivated by lust" or by "sexual animus toward women as women," his conduct was not discriminatory.

In applying this sexual animus test, the district court seemed to find it significant that Harvey did not seek "to drive [women] out of the organization so that their positions could be filled by men." He noted that the workplace was a teacher's union, in which women were traditionally not a minority. However, a pattern of abuse in the workplace directed at women, whether or not it is motivated by "lust" or by a desire to drive women out of the organization, can violate Title VII. Indeed, this case illustrates an alternative motivational theory in which an abusive bully takes advantage of a traditionally female workplace because he is more comfortable when bullying women than when bullying men. There is no logical reason why such a motive is any less because of sex than a motive involving sexual frustration, desire, or simply a motive to exclude or expel women from the workplace.

Whatever the motive, the ultimate question * * * is whether Harvey's behavior affected women more adversely than it affected men. Plaintiffs allege that Harvey's treatment of women employees was "more abusive" and that he treated "his female subordinates worse" by "subjecting the women to more severe, more frequent, more physically threatening abuse." Defendants deny this allegation. These charges and their denials make a triable question of fact.

We have previously held that it is error to conclude that harassing conduct is not because of sex merely because the abuser "consistently abused men and women alike." *Steiner v. Showboat Operating Co.,* 25 F.3d 1459, 1463 (9th Cir.1994). In that case, the sex- or gender-specific character of the abuse directed at female employees was fairly obvious, and summary judgment was clearly inappropriate. ("The numerous depositions of Showboat employees reveal that Trenkle was indeed abusive to men, but that his abuse of women was different. It relied on sexual epithets, offensive, explicit references to women's bodies and sexual conduct."). We went on to state that *even if* the supervisor had "used sexual epithets equal in intensity and in an equally degrading manner against male employees, he cannot thereby 'cure' his conduct toward women. *Ellison* unequivocally directs us to consider what is offensive and hostile to a reasonable *woman*."

We acknowledge that our invocation of the "reasonable woman" standard, which renders sex-specific differences in the subjective effects of objectively identical behavior sufficient to ground a claim of discrimination, was rooted in the context of explicitly sex- or gender-specific conduct or speech. We now hold that evidence of differences in subjective effects (along with, of course, evidence of differences in objective quality and quantity) is relevant to determining whether or not men and women were treated differently, even where the conduct is not facially sex- or gender-specific.

The record reveals at least a debatable question as to the objective differences in treatment of male and female employees, and strongly suggests that differences in subjective effects were very different for men and women. One male UniServ Director (the same position held by Christopher), apparently had a very different experience with Harvey than Christopher did. Mark Jones stated that Harvey raised his voice to him only on a "couple of occasions" and that they were "able to talk it out—I mean the period of raising the voice was very short" and that "[s]ince then I have not experienced any of that." Moreover, Christopher also testified that the character of Harvey's aggressiveness with male employees was different from that experienced by female employees: it had the quality of "bantering back and forth with somebody, and being with the boys ... at the end of the day, I would go in and he and Bob and Rich and Jeff are all laughing in Tom's office, talking, talking, talking, laughing, laughing." Similarly, Bhend stated that Harvey "shar[ed] a 'we're all guys here' relationship with male employees."

However, Cloutier testified to an incident with Harvey that "scared the hell out of" him, during which, at one point, Harvey "instantly [ ] was three inches from my nose-chin, he's a fairly short guy ... And I don't even remember what he was saying—very loud, spitting in my face, accusing me of being insubordinate." This is the only incident described in the record that seems to be comparable in magnitude with the multiple incidents involving female employees described by the plaintiffs. Moreover, there is no evidence in the record that any male employee manifested anywhere near the same severity of reactions (e.g., crying, feeling panicked and physically threatened, avoiding contact with Harvey, avoiding submitting overtime hours for fear of angering Harvey, calling the police, and ultimately resigning) to Harvey's conduct as many of the female employees have reported. A few instances of hostile behavior toward male employees-which the record suggests may have had a qualitatively different, "bantering" character—do not erase the possibility that a reasonable jury might find that the pattern of abuse directed at female employees was discriminatory.

The defendants argue that because Harvey had more regular contact with female than with male employees the differential effect on women was merely incidental. For example, Cloutier testified that the "men working in that office left lots of times to go to school buildings, to fly out of state. It was only the women that stayed there, and it was the women who felt most vulnerable."

At least two other circuits have held, as we now do, that an unbalanced distribution of men and women in relevant employment positions, and the fact that some men were also harassed, does not automatically defeat a showing of differential treatment. *See Kopp v. Samaritan Health Sys., Inc.,* 13 F.3d 264, 269 (8th Cir.1993) ("[T]he incidents of abuse Kopp has cited in the record involve primarily women.... [A]pproximately ten involved female employees; only four involved male employees."); *Haugerud v. Amery School Dist.,* 259 F.3d 678, 695 (7th Cir.2001) (reversing summary judgment on hostile work environment claim despite fact that "[d]etermining whether plaintiff was treated differently because of her sex, as opposed to some other reason ... is admittedly complicated by the fact that she is the only day custodian at the high school"). To hold otherwise would allow the accident of a mostly female workplace to insulate even a culpable employer from liability. The precise determination of how much qualitative and quantitative difference in treatment is enough circumstantial evidence to support a Title VII claim is a question for the jury. We leave open the possibility that in some cases, the quantitative comparison between male and female employees as classes will reveal differences too slight to survive summary judgment. In this case, however, summary judgment was not appropriate.

The facts already recited present a triable issue whether the work environment Harvey created was sufficiently severe to be illegal under Title VII. The rule is that "the required showing of severity or seriousness of the harassing conduct varies inversely with the pervasiveness or frequency of the conduct." *Ellison v. Brady,* 924 F.2d at 878. Where the conduct in question was allegedly a "daily thing," there can be little question that a reasonable juror might infer that Harvey's pattern of verbal and physical intimidation, as confirmed by a wide range of employees, was sufficiently severe to satisfy the statute. * * *

NOTES

1. ***Smith v. Hy–Vee,*** 622 F.3d 904 (8th Cir. 2010). A female employee on at least 60 distinct occasions was subjected to "rude, vulgar, and sexually charged behavior" by a female co-worker that included regular physical contact of a sexual nature: rubbing the plaintiff's body simulating a rape, smacking plaintiff on the buttocks, and simulated handling of, as well as discussion of, male genitalia. Barbie dolls were put in sexual explicit positions. The aggressive co-worker—a baker—on two occasions made dough in the shape of genitalia and shoved the dough into plaintiff's face with scatological suggestions. Plaintiff complained to at least 12 different managers, but

defendant took no remedial action. Nonetheless, the court affirmed a summary judgment in favor of the defendant on grounds that plaintiff failed to indicate that the co-worker's behavior was "motivated by a particular attraction" to the plaintiff or that the behavior demonstrated a "general hostility to women" at the work place. The court made this conclusion based in large part because the offending co-worker subjected others, both male and female, to similar "vulgar and inappropriate" behavior.

2. **Rene v. MGM Grand Hotel, Inc.,** 305 F.3d 1061 (9th Cir. 2002)((en banc) involved an openly gay male employee who was subject to a regular barrage of threatening acts by male co-workers, including grabbing the plaintiff's crotch, poking his anus, and threatening him with "rape." The very sexual nature of the conduct itself established the sex stereotype motivation for the harassment.

3. **USERRA** (38 U.S.C § 4311(a)) prohibits "denial of any benefit of employment" based on military service. This language, omitting "term or condition of employment," resulted in a conclusion that harassment of an employee because of his military service that did not affect a tangible job benefit was not proscribed, even though subsection (b) proscribing retaliation prohibits "discrimination" or taking "any adverse actions." **Carder v. Continental Airlines, Inc.,** 636 F.3d 172 (5th Cir. 2011).

MATHIRAMPUZHA v. POTTER, POSTMASTER GENERAL

United States Court of Appeals, Second Circuit, 2008
548 F.3d 70

SACK, CIRCUIT JUDGE:

Plaintiff Joseph Mathirampuzha appeals from a final judgment of the United States District Court for the District of Connecticut. This appeal arises principally from an alleged physical assault at a postal facility on September 29, 2003, by Ron Sacco, a supervisor, against the plaintiff, a postal employee. The plaintiff asserts claims under Title VII of the Civil Rights Act of 1964 ("Title VII"). * * *

With regard to the plaintiff's Title VII claims, the district court properly granted summary judgment. * * *

On September 29, 2003, the plaintiff was physically assaulted by Ron Sacco, a supervisor at the Wallingford plant. (Sacco was not the plaintiff's direct supervisor when the incident occurred.) Sacco grabbed the plaintiff's arm, punched him in the shoulder and the chest, spit in his face, and poked him in the eye. Sacco also shouted, "Joe, I['ll] never let you go to [the] Hartford plant."

The plaintiff's direct supervisor, Claudio Scirocco, quickly intervened—or, as the plaintiff phrased it, "came to save my life." A union representative promptly arrived on the scene and brought the plaintiff to the office of a higher-ranking Postal Service supervisor. But the supervisor laughed when the plaintiff told her what had happened. The plaintiff's union continued to advocate on his behalf, however, and Sacco was ultimately issued a "Letter of Warning" for "Conduct Unbecoming a Postal Supervisor" and was transferred to another work assignment for at least a year.

The plaintiff asserts that his confrontation with Sacco caused him physical injury and severe emotional distress. He suffered chest pains and contusions to his shoulder blade, required eye surgery, and fell into a depression.

* * * [P]laintiff seeks relief under Title VII for being subjected to a hostile work environment on the basis of his race, color, and national origin. His amended complaint may be fairly read also to seek relief under Title VII based upon the encounter with Sacco. * * *

1. Sacco's Aggressive Conduct Toward Plaintiff.

We agree with the district court that the plaintiff's "asserted treatment at the hands of Ron Sacco on September 29—while unprofessional and boorish—and the initially dismissive attitude of other supervisors when Sacco's behavior was brought to their attention, does not amount to an 'adverse employment action'...." An adverse employment action is "a materially adverse *change* in the terms and conditions of employment." * * *

Only in limited circumstances does a single, acute incident of abuse qualify as an adverse employment action. In the context of hostile work environment claims, we have stated that a single event, if "extraordinarily severe," could alter the conditions of a working environment. A "single incident of rape," for example, " 'sufficiently alters the conditions of the victim's employment and clearly creates an abusive work environment for purposes of Title VII liability' " for sex-based discrimination. *Ferris v. Delta Air Lines, Inc.*, 277 F.3d 128, 136 (2d Cir. 2001). But we require that the incident constitute an "intolerable alteration" of the plaintiff's working conditions, so as to substantially interfere with or impair his ability to do his job.

We conclude, in light of that authority, that Sacco's aggressive conduct toward the plaintiff on September 29, 2003, was not an adverse employment action. After the incident took place, the plaintiff continued to work at the Wallingford plant in the same position, at the same pay, and with the same responsibilities. Indeed, there is no evidence that the assault brought lasting harm to the plaintiff's ability to do his job. The physical encounter itself, while understandably upsetting, was not so severe as to alter materially the plaintiff's working conditions—unlike, for example, a rape or an obscene and humiliating verbal tirade that undermines the victim's authority in the workplace. The Postal Service's response to the incident, moreover, while not immediate, ultimately ameliorated the plaintiff's working conditions, as Sacco was eventually disciplined and transferred to another work assignment for at least one year. Although a more severe incident of harassment or abuse could constitute an adverse employment action, the brief incident in this case, however regrettable, does not meet the "extraordinarily severe" standard. The plaintiff has therefore failed to establish a *prima facie* case of employment discrimination based on that event.

NOTES

1. ***Clark County School Dist. v. Breeden,*** 532 U.S. 268, 121 S.Ct. 1508, 149 L.Ed.2d 509 (2001), reproduced *infra, p.* 450 held that a single repetition of an off color joke, followed by male employees, laughter could not, standing alone, adversely affect a female employee's working conditions.

2. *Compare:* ***Moring v. Arkansas Department of Correction,*** 243 F.3d 452 (8th Cir. 2001), where a single encounter in a hotel room where a supervisor attempted to kiss a female employee while grabbing her thigh and refused her repeated requests for him to leave her room created a hostile environment. Similarly, ***Collier v. Turner Indus. Group, LLC***, 2011 WL 5439160 (D.Idaho 2011), while recognizing that rarely will a single incident constitute actionable harassment, nonetheless, held that a single incident of a supervisor pushing the female plaintiff against the wall and verbally assaulted her for three or four minutes would permit a jury verdict in favor of the plaintiff.

3. ***EEOC v. Prospect Airport Services,*** 621 F.3d 991 (9th Cir. 2010), emphasized that activities of supervisors directed against those under their supervision are more likely to create an environment that a reasonable person would perceive as hostile, than would be similar actions committed by non-supervisory co-workers. Co-worker actions that are merely "offensive" normally will not create a hostile environment. An isolated incident of a co-worker, even if serious, "will rarely (if ever) give rise to a reasonable fear that sexual harassment has become a permanent feature of the employment relationship."

BILLINGS v. TOWN OF GRAFTON

United States Court of Appeals, First Circuit, 2008
515 F.3d 39

HOWARD, CIRCUIT JUDGE.

[A male supervisor (Connor) over approximately three years allegedly stared at the female plaintiff's chest for a few seconds during many of their conversations.]

* * *

The district court granted summary judgment for the Town and Connor on the hostile environment * * * claims, ruling that "the alleged harassing conduct here is insufficient as a matter of law to create an objectively hostile work environment because it is not sufficiently severe or pervasive."

* * *

To give rise to a sexual harassment claim, "a sexually objectionable environment must be both objectively and subjectively offensive, one that a reasonable person would find hostile or abusive, and one that the victim in fact did perceive to be so." *Faragher v. City of Boca Raton,* 524 U.S. 775, 787, 118 S.Ct. 2275, 141 L.Ed.2d 662 (1998).

* * *

The point at which a work environment becomes hostile or abusive does not depend on any "mathematically precise test." Instead, "the objective severity of harassment should be judged from the perspective of a reasonable person in the plaintiff's position, considering 'all the circumstances.'" *Oncale v. Sundowner Offshore Servs., Inc.,* 523 U.S. 75, 81, 118 S.Ct. 998, 140 L.Ed.2d 201 (1998). These circumstances "may include the frequency of the discriminatory conduct; its severity; whether it is physically threatening or humiliating, or a mere offensive utterance; and whether it unreasonably interferes with an employee's work performance," but are by no means limited to them, and "no single factor is required."

While the district court properly articulated this standard, we think it applied the standard in too rigid a manner. In particular, we think the court's analysis placed undue weight on the fact—undisputed though it was—that Connor's alleged behavior did not include touching, sexual advances, or "overtly sexual comments to or about her."

As we have just explained, the hostility vel non of a workplace does not depend on any particular kind of conduct; indeed, "[a] worker need not be propositioned, touched offensively, or harassed by sexual innuendo in order to have been sexually harassed."

Of course, behavior like fondling, come-ons, and lewd remarks is often the stuff of hostile environment claims, including several previously upheld by this Court.

* * *

"Prior cases in which we have concluded that a reasonable juror could find that the work environment was objectively hostile do not establish a baseline that subsequent plaintiffs must reach in order to prevail."

The highly fact-specific nature of a hostile environment claim tends to make it difficult to draw meaningful contrasts between one case and another for purposes of distinguishing between sufficiently and insufficiently abusive behavior. Conduct that amounts to sexual harassment under one set of circumstances may, in a different context, equate with the sort of "'merely offensive'" behavior that lies beyond the purview of Title VII, and vice versa. Again, we agree with the Second Circuit that "the fact that . . . actions did not constitute a hostile work environment in [one] case, when considered as part of all the circumstances there, does not establish a rule that similar actions in another context would not, as a matter of law, amount to one."

[I]n *Lee–Crespo v. Schering–Plough Del Caribe Inc.,* 354 F.3d 34 (1st Cir.2003), * * * we upheld summary judgment for the employer because the employee failed to prove she was subjected to a hostile work environment that was severe or pervasive. In *Lee–Crespo,* the plaintiff's supervisor "bothered [her] with meddlesome and prying questions about her personal life and made comments about her appearance and behavior," manifesting "a disregard for professional courtesy and a penchant for inquiring about the personal affairs of other workers (both male and female)." We held that this conduct—which we characterized as "a supervisor's unprofessional managerial approach and accompanying efforts to assert her authority"—was simply "not the focus of the discrimination laws."

Connor's complained-of behavior, however, does not lend itself to the same characterization. As the district court recognized, "for a male supervisor to stare repeatedly at a female subordinate's breasts . . . is inappropriate and offensive," not merely "unprofessional." Thus Connor's alleged staring is fundamentally different from the intrusive questions and comments at issue in *Lee–Crespo*. Furthermore, to the extent that actions so different in kind lend themselves to any comparison "in terms of degree," we believe that the degree of harassment allegedly experienced by Billings in this case exceeds that allegedly experienced by the plaintiff in *Lee–Crespo*. There, applying the *Harris* factors, we reasoned that "the complained of conduct was episodic, but not so frequent as to become pervasive; was never severe; was never physically threatening (though occasionally discomforting or mildly humiliating); and significantly, was never . . . an impediment to [the plaintiff's] work performance." We cannot make the same determinations about Connor's behavior here, particularly where the record permits competing conclusions about the frequency and intensity of Connor's alleged conduct.

* * *

NOTES

1. ***National R.R. Passenger Corp. v. Morgan,*** 536 U.S. 101, 122 S.Ct. 2061, 153 L.Ed.2d 106 (2002), confirms that a series of actions, no one of which would be actionable, can, in their aggregate, create an actionable "hostile environment."

2. *Contrast* the principal case with:

a. ***Alvarez v. Des Moines Bolt Supply, Inc.,*** 626 F.3d 410 (8th Cir. 2010), summary judgment for the defendant was affirmed notwithstanding the following:

(i) repeated and regular use of sexually explicit jokes and language,

(ii) solicitation of sex from plaintiff,

(iii) comments on plaintiff's breast size,

(iv) references to plaintiff's inability to lift the genitals of her harasser,

(v) slapping plaintiff's buttocks, brushing her body, squeezing her neck, and grabbing her hair

(vi) suggestions that plaintiff do a strip dance.

b. ***Williams v. CSX Transp. Co., Inc.***, 643 F.3d 502 (6th Cir. 2011), the following did not warrant a jury finding for a black woman:

(i) assigned filthy tasks (cleaning urine and feces) not assigned to white men,

(ii) refused reimbursements for expenses routinely given white men,

(iii) whose automobile on five occasions was vandalized.

(iv) confronted by supervisors who made various racist comments, such as referring to black political leaders as "monkeys" whose riddance would make the county better, and "blacks should go back to where they came from."

3. *Symbols, Grafitti & Displays:* Racially charged symbols such as placing over a black employee's desk a hangman's noose can create a hostile environment, requiring the employer to immediately remove the offensive display. *Rodgers v. Western–Southern Life Ins. Co.*, 12 F.3d 668 (7th Cir. 1993). Consider the effect on black employees of the display of the Confederate battle flag. *Watson v. CEVA Logistics U.S., Inc.*, 619 F.3d 936 (8th Cir. 2010).

Sexist graffiti or display of sexually explicit pictures can create a hostile environment for women. *Hoyle v. Freightliner, LLC*, 650 F.3d 321 (4th Cir. 2011). Consider co-worker displays of "Sports Illustrated" calendars featuring women in swimsuits. *Robinson v. Jacksonville Shipyards, Inc.*, 760 F.Supp. 1486 (M.D.Fla.1991).

4. *Harassment by Third Persons*: An employee of a nursing home was repeatedly harassed sexually by one of the patients in the nursing home. Held: the employee stated a claim against the nursing home employer for its failure to take reasonable remedial steps to protect the employee from non-employee harassment. *Aguiar v. Bartlesville Care Ctr.*, (10th Cir. 1/28/11) (unreported) 21 DLR A–7.

2. SUBJECTIVE REQUIREMENT: "VOLUNTARY" vs. "UNWELCOME"

a. ***MERITOR SAVINGS BANK v. VINSON***, 477 U.S. 57, 106 S.Ct. 2399, 91 L.Ed.2d 49 (1986):

The fact that the sex related conduct was " 'voluntary' in the sense that the complaint was not forced to participate against her will, is not a defence. * * * The gravamen of any sexual harassment claim is that the alleged sexual advances were 'unwelcome.' * * * [T]he question whether particular conduct was indeed unwelcome presents difficult problems of proof and turns largely on credibility determinations committed to the trier of fact. * * * While 'voluntariness' in the sense of consent is not a defense to such a claim, it does not follow that a complainant's sexually provocative speech or dress is irrelevant as a matter of law in determining whether he or she found particular sexual advances unwelcome. To the contrary such evidence is obviously relevant. * * *

[The Court of Appeals concluded] "that testimony about provocative dress and publicly expressed fantasies had no place in this litigation. [This was error.] While the District Court must carefully weigh the applicable considerations in deciding whether to admit evidence of this kind, there is no per se rule against its admissibility. * * *

---

b. *Plaintiff's Past:* Having appeared nude in a magazine does not establish that workplace sexual advances are "welcomed." *Burns McGegor Electronic Indus,* 989 F.2d 959 (8th Cir. 1993). Frequent use of sexually explicit language by the victim does not, in itself, welcome sexual advances. *Swentek v. USAIR, Inc.,* 830 F.2d 552 (4th Cir. 1987). Consensual sexual activity with one co-worker does not establish that suggestions for similar activity from others are being invited. *See, Sheffield v. Hilltop Sand & Gravel Co.,* 895 F.Supp. 105 (E.D.Va. 1995). Nonetheless, an employee who willingly joins in a ribald atmosphere—"giving as good as she got"—cannot be an unwilling victim. One who apparently welcomes sexual advances by making them cannot complain about their return delivery. *Holly D. v. California Inst. of Tech.,* 339 F.3d 1158 (9th Cir. 2003).

c. *Female harassment of males* is actionable. Moreover, it cannot be assumed that a male receiving a barrage of suggestive comments and solicitations from a female would welcome such aggressive behavior from this person. Nonetheless, it is incumbent on the victim to communicate to superiors that such conduct is taking place and indicate that it is "unwelcome." *EEOC v. Prospect Airport Services,* 621 F.3d 991 (9th Cir. 2010).

d. *Males Harassing Males:* **Oncale v. Sundowner Offshore Services, Inc.,** 523 U.S. 75, 118 S.Ct. 998, 140 L.Ed.2d 201 (1998), confirmed that male-on-male harassment could violate Title VII. Harassment must be "discrimination" in that plaintiff was treated differently than others, and this discrimination must be "because of sex." However, the Court implied, and lower courts have held, that the element of "sex" can be shown through the sexual nature of the acts of harassment. **Cherry v. Shaw Costal Inc.,** 668 F.3d 182 (5th Cir. 2012) (touching, suggestive comments, and provocative text messages).

D. "THE FARAGHER DEFENSE" AND CONSTRUCTIVE DISCHARGE

PENNSYLVANIA STATE POLICE v. SUDERS

Supreme Court of the United States, 2004
542 U.S. 129, 124 S.Ct. 2342, 159 L.Ed.2d 204

JUSTICE GINSBURG delivered the opinion of the Court

Plaintiff-respondent Nancy Drew Suders alleged sexually harassing conduct by her supervisors, officers of the Pennsylvania State Police (PSP), of such severity she was forced to resign. The question presented concerns the proof burdens parties bear when a sexual harassment/constructive discharge claim of that character is asserted under Title VII of the Civil Rights Act of 1964.

To establish hostile work environment, plaintiffs like Suders must show harassing behavior "sufficiently severe or pervasive to alter the conditions of [their] employment." "[T]he very fact that the discriminatory conduct was so severe or pervasive that it created a work environment abusive to employees because of their ... gender ... offends Title VII's broad rule of workplace equality." Beyond that, we hold, to establish "constructive discharge," the plaintiff must make a further showing: She must show that the abusive working environment became so intolerable that her resignation qualified as a fitting response. An employer may defend against such a claim by showing both (1) that it had installed a readily accessible and effective policy for reporting and resolving complaints of sexual harassment, and (2) that the plaintiff unreasonably failed to avail herself of that employer—provided preventive or remedial apparatus. This affirmative defense will not be available to the employer, however, if the plaintiff quits in reasonable response to an employer-sanctioned adverse action officially changing her employment status or situation, for example, a humiliating demotion, extreme cut in pay, or transfer to a position in which she would face unbearable working conditions. In so ruling today, we follow the path marked by our 1998 decisions in *Burlington Industries, Inc. v. Ellerth,* 524 U.S. 742, 118 S.Ct. 2257, 141 L.Ed.2d 633, and *Faragher v. Boca Raton,* 524 U.S. 775, 118 S.Ct. 2275, 141 L.Ed.2d 662.

I

* * * In March 1998, the PSP hired Suders as a police communications operator for the McConnellsburg barracks. Suders' supervisors were Sergeant Eric D. Easton, Station Commander at the McConnellsburg barracks, Patrol Corporal William D. Baker, and Corporal Eric B. Prendergast. Those three supervisors subjected Suders to a continuous barrage of sexual harassment that ceased only when she resigned from the force. Easton "would bring up [the subject of] people having sex with animals" each time Suders entered his office. He told Prendergast, in front of Suders, that young girls should be given instruction in how to gratify men with oral sex. Easton also would sit down near Suders, wearing spandex shorts, and spread his legs apart. Apparently imitating a move popularized by television wrestling, Baker repeatedly made an obscene gesture in Suders' presence by grabbing his genitals and shouting out a vulgar comment inviting oral sex. Baker made this gesture as many as five-to-ten times per night throughout Suders' employment at the barracks. Suders once told Baker she " 'd[id]n't think [he] should be doing this' "; Baker responded by jumping on a chair and again performing the gesture, with the accompanying vulgarity. Further, Baker would "rub his rear end in front of her and remark 'I have a nice ass, don't I?' " Prendergast told

Suders " 'the village idiot could do her job' "; wearing black gloves, he would pound on furniture to intimidate her.

In June 1998, Prendergast accused Suders of taking a missing accident file home with her. After that incident, Suders approached the PSP's Equal Employment Opportunity Officer, Virginia Smith–Elliott, and told her she "might need some help." Smith–Elliott gave Suders her telephone number, but neither woman followed up on the conversation. On August 18, 1998, Suders contacted Smith–Elliott again, this time stating that she was being harassed and was afraid. Smith–Elliott told Suders to file a complaint, but did not tell her how to obtain the necessary form. Smith–Elliott's response and the manner in which it was conveyed appeared to Suders insensitive and unhelpful.

Two days later, Suders' supervisors arrested her for theft, and Suders resigned from the force. The theft arrest occurred in the following circumstances. Suders had several times taken a computer-skills exam to satisfy a PSP job requirement. Each time, Suders' supervisors told her that she had failed. Suders one day came upon her exams in a set of drawers in the women's locker room. She concluded that her supervisors had never forwarded the tests for grading and that their reports of her failures were false. Regarding the tests as her property, Suders removed them from the locker room. Upon finding that the exams had been removed, Suders' supervisors devised a plan to arrest her for theft. The officers dusted the drawer in which the exams had been stored with a theft-detection powder that turns hands blue when touched. As anticipated by Easton, Baker, and Prendergast, Suders attempted to return the tests to the drawer, whereupon her hands turned telltale blue. The supervisors then apprehended and handcuffed her, photographed her blue hands, and commenced to question her. Suders had previously prepared a written resignation, which she tendered soon after the supervisors detained her. Nevertheless, the supervisors initially refused to release her. Instead, they brought her to an interrogation room, gave her warnings * * * and continued to question her. Suders reiterated that she wanted to resign, and Easton then let her leave. The PSP never brought theft charges against her.

In September 2000, Suders sued the PSP in Federal District Court, alleging, *inter alia,* that she had been subjected to sexual harassment and constructively discharged, in violation of Title VII of the Civil Rights Act of 1964. At the close of discovery, the District Court granted the PSP's motion for summary judgment. Suders' testimony, the District Court recognized, sufficed to permit a trier of fact to conclude that the supervisors had created a hostile work environment. The court nevertheless held that the PSP was not vicariously liable for the supervisors' conduct.

In so concluding, the District Court referred to our 1998 decision in *Faragher v. Boca Raton,* In *Faragher,* along with *Burlington Industries, Inc. v. Ellerth,* decided the same day, the Court distinguished between supervisor harassment unaccompanied by an adverse official act and supervisor harassment attended by "a tangible employment action." Both decisions hold that an employer is strictly liable for supervisor harassment that "culminates in a tangible employment action, such as discharge, demotion, or undesirable reassignment." But when no tangible employment action is taken, both decisions also hold, the employer may raise an affirmative defense to liability, subject to proof by a preponderance of the evidence: "The defense comprises two necessary elements: (a) that the employer exercised reasonable care to prevent and correct promptly any sexually harassing behavior, and (b) that the plaintiff employee unreasonably failed to take advantage of any preventive or corrective opportunities provided by the employer or to avoid harm otherwise."

Suders' hostile work environment claim was untenable as a matter of law, the District Court stated, because she "unreasonably failed to avail herself of the PSP's internal procedures for reporting any harassment." Resigning just two days after she first mentioned anything about harassment to Equal Employment Opportunity Officer Smith–Elliott, the court noted, Suders had "never given [the PSP] the opportunity to respond to [her] complaints." The District Court did not address Suders' constructive discharge claim.

The Court of Appeals for the Third Circuit reversed and remanded the case for disposition on the merits. The Third Circuit agreed with the District Court that Suders had presented evidence sufficient for a trier of fact to conclude that the supervisors had engaged in a "pattern of sexual harassment that was pervasive and regular." * * *

The Court of Appeals then made the ruling challenged here: It held that "a constructive discharge, when proved, constitutes a tangible employment action." Under *Ellerth* and *Faragher,* the court observed, such an action renders an employer strictly liable and precludes employer recourse to the affirmative defense announced in those decisions. * * *

This Court granted certiorari to resolve the disagreement among the Circuits on the question whether a constructive discharge brought about by supervisor harassment ranks as a tangible employment action and therefore precludes assertion of the affirmative defense articulated in *Ellerth* and *Faragher.* We conclude that an employer does not have recourse to the Ellerth/Faragher affirmative defense when a supervisor's official act precipitates the constructive discharge; absent such a "tangible employment action," however, the defense is available to the employer whose supervisors are charged with harassment. We therefore vacate the Third Circuit's judgment and remand the case for further proceedings.

II

A

Under the constructive discharge doctrine, an employee's reasonable decision to resign because of unendurable working conditions is assimilated to a formal discharge for remedial purposes. The inquiry is objective: Did working conditions become so intolerable that a reasonable person in the employee's position would have felt compelled to resign?

* * * The Courts of Appeals have recognized constructive discharge claims in a wide range of Title VII cases. And the Equal Employment Opportunity Commission (EEOC), the federal agency charged with implementing Title VII, has stated: An employer "is responsible for a constructive discharge in the same manner that it is responsible for the outright discriminatory discharge of a charging party."

Although this Court has not had occasion earlier to hold that a claim for constructive discharge lies under Title VII, we have recognized constructive discharge in the labor-law context. Furthermore, we have stated that "Title VII is violated by either explicit or constructive alterations in the terms or conditions of employment." "The phrase 'terms, conditions, or privileges of employment' [in Title VII] evinces a congressional intent to strike at the entire spectrum of disparate treatment of men and women in employment." We agree with the lower courts and the EEOC that Title VII encompasses employer liability for a constructive discharge.

B

This case concerns an employer's liability for one subset of Title VII constructive discharge claims: constructive discharge resulting from sexual harassment, or "hostile work environment," attributable to a supervisor. Our starting point is the framework Ellerth and Faragher established to govern employer liability for sexual harassment by supervisors. As earlier noted, those decisions delineate two categories of hostile work environment claims: (1) harassment that "culminates in a tangible employment action," for which employers are strictly liable, and harassment that takes place in the absence of a tangible employment action, to which employers may assert an affirmative defense. With the background set out above in mind, we turn to the key issues here at stake: which Ellerth/Faragher category do hostile-environment constructive discharge claims fall—and what proof burdens do the parties bear in such cases.
* * *

Ellerth and Faragher also clarified the parties' respective proof burdens in hostile environment cases. Title VII, the Court noted, "borrows from tort law the avoidable consequences doctrine," under which victims have "a duty 'to use such means as are reasonable under the circumstances to avoid or minimize the damages' that result from violations of the statute." The Ellerth/Faragher affirmative defense accommodates that doctrine by requiring plaintiffs reasonably to stave off avoidable harm. But both decisions place the burden squarely on the defendant to prove that the plaintiff unreasonably failed to avoid or reduce harm.

The constructive discharge here at issue stems from, and can be regarded as an aggravated case of, sexual harassment or hostile work environment. For an atmosphere of sexual harassment or hostility to be actionable, we reiterate, the offending behavior "must be sufficiently severe or pervasive to alter the conditions of the victim's employment and create an abusive working environment." A hostile-environment constructive discharge claim entails something more: A plaintiff who advances such a compound claim must show working conditions so intolerable that a reasonable person would have felt compelled to resign. *Perry v. Harris Chernin, Inc.,* 126 F.3d 1010, 1015 (C.A.7 1997) ("[U]nless conditions are beyond 'ordinary' discrimination, a complaining employee is expected to remain on the job while seeking redress.").[1]

Suders' claim is of the same genre as the hostile work environment claims the Court analyzed in *Ellerth* and *Faragher*. Essentially, Suders presents a "worse case" harassment scenario, harassment ratcheted up to the breaking point. Like the harassment considered in our pathmarking decisions, harassment so intolerable as to cause a resignation may be effected through co-worker conduct, unofficial supervisory conduct, or official company acts. Unlike an actual termination, which is *always* effected through an official act of the company, a constructive discharge need not be. A constructive discharge involves both an employee's decision to leave and precipitating conduct: The former involves no official action; the latter, like a harassment claim without any constructive discharge assertion, may or may not involve official action.

To be sure, a constructive discharge is functionally the same as an actual termination in damages-enhancing respects. As the Third Circuit observed, both "en[d] the employer-employee relationship," and both "inflic[t] ... direct economic harm." But when an official act does not underlie the constructive discharge, the *Ellerth* and *Faragher* analysis, we here hold, calls for extension of the affirmative defense to the employer. As those leading decisions indicate, official directions and declarations are the acts most likely to be brought home to the employer, the measures over which the employer can exercise greatest control. Absent "an official act of the enterprise," as the last straw, the employer ordinarily would have no particular reason to suspect that a resignation is not the typical kind daily occurring in the work force. And as *Ellerth* and *Faragher* further point out, an official act reflected in company records-a demotion or a reduction in compensation, for example-shows "beyond question" that the supervisor has used his managerial or controlling position to the employee's disadvantage. Absent such an official act, the extent to which the supervisor's misconduct has been aided by the agency relation, as we earlier recounted is less certain. That uncertainty, our precedent establishes, justifies affording the employer the chance to establish, through the *Ellerth/Faragher* affirmative defense, that it should not be held vicariously liable.

* * * We note, finally, two recent Court of Appeals decisions that indicate how the "official act" (or "tangible employment action") criterion should play out when constructive discharge is alleged. Both decisions advance the untangled approach we approve in this opinion. In *Reed v. MBNA Marketing Systems, Inc.,* 333 F.3d 27 (C.A.1 2003), the plaintiff claimed a

---

1. *Ellerth* and *Faragher* expressed no view on the employer liability standard for co-worker harassment. Nor do we.

constructive discharge based on her supervisor's repeated sexual comments and an incident in which he sexually assaulted her. The First Circuit held that the alleged wrongdoing did not preclude the employer from asserting the *Ellerth/Faragher* affirmative defense. As the court explained in *Reed,* the supervisor's behavior involved no official actions. Unlike, *"e.g.,* an extremely dangerous job assignment to retaliate for spurned advances," the supervisor's conduct in *Reed* "was exceedingly unofficial and involved no direct exercise of company authority"; indeed, it was "exactly the kind of wholly unauthorized conduct for which the affirmative defense was designed," In contrast, in *Robinson v. Sappington,* 351 F.3d 317 (C.A.7 2003), after the plaintiff complained that she was sexually harassed by the judge for whom she worked, the presiding judge decided to transfer her to another judge, but told her that "her first six months [in the new post] probably would be 'hell,' " and that it was in her " 'best interest to resign.' " The Seventh Circuit held that the employer was precluded from asserting the affirmative defense to the plaintiff's constructive discharge claim. The *Robinson* plaintiff's decision to resign, the court explained, "resulted, at least in part, from [the presiding judge's] official actio[n] in transferring" her to a judge who resisted placing her on his staff. The courts in *Reed* and *Robinson* properly recognized that *Ellerth* and *Faragher,* which divided the universe of supervisor-harassment claims according to the presence or absence of an official act, mark the path constructive discharge claims based on harassing conduct must follow.

* * * We see no cause for leaving the district courts thus unguided. Following *Ellerth* and *Faragher,* the plaintiff who alleges no tangible employment action has the duty to mitigate harm, but the defendant bears the burden to allege and prove that the plaintiff failed in that regard. The plaintiff might elect to allege facts relevant to mitigation in her pleading or to present those facts in her case in chief, but she would do so in anticipation of the employer's affirmative defense, not as a legal requirement.* * *

We hold * * * that the Court of Appeals erred in declaring the affirmative defense described in *Ellerth* and *Faragher* never available in constructive discharge cases. Accordingly, we vacate the Third Circuit's judgment and remand the case for further proceedings consistent with this opinion.

NOTES

1. ***FARAGHER v. CITY OF BOCA RATON,* 524 U.S. 775, 118 S.Ct. 2275, 141 L.Ed.2d 662 (1998):**

The defense [to a charge of hostile environmental harassment] comprises two necessary elements: (a) that the employer exercised reasonable care to prevent and correct promptly any sexually harassing, and (b) that the plaintiff employee unreasonable failed to take advantage of any preventive or corrective opportunities provided by the employer * * * While proof that an employer had promulgated an anti-harassment policy with complaint procedure is not necessary in every instance as a matter of law, the need for a stated policy suitable to the employment circumstances may appropriately be addressed in any case when litigating the first element of the defense. * * *

It appears from the record that any such avenue is closed. * * * The [defendant] had entirely failed to disseminate its policy against sexual harassment among the [relevant] employees and * * * its officials made no attempt to keep track of supervisors. [Defendant's] policy did not include any assurance that the harassing supervisors could be bypassed in registering complaints. * * * [W]e hold as a matter of law that [defendant] could not be found to have exercised reasonable care to prevent the supervisors' harassing conduct.

2. *BURLINGTON INDUSTRIES v. ELLERTH*, **524 U.S. 742, 118 S.Ct. 2257, 141 L.Ed.2d 633 (1998):**

During her tenure at Burlington, [plaintiff] Ellerth did not inform anyone in authority about [supervisor] Slavic's conduct, despite knowing Burlington had a policy against sexual harassment. In fact, she chose not to inform her immediate supervisor * * *

[W]hile proof that an employee failed to fulfill the corresponding obligation of reasonable care to avoid harm is not limited to showing any unreasonable failure to use any complaint procedure provided by the employer, a demonstration of such failure will normally suffice to satisfy the employer's burden under the second element of the defense.

3. *The Boss: Suders,* the principal case, noted that liability attaches through "official company acts." Where the harasser is the "alter ego" of the business in that he holds a sufficiently high management position to set company policies, there is no need to resort to the rules of agency to impute acts of "management" to the "employer." ***Ackel v. National Communications, Inc.,*** 339 F.3d 376 (5th Cir. 2003).

4. *Supervisors:* Where the harasser is a supervisor of the victim, his acts can be attributed to the "employer," but subject to the *Faragher* defense (which does not apply to a supervisor's "quid pro quo" denial of tangible benefits). However, harassment by an employee with general supervisory responsibilities, but not over the victim, will be treated as actions of fellow co-workers. A co-worker that has some leadership responsibilities is not considered a supervisor. *Montgomery v. American Airlines, Inc.,* 626 F.3d 382 (7th Cir. 2010)("crew chief" not a supervisor).

5. *Co–Workers:* In footnote 1, the *Suders* Court disclaimed addressing how and when harassment by co-workers would be attributable to the "employer." *Faragher and Ellerth, supra,* stated, however, that common law rules of agency should be the first reference, and that, "Negligence sets a minimum standard for employer liability under Title VII, [and the] employer is negligent with respect to sexual harassment if it knew or should have known about the conduct and failed to stop it." *See also, Wilson v. Moulison North Corp.,* 639 F.3d 1 (1st Cir. 2011); *EEOC Guidance on Vicarious Liability.*

   a. Notice:

Where there are open or recurring incidents such as undue horseplay, sexually graphic displays, or raucous behavior, the employer should be on inquiry, if not actual, notice that co-worker harassment is occurring. *Sandoval v. American Bld. Maint. Indus.*, 578 F.3d 787 (8th Cir. 2009). Actual complaints of harassment, whether or not the employer has a formalized grievance process, will put the employer on "inquiry" notice that would warrant a reasonable investigation of the charges. *Adams v. O'Reilly Automotive, Inc.*, 538 F.3d 926 (8th Cir. 2008).

b. *Failure to take "prompt, appropriate remedial action":*

Once the "employer" receives actual or constructive notice of the co-worker harassment, the employer's first obligation is to undertake a prompt investigation of the alleged harassment. Failure to act promptly in a reasonable way to ascertain the underlying facts can result in liability. *See, Sutherland v. Wal–Mart Stores, Inc.*, 632 F.3d 990 (7th Cir. 2011)(investigation reasonable even though it did not include questioning the alleged harasser).

If the investigation discloses probable harassment, the employer must take "appropriate" remedial steps. "Reasonableness" under the circumstances is an issue of fact. As a matter of law, "reasonable" remedial action requires more than jocular responses or informal oral disapproval (*i.e.*,"behave yourself!"). Employers generally may use a system of "progressive discipline," issuing formal warnings and/or imposing mandatory training for first time offenders and for relatively minor offenses, but with an obligation to use more prophylactic remedies, such as suspensions, demotions, or permanent pay reductions, when such warnings or reprimands prove ineffective. See, *Sutherland v. Wal–Mart Stores,* 632 F.3d 990 (7th Cir. 2011).

Transferring the *victim* of the harassment is *not* a reasonable response. *Paroline v. Unisys,* 879 F.2d 100 (4th Cir. 1989). Reasonable response to a pattern of harassment often requires the transfer of the *offender.* That the offender is "too important" to lose, or the victim is relatively "insignificant" does not justify employer inaction. *Cadena v. Pacesetter Corp.,* 224 F.3d 1203 (10th Cir. 2000). Moving the harasser to a different location that reduced, but did not eliminate, contact with the victim was "reasonable" even though it proved ineffective to stop future harassment. *Sutherland v. Wal–Mart Stores, Inc., supra.* Discharge of the harasser rarely is mandated on the first offenses. *Wilson v. Moulison North Corp.,* 639 F.3d 1 (1st Cir. 2011)(warning that continued behavior would result in dismissal was appropriate as a matter of law). However, for very serious misconduct, (such as rape) or for repeated injurious misconduct (such as regular use of racist threats), dismissal may be the only reasonable remedy. *See, Intlekofer v. Turnage,* 973 F.2d 773 (9th Cir. 1992).

6. *Constructive Discharge*: An employee is constructively discharged who resigns upon being told that she has a choice of resigning or being dismissed. *Kodish v. Oakbrook Terr. Fire Protection Dist.,* 604 F.3d 490 (7th Cir. 2010). An employee was discharged constructively when her belongings were removed from her office and the office converted into a storage room. *EEOC v. University of Chicago Hospitals*, 276 F.3d 326 (7th Cir. 2002).

When an employee resigns in response to harassment, the act of quitting will be considered a discharge, only if the employee has been subjected to discriminatory working conditions so "intolerable" that a reasonable person would have resigned rather than remain on the job. In evaluating whether working conditions have been made "intolerable" the courts will consider: (1) the extent of the pattern of racial or sexual harassment, (2) major demotion or significantly reduced job responsibilities and/or salary, (3) assignment of degrading or demeaning work, (4) reassignment to work under the supervision of younger or less experienced persons, (5) patterns of petty belittling or badgering, (6) relocation to patently inferior surroundings, (7) repeated encouragement to resign, (8) offering early retirement or risk future employment on significantly less favorable terms. *Dediol v. Best Chevrolet, Inc.*, 655 F.3d 435 (5th Cir. 2011).

CHAPTER 5

"TO DISCRIMINATE"

■ ■ ■

A. INDIVIDUAL vs. CLASS TREATMENT

CITY OF LOS ANGELES, DEPARTMENT OF WATER AND POWER v. MANHART

Supreme Court of the United States, 1978
435 U.S. 702, 98 S.Ct. 1370, 55 L.Ed.2d 657

JUSTICE STEVENS delivered the opinion of the Court.

As a class, women live longer than men. For this reason, the Los Angeles Department of Water and Power required its female employees to make larger contributions to its pension fund than its male employees. We granted certiorari to decide whether this practice discriminated against individual female employees because of their sex in violation of § 703(a)(1) of the Civil Rights Act of 1964.

For many years the Department has administered retirement, disability, and death-benefit programs for its employees. Upon retirement each employee is eligible for a monthly retirement benefit computed as a fraction of his or her salary multiplied by years of service. The monthly benefits for men and women of the same age, seniority, and salary are equal. Benefits are funded entirely by contributions from the employees and the Department, augmented by the income earned on those contributions. No private insurance company is involved in the administration or payment of benefits.

Based on a study of mortality tables and its own experience, the Department determined that its 2,000 female employees, on the average, will live a few years longer than its 10,000 male employees. The cost of a pension for the average retired female is greater than for the average male retiree because more monthly payments must be made to the average woman. The Department therefore required female employees to make monthly contributions to the fund which were 14.84% higher than the contributions required of comparable male employees. Because employee contributions were withheld from paychecks a female employee took home less pay than a male employee earning the same salary.[5]

* * * In 1973, respondents brought this suit in the United States District Court for the Central District of California on behalf of a class of women employed or formerly employed by the Department. They prayed for an injunction and restitution of excess contributions.

* * *

The Department and various *amici curiae* contend that: (1) the differential in take-home pay between men and women was not discrimination within the meaning of § 703(a)(1) because it was offset by a difference in the value of the pension benefits provided to the two classes of employees; (2) the differential was based on a factor "other than sex" within the meaning of the Equal Pay Act of 1963 and was therefore protected by the so-called Bennett Amendment; * * *.

I

There are both real and fictional differences between women and men. It is true that the average man is taller than the average woman; it is not true that the average woman driver is more accident prone than the average man. Before the Civil Rights Act of 1964 was enacted, an employer could fashion his personnel policies on the basis of assumptions about the differences between men and women, whether or not the assumptions were valid.

It is now well recognized that employment decisions cannot be predicated on mere "stereotyped" impressions about the characteristics of males or females. Myths and purely habitual assumptions about a woman's inability to perform certain kinds of work are no longer acceptable reasons for refusing to employ qualified individuals, or for paying them less. This case does not, however, involve a fictional difference between men and women. It involves a generalization that the parties accept as unquestionably true: Women, as a class, do live longer than men. The Department treated its women employees differently from its men employees because the two classes are in fact different. It is equally true, however, that all individuals in the respective classes do not share the characteristic that differentiates the average class representatives. Many women do not live as long as the average man and many men outlive the average woman. The question, therefore, is whether the existence or nonexistence of "discrimination" is to be determined by comparison of class characteristics or individual characteristics. A "stereotyped" answer to that question may not be the same as the answer that the language and purpose of the statute command.

The statute makes it unlawful "to discriminate against any *individual* with respect to his compensation, terms, conditions, or privileges of employment, because of such *individual's* race, color, religion, sex, or

---

5. The significance of the disparity is illustrated by the record of one woman whose contributions to the fund (including interest on the amount withheld each month) amounted to $18,171.40; a similarly situated male would have contributed only $12,843.53.

national origin." The statute's focus on the individual is unambiguous. It precludes treatment of individuals as simply components of a racial, religious, sexual, or national class. If height is required for a job, a tall woman may not be refused employment merely because, on the average, women are too short. Even a true generalization about the class is an insufficient reason for disqualifying an individual to whom the generalization does not apply.

That proposition is of critical importance in this case because there is no assurance that any individual woman working for the Department will actually fit the generalization on which the Department's policy is based. Many of those individuals will not live as long as the average man. While they were working, those individuals received smaller paychecks because of their sex, but they will receive no compensating advantage when they retire.

It is true, of course, that while contributions are being collected from the employees, the Department cannot know which individuals will predecease the average woman. Therefore, unless women as a class are assessed an extra charge, they will be subsidized, to some extent, by the class of male employees. It follows, according to the Department, that fairness to its class of male employees justifies the extra assessment against all of its female employees.

But the question of fairness to various classes affected by the statute is essentially a matter of policy for the legislature to address. Congress has decided that classifications based on sex, like those based on national origin or race, are unlawful. Actuarial studies could unquestionably identify differences in life expectancy based on race or national origin, as well as sex.[15] But a statute that was designed to make race irrelevant in the employment market, could not reasonably be construed to permit a take-home-pay differential based on a racial classification.

Even if the statutory language were less clear, the basic policy of the statute requires that we focus on fairness to individuals rather than fairness to classes. Practices that classify employees in terms of religion, race, or sex tend to preserve traditional assumptions about groups rather than thoughtful scrutiny of individuals. The generalization involved in this case illustrates the point. Separate mortality tables are easily interpreted as reflecting innate differences between the sexes; but a significant part of the longevity differential may be explained by the social fact that men are heavier smokers than women.

Finally, there is no reason to believe that Congress intended a special definition of discrimination in the context of employee group insurance coverage. It is true that insurance is concerned with events that are individually unpredictable, but that is characteristic of many employment decisions. Individual risks, like individual performance, may not be predicted by resort to classifications proscribed by Title VII. Indeed, the fact

---

15. For example, the life expectancy of a white baby in 1973 was 72.2 years; a nonwhite baby could expect to live 65.9 years, a difference of 6.3 years.

that this case involves a group insurance program highlights a basic flaw in the Department's fairness argument. For when insurance risks are grouped, the better risks always subsidize the poorer risks. Healthy persons subsidize medical benefits for the less healthy; unmarried workers subsidize the pensions of married workers; persons who eat, drink, or smoke to excess may subsidize pension benefits for persons whose habits are more temperate. Treating different classes of risks as though they were the same for purposes of group insurance is a common practice that has never been considered inherently unfair. To insure the flabby and the fit as though they were equivalent risks may be more common than treating men and women alike; but nothing more than habit makes one "subsidy" seem less fair than the other.[20]

An employment practice that requires 2,000 individuals to contribute more money into a fund than 10,000 other employees simply because each of them is a woman, rather than a man, is in direct conflict with both the language and the policy of the Act. Such a practice does not pass the simple test of whether the evidence shows "treatment of a person in a manner which but for that person's sex would be different." It constitutes discrimination and is unlawful unless exempted by the Equal Pay Act of 1963 or some other affirmative justification.

II

Shortly before the enactment of Title VII in 1964, Senator Bennett proposed an amendment providing that a compensation differential based on sex would not be unlawful if it was authorized by the Equal Pay Act, which had been passed a year earlier.[22] The Equal Pay Act requires employers to pay members of both sexes the same wages for equivalent work, except when the differential is pursuant to one of four specified exceptions.[23] The Department contends that the fourth exception applies

---

20. A variation on the Department's fairness theme is the suggestion that a gender-neutral pension plan would itself violate Title VII because of its disproportionately heavy impact on male employees. This suggestion has no force in the sex discrimination context because each retiree's total pension benefits are ultimately determined by his *actual life span*; any differential in benefits paid to men and women in the aggregate is thus "based on [a] factor other than sex," and consequently immune from challenge under the Equal Pay Act, 29 U.S.C. § 206(d); Even under Title VII itself-assuming disparate-impact analysis applies to fringe benefits,—the male employees would not prevail. Even a completely neutral practice will inevitably have *some* disproportionate impact on one group or another.* * *

22. The Bennett Amendment became part of § 703(h), which provides in part:

"It shall not be unlawful employment practice under this title for any employer to differentiate upon the basis of sex in determining the amount of the wages or compensation paid or to be paid to employees of such employer if such differentiation is authorized by the provisions of section 6(d) of the Fair Labor Standards Act of 1938, as amended (29 U.S.C. § 206(d))." 42 U.S.C. § 2000e–2(h).

23. The Equal Pay Act provides, in part:

"No employer having employees subject to any provisions of this section shall discriminate, within any establishment in which such employees are employed, between employees on the basis of sex by paying wages to employees in such establishment at a rate less than the rate at which he pays wages to employees of the opposite sex in such establishment for equal work on jobs the performance of which requires equal skill, effort, and responsibility, and which are performed under similar working conditions, except where such payment is made pursuant to (i) a seniority system; (ii) a merit system; (iii) a system which measures earnings by quantity or

here. That exception authorizes a "differential based on any other factor other than sex."

We need not decide whether retirement benefits or contributions to benefit plans are "wages" under the Act, because the Bennett Amendment extends the Act's four exceptions to all forms of "compensation" covered by Title VII. The Department's pension benefits, and the contributions that maintain them, are "compensation" under Title VII.

The Department argues that the different contributions exacted from men and women were based on the factor of longevity rather than sex. It is plain, however, that any individual's life expectancy is based on a number of factors, of which sex is only one. The record contains no evidence that any factor other than the employee's sex was taken into account in calculating the 14.84% differential between the respective contributions by men and women. We agree with Judge Duniway's observation that one cannot "say that an actuarial distinction based entirely on sex is 'based on any other factor other than sex.' Sex is exactly what it is based on." * * *

Although we conclude that the Department's practice violated Title VII, we do not suggest that the statute was intended to revolutionize the insurance and pension industries. All that is at issue today is a requirement that men and women make unequal contributions to an employer-operated pension fund. Nothing in our holding implies that it would be unlawful for an employer to set aside equal retirement contributions for each employee and let each retiree purchase the largest benefit which his or her accumulated contributions could command in the open market. Nor does it call into question the insurance industry practice of considering the composition of an employer's work force in determining the probable cost of a retirement or death benefit plan. * * *

CHIEF JUSTICE BURGER, concurring in part and dissenting in part.

* * * Gender-based actuarial tables have been in use since at least 1843, and their statistical validity has been repeatedly verified. The vast life insurance, annuity, and pension plan industry is based on these tables. As the Court recognizes, it is a fact that "women, as a class, do live longer than men." It is equally true that employers cannot know in advance when individual members of the classes will die. Yet, if they are to operate economically workable group pension programs, it is only rational to permit them to rely on statistically sound and proved disparities in longevity between men and women. Indeed, it seems to me irrational to assume Congress intended to outlaw use of the fact that, for whatever reasons or combination of reasons, women as a class outlive men.

The Court's conclusion that the language of the civil rights statute is clear, admitting of no advertence to the legislative history, such as there

---

quality of production; or (iv) a differential based on any other factor other than sex: *Provided,* That an employer who is paying a wage rate differential in violation of this subsection shall not, in order to comply with the provisions of this subsection, reduce the wage rate of any employee." 29 U.S.C. § 206(d).

was, is not soundly based. An effect upon pension plans so revolutionary and discriminatory-this time favorable to women at the expense of men-should not be read into the statute without either a clear statement of that intent in the statute, or some reliable indication in the legislative history that this was Congress' purpose. * * *

The reality of differences in human mortality is what mortality experience tables reflect. The difference is the added longevity of women. All the reasons why women statistically outlive men are not clear. But categorizing people on the basis of sex, the one acknowledged immutable difference between men and women, is to take into account all of the unknown reasons, whether biologically or culturally based, or both, which give women a significantly greater life expectancy than men. It is therefore true as the Court says, "that any individual's life expectancy is based on a number of factors, of which sex is only one." But it is not true that by seizing upon the only constant, "measurable" factor, no others were taken into account. All other factors, whether known but variable—or unknown—are the elements which automatically account for the actuarial disparity. And all are accounted for when the constant factor is used as a basis for determining the costs and benefits of a group pension plan. * * *

This is in no sense a failure to treat women as "individuals" in violation of the statute, as the Court holds. It is to treat them as individually as it is possible to do in the face of the unknowable length of each individual life. Individually, every woman has the same statistical possibility of outliving men. This is the essence of basing decisions on reliable statistics when individual determinations are infeasible or, as here, impossible.

Of course, women cannot be disqualified from, for example, heavy labor just because the generality of women are thought not as strong as men-a proposition which perhaps may sometime be statistically demonstrable, but will remain individually refutable. When, however, it is impossible to tailor a program such as a pension plan to the individual, nothing should prevent application of reliable statistical facts to the individual, for whom the facts cannot be disproved until long after planning, funding, and operating the program have been undertaken.

I find it anomalous, if not contradictory, that the Court's opinion tells us, in effect, that the holding is not really a barrier to responding to the complaints of men employees, as a group. The Court states that employers may give their employees precisely the same dollar amount and require them to secure their own annuities directly from an insurer, who, of course, is under no compulsion to ignore 135 years of accumulated, recorded longevity experience.

NOTE

***ARIZONA GOVERNING COMMITTEE v. NORRIS,* 463 U.S. 1073, 103 S.Ct. 3492, 77 L.Ed.2d 1236 (1983),** applied the logic in *Manhart* to an employer sponsored "defined contribution" program in which similarly situated employees paid into the plan the same amount, but upon retirement could receive a periodic annuity payment that could differ because of the employee's sex. That the employee could select non-discriminatory alternatives to the sex-based pay-out option—such as a lump sum payment or an annuity for fixed years—did not preclude a finding that plan was discriminatory. That the employee had retired upon selecting the discriminatory option and that the plan was administered by third party underwriters, selected by the employee, did not preclude attributing liability for the sex discrimination in the plan to the "employer." The plan was part of the benefit package provided by the employer to the working employee, with the employer deducting funds from the employee's salary and, by virtue of a contract between employer and the annuity company, remitting the withheld funds to the annuity company. This connection between "employer" and the nominally independent annuity company was sufficient to attribute a discriminatory option offered by the annuity company to the covered "employer."

The topic of compensation discrimination will be discussed in Chapter 10.

B.   ACTIVE vs. PASSIVE "DISCRIMINATION"

GOODMAN v. LUKENS STEEL CO.

Supreme Court of the United States, 1987
482 U.S. 656, 107 S.Ct. 2617, 96 L.Ed.2d 572

JUSTICE WHITE delivered the opinion of the Court.

In 1973, individual employees of Lukens Steel Company (Lukens) brought this suit on behalf of themselves and others, asserting racial discrimination claims under Title VII of the Civil Rights Act of 1964,[2] and 42 U.S.C. § 1981 against their employer and their collective-bargaining agents, the United Steelworkers of America and two of its local unions (Unions). * * * On the merits, the District Court found that Lukens had discriminated in certain respects, but that in others plaintiffs had not made out a case. The District Court concluded that the Unions were also guilty of discriminatory practices, specifically in failing to challenge discriminatory

---

2. The part of Title VII relevant to the suit against the Unions is 42 U.S.C. § 2000e–2(c), which provides:

"(c) Labor organization practices

"It shall be an unlawful employment practice for a labor organization—

"(1) to exclude or to expel from its membership, or otherwise to discriminate against, any individual because of his race, color, religion, sex, or national origin;

"(2) to limit, segregate, or classify its membership or applicants for membership, or to classify or fail or refuse to refer for employment any individual, in any way which would deprive or tend to deprive any individual of employment opportunities, or would limit such employment opportunities or otherwise adversely affect his status as an employee or as an applicant for employment, because of such individual's race, color, religion, sex, or national origin; or

"(3) to cause or attempt to cause an employer to discriminate against an individual in violation of this section."

The judgment against Lukens is not at issue in the cases brought here.

discharges of probationary employees, failing and refusing to assert instances of racial discrimination as grievances, and in tolerating and tacitly encouraging racial harassment.

The Court of Appeals * * * affirmed the liability judgment against the Unions.

The District Court proceeded to find that the company had violated Title VII in several significant respects, including the discharge of employees during their probationary period, the toleration of racial harassment by employees, initial job assignments, promotions, and decisions on incentive pay. The court also found that in these identical ways the company had also violated § 1981, a finding the court could not have made without concluding that the company had intentionally discriminated on a racial basis in these respects.

Similarly, the Unions were found to have discriminated on racial grounds in violation of both Title VII and § 1981 in certain ways: failing to challenge discriminatory discharges of probationary employees; failure and refusal to assert racial discrimination as a ground for grievances; and toleration and tacit encouragement of racial harassment.

* * * The Unions contend that the judgment against them rests on the erroneous legal premise that Title VII and § 1981 are violated if a union passively sits by and does not affirmatively oppose the employer's racially discriminatory employment practices. It is true that the District Court declared that mere union passivity in the face of employer discrimination renders the union liable under Title VII and, if racial animus is properly inferable, under § 1981 as well." We need not discuss this rather abstract observation, for the court went on to say that the evidence proves "far more" than mere passivity. As found by the court, the facts were that since 1965, the collective-bargaining contract contained an express clause binding both the employer and the Unions not to discriminate on racial grounds; that the employer was discriminating against blacks in discharging probationary employees, which the Unions were aware of but refused to do anything about by way of filing proffered grievances or otherwise; that the Unions had ignored grievances based on instances of harassment which were indisputably racial in nature; and that the Unions had regularly refused to include assertions of racial discrimination in grievances that also asserted other contract violations.[12]

In affirming the District Court's findings against the Unions, the Court of Appeals also appeared to hold that the Unions had an affirmative duty to combat employer discrimination in the workplace. But it, too, held that the case against the Unions was much stronger than one of mere acquiescence in that the Unions deliberately chose not to assert claims of racial discrimination by the employer. It was the Court of Appeals' view that

---

12. The District Court also found that although the Unions had objected to the company's use of certain tests, they had never done so on racial grounds, even though they "were certainly chargeable with knowledge that many of the tests" had a racially disparate impact.

these intentional and knowing refusals discriminated against the victims who were entitled to have their grievances heard.

The Unions submit that the only basis for any liability in this case under Title VII is § 703(c)(3), which provides that a Union may not "cause or attempt to cause an employer to discriminate against an individual in violation of this section," and that nothing the District Court found and the Court of Appeals accepted justifies liability under this prohibition. We need not differ with the Unions on the reach of § 703(c)(3), for § 703(c)(1) makes it an unlawful practice for a Union to "exclude or to expel from its membership, *or otherwise to discriminate against,* any individual because of his race, color, religion, sex, or national origin." Both courts below found that the Unions had indeed discriminated on the basis of race by the way in which they represented the workers, and the Court of Appeals expressly held that "[t]he deliberate choice not to process grievances also violated § 703(c)(1) of Title VII." The plain language of the statute supports this conclusion.

The Court of Appeals is also faulted for stating that the Unions had violated their duty of fair representation, which the Unions assert has no relevance to this case. But we do not understand the Court of Appeals to have rested its affirmance on this ground, for as indicated above, it held that the Unions had violated § 703.

The Unions insist that it was error to hold them liable for not including racial discrimination claims in grievances claiming other violations of the contract. The Unions followed this practice, it was urged, because these grievances could be resolved without making racial allegations and because the employer would "get its back up" if racial bias was charged, thereby making it much more difficult to prevail. The trial judge, although initially impressed by this seemingly neutral reason for failing to press race discrimination claims, ultimately found the explanation "unacceptable" because the Unions also ignored grievances which involved racial harassment violating the contract covenant against racial discrimination but which did not also violate another provision. The judge also noted that the Unions had refused to complain about racially based terminations of probationary employees, even though the express undertaking not to discriminate protected this group of employees, as well as others, and even though, as the District Court found, the Unions knew that blacks were being discharged at a disproportionately higher rate than whites. In the judgment of the District Court, the virtual failure by the Unions to file any race-bias grievances until after this lawsuit started, knowing that the employer was practicing what the contract prevented, rendered the Unions' explanation for their conduct unconvincing.

As we understand it, there was no suggestion below that the Unions held any racial animus against or denigrated blacks generally. Rather, it was held that a collective-bargaining agent could not, without violating Title VII and § 1981, follow a policy of refusing to file grievable racial discrimination claims however strong they might be and however sure the agent was that the employer was discriminating against blacks. The Unions, in effect, categorized racial grievances as unworthy of pursuit and, while pursuing thousands of other legitimate grievances, ignored racial discrimination claims on behalf of blacks, knowing that the employer was discriminating in violation of the contract. Such conduct, the courts below concluded, intentionally discriminated against blacks seeking a remedy for disparate treatment based on their race and violated both Title VII and § 1981. As the District Court said: "A union which intentionally avoids asserting discrimination claims, either so as not to antagonize the employer and thus improve its chances of success on other issues, or in deference to the perceived desires of its white membership, is liable under both Title [VII] and § 1981, regardless of whether, as a subjective matter, its leaders were favorably disposed toward minorities."

The courts below, in our view, properly construed and applied Title VII and § 1981. Those provisions do not permit a union to refuse to file any and all grievances presented by a black person on the ground that the employer looks with disfavor on and resents such grievances. It is no less violative of these laws for a union to pursue a policy of rejecting disparate-treatment grievances presented by blacks solely because the claims assert racial bias and would be very troublesome to process.

The judgment of the Court of Appeals is affirmed.

JUSTICE POWELL, with whom JUSTICE SCALIA joins, and with whom JUSTICE O'CONNOR joins as to Parts I through IV, concurring in part and dissenting in part.

* * *

II

A

As the Court recognizes, plaintiffs can recover under § 1981 only for intentional discrimination. The Court also recognizes that a valid claim under Title VII must be grounded on proof of disparate-treatment or disparate impact. A disparate treatment claim, like a § 1981 claim, requires proof of a discriminatory purpose. Of course, "[d]iscriminatory purpose' ... implies more than intent as volition or intent as awareness of consequences." *Personnel Administrator of Mass. v. Feeney,* 442 U.S. 256, 279, 99 S.Ct. 2282, 2296, 60 L.Ed.2d 870 (1979). It implies that the challenged action was taken "at least in part 'because of,' not merely 'in spite of,' its adverse effects upon an identifiable group." The Court concedes that "there was no suggestion below that the Unions held any racial animus against or denigrated blacks generally." It nevertheless concludes that the Unions violated Title VII and § 1981 because they "refuse[d] to file any and all grievances presented by a black person on the ground that the employer looks with disfavor on and resents such grievances," and "pursue[d] a policy of rejecting disparate-treatment grievances presented by blacks solely because the claims assert racial bias and would be very troublesome to process." In my view, this description of the Union's conduct, and thus the Court's legal conclusion, simply does not fit the facts found by the District Court.

The Unions offered a nondiscriminatory reason for their practice of withdrawing grievances that did not involve a discharge or lengthy suspension. According to the Unions, this policy, that is racially neutral on its face, was motivated by the Unions' nondiscriminatory interest in using the inadequate grievance system to assist members who faced the most serious economic harm. The District Court made no finding that the Unions' explanation was a pretext for racial discrimination. The Unions' policy against pursuing grievances on behalf of probationary employees also permitted the Unions to focus their attention on members with the most to lose. Similarly, the Unions' stated purpose for processing racial grievances on nonracial grounds—to obtain the swiftest and most complete relief possible for the claimant was not racially invidious. * * * Absent a finding that the Unions intended to discriminate against black members, the conclusion that the Unions are liable under § 1981 or the disparate-treatment theory of Title VII is unjustified.

* * *

III

The Court does not reach the question whether a union may be held liable under Title VII for "mere passivity" in the face of discrimination by the employer, because it agrees with the courts below that the record shows more than mere passivity on the part of the Unions. I disagree with that conclusion, and so must consider whether the judgment can be affirmed on the ground that Title VII imposes an affirmative duty on unions to combat discrimination by the employer.

The starting point for analysis of this statutory question is, as always, the language of the statute itself. Section 703(c), the provision of Title VII governing suits against unions, does not suggest that the union has a duty to take affirmative steps to remedy employer discrimination. Section 703(c)(1) makes it unlawful for a union "to exclude or to expel from its membership, or otherwise to discriminate against, any individual because of his race, color, religion, sex, or national origin." This subsection parallels § 703(a)(1), that applies to employers. This parallelism, and the reference to union membership, indicate that § 703(c)(1) prohibits direct discrimination by a union against its members; it does not impose upon a union an obligation to remedy discrimination by the *employer*. Moreover, § 703(c)(3) specifically addresses the union's interaction with the employer, by outlawing efforts by the union "to cause or attempt to cause an employer to discriminate against an individual in violation of this section.". If Congress had intended to impose on unions a duty to challenge discrimination by the employer, it hardly could have chosen language more ill suited to its purpose. First, "[t]o say that the union 'causes' employer discrimination simply by allowing it is to stretch the meaning of the word beyond its limits." Moreover, the language of § 703(c)(3) is taken *in haec verba* from § 8(b)(2) of the National Labor Relations Act (NLRA), 29 U.S.C. § 158(b)(2). That provision of the NLRA has been held not to impose liability for passive acquiescence in wrongdoing by the employer. Indeed, well before the enactment of Title VII, the Court held that even encouraging or inducing employer discrimination is not sufficient to incur liability under § 8(b)(2). *Electrical Workers v. NLRB*, 341 U.S. 694, 703, 71 S.Ct. 954, 959, 95 L.Ed. 1299 (1951).

* * *

[The opinion of JUSTICE BRENNAN, joined by JUSTICE MARSHALL and JUSTICE BLACKMUN, concurring in part and dissenting in part is omitted.]

NOTES

1. *"Duty of Fair Representation:"* The National Labor Relations Act and the Railway Labor Act implicitly impose on labor organizations certified to represent employees an obligation to represent all workers in the defined unit "without hostile discrimination, fairly, impartially, and in good faith." *Steele v. Louisville & Nashville R. Co.*, 323 U.S. 192, 65 S.Ct. 226, 89 L.Ed. 173 (1944). Union breach of this duty may be remedied either through charges filed with the National Labor Relations Board or private suit in the federal district courts. *Vaca v. Sipes*, 386 U.S. 171, 87 S.Ct. 903, 17 L.Ed.2d 842 (1967). The duty of fair representation has been construed not only to prohibit acts of invidious discrimination, but also to require unions to take positive steps to oppose such discrimination by employers with which the union has a bargaining relationship. *Local Union No. 12 United Rubber, Cork, Linoleum & Plastic Workers v. NLRB*, 368 F.2d 12 (5th Cir. 1966). Assuming that a union has a positive duty to act imposed by law (the NLRA), could not a failure to act as required by law be considered active discrimination under Title VII?

AMERICAN FEDERATION OF STATE, COUNTY, AND MUNICIPAL EMPLOYEES (AFSCME) v. STATE OF WASHINGTON

United States Court of Appeals, Ninth Circuit, 1985
770 F.2d 1401

KENNEDY, CIRCUIT JUDGE

In this class action affecting approximately 15,500 of its employees, the State of Washington was sued in the United States District Court for the Western District of Washington. The class comprises state employees who have worked or do work in job categories that are or have been at least seventy percent female. The action was commenced for the class members by two unions, the American Federation of State, County, and Municipal Employees (AFSCME) and the Washington Federation of State Employees (WFSE). * * * The district court found the State discriminated on the basis of sex in violation of Title VII of the Civil Rights Act of 1964, by compensating employees in jobs where females predominate at lower rates than employees in jobs where males predominate, if these jobs, though dissimilar, were identified by certain studies to be of comparable worth. The State appeals. We conclude a violation of Title VII was not established here, and we reverse.

The State of Washington has required [by statute] salaries of state employees to reflect prevailing market rates. Throughout the period in question, comprehensive biennial salary surveys were conducted to assess prevailing market rates. The surveys involved approximately 2,700 employers in the public and private sectors. The results were reported to state personnel boards, which conducted hearings before employee representatives and agencies and made salary recommendations to the State Budget Director. The Director submitted a proposed budget to the Governor, who in turn presented it to the state legislature. Salaries were fixed by enactment of the budget.

In 1974 the State commissioned a study by management consultant Norman Willis to determine whether a wage disparity existed between employees in jobs held predominantly by women and jobs held predominantly by men. The study examined sixty-two classifications in which at least seventy percent of the employees were women, and fifty-nine job classifications in which at least seventy percent of the employees were men. It found a wage disparity of about twenty percent, to the disadvantage of employees in jobs held mostly by women, for jobs considered of comparable worth. Comparable worth was calculated by evaluating jobs under four criteria: knowledge and skills, mental demands, accountability, and working conditions. A maximum number of points was allotted to each category: 280 for knowledge and skills, 140 for mental demands, 160 for accountability, and 20 for working conditions. Every job was assigned a numerical value under each of the four criteria. The State of Washington conducted similar studies in 1976 and 1980, and in 1983 the State enacted legislation providing for a compensation scheme based on comparable worth. The scheme is to take effect over a ten-year period.

* * *

AFSCME alleges sex-based wage discrimination throughout the state system, but its explanation and proof of the violation is, in essence, Washington's failure as early as 1979 to adopt and implement at once a comparable worth compensation program. The trial court adopted this theory as well. The comparable worth theory, as developed in the case before us, postulates that sex-based wage discrimination exists if employees in job classifications occupied primarily by women are paid less than employees in job classifications filled primarily by men, if the jobs are of equal value to the employer, though otherwise dissimilar.

Section 703(a) of Title VII states in pertinent part:

It shall be an unlawful employment practice for an employer—

(1) . . . to discriminate against any individual with respect to his compensation, terms, conditions, or privileges of employment, because of such individual's . . . sex . . . or

(2) to limit, segregate, or classify his employees or applicants for employment in any way *which would deprive or tend to deprive any individual of employment opportunities* ... because of such individual's ... sex....

* * *

Under the disparate treatment theory * * * an employer's intent or motive in adopting a challenged policy is an essential element of liability for a violation of Title VII. It is insufficient for a plaintiff alleging discrimination under the disparate treatment theory to show the employer was merely aware of the adverse consequences the policy would have on a protected group. *See Personnel Administrator of Massachusetts v. Feeney,* 442 U.S. 256, 279, 99 S.Ct. 2282, 2296, 60 L.Ed.2d 870 (1979) (discriminatory purpose implies more than awareness of consequences). The plaintiff must show the employer chose the particular policy because of its effect on members of a protected class (discriminatory intent implies selection of a particular course of action "at least in part 'because of,' not merely 'in spite of,' its adverse effects upon an identifiable group").

* * *

We consider next the allegations of disparate treatment. Under the disparate treatment theory, AFSCME was required to prove a prima facie case of sex discrimination by a preponderance of the evidence. As previously noted, liability for disparate treatment hinges upon proof of discriminatory intent. In an appropriate case, the necessary discriminatory animus may be inferred from circumstantial evidence. Our review of the record, however, indicates failure by AFSCME to establish the requisite element of intent by either circumstantial or direct evidence.

AFSCME contends discriminatory motive may be inferred from the Willis study, which finds the State's practice of setting salaries in reliance on market rates creates a sex-based wage disparity for jobs deemed of comparable worth. AFSCME argues from the study that the market reflects a historical pattern of lower wages to employees in positions staffed predominantly by women; and it contends the State of Washington perpetuates that disparity, in violation of Title VII, by using market rates in the compensation system. The inference of discriminatory motive which AFSCME seeks to draw from the State's participation in the market system fails, as the State did not create the market disparity and has not been shown to have been motivated by impermissible sex-based considerations in setting salaries.

The requirement of intent is linked at least in part to culpability. That concept would be undermined if we were to hold that payment of wages according to prevailing rates in the public and private sectors is an act that, in itself, supports the inference of a purpose to discriminate. Neither law nor logic deems the free market system a suspect enterprise. Economic reality is that the value of a particular job to an employer is but one factor influencing the rate of compensation for that job. Other considerations may include the availability of workers willing to do the job and the effectiveness of collective bargaining in a particular industry. * * * [E]mployers may be constrained by market forces to set salaries under prevailing wage rates for different job classifications, We find nothing in the language of Title VII or its legislative history to indicate Congress intended to abrogate fundamental economic principles such as the laws of supply and demand or to prevent employers from competing in the labor market.

While the Washington legislature may have the discretion to enact a comparable worth plan if it chooses to do so, Title VII does not obligate it to eliminate an economic inequality that it did not create. * * *

We have recognized that in certain cases an inference of intent may be drawn from statistical evidence. Though the comparability of wage rates in dissimilar jobs may be relevant to a determination of discriminatory animus, job evaluation studies and comparable worth statistics alone are insufficient to establish the requisite inference of discriminatory motive critical to the disparate treatment theory. The weight to be accorded such statistics is determined by the existence of independent corroborative evidence of discrimination. We conclude the independent evidence of discrimination presented by AFSCME is insufficient to support an inference of the requisite discriminatory motive under the disparate treatment theory.

AFSCME offered proof of isolated incidents of sex segregation as evidence of a history of sex-based wage discrimination. The evidence * * * consists of "help wanted" advertisements restricting various jobs to members of a particular sex. These advertisements were often placed in separate "help wanted-male" and "help wanted-female" columns in state newspapers between 1960 and 1973, though most were discontinued when Title VII became applicable to the states in 1972. At trial, AFSCME called expert witnesses to testify that a causal relationship exists between sex segregation practices and sex-based wage discrimination, and that the effects of sex segregation practices may persist even after the practices are discontinued. However, none of the individually named plaintiffs in the action ever testified regarding specific incidents of discrimination. The isolated incidents alleged by AFSCME are insufficient to corroborate the results of the Willis study and do not justify an inference of discriminatory motive by the State in the setting of salaries for its system as a whole. Given the scope of the alleged intentional act, and given the attempt to show the core principle of the State's market-based compensation system was adopted or maintained with a discriminatory purpose, more is required to support the finding of liability than these isolated acts, which had only an indirect relation to the compensation principle itself.

We also reject AFSCME's contention that, having commissioned the Willis study, the State of Washington was committed to implement a new system of compensation based on comparable worth as defined by the study. Whether comparable worth is a feasible approach to employee compensation is a matter of debate. Assuming, however, that like other job evaluation studies it may be useful as a diagnostic tool, we reject a rule that would penalize rather than commend employers for their effort and innovation in undertaking such a study. * * *

We hold there was a failure to establish a violation of Title VII under the disparate treatment theory of discrimination, and reverse the district court on this aspect of the case as well. * *

NOTE

1. Failure of a union to raise a claim of race discrimination during a grievance hearing over plaintiff's termination was not discrimination in violation of 42 U.S.C. § 1981 absent a demonstration that the union had a practice of ignoring race-related grievances. *Wesley v. General Drivers, Warehousemen and Helpers Local 745,* 660 F.3d 211 (5th Cir. 2011).

CHAPTER 6

"BECAUSE OF"

■ ■ ■

A. MOTIVE BASED DISPARATE TREATMENT

1. GENERALLY

HAZEN PAPER CO. v. BIGGINS, 507 U.S. 604, 113 S.Ct. 1701, 123 L.Ed.2d 338 (1993)

'Disparate treatment' . . . is the most easily understood type of discrimination. The employer simply treats some people less favorably than others because of their race, color, religion [or other protected characteristics.] Proof of discriminatory motive is critical, although it can in some situations be inferred from the mere fact of differences in treatment. . . .

* * *

In a disparate treatment case, liability depends on whether the protected trait actually motivated the employer's decision. The employer may have relied upon a formal, facially discriminatory policy requiring adverse treatment of employees with that trait. Or the employer may have been motivated by the protected trait on an ad hoc, informal basis. Whatever the employer's decisionmaking process, a disparate treatment claim cannot succeed unless the employee's protected trait actually played a role in that process and had a determinative influence on the outcome.

a. Reconsider **AFSCME v. STATE OF WASHINGTON,** *supra page 302,* which illustrated the close relationship between the objective act of "discrimination" and the subjective element behind the act's motivation.

b. *WASHINGTON v. DAVIS,* **426 U.S. 229, 96 S.Ct. 2040, 48 L.Ed.2d 597 (1976).** A government employer administered an objective test that white applicants passed in proportionately greater numbers than blacks, an outcome that was predictable. This did not establish a racial motivation for administering the test. The reason, or motive, was to select the most qualified workers, not to exclude persons of color.

c. ***PERSONNEL ADMINISTRATOR OF MASS. v. FEENEY***, **442 U.S. 256, 99 S.Ct. 2282, 60 L.Ed.2d 870 (1979).** The state employer had adopted an employment preference for military veterans which easily could be foreseen to disadvantage women applicants. The purpose, or motive, was to assist veterans, not harm women, and thus did not constitute sex discrimination. The Court stated:

"Discriminatory purpose * * * implies more than intent as volition or intent as awareness of consequences. It implies the decisionmaker * * * selected or reaffirmed a particular course of action at least in part 'because of,' not merely 'in spite of' its adverse effects upon an identifiable group."

2. RELATIONSHIP BETWEEN STATE OF MIND AND ACTION: CAUSATION

STAUB v. PROCTOR HOSPITAL

Supreme Court of the United States, 2011
___ U.S. ___, 131 S.Ct. 1186, 179 L.Ed.2d 144

JUSTICE SCALIA, delivered the opinion of the Court.

We consider the circumstances under which an employer may be held liable for employment discrimination based on the discriminatory animus of an employee who influenced, but did not make, the ultimate employment decision.

I

Petitioner Vincent Staub worked as an <u>angiography</u> technician for respondent Proctor Hospital until 2004, when he was fired. Staub and Proctor hotly dispute the facts surrounding the firing, but because a jury found for Staub in his claim of employment discrimination against Proctor, we describe the facts viewed in the light most favorable to him.

While employed by Proctor, Staub was a member of the United States Army Reserve, which required him to attend drill one weekend per month and to train full time for two to three weeks a year. Both Janice Mulally, Staub's immediate supervisor, and Michael Korenchuk, Mulally's supervisor, were hostile to Staub's military obligations. Mulally scheduled **Staub** for additional shifts without notice so that he would " 'pa[y] back the department for everyone else having to bend over backwards to cover [his] schedule for the Reserves.' " She also informed Staub's co-worker, Leslie Sweborg, that Staub's " 'military duty had been a strain on th[e] department,' " and asked Sweborg to help her " 'get rid of him.' " Korenchuk referred to Staub's military obligations as " 'a b[u]nch of smoking and joking and [a] waste of taxpayers['] money.' " He was also aware that Mulally was " 'out to get' " Staub.

* * *

On April 2, 2004, Angie Day, Staub's co-worker, complained to Linda Buck, Proctor's vice president of human resources, and Garrett McGowan, Proctor's chief operating officer, about Staub's frequent unavailability and abruptness. McGowan directed Korenchuk and Buck to create a plan that would solve Staub's "'availability' problems." But three weeks later, before they had time to do so, Korenchuk informed Buck that Staub had left his desk without informing a supervisor, in violation of the January Corrective Action. Staub now contends this accusation was false: he had left Korenchuk a voice-mail notification that he was leaving his desk. Buck relied on Korenchuk's accusation, however, and after reviewing Staub's personnel file, she decided to fire him. The termination notice stated that Staub had ignored the directive issued in the January 2004 Corrective Action.

Staub challenged his firing through Proctor's grievance process, claiming that Mulally had fabricated the allegation underlying the Corrective Action out of hostility toward his military obligations. Buck did not follow up with Mulally about this claim. After discussing the matter with another personnel officer, Buck adhered to her decision.

Staub sued Proctor under the Uniformed Services Employment and Reemployment Rights Act of 1994, 38 U.S.C. § 4301 *et seq.,* claiming that his discharge was motivated by hostility to his obligations as a military reservist. His contention was not that Buck had any such hostility but that Mulally and Korenchuk did, and that their actions influenced Buck's ultimate employment decision. A jury found that Staub's "military status was a motivating factor in [Proctor's] decision to discharge him," and awarded $57,640 in damages.

The Seventh Circuit reversed, holding that Proctor was entitled to judgment as a matter of law. The court observed that Staub had brought a "'cat's paw' case," meaning that he sought to hold his employer liable for the animus of a supervisor who was not charged with making the ultimate employment decision.[1] It explained that under Seventh Circuit precedent, a "cat's paw" case could not succeed unless the nondecisionmaker exercised such "'singular influence'" over the decisionmaker that the decision to terminate was the product of "blind reliance." It then noted that "Buck looked beyond what Mulally and Korenchuk said," relying in part on her conversation with Day and her review of Staub's personnel file. The court "admit[ted] that Buck's investigation could have been more robust," since it "failed to pursue Staub's theory that Mulally fabricated the write-up." But the court said that the "'singular influence'" rule "does not require the decisionmaker to be a paragon of independence": "It is enough that the decisionmaker is not wholly dependent on a single source of information and conducts her own investigation into the facts

---

1. The term "cat's paw" derives from a fable conceived by Aesop, put into verse by La Fontaine in 1679, and injected into United States employment discrimination law by Posner in 1990. In the fable, a monkey induces a cat by flattery to extract roasting chestnuts from the fire. After the cat has done so, burning its paws in the process, the monkey makes off with the chestnuts and leaves the cat with nothing. * * *

relevant to the decision. Because the undisputed evidence established that Buck was not wholly dependent on the advice of Korenchuk and Mulally, the court held that Proctor was entitled to judgment.

We granted certiorari.

II

The Uniformed Services Employment and Reemployment Rights Act (USERRA) provides in relevant part as follows:

> "A person who is a member of ... or has an obligation to perform service in a uniformed service shall not be denied initial employment, reemployment, retention in employment, promotion, or any benefit of employment by an employer on the basis of that membership, ... or obligation." 38 U.S.C. § 4311(a).

It elaborates further:

> "An employer shall be considered to have engaged in actions prohibited ... under subsection (a), if the person's membership ... is a motivating factor in the employer's action, unless the employer can prove that the action would have been taken in the absence of such membership." § 4311(c).

The statute is very similar to Title VII, which prohibits employment discrimination "because of ... race, color, religion, sex, or national origin" and states that such discrimination is established when one of those factors "was a motivating factor for any employment practice, even though other factors also motivated the practice." 42 U.S.C. §§ 2000e–2(a), (m).

The central difficulty in this case is construing the phrase "motivating factor in the employer's action." When the company official who makes the decision to take an adverse employment action is personally acting out of hostility to the employee's membership in or obligation to a uniformed service, a motivating factor obviously exists. The problem we confront arises when that official has no discriminatory animus but is influenced by previous company action that is the product of a like animus in someone else.

In approaching this question, we start from the premise that when Congress creates a federal tort it adopts the background of general tort law. Intentional torts such as this, "as distinguished from negligent or reckless torts, ... generally require that the actor intend 'the *consequences*' of an act,' not simply 'the act itself.' "

Staub contends that the fact that an unfavorable entry on the plaintiff's personnel record was caused to be put there, with discriminatory animus, by Mulally and Korenchuk, suffices to establish the tort, even if Mulally and Korenchuk did not intend to cause his dismissal. But discrimination was no part of Buck's reason for the dismissal; and while Korenchuk and Mulally acted with discriminatory animus, the act they committed—the mere making of the reports—was not a denial of "initial employment, reemployment, retention in employment, promotion, or any benefit of employment,'' as liability under USERRA requires. If dismissal was not the object of Mulally's and Korenchuk's reports, it may have been their result, or even their foreseeable consequence, but that is not enough to render Mulally or Korenchuk responsible.

Here, however, Staub is seeking to hold liable not Mulally and Korenchuk, but their employer. Perhaps, therefore, the discriminatory motive of one of the employer's agents (Mulally or Korenchuk) can be aggregated with the act of another agent (Buck) to impose liability on Proctor. * * *

Proctor, on the other hand, contends that the employer is not liable unless the *de facto* decisionmaker (the technical decisionmaker or the agent for whom he is the "cat's paw") is motivated by discriminatory animus. * * * We do not think that the ultimate decisionmaker's exercise of judgment automatically renders the link to the supervisor's bias "remote" or "purely contingent." The decisionmaker's exercise of judgment is *also* a proximate cause of the employment decision, but it is common for injuries to have multiple proximate causes. Nor can the ultimate decisionmaker's judgment be deemed a superseding cause of the harm. A cause can be thought "superseding" only if it is a "cause of independent origin that was not foreseeable."

Moreover, the approach urged upon us by Proctor gives an unlikely meaning to a provision designed to prevent employer discrimination. An employer's authority to reward, punish, or dismiss is often allocated among multiple agents. The one who makes the ultimate decision does so on the basis of performance assessments by other supervisors. Proctor's view would have the improbable consequence that if an employer isolates a personnel official from an employee's supervisors, vests the decision to take adverse employment actions in that official, and asks that official to review the employee's personnel file before taking the adverse action, then the employer will be effectively shielded from discriminatory acts and recommendations of supervisors that were *designed and intended* to produce the adverse action. That seems to us an implausible meaning of the text, and one that is not compelled by its words.

Proctor suggests that even if the decisionmaker's mere exercise of independent judgment does not suffice to negate the effect of the prior discrimination, at least the decisionmaker's independent investigation (and rejection) of the employee's allegations of discriminatory animus ought to do so. We decline to adopt such a hard-and-fast rule. As we have already acknowledged, the requirement that the biased supervisor's action be a causal factor of the ultimate employment action incorporates the traditional tort-law concept of proximate cause. Thus, if the employer's investigation results in an adverse action for reasons unrelated to the supervisor's original biased action (by the terms of USERRA it is the employer's burden to establish that), then the employer will not be liable. But the supervisor's biased report may remain a causal factor if the independent investigation takes it into account without determining that the adverse action was, apart from the supervisor's recommendation, entirely justified. We are aware of no principle in tort or agency law under which an employer's mere conduct of an independent investigation has a claim-preclusive effect. Nor do we think the independent investigation somehow relieves the employer of "fault." The employer is at fault because one of its agents committed an action based on discriminatory animus that was intended to cause, and did in fact cause, an adverse employment decision.

* * *

We therefore hold that if a supervisor performs an act motivated by antimilitary animus that is *intended* by the supervisor to cause an adverse employment action, and if that act is a proximate cause of the ultimate employment action, then the employer is liable under USERRA.[4]

III

Applying our analysis to the facts of this case, it is clear that the Seventh Circuit's judgment must be reversed. Both Mulally and Korenchuk were acting within the scope of their employment when they took the actions that allegedly caused Buck to fire Staub. A "reprimand ... for workplace failings" constitutes conduct within the scope of an agent's employment. As the Seventh Circuit recognized, there was evidence that Mulally's and Korenchuk's actions were motivated by hostility toward Staub's military obligations. There was also evidence that Mulally's and Korenchuk's actions were causal factors underlying Buck's decision to fire Staub. Buck's termination notice expressly stated that Staub was terminated because he had "ignored" the directive in the Corrective Action. Finally, there was evidence that both Mulally and Korenchuk had the specific intent to cause Staub to be terminated. Mulally stated she was trying to " 'get rid of' " Staub, and Korenchuk was aware that Mulally was " 'out to get' " Staub. Moreover, Korenchuk informed Buck, Proctor's personnel officer responsible for terminating employees, of Staub's alleged noncompliance with Mulally's Corrective Action, and Buck fired Staub immediately thereafter; a reasonable jury could infer that Korenchuk intended that Staub be fired. The Seventh Circuit therefore erred in holding that Proctor was entitled to judgment as a matter of law.

It is less clear whether the jury's verdict should be reinstated or whether Proctor is entitled to a new trial. The jury instruction did not hew precisely to the rule we adopt today; it required only that the jury find that "military status was a motivating factor in [Proctor's] decision to discharge him." Whether the variance between the instruction and our

---

4. Needless to say, the employer would be liable only when the supervisor acts within the scope of his employment, or when the supervisor acts outside the scope of his employment and liability would be imputed to the employer under traditional agency principles. We express no view as to whether the employer would be liable if a co-worker, rather than a supervisor, committed a discriminatory act that influenced the ultimate employment decision. We also observe that **Staub** took advantage of Proctor's grievance process, and we express no view as to whether Proctor would have an affirmative defense if he did not.

rule was harmless error or should mandate a new trial is a matter the Seventh Circuit may consider in the first instance.

* * *

The judgment of the Seventh Circuit is reversed, and the case is remanded for further proceedings consistent with this opinion.

[The concurring opinion of JUSTICE ALITO, joined by JUSTICE THOMAS, is omitted.]

NOTE

1. Where the operative language of USERRA and Title VII are similar, courts have tended to rely upon judicial interpretation of Title VII. *See, Knowles v. Citicorp,* 142 F.3d 1082 (8th Cir. 1998). However, in a number of aspects the language of USERRA differs from that in the core statutes, such as in prohibiting discharge of a returning veteran within one year except "for cause." As USERRA prohibits only "denial of any benefit of employment," one court has held that USERRA does not proscribe harassment based on military service that does not affect a tangible "benefit." *Carder v. Continental Airlines, Inc.,* 636 F.3d 172 (5th Cir. 2011).

McKENNON v. NASHVILLE BANNER PUBLISHING COMPANY

Supreme Court of the United States, 1995
513 U.S. 352, 115 S.Ct. 879, 130 L.Ed.2d 852

JUSTICE KENNEDY delivered the opinion of the Court.

The question before us is whether an employee discharged in violation of the Age Discrimination in Employment Act of 1967 is barred from all relief when, after her discharge, the employer discovers evidence of wrongdoing that, in any event, would have led to the employee's termination on lawful and legitimate grounds.

I

For some 30 years, petitioner Christine McKennon worked for respondent Nashville Banner Publishing Company. She was discharged, the Banner claimed, as part of a work force reduction plan necessitated by cost considerations. McKennon, who was 62 years old when she lost her job, thought another reason explained her dismissal: her age. She filed suit in the United States District Court for the Middle District of Tennessee, alleging that her discharge violated the Age Discrimination in Employment Act of 1967. * * *

McKennon sought a variety of legal and equitable remedies available under the ADEA, including backpay.

In preparation of the case, the Banner took McKennon's deposition. She testified that, during her final year of employment, she had copied several confidential documents bearing upon the company's financial condition.

She had access to these records as secretary to the Banner's comptroller. McKennon took the copies home and showed them to her husband. Her motivation, she averred, was an apprehension she was about to be fired because of her age. When she became concerned about her job, she removed and copied the documents for "insurance" and "protection." A few days after these deposition disclosures, the Banner sent McKennon a letter declaring that removal and copying of the records was in violation of her job responsibilities and advising her (again) that she was terminated. The Banner's letter also recited that had it known of McKennon's misconduct it would have discharged her at once for that reason.

* * * The District Court granted summary judgment for the Banner, holding that McKennon's misconduct was grounds for her termination and that neither backpay nor any other remedy was available to her under the ADEA. The United States Court of Appeals for the Sixth Circuit affirmed on the same rationale. We granted certiorari to resolve conflicting views among the Courts of Appeals on the question whether all relief must be denied when an employee has been discharged in violation of the ADEA and the employer later discovers some wrongful conduct that would have led to discharge if it had been discovered earlier. We now reverse.

II

We shall assume, as summary judgment procedures require us to assume, that the sole reason for McKennon's initial discharge was her age, a discharge violative of the ADEA. Our further premise is that the misconduct revealed by the deposition was so grave that McKennon's immediate discharge would have followed its disclosure in any event. * * * We do question the legal conclusion reached by those courts that after-acquired evidence of wrongdoing which would have resulted in discharge bars employees from any relief under the ADEA. That ruling is incorrect.

The Court of Appeals considered McKennon's misconduct, in effect, to be supervening grounds for termination. That may be so, but it does not follow, as the Court of Appeals said in citing one of its own earlier cases, that the misconduct renders it " 'irrelevant whether or not [McKennon] was discriminated against.' " We conclude that a violation of the ADEA cannot be so altogether disregarded.

* * * The ADEA incorporates some features of both Title VII and the Fair Labor Standards Act of 1938, which has led us to describe it as "something of a hybrid." The substantive, antidiscrimination provisions of the ADEA are modeled upon the prohibitions of Title VII. Its remedial provisions incorporate by reference the provisions of the Fair Labor Standards Act of 1938. When confronted with a violation of the ADEA, a district court is authorized to afford relief by means of reinstatement, backpay, injunctive relief, declaratory judgment, and attorney's fees. In the case of a willful violation of the Act, the ADEA authorizes an award of liquidated damages equal to the backpay award. 29 U.S.C. § 626(b). The Act also gives federal courts the discretion to "grant such legal or

equitable relief as may be appropriate to effectuate the purposes of [the Act]."

The ADEA and Title VII share common substantive features and also a common purpose: "the elimination of discrimination in the workplace." Congress designed the remedial measures in these statutes to serve as a "spur or catalyst" to cause employers "to self-examine and to self-evaluate their employment practices and to endeavor to eliminate, so far as possible, the last vestiges" of discrimination. Deterrence is one object of these statutes. Compensation for injuries caused by the prohibited discrimination is another. The ADEA, in keeping with these purposes, contains a vital element found in both Title VII and the Fair Labor Standards Act: It grants an injured employee a right of action to obtain the authorized relief. The private litigant who seeks redress for his or her injuries vindicates both the deterrence and the compensation objectives of the ADEA. It would not accord with this scheme if after-acquired evidence of wrongdoing that would have resulted in termination operates, in every instance, to bar all relief for an earlier violation of the Act.

The objectives of the ADEA are furthered when even a single employee establishes that an employer has discriminated against him or her. The disclosure through litigation of incidents or practices that violate national policies respecting nondiscrimination in the work force is itself important, for the occurrence of violations may disclose patterns of noncompliance resulting from a misappreciation of the Act's operation or entrenched resistance to its commands, either of which can be of industry-wide significance. The efficacy of its enforcement mechanisms becomes one measure of the success of the Act.

The Court of Appeals in this case relied upon two of its earlier decisions, and the opinion of the Court of Appeals for the Tenth Circuit in *Summers v. State Farm Mutual Automobile Ins. Co.,* 864 F.2d 700 (1988). * * * *Summers,* in turn, relied upon our decision in *Mt. Healthy City Bd. of Ed. v. Doyle,* 429 U.S. 274, 97 S.Ct. 568, 50 L.Ed.2d 471 (1977), but that decision is inapplicable here.

In *Mt. Healthy* we addressed a mixed-motives case, in which two motives were said to be operative in the employer's decision to fire an employee. One was lawful, the other (an alleged constitutional violation) unlawful. We held that if the lawful reason alone would have sufficed to justify the firing, the employee could not prevail in a suit against the employer. The case was controlled by the difficulty, and what we thought was the lack of necessity, of disentangling the proper motive from the improper one where both played a part in the termination and the former motive would suffice to sustain the employer's action.

That is not the problem confronted here. As we have said, the case comes to us on the express assumption that an unlawful motive was the sole basis for the firing. McKennon's misconduct was not discovered until after she had been fired. The employer could not have been motivated by knowledge it did not have and it cannot now claim that the employee was fired for the nondiscriminatory reason. Mixed motive cases are inapposite here, except to the important extent they underscore the necessity of determining the employer's motives in ordering the discharge, an essential element in determining whether the employer violated the federal antidiscrimination law. As has been observed, "proving that the same decision would have been justified ... is not the same as proving that the same decision would have been made."

Our inquiry is not at an end, however, for even though the employer has violated the Act, we must consider how the after-acquired evidence of the employee's wrongdoing bears on the specific remedy to be ordered. Equity's maxim that a suitor who engaged in his own reprehensible conduct in the course of the transaction at issue must be denied equitable relief because of unclean hands, a rule which in conventional formulation operated *in limine* to bar the suitor from invoking the aid of the equity court, has not been applied where Congress authorizes broad equitable relief to serve important national policies. We have rejected the unclean hands defense "where a private suit serves important public purposes." That does not mean, however, the employee's own misconduct is irrelevant to all the remedies otherwise available under the statute. The statute controlling this case provides that "the court shall have jurisdiction to grant such legal or equitable relief as may be appropriate to effectuate the purposes of this chapter, including without limitation judgments compelling employment, reinstatement or promotion, or enforcing the liability for [amounts owing to a person as a result of a violation of this chapter]." 29 U.S.C. § 626(b). In giving effect to the ADEA, we must recognize the duality between the legitimate interests of the employer and the important claims of the employee who invokes the national employment policy mandated by the Act. The employee's wrongdoing must be taken into account, we conclude, lest the employer's legitimate concerns be ignored. * * *

* * * We do conclude that here, and as a general rule in cases of this type, neither reinstatement nor front pay is an appropriate remedy. It would be both inequitable and pointless to order the reinstatement of someone the employer would have terminated, and will terminate, in any event and upon lawful grounds.

The proper measure of backpay presents a more difficult problem. Resolution of this question must give proper recognition to the fact that an ADEA violation has occurred which must be deterred and compensated without undue infringement upon the employer's rights and prerogatives. The object of compensation is to restore the employee to the position he or she would have been in absent the discrimination, * * *. Once an employer learns about employee wrongdoing that would lead to a legitimate discharge, we cannot require the employer to ignore the information, even if it is acquired during the course of discovery in a suit against the employer and even if the information might have gone undiscovered absent the suit. The beginning point in the trial court's formulation of a remedy should be calculation of backpay from the date of the unlawful discharge to the date the new information was discovered. In determining the appropriate order for relief, the court can consider taking into further account extraordinary equitable circumstances that affect the legitimate interests of either party. An absolute rule barring any recovery of backpay, however, would undermine the ADEA's objective of forcing employers to consider and examine their motivations, and of penalizing them for employment decisions that spring from age discrimination.

Where an employer seeks to rely upon after-acquired evidence of wrongdoing, it must first establish that the wrongdoing was of such severity that the employee in fact would have been terminated on those grounds alone if the employer had known of it at the time of the discharge. The concern that employers might as a routine matter undertake extensive discovery into an employee's background or performance on the job to resist claims under the Act is not an insubstantial one, but we think the authority of the courts to award attorney's fees, mandated under the statute, 29 U.S.C. §§ 216(b), 626(b), and to invoke the appropriate provisions of the Federal Rules of Civil Procedure will deter most abuses.

The judgment is reversed, and the case is remanded to the Court of Appeals for the Sixth Circuit for further proceedings consistent with this opinion.

NOTES

1. *Burdens:* To avoid full remedies of reinstatement and back pay it would seem that the burden is on the employer to prove that it would have discharged the employee upon discovery of the misconduct. *Rivera v. NIBCO,* 364 F.3d 1057 (9th Cir. 2004). If others had not been similarly disciplined for similar behavior it would be difficult, if not impossible, for the employer to carry that burden. Moreover, a significant time lapse between discovery of the misconduct and the employee's discharge undermines arguments that misconduct, not retaliation, motivated the employer.

2. *Resume fraud:* A related, but distinguishable, issue arises when an employer, in response to an employee's charge of discrimination, examines the employee's initial application for employment and discovers that the employee had misstated certain facts or failed to display candor (such as failing to list a former employer). The employer now (re-)dismisses the employee based on the discrepancy. The employer argues that, unlike *McKennon* who misbehaved on the job, had this employee been truthful in her initial application, she would *not have been hired.* Since the employee would not have been hired, the argument goes, the employee is not entitled to reinstatement or any backwages.

For this argument to have traction the employer must establish, not that the employee's application would have been rejected, but that the initial misrepresentation was sufficiently serious that the employee would be *discharged* upon the misstatement being discovered. *Shattuck v. Kinetic Concepts, Inc.,* 49 F.3d 1106 (5th Cir. 1995). Thus, if the employee had misrepresented an essential credential required for the job, such as a college degree for a teacher, this would justify denial of reinstatement or back wages for the period past the discovery of the employee's "fraud." However, if the initial misstatement was a minor inaccuracy, such as the employee's age or marital status, it would be difficult, if not impossible, for the employer to prove that the worker who had performed well would now be *dismissed* for such a misstatement. If the employer asserts that the employee is being dismissed simply because of "dishonesty" on his application, as a practical matter, the employer must establish that other employees are dismissed for similar acts of "dishonesty." *See, Calloway v. Partners Nat'l Health Plans,* 986 F.2d 446 (11th Cir. 1993).

3. *Retaliation?* Consider the argument that sleuthing into an employee's background because the employee filed an EEOC charge is an act of unlawful retaliation under § 704. The employer would not have discovered any discrepancy had the employee not exercised a protected right. Employees who have not been fully candid in the application process would be chilled in any future assertion of statutory protection for fear that long past picadillos would be disclosed and used to rationalize retaliation.

4. *Post-discharge misconduct:* After the employee has been illegally discharged, the former employee engages in behavior that normally would result in the employee being dismissed. As a general proposition such behavior would not be a basis for denying reinstatement and an award of full back pay. *See, Carr v. Woodbury County Juv. Det. Cn'tr,* 905 F.Supp. 619 (N.D.Iowa 1995) (denying admissibility of such evidence), *aff'd,* 97 F.3d 1456 (8th Cir. 1996). However, serious misconduct, such as violent behavior or illegal actions directed against the employer, may warrant denial of reinstatement. *McDonnell Douglas Corp. v. Green,* 411 U.S. 792, 93 S.Ct. 1817, 36 L.Ed.2d 668 (1973).

B. DISCRIMINATORY EFFECT IN THE ABSENCE OF MOTIVE

1. THE GENERAL PRINCIPLE

GRIGGS v. DUKE POWER CO.

Supreme Court of the United States, 1971
401 U.S. 424, 91 S.Ct. 849, 28 L.Ed.2d 158

CHIEF JUSTICE BURGER delivered the opinion of the Court.

We granted the writ in this case to resolve the question whether an employer is prohibited by the Civil Rights Act of 1964, Title VII, from requiring a high school education or passing of a standardized general intelligence test as a condition of employment in or transfer to jobs when (a) neither standard is shown to be significantly related to successful job performance, (b) both requirements operate to disqualify Negroes at a substantially higher rate than white applicants, and (c) the jobs in question formerly had been filled only by white employees as part of a longstanding practice of giving preference to whites.

* * * All the petitioners are employed at the Company's Dan River Steam Station, a power generating facility located at Draper, North Carolina. At

the time this action was instituted, the Company had 95 employees at the Dan River Station, 14 of whom were Negroes; 13 of these are petitioners here.

The District Court found that prior to July 2, 1965, the effective date of the Civil Rights Act of 1964, the Company openly discriminated on the basis of race in the hiring and assigning of employees at its Dan River plant. The plant was organized into five operating departments: (1) Labor, (2) Coal Handling, (3) Operations, (4) Maintenance, and (5) Laboratory and Test. Negroes were employed only in the Labor Department where the highest paying jobs paid less than the lowest paying jobs in the other four 'operating' departments in which only whites were employed. Promotions were normally made within each department on the basis of job seniority. Transferees into a department usually began in the lowest position.

In 1955 the Company instituted a policy of requiring a high school education for initial assignment to any department except Labor, and for transfer from the Coal Handling to any 'inside' department (Operations, Maintenance, or Laboratory). When the Company abandoned its policy of restricting Negroes to the Labor Department in 1965, completion of high school also was made a prerequisite to transfer from Labor to any other department. From the time the high school requirement was instituted to the time of trial, however, white employees hired before the time of the high school education requirement continued to perform satisfactorily and achieve promotions in the 'operating' departments. Findings on this score are not challenged.

The Company added a further requirement for new employees on July 2, 1965, the date on which Title VII became effective. To qualify for placement in any but the Labor Department it become necessary to register satisfactory scores on two professionally prepared aptitude tests, as well as to have a high school education. Completion of high school alone continued to render employees eligible for transfer to the four desirable departments from which Negroes had been excluded if the incumbent had been employed prior to the time of the new requirement. In September 1965 the Company began to permit incumbent employees who lacked a high school education to qualify for transfer from Labor or Coal Handling to an 'inside' job by passing two tests—the Wonderlic Personnel Test, which purports to measure general intelligence, and the Bennett Mechanical Comprehension Test. Neither was directed or intended to measure the ability to learn to perform a particular job or category of jobs. The requisite scores used for both initial hiring and transfer approximated the national median for high school graduates.

The District Court had found that while the Company previously followed a policy of overt racial discrimination in a period prior to the Act, such conduct had ceased. The District Court also concluded that Title VII was intended to be prospective only and, consequently, the impact of prior inequities was beyond the reach of corrective action authorized by the Act.

After careful analysis a majority of [the Court of Appeals] concluded that a subjective test of the employer's intent should govern, particularly in a close case, and that in this case there was no showing of a discriminatory purpose in the adoption of the diploma and test requirements. On this basis, the Court of Appeals concluded there was no violation of the Act.

The Court of Appeals reversed the District Court in part, rejecting the holding that residual discrimination arising from prior employment practices was insulated from remedial action.[4] The Court of Appeals noted, however, that the District Court was correct in its conclusion that there was no showing of a racial purpose or invidious intent in the adoption of the high school diploma requirement or general intelligence test and that these standards had been applied fairly to whites and Negroes alike. It held that, in the absence of a discriminatory purpose, use of such requirements was permitted by the Act. In so doing, the Court of Appeals rejected the claim that because these two requirements operated to render ineligible a markedly disproportionate number of Negroes, they were unlawful under Title VII unless shown to be job related. We granted the writ on these claims.

The objective of Congress in the enactment of Title VII is plain from the language of the statute. It was to achieve equality of employment opportunities and remove barriers that have operated in the past to favor an identifiable group of white employees over other employees. Under the Act, practices, procedures, or tests neutral on their face, and even neutral in terms of intent, cannot be maintained if they operate to 'freeze' the status quo of prior discriminatory employment practices.

The Court of Appeals' opinion, and the partial dissent, agreed that, on the record in the present case, 'whites register far better on the Company's alternative requirements' than Negroes.[6] This consequence would appear to be directly traceable to race. Basic intelligence must have the means of articulation to manifest itself fairly in a testing process. Because they are Negroes, petitioners have long received inferior education in segregated schools * * *. Congress did not intend by Title VII, however, to guarantee a job to every person regardless of qualifications. In short, the Act does not command that any person be hired simply because he was formerly

---

4. The Court of Appeals ruled that Negroes employed in the Labor Department at a time when there was no high school or test requirement for entrance into the higher paying departments could not now be made subject to those requirements, since whites hired contemporaneously into those departments were never subject to them. The Court of Appeals also required that the seniority rights of those Negroes be measured on a plantwide, rather than a departmental, basis. However, the Court of Appeals denied relief to the Negro employees without a high school education or its equivalent who were hired into the Labor Department after institution of the educational requirement.

6. In North Carolina, 1960 census statistics show that, while 34% of white males had completed high school, only 12% of Negro males had done so. U.S. Bureau of the Census, U.S. Census of Population: 1960, Vol. 1, Characteristics of the Population, pt. 35, Table 47.

Similarly, with respect to standardized tests, the EEOC in one case found that use of a battery of tests, including the Wonderlic and Bennett tests used by the Company in the instant case, resulted in 58% of whites passing the tests, as compared with only 6% of the blacks. Decision of EEOC, CCH Empl.Prac. Guide, 17,304.53 (Dec. 2, 1966). See also Decision of EEOC 70–552, CCH Empl.Prac. Guide, 6139 (Feb. 19, 1970).

the subject of discrimination, or because he is a member of a minority group. Discriminatory preference for any group, minority or majority, is precisely and only what Congress has proscribed. What is required by Congress is the removal of artificial, arbitrary, and unnecessary barriers to employment when the barriers operate invidiously to discriminate on the basis of racial or other impermissible classification.

Congress has now provided that tests or criteria for employment or promotion may not provide equality of opportunity merely in the sense of the fabled offer of milk to the stork and the fox. On the contrary, Congress has now required that the posture and condition of the job-seeker be taken into account. It has—to resort again to the fable—provided that the vessel in which the milk is proffered be one all seekers can use. The Act proscribes not only overt discrimination but also practices that are fair in form, but discriminatory in operation. The touchstone is business necessity. If an employment practice which operates to exclude Negroes cannot be shown to be related to job performance, the practice is prohibited.

On the record before us, neither the high school completion requirement nor the general intelligence test is shown to bear a demonstrable relationship to successful performance of the jobs for which it was used. Both were adopted, as the Court of Appeals noted, without meaningful study of their relationship to job-performance ability. Rather, a vice president of the Company testified, the requirements were instituted on the Company's judgment that they generally would improve the overall quality of the work force.

The evidence, however, shows that employees who have not completed high school or taken the tests have continued to perform satisfactorily and make progress in departments for which the high school and test criteria are now used. The promotion record of present employees who would not be able to meet the new criteria thus suggests the possibility that the requirements may not be needed even for the limited purpose of preserving the avowed policy of advancement within the Company. * * *

The Court of Appeals held that the Company had adopted the diploma and test requirements without any 'intention to discriminate against Negro employees.' We do not suggest that either the District Court or the Court of Appeals erred in examining the employer's intent; but good intent or absence of discriminatory intent does not redeem employment procedures or testing mechanisms that operate as 'built-in headwinds' for minority groups and are unrelated to measuring job capability.

The Company's lack of discriminatory intent is suggested by special efforts to help the undereducated employees through Company financing of two-thirds the cost of tuition for high school training. But Congress directed the thrust of the Act to the consequences of employment practices, not simply the motivation. More than that, Congress has placed on the employer the burden of showing that any given requirement must have a manifest relationship to the employment in question.

The facts of this case demonstrate the inadequacy of broad and general testing devices as well as the infirmity of using diplomas or degrees as fixed measures of capability. History is filled with examples of men and women who rendered highly effective performance without the conventional badges of accomplishment in terms of certificates, diplomas, or degrees. Diplomas and tests are useful servants, but Congress has mandated the commonsense proposition that they are not to become masters of reality.

The Company contends that its general intelligence tests are specifically permitted by § 703(h) of the Act.[8] That section authorizes the use of 'any professionally developed ability test' that is not 'designed, intended or used to discriminate because of race * * *.'

The Equal Employment Opportunity Commission, having enforcement responsibility, has issued guidelines interpreting § 703(h) to permit only the use of job-related tests. The administrative interpretation of the Act by the enforcing agency is entitled to great deference. Since the Act and its legislative history support the Commission's construction, this affords good reason to treat the guidelines as expressing the will of Congress.

* * *

From the sum of the legislative history relevant in this case, the conclusion is inescapable that the EEOC's construction of § 703(h) to require that employment tests be job related comports with congressional intent.

Nothing in the Act precludes the use of testing or measuring procedures; obviously they are useful. What Congress has forbidden is giving these devices and mechanisms controlling force unless they are demonstrably a reasonable measure of job performance. Congress has not commanded that the less qualified be preferred over the better qualified simply because of minority origins. Far from disparaging job qualifications as such, Congress has made such qualifications the controlling factor, so that race, religion, nationality, and sex become irrelevant. What Congress has commanded is that any tests used must measure the person for the job and not the person in the abstract.

The judgment of the Court of Appeals is, as to that portion of the judgment appealed from, reversed.

Notes

1. *Amendments to Title VII, § 703(k)(1)(A):* The 1991 Amendments codified the *Griggs* impact standard as follows:

An unlawful practice based on disparate impact is established under this title only if—

(i) a complaining party demonstrates that a respondent uses a particular employment practice that causes a disparate impact on the basis of race,

---

8. Section 703(h) applies only to tests. It has no applicability to the high school diploma requirement.

color, religion, sex, or national origin and the respondent fails to demonstrate that the challenged practice is job related for the position in question and consistent with businesses necessity.

The Amendments also clarified the burdens: "The term 'demonstrates' means meets the burden of production and persuasion." 42 U.S.C.§ 2000e(m).

2. *Americans With Disabilities Act:* "[T]he term 'discrimination' includes:

(6) using qualification standards, employment tests, or other selection criteria that screen out, or tend to screen out an individual with a disability or a class of individuals with disabilities unless the standard, test, or other selection criteria as used by the covered entity is shown to be job-related for the position in question and is consistent with business necessity." 42 U.S.C. § 12112(b)

3. *Age Discrimination in Employment Act:* No clarifying provisions similar to those now in Title VII and the ADA are in the ADEA. Moreover, the ADEA has a proviso, with no counterpart in Title VII, which specifically allows employers to make differentiations "based on reasonable factors other than age." 29 U.S.C. § 623(f)(1). These differences led some lower courts to conclude that under the ADEA disparate impact could not be a basis for liability, until:

SMITH v. CITY OF JACKSON, 544 U.S. 228, 125 S.Ct. 1536, 161 L.Ed.2d 410 (2005):

When Congress uses the same language in two statutes having similarly purposes * * * it is appropriate to presume that Congress intended the text to have the same meaning in both statutes. * * * Our unanimous interpretation of § 703(a)(2) of the Title VII in Griggs is therefore a precedent of compelling importance. * * *

While our opinion in *Griggs* relied primarily on the purposes of the Act, * * * *Griggs* which interpreted the identical text at issue here [in the ADEA] thus strongly suggests that a disparate impact theory should be cognizable under the ADEA. * * *

[Only] in cases involving disparate impact claims that the [623(f)(1) "factors other than age"] RFOA provision plays its principal role by precluding liability if the adverse impact is attributable to a nonage factor that was 'reasonable.' Rather than support an argument that disparate impact is unavailable under the ADEA, the RFOA provisions actually supports the contrary conclusion. * * *

The text of the statute, as interpreted by *Griggs*, the RFOA provision, and the EEOC regulations all support [plaintiff's] view. We therefore conclude that it was error for the Court of Appeals to hold that the disparate-impact theory of liability is categorically unavailable under the ADEA.

MEACHAM v. KNOLLS ATOMIC POWER LAB., 554 U.S. 84, 128 S.Ct. 2395, 171 L.Ed.2d 283 (2008):

The question is whether the employer facing a disparate impact claim and planning to defend on the basis of ["reasonable factor other than age"] must not only produce evidence raising the defense, but also persuade the factfinder of its merit. We hold that the employer must do both. * * *

* * * [W]e find it impossible to look at the text and structure of the ADEA and imagine that the ["reasonable factor other than age"] clause works differently from the BFOQ clause next to it. Both except otherwise illegal conduct by reference to a further item of proof, thereby creating a defense for which the burden of persuasion falls on the 'one who claims its benefits,' the 'party seeking relief,' and here, 'the employer.'

4. *Reconstruction Era Civil Rights Acts:*

a. The Fourteenth Amendment, which prohibits *state sanctioned* race discrimination, requires proof of racial motive. Liability of public employers under the Constitution may not be established by proving that a policy neutral in terms of intent, such as a pre-employment test, had an adverse impact on a distinct racial group. ***Washington v. Davis,*** 426 U.S. 229, 96 S.Ct. 2040, 48 L.Ed.2d 597 (1976).

b. The 1866 Civil Rights Act, 42 U.S.C. § 1981, was enacted under authority granted to Congress by section 2 of Amendment Thirteen. 42 U.S.C. § 1981 does not require state action. Nonetheless, 42 U.S.C. § 1981 requires plaintiff to establish racial motivation, and does not impose liability based solely upon adverse impact. ***General Bld Contr. Ass'n v. Pennsylvania,*** 458 U.S. 375, 102 S.Ct. 3141, 73 L.Ed.2d 835 (1982).

5. *Proving Violations:* Plaintiff's proof of adverse impact and the employer's responsive burden to establish "business necessity" will be explored *infra* Chapter 7.

2. THE SENIORITY EXCEPTION: MOTIVE RETURNS

INTERNATIONAL BROTHERHOOD OF TEAMSTERS v. UNITED STATES

Supreme Court of the United States, 1977
431 U.S. 324, 97 S.Ct. 1843, 52 L.Ed.2d 396

JUSTICE STEWART delivered the opinion of the Court.

[Defendant union is the representative of employees of the defendant employer. The United States is the plaintiff in a "pattern or practice" action alleging that the seniority system adopted and implemented by defendants in a collective bargaining agreement violates Title VII of the Civil Rights Act of 1964. The United States relied upon *Griggs v. Duke Power Co., supra,* arguing that the seniority system operated by defendants has an adverse impact on black and Hispanic employees that is not justified by "business necessity." Defendants argued that the analysis of *Griggs v. Duke Power Co., supra,* is not applicable to seniority systems because of the provision in s 703(h) of Title VII, 42 U.S.C. § 2000e–2(h). The District Court and the Court of Appeals found that the seniority system operated to violate Title VII based upon the impact of such systems on minority employees and the lack of any showing by defendants that seniority calculated within distinct employment units was a "business necessity."]

B

* * * For purposes of calculating benefits, such as vacations, pensions, and other fringe benefits, an employee's seniority under this system runs from the date he joins the company, and takes into account his total service in all jobs and bargaining units. For competitive purposes, however, such as determining the order in which employees may bid for particular jobs, are laid off, or are recalled from layoff, it is bargaining-unit seniority that controls. Thus, a line driver's seniority, for purposes of bidding for particular runs and protection against layoff, takes into account only the length of time he has been a line driver at a particular terminal The practical effect is that a city driver or serviceman who transfers to a line-driver job must forfeit all the competitive seniority he has accumulated in his previous bargaining unit and start at the bottom of the line drivers' "board."

The vice of this arrangement, as found by the District Court and the Court of Appeals, was that it "locked" minority workers into inferior jobs and perpetuated prior discrimination by discouraging transfers to jobs as line drivers. While the disincentive applied to all workers, including whites, it was Negroes and Spanish-surnamed persons who, those courts found, suffered the most because many of them had been denied the equal opportunity to become line drivers when they were initially hired, whereas whites either had not sought or were refused line-driver positions for reasons unrelated to their race or national origin.

The linchpin of the theory embraced by the District Court and the Court of Appeals was that a discriminatee who must forfeit his competitive seniority in order finally to obtain a line-driver job will never be able to "catch up" to the seniority level of his contemporary who was not subject to discrimination.[27] Accordingly, this continued, built-in disadvantage to the prior discriminatee who transfers to a line-driver job was held to constitute a continuing violation of Title VII, for which both the employer and the union who jointly created and maintain the seniority system were liable.

The union, while acknowledging that the seniority system may in some sense perpetuate the effects of prior discrimination, asserts that the system is immunized from a finding of illegality by reason of s 703(h) of Title VII, 42 U.S.C. § 2000e–2(h), which provides in part:

---

27. An example would be a Negro who was qualified to be a line driver in 1958 but who, because of his race, was assigned instead a job as a city driver, and is allowed to become a line driver only in 1971. Because he loses his competitive seniority when he transfers jobs, he is forever junior to white line drivers hired between 1958 and 1970. The whites, rather than the Negro, will henceforth enjoy the preferable runs and the greater protection against layoff. Although the original discrimination occurred in 1958 before the effective date of Title VII the seniority system operates to carry the effects of the earlier discrimination into the present.

"Notwithstanding any other provision of this subchapter, it shall not be an unlawful employment practice for an employer to apply different standards of compensation, or different terms, conditions, or privileges of employment pursuant to a bona fide seniority ... system, ... provided that such differences are not the result of an intention to discriminate because of race ... or national origin...."

It argues that the seniority system in this case is "bona fide" within the meaning of § 703(h) when judged in light of its history, intent, application, and all of the circumstances under which it was created and is maintained. More specifically, the union claims that the central purpose of § 703(h) is to ensure that mere perpetuation of pre-Act discrimination is not unlawful under Title VII. And, whether or not § 703(h) immunizes the perpetuation of post-Act discrimination, the union claims that the seniority system in this litigation has no such effect. Its position in this Court, as has been its position throughout this litigation, is that the seniority system presents no hurdle to post-Act discriminatees who seek retroactive seniority to the date they would have become line drivers but for the company's discrimination. Indeed, the union asserts that under its collective-bargaining agreements the union will itself take up the cause of the post-Act victim and attempt, through grievance procedures, to gain for him full "make whole" relief, including appropriate seniority.

The Government responds that a seniority system that perpetuates the effects of prior discrimination pre-Act or post-Act can never be "bona fide" under § 703(h); at a minimum Title VII prohibits those applications of a seniority system that perpetuate the effects on incumbent employees of prior discriminatory job assignments.

The issues thus joined are open ones in this Court.[28] We considered § 703(h) in Franks v. Bowman Transportation Co., 424 U.S. 747, 96 S.Ct. 1251, 47 L.Ed.2d 444, but there decided only that § 703(h) does not bar the award of retroactive seniority to job applicants who seek relief from an employer's post-Act hiring discrimination. We stated that "the thrust of (§ 703(h)) is directed toward defining what is and what is not an illegal discriminatory practice in instances in which the post-Act operation of a seniority system is challenged as perpetuating the effects of discrimination occurring prior to the effective date of the Act." Beyond noting the general purpose of the statute, however, we did not undertake the task of statutory construction required in this litigation.

* * *

---

28. Concededly, the view that § 703(h) does not immunize seniority systems that perpetuate the effects of prior discrimination has much support. It was apparently first adopted in Quarles v. Philip Morris, Inc., 279 F.Supp. 505 (ED Va.). The court there held that "a departmental seniority system that has its genesis in racial discrimination is not a bona fide seniority system." The Quarles view has since enjoyed wholesale adoption in the Courts of Appeals. Insofar as the result in Quarles and in the cases that followed it depended upon findings that the seniority systems were themselves "racially discriminatory" or had their "genesis in racial discrimination," the decisions can be viewed as resting upon the proposition that a seniority system that perpetuates the effects of pre-Act discrimination cannot be bona fide if an intent to discriminate entered into its very adoption.

(2)

What remains for review is the judgment that the seniority system unlawfully perpetuated the effects of pre-Act discrimination. We must decide, in short, whether § 703(h) validates otherwise bona fide seniority systems that afford no constructive seniority to victims discriminated against prior to the effective date of Title VII, and it is to that issue that we now turn.

The primary purpose of Title VII was "to assure equality of employment opportunities and to eliminate those discriminatory practices and devices which have fostered racially stratified job environments to the disadvantage of minority citizens. To achieve this purpose, Congress "proscribe(d) not only overt discrimination but also practices that are fair in form, but discriminatory in operation." Thus, the Court has repeatedly held that a prima facie Title VII violation may be established by policies or practices that are neutral on their face and in intent but that nonetheless discriminate in effect against a particular group. *Griggs v. Duke Power Co., supra.*

One kind of practice "fair in form, but discriminatory in operation" is that which perpetuates the effects of prior discrimination. As the Court held in Griggs: "Under the Act, practices, procedures, or tests neutral on their face, and even neutral in terms of intent, cannot be maintained if they operate to 'freeze' the status quo of prior discriminatory employment practices."

Were it not for § 703(h), the seniority system in this case would seem to fall under the *Griggs* rationale. The heart of the system is its allocation of the choicest jobs, the greatest protection against layoffs, and other advantages to those employees who have been line drivers for the longest time. Where, because of the employer's prior intentional discrimination, the line drivers with the longest tenure are without exception white, the advantages of the seniority system flow disproportionately to them and away from Negro and Spanish-surnamed employees who might by now have enjoyed those advantages had not the employer discriminated before the passage of the Act. This disproportionate distribution of advantages does in a very real sense "operate to 'freeze' the status quo of prior discriminatory employment practices." But both the literal terms of § 703(h) and the legislative history of Title VII demonstrate that Congress considered this very effect of many seniority systems extended a measure of immunity to them.

Throughout the initial consideration of H.R. 7152, later enacted as the Civil Rights Act of 1964, critics of the bill charged that it would destroy existing seniority rights. The consistent response of Title VII's congressional proponents and of the Justice Department was that seniority rights would not be affected, even where the employer had discriminated prior to the Act. An interpretive memorandum placed in the Congressional Record by Senators Clark and Case stated:

"Title VII would have no effect on established seniority rights. Its effect is prospective and not retrospective. Thus, for example, if a business has been discriminating in the past and as a result has an all-white working force, when the title comes into effect the employer's obligation would be simply to fill future vacancies on a non-discriminatory basis. He would not be obliged or indeed, permitted to fire whites in order to hire Negroes or to prefer Negroes for future vacancies, or, once Negroes are hired to give them special seniority rights at the expense of the white workers hired earlier.''

A Justice Department statement concerning Title VII placed in the Congressional Record by Senator Clark, voiced the same conclusion:

"Title VII would have no effect on seniority rights existing at the time it takes effect. If, for example, a collective bargaining contract provides that in the event of layoffs, those who were hired last must be laid off first, such a provision would not be affected in the least by title VII. This would be true even in the case where owing to discrimination prior to the effective date of the title, white workers had more seniority than Negroes."

* * * As the debates indicate, one of those ambiguities concerned Title VII's impact on existing collectively bargained seniority rights. It is apparent that § 703(h) was drafted with an eye toward meeting the earlier criticism on this issue with an explicit provision embodying the understanding and assurances of the Act's proponents, namely, that Title VII would not outlaw such differences in treatment among employees as flowed from a bona fide seniority system that allowed for full exercise of seniority accumulated before the effective date of the Act. It is inconceivable that s 703(h), as part of a compromise bill, was intended to vitiate the earlier representations of the Act's supporters by increasing Title VII's impact on seniority systems. * * *

In sum, the unmistakable purpose of § 703(h) was to make clear that the routine application of a bona fide seniority system would not be unlawful under Title VII. As the legislative history shows, this was the intended result even where the employer's pre-Act discrimination resulted in whites having greater existing seniority rights than Negroes. Although a seniority system inevitably tends to perpetuate the effects of pre-Act discrimination in such cases, the congressional judgment was that Title VII should not outlaw the use of existing seniority lists and thereby destroy or water down the vested seniority rights of employees simply because their employer had engaged in discrimination prior to the passage of the Act.

To be sure, § 703(h) does not immunize all seniority systems. It refers only to "bona fide" systems, and a proviso requires that any differences in treatment not be "the result of an intention to discriminate because of race ... or national origin ..." But our reading of the legislative history compels us to reject the Government's broad argument that no seniority system that tends to perpetuate pre-Act discrimination can be "bona fide." To accept the argument would require us to hold that a seniority system becomes illegal simply because it allows the full exercise of the pre-Act seniority rights of employees of a company that discriminated before

Title VII was enacted. It would place an affirmative obligation on the parties to the seniority agreement to subordinate those rights in favor of the claims of pre-Act discriminatees without seniority. The consequence would be a perversion of the congressional purpose. We cannot accept the invitation to disembowel § 703(h) by reading the words "bona fide" as the Government would have us do. Accordingly, we hold that an otherwise neutral, legitimate seniority system does not become unlawful under Title VII simply because it may perpetuate pre-Act discrimination. Congress did not intend to make it illegal for employees with vested seniority rights to continue to exercise those rights, even at the expense of pre-Act discriminatees.

That conclusion is inescapable even in a case, such as this one, where the pre-Act discriminatees are incumbent employees who accumulated seniority in other bargaining units. Although there seems to be no explicit reference in the legislative history to pre-Act discriminatees already employed in less desirable jobs, there can be no rational basis for distinguishing their claims from those of persons initially denied any job but hired later with less seniority than they might have had in the absence of pre-Act discrimination. We rejected any such distinction in Franks, finding that it had "no support anywhere in Title VII or its legislative history," As discussed above, Congress in 1964 made clear that a seniority system is not unlawful because it honors employees' existing rights, even where the employer has engaged in pre-Act discriminatory hiring or promotion practices. It would be as contrary to that mandate to forbid the exercise of seniority rights with respect to discriminatees who held inferior jobs as with respect to later hired minority employees who previously were denied any job. If anything, the latter group is the more disadvantaged. As in Franks, " 'it would indeed be surprising if Congress gave a remedy for the one (group) which it denied for the other.' "[41]

(3)

The seniority system in this litigation is entirely bona fide. It applies equally to all races and ethnic groups. To the extent that it "locks" employees into non-line-driver jobs, it does so for all. The city drivers and servicemen who are discouraged from transferring to line-driver jobs are not all Negroes or Spanish-surnamed Americans; to the contrary, the overwhelming majority are white. The placing of line drivers in a separate bargaining unit from other employees is rational in accord with the industry practice, and consistent with National Labor Relations Board precedents. It is conceded that the seniority system did not have its genesis in racial discrimination, and that it was negotiated and has been maintained free from any illegal purpose. In these circumstances, the

---

41. In addition, there is no reason to suppose that Congress intended in 1964 to extend less protection to legitimate departmental seniority systems than to plantwide seniority systems. Then, as now, seniority was measured in a number of ways, including length of time with the employer, in a particular plant, in a department, in a job, or in a line of progression. The legislative history contains no suggestion that any one system was preferred.

single fact that the system extends no retroactive seniority to pre-Act discriminatees does not make it unlawful.

Because the seniority system was protected by § 703(h), the union's conduct in agreeing to and maintaining the system did not violate Title VII. On remand, the District Court's injunction against the union must be vacated.

NOTES

1. *"System" defined: CALIFORNIA BREWERS ASS'N v. BRYANT,* **444 U.S. 598, 100 S.Ct. 814, 63 L.Ed.2d 55 (1980).** In order to claim the safe harbor of the seniority proviso, the decisions must be made pursuant to a:

> * * * scheme that, alone or in tandem with non-seniority criteria, allots ever improving employment rights and benefits as their relative length of employment increase. * * * The principal feature of any and every 'seniority system' is that preferential treatment is dispensed on the basis of some measure of time.

> [Nevertheless] by legislating with respect to 'systems' of seniority in § 703(h) Congress * * * quite evidently intended to exempt from the normal operation of Title VII more than simply those components of any particularly system that, viewed in isolation, embody or effectuate the principle that length of employment will be rewarded. In order for any seniority system to operate at all, it has to contain ancillary rules that accomplish certain necessary functions, but which may not themselves be directly related to length of employment. For instance, every seniority system must include rules that delineate how and when the seniority time clock begins ticking, as well as rules that specify how and when a particular person's seniority may be forfeited. Every seniority system must also have rules that define which passages of time will 'count' toward the accrual of seniority and which will not. Every seniority system must, moreover, contain rules that particularize the types of employment conditions that will be governed or influenced by seniority, and those that will not. Rules that serve these necessary purposes do not fall outside § 703(h) simply because they do not, in and of themselves, operate on the basis of some factor involving the passage of time.

---

2. *UNITED AIRLINES v. EVANS,* **431 U.S. 553, 97 S.Ct. 1885, 52 L.Ed.2d 571 (1977).** *Teamsters, supra,* sanctioned the application of non-time elements of the seniority system, in particular measuring the passage of time only within defined employee "units" and a loss of this unit seniority when an employee transferred to another unit. These non-time-measures were assumed in *Teamsters* to be protected elements of the system. In *Evans,* a companion to *Teamsters,* an airline flight attendant was forced to resign because of defendant's sexually discriminatory marriage rule. She did not, at the time, challenge the rule. A few years later plaintiff was re-employed by defendant. During an economic downturn defendant applied its seniority

system to determine the order of layoff ("last hired first fired"). The system specifically provided that "breaks in service" would result in the loss of accumulated seniority that could not be reclaimed upon re-employment. Pursuant to that rule plaintiff was not entitled to count her years of service that preceded her forced resignation. The Court held that the "break in service" rule requiring loss of seniority was a protected part of the "system," notwithstanding the fact that sex discrimination precipitated the employment break. Past illegal, but unchallenged, sex discrimination, the Court held,

> is merely an unfortunate event in history which has no present legal consequences. * * * [A] challenge to a neural system may not be predicated on the mere fact that a past event which has no present legal significance has affected the calculation of seniority credit, even if the past event might at one time have justified a valid claim against the employer.

3. *Objective elements of a "system:" the need for formalization.* To be protected the seniority system need not be contained in a legally binding contract or even formalized in an employee handbook or expressed employer policies. However, to be a "system" the practice must be more than ad hoc decisions that take into account in some imprecise way the length of service. A system does not exist where general guidelines are frequently ignored, or contain numerous exceptions. *Williams v. New Orleans S.S. Ass'n,* 673 F.2d 742 (5th Cir. 1982). *See in particular,* **US Airways Inc. v. Barnett,** 535 U.S. 391, 122 S.Ct. 1516, 152 L.Ed.2d 589 (2002), which held that the non-contractual but consistent practice of following seniority was preserved under the ADA even in the absence of a statutory equivalent to Title VII's § 703(h).

4. *Subjective "Bona Fides":* Plaintiff has the burden of proving that the system itself lacks bona fides, that is, that the *system* was adopted or applied to accomplish a proscribed discriminatory purpose. **American Tobacco Co. v. Patterson,** 456 U.S. 63, 102 S.Ct. 1534, 71 L.Ed.2d 748 (1982). *Teamsters* listed some non-exclusive factors that could be indicative of subjective "bona fides" (*e.g.*, rationality, industry practice, and NLRB certifications). Establishing the lack of bona fides of a seniority system mirrors plaintiff's burden in establishing motive generally. **Pullman–Standard v. Swint,** 456 U.S. 273, 102 S.Ct. 1781, 72 L.Ed.2d 66 (1982).

C. RELATIONSHIP BETWEEN MOTIVE AND IMPACT

RICCI v. DESTEFANO

Supreme Court of the United States, 2009
557 U.S. 557, 129 S.Ct. 2658, 174 L.Ed.2d 490

JUSTICE KENNEDY delivered the opinion of the Court.

In the fire department of New Haven, Connecticut—as in emergency-service agencies throughout the Nation—firefighters prize their promotion to and within the officer ranks. An agency's officers command respect within the department and in the whole community; and, of course, added responsibilities command increased salary and benefits. Aware of the intense competition for promotions, New Haven, like many cities, relies on objective examinations to identify the best qualified candidates.

In 2003, 118 New Haven firefighters took examinations to qualify for promotion to the rank of lieutenant or captain. Promotion examinations in New Haven (or City) were infrequent, so the stakes were high. The results would determine which firefighters would be considered for promotions during the next two years, and the order in which they would be considered. Many firefighters studied for months, at considerable personal and financial cost.

When the examination results showed that white candidates had outperformed minority candidates, the mayor and other local politicians opened a public debate that turned rancorous. Some firefighters argued the tests should be discarded because the results showed the tests to be discriminatory. They threatened a discrimination lawsuit if the City made promotions based on the tests. Other firefighters said the exams were neutral and fair. And they, in turn, threatened a discrimination lawsuit if the City, relying on the statistical racial disparity, ignored the test results and denied promotions to the candidates who had performed well. In the end the City took the side of those who protested the test results. It threw out the examinations.

Certain white and Hispanic firefighters who likely would have been promoted based on their good test performance sued the City and some of its officials. Theirs is the suit now before us. The suit alleges that, by discarding the test results, the City and the named officials discriminated against the plaintiffs based on their race, in violation of both Title VII of the Civil Rights Act of 1964. * * * The City and the officials defended their actions, arguing that if they had certified the results, they could have faced liability under Title VII for adopting a practice that had a disparate impact on the minority firefighters. The District Court granted summary judgment for the defendants, and the Court of Appeals affirmed.

We conclude that race-based action like the City's in this case is impermissible under Title VII unless the employer can demonstrate a strong basis in evidence that, had it not taken the action, it would have been liable under the disparate-impact statute. The respondents, we further determine, cannot meet that threshold standard. As a result, the City's action in discarding the tests was a violation of Title VII. * * *

Candidates took the examinations in November and December 2003. Seventy-seven candidates completed the lieutenant examination—43 whites, 19 blacks, and 15 Hispanics. Of those, 34 candidates passed—25 whites, 6 blacks, and 3 Hispanics. Eight lieutenant positions were vacant at the time of the examination. As the rule of three operated, this meant that the top 10 candidates were eligible for an immediate promotion to lieutenant. All 10 were white. Subsequent vacancies would have allowed at least 3 black candidates to be considered for promotion to lieutenant.

Forty-one candidates completed the captain examination—25 whites, 8 blacks, and 8 Hispanics. Of those, 22 candidates passed—16 whites, 3 blacks, and 3 Hispanics. Seven captain positions were vacant at the time of the examination. Under the rule of three, 9 candidates were eligible for an immediate promotion to captain–7 whites and 2 Hispanics. * * * * * *

[The Court gave extensive detail of public discussions held by the Civil Service Board (CSB) on whether the City should disregard or follow the results of the two examinations. What follows are brief excerpts]

Although they did not know whether they had passed or failed, some firefighter-candidates spoke at the first [Civil Service Board] CSB meeting in favor of certifying the test results. * * * Other firefighters spoke against certifying the test results. They described the test questions as outdated or not relevant to firefighting practices in New Haven. * * *

At a second CSB meeting, on February 5, the president of the New Haven firefighters' union asked the CSB to perform a validation study to determine whether the tests were job-related. Petitioners' counsel in this action argued that the CSB should certify the results. A representative of the International Association of Black Professional Firefighters, Donald Day from neighboring Bridgeport, Connecticut, "beseech[ed]" the CSB "to throw away that test," which he described as "inherently unfair" because of the racial distribution of the results. * * *

* * *

At the final CSB meeting, on March 18, Ude (the City's legal counsel) argued against certifying the examination results. Discussing the City's obligations under federal law, Ude advised the CSB that a finding of adverse impact "is the beginning, not the end, of a review of testing procedures" to determine whether they violated the disparate-impact provision of Title VII. Ude focused the CSB on determining "whether there are other ways to test for ... those positions that are equally valid with less adverse impact." Ude described Hornick as having said that the written examination "had one of the most severe adverse impacts that he had seen" and that "there are much better alternatives to identifying [firefighting] skills." Ude offered his "opinion that promotions ... as a result of these tests would not be consistent with federal law, would not be consistent with the purposes of our Civil Service Rules or our Charter[,] nor is it in the best interests of the firefighters ... who took the exams.". He stated that previous Department exams "have not had this kind of result," and that previous results had not been "challenged as having adverse impact, whereas we are assured that these will be."

* * *

At the close of witness testimony, the CSB voted on a motion to certify the examinations. With one member recused, the CSB deadlocked 2 to 2, resulting in a decision not to certify the results. * * *

The CSB's decision not to certify the examination results led to this lawsuit. The plaintiffs-who are the petitioners here-are 17 white firefighters and 1 Hispanic firefighter who passed the examinations but were denied a chance at promotions when the CSB refused to certify the test results. They include the named plaintiff, Frank Ricci, who addressed the CSB at multiple meetings.

* * *

The District Court granted summary judgment for respondents. It described petitioners' argument as "boil[ing] down to the assertion that if [respondents] cannot prove that the disparities on the Lieutenant and Captain exams were due to a particular flaw inherent in those exams, then they should have certified the results because there was no other alternative in place." The District Court concluded that, "[n]otwithstanding the shortcomings in the evidence on existing, effective alternatives, it is not the case that [respondents] *must* certify a test where they cannot pinpoint its deficiency explaining its disparate impact . . . simply because they have not yet formulated a better selection method." It also ruled that respondents' "motivation to avoid making promotions based on a test with a racially disparate impact . . . does not, as a matter of law, constitute discriminatory intent" under Title VII. The District Court rejected petitioners' equal protection claim on the theory that respondents had not acted because of "discriminatory animus" toward petitioners. It concluded that respondents' actions were not "based on race" because "all applicants took the same test, and the result was the same for all because the test results were discarded and nobody was promoted." * * * [T]he Court of Appeals affirmed. * * * We found it prudent and appropriate to grant certiorari. We now reverse.

* * *

A

Title VII of the Civil Rights Act of 1964, prohibits employment discrimination on the basis of race, color, religion, sex, or national origin. Title VII prohibits both intentional discrimination (known as "disparate treatment") as well as, in some cases, practices that are not intended to discriminate but in fact have a disproportionately adverse effect on minorities (known as "disparate impact").

As enacted in 1964, Title VII's principal nondiscrimination provision held employers liable only for disparate treatment. That section retains its original wording today. It makes it unlawful for an employer "to fail or refuse to hire or to discharge any individual, or otherwise to discriminate against any individual with respect to his compensation, terms, conditions, or privileges of employment, because of such individual's race, color, religion, sex, or national origin." Disparate-treatment cases present "the most easily understood type of discrimination," and occur where an employer has "treated [a] particular person less favorably than others because of" a protected trait. A disparate-treatment plaintiff must establish "that the defendant had a discriminatory intent or motive" for taking a job-related action.

The Civil Rights Act of 1964 did not include an express prohibition on policies or practices that produce a disparate impact. But in *Griggs v. Duke Power Co.*, the Court interpreted the Act to prohibit, in some cases, employers' facially neutral practices that, in fact, are "discriminatory in operation." The *Griggs* Court stated that the "touchstone" for disparate-impact liability is the lack of "business necessity": "If an employment practice which operates to exclude [minorities] cannot be shown to be related to job performance, the practice is prohibited." Under those precedents, if an employer met its burden by showing that its practice was job-related, the plaintiff was required to show a legitimate alternative that would have resulted in less discrimination.

Twenty years after *Griggs,* the Civil Rights Act of 1991 was enacted. The Act included a provision codifying the prohibition on disparate-impact discrimination. That provision is now in force along with the disparate-treatment section already noted. Under the disparate-impact statute, a plaintiff establishes a prima facie violation by showing that an employer uses "a particular employment practice that causes a disparate impact on the basis of race, color, religion, sex, or national origin." An employer may defend against liability by demonstrating that the practice is "job related for the position in question and consistent with business necessity." Even if the employer meets that burden, however, a plaintiff may still succeed by showing that the employer refuses to adopt an available alternative employment practice that has less disparate impact and serves the employer's legitimate needs.

B

Petitioners allege that when the CSB refused to certify the captain and lieutenant exam results based on the race of the successful candidates, it discriminated against them in violation of Title VII's disparate-treatment provision. The City counters that its decision was permissible because the tests "appear[ed] to violate Title VII's disparate-impact provisions."

Our analysis begins with this premise: The City's actions would violate the disparate-treatment prohibition of Title VII absent some valid defense. All the evidence demonstrates that the City chose not to certify the examination results because of the statistical disparity based on race—*i.e.,* how minority candidates had performed when compared to white candidates. As the District Court put it, the City rejected the test results because "too many whites and not enough minorities would be promoted were the lists to be certified." (respondents' "own arguments ... show that the City's reasons for advocating non-certification were related to the racial distribution of the results"). Without some other justification, this express, race-based decisionmaking violates Title VII's command that employers cannot take adverse employment actions because of an individual's race.

The District Court did not adhere to this principle, however. It held that respondents' "motivation to avoid making promotions based on a test with a racially disparate impact ... does not, as a matter of law, constitute discriminatory intent." And the Government makes a similar argument in this Court. It contends that the "structure of Title VII belies any claim that an employer's intent to comply with Title VII's disparate-impact provisions constitutes prohibited discrimination on the basis of race." But both of those statements turn upon the City's objective—avoiding disparate-impact liability—while ignoring the City's conduct in the name of reaching that objective. Whatever the City's ultimate aim—however well intentioned or benevolent it might have seemed—the City made its employment decision because of race. The City rejected the test results solely because the higher scoring candidates were white. The question is not whether that conduct was discriminatory but whether the City had a lawful justification for its race-based action.

We consider, therefore, whether the purpose to avoid disparate-impact liability excuses what otherwise would be prohibited disparate-treatment discrimination. Courts often confront cases in which statutes and principles point in different directions. Our task is to provide guidance to employers and courts for situations when these two prohibitions could be in conflict absent a rule to reconcile them. In providing this guidance our decision must be consistent with the important purpose of Title VII—that the workplace be an environment free of discrimination, where race is not a barrier to opportunity.

With these principles in mind, we turn to the parties' proposed means of reconciling the statutory provisions. Petitioners take a strict approach, arguing that under Title VII, it cannot be permissible for an employer to take race-based adverse employment actions in order to avoid disparate-impact liability—even if the employer knows its practice violates the disparate-impact provision. Petitioners would have us hold that, under Title VII, avoiding unintentional discrimination cannot justify intentional discrimination. That assertion, however, ignores the fact that, by codifying the disparate-impact provision in 1991, Congress has expressly prohibited both types of discrimination. We must interpret the statute to give effect to both provisions where possible. We cannot accept petitioners' broad and inflexible formulation.

Petitioners next suggest that an employer in fact must be in violation of the disparate-impact provision before it can use compliance as a defense in a disparate-treatment suit. Again, this is overly simplistic and too restrictive of Title VII's purpose. The rule petitioners offer would run counter to what we have recognized as Congress's intent that "voluntary compliance" be "the preferred means of achieving the objectives of Title VII." Forbidding employers to act unless they know, with certainty, that a practice violates the disparate-impact provision would bring compliance efforts to a near standstill. Even in the limited situations when this restricted standard could be met, employers likely would hesitate before taking voluntary action for fear of later being proven wrong in the course of litigation and then held to account for disparate treatment.

At the opposite end of the spectrum, respondents and the Government assert that an employer's good-faith belief that its actions are necessary to comply with Title VII's disparate-impact provision should be enough to justify race-conscious conduct. But the original, foundational prohibition of Title VII bars employers from taking adverse action "because of ... race." And when Congress codified the disparate-impact provision in 1991, it made no exception to disparate-treatment liability for actions taken in a good-faith effort to comply with the new, disparate-impact provision in subsection (k). Allowing employers to violate the disparate-treatment prohibition based on a mere good-faith fear of disparate-impact liability would encourage race-based action at the slightest hint of disparate impact. A minimal standard could cause employers to discard the results of lawful and beneficial promotional examinations even where there is little if any evidence of disparate-impact discrimination. That would amount to a *de facto* quota system, in which a "focus on statistics ... could put undue pressure on employers to adopt inappropriate prophylactic measures." Even worse, an employer could discard test results (or other employment practices) with the intent of obtaining the employer's preferred racial balance. That operational principle could not be justified, for Title VII is express in disclaiming any interpretation of its requirements as calling for outright racial balancing. The purpose of Title VII "is to promote hiring on the basis of job qualifications, rather than on the basis of race or color."

In searching for a standard that strikes a more appropriate balance, we note that this Court has considered cases similar to this one, albeit in the context of the Equal Protection Clause of the Fourteenth Amendment. The Court has held that certain government actions to remedy past racial discrimination-actions that are themselves based on race-are constitutional only where there is a " 'strong basis in evidence' " that the remedial actions were necessary. This suit does not call on us to consider whether the statutory constraints under Title VII must be parallel in all respects to those under the Constitution. That does not mean the constitutional authorities are irrelevant, however. * * *

The same interests are at work in the interplay between the disparate-treatment and disparate-impact provisions of Title VII. Congress has imposed liability on employers for unintentional discrimination in order to rid the workplace of "practices that are fair in form, but discriminatory in operation." But it has also prohibited employers from taking adverse employment actions "because of" race. Applying the strong-basis-in-evidence standard to Title VII gives effect to both the disparate-treatment and disparate-impact provisions, allowing violations of one in the name of compliance with the other only in certain, narrow circumstances. The standard leaves ample room for employers' voluntary compliance efforts, which are essential to the statutory scheme and to Congress's efforts to eradicate workplace discrimination. And the standard appropriately constrains employers' discretion in making race-based decisions: It limits that discretion to cases in which there is a strong basis in evidence of disparate-impact liability, but it is not so restrictive that it allows employers to act only when there is a provable, actual violation.

Resolving the statutory conflict in this way allows the disparate-impact prohibition to work in a manner that is consistent with other provisions of Title VII, including the prohibition on adjusting employment-related test scores on the basis of race. Examinations like those administered by the City create legitimate expectations on the part of those who took the tests. As is the case with any promotion exam, some of the firefighters here invested substantial time, money, and personal commitment in preparing for the tests. Employment tests can be an important part of a neutral selection system that safeguards against the very racial animosities Title VII was intended to prevent. Here, however, the firefighters saw their efforts invalidated by the City in sole reliance upon race-based statistics.

If an employer cannot rescore a test based on the candidates' race, then it follows *a fortiori* that it may not take the greater step of discarding the test altogether to achieve a more desirable racial distribution of promotion-eligible candidates-absent a strong basis in evidence that the test was deficient and that discarding the results is necessary to avoid violating the disparate-impact provision. * * *

For the foregoing reasons, we adopt the strong-basis-in-evidence standard as a matter of statutory construction to resolve any conflict between the disparate-treatment and disparate-impact provisions of Title VII.

* * * [O]nce that process has been established and employers have made clear their selection criteria, they may not then invalidate the test results, thus upsetting an employee's legitimate expectation not to be judged on the basis of race. Doing so, absent a strong basis in evidence of an impermissible disparate impact, amounts to the sort of racial preference that Congress has disclaimed, § 2000e–2(j), and is antithetical to the notion of a workplace where individuals are guaranteed equal opportunity regardless of race.

Title VII does not prohibit an employer from considering, before administering a test or practice, how to design that test or practice in order to provide a fair opportunity for all individuals, regardless of their race. And when, during the test-design stage, an employer invites comments to ensure the test is fair, that process can provide a common ground for open discussions toward that end. We hold only that, under Title VII, before an employer can engage in intentional discrimination for the asserted purpose of avoiding or remedying an unintentional disparate impact, the employer must have a strong basis in evidence to believe it will be subject to disparate-impact liability if it fails to take the race-conscious, discriminatory action.

C

The City argues that, even under the strong-basis-in-evidence standard, its decision to discard the examination results was permissible under Title VII. That is incorrect. Even if respondents were motivated as a subjective matter by a desire to avoid committing disparate-impact discrimination, the record makes clear there is no support for the conclusion that respondents had an objective, strong basis in evidence to find the tests inadequate, with some consequent disparate-impact liability in violation of Title VII.

* * *

The racial adverse impact here was significant, and petitioners do not dispute that the City was faced with a prima facie case of disparate-impact liability. On the captain exam, the pass rate for white candidates was 64 percent but was 37.5 percent for both black and Hispanic candidates. On the lieutenant exam, the pass rate for white candidates was 58.1 percent; for black candidates, 31.6 percent; and for Hispanic candidates, 20 percent. The pass rates of minorities, which were approximately one-half the pass rates for white candidates, fall well below the 80-percent standard set by the EEOC to implement the disparate-impact provision of Title VII. See 29 CFR § 1607.4(D) (2008) (selection rate that is less than 80 percent "of the rate for the group with the highest rate will generally be regarded by the Federal enforcement agencies as evidence of adverse impact") * * *

Based on the degree of adverse impact reflected in the results, respondents were compelled to take a hard look at the examinations to determine whether certifying the results would have had an impermissible disparate impact. The problem for respondents is that a prima facie case of disparate-impact liability—essentially, a threshold showing of a significant statistical disparity, and nothing more—is far from a strong basis in evidence that the City would have been liable under Title VII had it certified the results. That is because the City could be liable for disparate-impact discrimination only if the examinations were not job related and consistent with business necessity, or if there existed an equally valid, less-discriminatory alternative that served the City's needs but that the City refused to adopt. We conclude there is no strong basis in evidence to establish that the test was deficient in either of these respects. * * *

1

There is no genuine dispute that the examinations were job-related and consistent with business necessity. The City's assertions to the contrary are "blatantly contradicted by the record."

* * *

The City, moreover, turned a blind eye to evidence that supported the exams' validity. * * *

2

Respondents also lacked a strong basis in evidence of an equally valid, less-discriminatory testing alternative that the City, by certifying the examination results, would necessarily have refused to adopt. * * * The City used a 60/40 weighting as required by its contract with the New Haven firefighters' union. But respondents have produced no evidence to show that the 60/40 weighting was indeed arbitrary. In fact, because that formula was the result of a union-negotiated collective-bargaining agreement, we presume the parties negotiated that weighting for a rational reason. Nor does the record contain any evidence that the 30/70 weighting would be an equally valid way to determine whether candidates possess the proper mix of job knowledge and situational skills to earn promotions. Changing the weighting formula, moreover, could well have violated Title VII's prohibition of altering test scores on the basis of race. On this record, there is no basis to conclude that a 30/70 weighting was an equally valid alternative the City could have adopted.

* * *

3

On the record before us, there is no genuine dispute that the City lacked a strong basis in evidence to believe it would face disparate-impact liability if it certified the examination results. In other words, there is no evidence—let alone the required strong basis in evidence—that the tests were flawed because they were not job-related or because other, equally valid and less discriminatory tests were available to the City. Fear of litigation alone cannot justify an employer's reliance on race to the detriment of individuals who passed the examinations and qualified for promotions. The City's discarding the test results was impermissible under Title VII, and summary judgment is appropriate for petitioners on their disparate-treatment claim.

* * *

Our holding today clarifies how Title VII applies to resolve competing expectations under the disparate-treatment and disparate-impact provisions. If, after it certifies the test results, the City faces a disparate-impact suit, then in light of our holding today it should be clear that the City would avoid disparate-impact liability based on the strong basis in evidence that, had it not certified the results, it would have been subject to disparate-treatment liability.

Petitioners are entitled to summary judgment on their Title VII claim. The judgment of the Court of Appeals is reversed, and the cases are remanded for further proceedings consistent with this opinion.

JUSTICE GINSBURG, with whom JUSTICE STEVENS, JUSTICE SOUTER, and JUSTICE BREYER join, dissenting.

* * *

The white firefighters who scored high on New Haven's promotional exams understandably attract this Court's sympathy. But they had no vested right to promotion. Nor have other persons received promotions in preference to them. New Haven maintains that it refused to certify the test results because it believed, for good cause, that it would be vulnerable to a Title VII disparate-impact suit if it relied on those results. The Court today holds that New Haven has not demonstrated "a strong basis in evidence" for its plea. In so holding, the Court pretends that "[t]he City rejected the test results solely because the higher scoring candidates were white." That pretension, essential to the Court's disposition, ignores substantial evidence of multiple flaws in the tests New Haven used. The Court similarly fails to acknowledge the better tests used in other cities, which have yielded less racially skewed outcomes.

By order of this Court, New Haven, a city in which African–Americans and Hispanics account for nearly 60 percent of the population, must today be served—as it was in the days of undisguised discrimination—by a fire department in which members of racial and ethnic minorities are rarely seen in command positions. In arriving at its order, the Court barely acknowledges the pathmarking decision in *Griggs v. Duke Power Co.* which explained the centrality of the disparate-impact concept to effective enforcement of Title VII. The Court's order and opinion, I anticipate, will not have staying power.

I

A

The Court's recitation of the facts leaves out important parts of the story. Firefighting is a profession in which the legacy of racial discrimination casts an especially long shadow * * *

In a decision summarily affirmed by the Court of Appeals, the District Court granted summary judgment for respondents. Under Second Circuit precedent, the District Court explained, "the intent to remedy the disparate impact" of a promotional exam "is not equivalent to an intent to discriminate against non-minority applicants." Rejecting petitioners' pretext argument, the court observed that the exam results were sufficiently skewed "to make out a prima facie case of discrimination" under Title VII's disparate-impact provision. Had New Haven gone forward with certification and been sued by aggrieved minority test takers, the City would have been forced to defend tests that were presumptively invalid. And, * * * overcoming that presumption would have been no easy task. Given Title VII's preference for voluntary compliance, the court held, New Haven could lawfully discard the disputed exams even if the City had not definitively "pinpoint[ed]" the source of the disparity and "ha[d] not yet formulated a better selection method."

Respondents were no doubt conscious of race during their decisionmaking process, the court acknowledged, but this did not mean they had engaged in racially disparate treatment. The conclusion they had reached and the action thereupon taken were race-neutral in this sense: "[A]ll the test results were discarded, no one was promoted, and firefighters of every race will have to participate in another selection process to be considered for promotion." New Haven's action, which gave no individual a preference, "was 'simply not analogous to a quota system or a minority set-aside where candidates, on the basis of their race, are not treated uniformly.'"
* * *

* * * [T]he Court today sets at odds the statute's core directives. When an employer changes an employment practice in an effort to comply with Title VII's disparate-impact provision, the Court reasons, it acts "because of race"—something Title VII's disparate-treatment provision, generally forbids. This characterization of an employer's compliance-directed action shows little attention to Congress' design or to the *Griggs* line of cases Congress recognized as pathmarking.

* * *

To "reconcile" the supposed "conflict" between disparate treatment and disparate impact, the Court offers an enigmatic standard. Employers may attempt to comply with Title VII's disparate-impact provision, the Court declares, only where there is a "strong basis in evidence" documenting the necessity of their action. The Court's standard, drawn from inapposite equal protection precedents, is not elaborated. One is left to wonder what cases would meet the standard and why the Court is so sure this case does not.

* * *

The Court's decision in this litigation underplays a dominant Title VII theme. This Court has repeatedly emphasized that the statute "should not be read to thwart" efforts at voluntary compliance. The strong-basis-in-evidence standard, however, as barely described in general, and cavalierly applied in this case, makes voluntary compliance a hazardous venture.

As a result of today's decision, an employer who discards a dubious selection process can anticipate costly disparate-treatment litigation in which its chances for success-even for surviving a summary-judgment motion-are highly problematic. Concern about exposure to disparate-impact liability, however well grounded, is insufficient to insulate an employer from attack. Instead, the employer must make a "strong" showing that (1) its selection method was "not job related and consistent with business necessity," or (2) that it refused to adopt "an equally valid, less-discriminatory alternative." It is hard to see how these requirements differ from demanding that an employer establish "a provable, actual violation" *against itself.* * * *

[The concurring opinion of JUSTICE ALITO, joined by JUSTICE SCALIA and JUSTICE THOMAS, is omitted.]

NOTES

1. *Improperly motivated neutral policies: Griggs* implicitly held that if an otherwise neutral policy, such as test, is instituted for the purpose of disadvantaging a protected class, the improper motivation behind the facially neutral practice supplied the motive required by the statute. Defendant's proof of "job relatedness" is immaterial in the face of proscribed motivation. ***Albemarle Paper Co. v. Moody,*** 422 U.S. 405, 95 S.Ct. 2362, 45 L.Ed.2d 280 (1975). Accordingly, when a seniority system was amended for the purpose of disadvantaging female workers vis-a-vis male workers, and the system in fact

results in a disadvantage to a woman, there is discrimination "because of" her sex. That it was a reasonable system, uniform in application, and affected many men is not a defense to the sex motivation for adopting the system. Similarly, an employer had a "no rehire" policy applicable to all former employees. However, if the policy was adopted for the purpose of not re-hiring former workers who had disabilities, when the "no rehire" policy was in fact applied to a person with a disability, this was discrimination "because of" disability.

42 U.S.C. § 2000e–2(k)(2) reinforces this point:

"A demonstration that an employment practice is required by business necessity may not be used as a defense to a claim of intentional discrimination under this title."

2. *Affirmative action vs. contractual rights:*

a. Based on a finding of illegality, the defendant employer may be ordered to change its prior practices *See, Franks v. Bowman Transp. Co.,* 424 U.S. 747, 96 S.Ct. 1251, 47 L.Ed.2d 444 (1976). Or, an employer may be facing potential liability based on under-representation of certain classes in some job classification. Or, perhaps to comply with E.O. 11246, the employer may "voluntarily" alter its method of employee selection. Such employers may find that such a change in their prior practices affect the contractual rights of other employees. **W.R. Grace & Co. v. Local Union 759,** 461 U.S. 757, 103 S.Ct. 2177, 76 L.Ed.2d 298 (1983), acknowledged that employers making such changes may face two sets of conflicting obligations.

b. **United States v. Brennan,** 650 F.3d 65 (2d Cir. 2011), recognized the pressure *Ricci* created on affirmative action plans that may meet the standards of *Weber* and *Johnson, supra pages 234, 243.* The Second Circuit held that *Ricci* was applicable to a settlement agreement between the city employer and the U.S. Department of Justice which resulted in the employer altering its seniority system to the disadvantage of white employees. The court held that *Ricci* limited the *Weber/Johnson* standard to forward looking "plans" that provided relief to all members of the underrepresented class. When the employer was responding to the particular effects of an in-place system that affected some members of the class, *Ricci* was read to preclude a general "affirmative action" concern to override the operation of those systems. Only where there is a "strong basis in the evidence" that the system being disregarded to the detriment of identified workers violated Title VII, may the employer disregard the outcomes produced by the system.

3. *Claims of the black firefighters.* The question left unresolved by *Ricci* is whether the black firefighters—those disadvantaged by the test outcome— are precluded by *Ricci* from forcing the employer to establish the lack of job relatedness of the challenged test. The Second Circuit held that as non-parties to the *Ricci* litigation, minority plaintiffs could not be precluded from making such a challenge, concluding, "*Ricci* did not substantially change Title VII disparate-impact litigation * * *." **Briscoe v. City of New Haven,** 654 F.3d 200 (2d Cir. 2011).

PART 3

PROVING VIOLATIONS

■ ■ ■

CHAPTER 7

LIABILITY BASED UPON UNJUSTIFIED DISPARATE IMPACT

■ ■ ■

Review *Griggs v. Duke Power Co. supra p. 318.*

A. PLAINTIFF PROVING IMPACT

DOTHARD v. RAWLINSON, **433 U.S. 321, 97 S.Ct. 2720, 53 L.Ed.2d 786 (1977),** involved a challenge by female plaintiffs to a 5′2″ height requirement and 120 pound weight minimum for state prison guards:

"[The trial court] found that the 5′2″ requirement would operate to exclude 33.29% of the women in the United States between the ages of 18–79, while excluding only 1.28% of men between the same ages. The 120 pound weight restriction would exclude 22.29% of the women and 2.35% of the men in this age group. When the height and weight restrictions are combined, the Alabama statutory standards would exclude 41% of the female population while excluding less than one percent of the male population * * * We cannot say that the District Court was wrong in holding that the statutory height and weight standards had a discriminatory impact on women applicants. The plaintiffs in such a case are not required to exhaust every possible source of evidence, if the evidence actually presented on its face conspicuously demonstrates a job requirement's grossly discriminatory impact. If the employer discerns fallacies or deficiencies in the data offered by the plaintiff, is free to adduce countervailing evidence * * *.

JUSTICE WHITE dissented:

I have trouble agreeing that a prima facie case of sex discrimination was made out by statistics showing that the Alabama height and weight requirement would exclude a larger percentage of women in the United States than of men. * * * I am not now convinced that a larger percentage of the actual women applicants, or of those who are seriously interested in applying for prison guard positions would fail to satisfy the height and weight requirements.

WARDS COVE PACKING COMPANY, INC v. ATONIO

Supreme Court of the United States, 1989
490 U.S. 642, 109 S.Ct. 2115, 104 L.Ed.2d.733

JUSTICE WHITE delivered the opinion of the Court.

* * * *Griggs v. Duke Power Co.,* construed Title VII to proscribe "not only overt discrimination but also practices that are fair in form but discriminatory in practice." Under this basis for liability, which is known as the "disparate-impact" theory and which is involved in this case, a facially neutral employment practice may be deemed violative of Title VII without evidence of the employer's subjective intent to discriminate that is required in a "disparate-treatment" case.

I

The claims before us are disparate-impact claims, involving the employment practices of petitioners, two companies that operate salmon canneries in remote and widely separated areas of Alaska. The canneries operate only during the salmon runs in the summer months. They are inoperative and vacant for the rest of the year. In May or June of each year, a few weeks before the salmon runs begin, workers arrive and prepare the equipment and facilities for the canning operation. Most of these workers possess a variety of skills. When salmon runs are about to begin, the workers who will operate the cannery lines arrive, remain as long as there are fish to can, and then depart. The canneries are then closed down, winterized, and left vacant until the next spring. During the off-season, the companies employ only a small number of individuals at their headquarters in Seattle and Astoria, Oregon, plus some employees at the winter shipyard in Seattle.

The length and size of salmon runs vary from year to year, and hence the number of employees needed at each cannery also varies. Estimates are made as early in the winter as possible; the necessary employees are hired, and when the time comes, they are transported to the canneries. Salmon must be processed soon after they are caught, and the work during the canning season is therefore intense. For this reason, and because the canneries are located in remote regions, all workers are housed at the canneries and have their meals in company-owned mess halls.

Jobs at the canneries are of two general types: "cannery jobs" on the cannery line, which are unskilled positions; and "noncannery jobs," which fall into a variety of classifications. Most noncannery jobs are classified as skilled positions Cannery jobs are filled predominantly by nonwhites: Filipinos and Alaska Natives. The Filipinos are hired through, and dispatched by Local 37 of the International Longshoremen's and Warehousemen's Union pursuant to a hiring hall agreement with the local. The Alaska Natives primarily reside in villages near the remote cannery locations. Noncannery jobs are filled with predominantly white workers, who are hired during the winter months from the companies' offices in

Washington and Oregon. Virtually all of the noncannery jobs pay more than cannery positions. The predominantly white noncannery workers and the predominantly nonwhite cannery employees live in separate dormitories and eat in separate mess halls.

In 1974, respondents, a class of nonwhite cannery workers who were (or had been) employed at the canneries, brought this Title VII action against petitioners. Respondents alleged that a variety of petitioners' hiring/promotion practices—e.g., nepotism, a rehire preference, a lack of objective hiring criteria, separate hiring channels, a practice of not promoting from within—were responsible for the racial stratification of the work force and had denied them and other nonwhites employment as noncannery workers on the basis of race. Respondents also complained of petitioners' racially segregated housing and dining facilities. All of respondents' claims were advanced under both the disparate-treatment and disparate-impact theories of Title VII liability.

The District Court held a bench trial, after which * * * rejected the disparate-impact challenges involving the subjective employment criteria used by petitioners to fill these noncannery positions, on the ground that those criteria were not subject to attack under a disparate-impact theory. Petitioners' "objective" employment practices (e.g., an English language requirement, alleged nepotism in hiring, failure to post noncannery openings, the rehire preference, etc.) were found to be subject to challenge under the disparate-impact theory, but these claims were rejected for failure of proof. Judgment was entered for petitioners.

On appeal, a panel of the Ninth Circuit affirmed,, but * * * [t]he en banc hearing was ordered to settle an intra-circuit conflict over the question whether subjective hiring practices could be analyzed under a disparate-impact model; the Court of Appeals held—as this Court subsequently ruled in Watson v. Fort Worth Bank & Trust, 487 U.S. 977, 108 S.Ct. 2777, 101 L.Ed.2d 827 (1988)—that disparate-impact analysis could be applied to subjective hiring practices. The Ninth Circuit also concluded that in such a case, "[o]nce the plaintiff class has shown disparate impact caused by specific, identifiable employment practices or criteria, the burden shifts to the employer," to "prov[e the] business necessity" of the challenged practice. Because the en banc holding on subjective employment practices reversed the District Court's contrary ruling, the en banc Court of Appeals remanded the case to a panel for further proceedings.

On remand, the panel applied the en banc ruling to the facts of this case. It held that respondents had made out a prima facie case of disparate impact in hiring for both skilled and unskilled noncannery positions. The panel remanded the case for further proceedings, instructing the District Court that it was the employer's burden to prove that any disparate impact caused by its hiring and employment practices was justified by business necessity.

* * *

II

In holding that respondents had made out a prima facie case of disparate impact, the Court of Appeals relied solely on respondents' statistics showing a high percentage of nonwhite workers in the cannery jobs and a low percentage of such workers in the noncannery positions. Although statistical proof can alone make out a prima facie case, the Court of Appeals' ruling here misapprehends our precedents and the purposes of Title VII, and we therefore reverse.

* * *

It is clear to us that the Court of Appeals' acceptance of the comparison between the racial composition of the cannery work force and that of the noncannery work force, as probative of a prima facie case of disparate impact in the selection of the latter group of workers, was flawed for several reasons. Most obviously, with respect to the skilled noncannery jobs at issue here, the cannery work force in no way reflected "the pool of *qualified* job applicants" or the "*qualified* population in the labor force." Measuring alleged discrimination in the selection of accountants, managers, boat captains, electricians, doctors, and engineers-and the long list of other "skilled" noncannery positions found to exist by the District Court, by comparing the number of nonwhites occupying these jobs to the number of nonwhites filling cannery worker positions is nonsensical. If the absence of minorities holding such skilled positions is due to a dearth of qualified nonwhite applicants (for reasons that are not petitioners' fault), petitioners' selection methods or employment practices cannot be said to have had a "disparate impact" on nonwhites.

* * *

The Court of Appeals' theory, at the very least, would mean that any employer who had a segment of his work force that was—for some reason—racially imbalanced, could be hauled into court and forced to engage in the expensive and time-consuming task of defending the "business necessity" of the methods used to select the other members of his work force. The only practicable option for many employers would be to adopt racial quotas, insuring that no portion of their work forces deviated in racial composition from the other portions thereof; this is a result that Congress expressly rejected in drafting Title VII. The Court of Appeals' theory would "leave the employer little choice . . . but to engage in a subjective quota system of employment selection. This, of course, is far from the intent of Title VII."

The Court of Appeals also erred with respect to the unskilled noncannery positions. Racial imbalance in one segment of an employer's work force does not, without more, establish a prima facie case of disparate impact with respect to the selection of workers for the employer's other positions, even where workers for the different positions may have somewhat fungible skills (as is arguably the case for cannery and unskilled noncannery workers). As long as there are no barriers or practices deterring qualified nonwhites from applying for noncannery positions, if the percentage of selected applicants who are nonwhite is not significantly less than the percentage of qualified applicants who are nonwhite, the employer's selection mechanism probably does not operate with a disparate impact on minorities. Where this is the case, the percentage of nonwhite workers found in other positions in the employer's labor force is irrelevant to the question of a prima facie statistical case of disparate impact. As noted above, a contrary ruling on this point would almost inexorably lead to the use of numerical quotas in the workplace, a result that Congress and this Court have rejected repeatedly in the past.

Moreover, isolating the cannery workers as the potential "labor force" for unskilled noncannery positions is at once both too broad and too narrow in its focus. It is too broad because the vast majority of these cannery workers did not seek jobs in unskilled noncannery positions; there is no showing that many of them would have done so even if none of the arguably "deterring" practices existed. Thus, the pool of cannery workers cannot be used as a surrogate for the class of qualified job applicants because it contains many persons who have not (and would not) be noncannery job applicants. Conversely, if respondents propose to use the cannery workers for comparison purposes because they represent the "qualified labor population" generally, the group is too narrow because there are obviously many qualified persons in the labor market for noncannery jobs who are not cannery workers.

* * * Consequently, we reverse the Court of Appeals' ruling that a comparison between the percentage of cannery workers who are nonwhite and the percentage of noncannery workers who are nonwhite makes out a prima facie case of disparate impact. Of course, this leaves unresolved whether the record made in the District Court will support a conclusion that a prima facie case of disparate impact has been established on some basis other than the racial disparity between cannery and noncannery workers. This is an issue that the Court of Appeals or the District Court should address in the first instance.

III

Since the statistical disparity relied on by the Court of Appeals did not suffice to make out a prima facie case, any inquiry by us into whether the specific challenged employment practices of petitioners caused that disparity is pretermitted, as is any inquiry into whether the disparate impact that any employment practice may have had was justified by business considerations. Because we remand for further proceedings, however, on whether a prima facie case of disparate impact has been made in defensible fashion in this case, we address two other challenges petitioners have made to the decision of the Court of Appeals.

A

First is the question of causation in a disparate-impact case. The law in this respect was correctly stated by JUSTICE O'CONNOR's opinion last Term in *Watson v. Fort Worth Bank & Trust,* 487 U.S., at 994, 108 S.Ct., 2788–2789:

> "[W]e note that the plaintiff's burden in establishing a prima facie case goes beyond the need to show that there are statistical disparities in the employer's work force. The plaintiff must begin by identifying the specific employment practice that is challenged ... Especially in cases where an employer combines subjective criteria with the use of more rigid standardized rules or tests, the plaintiff is in our view responsible for isolating and identifying the specific employment practices that are allegedly responsible for any observed statistical disparities."

Indeed, even the Court of Appeals—whose decision petitioners assault on this score—noted that "it is ... essential that the practices identified by the cannery workers be linked causally with the demonstrated adverse impact." Notwithstanding the Court of Appeals' apparent adherence to the proper inquiry, petitioners contend that that court erred by permitting respondents to make out their case by offering "only [one] set of cumulative comparative statistics as evidence of the disparate impact of each and all of [petitioners' hiring] practices."

Our disparate-impact cases have always focused on the impact of *particular* hiring practices on employment opportunities for minorities. Just as an employer cannot escape liability under Title VII by demonstrating that, "at the bottom line," his work force is racially balanced (where particular hiring practices may operate to deprive minorities of employment opportunities), a Title VII plaintiff does not make out a case of disparate impact simply by showing that, "at the bottom line," there is racial *imbalance* in the work force. As a general matter, a plaintiff must demonstrate that it is the application of a specific or particular employment practice that has created the disparate impact under attack. Such a showing is an integral part of the plaintiff's prima facie case in a disparate-impact suit under Title VII.

Here, respondents have alleged that several "objective" employment practices (*e.g.,* nepotism, separate hiring channels, rehire preferences), as well as the use of "subjective decision making" to select noncannery workers, have had a disparate impact on nonwhites. Respondents base this claim on statistics that allegedly show a disproportionately low percentage of nonwhites in the at-issue positions. However, even if on remand respondents can show that nonwhites are underrepresented in the at-issue jobs in a manner that is acceptable under the standards set forth in Part II, *supra,* this alone will *not* suffice to make out a prima facie case of disparate impact. Respondents will also have to demonstrate that the disparity they complain of is the result of one or more of the employment practices that they are attacking here, specifically showing that each challenged practice has a significantly disparate impact on employment opportunities for whites and nonwhites. To hold otherwise would result in employers being potentially liable for "the myriad of innocent causes that may lead to statistical imbalances in the composition of their work forces."

Some will complain that this specific causation requirement is unduly burdensome on Title VII plaintiffs. But liberal civil discovery rules give plaintiffs broad access to employers' records in an effort to document their claims. Also, employers falling within the scope of the Uniform Guidelines on Employee Selection Procedures, 29 CFR § 1607.1 *et seq.* (1988), are required to "maintain . . . records or other information which will disclose the impact which its tests and other selection procedures have upon employment opportunities of persons by identifiable race, sex, or ethnic group[s]." This includes records concerning "the individual components of the selection process" where there is a significant disparity in the selection rates of whites and nonwhites. See § 1607.4(C). Plaintiffs as a general matter will have the benefit of these tools to meet their burden of showing a causal link between challenged employment practices and racial imbalances in the work force; respondents presumably took full advantage of these opportunities to build their case before the trial in the District Court was held.

Consequently, on remand, the courts below are instructed to require, as part of respondents' prima facie case, a demonstration that specific elements of the petitioners' hiring process have a significantly disparate impact on nonwhites.

B

If, on remand, respondents meet the proof burdens outlined above, and establish a prima facie case of disparate impact with respect to any of petitioners' employment practices, the case will shift to any business justification petitioners offer for their use of these practices. This phase of the disparate-impact case contains two components: first, a consideration of the justifications an employer offers for his use of these practices; and second, the availability of alternative practices to achieve the same business ends, with less racial impact. * * *

The judgment of the Court of Appeals is reversed, and the case is remanded * * *

JUSTICE BLACKMUN, with whom JUSTICE BRENNAN and JUSTICE MARSHALL, join dissenting.

Today a bare majority of the Court * * * bars the use of internal work force comparisons in the making of a prima facie case of discrimination, even where the structure of the industry in question renders any other statistical comparison meaningless. And it requires practice-by-practice statistical proof of causation, even where, as here, such proof would be impossible.

The harshness of these results is well demonstrated by the facts of this case. The salmon industry as described by this record takes us back to a kind of overt and institutionalized discrimination we have not dealt with in years: a total residential and work environment organized on principles of racial stratification and segregation, which * * * resembles a plantation economy. This industry long has been characterized by a taste for discrimination of the old-fashioned sort: a preference for hiring nonwhites to fill its lowest level positions, on the condition that they stay there. The majority's legal rulings essentially immunize these practices from attack under a Title VII disparate-impact analysis.

JUSTICE STEVENS, with whom JUSTICE BRENNAN, JUSTICE MARSHALL and JUSTICE BLACKMUN join, dissenting.

* * *

Statistical evidence of discrimination should compare the racial composition of employees in disputed jobs to that " 'of the qualified ... population in the relevant labor market.' " That statement leaves open the definition of the qualified population and the relevant labor market. Our previous opinions demonstrate that in reviewing statistical evidence, a court should not strive for numerical exactitude at the expense of the needs of the particular case.

The District Court's findings of fact depict a unique industry. Canneries often are located in remote, sparsely populated areas of Alaska. Most jobs are seasonal, with the season's length and the canneries' personnel needs varying not just year to year but day to day. To fill their employment requirements, petitioners must recruit and transport many cannery workers and noncannery workers from States in the Pacific Northwest. Most cannery workers come from a union local based outside Alaska or from Native villages near the canneries. Employees in the noncannery positions-the positions that are "at issue"-learn of openings by word of mouth; the jobs seldom are posted or advertised, and there is no promotion to noncannery jobs from within the cannery workers' ranks.

In general, the District Court found the at-issue jobs to require "skills," ranging from English literacy, typing, and "ability to use seam micrometers, gauges, and mechanic's hand tools" to "good health" and a driver's license. All cannery workers' jobs, like a handful of at-issue positions, are unskilled, and the court found that the intensity of the work during canning season precludes on-the-job training for skilled noncannery positions. It made no findings regarding the extent to which the cannery workers already are qualified for at-issue jobs: individual plaintiffs testified persuasively that they were fully qualified for such jobs, but the court neither credited nor discredited this testimony. Although there are no findings concerning wage differentials, the parties seem to agree that wages for cannery workers are lower than those for noncannery workers, skilled or unskilled. The District Court found that "nearly all" cannery workers are nonwhite, while the percentage of nonwhites employed in the entire Alaska salmon canning industry "has stabilized at about 47% to 50%." The precise stratification of the work force is not described in the findings, but the parties seem to agree that the noncannery jobs are predominantly held by whites.

* * *

* * * An undisputed requirement for employment either as a cannery or noncannery worker is availability for seasonal employment in the far reaches of Alaska. Many noncannery workers, furthermore, must be available for preseason work. Yet the record does not identify the portion of the general population in Alaska, California, and the Pacific Northwest that would accept this type of employment. This deficiency respecting a crucial job qualification diminishes the usefulness of petitioners' statistical evidence. In contrast, respondents' evidence, comparing racial compositions within the work force, identifies a pool of workers willing to work during the relevant times and familiar with the workings of the industry. Surely this is more probative than the untailored general population statistics on which petitioners focus. * * *:

Evidence that virtually all the employees in the major categories of at-issue jobs were white, whereas about two-thirds of the cannery workers were nonwhite, may not by itself suffice to establish a prima facie case of discrimination. But such evidence of racial stratification puts the specific employment practices challenged by respondents into perspective. Petitioners recruit employees for at-issue jobs from outside the work force rather than from lower paying, overwhelmingly nonwhite, cannery worker positions. Information about availability of at-issue positions is conducted by word of mouth; therefore, the maintenance of housing and mess halls that separate the largely white noncannery work force from the cannery workers, coupled with the tendency toward nepotistic hiring, are obvious barriers to employment opportunities for nonwhites. Putting to one side the issue of business justifications, it would be quite wrong to conclude that these practices have no discriminatory consequence. Thus I agree with the Court of Appeals that when the District Court makes the additional findings prescribed today, it should treat the evidence of racial stratification in the work force as a significant element of respondents' prima facie case.

NOTE

The City of Newark had a city residency requirement. A high percentage of city residents are black. The surrounding six county suburban area is predominately white. A white, non-resident job applicant is not considered. Held: The city residency rule had an adverse impact on white applicants. *Meditz v. City of Newark,* 658 F.3d 364 (3d Cir. 2011). A different demographic pattern can produce a different result. A city residency requirement can have an adverse impact on black applicants where the city's population is predominately white and neighboring areas have a significant minority population. *NAACP v. North Hudson Reg'l Fire & Rescue,* 665 F.3d 464 (3d Cir. 2011).

Consider, whether a residency requirement having the adverse racial impact could be justified as "job related consistent with business necessity." A public employer giving job preference to its own residents may be rational, but would not appear to be "*job* related." Would it make a difference if the residency requirement was for public safety positions, and rationalized as making the employee readily available for emergency duty? However, a residency requirement that applied only to hiring, and was not a continuing obligation, suggests an "emergency duty" justification was not a "necessity."

Is there a constitutional problem of governments imposing residency requirements on its employees?

NEW YORK CITY TRANSIT AUTHORITY v. BEAZER

Supreme Court of the United States, 1979
440 U.S. 568, 99 S.Ct. 1355, 59 L.Ed.2d 587

JUSTICE STEVENS delivered the opinion of the Court.

The New York City Transit Authority refuses to employ persons who use methadone. The District Court found that this policy violates the Equal Protection Clause of the Fourteenth Amendment. In a subsequent opinion, the court also held that the policy violates Title VII of the Civil Rights Act of 1964. The Court of Appeals affirmed without reaching the statutory question. The departure by those courts from the procedure normally followed in addressing statutory and constitutional questions in the same case, as well as concern that the merits of these important questions had been decided erroneously, led us to grant certiorari. We now reverse.

The Transit Authority (TA) operates the subway system and certain bus lines in New York City. It employs about 47,000 persons, of whom many-perhaps most-are employed in positions that involve danger to themselves or to the public. For example, some 12,300 are subway motormen, towermen, conductors, or bus operators. The District Court found that these jobs are attended by unusual hazards and must be performed by "persons of maximum alertness and competence." Certain other jobs, such as operating cranes and handling high-voltage equipment, are also considered "critical" or "safety sensitive," while still others, though classified as "noncritical," have a potentially important impact on the overall operation of the transportation system.

TA enforces a general policy against employing persons who use narcotic drugs. The policy is reflected in Rule 11(b) of TA's Rules and Regulations.

> "Employees must not use, or have in their possession, narcotics, tranquilizers, drugs of the Amphetamine group or barbiturate derivatives or paraphernalia used to administer narcotics or barbiturate derivatives, except with the written permission of the Medical Director–Chief Surgeon of the System."

Methadone is regarded as a narcotic within the meaning of Rule 11(b). No written permission has ever been given by TA's medical director for the employment of a person using methadone.

The District Court found that methadone is a synthetic narcotic and a central nervous system depressant. If injected into the bloodstream with a needle, it produces essentially the same effects as heroin. Methadone has been used legitimately in at least three ways-as a pain killer, in "detoxification units" of hospitals as an immediate means of taking addicts off of heroin, and in long-range "methadone maintenance programs" as part of an intended cure for heroin addiction. In such programs the methadone is taken orally in regular doses for a prolonged period. As so administered, it does not produce euphoria or any pleasurable effects associated with heroin; on the contrary, it prevents users from experiencing those effects when they inject heroin, and also alleviates the severe and prolonged discomfort otherwise associated with an addict's discontinuance of the use of heroin.

About 40,000 persons receive methadone maintenance treatment in New York City, of whom about 26,000 participate in the five major public or semipublic programs, and 14,000 are involved in about 25 private programs.[7] The sole purpose of all these programs is to treat the addiction of persons who have been using heroin for at least two years.

Methadone maintenance treatment in New York is largely governed by regulations promulgated by the New York State Drug Abuse Control Commission. Under the regulations, the newly accepted addict must first be detoxified, normally in a hospital. A controlled daily dosage of methadone is then prescribed. The regulations require that six doses a week be administered at a clinic, while the seventh day's dose may be taken at home. If progress is satisfactory for three months, additional doses may be taken away from the clinic, although throughout most of the program, which often lasts for several years, there is a minimum requirement of three clinic appearances a week. During these visits, the patient not only receives his doses but is also counseled and tested for illicit use of drugs.

The evidence indicates that methadone is an effective cure for the physical aspects of heroin addiction. But the District Court also found "that many persons attempting to overcome heroin addiction have psychological or life-style problems which reach beyond what can be cured by the physical taking of doses of methadone." The crucial indicator of successful methadone maintenance is the patient's abstinence from the illegal or excessive use of drugs and alcohol. The District Court found that the risk of reversion to drug or alcohol abuse declines dramatically after the first few months of treatment. Indeed, "the strong majority" of patients who have been on methadone maintenance for at least a year are free from illicit drug use. But a significant number are not. On this critical point, the evidence relied upon by the District Court reveals that even among participants with more than 12 months' tenure in methadone maintenance programs, the incidence of drug and alcohol abuse may often approach and even exceed 25%.

This litigation was brought by the four respondents as a class action on behalf of all persons who have been, or would in the future be, subject to discharge or rejection as employees of TA by reason of participation in a methadone maintenance program. Two of the respondents are former

---

7. "[V]ery little specific information was provided [at trial] regarding the private clinics." What evidence there was indicated that those clinics were likely to be less successful and less able to provide accurate information about their clients than the public clinics.

employees of TA who were dismissed while they were receiving methadone treatment. The other two were refused employment by TA, one both shortly before and shortly after the successful conclusion of his methadone treatment, and the other while he was taking methadone. Their complaint alleged that TA's blanket exclusion of all former heroin addicts receiving methadone treatment was illegal under the Civil Rights Act of 1866, 42 U.S.C. § 1981, Title VII of the Civil Rights Act of 1964, and the Equal Protection Clause of the Fourteenth Amendment.

The trial record contains extensive evidence concerning the success of methadone maintenance programs, the employability of persons taking methadone, and the ability of prospective employers to detect drug abuse or other undesirable characteristics of methadone users. In general, the District Court concluded that there are substantial numbers of methadone users who are just as employable as other members of the general population and that normal personnel-screening procedures—at least if augmented by some method of obtaining information from the staffs of methadone programs—would enable TA to identify the unqualified applicants on an individual basis. On the other hand, the District Court recognized that at least one-third of the persons receiving methadone treatment-and probably a good many more—would unquestionably be classified as unemployable.

After extensively reviewing the evidence, the District Court briefly stated its conclusion that TA's methadone policy is unconstitutional. * * *

The District Court * * * [r]ecognizing, however, the special responsibility for public safety borne by certain TA employees and the correlation between longevity in a methadone maintenance program and performance capability, * * * authorized TA to exclude methadone users from specific categories of safety-sensitive positions and also to condition eligibility on satisfactory performance in a methadone program for at least a year.

Almost a year later the District Court filed a supplemental opinion * * * determin[ed] * * * that TA's drug policy violated Title VII. Having already concluded that the blanket exclusion was not rationally related to any business needs of TA, the court reasoned that the statute is violated if the exclusionary policy has a discriminatory effect against blacks and Hispanics. That effect was proved, in the District Court's view, by two statistics: (1) of the employees referred to TA's medical consultant for suspected violation of its drug policy, 81% are black or Hispanic; (2) between 62% and 65% of all methadone-maintained persons in New York City are black or Hispanic. The court, however, did not find that TA's policy was motivated by any bias against blacks or Hispanics; indeed, it expressly found that the policy was not adopted with a discriminatory purpose.

The Court of Appeals affirmed * * *

II

The District Court's findings do not support its conclusion that TA's regulation prohibiting the use of narcotics, or its interpretation of that regulation to encompass users of methadone, violated Title VII of the Civil Rights Act.

A prima facie violation of the Act may be established by statistical evidence showing that an employment practice has the effect of denying the members of one race equal access to employment opportunities. Even assuming that respondents have crossed this threshold, when the entire record is examined it is clear that the two statistics on which they and the District Court relied do not prove a violation of Title VII.[25]

First, the District Court noted that 81% of the employees referred to TA's medical director for suspected violation of its narcotics rule were either black or Hispanic. But respondents have only challenged the rule to the extent that it is construed to apply to methadone users, and that statistic tells us nothing about the racial composition of the employees suspected of using methadone. Nor does the record give us any information about the number of black, Hispanic, or white persons who were dismissed for using methadone.[26]

Second, the District Court noted that about 63% of the persons in New York City receiving methadone maintenance in *public* programs—*i.e.*, 63% of the 65% of all New York City methadone users who are in such programs-are black or Hispanic. We do not know, however, how many of these persons ever worked or sought to work for TA. This statistic therefore reveals little if anything about the racial composition of the class of TA job applicants and employees receiving methadone treatment. More particularly, it tells us nothing about the class of otherwise-qualified applicants and employees who have participated in methadone mainte-nance programs for over a year—the only class improperly excluded by TA's policy under the District Court's analysis. The record demonstrates, in fact, that the figure is virtually irrelevant because a substantial portion of the persons included in it are either unqualified for other reasons—such as the illicit use of drugs and alcohol[28]—or have received successful

---

25. "Statistics are . . . competent in proving employment discrimination. We caution only that statistics are not irrefutable; they come in infinite variety and, like any other kind of evidence, they may be rebutted. In short, their usefulness depends on all the surrounding facts and circumstances." * * * Because of our conclusion on the merits of respondents' Title VII claim, we need not address the constitutional challenge made by TA to Title VII insofar as it authorizes relief against a municipal agency under the circumstances of this case.

26. Indeed, it is probable that none of the employees comprising this 81% were methadone users. The parties stipulated that:

"TA employees showing physical manifestations of drug abuse *other than* the definite presence of morphine or *methadone* or other illicit drug in the urine, are referred for consultation to [the medical director] . . ."

In view of this stipulation and the District Court's finding that few if any physical manifesta-tions of drug abuse characterize methadone-maintained persons, it seems likely that such persons would not be included in the statistical pool referred to by the District Court. It should also be noted that when the dissent refers to the rejection of almost 5% of all applicants "due to the rule," the reference is to all narcotics users rather than to methadone users. The record does not tell us how many methadone users were rejected.

28. To demonstrate employability, the District Court referred to a study indicating that 34% to 59% of the methadone users who have been in a maintenance program for a substantial period of time are employed. The evidence was inconclusive with respect to all methadone users. However, the director of the second largest program in New York City testified that only 33% of the entire methadone-patient population in that program were employable. * * *

assistance in finding jobs with employers other than TA.[29] Finally, we have absolutely no data on the 14,000 methadone users in the *private* programs, leaving open the possibility that the percentage of blacks and Hispanics in the class of methadone users is not significantly greater than the percentage of those minorities in the general population of New York City.

At best, respondents' statistical showing is weak; even if it is capable of establishing a prima facie case of discrimination, it is assuredly rebutted by TA's demonstration that its narcotics rule (and the rule's application to methadone users) is "job related."[31] The District Court's express finding that the rule was not motivated by racial animus forecloses any claim in rebuttal that it was merely a pretext for intentional discrimination. We conclude that respondents failed to prove a violation of Title VII. We therefore must reach the constitutional issue.

* * *

No matter how unwise it may be for TA to refuse employment to individual car cleaners, track repairmen, or bus drivers simply because they are receiving methadone treatment, the Constitution does not authorize a federal court to interfere in that policy decision. The judgment of the Court of Appeals is

Reversed.

JUSTICE BRENNAN, dissenting.

* * * I cannot agree with the Court's assertions that this evidence "reveals little if anything," "tells us nothing," and is "virtually irrelevant." There is not a shadow of doubt that methadone users do apply for employment with petitioners, and because 63% of all methadone users are black or Hispanic, there is every reason to conclude that a majority of methadone users who apply are also from these minority groups. Almost 5% of all applicants are rejected due to the rule, and undoubtedly many black and Hispanic methadone users are among those rejected. Why would proportionally fewer of them than whites secure work with petitioners absent the challenged practice? The Court gives no reason whatsoever for rejecting this sensible inference, and where the inference depends so much

---

29. Although "a statistical showing of disproportionate impact [need not] always be based on an analysis of the characteristics of actual applicants," *Dothard v. Rawlinson*, 433 U.S. 321, 330, 97 S.Ct. 2720, 2727, 53 L.Ed.2d 786, "evidence showing that the figures for the general population might not accurately reflect the pool of qualified job applicants" undermines the significance of such figures. *Teamsters v. United States, supra*, 431 U.S., at 340 n. 20, 97 S.Ct., at 1857 n. 20.

31. Respondents recognize, and the findings of the District Court establish, that TA's legitimate employment goals of safety and efficiency require the exclusion of all users of illegal narcotics, barbiturates, and amphetamines, and of a majority of all methadone users. The District Court also held that those goals require the exclusion of all methadone users from the 25% of its positions that are "safety sensitive." Finally, the District Court noted that those goals are significantly served by—even if they do not require—TA's rule as it applies to all methadone users including those who are seeking employment in nonsafety-sensitive positions. The record thus demonstrates that TA's rule bears a "manifest relationship to the employment in question." Whether or not respondents' weak showing was sufficient to establish a prima facie case, it clearly failed to carry respondents' ultimate burden of proving a violation of Title VII.

on local knowledge, I would accept the judgment of the District Court rather than purport to make an independent judgment from the banks of the Potomac. * * *

The Court complains that even if minority groups make up 63% of methadone-user applicants this statistic is an insufficient indicator of the composition of the group found by the District Court to have been wrongly excluded—that is, those who have been successfully maintained for a year or more. I cannot, however, presume with the Court that blacks or Hispanics will be less likely than whites to succeed on methadone. I would have thought the presumption, until rebutted, would be one of an equal chance of success, and there has been no rebuttal.

Finally, as to the racial composition of the patients at private clinics, I note first that the District Court found that "[b]etween 62% and 65% of methadone maintained persons in New York City are black and Hispanic . . ." The finding was for the total population, not just for public clinics. Even assuming that the Court wishes to overturn this finding of fact as clearly erroneous, I see no support for doing so. The evidence from the Methadone Information Center at Rockefeller University indicated that 61% of all patients in the metropolitan area were black or Puerto Rican (with 5.85% undefined). This was based on a 1,400–patient sample, which, according to the Center, "was drawn on a random basis and very accurately reflects the *total population* for Metropolitan New York City". There is no reason to believe that this study, which in its reporting of the total number of patients of all races included both public and private clinics, did not include private programs in its racial-composition figures. And even if everyone in the private clinics were white, a highly unlikely assumption at best, the challenged rule would still automatically exclude a substantially greater number of blacks and Hispanics than would a practice with a racially neutral effect.

With all due respect, I would accept the statistics as making a prima facie case of disparate impact. Obviously, the case could have been stronger, but this Court is unjustified in displacing the District Court's acceptance of uncontradicted, relevant evidence. * * *

NOTES

1.   *42 U.S.C. § 2000e–2(k)(1) (added to Title VII by 1991 Amendments)*:

   (A): An unlawful employment practice based on disparate impact is established under this title only if—

   (i) a complaining party demonstrates that a respondent uses a particular employment practice that causes a disparate impact, and respondent fails to demonstrate that the challenged practice is job related for the position and consistent with business necessity * * *

   (B) (i) With respect to demonstrating that a particular employment practice causes a disparate impact as described in subparagraph (A)(i), the complaining party shall demonstrate that each particular challenged employment practice causes a disparate impact, * * *.

(ii) If the respondent demonstrates that a specific employment practice does not cause the disparate impact, the respondent shall not be required to demonstrate that such practice is required by business necessity.

2. *Two measures of impact*:

a. *Applicant Pool* examines the impact a device has upon an identified "pool" of potential applicants from which the employer could be expected to select its employees. *Griggs v. Duke Power, supra, page 318* and *Dothard v. Rawlinson, supra page 346,* relied upon such "potential applicant pool" or general population evidence. Such "pool" data requires identifying the geographic area surrounding the work site, *and* the demographic make-up of employable persons by race and sex living within that geographic area. *Griggs* and *Dothard* both utilized state boundaries as the relevant geographic area from which the employers would draw applicants. *Hazelwood v. U.S., infra page 434,* utilized as the relevant area the St. Louis, Missouri, "standard metropolitan statistical area" (SMSA). *Tusing v. DeMoines Ind. Comm. Sch. Dist.,* 639 F.3d 507 (8th Cir. 2011). This pool type data is typically employed when the challenged device is a non-scored device such as an educational credential.

As the principal case held, raw pool data often must be refined to account for persons otherwise unqualified for the position. In *Hazelwood v. U.S., supra,* the relevant number was the percentage of black and white teachers in the to-be-defined St. Louis geographical area. Here plaintiffs had refined their data to those qualified by teaching credentials for the positions in question.

b. *Applicant Flow* measures the employer's actual experience in using the challenged device, comparing the passage rates of minority and non-minority applicants. *Beazer,* the principal case, analyzed but found inadequate, plaintiff's applicant flow data. The EEOC allows flow impact to be determined by a "Rule of 4/5" or 80%. A device will be assumed to have an impact if the success rate on the challenged device of the plaintiff's class is less than 80% of the success rate of the most successful class of applicants. 29 CFR § 1607.4D. Thus, if 50 white applicants take a test, and 25 of them pass, their pass rate is 50%. The device will be presumed to have an impact on black applicants if the passage rate of black applicants is less than 80% of the passage rate of whites. Thus, if black applicants pass at a rate of less than 40% (*e.g.,* of 20 black test-takers, only 5 pass = 25% rate), the device will be seen as having an adverse impact on black applicants. To be meaningful the "Rule of 4/5" requires a sufficient number of experiences in using the device so that a small change in the gross number involved would not produce a large change in the percentages. Thus, a half dozen test takers, 4 whites and 2 blacks, could not produce reliable evidence of impact regardless of the outcome.

A more statistically accurate measure would be to determine mathematically whether the difference in the success rates of the classes could be attributable to chance. The "expected" outcome would be identical pass rates for all classes. If chance is mathematically eliminated as an explanation for the "observed" disparity in the test results, then it may be assumed that the disparity is not a product of chance, but the result of the challenged device.

See discussion of statistical methodology, *supra p. 439. Shoben, "Differential Pass–Fail Rates in Employment Testing: Statistical Proof Under Title VII,* 91 Harv.L.Rev. 793 (1978).

3. *Which works best?* Generally, flow data is a more reliable measurement of the actual impact of a challenged device, and is generally relied upon when the challenged device is an objective test given to actual applicants. Pool data is inherently imprecise in that it requires setting an arbitrary definition of the pool's geographical boundaries and refining imprecisely the population to reflect those in the pool who are otherwise interested in and qualified for this kind of job. On the other hand, actual applicant flow may not reflect the true impact of a device where "otherwise qualified" people might be discouraged from applying because of a self-recognized inability to meet the very standards being challenged. *Dothard v. Rawlinson, supra, page 346.* For example, the very existence of a height requirement of 5′2″ would likely cause those shorter than the required height not to apply. The device itself would cause self-selection. Similarly, an announced high school diploma requirement would deter those without the credential from entering the "flow." Conversely, vigorous affirmative action efforts may produce a disproportionate number of marginally qualified minority applicants. Ultimately, the fact finder must determine which set of data is the most reliable indicator of impact under the unique circumstances of each case.

4. *Impact and the ADEA:* ***Clark v. Matthews International Corp.,*** 628 F.3d 462 (8th Cir. 2010), involved a reduction-in-force in which 14 of the 15 employees dismissed were over age 40. The court held that this flow data failed to prove the adverse impact of the criteria used to determine order of lay off. The proper statistic, the court held, was the pool consisting of all of the employer's non-management employees. The impact was established only by comparing the percentage of older workers at the plant before and after the force reduction. Using that standard, change in the percent of older workers retained was too small to establish the impact of the criteria used for retention.

5. *American's With Disabilities Act:* Recall that the ADA protects the disability of addiction (42 U.S.C. § 12114(a)), and proscribes use of selection criteria that tend to screen out individuals with disabilities unless the criteria are "job related and consistent with business necessity." 42 U.S.C. § 12112(b).

a. ***RAYTHEON CO. v. HERNANDEZ***, 540 U.S. 44, 124 S.Ct. 513, 157 L.Ed.2d 357 (2003), held that an employer relying on a broad "no-rehire" policy for employees who had been discharged for any cause did not violate the ADA when it refused to rehire a former employee who had previously been dismissed for failure to pass a drug test. The impact of the employer's "no rehire" policy on persons with an addiction disability could not be assumed. Note that the ADA provides:

> Nothing in this title shall be construed to encourage, prohibit, or authorize the conducting of drug testing for the illegal use of drugs by job applicants or employees or making employment decisions based on such test results. 42 U.S.C. 12114(d)(2).

b. While ADA excludes from protection discrimination based on an employee or applicant "currently engaged in the illegal use of drugs" (42

U.S.C. § 12114(a)), it goes on to provide that this exclusion does not apply to an otherwise qualified individual with the disability of addiction who "has successfully completed (or is participating in) a supervised drug rehabilitation program and is no longer engaging in the illegal use of drugs." 42 U.S.C. § 12114(b)(1) and (2). **Lopez v. Pacific Maritime Ass'n.,** 657 F.3d 762 (9th Cir. 2011), applied **Raytheon**, *supra,* to a required pre-employment drug test coupled with the employer's "one strike" policy whereby it would not consider anyone who had previously failed its drug test. Plaintiff, who had earlier failed the pre-employment drug test reapplied after undergoing rehabilitation treatment. He argued that the "one strike" policy virtually insured that addicts who had completed rehabilitation programs would not be hired. Nonetheless, the court refused to assume without supporting data that the policy had an adverse impact on rehabilitated addicts. Moreover, absent defendant having notice that plaintiff was in fact an addict who was in remission, there was no evidence of improper motivation in the employer's invoking the "one strike" policy to reject plaintiff's application.

    c.   Consider whether the policy under attack in the principal case violates the ADA. Recall that the ADA provides that an individual does not meet the employer's "qualification standards" if she poses a "direct threat to the health or safety of other individuals in the workplace." 42 U.S.C. § 12113(b). "Direct threat" is defined to mean "a significant risk to the health or safety of others that cannot be eliminated by reasonable accommodation." 42 U.S.C § 12111(3). In addition, the act specifically provides that employers subject to the jurisdiction of the Department of Transportation may test employees in *"safety sensitive"* positions for illegal drug use and on-duty impairment by alcohol and remove persons who test positive from *"safety sensitive duties."* 42 U.S.C. § 12114(e).

CONNECTICUT v. TEAL

Supreme Court of the United States, 1982
457 U.S. 440, 102 S.Ct. 2525, 73 L.Ed.2d 130

* * *

We consider here whether an employer sued for violation of Title VII of the Civil Rights Act of 1964 may assert a "bottom line" theory of defense. Under that theory, asserted in this case, an employer's acts of racial discrimination in promotions affected by an examination having disparate impact would not render the employer liable for racial discrimination suffered by employees barred from promotion if the "bottom line" result of the promotional process was an appropriate racial balance. We hold that the "bottom line" does not preclude respondent employees from establishing a prima facie case, nor does it provide petitioner employer with a defense to such a case.

[In filling supervisory positions defendant utilized a multi-tier selection process the first step of which was that all applicants must secure a passing score on a written examination. Plaintiffs, who were black, failed to achieve a passing score and thus were excluded from further consideration. Applicants who passed the test were placed on an "eligibility list." Plaintiffs established that a disproportionate percentage of black candidates failed to make a passing score on the test. Defendant failed to establish the "job relatedness" of the test. In filling vacancies defendant considered the past work performance, recommendations from supervisors, and the seniority of those who were on the "eligibility list" by virtue of their passing the initial test. The "bottom line" of defendant's selection process resulted in an outcome in which final selection rate for black and white candidates for the supervisory positions in fact was slightly more favorable to blacks than to whites. The Court affirmed a Court of Appeals holding:]

[T]hat where "an identifiable pass-fail barrier denies an employment opportunity to a disproportionate number of minorities and prevents them from proceeding to the next step in the selection process" that barrier must be shown to be job related. * * *

[W]e must address the suggestion of [defendant] and some *amicus curiae* that we recognize an exception, either in the nature of an additional burden on plaintiff's seeking to establish a prima face case on in the nature of an affirmative defense, for cases in which an employer has compensated for a discriminatory pass-fail barrier by hiring or promoting a significant number of black employees to reach a nondiscriminatory "bottom line." We reject this suggestion, which in essence is nothing more than a request that we redefine the protections guaranteed by Title VII. * * *

It is clear beyond cavil that the obligation imposed by Title VII is to provide an equal opportunity for *each* applicant regardless of race, without regard to whether members of the applicant's race are already proportionately represented in the work force.

* * *

NOTES

Possible Employer Response to Connecticut v. Teal:

a. *Adjust* the test scores along racial or gender lines to eliminate impact? § 703(*l*), 42 U.S.C. § 2000e–2(*l*) provides:

> It shall be an unlawful employment practice for a respondent, in connection with the selection or referral of applicants * * * for employment or promotion, to adjust the scores of, use different cutoff scores for, or otherwise alter the results of employment related tests on the basis of race, color, religion, sex, or national origin.

b. *Disregard* the test results and rely on the other criteria: education, experience, or subjective interviews? *Ricci v. DeStefano, supra page 331,* places significant obstacles to this approach.

c. *Revamp* by using the test as one of multiple components that produces a single overall score? 42 U.S.C. § 2000e–2(k)(1)(B)(i) provides:

> With respect to demonstrating that a particular employment practice causes a disparate impact * * * the complaining party shall demonstrate that each particular challenged employment practice causes a disparate impact, *except that if * * * the respondent's decision making processes are not capable of separation for analysis, the decision making process may be analyzed as one employment practice.*

B. DEFENDANT'S BURDEN: JUSTIFYING IMPACT

1. GENERALLY: "JOB RELATED CONSISTENT WITH BUSINESS NECESSITY"

ALBERMARLE PAPER CO. v. MOODY, **422 U.S. 405, 95 S.Ct. 2362, 45 L.Ed.2d 280 (1975),** *reproduced in part, infra, p. 367* in addressing scored tests shown to have an adverse impact on racial minorities interpreted *Griggs v. Duke Power Co., supra page 318,* to forbid "the use of employment tests that are discriminatory in effect unless the employer meets the burden of showing that any given requirement has a manifest relationship to the employment in question." The *Griggs* articulation— "the touchstone is business necessity"—was not mentioned. The *Albermarle* Court continued: "If an employer does then meet the burden of proving that its tests are 'job related,' it remains open to the complaining party to show that other tests or selection devices, without a similarly undesirable racial effect, would also serve the employer's legitimate interest in 'efficient and trustworthy workmanship.' Such a showing would be evidence that the employer was using its tests merely as a 'pretext' for discrimination."

Albermarle Paper thus de-emphasized "necessity" in favor of the simple "job relatedness" of the challenged device. The existence of a lesser discriminatory alternative, which would tend to show that the challenged device was not necessary, could be presented by plaintiff. When presented, however, this evidence would tend to prove—not the lack of necessity— but defendant's illegal motive in using the device.

DOTHARD v. RAWLINSON, **433 U.S. 321, 97 S.Ct. 2720, 53 L.Ed.2d 786 (1977),** addressed the "business necessity" of a minimum height and weight requirement for prison guards (or "correctional counselors") that was found to have an adverse impact on women. In its footnote 14 the Court, citing *Griggs v. Duke Power Co.,* stated, "[A] discriminatory employment practice must be shown to be necessary to safe and efficient job performance to survive a Title VII challenge." Applying that standard the Court rejected the argument that the physical size of a person was necessary to safe and efficient job performance. Moreover, while conceding that minimal levels of physical strength might be "essential" to perform safely as a prison guard, the Court was unwilling to assume that there was sufficient correlation between size and strength to satisfy the high standard of "business necessity" set by *Griggs.* Moreover, the Court emphasized:

> If the job-related quality [of physical size] that the appellants identify is bona fide, their purpose could be achieved by adopting and validating a test for applicants that measures strength directly. Such a test, fairly administered, would fully satisfy the standards of Title VII

because it would be one that 'measures the person for the job and not the person in the abstract.'

WARDS COVE PACKING v. ATONIO, 490 U.S. 642, 109 S.Ct. 2115, 104 L.Ed.2d 733 (1989), (in a segment omitted from the above), provided a relatively precise definition of defendant's burden upon plaintiff proving the adverse impact of a device. Defendant will satisfy its burden by establishing that:

> [T]he challenged device serves, in a significant way, the legitimate goals of the employer. * * * A mere insubstantial justification * * * will not suffice. At the same time, though, there is no requirement that the challenged practice be 'essential' or 'indispensible.'

The 1991 Amendments rejected the *Wards Cove Packing* formulation of "business necessity," but did nothing to define the two phrases coined in *Griggs*—"job related" and "business necessity." Indeed, the legislation expressly excluded from consideration any legislative history that discussed those terms, and directed that Congress was endorsing the judicial interpretations of "job relatedness" and "business necessity" *prior* to the decision in *Wards Cove Packing*. This left unresolved the question of the status of the law prior to *Wards Cove Packing*. Was it "job relatedness" stated in *Albermarle Paper Co. v. Moody,* or, the "necessary"/"essential" standard used in *Dothard v. Rawlinson*?

As the above excerpts indicated, *Albermarle Paper Co. v. Moody* and *Dothard v. Rawlinson* placed the burden of persuasion on the defendant. *Wards Cove Packing* indicated to the contrary. Once the adverse impact of the device was established by plaintiff, *Wards Cove Packing* stated that defendant's burden was one of *presenting evidence* of the business necessity, rather than the burden of convincing the fact finder of the device's "business necessity." The 1991 Amendments also rejected this aspect of the *Wards Cove Packing* decision, providing:

> An unlawful employment practice based on disparate impact is established under this title only if—(i) a complaining party demonstrates that a respondent uses a particular employment practice that causes a disparate impact on the basis of [a protected class] and the respondent fails to demonstrate that the challenged practice is job related for the position and consistent with business necessity. 42 U.S.C. § 2000e–2(k)(1)(A)(i)

"Demonstrate" was defined to mean: "meets the burdens of production and persuasion." 42 U.S.C. § 2000e(m).

2. "BUSINESS NECESSITY" APPLIED TO SCORED TESTS

ALBERMARLE PAPER CO. v. MOODY

Supreme Court of the United States, 1975
422 U.S. 405, 95 S.Ct. 2362, 45 L.Ed.2d 280

JUSTICE STEWART delivered the opinion of the Court.

These consolidated cases raise * * * important questions under Title VII of the Civil Rights Act of 1964, * * * What must an employer show to establish that pre-employment tests racially discriminatory in effect, though not in intent, are sufficiently 'job related' to survive challenge under Title VII?

I

The respondents—plaintiffs in the District Court—are a certified class of present and former Negro employees at a paper mill in Roanoke Rapids, N.C.; the petitioners—defendants in the District Court—are the plant's owner, the Albemarle Paper Co., and the plant employees' labor union, Halifax Local No. 425. * * *

The court * * * refused to enjoin or limit Albemarle's testing program. Albemarle had required applicants for employment in the skilled lines of progression to have a high school diploma and to pass two tests, the Revised Beta Examination, allegedly a measure of nonverbal intelligence, and the Wonderlic Personnel Test (available in alternative Forms A and B), allegedly a measure of verbal facility. After this Court's decision in, and on the eve of trial, Albemarle engaged an industrial psychologist to study the 'job relatedness' of its testing program. His study compared the test scores of current employees with supervisorial judgments of their competence in ten job groupings selected from the middle or top of the plant's skilled lines of progression. The study showed a statistically significant correlation with supervisorial ratings in three job groupings for the Beta Test, in seven job groupings for either Form A or Form B of the Wonderlic Test, and in two job groupings for the required battery of both the Beta and the Wonderlic Tests. The respondents' experts challenged the reliability of these studies, but the court concluded:

'The personnel tests administered at the plant have undergone validation studies and have been proven to be job related. The defendants have carried the burden of proof in proving that these tests are 'necessary for the safe and efficient operation of the business' and are, therefore, permitted by the Act. However, the high school education requirement used in conjunction with the testing requirements is unlawful in that the personnel tests alone are adequate to measure the mental ability and reading skills required for the job classifications.'

* * *

As for the pre-employment tests, the Court of Appeals held, that it was error

'to approve a validation study done without job analysis, to allow Albemarle to require tests for 6 lines of progression where there has been no validation study at all, and to allow Albemarle to require a person to pass two tests for entrance into 7 lines of progression when only one of those tests was validated for that line of progression.'

In so holding the Court of Appeals 'gave great deference' to the 'Guidelines on Employee Selection Procedures,' 29 CFR pt. 1607, which the EEOC has issued 'as a workable set of standards for employers, unions and employment agencies in determining whether their selection procedures conform with the obligations contained in title VII . . .'

We granted certiorari as to the showing required to establish the 'job relatedness' of pre-employment tests. * * *

III

In *Griggs v. Duke Power Co.* this Court unanimously held that Title VII forbids the use of employment tests that are discriminatory in effect unless the employer meets 'the burden of showing that any given requirement (has) . . . a manifest relationship to the employment in question.' This burden arises, of course, only after the complaining party or class has made out a prima facie case of discrimination, i.e. has shown that the tests in question select applicants for hire or promotion in a racial pattern significantly different from that of the pool of applicants. If an employer does then meet the burden of proving that its tests are 'job related,' it remains open to the complaining party to show that other tests or selection devices, without a similarly undesirable racial effect, would also serve the employer's legitimate interest in 'efficient and trustworthy workmanship.' Such a showing would be evidence that the employer was using its tests merely as a 'pretext' for discrimination. In the present case, however, we are concerned only with the question whether Albemarle has shown its tests to be job related.

The concept of job relatedness takes on meaning from the facts of the Griggs case. A power company in North Carolina had reserved its skilled jobs for whites prior to 1965. Thereafter, the company allowed Negro workers to transfer to skilled jobs, but all transferees-white and Negro-were required to attain national median scores on two tests:

'(T)he Wonderlic Personnel Test, which purports to measure general intelligence, and the Bennett Mechanical Comprehension Test. Neither was directed or intended to measure the ability to learn to perform a particular job or category of jobs . . .

'. . . Both were adopted, as the Court of Appeals noted, without meaningful study of their relationship to job-performance ability. Rather, a vice president of the Company testified, the requirements were instituted on the Company's judgment that they generally would improve the overall quality of the work force.'

The Court took note of 'the inadequacy of broad and general testing devices as well as the infirmity of using diplomas or degrees as fixed measures of capability,' and concluded:

> 'Nothing in the Act precludes the use of testing or measuring procedures; obviously they are useful. What Congress has forbidden is giving these devices and mechanisms controlling force unless they are demonstrably a reasonable measure of job performance.... What Congress has commanded is that any tests used must measure the person for the job and not the person in the abstract.'

Like the employer in *Griggs*, Albemarle uses two general ability tests, the Beta Examination, to test nonverbal intelligence, and the Wonderlic Test (Forms A and B), the purported measure of general verbal facility which was also involved in the Griggs case. Applicants for hire into various skilled lines of progression at the plant are required to score 100 on the Beta Exam and 18 on one of the Wonderlic Test's two alternative forms.

The question of job relatedness must be viewed in the context of the plant's operation and the history of the testing program. The plant, which now employs about 650 persons, converts raw wood into paper products. It is organized into a number of functional departments, each with one or more distinct lines of progression, the theory being that workers can move up the line as they acquire the necessary skills. The number and structure of the lines have varied greatly over time. * * * In this sense, at least, it is still possible to speak of relatively skilled and relatively unskilled lines.

In the 1950's while the plant was being modernized with new and more sophisticated equipment, the Company introduced a high school diploma requirement for entry into the skilled lines. Though the Company soon concluded that this requirement did not improve the quality of the labor force, the requirement was continued until the District Court enjoined its use. In the late 1950's, the Company began using the Beta Examination and the Bennett Mechanical Comprehension Test (also involved in the Griggs case) to screen applicants for entry into the skilled lines. The Bennett Test was dropped several years later, but use of the Beta Test continued.[23]

The Company added the Wonderlic Tests in 1963, for the skilled lines, on the theory that a certain verbal intelligence was called for by the increasing sophistication of the plant's operations. The Company made no attempt to validate the test for job relatedness, and simply adopted the national 'norm' score of 18 as a cut-off point for new job applicants. After 1964, when it discontinued overt segregation in the lines of progression, the Company allowed Negro workers to transfer to the skilled lines if they could pass the Beta and Wonderlic Tests, but few succeeded in doing so. Incumbents in the skilled lines, some of whom had been hired before

---

23. While the Company contends that the Bennett and Beta Tests were 'locally validated' when they were introduced, no record of this validation was made. Plant officials could recall only the barest outlines of the alleged validation. Job relatedness cannot be proved through vague and unsubstantiated hearsay.

adoption of the tests, were not required to pass them to retain their jobs or their promotion rights. The record shows that a number of white incumbents in high-ranking job groups could not pass the tests.[25]

Because departmental reorganization continued up to the point of trial, and has indeed continued since that point, the details of the testing program are less than clear from the record. The District Court found that, since 1963, the Beta and Wonderlic Tests have been used in 13 lines of progression, within eight departments. Albemarle contends that at present the tests are used in only eight lines of progression, within four departments.

Four months before this case went to trial, Albemarle engaged an expert in industrial psychology to 'validate' the job relatedness of its testing program. He spent a half day at the plant and devised a 'concurrent validation' study, which was conducted by plant officials, without his supervision. The expert then subjected the results to statistical analysis. The study dealt with 10 job groupings, selected from near the top of nine of the lines of progression. Jobs were grouped together solely by their proximity in the line of progression; no attempt was made to analyze jobs in terms of the particular skills they might require. All, or nearly all, employees in the selected groups participated in the study—105 employees in all, but only four Negroes. Within each job grouping the study compared the test scores of each employee with an independent 'ranking' of the employee, relative to each of his coworkers, made by two of the employee's supervisors. The supervisors, who did not know the test scores, were asked to

> determine which ones they felt irrespective of the job that they were actually doing, but in their respective jobs, did a better job than the person they were rating against. . . .

For each job grouping, the expert computed the 'Phi coefficient' of statistical correlation between the test scores and an average of the two supervisorial rankings. Consonant with professional conventions, the expert regarded as 'statistically significant' any correlation that could have occurred by chance only five times, or fewer in 100 trials. On the basis of these results, the District Court found that '(t)he personnel test administered at the plant have undergone validation studies and have been proven to be job related.' Like the Court of Appeals, we are constrained to disagree.

The EEOC has issued 'Guidelines' for employers seeking to determine, through professional validation studies, whether their employment tests are job related. 29 CFR pt. 1607. These Guidelines draw upon and make

---

25. In the course of a 1971 validation effort test scores were accumulated for 105 incumbent employees (101 of whom were white) working in relatively high-ranking jobs. Some of these employees apparently took the tests for the first time as part of this study. The Company's expert testified that the test cut-off scores originally used to screen these incumbents for employment or promotion 'couldn't have been . . . very high scores because some of these guys tested very low, as low as 8 in the Wonderlic test, and as low as 95 in the Beta. They couldn't have been using very high cut-off scores or they wouldn't have these low testing employees.'

reference to professional standards of test validation established by the American Psychological Association.[29] The EEOC Guidelines are not administrative regulations' promulgated pursuant to formal procedures established by the Congress. But, as this Court has heretofore noted, they do constitute '(t)he administrative interpretation of the Act by the enforcing agency,' and consequently they are 'entitled to great deference.'

The message of these Guidelines is the same as that of the Griggs case-that discriminatory tests are impermissible unless shown, by professionally acceptable methods, to be 'predictive of or significantly correlated with important elements of work behavior which comprise or are relevant to the job or jobs for which candidates are being evaluated.' 29 CFR § 1607.4(c).

Measured against the Guidelines, Albemarle's validation study is materially defective in several respects:

(1) Even if it had been otherwise adequate, the study would not have 'validated' the Beta and Wonderlic test battery for all of the skilled lines of progression for which the two tests are, apparently, now required. The study showed significant correlations for the Beta Exam in only three of the eight lines. Though the Wonderlic Test's Form A and Form B are in theory identical and interchangeable measures of verbal facility, significant correlations for one form but not for the other were obtained in four job groupings. In two job groupings neither form showed a significant correlation. Within some of the lines of progression, one form was found acceptable for some job groupings but not for others. Even if the study were otherwise reliable, this odd patchwork of results would not entitle Albemarle to impose its testing program under the Guidelines. A test may be used in jobs other than those for which it has been professionally validated only if there are 'no significant differences' between the studied and unstudied jobs. 29 CFR § 1607.4(c)(2). The study in this case involved no analysis of the attributes of, or the particular skills needed in, the studied job groups. There is accordingly no basis for concluding that 'no significant differences' exist among the lines of progression, or among distinct job groupings within the studied lines of progression. Indeed, the study's checkered results appear to compel the opposite conclusion.

(2) The study compared test scores with subjective supervisorial rankings. While they allow the use of supervisorial rankings in test validation, the Guidelines quite plainly contemplate that the rankings will be elicited with far more care than was demonstrated here.[30] Albemarle's supervisors were asked to rank employees by a 'standard' that was extremely vague and fatally open to divergent interpretations. As previously noted, each

---

29. American Psychological Association, Standards for Educational and Psychological Tests and Manuals (1966) (hereafter APA Standards). A volume of the same title, containing modifications, was issued in 1974. The EEOC Guidelines refer to the APA Standards at 29 CFR § 1607.5(a). Very similar guidelines have been issued by the Secretary of Labor for the use of federal contractors. 41 CFR § 60–3.1 et seq.

30. The Guidelines provide, at 29 CFR §§ 1607.5(b)(3) and (4):

'job grouping' contained a number of different jobs, and the supervisors were asked, in each grouping to

> '(3) The work behaviors or other criteria of employee adequacy which the test is intended to predict or identify must be fully described; and, additionally, in the case of rating techniques, the appraisal form(s) and instructions to the rater(s) must be included as a part of the validation evidence. Such criteria may include measures other than actual work proficiency, such as training time, supervisory ratings, regularity of attendance and tenure. Whatever criteria are used they must represent major or critical work behaviors as revealed by careful job analyses.

> '(4) In view of the possibility of bias inherent in subjective evaluations, supervisory rating techniques should be carefully developed, and the ratings should be closely examined for evidence of bias. In addition, minorities might obtain unfairly low performance criterion scores for reasons other than supervisor's prejudice, as when, as new employees, they have had less opportunity to learn job skills. The general point is that all criteria need to be examined to insure freedom from factors which would unfairly depress the scores of minority groups.'

determine which ones (employees) they felt irrespective of the job that they were actually doing, but in their respective jobs, did a better job than the person they were rating against. . . .

There is no way of knowing precisely what criteria of job performance the supervisors were considering, whether each of the supervisors was considering the same criteria or whether, indeed, any of the supervisors actually applied a focused and stable body of criteria of any kind.[32] There is, in short, simply no way to determine whether the criteria actually considered were sufficiently related to the Company's legitimate interest in job-specific ability to justify a testing system with a racially discriminatory impact.

(3) The Company's study focused, in most cases, on job groups near the top of the various lines of progression. In *Griggs v. Duke Power Co., supra,* the Court left open 'the question whether testing requirements that take into account capability for the next succeeding position or related future promotion might be utilized upon a showing that such long-range requirements fulfill a genuine business need.' The Guidelines take a sensible approach to this issue, and we now endorse it:

> If job progression structures and seniority provisions are so established that new employees will probably, within a reasonable period of time and in a great majority of cases, progress to a higher level, it may be considered that candidates are being evaluated for jobs at that higher level. However, where job progression is not so nearly auto-

---

32. It cannot escape notice that Albemarle's study was conducted by plant officials, without neutral, on-the-scene oversight, at a time when this litigation was about to come to trial. Studies so closely controlled by an interested party in litigation must be examined with great care.

matic, or the time span is such that higher level jobs or employees' potential may be expected to change in significant ways, it shall be considered that candidates are being evaluated for a job at or near the entry level. 29 CFR § 1607.4(c)(1).

The fact that the best of those employees working near the top of a line of progression score well on a test does not necessarily mean that that test, or some particular cutoff score on the test, is a permissible measure of the minimal qualifications of new workers entering lower level jobs. In drawing any such conclusion, detailed consideration must be given to the normal speed of promotion, to the efficacy of on-the-job training in the scheme of promotion, and to the possible use of testing as a promotion device, rather than as a screen for entry into low-level jobs. The District Court made no findings on these issues. The issues take on special importance in a case, such as this one, where incumbent employees are permitted to work at even high-level jobs without passing the company's test battery.

(4) Albemarle's validation study dealt only with job-experienced, white workers; but the tests themselves are given to new job applicants, who are younger, largely inexperienced, and in many instances nonwhite. The APA Standards state that it is 'essential' that

'(t)he validity of a test should be determined on subjects who are at the age or in the same educational or vocational situation as the persons for whom the test is recommended in practice.'

The EEOC Guidelines likewise provide that '(d)ate must be generated and results separately reported for minority and nonminority groups wherever technically feasible.' 29 CFR § 1607.5(b)(5). In the present case, such 'differential validation' as to racial groups was very likely not 'feasible,' because years of discrimination at the plant have insured that nearly all of the upper level employees are white. But there has been no clear showing that differential validation was not feasible for lower level jobs. More importantly, the Guidelines provide:

'If it is not technically feasible to include minority employees in validation studies conducted on the present work force, the conduct of a validation study without minority candidates does not relieve any person of his subsequent obligation for validation when inclusion of minority candidates becomes technically feasible.' 29 CFR § 1607.5(b)(1).

'. . . (E)vidence of satisfactory validity based on other groups will be regarded as only provisional compliance with these guidelines pending separate validation of the test for the minority group in question.' 29 CFR § 1607.5(b)(5).

For all these reasons, we agree with the Court of Appeals that the District Court erred in concluding that Albemarle had proved the job relatedness of its testing program * * *. We also note that the Guidelines authorize provisional use of tests, pending new validation efforts, in certain very limited circumstances. 29 CFR § 1607.9. Whether such circumstances now obtain is a matter best decided, in the first instance, by the District Court. That court will be free to take such new evidence, and to exercise such control of the Company's use and validation of employee selection procedures, as are warranted by the circumstances and by the controlling law.

Accordingly, the judgment is vacated, and these cases are remanded to the District Court for proceedings consistent with this opinion.

NOTE

Criterion, or Predictive, Validity: Albermarle Paper and EEOC Guidelines accept a method of test validation that with some statistical accuracy predicts future job performance based on identified job performance criteria. This requires the employer to identify and measure with some precision major "criteria" for successful job performance. Performance of test takers is compared to their performance on the job. There must be a positive statistical correlation between their performance on the job as measured by the established criteria and the test scores that were used to select employees for that particular job. Positive correlation does not require precise 100% correlation; outliers are inevitable and do not undermine predictive reliability. The correlation must only be strong enough to predict with some accuracy an applicant's likelihood of success performing job duties. Secondly, the positive correlation must have "statistical significance," meaning that defendant must demonstrate that the positive correlation between test and job performance is not a product of chance, that chance has been mathematically eliminated as an explanation for the positive correlation between test and job performance. Once a test has been validated as predicting job performance it may be used to select future employees for that job, but only that job. The content of a test need have no relationship to the content of the job. The LSAT would be an example of a test having predictive validity for the selection of law students even though the test questions have nothing to do with law.

ASSOCIATION OF MEXICAN–AMERICAN EDUCATORS v. CALIFORNIA

United States Court of Appeals, Ninth Circuit (en banc), 2000
231 F.3d 572

GRABER, CIRCUIT JUDGE.

Plaintiffs are a class of Mexican–American, Asian–American, and African–American educators and would-be educators in California. They appeal from an adverse judgment in their action against the State of California and its agency, challenging (1) the district court's holding that the California Basic Education Skills Test ("CBEST"), which is a prerequisite to employment in a variety of positions in the California public schools, violates neither Title VI nor Title VII of the Civil Rights Act of 1964
* * *.

FACTUAL AND PROCEDURAL BACKGROUND

Effective February 1, 1983, the California legislature amended the California Education Code to prohibit the California Commission on Teacher Credentialing ("CCTC") from issuing "any credential, permit, certificate, or renewal of an emergency credential to any person to serve in the public schools unless the person has demonstrated proficiency in basic reading, writing, and mathematics skills." At the same time, the legislature authorized the state's Superintendent of Public Instruction to "adopt an appropriate state test to measure proficiency in these basic skills." The Superintendent adopted the CBEST and, in May 1983, CCTC assumed responsibility for administering and revising the test.

The CBEST is a pass-fail examination consisting of three sections: reading, writing, and mathematics. The reading and mathematics sections each contain 50 multiple-choice questions, 40 of which are scored. The writing section consists of two essays. The CBEST was revised in 1995. * * * At that time, questions that tested "higher order" mathematical skills, such as geometry, were eliminated from the mathematics section of the test.

To pass the CBEST, a candidate must receive a "scaled" score of 123. Accordingly, a candidate passes by averaging 41 points on each of the three sections (out of a score range of 20 to 80). A scaled score of 41 on the reading section translates into a raw score of 28 out of 40 questions correct; on the mathematics section, a scaled score of 41 equates to a raw score of 26 out of 40 correct. Each of the two essays is graded by two readers, who give raw scores of between one and four points per essay. Thus, the range of possible scores for the writing section is between four and 16 points. A raw score of 12 points translates into a scaled score of 41 points. The CBEST employs a "compensatory scoring" model, under which a candidate passes the test with a scaled score lower than 41 on a particular section, so long as his or her total scaled score is at least 123.

A passing score on the CBEST is required for all public elementary and secondary school teachers in California. A passing score also is required for many nonteaching employees of the California public schools, including administrators, school counselors, and school librarians.

Since the CBEST's inception, minority candidates have disproportionately received failing scores. * * *

* * *

On appeal, Plaintiffs argue (1) that the district court erred in concluding, after trial, that the CBEST was validated properly and (2) that the court violated <u>Federal Rule of Evidence 706</u> by relying on the advice of an expert who was not subject to cross-examination and did not prepare a report. * * *

DISCUSSION

I. *Title VII*

A. Title VII Applies to the CBEST

* * *

Plaintiffs and Defendants do not have a direct employment relationship. Rather, Plaintiffs are employees and potential employees of individual school districts in California. That fact does not end our inquiry, however. A direct employment relationship is not a prerequisite to Title VII liability. Although "there must be some connection with an employment relationship for Title VII protections to apply," that "connection with employment need not necessarily be direct."

Among other things, we have held that an entity that is not the direct employer of a Title VII plaintiff nevertheless may be liable if it " 'interferes with an individual's employment opportunities with another employer.' " In *Gomez*, we held that the defendant hospital could be held liable under Title VII for its discriminatory treatment of the plaintiff, notwithstanding the fact that the plaintiff was employed by a third party, if the defendant had interfered with the plaintiff's employment by that third party. * * *

In concluding that Title VII applies in this case, the district court held that Defendants "interfere[d]" with Plaintiffs' employment opportunities with local school districts in California by requiring, implementing, and administering the CBEST. We agree. * * * We turn next to the question whether the CBEST violates the provisions of that Act.

B. The District Court Did Not Clearly Err in Concluding that the CBEST Was Properly Validated.

"[D]iscriminatory tests are impermissible unless shown, by professionally acceptable methods, to be predictive of or significantly correlated with important elements of work behavior which comprise or are relevant to the job or jobs for which candidates are being evaluated." *Albemarle Paper Co. v. Moody.* * * *

Because Plaintiffs have established a prima facie case, the burden shifts to Defendants to demonstrate that the CBEST was validated properly.[7] In its detailed and careful opinion, the district court concluded that Defendants had met their burden and that the test had been validated properly based on three studies: (1) the 1982 Wheeler and Elias study; (2) the 1985 Practitioners' Review; and (3) the 1995 Lundquist study. Plaintiffs challenge that conclusion.

* * * The question whether a test has been validated properly is primarily a factual question, which depends on underlying factual determinations regarding the content and reliability of the validation studies that a defendant utilized. Consistent with Clady, we review for clear error the

---

7. In cases in which a defendant establishes that a test is validated properly, the burden shifts back to the plaintiff to show the existence of other selection devices that also would "serve the employer's legitimate interest in efficient and trustworthy workmanship," but that are not discriminatory. *Albemarle Paper.* Here, Plaintiffs' challenge is limited to the validation of the test; they do not attempt on appeal to meet their burden of demonstrating the existence of preferable selection devices, assuming that the CBEST is validated.

district court's determination in this case that the CBEST was validated properly.

To demonstrate that the CBEST was validated properly, Defendants are required to "show that it has 'a manifest relationship to the employment in question.'" In cases in which a scored test, like this one, is challenged, we require that the test be "job related"—that is, "that it actually measures skills, knowledge, or ability required for successful performance of the job." In making determinations about job-relatedness, we follow a three-step approach: The employer must first specify the particular trait or characteristic which the selection device is being used to identify or measure. The employer must then determine that the particular trait or characteristic is an important element of work behavior. Finally, the employer must demonstrate by "professionally acceptable methods" that the selection device is "predictive of or significantly correlated" with the element of work behavior identified in the second step.[8]

We will analyze each of those three steps in turn. In addition, we will consider Plaintiffs' argument that the passing score on the writing component of the CBEST is set too high.

1. *Specific Traits or Characteristics*

The first step of our inquiry is to identify the trait or characteristic that the test is designed to measure. Here, the district court found that the test was being used to measure "basic skills in reading, writing, and mathematics, and Plaintiffs do not dispute that finding.

2. *Important Elements of Work Behavior*

Next, we consider whether basic skills in reading, writing, and mathematics are "important element[s] of work behavior," the public school jobs for which the test is required. The district court found that the tested skills were important to the jobs at issue. Plaintiffs challenge that finding on three grounds. First, they argue that the 1985 Practitioners' Review failed to identify any particular work behaviors or job duties and thus could not be used to assess whether the CBEST measured important elements of work behavior. Second, they argue that Lundquist's 1995 study failed to distinguish "important" skills from skills that are less important. Third, they argue that Defendants failed to demonstrate that the CBEST is job-related for the particular positions for which it is required. We address each of those arguments in turn.

---

8. Also relevant to our inquiry are the Equal Employment Opportunity Commission's ("EEOC") Uniform Guidelines on Employee Selection Procedures ("Guidelines"), which are codified at 29 C.F.R. pt. 1607. Although the Guidelines are not legally binding, they are "entitled to great deference." Failure to comply with the Guidelines, although not automatically fatal to an employment test, "diminishes the probative value of the defendants' validation study." The studies on which Defendants rely were content validity studies. Such studies establish whether the content of a test approximates the knowledge, skills, or abilities that an applicant will use on the job. "Evidence of the validity of a test or other selection procedure by a content validity study should consist of data showing that the content of the selection procedure is representative of important aspects of performance on the job for which the candidates are to be evaluated."

Plaintiffs first argue that the 1985 Practitioners' Review, conducted by Dr. Richard Watkins, was inadequate because it failed to identify specific job duties to which the CBEST skills could be correlated. We conclude that the district court did not clearly err in finding that the 1985 study adequately identified the "element[s] of work behavior," that the CBEST is designed to measure.

The district court found that the Review comprised the "pooled judgments" of knowledgeable persons, such as incumbents in the jobs, "about the relevance of the skills tested on the CBEST to the jobs for which it is required, an appropriate form of a job analysis under the professional standards of the time." Specifically, the Practitioners' Review consulted 234 teachers, administrators, and other public school employees, 36 percent of whom were members of minority groups. "The participants took part in nine review panels, in which they judged the relevance of both the skills assessed by the CBEST and the test items themselves." They were asked to rate how relevant each of the CBEST skills would be to the work of four groups: (1) elementary school teachers; (2) secondary school teachers; (3) librarians, counselors, and attendance officers; and (4) school administrators. The possible ratings ranged from "not relevant" to "very relevant."

Thus, the Practitioners' Review was designed to learn from teachers, administrators, and other school employees the categories of skills that they considered relevant to their own jobs. The skills measured by the study tracked the categories of skills measured by the CBEST, and the skills were described in some detail on the rating forms used by the panel members. For example, the broad skill category * * *

We next consider Plaintiff's second challenge under the "important elements" prong * * *. Plaintiffs do not challenge the 1995 Lundquist study's methodology for identifying job-related skills. They do, however, challenge that study's method for determining which skills are "important" to particular jobs.

Dr. Lundquist polled experts and interviewed and observed educators in order to develop a list of activities and skills used by educators. She then polled 1,330 teachers and administrators, asking them to rate the importance of those activities and skills on a four-point scale from 0 ("not applicable") to 3 ("critical"). Activities and skills were retained only if "at least 80 percent of the survey respondents rated the activity or skill as applicable to the job and the mean importance rating was 1.5 or higher." Applying those standards led to elimination of a number of the activities and skills from Dr. Lundquist's list. * * * Dr. Lundquist then formulated new specifications for all three sections of the test. In response to those specifications, Defendants revised the CBEST before they administered the August 1995 test.

Plaintiffs focus on the fact that Dr. Lundquist retained activities and skills on her list if they received a "mean importance rating" of 1.5 on a scale that designated 2 as "important" and 1 as "minor." By using a mean rating of 1.5, Plaintiffs argue, Dr. Lundquist retained skills and activities that were rated as "less than important" by the study's participants. Therefore, their argument proceeds, the study violated the requirement * * *that only "important" work skills be measured.

The district court rejected Plaintiffs' argument, finding that "Dr. Lundquist's decisions reflect manifestly reasonable professional judgments * * *

We agree that it is theoretically possible to imagine a circumstance that illustrates Plaintiffs' concerns on this point. * * * Plaintiffs present only a theoretical possibility that such "highly relevant but unimportant" skills remained on Dr. Lundquist's list. * * *

Validation studies "are by their nature difficult, expensive, time consuming and rarely, if ever, free of error." Plaintiffs' argument demonstrates, at most, that Dr. Lundquist's study may not be totally free of error. But the argument does not persuade us that the district court clearly erred in relying on Dr. Lundquist's study.

Finally, Plaintiffs argue that Defendants failed to conduct job-specific studies to determine that the CBEST is "job related for the position [s] in question." The CBEST is not intended to measure all the skills that are relevant to all the jobs for which it is required. (Indeed, it does not purport to measure *all* the skills of *any* of the jobs for which it is required.) Rather, the CBEST is intended to establish only a minimum level of competence in three areas of basic educational skills. The question is whether the validation studies in this case have satisfied the requirement that those skills be "job related" for all the positions in question. The district court found that the validation studies adequately analyzed the CBEST in terms of both the teaching and nonteaching jobs for which the test is required. The district court did not clearly err in so finding.

Both the 1985 and the 1995 validation studies contained adequate consideration of the specific positions for which the CBEST is required. The 1985 Practitioners' Review defined the positions that it analyzed as (1) elementary school teachers, (2) secondary school teachers, (3) librarians, counselors, and attendance officers, and (4) school administrators. All participants in the study were asked to judge the relevance of the CBEST skills by category for those jobs. Because the study's participants were asked to determine the relevance of the basic skills measured by the CBEST to the disparate groups of positions for which the test is required, we cannot say that the district court clearly erred in finding the job analysis in the Practitioners' Review to be sufficiently specific and particularized.

* * *

In sum, we hold that the district court did not clearly err in finding that the skills measured by the CBEST are "important element[s] of work behavior" with regard to the jobs for which the test is required.

3. *Actual Measurement of Skills*

The final step in this court's three-step analysis * * * is to determine whether Defendants have demonstrated by "professionally acceptable methods that the selection device is predictive of or significantly correlated with the element of work behavior" that it is designed to measure. The district court concluded that "the CBEST actually measures ... basic skills [in reading, writing, and mathematics]." Plaintiffs claim that the district court simply accepted the "facial" validity of the CBEST without any evidence that it actually measures the basic skills that it purports to test.

* * * "[A] key requirement of [the] third step, a requirement essential to proof of job relatedness generally, is that the validation method be professionally acceptable." Here, there is evidence in the record from an expert, Dr. William A. Mehrens, that supports the district court's findings on this issue. Dr. Mehrens reported:

> ETS [Educational Testing Service] personnel wrote some of the original items and assisted the test development committees in writing other items. ETS is well known and respected as a developer of standardized tests. They have well trained item writers and an impressive internal set of guidelines they follow with respect to item writing.

When asked whether "the CBEST development [was] appropriate with respect to writing and evaluating the items," he reported:

> It has been. Many of the items came from an existing ETS pool. Others were written specifically for CBEST by members of the test development committee in concert with ETS test development specialists. The individuals on the committees worked with specialists from ETS to further develop and define the content specifications, to review an existing ETS pool test item, to write new test items, and to review the items submitted by fellow committee members. In addition, the committees studied all of the data from the field testing, made recommendations for revisions as they felt necessary, and reviewed all final test results.

There also is additional evidence in the record that the test questions were "matched" to the skills that they were intended to measure. The district court referred to the "Curriculum Matching Project, in which two ETS employees matched CBEST test specifications to material found in textbooks purportedly used in the California public schools. The district court was somewhat critical of this study, but noted that "the study did support the overall conclusion that the kinds of skills tested on the CBEST can be found in elementary and secondary school textbooks."

In short, there is evidence-even if not overwhelming evidence-that the development and evaluation of the CBEST were appropriate and that the test measures the types of skills that it was designed to measure. We therefore hold that the district court did not clearly err in concluding that the test questions had been shown by professionally acceptable methods to be "predictive of or significantly correlated with the element of work behavior" that they were designed to measure.

In sum, we hold that the district court did not clearly err in concluding that the CBEST was validated properly.

4. *Standards for Passing Scores*

Plaintiffs also argue that the 12–out–of–16 passing score on the writing section of the CBEST is too high. According to Plaintiffs, the 1982 Wheeler and Elias study demonstrates that the proper passing score is 9 or 10 out of 16.

An employer is not required to validate separately the selection of particular passing scores on an employment test. Rather, the EEOC's Guidelines more generally provide: "Where cutoff scores are used, they should normally be set so as to be reasonable and consistent with normal expectations of acceptable proficiency within the work force." 29 C.F.R. § 1607.5(H). This court previously has applied that standard. In analyzing the Guidelines' scoring requirement, the Second Circuit has stated that an employer "might establish a valid cutoff score by using a professional estimate of the requisite ability levels, or, at the very least, by analyzing the test results to locate a logical 'break-point' in the distribution of scores." Guardians Ass'n of New York City Police Dep't, Inc. v. Civil Serv. Comm'n of New York, 630 F.2d 79, 105 (2d Cir.1980).

Here, the district court found that "the passing scores on the CBEST reflect reasonable judgments about the minimum level of basic skills competence that should be required of teachers. The evidence before the court revealed that the California Superintendent of Public Instruction, who was responsible for establishing the cutoff scores, relied on polling data created as part of the Wheeler and Elias study in setting the cutoff for the writing section of the test. As part of that study, 44 readers reviewed approximately 6,800 CBEST essays and made recommendations regarding the cutoff between passing and failing scores. The readers *unanimously* agreed that a raw score of 12 out of 16 was a "passing" score. Approximately 80 percent of the readers agreed that a score of 11 out of 16 could be a "passing" score. On that basis, the Superintendent established a passing score of 12 out of 16, with an absolute minimum of 11 out of 16 under the "compensatory scoring" system.

Those cutoff scores represent a "logical breakpoint" between passing and failing scores. Plaintiffs argue that the breakpoint should have been set at 9 or 10 out of 16, because a majority of the readers opined that 10 out of 16 was a "passing" score. But the Superintendent was not required to set the score at the lowest level that a majority of the readers considered to be "passing." Rather, he was required to set a cutoff that was logical, reasonable, and consistent with the data before him. He chose to set the cutoff at a level that all the readers agreed was "passing," and to set an absolute minimum at a level that 80 percent of the readers thought was "passing." The district court found that the Superintendent's decision to set the cutoff score at that level was consistent with the EEOC's Guidelines. We conclude that the district court did not clearly err in so finding.

* * *

AFFIRMED.

REINHARDT, CIRCUIT JUDGE, with whom CIRCUIT JUDGES SCHROEDER and THOMAS join, concurring in part and dissenting in part:

* * * I cannot agree with the majority's holding that the CBEST was properly validated under Title VII. * * * Despite Title VII's clear requirement that a test that has a disparate impact on minorities must be validated by reference to a particular job, the majority accepts validation studies that fail to differentiate among different school jobs, ranging from bilingual education teachers to mathematics teachers to physical education teachers. Further, even though Title VII demands that the defendants demonstrate "by professionally acceptable methods" that the test items are predictive of or significantly correlated to job-related skills, the majority finds that the CBEST met this requirement through a study that the district court found to be "unscientific" and "not particularly helpful."

* * *

The majority states that the CBEST establishes only "a minimum level of competence" in skills that are job related for all the positions in question. While it *may* be possible to construct a test that measures skills relevant for *all* teachers, *Albemarle* holds that such a test may only be used if it has been validated for each "particular job" involved or if there are "no significant differences" among the jobs at issue.

As the majority notes, the third step * * * requires employers to "demonstrate by 'professionally acceptable methods' that the selection device is 'predictive of or significantly correlated' with the element of work behavior identified [by the job analysis]." In other words, the employer must demonstrate not only that the skills identified in the job analysis are job related, but also that the test items actually measure those skills. * * * Here, even assuming that the job analysis was sufficiently specific to generate skills important for all the positions in question, the CBEST is invalid because the CTC failed to demonstrate in a professionally acceptable manner that the test actually measures the skills identified in the job analysis.

The majority appears to concede that neither the Practitioner's Review study nor the Lundquist study attempted to match the test items to the job skills as required. To support the district court's finding of validity, the majority cites evidence describing the process of test development employed by ETS. However, this evidence merely purports to show that the test items were expertly developed; it does *not* demonstrate * * * that the final version of the CBEST administered to job applicants is "predictive of or significantly correlated" with the skills identified in the job analysis as important for the job. Where an employer seeks to use a test that has a disparate impact on minorities, it must present evidence that the test actually measures the skills that have been identified as important for the job, and may not rely solely on the fact that it used a "well known and respected as a developer of standardized tests."

As evidence that the test questions were "matched" to the skills they were intended to measure, the majority points only to the Curriculum Matching Project, in which two ETS employees matched CBEST test specifications to material found in textbooks purportedly used in California public schools. The district court criticized this study as "unscientific" and "not particularly helpful," but nevertheless upheld the test. We have explicitly held that it is "essential" that the item validation method be professionally acceptable. "Unscientific" and "not particularly helpful" tests clearly do not meet that standard. Thus, even under a clear error standard, the district court's determination that step three * * * was satisfied requires reversal.

* * *

NOTES

1. *"Content Validity:"* The principal case illustrates the difficulty of validating tests that claim to have "content validity," in that the test itself attempts to measure critical elements of the job. Note that this methodology shares with "criterion validity" the problem of identifying and measuring critical elements of the job. But content validity tests performance of job elements, without reference to subsequent measurement of actual job performance. Thus, while typing may be skill needed by police officers to complete reports or legal documents, it would not be considered a skill critical to the officer's job. *See, Blake v. City of Los Angeles,* 595 F.2d 1367 (9th Cir. 1979). Common illustrations of content validity would be driving tests to select bus drivers and word processing efficiency tests to select administrative assistants. Bar examinations and medical board tests are further examples of tests asserting content validity. Content validation is used where it is relatively easy to identify job skills or necessary knowledge and it is difficult to measure actual performance on the job.

2. *Cut off v. Rank Order:* The principal case illustrates how setting minimum passing scores is arbitrary. Different issues are presented where the test is relied upon to select applicants on the rank order of their test performance. To illustrate, when a job regularly requires lifting of no more than 50 pounds, a test measuring the applicants' ability to lift 50 pounds would be content valid. However, if the employer selected an applicant who could lift 65 pounds over an applicant who could lift only 55 pounds, it would not be relying on content validity in that the employer is using the test to measure an ability that is not needed for the job. In the principal case, what if school systems selected teachers based on their rank order score on the CBEST test? Valid? Assuming adverse impact of such a practice, and that a college degree is deemed to have content validity for the particular job, is

selecting employees based on their college grade point averages or class rank a content valid practice?

3. *Dangerous or professional jobs:* Courts have been less demanding of precise validation where the jobs are professional (e.g., teachers or lawyers) or where unsatisfactory performance presents risks of harm to third persons (e.g., police officers, airplane crew, firefighters). ***Washington v. Davis,*** 426 U.S. 229, 96 S.Ct. 2040, 48 L.Ed.2d 597 (1976), for example, allowed a police department to use an examination that generally predicted a cadet's success in police academy even though the test had not been professionally validated as to actual on-job performance as a police officer. In *Lanning v. SEPTA,* 308 F.3d 286 (3d Cir. 2002), a test was given to applicants for transit police officer positions that required the candidate to run 1.5 miles in less than 12 minutes. Experts testified that such a test established a minimal aerobic capacity, and on this basis the court concluded that it was important for law enforcement officers to have this level of aerobic fitness even though the test measured but one aspect of the officer's job and was not required of current officers or those seeking promotions.

3. "BUSINESS NECESSITY" OF OBJECTIVE, NON–SCORED DEVICES

HAWKINS v. ANHEUSER–BUSCH, INC.

United States Court of Appeals, Eighth Circuit, 1983
697 F.2d 810

HEANEY, CIRCUIT JUDGE.

* * *

I.

BACKGROUND

Hawkins was initially employed by Anheuser–Busch on February 15, 1967 as a junior secretary (grade 4). Her duties were primarily clerical. In April of 1971, after a maternity leave, she was rehired as a junior secretary in the Operations Material Control Department.

* * *

In June of 1979, trades returns supervisor Forbes was transferred to a new position within the company. Again, Hawkins applied for the supervisor position, and again she was denied the promotion. The job was given to Thomas Sanders, a white male with a B.S. degree in management science. * * *

Hawkins relies on a disparate impact theory to support her claim that she was discriminatorily denied the trade returns supervisor position. Specifically, Hawkins contends that the requirement that applicants for the trade returns supervisor position have a college degree in business, industrial engineering, materials management, or a related field had a disparate impact on women.

* * *

Assuming, without deciding, that Hawkins established her prima facie case, the burden of persuasion shifted to the defendant to prove that the college degree requirement was justified by business necessity. To establish the business necessity defense, Anheuser–Busch carries a heavy burden. It must demonstrate that the college degree requirement had "a manifest relationship to the employment in question." A discriminatory employment practice cannot be "justified by routine business considerations;" the employer must demonstrate that there is a *"compelling need* * * * to maintain that practice."

The district court held that Anheuser–Busch established that its college degree requirement was justified by business necessity. While this Court might have reached a contrary result had it been the fact-finder, we cannot say that the district court's decision was a clearly erroneous one.

An employer cannot rely on purely conclusory testimony by company personnel to prove that a college degree is job-related and required by business necessity. Although Anheuser–Busch presented such testimony here, it did not rely exclusively on it. Its witnesses testified at length concerning the reasons why the college degree requirement was job-related and justified by business necessity.

A validation study would have strengthened the company's case. It is the preferred type of evidence in a disparate impact case. We cannot say, however, that validation studies are always required, and we are not willing to hold under the facts of this case that such evidence was required here.

Once the employer met its burden of demonstrating that the educational requirement was justified by business necessity, the plaintiff then had to show that another employment practice, which did not produce a similar discriminatory impact, would satisfy "the employer's legitimate interest in 'efficient and trustworthy workmanship.' " When the employer is shown an alternative selection method that has substantial validity and less adverse impact, it must choose the less discriminatory method. Uniform Guidelines on Employee Selection Procedures, 29 C.F.R. § 1607.3(B).

Here, Hawkins contended that her experience performing all or substantially all of the duties of the trade returns supervisor was an adequate alternative to the college degree requirement. We agree that such on-the-job experience with the company, if proven, would be a less-discriminatory alternative to the degree requirement, and that Anheuser–Busch would have had to recognize this selection method if it was available. The district court, however, found, that * * * Hawkins had not performed all, or even substantially all, of the duties of the trade returns supervisor during her tenure with Anheuser–Busch.

Although Hawkins testified that she in fact had performed all such duties, the company's witnesses testified that the supervisory functions performed by the plaintiff were at the direction and under the supervision of her superiors. They further testified that Hawkins did not make supervisory decisions, but rather executed the decisions made by her superiors. In light of this contradictory testimony, we cannot say, after carefully reviewing the record as a whole, that the district court erred in concluding that Hawkins had not been performing the principal duties of the trade returns supervisor prior to the time she was rejected for that position. Since Hawkins advanced no other selection criteria than her own previous experience, she has not shown that Anheuser–Busch had available an alternative selection method that was valid and less discriminatory than its degree requirement. Accordingly, we hold that the district court did not err in finding against Hawkins on her trade returns supervisor claim.

NOTE

Lesser Discriminatory Alternatives (again): The 1991 Amendments leave unclear what role, if any, is played by the presence of alternative selection devices that served the employer's business needs equally well but had less of a discriminatory effect on the protected class. 42 U.S.C. § 2000e–2((k)(1)(A) provides:

> An unlawful employment practice based on disparate impact is established under this title only if—* * *

> (ii) the complaining party makes the demonstration in subparagraph (C) with respect to an alternative employment practice and the respondent refuses to adopt such alternative employment practice.

Subparagraph (C) states:

> The demonstration referred to by subparagraph (A)(ii) shall be in accordance with law as it existed on June 4, 1989 with respect to the concept of "alternative employment practices."

This suggests that, rather than being an element of "business necessity," or even evidence of improper motive in implementing the device, the unlawful employment practice flows from the employer's refusal to adopt a lesser discriminatory alternative that the employee has suggested. *See, Adams v. City of Chicago,* 469 F.3d 609 (7th Cir. 2006).

BRADLEY v. PIZZACO OF NEBRASKA

United States Court of Appeals, Eighth Circuit, 1993
7 F.3d 795

BOWMAN, CIRCUIT JUDGE.

* * *

I.

The EEOC appeals a judgment entered in favor of defendants Pizzaco of Nebraska, Inc., and Domino's Pizza, Inc. (collectively "Domino's"). This action arose out of a Title VII employment discrimination claim brought by Langston Bradley, a former Domino's delivery man. Bradley alleged that Domino's discriminated against him on the basis of race when it fired him for failure to appear clean-shaven in compliance with the company's no-beard policy. The no-beard policy is established nationwide by Pizzaco's franchisor, Domino's Pizza, Inc. Bradley alleged that he suffered from pseudofolliculitis barbae ("PFB"), a skin condition affecting approximately fifty percent of African American males, half of which number cannot shave at all. Bradley claimed that the no-beard policy deprived him and other African American males suffering from PFB of equal employment opportunities in violation of Title VII of the Civil Rights Act of 1964.

After a trial of the entire case, including the question of Domino's business justification for its strict no-beard policy, the District Court ruled in favor of Domino's, finding that Bradley and the EEOC failed to show the no-beard policy has a disparate impact on African American males. The court's opinion did not reach the business justification issue. On appeal, in *Bradley v. Pizzaco of Neb., Inc (I)*, we reversed the District Court's finding of no disparate impact. We held that the evidence presented by the EEOC clearly established a prima facie case of disparate impact on African American males and that the District Court erred in finding otherwise. * * *

The EEOC contends that the record conclusively demonstrates that Domino's has failed to show business justification under *Griggs* for its inflexible no-beard policy and that we need not remand to the District Court for a determination of that issue. We agree.* * *

We apply *Griggs* to Domino's evidence concerning the business justification defense. Domino's offered the testimony of Paul D. Black, Domino's vice president for operations. Black said it was "common sense" that "the better our people look, the better our sales will be." Black also cited a public opinion survey indicating that up to twenty percent of customers would "have a negative reaction" to a delivery person wearing a beard. Further, Black speculated that Domino's would encounter difficulty enforcing any exceptions to their dress and grooming code. Black did not offer evidence of any particular exception that was tried without success; rather, he merely stated that monitoring the hair length and moustaches of employees at five thousand Domino's locations is difficult.

Black's testimony was largely speculative and conclusory. Such testimony, without more, does not prove the business necessity of maintaining the strict no-beard policy. "An employer cannot rely on purely conclusory testimony by company personnel to prove that a [challenged practice] is job-related and required by business necessity."

In addition to Black's testimony, Domino's offered the results of a public opinion survey it commissioned. The survey purported to measure public reaction to beards on pizza shop employees. The survey showed that up to twenty percent of those surveyed would react negatively to a delivery man wearing a beard. Even if the survey results indicated a significant customer apprehension regarding beards, which they do not, the results would not constitute evidence of a sufficient business justification defense for

Domino's strict no-beard policy. Although this Circuit has not directly addressed customer preference as a business justification for policies having a disparate impact on a protected class, cases from other circuits have not looked favorably on this kind of evidence. *See Diaz v. Pan Am. World Airways, Inc.,* 442 F.2d 385, 388–89 (5th Cir.) (customer preference may only be taken into account when it goes to a matter affecting the company's ability to perform the primary necessary function or service it offers, rather than a tangential aspect of that service or function),; *Gerdom v. Continental Airlines, Inc.,* 692 F.2d 602 (9th Cir.1982) (holding that customer preference for slim female flight attendants did not justify a discriminatory policy where weight was unrelated to job performance). The existence of a beard on the face of a delivery man does not affect in any manner Domino's ability to make or deliver pizzas to their customers. Customer preference, which is at best weakly shown by Domino's survey, is clearly not a colorable business justification defense in this case. Significantly, the survey makes no showing that customers would order less pizza in the absence of a strictly enforced no-beard rule.

* * * Domino's has * * * failed to prove a compelling need for the strict no-beard policy as applied to those afflicted with PFB and has failed to present any evidence suggesting that the current policy is without workable alternatives or that it has a manifest relationship to the employment in question. Domino's is free to establish any grooming and dress standards it wishes; we hold only that reasonable accommodation must be made for members of the protected class who suffer from PFB. We note that the burden of a narrow medical exception for African American males who cannot shave because of PFB appears minimal. The employer, of course, should not be precluded from requiring that any beards permitted under this narrow medical exception be neatly trimmed, clean, and not in excess of a specified length.

We reverse the District Court's finding of business justification for Domino's no-beard policy as applied to PFB sufferers and remand to the District Court for entry of an injunction granting the EEOC the narrow prospective relief it seeks. The injunction shall be carefully tailored to place Domino's under the minimal burden of recognizing a limited exception to its no-beard policy for African American males who suffer from PFB and as a result of this medical condition are unable to shave. * * *

NOTES

1. *Content valid credentials:* Objective requirements that have a strong content relationship to the job are generally accepted as being job related without defendant providing professional validation studies. Thus, for example, a library degree for librarians, an education degree for a teacher, a law degree for an attorney, all would be "content valid" credentials. Consider again using class rank as either a minimum credential ("applicants must be in top 20% of their class"), or basing decisions on relative grade point averages of the applicants.

2. *Risks of harm: Griggs v. Duke Power Co., supra,* rejected the possession of a high school diploma for manual workers as being "job related." Nonetheless, **Spurlock v. United Airlines, Inc.,** 475 F.2d 216 (10th Cir. 1972), in sustaining both experience and educational minima for airline pilots explained:

> When a job requires a small amount of skill and training and the consequences of hiring an unqualified applicant are insignificant, the courts should examine closely any pre-employment standard or criteria which disproportionately discriminates against minorities * * * On the other hand, when the job clearly requires a high degree of skill, and the economic and human risks involved in hiring an unqualified applicant are great, the employer bears a correspondingly lighter burden to show that his employment criteria are job related.

Thus, general educational requirements for public safety officers have been sustained. *Davis v. Dallas,* 777 F.2d 205 (5th Cir. 1985). Where facial hair might present a risk that a firefighter might not be able to perform his job without risk, not only to himself, but to others, "clean shaven" has been held to be a "business necessity." *Fitzpatrick v. City of Atlanta,* 2 F.3d 1112 (11th Cir. 1993). In semi-skilled jobs, such as driving a "big rig" truck, the requirement of "prior experience" was accepted as being "job related." *Kilgo v. Bowman Transp. Co.,* 789 F.2d 859 (11th Cir. 1986).

4. "BUSINESS NECESSITY" OF SUBJECTIVE SYSTEMS

WATSON v. FORT WORTH BANK & TRUST, 487 U.S. 977, 108 S.Ct. 2777, 101 L.Ed.2d 827 (1988):

* * *

We are persuaded that our decisions in *Griggs* and succeeding cases could largely be nullified if disparate impact analysis were applied only to standardized selection devices. * * * We are also persuaded that disparate impact analysis is in principle no less applicable to subjective employment criteria than to objective or standardized tests.

* * *

The plaintiff must begin by identifying the specific employment practice that is challenged. Although this has been relatively easy to do in challenges to standardized tests, it may sometimes be more difficult when subjective selection criteria are at issue. * * * [T]he plaintiff is in our view responsible for isolating and identifying the specific employment practices that are allegedly responsible for any observed statistical disparities.

Once the employment practice at issue has been identified, causation must be proved; that is, the plaintiff must offer statistical evidence of a kind and degree sufficient to show that the practice in question has caused the exclusion of applicants for jobs or promotions because of their membership in a protected group. Our formulations, which have never been framed in terms of any rigid mathematical formula, have consistently stressed that statistical disparities must be sufficiently substantial that they raise such an inference of causation. * * *

A second constraint on the application of disparate impact theory lies in the nature of the "business necessity" or "job relatedness" defense. * * * Factors such as costs or other burdens of proposed alternative selection devices are relevant in determining whether they would be equally effective as the challenged device in serving the employer's legitimate business goals. * * *

In the context of subjective or discretionary employment decision, the employer will often find it easier than in the case of standardized tests to produce evidence of a 'manifest relationship to the employment in question.' It is self-evident that many jobs, for example those involving managerial responsibilities, require personal qualities that have never been considered amenable to standardized testing. In evaluating claims that discretionary employment practices are insufficiently related to legitimate business purposes, it must be borne in mind that 'courts are generally less competent than employers to restructure business practices * * *. Some qualities—for example, common sense, good judgment, originality, ambition, [L]oyalty, and tact—cannot be measured accurately through standardized testing techniques. Moreover, success at many jobs in which such qualities are crucial cannot itself be measured directly. Opinions often differ when managers and supervisors are evaluated, and the same can be said for many jobs that involve close cooperation with one's co-workers or complex and subtle tasks like the provision of professional services or personal counseling.

'It would be a most radical interpretation of Title VII for a court to enjoin use of an historically settled process and plainly relevant criteria largely because they lead to decisions which are difficult for a court to review.'

NOTES

Subjective Prejudice: Lesser Discriminatory Alternatives and Evidence of Pretext (again!) Where subjective selection is unavoidable—even necessary— the employer may be faced with the follow-up argument that the unchecked discretion of the individual white-male decision-maker is producing adverse effects that are unjustified when the impact of unchecked subjectivity could be reduced or eliminated by systems that include checks to insure that subjective evaluations are made as free as possible from conscious or unconscious considerations of race, sex, age or disability. This can be accomplished by the employer setting standardized interview criteria, uniformly followed; use of multiple interviewers who are balanced by race, sex, and age; numerical scoring of responses; requiring interviewers to explain their scores; recommendations reviewed by a decision-maker who does not know the race, sex and age of the candidates. Absence of such safeguards can be seen either as proof that the unchecked system was not "necessary," or that failure to implement such known checks against prejudice is itself a violation. Some authority indicates, however, that rather than establishing lack of necessity, undue subjectivity lacking safeguards is merely evidence of a pretextual motive. *See, Torgerson v. City of Rochester,* 605 F.3d 584 (8th Cir. 2010).

To illustrate, no one would deny that a high degree of subjective judgment is necessary in selecting musicians for an orchestra. Nonetheless, there are documented examples where unguarded subjectivity produced an adverse impact on highly capable women musicians. However, when physical screens were used to hide the identity of the musicians being auditioned, there were dramatically different outcomes, producing more women in orchestras and presumably better orchestras. *See, M. Gladwell, "Blink" pp. 245–54 (Back Bay Books, 2005).*

CHAPTER 8

PROVING DISPARATE TREATMENT

■ ■ ■

A. INTRODUCTION: A MATTER OF EVIDENCE

The statutes require that discrimination against the plaintiff be "because of" plaintiff's classification. Plaintiff carries the ultimate burden of proving that critical element for defendant's liability. When the defendant establishes policy differences between protected classes, as in the cases of *Los Angeles Power v. Manhart, supra, page* 291 (sex-based retirement benefits) and *Johnson Controls, supra, page* 51 (refusal to hire fertile women), the differences are apparent on the face of the rule or policy, truncating any need to establish the defendant's motive behind the policy or action. However, when the distinction made by the employer is neutral on its face and plaintiff asserts an invidious motivation for the distinction, while defendant counters that its actions were based on elements not proscribed by the statutes, the factual issue of defendant's motive is joined. Review, *supra* pages 307–313.

In embarking on this inquiry two facts will be critical: (1) defendant's state of mind or animus, and (2) whether the action was "because of" or motivated by the animus. Both facts are extremely difficult, if not impossible, to determine with certainty. Nonetheless, they are questions of fact to be resolved by the jury. Here employment discrimination law merges with the complex law of evidence. There are various methods a plaintiff might use in establishing defendant's state of mind and that plaintiff's treatment was "because of" that state of mind:

1. Direct evidence: Oral or written evidence, which, if credited, tends to prove the issue in question without reliance upon an inference or presumption. True "direct evidence" is tantamount to an expressed, facial policy; it is a statement or confession by defendant that proscribed animus caused the challenged treatment.

2. "A convincing mosaic" of circumstantial evidence which may consist of:

    a. Suspicious timing of the employer's actions,

b. Behavior toward or comments directed at plaintiff and other persons in plaintiff's protected class indicating a class animus (but requiring an inference that the animus motivated the challenged decision),

c. "Bits and pieces" of evidence from which an inference of discriminatory intent might be drawn, including ambiguous comments, adverse treatment of other members of plaintiff's class, failure to follow traditional procedures, and suspicious numerical imbalances,

d. Better treatment of similarly situated persons outside plaintiff's protected class than the treatment accorded plaintiff,

e. The reason given for the adverse treatment of plaintiff was inconsistent or appeared pretextual,

f. Statistical methodology eliminating chance as an explanation for defendant's behavior.

B. VERBAL EVIDENCE

KING v. HARDESTY

United States Court of Appeals, Eighth Circuit, 2008
517 F.3d 1049

SMITH, CIRCUIT JUDGE.

* * *

Within three days of beginning her employment [with the co-defendant District school system]* * * Hardesty [plaintiff's supervisor] began making racial remarks to [plaintiff] King. Among other things, King claims that Hardesty: (1) asked King if she had white in her blood because she was light-skinned; (2) told King that his family had been slaveholders; (3) told King that "white people teach black kids, African–American students, better than someone from their own race"; (4) asked King how she felt about the word "nigger" and used the word in King's presence; (5) asked King if she dated white males and said "once you go black, you never go back"; (6) told racial jokes in the office; (7) referred to African–American male employees as "big black bucks" and "my boys"; (8) referred to African–American students as "slaves," "crack babies," and "ghetto kids"; (9) used the words "ho" and "whore" to refer to female African–American students; and (10) made racially derogatory statements about the parents of African–American students. King was offended by Hardesty's comments and asked him, on multiple occasions, to refrain from making such comments, but Hardesty would respond: "I can run this school any way I want to"; "no one questions my actions because I am the administrator"; or "I can run [the school] any damn way I please."

* * * "At the summary judgment stage, the issue is whether the plaintiff has sufficient evidence that unlawful discrimination was *a* motivating factor in the defendant's adverse employment action. If so, the presence of additional legitimate motives will not entitle the defendant[s] to summary judgment." "Therefore, evidence of additional motives, and the question whether the presence of mixed motives defeats all or some part of plaintiff's claim, are trial issues, not summary judgment issues." "Evidence of the employer's motives for the action, and whether the presence of ... mixed motives defeats the plaintiff's claim, is a trial issue, not intended for summary judgment".

The district court acknowledged that Hardesty had made offensive racial remarks to King, but concluded that nothing in the record created an inference that Hardesty's racial animus motivated any adverse employment action suffered by King. * * *

Price Waterhouse defined the term "direct evidence" negatively to exclude "stray remarks in the workplace," "statements by nondecisionmakers," or "statements by decisionmakers unrelated to the decisional process itself." *Price Waterhouse,* 490 U.S. at 277, 109 S.Ct. 1775 (O'Connor, J., concurring). We have held that direct evidence within the meaning of *Price Waterhouse* may include "evidence of actions or remarks of the employer that reflect a discriminatory attitude," "comments which demonstrate a discriminatory animus in the decisional process," or comments "uttered by individuals closely involved in employment decisions." Given these benchmarks, we hold that the district court erred in finding that King had not provided any direct evidence of discrimination and by not analyzing King's termination and nonassignment of homebound instruction claims under the *Price Waterhouse* approach.

Many of Hardesty's alleged racial comments fall into the "stray remarks" or "statements by decisionmakers unrelated to the decisional process" categories of comments that are insufficient for a finding of direct evidence; however, we conclude that Hardesty's statement to King—an African–American teacher—that "white people teach black kids ... better than someone from their own race," is evidence that may be viewed as directly reflecting Hardesty's alleged discriminatory attitude. With such evidence, the factfinder could find that a discriminatory attitude was more likely than not a motivating factor in Hardesty's decisions because Hardesty may believe white teachers on the basis of their race would do a better job than King, an African–American. *See* Browning v. President Riverboat Casino–Missouri, Inc., 139 F.3d 631, 635 (8th Cir.1998) (holding that supervisor's "reference to [plaintiff] as 'that white boy' in context of [plaintiff's] employment warrant[ed] an inference of discriminatory attitude sufficient to permit the factfinder to conclude that race was a motivating factor in the subsequent decision to terminate [plaintiff]").[8]

---

8. See also Stacks v. Southwestern Bell Yellow Pages, Inc., 27 F.3d 1316, 1324 (8th Cir.1994) (holding that supervisor's comment that "women were the worst thing that had happened to this company" was direct evidence that an illegitimate criteria (gender) was a motivating factor in company's adverse employment action against plaintiff, even though the statement was not made during the decisional process); EEOC v. Alton Packaging Corp., 901 F.2d 920, 924 (11th Cir.1990) (holding manager's statement that "if it were his company he would not hire blacks" was direct evidence of discrimination in plaintiff's failure to promote claim; statement indicated "a decidedly negative attitude toward black people" on the part of a decisionmaker and there was "no reason to think [his] attitude[ ] differ[ed] from hiring to promotion").

Following King's termination, her former student was placed into a white teacher's classroom. Hardesty's "white people teach black kids better" comment revealed "a decidedly negative attitude toward [African–American] people on the part of [a person] responsible for [the employment decision]."

Therefore, we conclude that the district court erred in finding that King had not adduced direct evidence that race *was a* motivating factor in Hardesty's decision to terminate her from Bearfield [assignments] and not assign her homebound instructions hours. We reverse the summary judgment on those claims and remand them for further proceedings because "evidence of additional motives, and the question whether the presence of mixed motives defeats all or some part of plaintiff's claim, are trial issues, not summary judgment issues."

King did not produce direct evidence for her remaining discrimination claims: the District's failure to pay her the long-term substitute rate, failure to assign her substitute teaching assignments, and failure to hire her as a home school communicator. She also did not establish that Hardesty [who had made the offending remarks] was a decisionmaker or that he was involved in the decisionmaking processes relating to these claims. Thus, King failed to establish any direct evidence in support of those claims * * *.

NOTES

1. *Four Levels:* Courts will view plaintiff's verbal evidence on four levels:

a. *Are the Words Admissible?* The court must initially determine whether the proffered verbal evidence is relevant, and if so, does its probative value outweigh unwarranted impact on the fact finder. Trial courts have wide discretion in determining admissibility of evidence deemed to be unduly prejudicial. *"Stray Remarks"* is the label often given to words that have little, if any, probative value but could inflame the jury to an unwarranted prejudice.

(i) *Decision-maker?* Comments made by persons other than the person responsible for plaintiff's treatment often are excluded as lacking probative value, particularly when balanced against possible misinterpretation by a jury. *Girten v. McRentals,* 337 F.3d 979 (8th Cir. 2003).

(ii) *Evaluative?* Comments that refer to sex, race, or age seen as "descriptive," rather than "evaluative," may be excluded as having little probative value and can be misleading, if not inflammatory. Only pejorative or "evaluative" use of terms carries an inference that the speaker harbors a significant animus against plaintiff's class. For example: describing an incident that involved a "very large, very strong, very muscular black man" allegedly attempting to intimidate "three smaller white men" was held to be descriptive of an event and non-indicative of a racial animus. *Evans v. McClain of Georgia, Inc.,* 131 F.3d 957 (11th Cir. 1997). Referring to the defendant as an "old fart" was seen as a common descriptive colloquialism that did not evidence age animus. *Montgomery v.*

John Deere & Co., 169 F.3d 556 (8th Cir. 1999). Even the pejorative "bitch" was seen by one court as a descriptive "opinion" that did not disclose an animus against women. *Neuren v. Adduci, Mastriani, Meeks & Schill,* 43 F.3d 1507 (D.C.Cir. 1995). However, derogatory references, not directed at the plaintiff and not used to describe the challenged action, such as referring to Italian–Americans generally as "dirty wops," or to Chinese as "chinks" are admissible indicia of the speaker's mind set from which an impermissible motive for the challenged action might be inferred. *DiCarlo v. Potter,* 358 F.3d 408 (6th Cir. 2004).

(iii) *Temporal Proximity?* Even evaluative remarks such as strong racist insults, when isolated in nature or uttered at a time contextually removed from the decision making process, may be excluded. The issue before the judge will be whether the probative value of remote, isolated, or out-of context expletives are outweighed by the potential inflammatory impact they would have on the jury. For example, use of the expletive "nigger" four years earlier was seen as a "stray remark" and properly excluded from jury consideration. *Manning v. Chevron Chemical Co., LLC,* 332 F.3d 874 (5th Cir. 2003). "Old grey haired fart" made a year earlier was a "stray remark" not sufficient to create a jury issue when the 69 year old plaintiff was dismissed. *Jackson v. Cal-Western Packaging Co.,* 602 F.3d 374 (5th Cir. 2010).

b. Were the words said? The employer may deny that the words introduced by plaintiff were even uttered. When the employer denies making the statement this factual issue must be resolved. Only if the fact finder concludes that the words in fact were said will the inquiry continue.

c. Are the words sufficient to support a verdict? Remarks admitted into evidence may be insufficient, *standing alone,* to support a jury verdict for plaintiff. The issue of legal sufficiency is raised prior to trial on a defendant's motion for summary judgment or after trial on a motion for a directed verdict. Contrast:

Heim v. State of Utah, 8 F.3d 1541 (10th Cir. 1993), the angry outburst: "Fucking women, I hate having fucking women in the office," was insufficient to support a finding that the female plaintiff was a victim of sex discrimination.

Stacks v. Southwestern Bell Yellow Pages, Inc., 27 F.3d 1316, 1324 (8th Cir.1994), a supervisor's more measured evaluation that "women were the worst thing that had happened to [this company]" would support a finding that sex was a motivating factor in the company's adverse employment action against plaintiff, even though the statement was not made during the decisional process.

d. Do the words compel a verdict? At some level the weight of the verbal evidence may be so compelling that no reasonable jury could find that defendant was not motivated by race, warranting judgment as a matter of law for plaintiff. For example:

Brown v. East Mississippi Electric Power Ass'n, 989 F.2d 858 (5th Cir. 1993):

* * * It is uncontroverted that Pippin [the supervisor] used the term "nigger" both to refer to Brown [the plaintiff] in particular and to black persons in general. According to Kim Culpepper, a white serviceman, Pippen used the term "basically any time there was a reference to a black." Pippen testified that he stopped after Murray reprimanded him in August 1988 but Culpepper disagreed; he testified that he observed no change whatever.

Brown offered evidence of the following instances of racial remarks by Pippen. Thomas Hamner, a retired white line foreman, testified that Pippen had told him, "I had to dust my little nigger again today," with reference to Brown. Jimmy Gressett, a white right-of-way supervisor, testified that Pippen had said the same to him. Louvenia Ford, a black service clerk, complained to Murray in August 1988 after she overheard Pippen say "I haven't seen my little nigger friend this morning" and two cashiers told her Pippen had used the slur with reference to her. In addition to the threat to say "What do you want, nigger?" over the radio, Brown testified to overhearing Pippen, discussing a recent car accident, say "I felt like getting my gun and killing that nigger," and, talking with a white serviceman, "You should have hooked that power up for that nigger. You know how they are." * * *

That Pippen usually was circumspect in using the term in the presence of African–Americans underscores that he knew it was insulting. Nonetheless, he persisted in demeaning African–Americans by using it among whites. This is racism. * * *

The court concluded, as a matter of law, that "Pippen's racism infected the disciplinary decisions of which Brown complains." Even though the racist remarks of the supervisor were neither directed toward plaintiff nor uttered in connection with the employment decision, the court considered these statements were sufficient to compel judgment for the plaintiff. No reasonable jury could conclude that defendant was motivated by legitimate reasons.

2. *"Direct Evidence:"* Properly defined, direct evidence is that which establishes the ultimate issue without the use of an inference. *DiCarlo v. Potter,* 358 F.3d 408 (6th Cir. 2004). When the decision maker expresses that the race, sex, national origin, age, religion, or impairment of the plaintiff served as a basis for the challenged decision, this is a confession of the motivation behind the action. For example, if an interviewer notes on the plaintiff's application, "too old for this job; we need a younger person," no inference was needed to compel a conclusion as to the employer's motive. The employer stated its motive for its action. *See, e.g., Van Voorhis v. Hillsborough County,* 512 F.3d 1296 (11th Cir. 2008); *Dixon v. Hallmark Companies,* 627 F.3d 849 (11th Cir. 2010).

Recall the Supreme Court case of *Price Waterhouse v. Hopkins supra p. 80.* Plaintiff presented uncontested evidence that sex stereotype words were used by the persons responsible for the denial of her promotion, and this expressed bias played a direct role in the final decision. It was written on the evaluation forms: "too macho "overcompensated for being a woman," and "a lady using foul language." Plaintiff's rejection notice contained her supervisors' advice for future advancement, "be more ladylike." On these written statements alone, the Court accepted that sex was "a" motive for rejecting plaintiff and proceeded to address how defendant might avoid liability for its sex motivated decision by carrying a burden of persuading the fact finder that the employer would have made the same decision on legitimate grounds even in the absence of the illegal sex motive. The evidence the Court was considering was traditional "direct evidence."

By contrast, a supervisor's general use of racial or ethnic slurs, while very probative of the speaker's underlying racist animus still requires an inference to conclude that this expressed animus motivated an adverse action against the particular plaintiff. As such, technically, this would not be direct evidence of illegal motive. If uttered by a person responsible for the decision and at a time and place not remote from the decision the expletives are probative, but not "direct" evidence. Nonetheless, as in the principal case and in *Brown v. East Mississippi Electric, supra,* courts often label all strong verbal evidence of animus as "direct." This technical distinction between true direct evidence and verbal evidence of animus could have practical consequences.

Based on *Price Waterhouse,* true "direct evidence" should compel a fact finder to conclude that at least "a" motive for the decision was proscribed. *See, e.g., Dixon v. Hallmark Companies,* 627 F.3d 849 (11th Cir. 2010). But here again the decisions are not consistent. In *Lewis v. City of Chicago,* 496 F.3d 645 (7th Cir. 2007), plaintiff's supervisor denied her a requested assignment. Plaintiff alleged that she was told by the supervisor that it was "because she was a female," that the assignment would be "dangerous, and that [she] would "thank him later" for denying it to her. The supervisor denied saying these words. The court rightfully held that whether the supervisor said the words was a disputed fact that must be resolved by the jury. The court indicated, however, that even if the supervisor said those words this would not compel a judgment for the plaintiff.

When evidence merely indicates the speaker's general animus toward the plaintiff's class ("I hate women") thus requiring an inference to conclude that the expressed animus motivated the particular decision regarding female plaintiff, it is more difficult, but not impossible, to reach a conclusion that a reasonable jury must draw such an inference. *Cf. Brown v. East Mississippi Electric, supra page 396.*

ASH v. TYSON FOODS, INC.

Supreme Court of the United States, 2006
546 U.S. 454, 126 S.Ct. 1195, 163 L.Ed.2d 1053

PER CURIAM.

Petitioners Anthony Ash and John Hithon were superintendents at a poultry plant owned and operated by respondent Tyson Foods, Inc. Petitioners, who are African–American, sought promotions to fill two open shift manager positions, but two white males were selected instead. Alleging that Tyson had discriminated on account of race, petitioners sued under 42 U.S.C. § 1981, and Title VII of the Civil Rights Act of 1964.

A trial proceeded in the United States District Court for the Northern District of Alabama. At the close of the plaintiffs' evidence, Tyson moved for judgment as a matter of law. The District Court denied the motion, and the jury found for petitioners, awarding compensatory and punitive damages. The employer renewed its motion for judgment under Rule 50(b) [Fed.Rule Civ.Pro] The District Court granted the motion and, in the alternative, ordered a new trial as to both plaintiffs under Rule 50(c).

The United States Court of Appeals for the Eleventh Circuit affirmed in part and reversed in part. * * *

The judgment of the Court of Appeals, and the trial court rulings it affirmed, may be correct in the final analysis. In the course of its opinion, however, the Court of Appeals erred in two respects, requiring that its judgment now be vacated and the case remanded for further consideration.

First, there was evidence that Tyson's plant manager, who made the disputed hiring decisions, had referred on some occasions to each of the petitioners as "boy." Petitioners argued this was evidence of discriminatory animus. The Court of Appeals disagreed, holding that "[w]hile the use of 'boy' when modified by a racial classification like 'black' or 'white' is evidence of discriminatory intent, the use of 'boy' alone is not evidence of discrimination." Although it is true the disputed word will not always be evidence of racial animus, it does not follow that the term, standing alone, is always benign. The speaker's meaning may depend on various factors including context, inflection, tone of voice, local custom, and historical usage. Insofar as the Court of Appeals held that modifiers or qualifications are necessary in all instances to render the disputed term probative of bias, the court's decision is erroneous.

* * *

C. "CIRCUMSTANTIAL (OR INDIRECT) EVIDENCE"

1. THE ANALYTICAL FRAMEWORK: "A THREE STEP DANCE"

McDONNELL DOUGLAS CORPORATION v. GREEN

Supreme Court of the United States, 1973
411 U.S. 792, 93 S.Ct. 1817, 36 L.Ed.2d 668

JUSTICE POWELL delivered the opinion for a unanimous Court.

The case before us raises significant questions as to the proper order and nature of proof in actions under Title VII of the Civil Rights Act of 1964.

Petitioner, McDonnell Douglas Corp., is an aerospace and aircraft manufacturer headquartered in St. Louis, Missouri, where it employs over 30,000 people. Respondent, a black citizen of St. Louis, worked for petitioner as a mechanic and laboratory technician from 1956 until August 28, 1964 when he was laid off in the course of a general reduction in petitioner's work force.

Respondent, a long-time activist in the civil rights movement, protested vigorously that his discharge and the general hiring practices of petitioner were racially motivated. As part of this protest, respondent and other members of the Congress on Racial Equality illegally stalled their cars on the main roads leading to petitioner's plant for the purpose of blocking access to it at the time of the morning shift change. * * *

On July 2, 1965, a 'lock-in' took place wherein a chain and padlock were placed on the front door of a building to prevent the occupants, certain of petitioner's employees, from leaving. Though respondent apparently knew beforehand of the 'lock-in,' the full extent of his involvement remains uncertain.

Some three weeks following the 'lock-in,' on July 25, 1965, petitioner publicly advertised for qualified mechanics, respondent's trade, and respondent promptly applied for re-employment. Petitioner turned down respondent, basing its rejection on respondent's participation in the 'stall-in' and 'lock-in.' Shortly thereafter, respondent filed a formal complaint with the Equal Employment Opportunity Commission * * *

The critical issue before us concerns the order and allocation of proof in a private, non-class action challenging employment discrimination. The language of Title VII makes plain the purpose of Congress to assure equality of employment opportunities and to eliminate those discriminatory practices and devices which have fostered racially stratified job environments to the disadvantage of minority citizens.

'Congress did not intend by Title VII, however, to guarantee a job to every person regardless of qualifications. In short, the Act does not command that any person be hired simply because he was formerly the subject of discrimination, or because he is a member of a minority group. Discriminatory preference for any group, minority or majority, is precisely and only what Congress has proscribed. * * *

In this case respondent, the complainant below, charges that he was denied employment 'because of his involvement in civil rights activities' and 'because of his race and color.' Petitioner denied discrimination of any kind, asserting that its failure to re-employ respondent was based upon and justified by his participation in the unlawful conduct against it. Thus, the issue at the trial on remand is framed by those opposing factual contentions. We now address this problem.

The complainant in a Title VII trial must carry the initial burden under the statute of establishing a prima facie case of racial discrimination. This may be done by showing (i) that he belongs to a racial minority; (ii) that he applied and was qualified for a job for which the employer was seeking applicants; (iii) that, despite his qualifications, he was rejected; and (iv) that, after his rejection, the position remained open and the employer continued to seek applicants from persons of complainant's qualifications.[13] In the instant case, we agree with the Court of Appeals that

---

13. The facts necessarily will vary in Title VII cases, and the specification above of the prima facie proof required from respondent is not necessarily applicable in every respect to differing factual situations.

respondent proved a prima facie case. Petitioner sought mechanics, respondent's trade, and continued to do so after respondent's rejection. Petitioner, moreover, does not dispute respondent's qualifications[14] and acknowledges that his past work performance in petitioner's employ was 'satisfactory.'

The burden then must shift to the employer to articulate some legitimate, nondiscriminatory reason for the employee's rejection. We need not attempt in the instant case to detail every matter which fairly could be recognized as a reasonable basis for a refusal to hire. Here petitioner has assigned respondent's participation in unlawful conduct against it as the cause for his rejection. We think that this suffices to discharge petitioner's burden of proof at this stage and to meet respondent's prima facie case of discrimination.

The Court of Appeals intimated, however, that petitioner's stated reason for refusing to rehire respondent was a 'subjective' rather than objective criterion which 'carr[ies] little weight in rebutting charges of discrimination,' This was among the statements which caused the dissenting judge to read the opinion as taking 'the position that such unlawful acts as Green committed against McDonnell would not legally entitle McDonnell to refuse to hire him, even though no racial motivation was involved . . . .'. Regardless of whether this was the intended import of the opinion, we think the court below seriously underestimated the rebuttal weight to which petitioner's reasons were entitled. Respondent admittedly had taken part in a carefully planned 'stall-in,' designed to tie up access to and egress from petitioner's plant at a peak traffic hour. Nothing in Title VII compels an employer to absolve and rehire one who has engaged in such deliberate, unlawful activity against it. * * *

Petitioner's reason for rejection thus suffices to meet the prima facie case, but the inquiry must not end here. While Title VII does not, without more, compel rehiring of respondent, neither does it permit petitioner to use respondent's conduct as a pretext for the sort of discrimination prohibited by § 703(a)(1). On remand, respondent must, as the Court of Appeals recognized, be afforded a fair opportunity to show that petitioner's stated reason for respondent's rejection was in fact pretext. Especially relevant to such a showing would be evidence that white employees involved in acts against petitioner of comparable seriousness to the 'stall-in' were nevertheless retained or rehired. Petitioner may justifiably refuse to rehire one who was engaged in unlawful, disruptive acts against it, but only if this criterion is applied alike to members of all races.

Other evidence that may be relevant to any showing of pretext includes facts as to the petitioner's treatment of respondent during his prior term of employment; petitioner's reaction, if any, to respondent's legitimate

---

14. We note that the issue of what may properly be used to test qualifications for employment is not present in this case. Where employers have instituted employment tests and qualifications with an exclusionary effect on minority applicants, such requirements must be 'shown to bear a demonstrable relationship to successful performance of the jobs' for which they were used, *Griggs v. Duke Power Co.*, 401 U.S. 424, 431, 91 S.Ct. 849, 853, 28 L.Ed.2d 158 (1971).

civil rights activities; and petitioner's general policy and practice with respect to minority employment. On the latter point, statistics as to petitioner's employment policy and practice may be helpful to a determination of whether petitioner's refusal to rehire respondent in this case conformed to a general pattern of discrimination against blacks.[19] In short, on the retrial respondent must be given a full and fair opportunity to demonstrate by competent evidence that the presumptively valid reasons for his rejection were in fact a coverup for a racially discriminatory decision.

The court below appeared to rely upon *Griggs v. Duke Power Co., supra,* in which the Court stated: 'If an employment practice which operates to exclude Negroes cannot be shown to be related to job performance, the practice is prohibited.' But *Griggs* differs from the instant case in important respects. It dealt with standardized testing devices which, however neutral on their face, operated to exclude many blacks who were capable of performing effectively in the desired positions. *Griggs* was rightly concerned that childhood deficiencies in the education and background of minority citizens, resulting from forces beyond their control, not be allowed to work a cumulative and invidious burden on such citizens for the remainder of their lives. Respondent, however, appears in different clothing. He had engaged in a seriously disruptive act against the very one from whom he now seeks employment. And petitioner does not seek his exclusion on the basis of a testing device which overstates what is necessary for competent performance, or through some sweeping disqualification of all those with any past record of unlawful behavior, however remote, insubstantial, or unrelated to applicant's personal qualifications as an employee. Petitioner assertedly rejected respondent for unlawful conduct against it and, in the absence of proof of pretext or discriminatory application of such a reason, this cannot be thought the kind of 'artificial, arbitrary, and unnecessary barriers to employment' which the Court found to be the intention of Congress to remove.[21]

III

In sum, respondent should have been allowed to pursue his claim under § 703(a)(1). If the evidence on retrial is substantially in accord with that before us in this case, we think that respondent carried his burden of establishing a prima facie case of racial discrimination and that petitioner

---

19. The District Court may, for example, determine, after reasonable discovery that 'the (racial) composition of defendant's labor force is itself reflective of restrictive or exclusionary practices.' We caution that such general determinations, while helpful, may not be in and of themselves controlling as to an individualized hiring decision, particularly in the presence of an otherwise justifiable reason for refusing to rehire.

21. It is, of course, a predictive evaluation, resistant to empirical proof, whether 'an applicant's past participation in unlawful conduct directed at his prospective employer might indicate the applicant's lack of a responsible attitude toward performing work for that employer.' But in this case, given the seriousness and harmful potential of respondent's participation in the 'stall-in' and the accompanying inconvenience to other employees, it cannot be said that petitioner's refusal to employ lacked a rational and neutral business justification. As the Court has noted elsewhere: 'Past conduct may well relate to present fitness; past loyalty may have a reasonable relationship to present and future trust.'

successfully rebutted that case. But this does not end the matter. On retrial, respondent must be afforded a fair opportunity to demonstrate that petitioner's assigned reason for refusing to re-employ was a pretext or discriminatory in its application. If the District Judge so finds, he must order a prompt and appropriate remedy. In the absence of such a finding, petitioner's refusal to rehire must stand.

The cause is hereby remanded to the District Court for reconsideration in accordance with this opinion.

2. THE FIRST STEP: PLAINTIFF'S PRIMA FACIE SHOWING

REEVES v. SANDERSON PLUMBING PRODUCTS, INC.

Supreme Court of the United States, 2000
530 U.S. 133, 120 S.Ct. 2097, 147 L.Ed.2d 105

JUSTICE O'CONNOR delivered the opinion of the Court.

* * *

II

Under the ADEA, it is "unlawful for an employer . . . to fail or refuse to hire or to discharge any individual or otherwise discriminate against any individual with respect to his compensation, terms, conditions, or privileges of employment, because of such individual's age." When a plaintiff alleges disparate treatment, "liability depends on whether the protected trait (under the ADEA, age) actually motivated the employer's decision." That is, the plaintiff's age must have "actually played a role in [the employer's decisionmaking] process and had a determinative influence on the outcome." Recognizing that "the question facing triers of fact in discrimination cases is both sensitive and difficult," and that "[t]here will seldom be 'eyewitness' testimony as to the employer's mental processes," the Courts of Appeals, including the Fifth Circuit in this case, have employed some variant of the framework articulated in *McDonnell Douglas* to analyze ADEA claims that are based principally on circumstantial evidence. This Court has not squarely addressed whether the *McDonnell Douglas* framework, developed to assess claims brought under § 703(a)(1) of Title VII of the Civil Rights Act of 1964, also applies to ADEA actions. Because the parties do not dispute the issue, we shall assume, *arguendo,* that the *McDonnell Douglas* framework is fully applicable here.

McDonnell Douglas and subsequent decisions have "established an allocation of the burden of production and an order for the presentation of proof in . . . discriminatory-treatment cases." First, the plaintiff must establish a prima facie case of discrimination. It is undisputed that petitioner satisfied this burden here: (i) at the time he was fired, he was a member of the class protected by the ADEA ("individuals who are at least 40 years of age," 29 U.S.C. § 631(a)), (ii) he was otherwise qualified for the position of Hinge Room supervisor, (iii) he was discharged by respondent, and (iv) respondent successively hired three persons in their thirties to fill petitioner's position. The burden therefore shifted to respondent to "produc[e] evidence that the plaintiff was rejected, or someone else was preferred, for a legitimate, nondiscriminatory reason." This burden is one of production, not persuasion; it "can involve no credibility assessment." Respondent met this burden by offering admissible evidence sufficient for the trier of fact to conclude that petitioner was fired because of his failure to maintain accurate attendance records. Accordingly, "the *McDonnell Douglas* framework—with its presumptions and burdens"—disappeared, and the sole remaining issue was "discrimination *vel non.*"

Although intermediate evidentiary burdens shift back and forth under this framework, "[t]he ultimate burden of persuading the trier of fact that the defendant intentionally discriminated against the plaintiff remains at all times with the plaintiff." And in attempting to satisfy this burden, the plaintiff—once the employer produces sufficient evidence to support a nondiscriminatory explanation for its decision—must be afforded the "opportunity to prove by a preponderance of the evidence that the legitimate reasons offered by the defendant were not its true reasons, but were a pretext for discrimination. That is, the plaintiff may attempt to establish that he was the victim of intentional discrimination "by showing that the employer's proffered explanation is unworthy of credence." Moreover, although the presumption of discrimination "drops out of the picture" once the defendant meets its burden of production, the trier of fact may still consider the evidence establishing the plaintiff's prima facie case "and inferences properly drawn therefrom . . . on the issue of whether the defendant's explanation is pretextual,"

NOTES

1. *Swierkiewicz v. Sorema N. A.*, **534 U.S. 506, 122 S.Ct. 992, 152 L.Ed.2d 1 (2002),** in holding that the *McDonnell Douglas* model did not impose a pleading obligation on plaintiff, cautioned:

> [T]he *McDonnell Douglas* framework does not apply in every employment discrimination case. For instance, if a plaintiff is able to produce direct evidence of discrimination, he may prevail without proving all the elements of a prima facie case. * * * Moreover, the precise requirements of a prima facie case can vary depending on the context and were "never intended to be rigid, mechanized, or ritualistic."

2. *"Protected Class:"* To create an inference of illegal motivation, it is incumbent on the plaintiff to establish that the decision-maker was aware of plaintiff's status. *Norman–Nunnery v. Madison Area Tech. College*, 625 F.3d 422 (7th Cir. 2010).

3. *"Qualified?"* The element of "qualified" in discharge cases remains confused (even in the same circuit). Some courts have held that when an employee has a record of inadequate job performance, the employee has failed to prove that she is "qualified," and thus has not established a prima facie case. Other courts have held that plaintiff is "qualified" if she possesses the

objective "basic skills necessary." Alleged inadequate performance is the "legitimate reason" that must be "articulated" by the defendant through presenting admissible evidence of plaintiff's unacceptable performance. *Haigh v. Gelita, USA, Inc.,* 632 F.3d 464 (8th Cir. 2011).

In cases arising in a broad reduction in force, there may be no hiring of a person from another class that would create the initial inference that the action is improperly motivated. In such cases, lower courts have held that plaintiff must point to suspicious behavior, such as retention of persons significantly younger, or if alleged misconduct was involved, that other persons were not similarly treated. Recall, *McDonald v. Santa Fe Trails Transp., supra page 29.* Most courts indicate that in economically motivated general layoffs plaintiff must show that persons of other classes were not similarly treated or were retained even though they performed at a lower level than the plaintiff. *Mitchell v. Data General Corp.,* 12 F.3d 1310 (4th Cir. 1993). In ADEA cases some require "additional evidence" of age motivation that goes beyond retention of younger workers and isolated incidents of other older workers being laid off. *Schoonmaker v. Spartan Graphics Leasing, LLC,* 595 F.3d 261 (6th Cir. 2010).

4. *Suspicious Disparate Treatment:* **O'CONNOR v. CONSOLIDATED COIN CATERERES CORP., 517 U.S. 308, 116 S.Ct. 1307, 134 L.Ed.2d 433 (1996).** Plaintiff was age 56. He was fired and replaced by a person slightly over 40 years old. The lower court had held that because plaintiff and the favored person were over age 40, placing them both in the protected 40 and over age group, plaintiff had failed to create an inference of illegal age discrimination. The Court reversed. Evidence that "plaintiff was replaced by someone *outside the protected class* is not a proper element of the *McDonnell Douglas* prima face case." All that is required is proof that the favored person, even if over age 40, was *"significantly younger"* than the plaintiff. The 16 year age difference in *O'Connor* was a "significant" difference, and thus created a prima facie showing of age motivation.

McDonnell Douglas, the principal case, required plaintiff to establish not only his own "application for a vacancy" but also the failure of defendant to fill the vacancy, leaving the vacancy unfilled. Rarely is an inference of illegal motivation possible where the individual selected to fill the vacancy is of the same race and sex as plaintiff. *Jones v. Western Geophysical Co.,* 669 F.2d 280 (5th Cir. 1982).

3.　DEFENDANT'S REQUIRED RESPONSE: STEP 2 IN THE "DANCE"

FURNCO CONSTRUCTION CORP. v. WATERS, 438 U.S. 567, 98 S.Ct. 2943, 57 L.Ed.2d 957 (1978). The Court first made it clear that the employer's statistically balanced work force could not substitute for its obligation to "articulate a legitimate, nondiscriminatory reason" for its treatment of plaintiff in response to plaintiff's prima facie showing. The Court continued:

> The Court of Appeals * * * thought [defendant's] hiring procedures * * * must be the method which allows the employer to consider the

qualifications of the largest number of minority applicants. We think the imposition of that * * * requirement simply finds no support either in the nature of the prima face case or the purpose of Title VII. * * *

The method suggested in *McDonnell Douglas* [was] * * *an orderly way to evaluate the evidence in light of common experience as it bears on the critical issue of discrimination. A prima facie case under *McDonnell Douglas* raises an inference of discrimination only because we presume these acts, if otherwise unexplained, are more likely than not base on consideration of impermissible factors. And we are willing to presume this largely because we know from our experience that more often than not people do not act in a totally arbitrary manner, without any underlying reasons, especially in a business setting. * * * [I]t is apparent that the burden which shifts to the employer is merely proving that he based his employment decision on a legitimate consideration, and not an illegitimate one such as race. To prove that, he need not prove that he pursued the course which would both enable him to achieve his own business goal *and* allow him to consider the *most* employment applications. Title VII * * * does not impose a duty to adopt a hiring procedure that maximizes hiring of minority employees. * * * Proof [by defendant] that his work force was racially balanced or that it contained a disproportionately high percentage of minority workers is not wholly irrelevant on the issue of intent. * * * We cannot say that such proof would have absolutely no probative value in determining whether the otherwise unexplained rejection of minority applicants was discriminatorily motivated. * * * [T]he district court was entitled to consider the racial mix of the work force when trying to make the determination as to motivation.

TEXAS DEP'T OF COMMUNITY AFFAIRS v. BURDINE, 450 U.S. 248, 101 S.Ct. 1089, 67 L.Ed.2d 207 (1981):

The burden of [plaintiff] establishing a prima face case of disparate treatment is not onerous. * * * The prima face case serves an important function in the litigation: It eliminates the most common non-discriminatory reasons for plaintiff's rejection. * * * If the trier of fact believes the plaintiff's evidence, and if the employer remains silent in the face of the presumption, the court must enter a judgment for the plaintiff because no issue of fact remains in the case.

The burden that shifts to the defendant, therefore, is to rebut the presumption. * * * Defendant need not persuade the court that it was actually motivated by the proffered reasons. It is sufficient if the defendant's evidence raises a genuine issue of fact as to whether it discriminated against the plaintiff. To accomplish this, the defendant must clearly set forth, through admissible evidence, the reasons for plaintiff's rejection. An articulation not admitted into evidence will not suffice. Thus, the defendant cannot meet its burden merely through an answer to the complaint or argument of counsel. * * *

When the plaintiff has proved a prima facie case of discrimination, defendant bears only the burden of explaining clearly the non-discriminatory reasons for its actions.

Placing this burden of production on the defendant thus serves simultaneously to meet the plaintiff's prima face case by presenting a legitimate reason for the action and to frame the factual issue with sufficient clarity so that the plaintiff will have a full and fair opportunity to demonstrate pretext. The sufficiency of the defendant's evidence should be evaluated by the extent to which it fulfills these functions.

The plaintiff retains the burden of persuasion. She must now have the opportunity to demonstrate that the proffered reason was not the true reason for the employment decision. * * * She may succeed in this either directly by persuading the court that a discriminatory reason more likely motivated the employer or indirectly by showing that the employer's proffered explanation is unworthy of credence.

In summary, the Court of Appeals erred by requiring the defendant to prove by a preponderance of the evidence the existence of non-discriminatory reasons for terminating the [plaintiff] and that the person retained in her stead had superior objective qualifications for the position. When the plaintiff has proved a prima facie case of discrimination, the defendant bears only the burden of explaining clearly the non discriminatory reasons for its actions.

PATTERSON v. McLEAN CREDIT UNION, 491 U.S. 164, 109 S.Ct. 2363, 105 L.Ed.2d 132 (1989). The trial court had held that if the defendant articulated as its reason for rejecting the plaintiff "superior qualifications" of the person actually selected, the plaintiff had to prove that she was better qualified than the white employee who received the promotion. The Court held that this was error:

Although [plaintiff] retains the ultimate burden of persuasion * * * she must also have the opportunity to demonstrate that [defendant's] proffered reasons for its decision were not its true reasons. In doing so, [plaintiff] is not limited to presenting a certain type of evidence. * * * The evidence which [plaintiff] can present in an attempt to establish that [defendant's] stated reasons are pretextual may take a variety of forms. Indeed, she may seek to demonstrate that [defendant's] claim was pretextual by showing that she was in fact better qualified than the person chosen for the position. The district court erred, however, in instructing the jury that in order to succeed [plaintiff] was *required* to make such a showing. There are certainly other ways in which [plaintiff] could seek to prove that [defendant's] reasons were pretextual. Thus, for example, [plaintiff] could seek to persuade the jury that respondent had not offered the true reason for its promotion decision by presenting evidence of [defendant's] past treatment of petitioner, including the instances of racial harassment which she alleges and [defendant's] failure to train her for [such a position]. While we do not intend to say this evidence necessarily would carry the day, it cannot be denied that it is one of the various ways in which [plaintiff] might seek to prove intentional discrimination * * *.

ST. MARY'S HONOR CENTER v. HICKS, 509 U.S. 502, 113 S.Ct. 2742, 125 L.Ed.2d 407 (1993).

[The Court of Appeals reasoned:] Because all of defendants' proffered reasons were discredited, defendants were in a position of having offered no legitimate reason for their actions. In other words, defendants were in no better position than if they had remained silent, offering no rebuttal to an established inference that they had unlawfully discriminated against plaintiff on the basis of his race." That is not so. By producing evidence (whether ultimately persuasive or not) of non-discriminatory reasons, [defendants] sustained their burden of production, and thus placed themselves in a better position than if they had remained silent.

NOTES

1. *"Legitimate" Reason Revisited:*

a. *"Job–Related," "Rational," or "Trivial"?* **McDonnell Douglas, Furnco Construction Corp.,** *supra* and **Texas** *Dep't of Community Affairs, supra* all rejected a requirement that "legitimate" reasons must have a manifest relationship to actual job performance. Nonetheless, *McDonnell Douglas* and *Furnco* seemed to reject as "legitimate" reasons that were "arbitrary" with no business relationship, "because we know from our experience that more often than not people do not act in a totally arbitrary manner, without any underlying reasons, especially in a business setting." *Budine* stated:

[The alleged] legitimate reason for the action * * * [should] frame the factual issue with sufficient clarity so that the plaintiff will have a full and fair opportunity to demonstrate pretext. The sufficiency of the defendant's evidence should be evaluated by the extent to which it fulfills these functions."

Nonetheless, lower courts have tended to dilute defendant's burden, allowing the burden to be carried by articulating reasons that are "foolish, trivial, or even baseless." *See, e.g., Balderston v. Fairbanks Morse Engine,* 328 F.3d 309 (7th Cir. 2003).

b. *"Legitimate subjectivity:"* The reason "articulated" by defendant in *Budine, supra,* was a conclusion that the "person hired or promoted was more qualified than the plaintiff." The court of appeals in *Burdine* had imposed an obligation on the defendant/employer to prove with objective evidence the actual "superiority" of the qualifications of the favoured employees. In reversing, *Burdine* signalled that the employer might satisfy its evidentiary burden by proffering a subjective *conclusion,* leaving for the plaintiff on rebuttal to challenge the factual basis for that conclusion.

While giving lip service to the truism that "subjectivity is suspect because it is easily fabricated" (*Barber v. CI Truck Driver Training, LLC*, 656 F.3d 782 (8th Cir. 2011), increasingly, courts have accepted as "legitimate" extremely subjective and vague reasons, such as defendant *"did not like"* the plaintiff; that plaintiff lacked *"people skills;"* or that defendant *"assumed"* that plaintiff would not be interested in the vacant job. *Balderston v. Fairbanks*, 328 F.3d 309 (7th Cir. 2003), *Loeb v. Best Buy, Inc.*, 537 F.3d 867 (8th Cir. 2008); *Brooks v. Ameren UE.*, 345 F.3d 986 (8th Cir. 2003). Moreover, the courts have pointed out that it is not the objective existence of the articulated reason that is the critical focus, but defendant's subjective *belief* in the reason's existence. *Russell v. University of Toledo*, 537 F.3d 596 (6th Cir. 2008).

     c. *"Non–Discriminatory:"*

     (1) *Adverse impact:* **RAYTHEON CO. v. HERNANDEZ,** 540 U.S. 44, 124 S.Ct. 513, 157 L.Ed.2d 357 (2003), re-affirmed, **Furnco,** *supra page 405,* that a reason could be legitimate and "non-discriminatory" even though its use might have an adverse impact on plaintiff's class. The employer in *Raytheon,* had a policy of not rehiring dismissed employees. The "no rehire" policy was held to be a legitimate reason for refusing to rehire an individual with a disability notwithstanding its possible impact on persons with plaintiff's disability.

     (2) *Legality:* As incredible as it may seem, reasons may be "legitimate" even if illegal! Recall, **Hazen Paper Co. v. Biggins,** 507 U.S. 604, 113 S.Ct. 1701, 123 L.Ed.2d 338 (1993), *supra, p. 131,* where the employer articulated that it had discharged plaintiff, because of the number of years of his employment, which would cause the plaintiff's pension rights to vest. The Court conceded that dismissing plaintiff to avoid the vesting of pensions would violate the federal ERISA statute. Nonetheless, illegal pension avoidance by the employer appeared to be a "legitimate" reason, sufficient for defendant to refute an inference of age motivation.

4. PLAINTIFF'S RESPONSIVE STEP: PRESENTATION OF "PRETEXT"

REEVES v. SANDERSON PLUMBING PRODUCTS, INC.

Supreme Court of the United States, 2000
530 U.S. 133, 120 S.Ct. 2097, 147 L.Ed.2d 105

JUSTICE O'CONNOR delivered the opinion of the Court.

This case concerns the kind and amount of evidence necessary to sustain a jury's verdict that an employer unlawfully discriminated on the basis of age. Specifically, we must resolve whether a defendant is entitled to judgment as a matter of law when the plaintiff's case consists exclusively of a prima facie case of discrimination and sufficient evidence for the trier of fact to disbelieve the defendant's legitimate, nondiscriminatory explanation for its action. We must also decide whether the employer was entitled to judgment as a matter of law under the particular circumstances presented here.

I

In October 1995, petitioner Roger Reeves was 57 years old and had spent 40 years in the employ of respondent, Sanderson Plumbing Products, Inc., a manufacturer of toilet seats and covers. Petitioner worked in a department known as the "Hinge Room," where he supervised the "regular line." Joe Oswalt, in his mid-thirties, supervised the Hinge Room's "special line," and Russell Caldwell, the manager of the Hinge Room and age 45, supervised both petitioner and Oswalt. Petitioner's responsibilities included recording the attendance and hours of those under his supervision, and reviewing a weekly report that listed the hours worked by each employee.

In the summer of 1995, Caldwell informed Chesnut, the director of manufacturing and the husband of company president Sandra Sanderson, that "production was down" in the Hinge Room because employees were often absent and were "coming in late and leaving early." Because the monthly attendance reports did not indicate a problem, Chesnut ordered an audit of the Hinge Room's timesheets for July, August, and September of that year. According to Chesnut's testimony, that investigation revealed "numerous timekeeping errors and misrepresentations on the part of Caldwell, Reeves, and Oswalt." Following the audit, Chesnut, along with Dana Jester, vice president of human resources, and Tom Whitaker, vice president of operations, recommended to company president Sanderson that petitioner and Caldwell be fired. In October 1995, Sanderson followed the recommendation and discharged both petitioner and Caldwell.

In June 1996, petitioner filed suit in the United States District Court for the Northern District of Mississippi, contending that he had been fired because of his age in violation of the Age Discrimination in Employment Act of 1967 (ADEA). At trial, respondent contended that it had fired petitioner due to his failure to maintain accurate attendance records, while petitioner attempted to demonstrate that respondent's explanation was pretext for age discrimination. Petitioner introduced evidence that he had accurately recorded the attendance and hours of the employees under his supervision, and that Chesnut, whom Oswalt described as wielding "absolute power" within the company, had demonstrated age-based animus in his dealings with petitioner.

During the trial, the District Court twice denied oral motions by respondent for judgment as a matter of law under Rule 50 of the Federal Rules of Civil Procedure, and the case went to the jury. The court instructed the jury that "[i]f the plaintiff fails to prove age was a determinative or motivating factor in the decision to terminate him, then your verdict shall be for the defendant." So charged, the jury returned a verdict in favor of petitioner, awarding him $35,000 in compensatory damages, and found that respondent's age discrimination had been "willfu[l]." The District Court accordingly entered judgment for petitioner in the amount of $70,000, which included $35,000 in liquidated damages based on the jury's finding of willfulness. Respondent then renewed its motion for judgment as a matter of law and alternatively moved for a new trial, while petitioner moved for front pay. The District Court denied respondent's motions and granted petitioner's, awarding him $28,490.80 in front pay for two years' lost income.

The Court of Appeals for the Fifth Circuit reversed, holding that petitioner had not introduced sufficient evidence to sustain the jury's finding of unlawful discrimination. * * *

We granted certiorari, to resolve a conflict among the Courts of Appeals as to whether a plaintiff's prima facie case of discrimination (as defined in *McDonnell Douglas Corp. v. Green*), combined with sufficient evidence for a reasonable factfinder to reject the employer's nondiscriminatory explanation for its decision, is adequate to sustain a finding of liability for intentional discrimination.

II

[The segment of the opinion discussing the *McDonnell Douglas* model of proof was reproduced, *supra* p. 403.] * * *

In this case, the evidence supporting respondent's explanation for petitioner's discharge consisted primarily of testimony by Chesnut and Sanderson and documentation of petitioner's alleged "shoddy record keeping." * * * He and Sanderson also stated that petitioner's errors, by failing to adjust for hours not worked, cost the company overpaid wages. Sanderson testified that she accepted the recommendation to discharge petitioner because he had "intentionally falsif[ied] company pay records."

Petitioner, however, made a substantial showing that respondent's explanation was false. First, petitioner offered evidence that he had properly maintained the attendance records. Most of the timekeeping errors cited by respondent involved employees who were not marked late but who were recorded as having arrived at the plant at 7 a.m. for the 7 a.m. shift. Respondent contended that employees arriving at 7 a.m. could not have been at their workstations by 7 a.m., and therefore must have been late. But both petitioner and Oswalt testified that the company's automated timeclock often failed to scan employees' timecards, so that the timesheets would not record any time of arrival. On these occasions, petitioner and Oswalt would visually check the workstations and record whether the employees were present at the start of the shift. They stated that if an employee arrived promptly but the timesheet contained no time of arrival, they would reconcile the two by marking "7 a.m." as the employee's arrival time, even if the employee actually arrived at the plant earlier. On cross-examination, Chesnut acknowledged that the timeclock sometimes malfunctioned, and that if "people were there at their work station[s]" at the start of the shift, the supervisor "would write in seven o'clock." Petitioner also testified that when employees arrived before or stayed after their shifts, he would assign them additional work so they would not be overpaid.

Petitioner similarly cast doubt on whether he was responsible for any failure to discipline late and absent employees. Petitioner testified that his job only included reviewing the daily and weekly attendance reports, and that disciplinary writeups were based on the monthly reports, which were reviewed by Caldwell. Sanderson admitted that Caldwell, and not petitioner, was responsible for citing employees for violations of the company's attendance policy. Further, Chesnut conceded that there had never been a union grievance or employee complaint arising from petitioner's record-keeping, and that the company had never calculated the amount of overpayments allegedly attributable to petitioner's errors. Petitioner also testified that, on the day he was fired, Chesnut said that his discharge was due to his failure to report as absent one employee, Gina Mae Coley, on two days in September 1995. But petitioner explained that he had spent those days in the hospital, and that Caldwell was therefore responsible for any overpayment of Coley. Finally, petitioner stated that on previous occasions that employees were paid for hours they had not worked, the company had simply adjusted those employees' next paychecks to correct the errors.

Based on this evidence, the Court of Appeals concluded that petitioner "very well may be correct" that "a reasonable jury could have found that [respondent's] explanation for its employment decision was pretextual." Nonetheless, the court held that this showing, standing alone, was insufficient to sustain the jury's finding of liability: "We must, as an essential final step, determine whether Reeves presented sufficient evidence that his age motivated [respondent's] employment decision." And in making this determination, the Court of Appeals ignored the evidence supporting petitioner's prima facie case and challenging respondent's explanation for its decision. The court confined its review of evidence favoring petitioner to that evidence showing that Chesnut had directed derogatory, age-based comments at petitioner, and that Chesnut had singled out petitioner for harsher treatment than younger employees. It is therefore apparent that the court believed that only this additional evidence of discrimination was relevant to whether the jury's verdict should stand. That is, the Court of Appeals proceeded from the assumption that a prima facie case of discrimination, combined with sufficient evidence for the trier of fact to disbelieve the defendant's legitimate, nondiscriminatory reason for its decision, is insufficient as a matter of law to sustain a jury's finding of intentional discrimination.

In so reasoning, the Court of Appeals misconceived the evidentiary burden borne by plaintiffs who attempt to prove intentional discrimination through indirect evidence. This much is evident from our decision in *St. Mary's Honor Center*. There we held that the factfinder's rejection of the employer's legitimate, nondiscriminatory reason for its action does not *compel* judgment for the plaintiff. The ultimate question is whether the employer intentionally discriminated, and proof that "the employer's proffered reason is unpersuasive, or even obviously contrived, does not necessarily establish that the plaintiff's proffered reason ... is correct."

In other words, "[i]t is not enough ... to *dis* believe the employer; the factfinder must *believe* the plaintiff's explanation of intentional discrimination."

In reaching this conclusion, however, we reasoned that it is *permissible* for the trier of fact to infer the ultimate fact of discrimination from the falsity of the employer's explanation. Specifically, we stated:

> "The factfinder's disbelief of the reasons put forward by the defendant (particularly if disbelief is accompanied by a suspicion of mendacity) may, together with the elements of the prima facie case, suffice to show intentional discrimination. Thus, rejection of the defendant's proffered reasons will *permit* the trier of fact to infer the ultimate fact of intentional discrimination."

Proof that the defendant's explanation is unworthy of credence is simply one form of circumstantial evidence that is probative of intentional discrimination, and it may be quite persuasive. ("[P]roving the employer's reason false becomes part of (and often considerably assists) the greater enterprise of proving that the real reason was intentional discrimination"). In appropriate circumstances, the trier of fact can reasonably infer from the falsity of the explanation that the employer is dissembling to cover up a discriminatory purpose. Such an inference is consistent with the general principle of evidence law that the factfinder is entitled to consider a party's dishonesty about a material fact as "affirmative evidence of guilt." Moreover, once the employer's justification has been eliminated, discrimination may well be the most likely alternative explanation, especially since the employer is in the best position to put forth the actual reason for its decision. ("[W]hen all legitimate reasons for rejecting an applicant have been eliminated as possible reasons for the employer's actions, it is more likely than not the employer, who we generally assume acts with *some* reason, based his decision on an impermissible consideration"). Thus, a plaintiff's prima facie case, combined with sufficient evidence to find that the employer's asserted justification is false, may permit the trier of fact to conclude that the employer unlawfully discriminated.

This is not to say that such a showing by the plaintiff will *always* be adequate to sustain a jury's finding of liability. Certainly there will be instances where, although the plaintiff has established a prima facie case and set forth sufficient evidence to reject the defendant's explanation, no rational factfinder could conclude that the action was discriminatory. For instance, an employer would be entitled to judgment as a matter of law if the record conclusively revealed some other, nondiscriminatory reason for the employer's decision, or if the plaintiff created only a weak issue of fact as to whether the employer's reason was untrue and there was abundant and uncontroverted independent evidence that no discrimination had occurred. *Fisher v. Vassar College,* 114 F.3d, at 1338 ("[I]f the circumstances show that the defendant gave the false explanation to conceal something other than discrimination, the inference of discrimination will be weak or nonexistent"). To hold otherwise would be effectively to insulate an entire category of employment discrimination cases from review under Rule 50, and we have reiterated that trial courts should not " 'treat discrimination differently from other ultimate questions of fact.' "

Whether judgment as a matter of law is appropriate in any particular case will depend on a number of factors. Those include the strength of the plaintiff's prima facie case, the probative value of the proof that the employer's explanation is false, and any other evidence that supports the employer's case and that properly may be considered on a motion for judgment as a matter of law. For purposes of this case, we need not-and could not-resolve all of the circumstances in which such factors would entitle an employer to judgment as a matter of law. It suffices to say that, because a prima facie case and sufficient evidence to reject the employer's explanation may permit a finding of liability, the Court of Appeals erred in proceeding from the premise that a plaintiff must always introduce additional, independent evidence of discrimination.

III

A

The remaining question is whether, despite the Court of Appeals' misconception of petitioner's evidentiary burden, respondent was nonetheless entitled to judgment as a matter of law. Under Rule 50, a court should render judgment as a matter of law when "a party has been fully heard on an issue and there is no legally sufficient evidentiary basis for a reasonable jury to find for that party on that issue." Fed. Rule Civ. Proc. 50(a). The Courts of Appeals have articulated differing formulations as to what evidence a court is to consider in ruling on a Rule 50 motion. Some decisions have stated that review is limited to that evidence favorable to the nonmoving party, while most have held that review extends to the entire record, drawing all reasonable inferences in favor of the nonmovant.

* * * It therefore follows that, in entertaining a motion for judgment as a matter of law, the court should review all of the evidence in the record.

In doing so, however, the court must draw all reasonable inferences in favor of the nonmoving party, and it may not make credibility determinations or weigh the evidence. "Credibility determinations, the weighing of the evidence, and the drawing of legitimate inferences from the facts are jury functions, not those of a judge." Thus, although the court should review the record as a whole, it must disregard all evidence favorable to the moving party that the jury is not required to believe. That is, the court should give credence to the evidence favoring the nonmovant as well as that "evidence supporting the moving party that is uncontradicted and unimpeached, at least to the extent that that evidence comes from disinterested witnesses."

B

Applying this standard here, it is apparent that respondent was not entitled to judgment as a matter of law. In this case, in addition to establishing a prima facie case of discrimination and creating a jury issue as to the falsity of the employer's explanation, petitioner introduced additional evidence that Chesnut was motivated by age-based animus and was principally responsible for petitioner's firing. Petitioner testified that Chesnut had told him that he "was so old [he] must have come over on the Mayflower" and, on one occasion when petitioner was having difficulty starting a machine, that he "was too damn old to do [his] job." According to petitioner, Chesnut would regularly "cuss at me and shake his finger in my face." Oswalt, roughly 24 years younger than petitioner, corroborated that there was an "obvious difference" in how Chesnut treated them. He stated that, although he and Chesnut "had [their] differences," "it was nothing compared to the way [Chesnut] treated Roger." Oswalt explained that Chesnut "tolerated quite a bit" from him even though he "defied" Chesnut "quite often," but that Chesnut treated petitioner "[i]n a manner, as you would ... treat ... a child when ... you're angry with [him].". Petitioner also demonstrated that, according to company records, he and Oswalt had nearly identical rates of productivity in 1993. Yet respondent conducted an efficiency study of only the regular line, supervised by petitioner, and placed only petitioner on probation. Chesnut conducted that efficiency study and, after having testified to the contrary on direct examination, acknowledged on cross-examination that he had recommended that petitioner be placed on probation following the study.

Further, petitioner introduced evidence that Chesnut was the actual decisionmaker behind his firing. Chesnut was married to Sanderson, who made the formal decision to discharge petitioner. Although Sanderson testified that she fired petitioner because he had "intentionally falsif[ied] company pay records," respondent only introduced evidence concerning the inaccuracy of the records, not their falsification. A 1994 letter authored by Chesnut indicated that he berated other company directors, who were supposedly his coequals, about how to do their jobs. Moreover, Oswalt testified that all of respondent's employees feared Chesnut, and that Chesnut had exercised "absolute power" within the company for "[a]s long as [he] can remember."

In holding that the record contained insufficient evidence to sustain the jury's verdict, the Court of Appeals misapplied the standard of review dictated by Rule 50. Again, the court disregarded critical evidence favorable to petitioner—namely, the evidence supporting petitioner's prima facie case and undermining respondent's nondiscriminatory explanation. The court also failed to draw all reasonable inferences in favor of petitioner. For instance, while acknowledging "the potentially damning nature" of Chesnut's age-related comments, the court discounted them on the ground that they "were not made in the direct context of Reeves's termination." And the court discredited petitioner's evidence that Chesnut was the actual decisionmaker by giving weight to the fact that there was "no evidence to suggest that any of the other decision makers were motivated by age." Moreover, the other evidence on which the court relied-that Caldwell and Oswalt were also cited for poor recordkeeping, and that respondent employed many managers over age 50—although relevant, is certainly not dispositive. See *Furnco,* 438 U.S., at 580, 98 S.Ct. 2943 (evidence that employer's work force was racially balanced, while "not wholly irrelevant," was not "sufficient to *conclusively* demonstrate that [the employer's] actions were not discriminatorily motivated"). In concluding that these circumstances so overwhelmed the evidence favoring petitioner that no rational trier of fact could have found that petitioner was fired because of his age, the Court of Appeals impermissibly substituted its judgment concerning the weight of the evidence for the jury's.

The ultimate question in every employment discrimination case involving a claim of disparate treatment is whether the plaintiff was the victim of intentional discrimination. Given the evidence in the record supporting petitioner, we see no reason to subject the parties to an additional round of litigation before the Court of Appeals rather than to resolve the matter here. The District Court plainly informed the jury that petitioner was required to show "by a preponderance of the evidence that his age was a determining and motivating factor in the decision of [respondent] to terminate him." The court instructed the jury that, to show that respondent's explanation was a pretext for discrimination, petitioner had to demonstrate "1, that the stated reasons were not the real reasons for [petitioner's] discharge; *and* 2, that age discrimination was the real reason for [petitioner's] discharge." Given that petitioner established a prima facie case of discrimination, introduced enough evidence for the jury to reject respondent's explanation, and produced additional evidence of age-based animus, there was sufficient evidence for the jury to find that respondent had intentionally discriminated. The District Court was therefore correct to submit the case to the jury, and the Court of Appeals erred in overturning its verdict.

For these reasons, the judgment of the Court of Appeals is reversed.

NOTE

1. *Sufficient v. Compelling: Reeves* strongly suggested that while the evidence was sufficient to *permit* a jury finding for plaintiff, the evidence did not *compel* such a finding entitling plaintiff to a judgment as a matter of law. If disbelief of the sole reason articulated by defendant, plus acceptance of the compelling verbal (if not direct) evidence of age motivation, plus additional examples of differential treatment of plaintiff and younger workers does not compel a judgment for plaintiff, one might ask: how strong must plaintiff's evidence be to secure a judgment as a matter of law?

ASH v. TYSON FOODS, INC.

Supreme Court of the United States, 2006
546 U.S. 454, 126 S.Ct. 1195, 163 L.Ed.2d 1053

PER CURIAM.

[The facts are reproduced, *supra, p. 398*] * * *

[T]he Court of Appeals erred in articulating the standard for determining whether the asserted nondiscriminatory reasons for [defendant] Tyson's hiring decisions were pretextual. Petitioners had introduced evidence that their qualifications were superior to those of the two successful applicants. (Part of the employer's defense was that the plant with the openings had performance problems and petitioners already worked there in a supervisory capacity.) The Court of Appeals, in finding petitioners' evidence insufficient, "Pretext can be established through comparing qualifications only when 'the disparity in qualifications is so apparent as virtually to jump off the page and slap you in the face.'"

Under this Court's decisions, qualifications evidence may suffice, at least in some circumstances, to show pretext. * * * [A] plaintiff "might seek to demonstrate that respondent's claim to have promoted a better qualified applicant was pretextual by showing that she was in fact better qualified than the person chosen for the position" "The fact that a court may think that the employer misjudged the qualifications of the applicants does not in itself expose him to Title VII liability, although this may be probative of whether the employer's reasons are pretexts for discrimination." Cf. *Reeves v. Sanderson Plumbing Products, Inc.,* ("[A] plaintiff's prima facie case, combined with sufficient evidence to find that the employer's asserted justification is false, may permit the trier of fact to conclude that the employer unlawfully discriminated").

The visual image of words jumping off the page to slap you (presumably a court) in the face is unhelpful and imprecise as an elaboration of the standard for inferring pretext from superior qualifications. Federal courts, including the Court of Appeals for the Eleventh Circuit in a decision it cited here, have articulated various other standards, noting that "disparities in qualifications must be of such weight and significance that no reasonable person, in the exercise of impartial judgment, could have chosen the candidate selected over the plaintiff for the job in question." *Raad v. Fairbanks North Star Borough School Dist.,* 323 F.3d 1185, 1194 (C.A.9 2003) (holding that qualifications evidence standing alone may establish pretext where the plaintiff's qualifications are " 'clearly superior' " to those of the selected job applicant); *Aka v. Washington Hospital Center,* 156 F.3d 1284, 1294 (C.A.D.C.1998) (en banc) (concluding the factfinder may infer pretext if "a reasonable employer would have found the plaintiff to be significantly better qualified for the job"), and in this case the Court of Appeals qualified its statement by suggesting that superior qualifications may be probative of pretext when combined with other evidence. This is not the occasion to define more precisely what standard should govern pretext claims based on superior qualifications. Today's decision, furthermore, should not be read to hold that petitioners' evidence necessarily showed pretext. The District Court concluded otherwise. It suffices to say here that some formulation other than the test the Court of Appeals articulated in this case would better ensure that trial courts reach consistent results.

The Court of Appeals should determine in the first instance whether the two aspects of its decision here determined to have been mistaken were essential to its holding. On these premises, certiorari is granted, the judgment of the Court of Appeals is vacated, and the case is remanded for further proceedings consistent with this opinion.

Notes

1. *Qualifications "Gap:"* **Calhoun v. Johnson,** 632 F.3d 1259 (D.C.Cir. 2011), held that a difference in qualifications between plaintiff and the person hired will support an inference of improper motivation only if the difference is "substantial," or those of the plaintiff are "markedly superior." Superiority in one factor can be offset by the favored employee having better qualifications in another area. Moreover, when objective qualifications of applicants are "similar," no inference of improper motivation can be drawn from the decision maker relying on a properly structured subjective judgment. *Torgerson v. City of Rochester,* 643 F.3d 1031 (8th Cir. 2011) (uniform criteria for interviews established in advance, candidates awarded numerical scores, and interviewers explained their scores).

2. *"Me too:"* Plaintiffs may offer evidence of *individual acts* of alleged discrimination against *other workers* to support an inference that plaintiff, too, was subject to similar discrimination. *Sanderson, supra,* noted that examples of similar discrimination against other individuals in plaintiff's class might be some evidence of improper motive in the treatment of the plaintiff. Such proof raises three constraints: (1) the danger of going far afield to litigate disputed facts of other cases, particularly where the collateral examples are only remotely related to plaintiff's claim; (2) the potential for jury confusion of the issues; and (3) the possibility of the jury drawing a "bad man" inference, in that it might give defendant's past misconduct greater weight than its probative value.

On these grounds a trial court had a *per se* rule excluding "me too" evidence. **SPRINT/UNITED MANAGEMENT CO. v. MENDELSOHN,** 552 U.S. 379, 128 S.Ct. 1140, 170 L.Ed.2d 1 (2008), reversed, holding that there is no absolute rule either prohibiting or requiring jury consideration of the employer's collateral acts of discrimination against third parties. Trial courts have the discretion to allow or to exclude such evidence. *See, Mendelsohn v. United Sprint Mgt. Co.,* on remand, 402 Fed.Appx. 337 (10th Cir. 2010), affirming the trial court's exercise of discretion to exclude such evidence. *Contrast, Bennett v. Nucor Corp.,* 656 F.3d 802 (8th Cir. 2011), which affirmed trial court admission into evidence prior EEOC charges of others against the employer, letters of complaint to the EEOC, and various affidavits by nonparty employees gathered in anticipation of litigation, all of which outlined perceived discriminatory treatment they had suffered at the hands of the employer. Rejecting first, challenges that these documents constituted inadmissible hearsay, the court concluded that the relevance of such documents was particularly probative when, as here, plaintiff was alleging harassment and concluded that the trial court did not abuse its discretion in concluding that the probative value of co-worker allegations of discrimination outweighed any unwarranted prejudicial effect they might have on a jury. *See,* Fed.R.Evidence, 403.

3. *Inconsistency:"* In **Jones v. National Am. Univ,** 608 F.3d 1039 (8th Cir. 2010), defendant's response to the EEOC charge was that plaintiff was not promoted because she had "struggled with her *performance."* At trial defendant articulated that it was plaintiff's lack of managerial and marketing *experience* that warranted her non-selection. Defendant presented no evidence of the first asserted reason (plaintiff's deficient job performance). This shifting justification cast doubt on whether the employer actually relied on the subsequently articulated reason (lack of experience) when it made its decision. Moreover, as to this second explanation, plaintiff demonstrated that the person who was promoted also lacked extensive managerial experience. Such inconsistency permitted the fact finder to conclude that the reason articulated by defendant at trial was a pretext for improper motive. Moreover, failure of the employer to follow established procedures in its treatment of plaintiff can be evidence of improper motive. **Rahlf v. Mo–Tech Corp., Inc.,** 642 F.3d 633 (8th Cir. 2011).

4. *Destruction or Loss of Evidence* (particularly if contrary to EEOC rules requiring the retention of records or contrary to company rules or practices) gives rise to an inference that the information contained therein is harmful to the defendant. While not sufficient standing alone to prove pretext of a proffered reason, unexplained destruction of documentation of reasons given at the time can be a part of an evidentiary "mosaic." **Talavera v. Shah,** 638 F.3d 303 (D.C.Cir. 2011).

5. *Statistics:* Imbalance in the work force, a statistical pattern of hiring or discharges, or similar numerical presentations that fall short of being statistically significant do not, standing alone, establish that a "legitimate" reason articulated by defendant was pretextual. *Jackson v. Watkins,* 619 F.3d 463 (5th Cir. 2010). Nonetheless, suspicious patterns often will be admitted as a piece of the "mosaic" suggesting pretext. *Lewis v. City of Chicago,* 496 F.3d 645 (7th Cir. 2007); *Sanders v. Southwestern Bell Tel., L.P.,* 544 F.3d 1101 (10th Cir. 2008).

5. PLAINTIFF'S ULTIMATE BURDEN OF PERSUASION

DESERT PALACE, INC. v. COSTA, 539 U.S. 90, 123 S.Ct. 2148, 156 L.Ed.2d 84 (2003), interpreted Title VII, as amended in 1991 by adding §§ 703(m) and 705(g)(2)(B). The Court, in an opinion by JUSTICE THOMAS, quoted with approval the following trial court instruction to the jury on "mixed motives" under Title VII:

> You have heard evidence that defendant's treatment of the plaintiff was motivated by the plaintiff's sex and also by other lawful reasons.

If you find that plaintiff's sex was a motivating factor in the defendant's treatment of the plaintiff, the plaintiff is entitled to your verdict, even if you find that defendant's conduct was also motivated by lawful reasons.

However, if you find the defendant's treatment of the plaintiff was motivated by both gender and lawful reasons, you must decide whether plaintiff is entitled to damages. The plaintiff is entitled to damages unless the defendant proves by a preponderance of the evidence that the defendant would have treated plaintiff similarly even if the plaintiff's gender had played no role in the employment decision.

Petitioner [defendant employer] unsuccessfully objected to this instruction claiming that respondent [plaintiff] had failed to adduce 'direct evidence' that sex was a motivating factor in her dismissal * * *. The jury rendered a verdict for respondent [plaintiff] awarding backpay, compensatory, and punitive damages. * * *

The question before us in this case is whether a plaintiff must present direct evidence of discrimination in order to obtain a mixed-motive instruction under [42 U.S.C. § 2000e–2(m)] We hold that direct evidence is not required. * * *

[W]e agree with the Court of Appeals that no heightened showing is required under § 2000e–2(m). * * *

In order to obtain an instruction under § 2000e–2(m) a plaintiff need only present sufficient evidence for a reasonable jury to conclude, by a preponderance of the evidence, that "race, color, religion, sex, or national origin, was a motivating factor for any employment practice." Because direct evidence of discrimination is not required in mixed-motive cases, the Court of Appeals correctly concluded that the District Court did not abuse its discretion in giving a mixed-motive instruction to the jury. * * *

GROSS v. FBL FINANCIAL SERVICES, INC.

Supreme Court of the United States, 2009
557 U.S. 167, 129 S.Ct. 2343, 174 L.Ed.2d 119

JUSTICE THOMAS delivered the opinion of the Court.

* * *

Petitioner Jack Gross began working for respondent FBL Financial Group, Inc. (FBL), in 1971. As of 2001, Gross held the position of claims administration director. But in 2003, when he was 54 years old, Gross was reassigned to the position of claims project coordinator. At that same time, FBL transferred many of Gross' job responsibilities to a newly created position-claims administration manager. That position was given to Lisa Kneeskern, who had previously been supervised by Gross and who was then in her early forties. Although Gross (in his new position) and Kneeskern received the same compensation, Gross considered the reassignment a demotion because of FBL's reallocation of his former job responsibilities to Kneeskern.

In April 2004, Gross filed suit in District Court, alleging that his reassignment to the position of claims project coordinator violated the ADEA, which makes it unlawful for an employer to take adverse action against an employee "because of such individual's age." The case proceeded to trial, where Gross introduced evidence suggesting that his reassignment was based at least in part on his age. FBL defended its decision on the grounds that Gross' reassignment was part of a corporate restructuring and that Gross' new position was better suited to his skills.

[T]he District Court instructed the jury that it must return a verdict for Gross if he proved, by a preponderance of the evidence, that FBL "demoted [him] to claims projec[t] coordinator" and that his "age was a motivating factor" in FBL's decision to demote him. The jury was further instructed that Gross' age would qualify as a " 'motivating factor,' if [it] played a part or a role in [FBL]'s decision to demote [him]." The jury was also instructed regarding FBL's burden of proof. According to the District Court, the "verdict must be for [FBL] ... if it has been proved by the preponderance of the evidence that [FBL] would have demoted [Gross] regardless of his age." The jury returned a verdict for Gross, awarding him $46,945 in lost compensation.

FBL challenged the jury instructions on appeal. The United States Court of Appeals for the Eighth Circuit reversed and remanded for a new trial, holding that the jury had been incorrectly instructed under the standard established in *Price Waterhouse v. Hopkins,* 490 U.S. 228, 109 S.Ct. 1775, 104 L.Ed.2d 268 (1989). In *Price Waterhouse,* this Court addressed the proper allocation of the burden of persuasion in cases brought under Title VII of the Civil Rights Act of 1964 when an employee alleges that he suffered an adverse employment action because of both permissible and impermissible considerations—*i.e.,* a "mixed-motives" case. The *Price Waterhouse* decision was splintered. Four Justices joined a plurality opinion. Justices White and O'Connor separately concurred in the judgment, (opinion of O'CONNOR, J.), and three Justices dissented (opinion of KENNEDY, J.). Six Justices ultimately agreed that if a Title VII plaintiff shows that discrimination was a "motivating" or a " 'substantial' " factor in the employer's action, the burden of persuasion should shift to the employer to show that it would have taken the same action regardless of that impermissible consideration. (plurality opinion); (opinion of O'Connor, J.). Justice O'Connor further found that to shift the burden of persuasion to the employer, the employee must present "direct evidence that an illegitimate criterion was a substantial factor in the [employment] decision."
* * *

The Court of Appeals thus concluded that the District Court's jury instructions were flawed because they allowed the burden to shift to FBL upon a presentation of a preponderance of *any* category of evidence showing that age was a motivating factor-not just "direct evidence" related to FBL's alleged consideration of age. Because Gross conceded that he had not presented direct evidence of discrimination, the Court of Appeals held that the District Court should not have given the mixed-motives instruction. Rather, Gross should have been held to the burden of persuasion applicable to typical, non-mixed-motives claims; the jury thus should have been instructed only to determine whether Gross had carried his burden of "prov[ing] that age was the determining factor in FBL's employment action."

We granted certiorari, and now vacate the decision of the Court of Appeals.

II

* * * [W]e must first determine whether the burden of persuasion ever shifts to the party defending an alleged mixed-motives discrimination claim brought under the ADEA. We hold that it does not.

A

Petitioner relies on this Court's decisions construing Title VII for his interpretation of the ADEA. Because Title VII is materially different with respect to the relevant burden of persuasion, however, these decisions do not control our construction of the ADEA.

In *Price Waterhouse,* a plurality of the Court and two Justices concurring in the judgment determined that once a "plaintiff in a Title VII case proves that [the plaintiff's membership in a protected class] played a motivating part in an employment decision, the defendant may avoid a finding of liability only by proving by a preponderance of the evidence that it would have made the same decision even if it had not taken [that factor] into account." But as we explained in *Desert Palace, Inc. v. Costa,* 539 U.S. 90, 94–95, 123 S.Ct. 2148, 156 L.Ed.2d 84 (2003), Congress has since amended Title VII by explicitly authorizing discrimination claims in which an improper consideration was "a motivating factor" for an adverse employment decision. See 42 U.S.C. § 2000e–2(m) (providing that "an unlawful employment practice is established when the complaining party demonstrates that race, color, religion, sex, or national origin was *a motivating factor* for any employment practice, even though other factors also motivated the practice" (emphasis added)); § 2000e–5(g)(2)(B) (restricting the remedies available to plaintiffs proving violations of § 2000e–2(m)).

This Court has never held that this burden-shifting framework applies to ADEA claims. And, we decline to do so now. When conducting statutory interpretation, we "must be careful not to apply rules applicable under one statute to a different statute without careful and critical examination." Unlike Title VII, the ADEA's text does not provide that a plaintiff may establish discrimination by showing that age was simply a motivating factor. Moreover, Congress neglected to add such a provision to the ADEA when it amended Title VII to add §§ 2000e–2(m) and 2000e–5(g)(2)(B), even though it contemporaneously amended the ADEA in several ways.

We cannot ignore Congress' decision to amend Title VII's relevant provisions but not make similar changes to the ADEA. When Congress amends one statutory provision but not another, it is presumed to have acted intentionally. Furthermore, as the Court has explained, "negative implications raised by disparate provisions are strongest" when the provisions were "considered simultaneously when the language raising the implication was inserted." As a result, the Court's interpretation of the ADEA is not governed by Title VII decisions such as *Desert Palace* and *Price Waterhouse.*

B

Our inquiry therefore must focus on the text of the ADEA to decide whether it authorizes a mixed-motives age discrimination claim. It does not. "Statutory construction must begin with the language employed by Congress and the assumption that the ordinary meaning of that language accurately expresses the legislative purpose." The ADEA provides, in relevant part, that "[i]t shall be unlawful for an employer . . . to fail or refuse to hire or to discharge any individual or otherwise discriminate against any individual with respect to his compensation, terms, conditions, or privileges of employment, *because of* such individual's age."

The words "because of" mean "by reason of: on account of." 1 Webster's Third New International Dictionary 194 (1966); see also 1 Oxford English Dictionary 746 (1933) (defining "because of" to mean "By reason *of,* on account *of*"); The Random House Dictionary of the English Language 132 (1966) (defining "because" to mean "by reason; on account"). Thus, the ordinary meaning of the ADEA's requirement that an employer took adverse action "because of" age is that age was the "reason" that the employer decided to act. See *Hazen Paper Co. v. Biggins,* 507 U.S. 604, 610, 113 S.Ct. 1701, 123 L.Ed.2d 338 (1993) (explaining that the claim "cannot succeed unless the employee's protected trait actually played a role in [the employer's decisionmaking] process *and had a determinative influence on the outcome*"). To establish a disparate-treatment claim under the plain language of the ADEA, therefore, a plaintiff must prove that age was the "but-for" cause of the employer's adverse decision.

It follows, then, that under § 623(a)(1), the plaintiff retains the burden of persuasion to establish that age was the "but-for" cause of the employer's adverse action. Indeed, we have previously held that the burden is allocated in this manner in ADEA cases. And nothing in the statute's text indicates that Congress has carved out an exception to that rule for a subset of ADEA cases. Where the statutory text is "silent on the allocation of the burden of persuasion," we "begin with the ordinary default rule that plaintiffs bear the risk of failing to prove their claims." We have no warrant to depart from the general rule in this setting.

Hence, the burden of persuasion necessary to establish employer liability is the same in alleged mixed-motives cases as in any other ADEA disparate-treatment action. A plaintiff must prove by a preponderance of the evidence (which may be direct or circumstantial), that age was the "but-for" cause of the challenged employer decision.[4]

III

Finally, we reject petitioner's contention that our interpretation of the ADEA is controlled by *Price Waterhouse,* which initially established that the burden of persuasion shifted in alleged mixed-motives Title VII claims. In any event, it is far from clear that the Court would have the same approach were it to consider the question today in the first instance.

Whatever the deficiencies of *Price Waterhouse* in retrospect, it has become evident in the years since that case was decided that its burden-shifting framework is difficult to apply. For example, in cases tried to a jury, courts have found it particularly difficult to craft an instruction to explain its burden-shifting framework. Thus, even if *Price Waterhouse* was doctrinally sound, the problems associated with its application have eliminated any perceivable benefit to extending its framework to ADEA claims.[6]

IV

We hold that a plaintiff bringing a disparate-treatment claim pursuant to the ADEA must prove, by a preponderance of the evidence, that age was the "but-for" cause of the challenged adverse employment action. The burden of persuasion does not shift to the employer to show that it would have taken the action regardless of age, even when a plaintiff has produced some evidence that age was one motivating factor in that decision. Accordingly, we vacate the judgment of the Court of Appeals and remand the case for further proceedings consistent with this opinion.

JUSTICE STEVENS, with whom JUSTICE SOUTER, JUSTICE GINSBURG, and JUSTICE BREYER join, dissenting.

* * * The "but-for" causation standard endorsed by the Court today was advanced in JUSTICE KENNEDY'S dissenting opinion in *Price Waterhouse v. Hopkins,* a case construing identical language in Title VII of the Civil Rights Act of 1964. Not only did the Court reject the but-for standard in that case, but so too did Congress when it amended Title VII in 1991.

---

4. Because we hold that ADEA plaintiffs retain the burden of persuasion to prove all disparate-treatment claims, we do not need to address whether plaintiffs must present direct, rather than circumstantial, evidence to obtain a burden-shifting instruction. There is no heightened evidentiary requirement for ADEA plaintiffs to satisfy their burden of persuasion that age was the "but-for" cause of their employer's adverse action, see 29 U.S.C. § 623(a), and we will imply none. "Congress has been unequivocal when imposing heightened proof requirements" in other statutory contexts, including in other subsections within Title 29, when it has seen fit.

6. Gross points out that the Court has also applied a burden-shifting framework to certain claims brought in contexts other than pursuant to Title VII. citing, *inter alia, NLRB v. Transportation Management Corp.,* 462 U.S. 393, 401–403, 103 S.Ct. 2469, 76 L.Ed.2d 667 (1983) (claims brought under the National Labor Relations Act (NLRA)); *Mt. Healthy City Bd. of Ed. v. Doyle,* 429 U.S. 274, 287, 97 S.Ct. 568, 50 L.Ed.2d 471 (1977) (constitutional claims)). These cases, however, do not require the Court to adopt his contra statutory position. * * *

Given this unambiguous history, it is particularly inappropriate for the Court, on its own initiative, to adopt an interpretation of the causation requirement in the ADEA that differs from the established reading of Title VII. * * *

The Court asks whether a mixed-motives instruction is ever appropriate in an ADEA case. As it acknowledges, this was not the question we granted certiorari to decide. * * * Yet the Court is unconcerned that the question it chooses to answer has not been briefed by the parties or interested *amici curiae.* Its failure to consider the views of the United States, which represents the agency charged with administering the ADEA, is especially irresponsible.

Unfortunately, the majority's inattention to prudential Court practices is matched by its utter disregard of our precedent and Congress' intent. The ADEA provides that "[i]t shall be unlawful for an employer . . . to fail or refuse to hire or to discharge any individual or otherwise discriminate against any individual with respect to his compensation, terms, conditions, or privileges of employment, *because of* such individual's age." As we recognized in *Price Waterhouse* when we construed the identical "because of" language of Title VII, the most natural reading of the text proscribes adverse employment actions motivated in whole or in part by the age of the employee.

In *Price Waterhouse,* we concluded that the words " 'because of' such individual's . . . sex . . . mean that gender must be irrelevant to employment decisions." To establish a violation of Title VII, we therefore held, a plaintiff had to prove that her sex was a motivating factor in an adverse employment decision. We recognized that the employer had an affirmative defense: It could avoid a finding of liability by proving that it would have made the same decision even if it had not taken the plaintiff's sex into account. But this affirmative defense did not alter the meaning of "because of." As we made clear, when "an employer considers both gender and legitimate factors at the time of making a decision, that decision was 'because of' sex." We readily rejected the dissent's contrary assertion. "To construe the words 'because of' as colloquial shorthand for 'but-for' causation," we said, "is to misunderstand them."

Today, however, the Court interprets the words "because of" in the ADEA "as colloquial shorthand for 'but-for' causation." That the Court is construing the ADEA rather than Title VII does not justify this departure from precedent. The relevant language in the two statutes is identical, and we have long recognized that our interpretations of Title VII's language apply "with equal force in the context of age discrimination, for the substantive provisions of the ADEA 'were derived *in haec verba* from Title VII.' " * * *

The conclusion that "because of" an individual's age means that age was a motivating factor in an employment decision is bolstered by Congress' reaction to *Price Waterhouse* in the 1991 Civil Rights Act. As part of its response to "a number of recent decisions by the United States Supreme

Court that sharply cut back on the scope and effectiveness of [civil rights] laws," Congress eliminated the affirmative defense to liability that *Price Waterhouse* had furnished employers and provided instead that an employer's same-decision showing would limit only a plaintiff's remedies. See § 2000e–5(g)(2)(B). Importantly, however, Congress ratified *Price Waterhouse*'s interpretation of the plaintiff's burden of proof, rejecting the dissent's suggestion in that case that but-for causation was the proper standard. See § 2000e–2(m) ("[A]n unlawful employment practice is established when the complaining party demonstrates that race, color, religion, sex, or national origin was a motivating factor for any employment practice, even though other factors also motivated the practice").

Because the 1991 Act amended only Title VII and not the ADEA with respect to mixed-motives claims, the Court reasonably declines to apply the amended provisions to the ADEA. But it proceeds to ignore the conclusion compelled by this interpretation of the Act: *Price Waterhouse*'s construction of "because of" remains the governing law for ADEA claims.

* * *

JUSTICE BREYER, with whom JUSTICE SOUTER and JUSTICE GINSBURG join, dissenting.

I agree with JUSTICE STEVENS that mixed-motive instructions are appropriate in the Age Discrimination in Employment Act context. And I join his opinion. The Court rejects this conclusion on the ground that the words "because of" require a plaintiff to prove that age was the "but-for" cause of his employer's adverse employment action. But the majority does not explain why this is so. The words "because of" do not inherently require a showing of "but-for" causation, and I see no reason to read them to require such a showing.

It is one thing to require a typical tort plaintiff to show "but-for" causation. In that context, reasonably objective scientific or commonsense theories of physical causation make the concept of "but-for" causation comparatively easy to understand and relatively easy to apply. But it is an entirely different matter to determine a "but-for" relation when we consider, not physical forces, but the mind-related characterizations that constitute motive. Sometimes we speak of *determining* or *discovering* motives, but more often we *ascribe* motives, after an event, to an individual in light of the individual's thoughts and other circumstances present at the time of decision. In a case where we characterize an employer's actions as having been taken out of multiple motives, say, both because the employee was old and because he wore loud clothing, to apply "but-for" causation is to engage in a hypothetical inquiry about what would have happened if the employer's thoughts and other circumstances had been different. The answer to this hypothetical inquiry will often be far from obvious, and, since the employee likely knows less than does the employer about what the employer was thinking at the time, the employer will often be in a stronger position than the employee to provide the answer.

All that a plaintiff can know for certain in such a context is that the forbidden motive did play a role in the employer's decision. And the fact that a jury has found that age did play a role in the decision justifies the use of the word "because," *i.e.*, the employer dismissed the employee because of his age (and other things). I therefore would see nothing wrong in concluding that the plaintiff has established a violation of the statute.

But the law need not automatically assess liability in these circumstances. In *Price Waterhouse*, the plurality recognized an affirmative defense where the defendant could show that the employee would have been dismissed regardless. The law permits the employer this defense, not because the forbidden motive, age, had no role in the *actual* decision, but because the employer can show that he would have dismissed the employee anyway in the *hypothetical* circumstance in which his age-related motive was absent. And it makes sense that this would be an affirmative defense, rather than part of the showing of a violation, precisely because the defendant is in a better position than the plaintiff to establish how he would have acted in this hypothetical situation. I can see nothing unfair or impractical about allocating the burdens of proof in this way. * * *

NOTES

1. *Reconcile Gross and Sanderson Plumbing: Sanderson Plumbing, supra,* held that under Title VII a finding that defendant's proffered reason did not exist is sufficient, standing alone, to *permit* the fact finder to conclude that defendant was illegally motivated. Does *Gross* suggest a different result under the ADEA? That is, to permit a jury to conclude that age was *the* motive need plaintiff prove, not only that the proffered reason was false, but also present *additional evidence* of age motivation? Some authority so indicates. *Tusing v. DeMoines Ind. Comm. Sch. Dist,* 639 F.3d 507 (8th Cir. 2011).

2. *The Turbulent Wake of Gross:*

a. *Title VII Retaliation:* Literally, § 703e–2(m), does not apply to claims of retaliation brought under § 704. Some courts have held that this omission is critical and have continued to apply the mixed motive approach of *Price Waterhouse* (discussed in *Gross*). Thus, an employer that proves that it would have made the same decision in the absence of a retaliatory motive is absolved from liability. *Matima v. Celli,* 228 F.3d 68 (2d Cir. 2000). Others have held that notwithstanding the linguistic omission, the 1991 Amendments should be applied to § 704 retaliation claims. Accordingly, these courts do not absolve defendant from liability upon defendant proving that it would have made the same decision absent a retaliatory motive. This proof only prohibits the court from awarding reinstatement and back pay. *Stegall v. Citadel Broad. Co.,* 350 F.3d 1061 (9th Cir. 2003). *Gross* adds to the disarray. The Seventh Circuit applies the *Gross, "but for"* requirement to all retaliation claims. *Serwatka v. Rockwell Automation,* 591 F.3d 957 (7th Cir. 2010). The Fifth Circuit limits *Gross* to the ADEA. *Smith v. Xerox, Corp.,* 602 F.3d 320 (5th Cir. 2010).

b. *42 U.S.C. § 1981.* The Reconstruction Era Civil Rights Acts requires plaintiff to establish the racial motive of the defendant. When faced with possible dual or mixed motives in claims arising under the Fourteenth Amendment, **Mt. Healthy City Bd. of Ed. v. Doyle**, 429 U.S. 274, 287, 97 S.Ct. 568, 576, 50 L.Ed.2d 471 (1977), adopted a shifting burden approach similar to that which had been used under Title VII as construed by *Price Waterhouse* prior to the 1991 Amendments. After the 1991 Amendments, but prior to *Gross,* the courts were divided. Some held that the 1991 Amendments applied to § 1981 actions. *Metoyer v. Chassman,* 504 F.3d 919 (9th Cir. 2007). Others determined that the Amendments were not applicable to § 1981 claims, but in the absence of statutory guidance, the courts applied the shifting burden analysis of either *Mt. Healthy* or *Price Waterhouse. Mabra v. United Food Workers, Local 1996,* 176 F.3d 1357 (11th Cir. 1999).

c. *ADA:* The 1991 Amendments to Title VII do not expressly apply to the ADA. Moreover, the Rehabilitation Act, which preceded the ADA, requires that disability must be the "sole" reason for the discrimination, and the ADA incorporates consistent elements of the Rehabilitation Act. Accordingly, some courts have concluded that plaintiff must prove that the discrimination was based *"solely"* on plaintiff's disability. *Hedrick v. Western Reserve Care Syst.,* 355 F.3d 444 (6th Cir. 2004). This would seem similar to the "but for" analysis in *Gross.* Most courts, however, have not read "solely" into the ADA, and thus, prior to *Gross,* applied a mixed-motive analysis utilized in *Price Waterhouse. Parker v. Columbia Pictures Industries,* 204 F.3d 326 (2d Cir. 2000).

d. *USERRA:* Neither the language of Title VII, nor the interpretation by *Gross* of the ADEA, may be applicable to USERRA. *Lisdahl v. Mayo Foundation,* 633 F.3d 712 (8th Cir. 2011), held that plaintiff has the burden of proving that *"a"* motivating factor was plaintiff's military service. Defendant will avoid liability, however, only if it carries the burden of convincing the jury that it would have made the same decision regarding plaintiff even had it not been motivated by plaintiff's military service, in effect applying *Price Waterhouse.*

e. *State law:* State courts may interpret their statutory prohibition of age discrimination to require only that plaintiff prove that age was "a" motivating factor, leaving to defendant to prove that it would have made the same decision notwithstanding age being a consideration. *Tusing v. Des Moines Ind. Comm. Sch. Dist.,* 639 F.3d 507 (8th Cir. 2011) (Iowa state law).

f. *Reform? The Protecting Older Workers Against Discrimination Act* (H.R. 3721, 111th Cong.), introduced in 2009, would have amended the ADEA to mirror Title VII. Hearings were held in early 2010, but no action has been taken.

3. *Appellate Review:* **Anderson v. City of Bessemer, 470 U.S. 564, 105 S.Ct. 1504, 84 L.Ed.2d 518 (1985).** The trial court, as a fact finder, concluded that the employer's explanation for preferring a male applicant over the female plaintiff was pretextual based in part on its finding that plaintiff was better qualified for the position than the male candidate who was awarded the job. The Court of Appeals reversed based upon its reading of the evidence, concluding that the male candidate was better qualified than the plaintiff. The Supreme Court reversed:

Based on our own reading of the record, we cannot say that either interpretation of the facts is illogical or implausible. Each has support in inferences that may be drawn from the facts on the record; and if either interpretation had been drawn by a district court on the record before us, we would not be inclined to find it clearly erroneous. The question we must answer, however, is not whether the [Court of Appeals'] interpretation of the facts was clearly erroneous, but whether the District Court's finding was clearly erroneous. The District Court determined that [plaintiff] was better qualified, and * * * such a finding is entitled to deference notwithstanding that it is not based on credibility determinations. * * *

D. NUMERICALLY BASED CIRCUMSTANTIAL EVIDENCE: STATISTICS

INTERNATIONAL BROTHERHOOD OF TEAMSTERS v. UNITED STATES

Supreme Court of the United States, 1977
431 U.S. 324, 97 S.Ct. 1843, 52 L.Ed.2d 396

JUSTICE STEWART delivered the opinion of the Court.

[Defendant union is the exclusive representative of the defendant employer. The employer operates a nationwide freight transportation system] * * *

Consideration of the question whether the company engaged in a pattern or practice of discriminatory hiring practices involves controlling legal principles that are relatively clear. The Government's theory of discrimination was simply that the company, in violation of § 703(a) of Title VII, regularly and purposefully treated Negroes and Spanish-surnamed Americans less favorably than white persons. The disparity in treatment allegedly involved the refusal to recruit, hire, transfer, or promote minority group members on an equal basis with white people, particularly with respect to line-driving positions. The ultimate factual issues are thus simply whether there was a pattern or practice of such disparate treatment and, if so, whether the differences were "racially premised."[15]

As the plaintiff, the Government bore the initial burden of making out a prima facie case of discrimination. And, because it alleged a systemwide pattern or practice of resistance to the full enjoyment of Title VII rights, the Government ultimately had to prove more than the mere occurrence of isolated or "accidental" or sporadic discriminatory acts. It had to

---

15. "Disparate treatment" such as is alleged in the present case is the most easily understood type of discrimination. The employer simply treats some people less favorably than others because of their race, color, religion, sex, or national origin. Proof of discriminatory motive is critical, although it can in some situations be inferred from the mere fact of differences in treatment. Undoubtedly disparate treatment was the most obvious evil Congress had in mind when it enacted Title VII.

Claims of disparate treatment may be distinguished from claims that stress "disparate impact." The latter involve employment practices that are facially neutral in their treatment of different groups but that in fact fall more harshly on one group than another and cannot be justified by business necessity. Either theory may, of course, be applied to a particular set of facts.

establish by a preponderance of the evidence that racial discrimination was the company's standard operating procedure the regular rather than the unusual practice.

We agree with the District Court and the Court of Appeals that the Government carried its burden of proof. As of March 31, 1971, shortly after the Government filed its complaint alleging systemwide discrimination, the company had 6,472 employees. Of these, 314 (5%) were Negroes and 257 (4%) were Spanish-surnamed Americans. Of the 1,828 line drivers, however, there were only 8 (0.4%) Negroes and 5 (0.3%) Spanish-surnamed persons, and all of the Negroes had been hired after the litigation had commenced. With one exception, a man who worked as a line driver at the Chicago terminal from 1950 to 1959, the company and its predecessors did not employ a Negro on a regular basis as a line driver until 1969. And, as the Government showed, even in 1971 there were terminals in areas of substantial Negro population where all of the company's line drivers were white.[17] A great majority of the Negroes (83%) and Spanish-surnamed Americans 78%) who did work for the company held the lower paying city operations and serviceman jobs, whereas only 39% of the nonminority employees held jobs in those categories.

The Government bolstered its statistical evidence with the testimony of individuals who recounted over 40 specific instances of discrimination. Upon the basis of this testimony the District Court found that "(n)umerous qualified black and Spanish-surnamed American applicants who sought line driving jobs at the company over the years, either had their requests ignored, were given false or misleading information about requirements, opportunities, and application procedures, or were not considered and hired on the same basis that whites were considered and hired." Minority employees who wanted to transfer to line-driver jobs met with similar difficulties.

The company's principal response to this evidence is that statistics can never in and of themselves prove the existence of a pattern or practice of discrimination, or even establish a prima facie case shifting to the employer the burden of rebutting the inference raised by the figures. But, as even our brief summary of the evidence shows, this was not a case in which the Government relied on "statistics alone." The individuals who testified about their personal experiences with the company brought the cold numbers convincingly to life.

In any event, our cases make it unmistakably clear that "(s)tatistical analyses have served and will continue to serve an important role" in cases in which the existence of discrimination is a disputed issue. We have

---

17. In Atlanta, for instance, Negroes composed 22.35% of the population in the surrounding metropolitan area and 51.31% of the population in the city proper. The company's Atlanta terminal employed 57 line drivers. All were white. In Los Angeles, 10.84% of the greater metropolitan population and 17.88% of the city population were Negro. But at the company's two Los Angeles terminals there was not a single Negro among the 374 line drivers. The proof showed similar disparities in San Francisco, Denver, Nashville, Chicago, Dallas, and at several other terminals.

repeatedly approved the use of statistical proof, where it reached proportions comparable to those in this case, to establish a prima facie case of racial discrimination in jury selection cases.[20] We caution only that statistics are not irrefutable; they come in infinite variety and, like any other kind of evidence, they may be rebutted. In short, their usefulness depends on all of the surrounding facts and circumstances.

In addition to its general protest against the use of statistics in Title VII cases, the company claims that in this case the statistics revealing racial imbalance are misleading because they fail to take into account the company's particular business situation as of the effective date of Title VII. The company concedes that its line drivers were virtually all white in July 1965, but it claims that thereafter business conditions were such that its work force dropped. Its argument is that low personnel turnover, rather than post-Act discrimination, accounts for more recent statistical disparities. It points to substantial minority hiring in later years, especially after 1971, as showing that any pre-Act patterns of discrimination were broken.

The argument would be a forceful one if this were an employer who, at the time of suit, had done virtually no new hiring since the effective date of Title VII. But it is not. Although the company's total number of employees apparently dropped somewhat during the late 1960's, the record shows that many line drivers continued to be hired throughout this period, and that almost all of them were white. To be sure, there were improvements in the company's hiring practices. The Court of Appeals commented that "T.I.M.E.–D.C.'s recent minority hiring progress stands

---

20. Petitioners argue that statistics, at least those comparing the racial composition of an employer's work force to the composition of the population at large, should never be given decisive weight in a Title VII case because to do so would conflict with s 703(j) of the Act, 42 U.S.C. s 2000e–2(j). That section provides:

"Nothing contained in this subchapter shall be interpreted to require any employer . . . to grant preferential treatment to any individual or to any group because of the race . . . or national origin of such individual or group on account of an imbalance which may exist with respect to the total number or percentage of persons of any race . . . or national origin employed by any employer . . . in comparison with the total number or percentage of persons of such race . . . or national origin in any community, State, section, or other area, or in the available work force in any community, State, section, or other area."

The argument fails in this case because the statistical evidence was not offered or used to support an erroneous theory that Title VII requires an employer's work force to be racially balanced. Statistics showing racial or ethnic imbalance are probative in a case such as this one only because such imbalance is often a telltale sign of purposeful discrimination; absent explanation, it is ordinarily to be expected that nondiscriminatory hiring practices will in time result in a work force more or less representative of the racial and ethnic composition of the population in the community from which employees are hired. Evidence of longlasting and gross disparity between the composition of a work force and that of the general population thus may be significant even though s 703(j) makes clear that Title VII imposes no requirement that a work force mirror the general population. Considerations such as small sample size may, of course, detract from the value of such evidence, and evidence showing that the figures for the general population might not accurately reflect the pool of qualified job applicants would also be relevant.

"Since the passage of the Civil Rights Act of 1964, the courts have frequently relied upon statistical evidence to prove a violation. . . . In many cases the only available avenue of proof is the use of racial statistics to uncover clandestine and covert discrimination by the employer or union involved."

as a laudable good faith effort to eradicate the effects of past discrimination in the area of hiring and initial assignment."[22] But the District Court and the Court of Appeals found upon substantial evidence that the company had engaged in a course of discrimination that continued well after the effective date of Title VII. The company's later changes in its hiring and promotion policies could be of little comfort to the victims of the earlier post-Act discrimination, and could not erase its previous illegal conduct or its obligation to afford relief to those who suffered because of it.[23]

The District Court and the Court of Appeals, on the basis of substantial evidence, held that the Government had proved a prima facie case of systematic and purposeful employment discrimination, continuing well beyond the effective date of Title VII. The company's attempts to rebut that conclusion were held to be inadequate. For the reasons we have summarized, there is no warrant for this Court to disturb the findings of the District Court and the Court of Appeals on this basic issue.

* * *

[The Court discusses how liability and remedies are established for individual members of the class]

The company and union seize upon the *McDonnell Douglas* pattern as the only means of establishing a prima facie case of individual discrimination. Our decision in that case, however, did not purport to create an inflexible formulation. * * * The importance of *McDonnell Douglas* lies, not in its specification of the discrete elements of proof required, but in its recognition of the general principle that any Title VII plaintiff must carry the initial burden of offering evidence adequate to create an inference that the employment decision was based on a discriminatory criterion illegal under the Act. * * *

---

22. For example, in 1971 the company hired 116 new line drivers, of whom 16 were Negro or Spanish-surnamed Americans. Minority employees composed 7.1% of the company's systemwide work force in 1967 and 10.5% in 1972. Minority hiring increased greatly in 1972 and 1973, presumably due at least in part to the existence of the consent decree.

23. The company's narrower attacks upon the statistical evidence that there was no precise delineation of the areas referred to in the general population statistics, that the Government did not demonstrate that minority populations were located close to terminals or that transportation was available, that the statistics failed to show what portion of the minority population was suited by age, health, or other qualifications to hold trucking jobs, etc. are equally lacking in force. At best, these attacks go only to the accuracy of the comparison between the composition of the company's work force at various terminals and the general population of the surrounding communities. They detract little from the Government's further showing that Negroes and Spanish-surnamed Americans who were hired were overwhelmingly excluded from line-driver jobs. Such employees were willing to work, had access to the terminal, were healthy and of working age, and often were at least sufficiently qualified to hold city-driver jobs. Yet they became line drivers with far less frequency than whites. (of 2,919 whites who held driving jobs in 1971, 1,802 (62%) were line drivers and 1,117 (38%) were city drivers; of 180 Negroes and Spanish-surnamed Americans who held driving jobs, 13 (7%) were line drivers and 167 (93%) were city drivers).

In any event, fine tuning of the statistics could not have obscured the glaring absence of minority line drivers. As the Court of Appeals remarked, the company's inability to rebut the inference of discrimination came not from a misuse of statistics but from "the inexorable zero."

The plaintiff in a pattern-or-practice action is the Government, and its initial burden is to demonstrate that unlawful discrimination has been a regular procedure or policy followed by an employer or group of employers. At the initial, "liability" stage of a pattern-or-practice suit the Government is not required to offer evidence that each person for whom it will ultimately seek relief was a victim of the employer's discriminatory policy. Its burden is to establish a prima facie case that such a policy existed. The burden then shifts to the employer to defeat the prima facie showing of a pattern or practice by demonstrating that the Government's proof is either inaccurate or insignificant. An employer might show, for example, that the claimed discriminatory pattern is a product of pre-Act hiring rather than unlawful post-Act discrimination, or that during the period it is alleged to have pursued a discriminatory policy it made too few employment decisions to justify the inference that it had engaged in a regular practice of discrimination.[46]

If an employer fails to rebut the inference that arises from the Government's prima facie case, a trial court may then conclude that a violation has occurred and determine the appropriate remedy. Without any further evidence from the Government, a court's finding of a pattern or practice justifies an award of prospective relief. Such relief might take the form of an injunctive order against continuation of the discriminatory practice, an order that the employer keep records of its future employment decisions and file periodic reports with the court, or any other order "necessary to ensure the full enjoyment of the rights" protected by Title VII.

When the Government seeks individual relief for the victims of the discriminatory practice, a district court must usually conduct additional proceedings after the liability phase of the trial to determine the scope of individual relief. The petitioners' contention in this case is that if the Government has not, in the course of proving a pattern or practice, already brought forth specific evidence that each individual was discriminatorily denied an employment opportunity, it must carry that burden at the second, "remedial" stage of trial. * * * [A]s is typical of Title VII pattern-or-practice suits, the question of individual relief does not arise until it has been proved that the employer has followed an employment policy of unlawful discrimination. The force of that proof does not dissipate at the remedial stage of the trial. The employer cannot, therefore, claim that there is no reason to believe that its individual employment decisions were discriminatorily based; it has already been shown to have maintained a policy of discriminatory decisionmaking.

---

46. The employer's defense must, of course, be designed to meet the prima facie case of the Government. We do not mean to suggest that there are any particular limits on the type of evidence an employer may use. The point is that at the liability stage of a pattern-or-practice trial the focus often will not be on individual hiring decisions, but on a pattern of discriminatory decisionmaking. While a pattern might be demonstrated by examining the discrete decisions of which it is composed, the Government's suits have more commonly involved proof of the expected result of a regularly followed discriminatory policy. In such cases the employer's burden is to provide a nondiscriminatory explanation for the apparently discriminatory result.

The proof of the pattern or practice supports an inference that any particular employment decision, during the period in which the discriminatory policy was in force, was made in pursuit of that policy. The Government need only show that an alleged individual discriminatee unsuccessfully applied for a job and therefore was a potential victim of the proved discrimination. * * * [T]he burden then rests on the employer to demonstrate that the individual applicant was denied an employment opportunity for lawful reasons.

* * * [W]e have held that the District Court and Court of Appeals were not in error in finding that the Government had proved a systemwide pattern and practice of racial and ethnic discrimination on the part of the company. On remand, therefore, every post-Act minority group applicant for a line-driver position will be presumptively entitled to relief, subject to a showing by the company that its earlier refusal to place the applicant in a line-driver job was not based on its policy of discrimination.[50]

HAZELWOOD SCHOOL DISTRICT v. UNITED STATES

Supreme Court of the United States, 1977
433 U.S. 299, 97 S.Ct. 2736, 53 L.Ed.2d 768

JUSTICE STEWART delivered the opinion of the Court.

The petitioner Hazelwood School District covers 78 square miles in the northern part of St. Louis County, Mo. In 1973 the Attorney General brought this lawsuit against Hazelwood and various of its officials, alleging that they were engaged in a 'pattern or practice' of employment discrimination in violation of Title VII of the Civil Rights Act of 1964. The complaint asked for an injunction requiring Hazelwood to cease its discriminatory practices, to take affirmative steps to obtain qualified Negro faculty members, and to offer employment and give backpay to victims of past illegal discrimination.

Hazelwood was formed from 13 rural school districts between 1949 and 1951 by a process of annexation. By the 1967–1968 school year, 17,550 students were enrolled in the district, of whom only 59 were Negro; the number of Negro pupils increased to 576 of 25,166 in 1972–1973, a total of just over 2%.

From the beginning, Hazelwood followed relatively unstructured procedures in hiring its teachers. [There were no formal procedures for reviewing all qualified applicants before choosing whom to interview, and the interview process was highly subjective. While "applicants with student teaching experience at Hazelwood were given preference if their performance had been satisfactory," it was "undisputed that each school principal possessed virtually unlimited discretion in hiring teachers for his school."]

In the early 1960's Hazelwood found it necessary to recruit new teachers, and for that purpose members of its staff visited a number of colleges and

---

50. Any nondiscriminatory justification offered by the company will be subject to further evidence by the Government that the purported reason for an applicant's rejection was in fact a pretext for unlawful discrimination.

universities in Missouri and bordering States. All the institutions visited were predominantly white, and Hazelwood did not seriously recruit at either of the two predominantly Negro four-year colleges in Missouri. As a buyer's market began to develop for public school teachers, Hazelwood curtailed its recruiting efforts. For the 1971–1972 school year, 3,127 persons applied for only 234 teaching vacancies; for the 1972–1973 school year, there were 2,373 applications for 282 vacancies. A number of the applicants who were not hired were Negroes.

Hazelwood hired its first Negro teacher in 1969. The number of Negro faculty members gradually increased in successive years: 6 of 957 in the 1970 school year; 16 of 1,107 by the end of the 1972 school year; 22 of 1,231 in the 1973 school year. By comparison, according to 1970 census figures, of more than 19,000 teachers employed in that year in the St. Louis area, 15.4% were Negro. That percentage figure included the St. Louis City School District, which in recent years has followed a policy of attempting to maintain a 50% Negro teaching staff. Apart from that school district, 5.7% of the teachers in the county were Negro in 1970.

Drawing upon these historic facts, the Government mounted its 'pattern or practice' attack in the District Court upon four different fronts. It adduced evidence of (1) a history of alleged racially discriminatory practices, (2) statistical disparities in hiring, (3) the standardless and largely subjective hiring procedures, and (4) specific instances of alleged discrimination against 55 unsuccessful Negro applicants for teaching jobs. Hazelwood offered virtually no additional evidence in response, relying instead on evidence introduced by the Government, perceived deficiencies in the Government's case, and its own officially promulgated policy 'to hire all teachers on the basis of training, preparation and recommendations, regardless of race, color or creed.'

The District Court ruled that the Government had failed to establish a pattern or practice of discrimination. * * * [The court found "nothing illegal or suspect in the teaching hiring procedures that Hazelwood had followed."]

The Court of Appeals for the Eighth Circuit [rejected the trial court's analysis of the statistical data, in particular the trial court had made "an irrelevant comparison of Negro teachers to Negro pupils in Hazelwood. The Court of Appeals held that the proper comparison was "one between Negro teachers in Hazelwood and Negro teachers in the relevant labor market area"]

In addition, the Court of Appeals reasoned that the trial court had erred in failing to measure the 55 instances in which Negro applicants were denied jobs against the four-part standard for establishing a prima facie case of individual discrimination set out in this Court's opinion in *McDonnell Douglas Corp. v. Green* Applying that standard, the appellate court found 16 cases of individual discrimination, which 'buttressed' the statistical proof. Because Hazelwood had not rebutted the Government's prima facie case of a pattern or practice of racial discrimination, the Court of

Appeals directed judgment for the Government and prescribed the remedial order to be entered.

* * *

This Court's recent consideration in *International Brotherhood of Teamsters v. United States* of the role of statistics in pattern-or-practice suits under Title VII provides substantial guidance in evaluating the arguments advanced by the petitioners. In that case we stated that it is the Government's burden to 'establish by a preponderance of the evidence that racial discrimination was the (employer's) standard operating procedure the regular rather than the unusual practice.' We also noted that statistics can be an important source of proof in employment discrimination cases, since

> 'absent explanation, it is ordinarily to be expected that nondiscriminatory hiring practices will in time result in a work force more or less representative of the racial and ethnic composition of the population in the community from which employees are hired. Evidence of long-lasting and gross disparity between the composition of a work force and that of the general population thus may be significant even though § 703(j) makes clear that Title VII imposes no requirement that a work force mirror the general population.'

There can be no doubt, in light of the *Teamsters* case, that the District Court's comparison of Hazelwood's teacher work force to its student population fundamentally misconceived the role of statistics in employment discrimination cases. The Court of Appeals was correct in the view that a proper comparison was between the racial composition of Hazelwood's teaching staff and the racial composition of the qualified public school teacher population in the relevant labor market.[13] The percentage of Negroes on Hazelwood's teaching staff in 1972–1973 was 1.4% and in 1973–1974 it was 1.8% By contrast, the percentage of qualified Negro teachers in the area was, according to the 1970 census, at least 5.7%.[14]

---

13. In *Teamsters*, the comparison between the percentage of Negroes on the employer's work force and the percentage in the general areawide population was highly probative, because the job skill there involved the ability to drive a truck is one that many persons possess or can fairly readily acquire. When special qualifications are required to fill particular jobs, comparisons to the general population (rather than to the smaller group of individuals who possess the necessary qualifications) may have little probative value. The comparative statistics introduced by the Government in the District Court, however, were properly limited to public school teachers, and therefore this is not a case like *Mayor v. Educational Equality League,* 415 U.S. 605, 94 S.Ct. 1323, 39 L.Ed.2d 630, in which the racial-composition comparisons failed to take into account special qualifications for the position in question.

Although the petitioners concede as a general matter the probative force of the comparative work-force statistics, they object to the Court of Appeals' heavy reliance on these data on the ground that applicant-flow data, showing the actual percentage of white and Negro applicants for teaching positions at Hazelwood, would be firmer proof. As we have noted, see n. 5, supra, there was no clear evidence of such statistics. We leave it to the District Court on remand to determine whether competent proof of those data can be adduced. If so, it would, of course, be very relevant.

14. As is discussed below, the Government contends that a comparative figure of 15.4%, rather than 5.7%, is the appropriate one. But even assuming, arguendo, that the 5.7% figure urged by the petitioners is correct, the disparity between that figure and the percentage of Negroes on Hazelwood's teaching staff would be more than fourfold for the 1972–1973 school year, and threefold for the 1973–1974 school year. A precise method of measuring the significance of such statistical disparities was explained in *Castaneda v. Partida,* 430 U.S. 482, 496–497, n. 17,

Although these differences were on their face substantial, the Court of Appeals erred in substituting its judgment for that of the District Court and holding that the Government had conclusively proved its 'pattern or practice' lawsuit.

The Court of Appeals totally disregarded the possibility that this prima facie statistical proof in the record might at the trial court level be rebutted by statistics dealing with Hazelwood's hiring after it became subject to Title VII. Racial discrimination by public employers was not made illegal under Title VII until March 24, 1972. * * *

The record in this case showed that for the 1972–1973 school year, Hazelwood hired 282 new teachers, 10 whom (3.5%) were Negroes; for the following school year it hired 123 new teachers, 5 of whom (4.1%) were Negroes. Over the two-year period, Negroes constituted a total of 15 of the 405 new teachers hired (3.7%). Although the Court of Appeals briefly mentioned these data in reciting the facts, it wholly ignored them in discussing whether the Government had shown a pattern or practice of discrimination. And it gave no consideration at all to the possibility that post-Act data as to the number of Negroes hired compared to the total number of Negro applicants might tell a totally different story.

What the hiring figures prove obviously depends upon the figures to which they are compared. The Court of Appeals accepted the Government's argument that the relevant comparison was to the labor market area of St. Louis County and the city of St. Louis, in which, according to the 1970 census, 15.4% of all teachers were Negro. The propriety of that comparison was vigorously disputed by the petitioners, who urged that because the city of St. Louis has made special attempts to maintain a 50% Negro teaching staff, inclusion of that school district in the relevant market area distorts the comparison. Were that argument accepted, the percentage of Negro teachers in the relevant labor market area (St. Louis County alone) as shown in the 1970 census would be 5.7% rather than 15.4%.

The difference between these figures may well be important; the disparity between 3.7% (the percentage of Negro teachers hired by Hazelwood in 1972–1973 and 1973–1974) and 5.7% may be sufficiently small to weaken the Government's other proof, while the disparity between 3.7% and 15.4% may be sufficiently large to reinforce it.[17] In determining which of

---

97 S.Ct. 1272, 1281, 51 L.Ed.2d 498. It involves calculation of the 'standard deviation' as a measure of predicted fluctuations from the expected value of a sample. Using the 5.7% figure as the basis for calculating the expected value, the expected number of Negroes on the Hazelwood teaching staff would be roughly 63 in 1972–1973 and 70 in 1973–1974. The observed number in those years was 16 and 22, respectively. The difference between the observed and expected values was more than six standard deviations in 1972–1973 and more than five standard deviations in 1973–1974. The Court in Castaneda noted that '(a)s a general rule for such large samples, if the difference between the expected value and the observed number is greater than two or three standard deviations,' then the hypothesis that teachers were hired without regard to race would be suspect.

17. Indeed, under the statistical methodology explained in Castaneda v. Partida, supra, involving the calculation of the standard deviation as a measure of predicted fluctuations, the difference between using 15.4% and 5.7% as the areawide figure would be significant. If the 15.4% figure is taken as the basis for comparison, the expected number of Negro teachers hired by

the two figures or, very possibly, what intermediate figure provides the most accurate basis for comparison to the hiring figures at Hazelwood, it will be necessary to evaluate such considerations as (i) whether the racially based hiring policies of the St. Louis City School District were in effect as far back as 1970, the year in which the census figures were taken; (ii) to what extent those policies have changed the racial composition of that district's teaching staff from what it would otherwise have been; (iii) to what extent St. Louis' recruitment policies have diverted to the city, teachers who might otherwise have applied to Hazelwood;[19] (iv) to what extent Negro teachers employed by the city would prefer employment in other districts such as Hazelwood; and (v) what the experience in other school districts in St. Louis County indicates about the validity of excluding the City School District from the relevant labor market.

It is thus clear that a determination of the appropriate comparative figures in this case will depend upon further evaluation by the trial court. As this Court admonished in *Teamsters*: '(S)tatistics . . . come in infinite variety. . . . (T)heir usefulness depends on all of the surrounding facts and circumstances.' Only the trial court is in a position to make the appropriate determination after further findings. And only after such a determination is made can a foundation be established for deciding whether or not Hazelwood engaged in a pattern or practice of racial discrimination in its employment practices in violation of the law.[20]

We hold, therefore, that the Court of Appeals erred in disregarding the post-Act hiring statistics in the record, and that it should have remanded the case to the District Court for further findings as to the relevant labor market area and for an ultimate determination of whether Hazelwood engaged in a pattern or practice of employment discrimination after

Hazelwood in 1972–1973 would be 43 (rather than the actual figure of 10) of a total of 282, a difference of more than five standard deviations; the expected number of 1973–1974 would be 19 (rather than the actual figure 5) of a total of 123, a difference of more than three standard deviations. For the two years combined, the difference between the observed number of 15 Negro teachers hired (of a total of 405) would vary from the expected number of 62 by more than six standard deviations. Because a fluctuation of more than two or three standard deviations would undercut the hypothesis that decisions were being made randomly with respect to race, each of these statistical comparisons would reinforce rather than rebut the Government's other proof. If, however, the 5.7% areawide figure is used, the expected number of Negro teachers hired in 1972–1973 would be roughly 16, less than two standard deviations from the observed number of 10; for 1973–1974, the expected value would be roughly seven, less than one standard deviation from the observed value of 5; and for the two years combined, the expected value of 23 would be less than two standard deviations from the observed total of 15. A more precise method of analyzing these statistics confirms the results of the standard deviation analysis.

These observations are not intended to suggest that precise calculations of statistical significance are necessary in employing statistical proof, but merely to highlight the importance of the choice of the relevant labor market area.

19.   The petitioners observe, for example, that Harris Teachers College in St. Louis, whose 1973 graduating class was 60% Negro, is operated by the city. It is the petitioners' contention that the city's public elementary and secondary schools occupy an advantageous position in the recruitment of Harris graduates.

20.   Because the District Court focused on a comparison between the percentage of Negro teachers and Negro pupils in Hazelwood, it did not undertake an evaluation of the relevant labor market, and its casual dictum that the inclusion of the city of St. Louis 'distorted' the labor market statistics was not based upon valid criteria.

March 24, 1972.[21] Accordingly, the judgment is vacated, and the case is remanded to the District Court for further proceedings consistent with this opinion.

A (Very) Little Bit More on Statistical Techniques

1. Standard Deviation and the Rule of Exclusion:

Reduced to its simplest terms statistical proof is based on a mathematical analysis of probabilities. It begins with a comparison between an outcome that is "observed" with an outcome that would be "expected." An "observed" outcome is a simple counting. The appropriate "expected" outcome, as *Hazelwood* demonstrated, can become a difficult "battle of the experts" fraught with complex questions, such as the appropriate geographical area to be used in the study and the level of refinement of the populations based on interests and qualifications.

Once the "observed" and "expected" outcomes are determined, analysis of the comparison is based on an assumption known as the "null hypothesis," which is that ordinarily there should be no difference between "expected" and "observed" outcomes (i.e., the difference between observed and expected outcomes should be nothing, or "null"). To illustrate, if one flips a coin 100 times the expected outcome is that the result will be 50 heads and 50 tails (or "nil"). Yet, experience teaches that while 50 heads and 50 tails are "expected," variations from that outcome occur randomly, say an "observed outcome" of 48 heads and 52 tails. Such small differences easily can be attributed to a chance, or random, outcome. The null hypothesis states that any difference between the "expected outcome" (50–50) and the "observed outcome" (48–52), unless shown otherwise, should be attributed to chance. The person challenging chance as an explanation for the "observed outcome" has the burden of disproving the "null hypothesis" of a random outcome.

When there is a significant difference between "expected" and "observed" outcomes, the statisticians can state in mathematical terms the probabilities that the null hypothesis of random outcomes has been disproved. The null hypothesis will be rejected as an explanation for the outcome when the difference between "expected" and "observed" outcomes is "highly unlikely." The degree of "likelihood" in the "observed" outcome is stated mathematically as a "confidence level." The "confidence level" is the degree of risk that the null hypothesis operated to produce the observed result. Confidence levels are stated in degrees on a 100 scale. A "confidence level" of .01 means that chance could explain a given outcome in only one outcome out of 100. Generally, statisticians agree that a confidence level of .01 renders the null hypothesis mathematically disproved.

---

21. It will also be open to the District Court on remand to determine whether sufficiently reliable applicant-flow data are available to permit consideration of the petitioners' argument that those data may undercut a statistical analysis dependent upon hirings alone.

At this point chance cannot be relied upon to explain the observed outcome.

The confidence level is accomplished by applying a relatively simple formula that calculates the number of "standard deviations" between the observed and the expected outcomes. A confidence level of .01 (or 1 chance in 100) is reached at 2.57 standard deviations.

Standing alone, disproving the null hypothesis does nothing more than eliminate chance as an explanation for the difference between "observed" and "expected" outcomes. However, in the employment context elimination of chance as an explanation requires the employer to explain in neutral terms a reason that might explain the race or sex imbalance. In the absence of an explanation for the observed disparity courts will infer that the observed imbalance is a product of illegal motive.

To illustrate further using a deck of standard playing cards: if fairly shuffled there would be a 50% likelihood of randomly drawing a red card from the deck and a 25% chance of drawing a card from the diamond suit. If the cards were reshuffled after each draw and a single card drawn 100 times, the most likely, or expected, outcome of this process would be 50 red cards, 50 black cards and 25 cards of each of the four suits. Step 1 of the null hypothesis is that observed outcome will mirror this expected result.

Intuitively we know that 100 shuffles and draws often may not result in a total of 50 red cards or 25 cards of each suit. Random chance could easily explain an "observed" outcome on both sides of 50 (e.g., 52 red and 48 black, or 53 black and 47 red) or a slightly unequal division among the suits (e.g., 24 diamonds, 27, hearts, 25 spades, and 24 clubs).

The null hypothesis of random selection is disproved only if chance as a possible explanation for the difference in values is mathematically eliminated. If, the result is 10 black cards and 90 red cards, we know intuitively, and without resort to a mathematical formula, that chance as an explanation has been eliminated. Perhaps the shuffle was inadequate, the card handler dishonest, or cards were sticking to each other. The only assumption to be made at this point is that the dealer cannot defend the proposition that the imbalance was simply the "the luck of the draw."

Apply this playing card illustration to the workplace. Assume that the qualified and available work force in the geographical area in which the employer draws its workers is 50% female and 25% Hispanic. The "expected" outcome of this employer's work force would be 50% female and 25% Hispanic. Now the plaintiff simply counts the number of female and Hispanic workers to secure the "observed" outcome. If this count reveals that there are 48% women and 24% Hispanic, the difference between observed outcomes and the expected outcomes could well be within the null hypothesis; random selection remains a viable possibility. The employer is not obligated to give an explanation of such a small deviation. However, if similar to *Teamsters*, 8% of the employees were women and 3% were Hispanic, there is little need of a mathematical formula to reveal that such a disparity could not be the product of a random selection system. Something other than chance produced this observed outcome. The employer's burden is to show what, other than sex and national origin, could have produced this result.

The difficulty arises where, for example, the employer's "observed" work force was 40% women and 18% Hispanic. In such case the difference between "observed" and "expected" outcomes is facially suspect. It is here the standard deviation formula explains level of confidence that this difference was not produced by chance. If there is no more than 1 chance in 100 (confidence level of 0.01), which is reached at 2.57 standard deviations, statisticians would conclude that the employer cannot rely on chance as a viable explanation for the disparity, and therefore has the obligation of presenting neutral objective reasons for the disparity.

     2. *Multiple Regression*: When the employer offers one or more legitimate explanations for the observed disparity, such as education and/or experience, standard deviation analysis is rendered largely meaningless. As explained above, standard deviation only excludes chance as a hypothesis. Once an employer presents legitimate factors, a possible explanation for even significant disparities has been provided.

However, the mathematical technique known as "multiple regression" studies the influence on the outcomes of a number of possible factors as possible explanations. These articulated legitimate factors allegedly relied upon are known as "variables."

At its basic level the technique used is one of "matching pairs." Assume two applicants with similar education. One applicant is black; the other is white. The white applicant is selected. Repeat this comparison over a large number of hiring decisions. If selection is statistically related more to the applicant's race than to the applicant's education, "education" can be eliminated as a viable explanation. Multiple regression typically expands this concept on a three dimensional level to compare the influence of multiple variables among a group of applicants or employees (e.g., education, experience, seniority, prior performance evaluations, etc.). Once the employer articulates the factors or variables that it says it takes into account in making decisions, multiple regression holds those factors constant and determines whether race or sex is the most statistically significant of the possible factors. This is a complex methodology that requires for reliability a large number of experiences and depends upon expert, computer driven calculations.

CHAPTER 9

RETALIATION (REPRISAL) FOR "PARTICIPATION" OR "OPPOSITION"

■ ■ ■

A. GENERALLY

Retaliation is the most common charge filed with the EEOC (36,000 in 2010). Providing protection against retaliation has importance that goes beyond fairness to the victim. First, implementation of the public policy of eradicating invidious work place discrimination depends almost exclusively upon private initiative in filing charges with the EEOC, providing information to the EEOC, and in initiating enforcement litigation after exhaustion of the EEOC processes. Second, the policy of encouraging informal resolution of possible violations requires protection for workers who, rather than filing formal charges, informally bring questionable activity to the attention of their superiors in the anticipation of informal resolution.

Retaliation is proscribed in sections distinct from the substantive prohibitions. They read:

> It shall be an unlawful employment practice for an employer to discriminate against any of his employees or applicants for employment * * * because he has opposed any practice made an unlawful employment practice by this title, or because he has made a charge, testified, or participated in any manner in an investigation, proceeding or hearing under this title. 42 U.S.C.A. s 2000e–3

Where statutes do not expressly proscribe retaliation, such proscription is implicit. ***CBOCS West v. Humphries***, 553 U.S. 442, 128 S.Ct. 1951, 170 L.Ed.2d 864 (2008)(42 U.S.C. § 1981); ***Gomez–Perez v. Potter***, 553 U.S. 474, 128 S.Ct. 1931, 170 L.Ed.2d 887 (2008)(federal employee protection against retaliation under the ADEA).

THOMPSON v. NORTH AMERICAN STAINLESS, LP

Supreme Court of the United States, 2011
___ U.S. ___, 131 S.Ct. 863, 178 L.Ed.2d 694

JUSTICE SCALIA delivered the opinion of the Court.

[Plaintiff, Thompson, and his fiancée both worked for defendant NAS. Plaintiff's fiancée filed an EEOC charge against defendant. Soon after defendant was notified of the fiancée's charge, plaintiff, who in no way was associated with the charge or the proceedings, was discharged by defendant. Plaintiff alleged a violation of § 704. The lower courts held that as a matter of law plaintiff stated no claim in that he had not "made a charge, testified, or participated in * * * a proceeding." The Court reversed:]

[W]e have little difficulty concluding, that the firing of Thompson violated Title VII. * * * Title VII's anti-retaliation provision must be construed to cover a broad range of employer conduct. * * * Title VII's antiretaliation provision prohibits an employer from 'discriminating against any of his employees' for engaging in protected conduct, without specifying the employer acts that are prohibited. * * * [The] antiretaliation provision prohibits any employer action that 'might well have dissuaded a reasonable worker from making or supporting a charge of discrimination.' "

We think it obvious that a reasonable worker might be dissuaded from engaging in protected activity if she knew her fiancée would be fired.

[The Court thus looked at the foreseeable impact upon the employee filing a charge of a retaliatory action against an uninvolved co-worker. Rather than giving upon a narrow reading of § 704, the Court relied upon the broader language of 42 U.S.C. § 2000e–5(b), (f)(1), which authorizes a civil action to be commenced by "by the person aggrieved by the alleged unlawful employment practice." The Court continued:]

NAS [the employer] raises the concern, however, that prohibiting reprisals against third parties will lead to difficult line-drawing problems concerning the types of relationships entitled to protection. Perhaps retaliating against an employee by firing his fiancée would dissuade the employee from engaging in protected activity, but what about firing an employee's girlfriend, close friend, or trusted co-worker? * * * NAS argues [that this] will place the employer at risk any time it fires any employee who happens to have a connection to a different employee who filed a charge with the EEOC.

Although we acknowledge the force of this point, we do not think it justifies a categorical rule that third-party reprisals do not violate Title VII. * * *

We must also decline to identify a fixed class of relationships for which third party reprisals are unlawful. We expect that firing a close family member will almost always meet [this] standard, and inflicting a milder reprisal on a mere acquaintance will almost never do so, but beyond that we are reluctant to generalize. * * * Given the broad statutory text and the variety of workplace contexts in which retaliation may occur, Title VII's antiretaliation provision is simply not reducible to a comprehensive set of clear rules. We emphasize, however, that 'the provision's standard for judging harm must be objective,' so as to 'avoid the uncertainties and unfair discrepancies that can plague a judicial effort to determine a plaintiff's unusual subjective feelings.' " * * *

[The concurring opinion of JUSTICE GINSBURG, joined by JUSTICE BREYER, is omitted.]

NOTES

1. *References and Third Parties:* As seen in Chapter 1, a former "employer" who provides unfavorable references in retaliation for the employee's filing charges or opposing employer practices violates § 704. *Robinson v. Shell Oil Co.,* 519 U.S. 337, 117 S.Ct. 843, 136 L.Ed.2d 808 (1997). Even informing other employers that the former employee had filed EEOC charges has been held to be unlawful retaliation in that it tends to chill such participation. *See, Smith v. Secretary of the Navy,* 659 F.2d 1113 (D.C. Cir. 1981).

B. "PARTICIPATION"

1. Defined: "Participation" applies to activities which occur in conjunction with the filing of a charge or judicial action or actions that take place as part of, or in response to, the formal charge or related legal proceedings. Even informal communications to enforcement agencies, state or federal, such as letters or inquiries, are considered "participation." *Pettway v. American Cast Iron Pipe Co.,* 411 F.2d 998 (5th Cir. 1969).

KASTEN v. SAINT–GOBAIN PERFORMANCE PLASTICS CORP., ___ U.S. ___, 131 S.Ct. 1325 179 L.Ed.2d 379 (2011), construed similar provisions against retaliation found in the Fair Labor Standards Act, 29 U.S.C.A. § 215(a)(3). The Court reversed the Seventh Circuit which had held that the term "filing" required a written complaint to the enforcement agency. The Court concluded: "[T]he statutory term 'filed any complaint' includes oral as well as written complaints within its scope."

Generally stated, employee complaints *to the employer,* participating in an employer investigation *prior* to any EEOC charge being filed, or threats to file a formal charge, while possibly protected "opposition," are not "participation." However, if the employer investigation is precipitated by the EEOC charge, involvement in post-charge employer investigations may be considered "participation." *EEOC v. Total System Services, Inc.,* 221 F.3d 1171 (11th Cir. 2000). *But see, Hatmaker v. Memorial Med. Ctr.,* 619 F.3d 741 (7th Cir. 2010).

2. The "Privilege" Accorded "Participation:" Identification of activity as "participation," as opposed to "opposition," defines the level of protection accorded. It is generally agreed that "participation" is entitled to greater protection than is "opposition." However, there is no accord as to the precise level of protection granted "participation."

(a) Absolute: Leading early authority held that "participation" is absolutely privileged, even if the participatory activity was conducted in bad faith. *Pettway v. American Cast Iron Pipe Co.,* 411 F.2d 998 (5th Cir. 1969), held that a letter to the EEOC charging the employer with perjury in a concluded EEOC proceeding was a "motion for reconsideration" protected against retaliation even though the letter contained defamatory language and was perhaps made in bad faith. Any inquiry into the subjective mind set of the participant, the court reasoned, could inherently chill resort to statutory protections. *Accord: Booker v. Brown & Williamson Tobacco Co.,* 879 F.2d 1304 (6th Cir. 1989):

> Protection is not lost if the employee is wrong on the merits of the charge, nor is protection lost if the contents of the charge are malicious as well as wrong. Thus, once the activity in question is found to be within the scope of the participation clause, the employee is generally protected from retaliation.

(b) Qualified privilege requiring subjective good faith: A number of circuits have held that statements made as part of "participation in proceedings" are not protected against retaliation if the statements were made frivolously or in bad faith. This accords "participation" with a privilege that is "qualified" by requiring proof of the subjective bad faith of the participant. *Mattson v. Caterpillar, Inc.,* 359 F.3d 885 (7th Cir. 2004). "[I]t "cannot be true that a plaintiff can file false charges, lie to an investigator, and possibly defame co-employees, without suffering repercussions." *Gilooly v. Missouri Dept. of Health & Senior Services,* 421 F.3d 734, 740 (8th Cir.2005).

(c) Objective reasonableness? **Clark County School District v. Breeden**, *infra page 450,* suggests that good faith allegations in EEOC charges need not be reasonably based to receive statutory protection against retaliation. Accord: *Glover v. South Carolina Law Enf.,* 170 F.3d 411 (4th Cir. 1999). However, some courts appear to allow the employer to dismiss the employee for good faith participation if that participation violated otherwise legitimate employer rules. *Vaughn v. Epworth Villa,* 537 F.3d 1147 (10th Cir. 2008)(supplying the EEOC with documents supporting plaintiff's claim violated employer privacy interests and thus was unprotected). *Hatmaker v. Memorial Med. Ctr.,* 619 F.3d 741 (7th Cir. 2010)("[P]articipation doesn't insulate an employee from being discharged for conduct that, if it occurred outside an investigation, would warrant termination."). *Johnson v. ITT Aerospace,* 272 F.3d 498 (7th Cir. 2001) ("completely groundless" charges are unprotected.)

C. "OPPOSITION"

1. WHAT IT IS

CRAWFORD v. METROPOLITAN GOVERNMENT OF NASHVILLE

Supreme Court of the United States, 2009
555 U.S. 271, 129 S.Ct. 846, 172 L.Ed.2d 650

JUSTICE SOUTER delivered the opinion of the Court.

Title VII of the Civil Rights Act of 1964 forbids retaliation by employers against employees who report workplace race or gender discrimination. The question here is whether this protection extends to an employee who speaks out about discrimination not on her own initiative, but in answering questions during an employer's internal investigation. We hold that it does.

I

In 2002, respondent Metropolitan Government of Nashville and Davidson County, Tennessee (Metro), began looking into rumors of sexual harassment by the Metro School District's employee relations director, Gene Hughes. When Veronica Frazier, a Metro human resources officer, asked petitioner Vicky Crawford, a 30–year Metro employee, whether she had witnessed "inappropriate behavior" on the part of Hughes, Crawford described several instances of sexually harassing behavior: once, Hughes had answered her greeting, " 'Hey Dr. Hughes, what's up?,' " by grabbing his crotch and saying " '[Y]ou know what's up' "; he had repeatedly " 'put his crotch up to [her] window' "; and on one occasion he had entered her office and " 'grabbed her head and pulled it to his crotch,' " Two other employees also reported being sexually harassed by Hughes. Although Metro took no action against Hughes, it did fire Crawford and the two other accusers soon after finishing the investigation, saying in Crawford's case that it was for embezzlement. Crawford claimed Metro was retaliating for her report of Hughes's behavior and filed a charge of a Title VII violation with the Equal Employment Opportunity Commission (EEOC), followed by this suit in the United States District Court for the Middle District of Tennessee.

The Title VII antiretaliation provision has two clauses, making it "an unlawful employment practice for an employer to discriminate against any of his employees ... [1] because he has opposed any practice made an unlawful employment practice by this subchapter, or [2] because he has made a charge, testified, assisted, or participated in any manner in an investigation, proceeding, or hearing under this subchapter." 42 U.S.C. § 2000e–3(a). The one is known as the "opposition clause," the other as the "participation clause," and Crawford accused Metro of violating both.

The District Court granted summary judgment for Metro. It held that Crawford could not satisfy the opposition clause because she had not "instigated or initiated any complaint," but had "merely answered questions by investigators in an already-pending internal investigation, initiated by someone else." It concluded that her claim also failed under the participation clause, which Sixth Circuit precedent confined to protecting " 'an employee's participation in an employer's internal investigation . . . where that investigation occurs pursuant to a pending EEOC charge' " (not the case here).

The Court of Appeals affirmed on the same grounds, holding that the opposition clause " 'demands active, consistent "opposing" activities to warrant . . . protection against retaliation,' " whereas Crawford did "not claim to have instigated or initiated any complaint prior to her participation in the investigation, nor did she take any further action following the investigation and prior to her firing." Again like the trial judge, the Court of Appeals understood that Crawford could show no violation of the participation clause because her " 'employer's internal investigation' " was not conducted " 'pursuant to a pending EEOC charge.' "

Because the Sixth Circuit's decision conflicts with those of other Circuits, particularly as to the opposition clause we granted Crawford's petition for certiorari. We now reverse and remand for further proceedings.

II

The opposition clause makes it "unlawful . . . for an employer to discriminate against any . . . employe[e] . . . because he has opposed any practice made . . . unlawful . . . by this subchapter." The term "oppose," being left undefined by the statute, carries its ordinary meaning, "to resist or antagonize . . .; to contend against; to confront; resist; withstand," Although these actions entail varying expenditures of energy, "RESIST frequently implies more active striving than OPPOSE."

The statement Crawford says she gave to Frazier is thus covered by the opposition clause, as an ostensibly disapproving account of sexually obnoxious behavior toward her by a fellow employee, an answer she says antagonized her employer to the point of sacking her on a false pretense. Crawford's description of the louche goings-on would certainly qualify in the minds of reasonable jurors as "resist[ant]" or "antagoni[stic]" to Hughes's treatment, if for no other reason than the point argued by the Government and explained by an EEOC guideline: "When an employee communicates to her employer a belief that the employer has engaged in . . . a form of employment discrimination, that communication" virtually always "constitutes the employee's *opposition* to the activity." It is true that one can imagine exceptions, like an employee's description of a supervisor's racist joke as hilarious, but these will be eccentric cases, and this is not one of them.

The Sixth Circuit thought answering questions fell short of opposition, taking the view that the clause " 'demands active, consistent "opposing" activities to warrant . . . protection against retaliation,' " and that an employee must "instigat[e] or initiat[e]" a complaint to be covered. But though these requirements obviously exemplify opposition as commonly understood, they are not limits of it.

"Oppose" goes beyond "active, consistent" behavior in ordinary discourse, where we would naturally use the word to speak of someone who has taken no action at all to advance a position beyond disclosing it. Countless people were known to "oppose" slavery before Emancipation, or are said to "oppose" capital punishment today, without writing public letters, taking to the streets, or resisting the government. And we would call it "opposition" if an employee took a stand against an employer's discriminatory practices not by "instigating" action, but by standing pat, say, by refusing to follow a supervisor's order to fire a junior worker for discriminatory reasons. There is, then, no reason to doubt that a person can "oppose" by responding to someone else's question just as surely as by provoking the discussion, and nothing in the statute requires a freakish rule protecting an employee who reports discrimination on her own initiative but not one who reports the same discrimination in the same words when her boss asks a question.

Metro and its *amici* support the Circuit panel's insistence on "active" and "consistent" opposition by arguing that the lower the bar for retaliation claims, the less likely it is that employers will look into what may be happening outside the executive suite. As they see it, if retaliation is an easy charge when things go bad for an employee who responded to enquiries, employers will avoid the headache by refusing to raise questions about possible discrimination.

The argument is unconvincing, for we think it underestimates the incentive to enquire that follows from our decisions in *Burlington Industries, Inc. v. Ellerth,* 524 U.S. 742, 118 S.Ct. 2257, 141 L.Ed.2d 633 (1998), and *Faragher v. Boca Raton,* 524 U.S. 775, 118 S.Ct. 2275, 141 L.Ed.2d 662 (1998), [which] hold "[a]n employer ... subject to vicarious liability to a victimized employee for an actionable hostile environment created by a supervisor with ... authority over the employee." Although there is no affirmative defense if the hostile environment "culminates in a tangible employment action" against the employee, an employer does have a defense "[w]hen nontangible employment action is taken" if it "exercised reasonable care to prevent and correct promptly any" discriminatory conduct and "the plaintiff employee unreasonably failed to take advantage of any preventive or corrective opportunities provided by the employer or to avoid harm otherwise." Employers are thus subject to a strong inducement to ferret out and put a stop to any discriminatory activity in their operations as a way to break the circuit of imputed liability. The possibility that an employer might someday want to fire someone who might charge discrimination traceable to an internal investigation does not strike us as likely to diminish the attraction of an *Ellerth–Faragher* affirmative defense.

That aside, we find it hard to see why the Sixth Circuit's rule would not itself largely undermine the *Ellerth–Faragher* scheme, along with the statute's " 'primary objective' " of "avoid[ing] harm" to employees. If it were clear law that an employee who reported discrimination in answering an employer's questions could be penalized with no remedy, prudent employees would have a good reason to keep quiet about Title VII offenses against themselves or against others. This is no imaginary horrible given the documented indications that "[f]ear of retaliation is the leading reason why people stay silent instead of voicing their concerns about bias and discrimination." The appeals court's rule would thus create a real dilemma for any knowledgeable employee in a hostile work environment if the boss took steps to assure a defense under our cases. If the employee reported discrimination in response to the enquiries, the employer might well be free to penalize her for speaking up. But if she kept quiet about the discrimination and later filed a Title VII claim, the employer might well escape liability, arguing that it "exercised reasonable care to prevent and correct [any discrimination] promptly" but "the plaintiff employee unreasonably failed to take advantage of ... preventive or corrective opportunities provided by the employer." Nothing in the statute's text or our precedent supports this catch–22.

Because Crawford's conduct is covered by the opposition clause, we do not reach her argument that the Sixth Circuit misread the participation clause as well. * * *

III

The judgment of the Court of Appeals for the Sixth Circuit is reversed, and the case is remanded for further proceedings consistent with this opinion.

JUSTICE ALITO, with whom JUSTICE THOMAS joins, concurring in the judgment.

* * * I agree with the Court that the "opposition clause" of § 2000e–3(a) (2000 ed.) prohibits retaliation for such conduct. I also agree with the Court's primary reasoning, which is based on "the point argued by the Government and explained by an EEOC guideline: 'When an employee communicates to her employer a belief that the employer has engaged in ... a form of employment discrimination, that communication' virtually always 'constitutes the employee's *opposition* to the activity.' " I write separately to emphasize my understanding that the Court's holding does not and should not extend beyond employees who testify in internal investigations or engage in analogous purposive conduct.

* * *

In order to decide the question that is before us, we have no need to adopt a definition of the term "oppose" that is broader than the definition that petitioner advances. But in dicta, the Court defin[es] "oppose" to mean " 'to be hostile or adverse to, *as in opinion.*' " Thus, this definition embraces silent opposition.

While this is certainly *an* accepted usage of the term "oppose," the term is not always used in this sense, and it is questionable whether silent opposition is covered by the opposition clause. * * *

NOTES

1. A black employee removes a hangman's noose that has been left dangling in the workplace. Presumably his removal of the noose is a protected opposition to the harassing act and cannot be punished. *Brown v. Peterson*, 2006 WL 349805 (N.D. Tex. 2006).

2. *Silent Moral Support:* A supervisor accompanied a worker to the employer's human resources department where the worker lodged a sexual harassment charge. The supervisor said nothing. This was sufficient "opposition" to protect the supervisor against retaliation. *Collazo v. Bristol–Meyer Squibb Mfg. Inc.*, 617 F.3d 39 (1st Cir. 2010).

3. *Forcing Settlement:* An employer unlawfully retaliates by dismissing an employee for his refusal to settle or waive discrimination claims pending before the EEOC or courts. *Goldsmith v. Bagby Elevator Co.*, 513 F.3d 1261 (11th Cir. 2008). However, it is not unlawful retaliation for an employer to discriminate against an individual because the individual refuses to agree to submit *future* disputes between employer and employee to private arbitration. *Weeks v. Harden Mfg. Corp.*, 291 F.3d 1307 (11th Cir. 2002).

4. *Employment Practices:* Opposition directed toward employer activity, other than employment, is not protected. For example, a teacher objecting to the school's perceived discrimination against its *students* would not be considered opposition protected by Title VII. *Artis v. Francis Howell N. Band Booster Ass'n, Inc.*, 161 F.3d 1178 (8th Cir. 1998). An employee's release of a police department report critical primarily of the department's policing policies is unprotected. *Bonn v. City of Omaha*, 623 F.3d 587 (8th Cir. 2010).

2. THE "CONSCIENTIOUS (BUT UNREASONABLE) OBJECTOR"

CLARK COUNTY SCHOOL DISTRICT v. BREEDEN

Supreme Court of the United States, 2001
532 U.S. 268, 121 S.Ct. 1508, 149 L.Ed.2d 509

PER CURIAM

Under Title VII of the Civil Rights Act of 1964, it is unlawful "for an employer to discriminate against any of his employees ... because [the employee] has opposed any practice made an unlawful employment practice by [Title VII], or because [the employee] has made a charge, testified, assisted, or participated in any manner in an investigation, proceeding, or hearing under [Title VII]." In 1997, respondent filed a § 2000e–3(a) retaliation claim against petitioner Clark County School District. The claim as eventually amended alleged that petitioner had taken two separate adverse employment actions against her in response to two different protected activities in which she had engaged. The District Court granted summary judgment to petitioner, but a panel of the Court of Appeals for the Ninth Circuit reversed * * * . We grant the writ of certiorari and reverse.

On October 21, 1994, respondent's male supervisor met with respondent and another male employee to review the psychological evaluation reports of four job applicants. The report for one of the applicants disclosed that the applicant had once commented to a co-worker, "I hear making love to you is like making love to the Grand Canyon." At the meeting respondent's supervisor read the comment aloud, looked at respondent and stated, "I don't know what that means." The other employee then said, "Well, I'll tell you later," and both men chuckled. Respondent later complained about the comment to the offending employee, to Assistant Superintendent George Ann Rice, the employee's supervisor, and to another assistant superintendent of petitioner. Her first claim of retaliation asserts that she was punished for these complaints.

The Court of Appeals for the Ninth Circuit has applied § 2000e–3(a) to protect employee "oppos[ition]" not just to practices that are actually "made ... unlawful" by Title VII, but also to practices that the employee could reasonably believe were unlawful. (stating that respondent's opposition was protected "if she had a reasonable, good faith belief that the incident involving the sexually explicit remark constituted unlawful sexual harassment"); *Trent v. Valley Electric Assn. Inc.*, 41 F.3d 524, 526 (C.A.9 1994). We have no occasion to rule on the propriety of this interpretation, because even assuming it is correct, no one could reasonably believe that the incident recounted above violated Title VII.

Title VII forbids actions taken on the basis of sex that "discriminate against any individual with respect to his compensation, terms, conditions, or privileges of employment." Just three Terms ago, we reiterated, what was plain from our previous decisions, that sexual harassment is actionable under Title VII only if it is "so 'severe or pervasive' as to 'alter the conditions of [the victim's] employment and create an abusive working environment.' " Workplace conduct is not measured in isolation; instead, "whether an environment is sufficiently hostile or abusive" must be judged "by 'looking at all the circumstances,' including the 'frequency of the discriminatory conduct; its severity; whether it is physically threatening or humiliating, or a mere offensive utterance; and whether it unreasonably interferes with an employee's work performance.' " Hence, "[a] recurring point in [our] opinions is that simple teasing, offhand comments, and isolated incidents (unless extremely serious) will not amount to discriminatory changes in the 'terms and conditions of employment.' "

No reasonable person could have believed that the single incident recounted above violated Title VII's standard. The ordinary terms and conditions of respondent's job required her to review the sexually explicit statement in the course of screening job applicants. Her co-workers who participated in the hiring process were subject to the same requirement, and indeed, in the District Court respondent "conceded that it did not bother or upset her" to read the statement in the file. Her supervisor's comment, made at a meeting to review the application, that he did not know what the statement meant; her co-worker's responding comment; and the chuckling of both are at worst an "isolated inciden[t]" that cannot remotely be considered "extremely serious," as our cases require. The holding of the Court of Appeals to the contrary must be reversed.

Besides claiming that she was punished for complaining to petitioner's personnel about the alleged sexual harassment, respondent also claimed that she was punished for filing charges against petitioner with the Nevada Equal Rights Commission and the Equal Employment Opportunity Commission (EEOC) and for filing the present suit. Respondent filed her lawsuit on April 1, 1997; on April 10, 1997, respondent's supervisor, Assistant Superintendent Rice, "mentioned to Allin Chandler, Executive Director of plaintiff's union, that she was contemplating transferring plaintiff to the position of Director of Professional Development Education," and this transfer was "carried through" in May. In order to show, as her defense against summary judgment required, the existence of a causal connection between her protected activities and the transfer, respondent "relie[d] wholly on the temporal proximity of the filing of her complaint on April 1, 1997 and Rice's statement to plaintiff's union representative on April 10, 1997 that she was considering transferring plaintiff to the [new] position." * * *

[The trial court granted summary judgment to the employer.] The Court of Appeals reversed, relying on two facts: The EEOC had issued a right-to-sue letter to respondent three months before Rice announced she was contemplating the transfer, and the actual transfer occurred one month after Rice learned of respondent's suit. The latter fact is immaterial in light of the fact that petitioner concededly was contemplating the transfer before it learned of the suit. Employers need not suspend previously planned transfers upon discovering that a Title VII suit has been filed, and their proceeding along lines previously contemplated, though not yet definitively determined, is no evidence whatever of causality.

* * * [T]he opinion suggests that the letter provided petitioner with its first notice of respondent's charge before the EEOC, and hence allowed the inference that the transfer proposal made three months later was petitioner's reaction to the charge. This will not do.

First, there is no indication that Rice even knew about the right-to-sue letter when she proposed transferring respondent. And second, if one presumes she knew about it, one must also presume that she (or her predecessor) knew *almost two years earlier* about the protected action (filing of the EEOC complaint) that the letter supposedly disclosed. (The complaint had been filed on August 23, 1995, and both Title VII and its implementing regulations require that an employer be given notice within 10 days of filing. The cases that accept mere temporal proximity between an employer's knowledge of protected activity and an adverse employment action as sufficient evidence of causality to establish a prima facie case uniformly hold that the temporal proximity must be "very close," See, e.g., *Richmond v. ONEOK, Inc.*, 120 F.3d 205, 209 (C.A.10 1997) (3–month period insufficient); *Hughes v. Derwinski*, 967 F.2d 1168, 1174–1175 (C.A.7 1992) 4–month period insufficient). Action taken (as here) 20 months later suggests, by itself, no causality at all.

* * * The judgment of the Court of Appeals is reversed.

NOTE

Temporal Proximity: In the principal case plaintiff's "participation" claim failed for lack of evidence of discriminatory motive. For an inference that the protected activity motivated the discriminatory treatment, the Court accepted that "temporal proximity" between the two events would create an inference that the former motivated the latter. However, the 20 month gap between protected activity (the filing of the charge) and her adverse treatment was simply too great to allow such an inference. Lower courts have narrowed even more the required "proximity." *See, e.g., Smith v. Fairview Ridges Hosp.*, 625 F.3d 1076 (8th Cir. 2010), which held that one month between protected act and adverse treatment was insufficiently "proximate" to create an inference of retaliatory motive.

BUTLER v. ALABAMA DEP'T OF TRANSP.

United States Court of Appeals, Eleventh Circuit, 2008
536 F.3d 1209

CARNES, CIRCUIT JUDGE

Alvarene Butler is black and Karen Stacey is white. They both worked for the Alabama Department of Transportation (ALDOT). One work day in January of 2005 they were going to lunch together. Stacey was driving a pickup truck, and Butler was the only passenger.

On the way to lunch, the truck collided with another vehicle, which was driven by a black male. After the collision, Stacey turned to Butler and asked: "Did you see that? Did you see that stupid mother fucking nigger hit me?" A few minutes later, when the driver of the other vehicle was attempting to re-route traffic around the accident, Stacey said: "Look at him now. Now that stupid ass nigger down there is trying to direct traffic. I hope something come [sic] over that hill and run over his ass and kill him." Butler understandably found Stacey's use of racial epithets offensive. She did not, however, believe that Stacey's words were directed at her.

Later that day, while she was at the hospital receiving treatment for chest pains caused by the accident, Butler tried to inform her immediate supervisor, Patrick Jackson, about Stacey's offensive language. As Butler was trying to tell Jackson what happened, he interrupted her and told her to stop. * * *

On April 12, 2005, Butler received an unfavorable annual evaluation from Jackson. The next day she filed a departmental grievance, contending that the reason she had received that evaluation was that she had accused Stacey of using racial epithets. After Butler filed this grievance other bad things happened to her * * * [S]he had previously approved leave taken away; she received a letter of reprimand based on her failure to correctly complete a training form; she received a "letter of written counsel" regarding excessive absenteeism; and she received a "letter of written counsel" for failing to follow call-in procedures for unscheduled absences. Butler, however, was never suspended or demoted. Butler did have to perform manual labor while Stacey, who held the same job title, did not. * * *

[T]he only claims remaining for trial were Butler's retaliation claims against ALDOT and her racially disparate treatment claims against AL-DOT, Waits, and Jackson. Those * * * retaliation and discrimination claims were based on the allegations that Butler had been: (1) forced to perform manual labor at job sites while Stacey, a white co-worker, was excused from doing the same work; (2) required to report to work at 7:00 a.m. while Stacey was permitted to arrive at 7:30 a.m.; (3) disciplined for violating the "call-in" rule for unscheduled absences while Stacey, who also violated this rule, was not; (4) "docked" pay for days she was absent even though she was approved for leave with pay; and (5) denied a promotion to the civil engineer position, while Stacey was considered for the position (but never got it).

The case proceeded to trial. * * * The jury returned a special verdict form finding that: (1) ALDOT had retaliated against Butler in violation of Title VII * * * The jury awarded Butler $25,000 for lost benefits and earnings and $25,000 for her emotional distress and suffering. The jury also returned an award of punitive damages in the amount of $150,000. * * *

ALDOT, Waits, and Jackson appeal, contending that: (1) they were entitled to judgment as a matter of law on Butler's retaliation claims * * *.

II

As it comes to us, Butler's retaliation claim rests solely on her contention that she was retaliated against for reporting to Jackson in April of 2005 that Stacey had used racial epithets in her presence the day they had the accident while on lunch break. She characterizes her statements to Jackson as opposition to an unlawful employment practice within the meaning of Title VII's opposition clause. * * *

We previously have recognized that a plaintiff can establish a prima facie case of retaliation under the opposition clause of Title VII if he shows that he had a good faith, reasonable belief that the employer was engaged in unlawful employment practices. It is critical to emphasize that a plaintiff's burden under this standard has both a subjective and an objective component. A plaintiff must not only show that he *subjectively* (that is, in good faith) believed that his employer was engaged in unlawful employment practices, but also that his belief was *objectively* reasonable in light of the facts and record presented. It thus is not enough for a plaintiff to allege that his belief in this regard was honest and bona fide; the allegations and record must also indicate that the belief, though perhaps mistaken, was objectively reasonable.

Butler never testified that she believed Stacey's use of vile language amounted to an unlawful employment practice by ALDOT. Instead, Butler argues that the fact that she eventually did tell Jackson what happened is enough to prove that she believed it was an unlawful employment practice. We have our doubts about that, but we need not decide whether there is enough evidence in the record to satisfy the subjective belief component of the retaliation claim because it is clear the claim fails to meet the objective reasonableness requirement.

Assuming that Butler did believe that Stacey's words immediately after the wreck amounted to an unlawful employment practice by ALDOT, her belief is not objectively reasonable. It is not even close. The incident consisted of Stacey's use of a racial epithet twice a few minutes apart. What Stacey said was, as Butler testified, "uncalled for" and "ugly." But not every uncalled for, ugly, racist statement by a co-worker is an unlawful employment practice. This incident occurred away from work. It did not happen within the hearing of any supervisors. Butler admits that she never thought the epithets, deplorable as they are, were aimed at her. She has never even suggested that this one-time use of vile language away from work created a hostile work environment. She also conceded during cross-examination that the incident did not affect her ability to do her job.

The incident that gave rise to this case is nowhere near enough to create a racially hostile environment. * * * [A] racially derogatory remark by a co-worker, without more, does not constitute an unlawful employment practice* * * and opposition to such a remark, consequently, is not statutorily protected conduct.

* * *

While a plaintiff can prevail on a retaliation claim based on opposition to an employment practice that is not actually unlawful, we have to consider the controlling substantive law in this circuit when we assess whether a plaintiff's mistaken belief is objectively reasonable. Where binding precedent squarely holds that particular conduct is not an unlawful employment practice by the employer, and no decision of this Court or of the Supreme Court has called that precedent into question or undermined its reasoning, an employee's contrary belief that the practice is unlawful is unreasonable. *Weeks v. Harden Mfg. Corp.,* 291 F.3d 1307, 1317 (11th Cir.2002) ("Finally, the plaintiffs may not stand on their ignorance of the substantive law to argue that their belief was reasonable. As we have stated previously, if the plaintiffs are free to disclaim knowledge of the substantive law, the reasonableness inquiry becomes no more than speculation regarding their subjective knowledge.''

Assuming that Butler actually believed that Stacey's offensive statements constituted an unlawful employment practice of ALDOT, that belief was not objectively reasonable. It follows that her retaliation claim fails as a matter of law and judgment should have been entered for ALDOT on it. * * *

NOTES

1. *Mistakes of Law:*

a. ***Crawford v. Metro Government of Nashville,*** *supra page 446,* quoting with approval EEOC guidance:

> When an employee communicates to her employer a belief that the employer has engaged in ... a form of employment discrimination, that communication virtually always "constitutes the employee's *opposition* to the activity." It is true that one can imagine exceptions, like an employee's description of a supervisor's racist joke as hilarious, but these will be eccentric cases, and this is not one of them.

b. Apply ***Butler v. Alabama Dep't of Transp.***, the principal case, to a black employee who asks her employer to implement an affirmative action plan or perhaps complains that the employer which has such a plan is failing to follow it. The employee is discharged for complaining. *Holden v. Owens–Illinois,* 793 F.2d 745 (6th Cir. 1986). Alternatively, a white male employee complains about the employer adopting and implementing an affirmative action plan that meets the standards of *Steelworkers v. Weber, supra p. 234. See, Tanca v. Nordberg,* 98 F.3d 680 (1st Cir. 1996).

Assume sexual orientation discrimination is not protected by Title VII, but is proscribed by state law. *See supra,* Chapter 2.C.4. Plaintiff objects to perceived hostile treatment of homosexuals, and is discharged for this objection. *Compare, Hamner v. St. Vincent Hospital & Health Care Ctr.,* 224 F.3d 701 (7th Cir. 2000) *with Martin v. New York State Dep't of Correction Services,* 224 F.Supp.2d 434 (N.D.N.Y. 2002).

2. *Subjective Element:* ***Tate v. Executive Management Services***, 546 F.3d 528 (7th Cir. 2008), assumed that the sexual harassment of the plaintiff probably violated Title VII. However, plaintiff's expressed opposition to the harassment was unprotected because his opposition was to the supervisor's *behavior*, not to plaintiff's perception that the behavior was a violation of Title VII. Consider the ramifications of *Tate* and *Butler,* the principal case: A black worker objects to a racial slur directed at him. He does so at his peril in that: (1) the court might hold that the status of the law in that circuit is that a single racial slur cannot constitute actionable harassment (*Butler*) or (2) that the employee was objecting to the slur and not to the perception that the slur was illegal (*Tate*). The courts require the employee to simply "smile" and

"take it" until that ill defined moment when the law in his circuit allows that the slurs have reached the point of affecting adversely a "term or condition of employment," and then carefully express his "opposition" in terms of the illegality of the behavior!

3. *Employer response as "discrimination:"* **BURLINGTON NORTH-ERN & SANTA FE RR v. WHITE,** 548 U.S. 53, 126 S.Ct. 2405, 165 L.Ed.2d 345 (2006), reproduced, *supra,* p. 253, held that § 704 requires plaintiff to demonstrate "that a reasonable employee would have found the challenged action [by the employer] materially adverse, 'which in this context means it might well have dissuaded a reasonable worker from making or supporting a charge of discrimination.' " The Court concluded that reassignment to job duties that were more arduous, dirtier, and resulted in a loss of prestige was a materially adverse job action that could have dissuaded a reasonable worker from asserting rights under the statute. In addition, a 37–day suspension without pay, but which was later rescinded by the employer with back pay likewise was materially adverse. "Many reasonable employees would find a month without a paycheck to be a serious hardship." * * * That is to say, an indefinite suspension without pay could well act as a deterrent, even if the suspended employee eventually received backpay."

4. *"Concerted Activity" and the National Labor Relations Legislation:* The National Relations Act, 29 U.S.C. §§ 157 and 158 protects "concerted activity" for "mutual aid and protection," and prohibits discrimination against employees who peacefully protest the treatment of themselves and fellow workers, including the employer's treatment of women and minorities. *New Negro Alliance v. Sanitary Grocery Co.,* 303 U.S. 552, 58 S.Ct. 703, 82 L.Ed. 1012 (1938). The statute does not protect purely individual activity. Thus, if Ms. Butler in the principal case had been joined by another employee in complaining about racist comments of a co-worker, this complaint probably would have been protected by the labor relations statutes. Even where activity is individual, if undertaken with the authority of other employees and not solely by and on behalf of the lone employee, the activity will be protected. *NLRB v. City Disposal Systems,* 465 U.S. 822, 104 S.Ct. 1505, 79 L.Ed.2d 839 (1984). Accordingly, an employee who had discussions with other employees about obtaining maternity leave for the group, and requested the employer provide such leave, while perhaps not protected by Title VII, would be engaged in "concerted activity" protected by the National Labor Relations Act. *Boese Hilburn Electric Service Co.* 313 N.L.R.B. 372 (1993).

Efforts to organize legislative action that would provide protection in the workplace to otherwise unprotected individuals, such as advocating legislation protecting sexual orientation, may be protected "concerted activity." *See, Eastex Inc. v. NLRB,* 437 U.S. 556, 98 S.Ct. 2505, 57 L.Ed.2d 428 (1978). An individual invoking protections of a contract that protects the employees likewise may be considered engaged in protected "concerted activities" for "mutual aid and protection." *NLRB v. City Disposal Systems, Inc.,* 465 U.S. 822, 104 S.Ct. 1505, 79 L.Ed.2d 839 (1984).

3. REASONABLE OBJECTIONS, UNREASONABLE MEANS: OVERZEALOUS OBJECTORS

JENNINGS v. TINLEY PARK COMMUNITY CONSOL. SCHOOL DIST. NO. 146

United States Court of Appeals, Seventh Circuit, 1988
864 F.2d 1368

CUMMINGS, CIRCUIT JUDGE.

Plaintiff Kathryn Jennings appeals the district court's denial of her claim of retaliatory discharge as proscribed by Title VII of the Civil Rights Act of 1964. [T]he district court ruled in favor of the defendants on the retaliatory discharge claim. Jennings now appeals this ruling.

I. FACTS AND PROCEEDINGS BELOW

Jennings was employed by the Tinley Park (Illinois) Community Consolidated School District No. 146 from November 1973 until June 1979, serving as secretary to the Superintendent of the School District, Robert Procunier. Jennings' employment ended on June 15, 1979, when she was discharged by Procunier due to events and conduct surrounding a protest of alleged unlawful discrimination based upon sex.

The alleged sex discrimination concerned a disparity in pay between the School District's secretaries and custodians. During this period in issue, the School District designated the two groups of employees, secretaries and custodians, as "Class I" employees. Class I employees were full-time, salaried, non-certified employees. All secretaries were female; all custodians were male. Custodians were paid one and one-half times their hourly rate for overtime work as approved by a supervisor. Secretaries were not paid for overtime work. Defendants argued that secretaries were not required to work overtime.

Beginning in February 1979, the secretaries as a group first voiced concern over the perceived disparity in compensation between themselves and the custodians. At this time the School Board rejected a proposal by Procunier which would have vested in him the discretion to determine which district employees would be required to work on days that the schools would not open due to inclement weather. The School Board instead adopted a policy whereby every employee was expected to report to work on such days, and those that failed to report would be docked a day's pay. At Procunier's direction Jennings convened a meeting of the secretaries to elicit their reaction to the School Board's new policy. The secretaries objected to the new policy and were particularly disturbed that while they could be docked a day's pay due to inclement weather, they were ineligible for overtime pay. The secretaries embodied their views in a letter to the School Board, which was given to Procunier to present.

The secretaries remained disillusioned with the compensation policies of the School District and requested permission from Procunier to meet on a bimonthly basis, beginning in March 1979. Procunier granted the secretaries' request but declined their invitation to attend, sending in his stead Noel Swinford, the Assistant Superintendent. The secretaries held the March meeting as scheduled and provided Procunier with the minutes of the meeting. Jennings also spoke to Procunier about the secretaries' concerns.

At the secretaries' next regularly scheduled meeting, on May 23, 1979, Swinford presented a salary schedule proposed by Procunier and to be presented to the School Board at its next meeting, which was on the following day. The secretaries had never before been presented with a salary schedule in advance. The proposed salary schedule was opposed by the secretaries, primarily because of the perceived continuation of pay disparities between them and the custodians. Consequently, the secretaries decided to form an ad hoc committee to attend the School Board meeting on the following day, May 24. Again, minutes of the secretaries' meeting were delivered to Procunier, and Jennings and he discussed the secretaries' concerns.

The following day during the School Board meeting Procunier proposed his salary schedule as planned. The secretaries' ad hoc committee was in attendance and, after Procunier presented his salary schedule, explained the secretaries' opposition thereto. The School Board passed the salary schedule despite the secretaries' opposition.

In response to the School Board action on the salary schedule proposed by Procunier, the secretaries decided to prepare their own salary schedule, one that would contradict Procunier's. Jennings was the principal draftsman. The final draft, entitled "P.S. Salary Study" and consisting of the secretaries' proposed salary schedule and the minutes of their March and May meetings, was set for distribution on June 1, 1979. The P.S. Salary Study was signed collectively by the Committee of Concerned Secretaries, and individually by, among others, Jennings. This action, in contrast to the other meetings and activities, was done without Procunier's knowledge.

Rather than deliver the P.S. Salary Study to Procunier and instruct him to present it to the School Board at the next meeting (apparently scheduled for June 19th), as they had done previously, the secretaries decided to deliver individually the P.S. Salary Study to each Board member on June 1. Jennings was responsible for delivering a copy to Procunier, who heretofore was unaware of the P.S. Salary Study. Although delivery of the P.S. Salary Study to School Board members began at 2:00 P.M., and despite seeing and speaking to Procunier throughout the day-in fact Procunier asked Jennings to arrange a meeting with the secretaries so that Procunier could address their concerns-she did not deliver a copy to Procunier, nor inform him of its existence, until 3:50 P.M. that same day. Because of the timing of the delivery, Procunier was unable to respond to individual School Board members' inquiries which began that same day.

Following receipt of the P.S. Salary Study, the working relationship between Procunier and Jennings deteriorated. Procunier distanced himself from Jennings. Whereas prior to June 1, the delivery date of the P.S. Salary Study, Procunier had Jennings open the mail and the two would then review it together, after June 1 Procunier instructed her to leave the unopened mail in his office. He also instructed her not to answer phone calls on his personal line, as she had done in the past. A chair was removed from Procunier's office, apparently so that Jennings would have no place to sit.

On June 13, Procunier met with Jennings to discuss the timing and direct delivery of the P.S. Salary Study to Board members. Procunier expressed his displeasure at not being informed of its preparation and especially at not receiving a copy sooner. Jennings responded that some of the secretaries did not trust Procunier to present the P.S. Salary Study to the School Board, and thus the reason for the extraordinary delivery to Board members. Procunier replied that if such was the case, he expected Jennings to stand up and vouch for his trustworthiness, and if Jennings was unable to do this, then he could not in turn trust her.

On June 15, Procunier again met with Jennings and informed her that because she had not been loyal and supportive, he would recommend to the School Board that she be terminated. * * *

The sole rationale for Jennings' termination was her conduct arising out of the preparation and delivery of the P.S. Salary Study as it related to Procunier, her supervisor. No other secretary was terminated or disciplined for participating in the P.S. Salary Study or for delivering it directly to Board members.

* * *

In his written order, [trial] Judge Norgle lists as findings of fact several significant items. The essential ones are: mutual trust and confidence between Procunier and Jennings were essential to the proper functioning of the workplace; Jennings told Procunier she did not trust him to deliver the salary study to the School Board; Jennings' belief that Procunier would not deliver the salary study to the School Board was unreasonable; the salary study was not presented to Procunier prior to being delivered to members of the School Board in order to enhance its effectiveness; Procunier discharged Jennings because of the form of her protest, *i.e.,* not informing Procunier of the salary study or giving him a copy before it was delivered to the School Board; Jennings' discharge was based upon a loss of trust and confidence by Procunier, which was reasonable under the circumstances. * * *

In *Jennings I* [the previous proceeding] this Court expressed some doubt as to whether mere "disloyalty" can ever be the sole legitimate nondiscriminatory reason for discharging an employee protesting unlawful employment practices. Noting the Ninth Circuit's opinion in *Crown Zellerbach,* [720 F.2d at 1014] the panel majority observed that almost every form of opposition to an employment practice is in some sense disloyal.

In *Crown Zellerbach,* a group of minority employees, seeking to remedy what they perceived to be unlawful employment discrimination, filed complaints with the Equal Employment Opportunity Commission and engaged in other forms of protest activity. In particular, the group wrote letters not only to the employer's corporate parent requesting an open meeting to discuss the situation, but also to local officials, protesting the failure of public officials to investigate. The group picketed the office of the Mayor of Los Angeles. The group also lodged an administrative complaint with the Office of Federal Contract Compliance, charging that the employer's practices did not conform to Executive Order 11246, and this was later borne out by a General Services Administration investigation. All of this activity apparently was readily known by the employer. Finally, the group discovered through the company newspaper that the employer was to receive an award from the Los Angeles School District, a significant customer, for sponsorship of a program designed to provide career guidance to students at a predominantly Hispanic school. The group, believing that the employer did not merit an award for undertaking affirmative action, then wrote a letter to the School Board, composed of elected officials, to inform it of the "bigoted position of racism" and of various discrimination charges that had been filed against the company. As a consequence, the employer fired the group of employees for "disloyalty."

The Ninth Circuit applied a reasonableness test to determine whether the conduct could provide a legitimate nondiscriminatory basis for the discharge. Holding for the employees, the court determined that disloyalty alone would not suffice as reason for discharge, remarking that otherwise virtually any opposition, no matter how reasonable, could be chilled in that opposition by definition connotes overtures of disloyalty. Rather, the court determined that the letter to the School Board was an appropriate response to a decision by a body of elected officials to bestow an affirmative action award upon the employer.

The Ninth Circuit carefully distinguished cases in which an employee's opposition to perceived unlawful employment practices was determined to be unreasonable. In particular, the court distinguished *Hochstadt v. Worcester Foundation for Experimental Biology,* 545 F.2d 222 (1st Cir. 1976), where the manner of opposition by an employee was held unreasonable. Although the First Circuit in *Hochstadt* expressly determined that the employee's conduct was "disloyal," it was also clear that the employee's conduct resulted in her poor work performance and also in fellow employees' diminished performance and reduced morale. * * *

The standard adopted in *Crown Zellerbach* remains applicable in this case. The issue before us is whether Jennings' conduct gave rise to a legitimate nondiscriminatory reason for her discharge, despite the fact that the substance of her protest was protected. Although the district court held that "objection to the form of the protest cannot be easily divorced from an objection to the protest itself," that is exactly the result compelled by *Crown Zellerbach.* The substance of the secretaries' protest, unlawful sex discrimination, is of course protected. But the outcome here depends on whether in pursuing her protest, Jennings exceeded the cloak of statutory protection by engaging in unreasonable conduct.

The district court found, and we do not question, that in order to enhance its effectiveness Procunier was not informed of the P.S. Salary Study, nor given an advance copy. Despite seeing and speaking to Procunier throughout the day, Jennings deliberately chose to keep him in the dark instead of following past practice of letting him present such a study to the Board. Accordingly Procunier, the proponent of the competing salary schedule, was not given an opportunity to respond promptly to the School Board members' inquiries. Judge Norgle determined that the decision to withhold notice from Procunier and then surprise him with the P.S. Salary Study after the School Board members had been receiving their own copies, was unreasonable. Judge Norgle's findings compel the conclusion that Jennings' decision was a conscious effort to hamper a supervisor's ability to respond to his superiors for the purpose of accomplishing her own ends.

* * * As in *Hochstadt,* when an employee engaged in opposition to a perceived unlawful employment practice participates in conduct which does not further the protest, but rather merely hinders another person's ability to perform his job, that employee relinquishes statutory protection.

Here Jennings relinquished Title VII statutory protection. The substance of her protest was protected; she could not have been disciplined for her opposition to a reasonably perceived unlawful employment practice. Her decision to sandbag Procunier, however, was not entitled to protection. Perhaps if she had shown that Procunier was initially unresponsive, hostile or adversarial, such action might have been reasonable. But such was not the case. The facts indicate that Procunier was responsive, albeit his responses were not what the secretaries wanted to hear. The work environment was not disturbed because Procunier lessened Jennings' responsibilities; rather the environment was disturbed due to her decision to hinder her supervisor's ability to do his job. The record before Judge Norgle supports his conclusion that an adversarial relationship developed because of Jennings' unreasonable conduct.

An employee need not always inform a supervisor of her plans to, and substance of, protest. There are doubtless times where such a requirement would chill the rights of employees to engage in reasonable protest. Rather, we hold only that an employee may not use legitimate opposition to perceived unlawful employment discrimination as a gratuitous opportunity to embarrass a supervisor or thwart his ability to perform his job. Jennings' actions to hinder Procunier's ability to perform his job were purely gratuitous. If Procunier had been likely to disrupt or prevent legitimate opposition, contrary to what the district court found, the outcome of this litigation might be different.

Today's decision is not an affirmation of the "loyalty" defense that was questioned in *Jennings I.* It is doubtful whether loyalty alone can be a legitimate, nondiscriminatory reason for disciplining an employee engaged in opposition to an unlawful employment practice. The issue here is not simply loyalty; it is whether a supervisor can discipline an employee who deliberately interferes with the supervisor's efficacy in relationship to his superiors, particularly when the employee is in a position to repeat the interference. This decision recognizes that it is not unreasonable for a supervisor who has been thwarted once vis à vis his superiors to expect a repetition and to take action to avoid another attempt. An employer may in such circumstances discipline the employee, not because of her opposition, not because of a sense of disloyalty, but rather because of the employee's deliberate decision to disrupt the work environment, including her superior's standing with his own superiors.

The decision of the district court is affirmed.

Notes

1. Judicial interpretations of the scope of protection accorded by the labor relations legislation to "concerted activity" has guided courts in determining whether the opposition is reasonable and thus protected by the employment discrimination statutes. *Hochstadt v. Worcester Foundation,* 545 F.2d 222 (1st Cir. 1976).

2. *Disloyalty:* As a general proposition, opposition directed at the *employer's treatment of its employees,* even when the employees publicizes their views to the public—such as distributing handbills or making comments to the press—asking the public not to patronize the employer because of the employer's treatment of employees is likely protected as "loyal opposition." *Wrighten v. Metropolitan Hospitals, Inc.,* 726 F.2d 1346 (9th Cir. 1984). However, employee attacks on the quality of the employer's products, goods, or services will be unprotected *disloyal* behavior. *See NLRB v. Local 1229 IBEW (Jefferson Standard Broadcasting),* 346 U.S. 464, 74 S.Ct. 172, 98 L.Ed. 195 (1953)(NLRA).

3. *Determining "Reasonableness:"* **Hochstadt v. Worcester Foundation,** 545 F.2d 222 (1st Cir. 1976) explained the process:

> [W]e think courts have in each case to *balance* the purpose of the Act to protect persons engaging *reasonably* in activities opposing * * * discrimination, against Congress's equally manifest desire not to tie the hands of employers in the objective * * * control of personnel. Allowing the employee to invoke the protection of section 704(a) for conduct aimed at purely ulterior motives, or for conduct aimed at achieving proper objectives through the use of improper means, could have an effect directly contrary to Congress' goal. * * *

The court noted a pattern of opposition that included: (1) interfering with the work of fellow employees, (2) circulating false rumors that the employer was in danger of losing its funding, (3) engaging in covert "studies" that were sent to members of Congress, (4) supplying confidential salary information to a news reporter, and (5) use of working time and the employer's equipment to mount the opposition. The court held that the trial court properly concluded that the employee "went too far in her particular employment setting."

4. *Unlawful Acts:* In **McDonnell Douglas Corp. v. Green,** 411 U.S. 792, 93 S.Ct. 1817, 36 L.Ed.2d 668 (1973), an employee undertook a comprehensive, vocal public protest about the employer's perceived pattern of racial discrimination. As part of his protest the employee forcefully blocked the entrance to the workplace. In holding the refusal to rehire the employee was "legitimate and non-discriminatory" the Court stated: "Nothing in Title VII compels an employer to absolve and rehire one who has engaged in * * * deliberate, unlawful activity against it." There has arisen from this holding a presumption that illegal behavior cannot be protected opposition. *See, Cruz v. Coach Stores, Inc.,* 202 F.3d 560 (2d Cir. 2000)(striking a fellow employee unprotected). **Local 833 v. NLRB,** 300 F.2d 699 (D.C.Cir. 1962), articulated a more nuanced approach that is followed in the labor relations context:

> [W]here an employer who has committed [illegal acts] discharges employees for unprotected acts of misconduct, the [fact finder] must consider both the seriousness of the employer's unlawful acts and the seriousness of the employees' misconduct. * * * To hold that employee misconduct automatically precludes compulsory reinstatement ignores two considerations which we think important. First, the employer's antecedent [unlawful acts] may have been so blatant that it provoked employees to resort to unprotected action. Second, reinstatement is the only sanction which prevents an employer from benefiting from its illegal activity through discharges * * *.

5. *Insubordination and work stoppage:* Refusal to perform one's job assignment or performing in a slovenly manner is not protected. *See, NLRB v. Montgomery Ward,* 157 F.2d 486 (8th Cir. 1946)(NLRA); *Robinson v. Sappington,* 351 F.3d 317 (7th Cir. 2003). However, if the employee of a non-government employer joins with other employees who engage in a *total* work stoppage, such "concerted activity" would be protected under national labor relations legislation. *NLRB v. Washington Aluminum Co.,* 370 U.S. 9, 82 S.Ct. 1099, 8 L.Ed.2d 298 (1962).

6. *Confidential information:* Protected opposition is not a "license to engage in dubious self-help tactics or work place espionage in order to gain evidence of discrimination." *Argyropoulos v. City of Alton,* 539 F.3d 724 (7th Cir. 2008). Thus, even gaining unauthorized *access* to information the employer has designated as "confidential" or the unauthorized copying of such information is unlikely to be protected. *See, McKennon v. Nashville Banner Pub. Co.,* 513 U.S. 352, 115 S.Ct. 879, 130 L.Ed.2d 852 (1995). Moreover, unauthorized *distribution* of "confidential" materials to which the employee has access may be unprotected. *Niswander v. Cincinnati Ins. Co.,* 529 F.3d 714 (6th Cir. 2008) (confidential materials given to attorney to support EEOC charge unprotected).

7. *National Labor Relations statutes* place limits on employee collective activity by proscribing "secondary boycotts," picketing in some instances for organizational purposes, and splinter groups, such as civil rights organizations, exerting pressure on an employer to bargain over alleged discrimination

when the employer is under a statutory obligation to bargain exclusively with a certified bargaining agent (i.e., union). Individuals opposing employer practices by utilizing tactics deemed unlawful or even unprotect by labor relations statutes may find that their opposition is likewise unprotected by Title VII. *See, Emporium Capwell Co. v. Western Addition Community Org.*, 420 U.S. 50, 95 S.Ct. 977, 43 L.Ed.2d 12 (1975).

CHAPTER 10

COMPENSATION: WAGES AND BENEFITS

■ ■ ■

A. THE EQUAL PAY ACT

CORNING GLASS WORKS v. BRENNAN

Supreme Court of the United States, 1974
417 U.S. 188, 94 S.Ct. 2223, 41 L.Ed.2d 1

JUSTICE MARSHALL delivered the opinion of the Court.

These cases arise under the Equal Pay Act of 1963, 29 U.S.C. § 206(d)(1),[1] which added to § 6 of the Fair Labor Standards Act of 1938 the principle of equal pay for equal work regardless of sex. The principal question posed is whether Corning Glass Works violated the Act by paying a higher base wage to male night shift inspectors than it paid to female inspectors performing the same tasks on the day shift, where the higher wage was paid in addition to a separate night shift differential paid to all employees for night work. In No. 73–29, the Court of Appeals for the Second Circuit, in a case involving several Corning plants in Corning, New York, held that this practice violated the Act. In No. 73–695, the Court of Appeals for the Third Circuit, in a case involving a Corning plant in Wellsboro, Pennsylvania, reached the opposite conclusion. We granted certiorari and consolidated the cases to resolve this unusually direct conflict between two circuits. Finding ourselves in substantial agreement with the analysis of the Second Circuit, we affirm in No. 73–29 and reverse in No. 73–695.

I

Prior to 1925, Corning operated its plants in Wellsboro and Corning only during the day, and all inspection work was performed by women. Be-

---

1. 'No employer having employees subject to any provisions of this section shall discriminate, within any establishment in which such employees are employed, between employees on the basis of sex by paying wages to employees in such establishment at a rate less than the rate at which he pays wages to employees of the opposite sex in such establishment for equal work on jobs the performance of which requires equal skill, effort, and responsibility, and which are performed under similar working conditions, except where such payment is made pursuant to (i) a seniority system; (ii) a merit system; (iii) a system which measures earnings by quantity or quality of production; or (iv) a differential based on any other factor other than sex: Provided, That an employer who is paying a wage rate differential in violation of this subsection shall not, in order to comply with the provisions of this subsection, reduce the wage rate of any employee.'

tween 1925 and 1930, the company began to introduce automatic production equipment which made it desirable to institute a night shift. During this period, however, both New York and Pennsylvania law prohibited women from working at night. As a result, in order to fill inspector positions on the new night shift, the company had to recruit male employees from among its male dayworkers. The male employees so transferred demanded and received wages substantially higher than those paid to women inspectors engaged on the two day shifts. During this same period, however, no plant-wide shift differential existed and male employees working at night, other than inspectors, received the same wages as their day shift counterparts. Thus a situation developed where the night inspectors were all male, the day inspectors all female, and the male inspectors received significantly higher wages.

In 1944, Corning plants at both locations were organized by a labor union and a collective-bargaining agreement was negotiated for all production and maintenance employees. This agreement for the first time established a plantwide shift differential, but this change did not eliminate the higher base wage paid to male night inspectors. Rather, the shift differential was superimposed on the existing difference in base wages between male night inspectors and female day inspectors.

Prior to June 11, 1964, the effective date of the Equal Pay Act the law in both Pennsylvania and New York was amended to permit women to work at night. It was not until some time after the effective date of the Act, however, that Corning initiated efforts to eliminate the differential rates for male and female inspectors. Beginning in June 1966, Corning started to open up jobs on the night shift to women. Previously separate male and female seniority lists were consolidated and women became eligible to exercise their seniority, on the same basis as men, to bid for the higher paid night inspection jobs as vacancies occurred.

On January 20, 1969, a new collective-bargaining agreement went into effect, establishing a new 'job evaluation' system for setting wage rates. The new agreement abolished for the future the separate base wages for day and night shift inspectors and imposed a uniform base wage for inspectors exceeding the wage rate for the night shift previously in effect. All inspectors hired after January 20, 1969, were to receive the same base wage, whatever their sex or shift. The collective-bargaining agreement further provided, however, for a higher 'red circle' rate for employees hired prior to January 20, 1969, when working as inspectors on the night shift. This 'red circle' rate served essentially to perpetuate the differential in base wages between day and night inspectors.

The Secretary of Labor brought these cases to enjoin Corning from violating the Equal Pay Act and to collect back wages allegedly due female employees because of past violations. Three distinct questions are presented: (1) Did Corning ever violate the Equal Pay Act by paying male night shift inspectors more than female day shift inspectors? (2) If so, did Corning cure its violation of the Act in 1966 by permitting women to work as night shift inspectors? (3) Finally, if the violation was not remedied in 1966, did Corning cure its violation in 1969 by equalizing day and night inspector wage rates but establishing higher 'red circle' rates for existing employees working on the night shift?

II

Congress' purpose in enacting the Equal Pay Act was to remedy what was perceived to be a serious and endemic problem of employment discrimination in private industry—the fact that the wage structure of 'many segments of American industry has been based on an ancient but outmoded belief that a man, because of his role in society, should be paid more than a woman even though his duties are the same.' The solution adopted was quite simple in principle: to require that 'equal work will be rewarded by equal wages.'

The Act's basic structure and operation are similarly straightforward. In order to make out a case under the Act, the Secretary must show that an employer pays different wages to employees of opposite sexes 'for equal work on jobs the performance of which requires equal skill, effort, and responsibility, and which are performed under similar working conditions.' Although the Act is silent on this point, its legislative history makes plain that the Secretary has the burden of proof on this issue, as both of the courts below recognized.

The Act also establishes four exceptions—three specific and one a general catchall provision—where different payment to employees of opposite sexes 'is made pursuant to (i) a seniority system; (ii) a merit system; (iii) a system which measures earnings by quantity or quality of production; or (iv) a differential based on any other factor other than sex.' Again, while the Act is silent on this question, its structure and history also suggest that once the Secretary has carried his burden of showing that the employer pays workers of one sex more than workers of the opposite sex for equal work, the burden shifts to the employer to show that the differential is justified under one of the Act's four exceptions. All of the many lower courts that have considered this question have so held, and this view is consistent with the general rule that the application of an exemption under the Fair Labor Standards Act is a matter of affirmative defense on which the employer has the burden of proof.

The contentions of the parties in this case reflect the Act's underlying framework. Corning argues that the Secretary has failed to prove that Corning ever violated the Act because day shift work is not 'performed under similar working conditions' as night shift work. The Secretary maintains that day shift and night shift work are performed under 'similar working conditions' within the meaning of the Act. Although the Secretary recognizes that higher wages may be paid for night shift work, the Secretary contends that such a shift differential would be based upon a 'factor other than sex' within the catch-all exception to the Act and that Corning has failed to carry its burden of proof that its higher base wage for male night inspectors was in fact based on any factor other than sex.

The courts below relied in part on conflicting statements in the legislative history having some bearing on this question of statutory construction. The Third Circuit found particularly significant a statement of Congressman Goodell, a sponsor of the Equal Pay bill, who, in the course of explaining the bill on the floor of the House, commented that 'standing as opposed to sitting, pleasantness or unpleasantness of surroundings, periodic rest periods, hours of work, difference in shift, all would logically fall within the working condition factor.' The Second Circuit, in contrast, relied on a statement from the House Committee Report which, in describing the broad general exception for differentials 'based on any other factor other than sex,' stated: 'Thus, among other things, shift differentials ... would also be excluded....'

We agree with Judge Friendly, however, that in this case a better understanding of the phrase 'performed under similar working conditions' can be obtained from a consideration of the way in which Congress arrived at the statutory language than from trying to reconcile or establish preferences between the conflicting interpretations of the Act by individual legislators or the committee reports. As Mr. Justice Frankfurter remarked in an earlier case involving interpretation of the Fair Labor Standards Act, 'regard for the specific history of the legislative process that culminated in the Act now before us affords more solid ground for giving it appropriate meaning.'

The most notable feature of the history of the Equal Pay Act is that Congress recognized early in the legislative process that the concept of equal pay for equal work was more readily stated in principle than reduced to statutory language which would be meaningful to employers and workable across the broad range of industries covered by the Act. As originally introduced, the Equal Pay bill required equal pay for 'equal work on jobs the performance of which requires equal skills.' There were only two exceptions-for differentials 'made pursuant to a seniority or merit increase system which does not discriminate on the basis of sex....'

In both the House and Senate committee hearings, witnesses were highly critical of the Act's definition of equal work and of its exemptions. Many noted that most of American industry used formal, systematic job evaluation plans to establish equitable wage structures in their plants. Such systems, as explained coincidentally by a representative of Corning Glass Works who testified at both hearings, took into consideration four separate factors in determining job value-skill, effort, responsibility and working conditions-and each of these four components was further systematically divided into various subcomponents. Under a job evaluation plan, point values are assigned to each of the subcomponents of a given job, resulting in a total point figure representing a relatively objective measure of the job's value.

In comparison to the rather complex job evaluation plans used by industry, the definition of equal work used in the first drafts of the Equal Pay bill was criticized as unduly vague and incomplete. Industry representatives feared that as a result of the bill's definition of equal work, the Secretary of Labor would be cast in the position of second-guessing the validity of a company's job evaluation system. They repeatedly urged that the bill be amended to include an exception for job classification systems, or otherwise to incorporate the language of job evaluation into the bill. * * *

We think it plain that in amending the bill's definition of equal work to its present form, the Congress acted in direct response to these pleas. Spokesmen for the amended bill stated, for example, during the House debates:

> 'The concept of equal pay for jobs demanding equal skill has been expanded to require also equal effort, responsibility, and similar working conditions. These factors are the core of all job classification systems. They form a legitimate basis for differentials in pay.'

Indeed, the most telling evidence of congressional intent is the fact that the Act's amended definition of equal work incorporated the specific language of the job evaluation plan described at the hearings by Corning's own representative—that is, the concepts of 'skill,' 'effort,' 'responsibility,' and 'working conditions.'

Congress' intent, as manifested in this history, was to use these terms of incorporate into the new federal Act the well-defined and well-accepted principles of job evaluation so as to ensure that wage differentials based upon bona fide job evaluation plans would be outside the purview of the Act. * * *

It is in this light that the phrase 'working conditions' must be understood, for where Congress has used technical words or terms of art, 'it (is) proper to explain them by reference to the art or science to which they (are) appropriate.' This principle is particularly salutary where, as here, the legislative history reveals that Congress incorporated words having a special meaning within the field regulated by the statute so as to overcome objections by industry representatives that statutory definitions were vague and incomplete.

While a layman might well assume that time of day worked reflects one aspect of a job's 'working conditions,' the term has a different and much more specific meaning in the language of industrial relations. As Corning's own representative testified at the hearings, the element of working conditions encompasses two subfactors: 'surroundings' and 'hazards.' 'Surroundings' measures the elements, such as toxic chemicals or fumes, regularly encountered by a worker, their intensity, and their frequency. 'Hazards' takes into account the physical hazards regularly encountered, their frequency, and the severity of injury they can cause. This definition of 'working conditions' is not only manifested in Corning's own job evaluation plans but is also well accepted across a wide range of American industry.

Nowhere in any of these definitions is time of day worked mentioned as a relevant criterion. The fact of the matter is that the concept of 'working conditions,' as used in the specialized language of job evaluation systems, simply does not encompass shift differentials. Indeed, while Corning now argues that night inspection work is not equal to day inspection work, all of its own job evaluation plans, including the one now in effect, have consistently treated them as equal in all respects, including working conditions. And Corning's Manager of Job Evaluation testified in No. 73–29 that time of day worked was not considered to be a 'working condition.' Significantly, it is not the Secretary in this case who is trying to look behind Corning's bona fide job evaluation system to require equal pay for jobs which Corning has historically viewed as unequal work. Rather, it is Corning which asks us to differentiate between jobs which the company itself has always equated. We agree with the Second Circuit that the inspection work at issue in this case, whether performed during the day or night, is 'equal work' as that term is defined in the Act.[24]

This does not mean, of course, that there is no room in the Equal Pay Act for nondiscriminatory shift differentials. Work on a steady night shift no doubt has psychological and physiological impacts making it less attractive than work on a day shift. The Act contemplates that a male night worker may receive a higher wage than a female day worker, just as it contemplates that a male employee with 20 years' seniority can receive a higher wage than a woman with two years' seniority Factors such as these play a role under the Act's four exceptions-the seniority differential under the specific seniority exception, the shift differential under the catch-all exception for differentials 'based on any other factor other than sex.'

The question remains, however, whether Corning carried its burden of proving that the higher rate paid for night inspection work, until 1966 performed solely by men, was in fact intended to serve as compensation for night work, or rather constituted an added payment based upon sex. We agree that the record amply supports the District Court's conclusion that Corning had not sustained its burden of proof. As its history revealed, 'the higher night rate was in large part the product of the generally higher wage level of male workers and the need to compensate them for performing what were regarded as demeaning tasks.' The differential in base wages originated at a time when no other night employees received higher pay than corresponding day workers, and it was maintained long after the company instituted a separate plant-wide shift differential which was thought to compensate adequately for the additional burdens of night work. The differential arose simply because men would not work at the low rates paid women inspectors, and it reflected a job market in which

---

24. In No. 73–29, Corning also claimed that the night inspection work was not equal to day shift inspection work because night shift inspectors had to do a certain amount of packing, lifting, and cleaning which was not performed by day shift inspectors. Noting that it is now well settled that jobs need not be identical in every respect before the Equal Pay Act is applicable, the Court of Appeals concluded that the extra work performed by night inspectors was of so little consequence that the jobs remained substantially equal. The company has not pursued this issue here.

Corning could pay women less than men for the same work. That the company took advantage of such a situation may be understandable as a matter of economics, but its differential nevertheless became illegal once Congress enacted into law the principle of equal pay for equal work.

III

We now must consider whether Corning continued to remain in violation of the Act after 1966 when, without changing the base wage rates for day and night inspectors, it began to permit women to bid for jobs on the night shift as vacancies occurred. It is evident that this was more than a token gesture to end discrimination, as turnover in the night shift inspection jobs was rapid. The record in No. 73–29 shows, for example, that during the two-year period after June 1, 1966, the date women were first permitted to bid for night inspection jobs, women took 152 of the 278 openings, and women with very little seniority were able to obtain positions on the night shift. Relying on these facts, the company argues that it ceased discriminating against women in 1966, and was no longer in violation of the Equal Pay Act.

But the issue before us is not whether the company, in some abstract sense, can be said to have treated men the same as women after 1966. Rather, the question is whether the company remedied the specific violation of the Act which the Secretary proved. We agree with the Second Circuit, as well as with all other circuits that have had occasion to consider this issue, that the company could not cure its violation except by equalizing the base wages of female day inspectors with the higher rates paid the night inspectors. This result is implicit in the Act's language, its statement of purpose, and its legislative history.

* * *

To achieve this end, Congress required that employers pay equal pay for equal work and then specified:

> 'provided, That an employer who is paying a wage rate differential in violation of this subsection shall not, in order to comply with the provisions of this subsection, reduce the wage rate of any employee.' 29 U.S.C. s 206(d) (1).

* * *

By proving that after the effective date of the Equal Pay Act, Corning paid female day inspectors less than male night inspectors for equal work, the Secretary implicitly demonstrated that the wages of female day shift inspectors were unlawfully depressed and that the fair wage for inspection work was the base wage paid to male inspectors on the night shift. The whole purpose of the Act was to require that these depressed wages be raised, in part as a matter of simple justice to the employees themselves, but also as a matter of market economics, since Congress recognized as well that discrimination in wages on the basis of sex 'constitutes an unfair method of competition.'

We agree with Judge Friendly that

> 'In light of this apparent congressional understanding, we cannot hold that Corning, by allowing some—or even many—women to move into the higher paid night jobs, achieved full compliance with the Act. Corning's action still left the inspectors on the day shift—virtually all women—earning a lower base wage than the night shift inspectors because of a differential initially based on sex and still not justified by any other consideration; in effect, Corning was still taking advantage of the availability of female labor to fill its day shift at a differentially low wage rate not justified by any factor other than sex.'

The Equal Pay Act is broadly remedial, and it should be construed and applied so as to fulfill the underlying purposes which Congress sought to achieve. If, as the Secretary proved, the work performed by women on the day shift was equal to that performed by men on the night shift, the company became obligated to pay the women the same base wage as their male counterparts on the effective date of the Act. To permit the company to escape that obligation by agreeing to allow some women to work on the night shift at a higher rate of pay as vacancies occurred would frustrate, not serve, Congress' ends.

The company's final contention—that it cured its violation of the Act when a new collective-bargaining agreement went into effect on January 20, 1969—need not detain us long. While the new agreement provided for equal base wages for night or day inspectors hired after that date, it continued to provide unequal base wages for employees hired before that date, a discrimination likely to continue for some time into the future because of a large number of laid-off employees who had to be offered re-employment before new inspectors could be hired. After considering the rather complex method in which the new wage rates for employees hired prior to January 1969 were calculated and the company's stated purpose behind the provisions of the new agreement, the District Court in No. 73–29 concluded that the lower base wage for day inspectors was a direct product of the company's failure to equalize the base wages for male and female inspectors as of the effective date of the Act. We agree it is clear from the record that had the company equalized the base-wage rates of male and female inspectors on the effective date of the Act, as the law required, the day inspectors in 1969 would have been entitled to the same higher 'red circle' rate the company provided for night inspectors. We therefore conclude that on the facts of this case, the company's continued discrimination in base wages between night and day workers, though phrased in terms of a neutral factor other than sex, nevertheless operated to perpetuate the effects of the company's prior illegal practice of paying women less than men for equal work.

The judgment in No. 73–29 is affirmed. The judgment in No. 73–695 is reversed and the case remanded to the Court of Appeals for further proceedings consistent with this opinion.

NOTES

1. *Equal Work* first requires comparing the actual content of the two jobs. Three content elements are examined: (1) skill, (2) effort, and (3) responsibility, all three of which must be "equal." In footnote 24 the Court noted that "equal" does not mean "identical." But content of the jobs must be more than just "similar" or "comparable." "Equal" thus means "substantially equal." *Hein v. Oregon College of Educ,* 718 F.2d 910 (9th Cir. 1983). Equality must be both qualitative and quantitaive. For example, *Usery v. Columbia Univ.,* 568 F.2d 953 (2d Cir. 1977), held that "heavy cleaning" of small areas was not "equal" to light cleaning of large areas even though the janitorial duties were substantially equal in terms of skill level, responsibility, and the total effort expended. The two jobs were not "equal" because they were "different jobs" in that they lacked qualitative equality.

The fourth element of job equality goes not to job content but to the "working conditions" under which the equal jobs are performed. "Working conditions" which need only be "similar," and as the principal case pointed out, applies to physical surroundings or hazards, not to the time of day the work is performed.

2. *Unequal rates of pay*: For jobs that are "equal" the *rates* of pay for the men and women performing them must be equal. It is no defense that take-home pay, or gross pay, is the same for the men and women performing equal work. In *Bence v. Detroit Health Corp.,* 712 F.2d 1024 (6th Cir. 1983), a commission rate of pay for managers was based on a percentage of gross receipts. Commission rates for male managers were higher than the commission rates for female managers. Even though the different commission rates produced similar net income for men and women, the *"rate"* of pay was not equal.

3. *Between men and women.* The Equal Pay Act applies only to pay differences between men and women, protecting men as well as women. It is an objective standard that does not require plaintiff to establish sex motivation for the pay difference. As *Corning Glass* held, compliance is not accomplished by lowering the rate of the higher paid employee. The difference in pay is unpaid wages that must be paid to the lower paid worker, with the rate of pay of the lower paid employee increased to match that of the higher paid employee.

4. *Comparator:* When an employer has both men and women performing equal work, but some men make more, and others less, than the female plaintiff, the calculation is complicated. Comparisons need not be limited to current workers, but can be made to either predecessors or successors of the plaintiff. *Lawrence v. CNF Transp., Inc.,* 340 F.3d 486 (8th Cir. 2003). Literally, if any person of the opposite sex is, or has been, doing work equal to the plaintiff and is paid at a higher rate, the plaintiff has established a prima facie violation of the EPA, leaving the burden on defendant to establish that the pay differences between individuals were based on a "factor other than sex." *Mitchell v. Jefferson County Bd. of Educ.,* 936 F.2d 539 (11th Cir. 1991). Some authority indicates, however, that where substantial numbers of both

sexes doing equal work make both more and less than the plaintiff there is no EPA violation. *Yant v. United States,* 85 Fed.Cl. 264 (2009). Others compare *average* pay rates of male and female employees performing the equal work. *Heymann v. Tetra Plastics Corp.,* 640 F.2d 115 (8th Cir. 1981). Still others attempt to identify a *"comparator"* of the opposite sex who has credentials most like those possessed by the plaintiff. *Houck v. VPI,* 10 F.3d 204 (4th Cir. 1993).

5. *"Establishment" vs. "Employer:"* Coverage of the EPA is dramatically different than Title VII coverage. The EPA requires only employee contact with interstate commerce or an employer whose size is based upon the dollar amount of "annual sales made or business done" ($500,000). Accordingly, relatively small employers, with as few as two employees (one male and one female), can be covered. However, the EPA requires the equal work to be performed within the same "establishment" of a covered employer. "Establishment" generally, but not necessarily, refers to distinct physical locations within an employer. Thus, departments within a location in most cases would be considered within the same "establishment." However, unless centralized management controls pay and personnel decisions at remote locations each physically separate site of the employer will be considered a distinct "establishment." Pay differences for equal work in different "establishments" will not violate the EPA. 29 C.F.R. § 1620.9. (If improperly motivated, the difference will violate Title VII.)

6. *Defenses:* The EPA sets forth four defenses to unequal pay for equal work, defenses that the employer has the burden of establishing, three of which must be based on employer *"systems"* of (1) seniority, (2) merit, (3) and which measure quality or quantity of work. To qualify as a "system" it must be a fixed, objective, and consistently followed practice that has been communicated to the workers. Haphazard, idiosyncratic pay patterns that the employer attempts to rationalize after the fact will not be a "system." *Brock v. Georgia Southwestern College,* 765 F.2d 1026 (11th Cir. 1985).

The fourth is a catch-all defense which allows employers to set different rates of pay if they are based on "any other factor other than sex." This fourth defense has received the most attention.

a. Subjective Bona Fides: Los Angeles Dep't of Water & Power v. Manhart, supra p. 291 required that to qualify for the defense the "system" or "factor" had to be sex-neutral. The Court held that a sex-based mortality table used to set pension returns cannot qualify as a "factor other than sex," because sex is precisely what the table is based upon. The requirement of sex neutrality was affirmed in *Corning Glass Works v. Brennan, supra,* where a premium payment for night work, which otherwise would be a legitimate "factor," did not qualify under the facts of that case because the shift premium perpetuated past segregation of women by this employer. A training program that excludes women, and provides premium pay to "trainees" could not qualify as a "factor other than sex." *Shultz v. First Victoria Nat. Bank,* 420 F.2d 648 (5th Cir. 1969).

b. Objective Job Relatedness: The "factor" relied upon to justify the wage rate difference need not meet the more rigorous *Griggs* standard of being a "business necessity." *See, Meacham v. Knolls Atomic Power Lab.,* 554

U.S. 84, 128 S.Ct. 2395, 171 L.Ed.2d 283 (2008) (similar language in the ADEA). Thus, objective tests measuring mental or physical performance or credentials such as education or experience need not be directly related to job content or performance. However, some courts have held that to satisfy the defense, the "factor" must be shown by the employer to be derived from the unique characteristics of the job, the individuals' relative training, experience, or ability, or from special circumstances connected with the employer's business. It is not sufficient that the "reason" is simply rational. *Glenn v. General Motors Corp.* 841 F.2d 1567 (11th Cir. 1988).

Other courts have held that as long as the "factor" is rational the "factor" need not be connected to employee performance or serve actual business needs of the employer. Under this standard a program that provided premium pay to employees who were "heads" of their household would be a "factor other than sex," even though the policy had no immediate business purpose. *EEOC v. J.C. Penney Co.,* 843 F.2d 249 (6th Cir. 1988).

The courts generally agree that an employer may respond to external market demands in setting salary, such as paying premiums to attract new workers or to retain incumbents. Prior salary earned elsewhere is a legitimate "factor" in setting a new employee's salary. *AFSME v. State of Washington, supra p. 302; Kouba v. Allstate Ins. Co.,* 691 F.2d 873 (9th Cir. 1982). Additional "factors other than sex" would be shift differentials paid for evening or week-end work and "red circling" of higher pay for workers temporarily assigned to lower paying jobs held by persons of the opposite sex. *See, Corning Glass v. Brennan, supra p. 466.*

Again, the employer must prove the sex neutrality of such factors. For example, *King v. Acosta Sales & Mktg., Inc.,* ___ F.3d ___, 2012 WL 807199 (7th Cir. 2012), 49 DLR AA–1, held that differences in education and past experience might explain pay discrepancies in initial *starting* salaries. These "factors" did not, however, explain a difference in the percentage *increases* in salary where the female workers had higher job performance rating s than did their male counterparts. The unexplained granting of higher rates of raise *Increases* to the under-performing men was sufficient to allow a jury to conclude that sex, rather than the stated "factors," motivated the current pay discrepancies between similarly situated male and female workers.

    7. *Back wages and liquidated damages:* The EPA treats the difference between the higher paid employee and the lower paid employee of the opposite sex as a wage obligation of the employer which may be recovered for up to two years of past underpayments, or three years if the plaintiff can prove that the violation was "willful." 29 U.S.C. § 255(a). In addition, the underpaid employee may collect an additional amount equal to unpaid wages as statutory liquidated damages (resulting in double back pay). However, the trial court has discretion to reduce the "liquidated damage" award where the employer establishes that the violation of the Act was done in good faith with a reasonable basis for believing that the pay differences were lawful. 29 U.S.C. §§ 216(b) and 260.

B. RECONCILING TITLE VII AND THE EQUAL PAY ACT

1. THE "BENNETT AMENDMENT"

WASHINGTON COUNTY v. GUNTHER

Supreme Court of the United States, 1981
452 U.S. 161, 101 S.Ct. 2242, 68 L.Ed.2d 751

JUSTICE BRENNAN delivered the opinion of the Court.

The question presented is whether § 703(h) of Title VII of the Civil Rights Act of 1964, 42 U.S.C. § 2000e–2(h), restricts Title VII's prohibition of sex-based wage discrimination to claims of equal pay for equal work.

I

This case arises over the payment by petitioner, County of Washington, Or. of substantially lower wages to female guards in the female section of the county jail than it paid to male guards in the male section of the jail. Respondents are four women who were employed to guard female prisoners and to carry out certain other functions in the jail.[2] In January 1974, the county eliminated the female section of the jail, transferred the female prisoners to the jail of a nearby county, and discharged respondents.

Respondents filed suit against petitioners in Federal District Court under Title VII, seeking backpay and other relief.[3] They alleged that they were paid unequal wages for work substantially equal to that performed by male guards, and in the alternative, that part of the pay differential was attributable to intentional sex discrimination. The latter allegation was based on a claim that, because of intentional discrimination, the county set the pay scale for female guards, but not for male guards, at a level lower than that warranted by its own survey of outside markets and the worth of the jobs.

After trial, the District Court found that the male guards supervised more than 10 times as many prisoners per guard as did the female guards, and that the females devoted much of their time to less valuable clerical duties. It therefore held that respondents' jobs were not substantially equal to those of the male guards, and that respondents were thus not entitled to equal pay. The Court of Appeals affirmed on that issue, and respondents do not seek review of the ruling.

The District Court also dismissed respondents' claim that the discrepancy in pay between the male and female guards was attributable in part to

---

2. Oregon requires that female inmates be guarded solely by women, and the District Court opinion indicates that women had not been employed to guard male prisoners. For purposes of this litigation, respondents concede that gender is a bona fide occupational qualification for some of the female guard positions. * * *

3. Respondents could not sue under the Equal Pay Act because the Equal Pay Act did not apply to municipal employees until passage of the Fair Labor Standards Amendments of 1974, Title VII has applied to such employees since passage of the Equal Employment Opportunity Act of 1972.

intentional sex discrimination. It held as a matter of law that a sex-based wage discrimination claim cannot be brought under Title VII unless it would satisfy the equal work standard of the Equal Pay Act of 1963. The court therefore permitted no additional evidence on this claim, and made no findings on whether petitioner county's pay scales for female guards resulted from intentional sex discrimination.

The Court of Appeals reversed, holding that persons alleging sex discrimination "are not precluded from suing under Title VII to protest ... discriminatory compensation practices" merely because their jobs were not equal to higher paying jobs held by members of the opposite sex. The court remanded to the District Court with instructions to take evidence on respondents' claim that part of the difference between their rate of pay and that of the male guards is attributable to sex discrimination. We granted certiorari, and now affirm.

We emphasize at the outset the narrowness of the question before us in this case. Respondents' claim is not based on the controversial concept of "comparable worth,"[8] under which plaintiffs might claim increased compensation on the basis of a comparison of the intrinsic worth or difficulty of their job with that of other jobs in the same organization or community. Rather, respondents seek to prove, by direct evidence, that their wages were depressed because of intentional sex discrimination, consisting of setting the wage scale for female guards, but not for male guards, at a level lower than its own survey of outside markets and the worth of the jobs warranted. The narrow question in this case is whether such a claim is precluded by the last sentence of § 703(h) of Title VII, called the "Bennett Amendment."

II

Title VII makes it an unlawful employment practice for an employer "to discriminate against any individual with respect to his compensation, terms, conditions, or privileges of employment, because of such individual's ... sex...." 42 U.S.C. § 2000e–2(a). The Bennett Amendment to Title VII, however provides:

> "It shall not be an unlawful employment practice under this subchapter for any employer to differentiate upon the basis of sex in determining the amount of the wages or compensation paid or to be paid to employees of such employer if such differentiation is authorized by the provisions of [The Equal Pay Act]." 42 U.S.C. § 2000e–2(h).

To discover what practices are exempted from Title VII's prohibitions by the Bennett Amendment, we must turn to the Equal Pay Act—which provides in relevant part:

---

8. We are not called upon in this case to decide whether respondents have stated a prima facie case of sex discrimination under Title VII or to lay down standards for the further conduct of this litigation. The sole issue we decide is whether respondents' failure to satisfy the equal work standard of the Equal Pay Act in itself precludes their proceeding under Title VII.

No employer having employees subject to any provisions of this section shall discriminate, within any establishment in which such employees are employed, between employees on the basis of sex by paying wages to employees in such establishment at a rate less than the rate at which he pays wages to employees of the opposite sex in such establishment for equal work on jobs the performance of which requires equal skill, effort, and responsibility, and which are performed under similar working conditions, except where such payment is made pursuant to (i) a seniority system; (ii) a merit system; (iii) a system which measures earnings by quantity or quality of production; or (iv) a differential based on any other factor other than sex." 29 U.S.C. § 206(d)(1).

On its face, the Equal Pay Act contains three restrictions pertinent to this case. First, its coverage is limited to those employers subject to the Fair Labor Standards Act. Thus, the Act does not apply, for example, to certain businesses engaged in retail sales, fishing, agriculture, and newspaper publishing. See 29 U.S.C. §§ 203(s), 213(a) (1976 ed. and Supp.III). Second, the Act is restricted to cases involving "equal work on jobs the performance of which requires equal skill, effort, and responsibility, and which are performed under similar working conditions." Third, the Act's four affirmative defenses exempt any wage differentials attributable to seniority, merit, quantity or quality of production, or "any other factor other than sex."

Petitioners argue that the purpose of the Bennett Amendment was to restrict Title VII sex-based wage discrimination claims to those that could also be brought under the Equal Pay Act, and thus that claims not arising from "equal work" are precluded. Respondents, in contrast, argue that the Bennett Amendment was designed merely to incorporate the four affirmative defenses of the Equal Pay Act into Title VII for sex-based wage discrimination claims. Respondents thus contend that claims for sex-based wage discrimination can be brought under Title VII even though no member of the opposite sex holds an equal but higher paying job, provided that the challenged wage rate is not based on seniority, merit, quantity or quality of production, or "any other factor other than sex." The Court of Appeals found respondents' interpretation the "more persuasive." While recognizing that the language and legislative history of the provision are not unambiguous, we conclude that the Court of Appeals was correct.

A

The language of the Bennett Amendment suggests an intention to incorporate only the affirmative defenses of the Equal Pay Act into Title VII. The Amendment bars sex-based wage discrimination claims under Title VII where the pay differential is "authorized" by the Equal Pay Act. Although the word "authorize" sometimes means simply "to permit," it ordinarily denotes affirmative enabling action. Black's Law Dictionary 122 (5th ed. 1979) defines "authorize" as "[t]o empower; to give a right or authority to act." The question, then, is what wage practices have been affirmatively authorized by the Equal Pay Act.

The Equal Pay Act is divided into two parts: a definition of the violation, followed by four affirmative defenses. The first part can hardly be said to "authorize" anything at all: it is purely prohibitory. The second part, however, in essence "authorizes" employers to differentiate in pay on the basis of seniority, merit, quantity or quality of production, or any other factor other than sex, even though such differentiation might otherwise violate the Act. It is to these provisions, therefore, that the Bennett Amendment must refer.

Petitioners argue that this construction of the Bennett Amendment would render it superfluous. Petitioners claim that the first three affirmative defenses are simply redundant of the provisions elsewhere in § 703(h) of Title VII that already exempt bona fide seniority and merit systems and systems measuring earnings by quantity or quality of production,[10] and that the fourth defense—"any other factor other than sex"—is implicit in Title VII's general prohibition of sex-based discrimination.

We cannot agree. The Bennett Amendment was offered as a "technical amendment" designed to resolve any potential conflicts between Title VII and the Equal Pay Act. Thus, with respect to the first three defenses, the Bennett Amendment has the effect of guaranteeing that courts and administrative agencies adopt a consistent interpretation of like provisions in both statutes. Otherwise, they might develop inconsistent bodies of case law interpreting two sets of nearly identical language.

More importantly, incorporation of the fourth affirmative defense could have significant consequences for Title VII litigation. Title VII' s prohibition of discriminatory employment practices was intended to be broadly inclusive, proscribing "not only overt discrimination but also practices that are fair in form, but discriminatory in operation." *Griggs v. Duke Power Co.*, 401 U.S. 424, 431, 91 S.Ct. 849, 853, 28 L.Ed.2d 158 (1971). The structure of Title VII litigation, including presumptions, burdens of proof, and defenses, has been designed to reflect this approach. The fourth affirmative defense of the Equal Pay Act, however, was designed differently, to confine the application of the Act to wage differentials attributable to sex discrimination. Equal Pay Act litigation, therefore, has been structured to permit employers to defend against charges of discrimination where their pay differentials are based on a bona fide use of "other factors other than sex." Under the Equal Pay Act, the courts and administrative agencies are not permitted to "substitute their judgment for the judgment of the employer ... who [has] established and applied a bona fide job rating system," so long as it does not discriminate on the basis of sex.

---

10. Section 703(h), as set forth in 42 U.S.C. § 2000e–2(h), provides in relevant part:

"Notwithstanding any other provision of this subchapter, it shall not be an unlawful employment practice for an employer to apply different standards of compensation, or different terms, conditions, or privileges of employment *pursuant to a bona fide seniority or merit system, or a system which measures earnings by quantity or quality of production* ... provided that such differences are not the result of an intention to discriminate because of ... sex...."

Although we do not decide in this case how sex-based wage discrimination litigation under Title VII should be structured to accommodate the fourth affirmative defense of the Equal Pay Act, we consider it clear that the Bennett Amendment, under this interpretation, is not rendered superfluous.

We therefore conclude that only differentials attributable to the four affirmative defenses of the Equal Pay Act are "authorized" by that Act within the meaning of § 703(h) of Title VII.

B

The legislative background of the Bennett Amendment is fully consistent with this interpretation.

Title VII was the second bill relating to employment discrimination to be enacted by the 88th Congress. Earlier, the same Congress passed the Equal Pay Act "to remedy what was perceived to be a serious and endemic problem of [sex-based] employment discrimination in private industry" Any possible inconsistency between the Equal Pay Act and Title VII did not surface until late in the debate over Title VII in the House of Representatives, because, until then, Title VII extended only to discrimination based on race, color, religion, or national origin, while the Equal Pay Act applied only to sex discrimination. Just two days before voting on Title VII, the House of Representatives amended the bill to proscribe sex discrimination, but did not discuss the implications of the overlapping jurisdiction of Title VII, as amended, and the Equal Pay Act. The Senate took up consideration of the House version of the Civil Rights bill without reference to any committee. Thus, neither House of Congress had the opportunity to undertake formal analysis of the relation between the two statutes.

Several Senators expressed concern that insufficient attention had been paid to possible inconsistencies between the statutes. In an attempt to rectify the problem, Senator Bennett proposed his amendment. The Senate leadership approved the proposal as a "technical amendment" to the Civil Rights bill, and it was taken up on the floor on June 12, 1964, after cloture had been invoked. The Amendment engendered no controversy, and passed without recorded vote. * * *

Senator Bennett proposed the Amendment because of a general concern that insufficient attention had been paid to the relation between the Equal Pay Act and Title VII, rather than because of a *specific* potential conflict between the statutes. His explanation that the Amendment assured that the provisions of the Equal Pay Act "shall not be nullified" in the event of conflict with Title VII may be read as referring to the affirmative defenses of the Act. Indeed, his emphasis on the "technical" nature of the Amendment and his concern for not disrupting the "effective administration" of the Equal Pay Act are more compatible with an interpretation of the Amendment as incorporating the Act's affirmative defenses, as administratively interpreted, than as engrafting all the restrictive features of the Equal Pay Act onto Title VII.

* * *

Thus, although the few references by Members of Congress to the Bennett Amendment do not explicitly confirm that its purpose was to incorporate into Title VII the four affirmative defenses of the Equal Pay Act in sex-based wage discrimination cases, they are broadly consistent with such a reading, and do not support an alternative reading.

C

The interpretations of the Bennett Amendment by the agency entrusted with administration of Title VII—the Equal Employment Opportunity Commission—do not provide much guidance in this case. * * * but the EEOC now supports respondents' position in its capacity as *amicus curiae*. In light of this history, we feel no hesitation in adopting what seems to us the most persuasive interpretation of the Amendment, in lieu of that once espoused, but not consistently followed, by the Commission.

D

Our interpretation of the Bennett Amendment draws additional support from the remedial purposes of Title VII and the Equal Pay Act. Section 703(a) of Title VII makes it unlawful for an employer "to fail or refuse to hire or to discharge any individual, or *otherwise to discriminate* against any individual with respect to his compensation, terms, conditions, or privileges of employment" because of such individual's sex. As Congress itself has indicated, a "broad approach" to the definition of equal employment opportunity is essential to overcoming and undoing the effect of discrimination. We must therefore avoid interpretations of Title VII that deprive victims of discrimination of a remedy, without clear congressional mandate.

Under petitioners' reading of the Bennett Amendment, only those sex-based wage discrimination claims that satisfy the "equal work" standard of the Equal Pay Act could be brought under Title VII. In practical terms, this means that a woman who is discriminatorily underpaid could obtain no relief-no matter how egregious the discrimination might be—unless her employer also employed a man in an equal job in the same establishment, at a higher rate of pay. Thus, if an employer hired a woman for a unique position in the company and then admitted that her salary would have been higher had she been male, the woman would be unable to obtain legal redress under petitioners' interpretation. Similarly, if an employer used a transparently sex-based system for wage determination, women holding jobs not equal to those held by men would be denied the right to prove that the system is a pretext for discrimination. Moreover, to cite an example arising from a recent case, *Los Angeles Dept. of Water & Power v. Manhart*, 435 U.S. 702, 98 S.Ct. 1370, 55 L.Ed.2d 657 (1978), if the employer required its female workers to pay more into its pension program than male workers were required to pay, the only women who could bring a Title VII action under petitioners' interpretation would be those who could establish that a man performed equal work: a female auditor thus might have a cause of action while a female secretary might not. Congress surely did not intend the Bennett Amendment to insulate such blatantly discriminatory practices from judicial redress under Title VII.

Moreover, petitioners' interpretation would have other far-reaching consequences. Since it rests on the proposition that any wage differentials not prohibited by the Equal Pay Act are "authorized" by it, petitioners' interpretation would lead to the conclusion that discriminatory compensation by employers not covered by the Fair Labor Standards Act is "authorized"—since not prohibited—by the Equal Pay Act. Thus it would deny Title VII protection against sex-based wage discrimination by those employers not subject to the Fair Labor Standards Act but covered by Title VII. There is no persuasive evidence that Congress intended such a result, and the EEOC has rejected it since at least 1965. Indeed, petitioners themselves apparently acknowledge that Congress intended Title VII's broader coverage to apply to equal pay claims under Title VII, thus impliedly admitting the fallacy in their own argument.

Petitioners' reading is thus flatly inconsistent with our past interpretations of Title VII as "prohibit[ing] all practices in whatever form which create inequality in employment opportunity due to discrimination on the basis of race, religion, sex, or national origin." As we said in *Los Angeles Dept. of Water & Power v. Manhart,* "In forbidding employers to discriminate against individuals because of their sex, Congress intended to strike at the *entire spectrum* of disparate treatment of men and women resulting from sex stereotypes." We must therefore reject petitioners' interpretation of the Bennett Amendment.

III

Petitioners argue strenuously that the approach of the Court of Appeals places "the pay structure of virtually every employer and the entire economy ... at risk and subject to scrutiny by the federal courts." They raise the specter that "Title VII plaintiffs could draw any type of comparison imaginable concerning job duties and pay between any job predominantly performed by women and any job predominantly performed by men." But whatever the merit of petitioners' arguments in other contexts, they are inapplicable here, * * *. Respondents contend that the County of Washington evaluated the worth of their jobs; that the county determined that they should be paid approximately 95% as much as the male correctional officers; that it paid them only about 70% as much, while paying the male officers the full evaluated worth of their jobs; and that the failure of the county to pay respondents the full evaluated worth of their jobs can be proved to be attributable to intentional sex discrimination. Thus, respondents' suit does not require a court to make its own subjective assessment of the value of the male and female guard jobs, or to attempt by statistical technique or other method to quantify the effect of sex discrimination on the wage rates.

We do not decide in this case the precise contours of lawsuits challenging sex discrimination in compensation under Title VII. It is sufficient to note that respondents' claims of discriminatory undercompensation are not barred by § 703(h) of Title VII merely because respondents do not perform work equal to that of male jail guards. The judgment of the Court of Appeals is therefore *Affirmed*.

J**USTICE** R**EHNQUIST**, with whom C**HIEF** J**USTICE** B**URGER**, J**USTICE** S**TEWART**, and J**USTICE** P**OWELL** join, dissenting.

The Court today holds a plaintiff may state a claim of sex-based wage discrimination under Title VII without even establishing that she has performed "equal or substantially equal work" to that of males as defined in the Equal Pay Act. Because I believe that the legislative history of both the Equal Pay Act of 1963 and Title VII clearly establishes that there can be no Title VII claim of sex-based wage discrimination without proof of "equal work," I dissent.

* * *

The Equal Pay Act

The starting point for any discussion of sex-based wage discrimination claims must be the Equal Pay Act of 1963 * * *. It was there that Congress, after 18 months of careful and exhaustive study, specifically addressed the problem of sex-based wage discrimination. The Equal Pay Act states that employers shall not discriminate on the basis of sex by paying different wages for jobs that require equal skill, effort, and responsibility. In adopting the "equal pay for equal work" formula, Congress carefully considered and ultimately rejected the "equal pay for comparable worth" standard advanced by respondents and several *amici*. As the legislative history of the Equal Pay Act amply demonstrates, Congress realized that the adoption of the comparable-worth doctrine would ignore the economic realities of supply and demand and would involve both governmental agencies and courts in the impossible task of ascertaining the worth of comparable work, an area in which they have little expertise.

* * *

The legislative history of the Equal Pay Act clearly reveals that Congress was unwilling to give either the Federal Government or the courts broad authority to determine comparable wage rates. Congress recognized that the adoption of such a theory would ignore economic realities and would result in major restructuring of the American economy. Instead, Congress concluded that governmental intervention to equalize wage differentials was to be undertaken only within one circumstance: when men's and women's jobs were identical or nearly so, hence unarguably of equal worth. It defies common sense to believe that the same Congress-which, after 18 months of hearings and debates, had decided in 1963 upon the extent of federal involvement it desired in the area of wage rate claims-intended *sub silentio* to reject all of this work and to abandon the limitations of the equal work approach just one year later, when it enacted Title VII.

Title VII

Congress enacted the Civil Rights Act of 1964, one year after passing the Equal Pay Act. Title VII prohibits discrimination in employment on the basis of race, color, national origin, religion, and sex. The question is whether Congress intended to completely turn its back on the "equal work" standard enacted in the Equal Pay Act of 1963 when it adopted Title VII only one year later.

The Court answers that question in the affirmative, concluding that Title VII must be read more broadly than the Equal Pay Act. In so holding, the majority wholly ignores this Court's repeated adherence to the doctrine of *in pari materia*, namely, that "[w]here there is no clear intention otherwise, a specific statute will not be controlled or nullified by a general one, regardless of the priority of enactment." * * *

When those principles are applied to this case, there can be no doubt that the Equal Pay Act and Title VII should be construed *in pari materia*. The Equal Pay Act is the more specific piece of legislation, dealing solely with sex-based wage discrimination, and was the product of exhaustive congressional study. Title VII, by contrast, is a general antidiscrimination provision, passed with virtually no consideration of the specific problem of sex-based wage discrimination. * * *

In order to reach the result it so desperately desires, the Court neatly solves the problem of this contrary legislative history by simply giving it "no weight." * * *

In sum, Title VII and the Equal Pay Act, read together, provide a balanced approach to resolving sex-based wage discrimination claims. Title VII guarantees that qualified female employees will have access to all jobs, and the Equal Pay Act assures that men and women performing the same work will be paid equally. Congress intended to remedy wage discrimination through the Equal Pay Act standards, whether suit is brought under that statute or under Title VII. What emerges is that Title VII would have been construed *in pari materia* even without the Bennett Amendment, and that the Amendment serves simply to insure that the equal work standard would be the standard by which all wage compensation claims would be judged.

* * *

Even though today's opinion reaches what I believe to be the wrong result, its narrow holding is perhaps its saving feature. The opinion does not endorse to so-called "comparable worth" theory: though the Court does not indicate how a plaintiff might establish a prima facie case under Title VII, the Court does suggest that allegations of unequal pay for unequal, but comparable, work will not state a claim on which relief may be granted. The Court, for example, repeatedly emphasizes that this is not a case where plaintiffs ask the court to compare the value of dissimilar jobs or to quantify the effect of sex discrimination on wage rates.

2. PROVING SEX–BASED PAY DISCRIMINATION

a. Title VII

Re-read: AFSME v. STATE OF WASHINGTON, page 302.

NOTES

1. The rejection of "comparable worth" theory of liability has been challenged by critics (*See e.g.,* Clauss, *Comparable Worth * * *,* 20 U.Mich. J.L.Ref. 7 (1986)), but followed in the courts. *International Union UAW v. Michigan,* 886 F.2d 766 (6th Cir. 1989). A few state statutes, however, include comparable worth theories of liability. (*e.g.,* Minn. Stat. 471.991).

2. **AFSME** highlights the intersection of the Equal Pay Act with Title VII. There could be no Equal Pay Act violation here because the jobs evaluated admittedly were not "equal." However, as we saw in **Washington County v. Gunther,** *supra,* Title VII is violated by plaintiff proving improper motivation for compensation differences even where the work performed is not "equal." Thus, while unequal pay for equal work may be circumstantial evidence of improper motivation, Title VII's "because of" language is not limited by the objective "equal work" standard. **AFSME** re-emphasized this Title VII requirement for plaintiff to prove improper motive, restated that the mere failure to act is "discrimination" only if defendant's inertia is improperly motivated, and concluded that mere awareness of the possible consequences, or even the unfairness, of inaction is not motivation proscribed by Title VII. Inaction here was not "because of sex" but because of empty coffers.

3. *Impact and Compensation:* While **Washington County v. Gunther,** *supra,* holds out the possibility of Title VII liability based solely on the adverse impact of particular practice, **AFSME** demonstrates the practical difficulty, if not impossibility, of successfully using impact analysis to establish liability based compensation differences. First, plaintiffs will have difficulty in identifying a particular objective factor that caused the pattern of pay differences. Mere differences in class outcomes without identifying with precision the cause for those outcomes do not establish an impact claim. **WARDS COVE PACKING CO. v. ATONIO,** *supra, p. 347.* Second, as **Gunther** illustrated, the "Bennett Amendment" precludes Title VII liability were the employer demonstrates that an element influencing pay differences is a "factor other than sex," a significantly less onerous burden than "business necessity." Lower courts have held that education, prior experience, past salary not based on sex, and even sex-neutral market pressures can be "factors other than sex" that justify pay differentials between men and women. *See, Kouba v. Allstate Ins. Co.,* 691 F.2d 873 (9th Cir. 1982).

b. Objective Circumstantial Evidence

MIRANDA v. B & B CASH GROCERY STORE, INC.

United States Court of Appeals, Eleventh Circuit, 1992
975 F.2d 1518

KRAVITCH, CIRCUIT JUDGE

This case consists of two consolidated appeals resulting from a lawsuit filed by Karen Miranda Hopewell ("Miranda" or "plaintiff") against B & B Cash Grocery Store, Inc. ("B & B" or "defendant"), alleging gender-based discrimination in violation of Title VII of the Civil Rights Act of 1964 and the Equal Pay Act of 1963. * * *

Defendant moved for partial summary judgment on plaintiff's claims grounded in the Equal Pay Act * * * The Magistrate–Judge granted defendant's motion on both counts, holding that the plaintiff did not sustain her burden of establishing a *prima facie* case of sex-based wage discrimination under the Equal Pay Act. The Magistrate–Judge held a bench trial on the claims under Title VII, found that the defendant had discriminated against Miranda on the basis of her sex, and awarded the plaintiff backpay in the amount of $52,765.83.

Miranda appeals the grant of summary judgment to the defendant on her Equal Pay Act claim; B & B cross-appeals the finding of sex-based discrimination under Title VII. For the reasons discussed below, we REVERSE the Order of the Magistrate granting summary judgment to the defendant under the Equal Pay Act, AFFIRM the judgment in favor of the plaintiff under Title VII and the damages awarded to her, and REMAND to the district court for a trial on the Equal Pay Act claim.

Facts

B & B Cash Grocery Stores, Inc. is a family-owned business of twenty-four supermarkets operating under the name of U–Save in central and southwest Florida. In 1988, B & B's enterprise employed 1,900 workers. * * *

Buyers work out of the main office in downtown Tampa and have responsibility for buying either grocery, meat, dairy or non-food items for all of the stores. A separate buyer works with vendors who sold such items as soft drinks, bread, soda, wine and beer directly to the stores. The buyers are responsible for meeting with vendors, maintaining appropriate inventories of items assigned to them, replenishing supplies, and ordering new items. * * *

[James Duffy was B & B's grocery buyer and warehouse distribution director] resigned from B & B in June, 1986. He told Miranda that he would recommend that she succeed him as grocery buyer at a salary comparable with what the other buyers were paid. The president of B & B, C.C. Bever, Jr., decided to split Duffy's grocery buyer job into two separate positions and add an assistant dairy buyer position. Miranda was offered one of the grocery buyer positions, and Donald Kelley, a store manager, was offered the other.

Duffy had been paid approximately $600.00 per week as a grocery buyer, and had also received a "salary adjustment" at the end of the year. Miranda assumed that she would receive a comparable salary, but instead Bever told her that her starting salary would be $400.00 per week, which was only $34.00 more than she had earned as an inventory control clerk working for Duffy. When plaintiff told Bever that he could not hire a buyer for that position at that salary, Bever replied that "any third man would be astounded to hold the title that I am giving you." At trial, Bever explained the salary disparity between Miranda and the other buyers as due to budgetary constraints. All other buyers were paid between $600.00 and $650.00 per week.

* * *

Miranda testified that although she was displeased with the salary offered to her, she agreed to accept the buyer position in July, 1986, because she thought the company would reevaluate her pay after she had a chance to prove herself at the job. In September, 1986, Miranda's weekly salary was increased from $400.00 to $420.00; it remained at this level until her buying job was eliminated and she left defendant's employment in July, 1988.

The trial court found that Miranda's job was similar to that of the other buyers employed by defendant except that the initial assignment of grocery buying duties between plaintiff and Kelley resulted in Miranda being assigned substantially fewer grocery items. Miranda was responsible for approximately one-third of the items; Kelley was responsible for approximately two-thirds. Kelley was also assigned a larger number of higher velocity (turnover) items to purchase, which was consistent with Bever's plan that Kelley handle the more difficult items because of his buying experience as a store manager. Duffy, however, denied at trial that he intentionally gave Kelley more items or more responsibility. He testified that he simply roughly divided the number of vendors between the two buyers, a division that Miranda and Kelley would refine as necessary.

Plaintiff protested the unequal distribution of work, but the situation remained unchanged until approximately May 23, 1988. At that point, Harold Tidwell, who had replaced Duffy as head buyer, assigned her the additional items she requested. With the addition of these responsibilities, Miranda and Kelley had an approximately equal number of items to purchase. However, from the end of May, 1988, until her position was eliminated in July, 1988, Miranda never received a salary increase.

* * *

On July 25, 1988, Phillips, Tidwell, and Bever told Miranda that B & B could not afford two grocery buyers and that her position would be terminated effective the following Monday. Bever told her that they had a position available as head cashier at $8.00 per hour, but because she had no experience supervising people, a store manager or supervisory position was not available. Bever also told her that she had done an outstanding job, that she would be provided references if she decided to look elsewhere, and that with her youth and her ability, she should be able to find what she wanted. Plaintiff refused the position as head cashier and terminated her employment with B & B. Ten weeks later she was hired as a buyer by Kash 'n' Karry, a competing grocery chain.

* * *

The only two buyers whose positions were terminated were female. Five other B & B employees, all men, were demoted to positions they had occupied previously. Two supervisory positions occupied by men were eliminated and both workers returned to work as store managers. Neither, however, received a pay cut with the reassignment. In addition, four other men were demoted, but it is unclear whether they received a reduction in pay.

Within eight to ten months after Miranda's and Sholes' buyer positions were eliminated, Don Kelley's weekly salary increased from $625.00 to $750.00 per week, and many other executives received pay raises. The trial court noted, however, that these workers had not received any significant pay increases for approximately two years.

The trial court found as an undisputed fact that Miranda performed her job as a grocery buyer reasonably well. At the time that she took the job, she knew Duffy's system of ordering and the necessary paperwork better than anyone else in the company. She taught Kelley the computer format and the paperwork involved in the job. The plaintiff was formally evaluated only once, in 1988, at which point she received an "average" rating; Don Kelley was rated slightly "above average." B & B management testified, however, that they did not rely upon that evaluation in deciding to eliminate Miranda's position.

* * *

Analysis

I. Introduction: Gender–Based Discrimination in the Workplace

* * * The trial court held that the plaintiff failed to establish a claim under the Equal Pay Act, but that she proved that B & B violated Title VII. The defendant contends, however, *inter alia,* that a finding that a plaintiff has not presented a *prima facie* case of gender-based discrimination under the Equal Pay Act conclusively establishes that the plaintiff was not a victim of discrimination under Title VII. Thus, we must determine not only the individual applicability of each statute to B & B's actions, but the interaction between the two.

Gender-based discrimination in rates of pay to employees, whether male or female, is prohibited by the Equal Pay Act of 1963, as well as by Title VII of the Civil Rights Act of 1964. The Equal Pay Act was directed only at wage discrimination between the sexes and forbids the specific practice of paying unequal wages for equal work to employees of the opposite sex. Title VII, on the other hand, forbids discrimination on the basis of gender, race, or national origin in a wide range of employment practices, including hiring, firing, training, and promoting. The legislative history of Title VII demonstrates that it was enacted primarily to counter racial discrimination; the prohibition against gender-based bias was added to the legislation at the last moment, and, according to some theories, in an effort to thwart passage of the Civil Rights Act.

The burdens of proof are different under the two laws. A plaintiff suing under the Equal Pay Act must meet the fairly strict standard of proving that she performed substantially similar work for less pay. The burden then falls to the employer to establish one of the four affirmative defenses provided in the statute. Under the disparate treatment approach of Title VII, however, there is a relaxed standard of similarity between male and female-occupied jobs, but a plaintiff has the burden of proving an intent to discriminate on the basis of sex (or race or national origin).[11]

Under the Equal Pay Act, an additional amount equal to backpay may be awarded as liquidated damages unless the employer shows that the violation was in good faith. * * * The statute of limitations for backpay relief is also more generous under the Equal Pay Act than under Title VII. Further, the Equal Pay Act, unlike Title VII, does not require exhaustion of administrative remedies. * * *

Title VII and the Equal Pay Act exist side by side in the effort to rid the workforce of gender-based discrimination. Plaintiffs have two tools for relief, each of which provides different burdens of proof and may produce different amounts of compensation. If a defendant has both violated the Equal Pay Act and denied a woman a promotion because of her sex, the plaintiff may sue for relief under both statutes and is entitled to recovery for both injuries, if she satisfies the requirements of both laws.

* * *

II. *Gender–Based Wage Discrimination Under Title VII*

B & B contends that Title VII does not encompass a claim for sex-based wage discrimination and that Miranda can only bring her claim under the Equal Pay Act. Therefore, defendant argues, Miranda's failure to establish a *prima facie* case under the Equal Pay Act precludes her from bringing a claim under Title VII. This approach rests on the assumption that Title VII merely reiterates the intent of the Equal Pay Act, and goes no further. In *County of Washington v. Gunther,* the Supreme Court explicitly rejected this interpretation.

* * *

The issue remaining after *Gunther* is the method for establishing gender-based wage discrimination under Title VII, specifically whether the tradi-

---

11. We refer here only to the "disparate treatment" model of Title VII. Under some instances, plaintiffs can recover for the disparate impact of a defendant's facially neutral employment practices.

tional Title VII method of proof or the framework established by the Equal Pay Act applies. The Supreme Court has not revisited this question since *Gunther.*

This is also an issue of first impression for the Eleventh Circuit. * * * After considering the Supreme Court's decision in *Gunther,* and the legislative history of Title VII and the Equal Pay Act, we believe that the *McDonnell Douglas/Burdine* approach to disparate treatment is the appropriate framework for evaluating Miranda's claim of gender-based wage discrimination.

* * *

We agree with the trial court that Miranda carried her burden of proof and established that B & B discriminated against her because of her gender. The plaintiff establishes a *prima facie* case of sex discrimination under Title VII by demonstrating that she is female and that the job she occupied was similar to higher paying jobs occupied by males. The trial court found that Miranda's description of the type of duties she performed as a buyer, as well as testimony from defendant's witnesses established that she shared the same type of tasks as the other buyers.[15] The evidence demonstrated that the male buyers all received a weekly salary of $625 to $650 per week while the plaintiff received $400 to $420 per week. Accordingly, Miranda established a prima facie case of discrimination, thus shifting to the defendant the burden of producing a legitimate, non-discriminatory reason for the pay disparity.

Defendant's burden of production in rebutting the *prima facie* case is "exceedingly light." The trial court determined that B & B justified its decision to pay Miranda less than the other male buyers on the following:

> 1.   The company's budget was limited and it paid the plaintiff all that it could afford for the new position when the grocery buyer position was split into two positions.

> 2.   In-house promotions to grocery buyer were generally lateral transfers in terms of pay.

On the surface, these reasons appear legitimate, thus the burden returns to the plaintiff to establish by a preponderance of the evidence that the proffered justifications are actually a pretext for gender-based discrimination. In other words, Miranda must demonstrate that a discriminatory reason more likely than not motivated B & B to pay her less, or that B & B's explanation is not worthy of belief.

The trial court found that the plaintiff bore her burden of demonstrating that B & B's explanation was a pretext for gender-based discrimination and that the defendant intentionally discriminated against Miranda. That determination is a finding of fact that is binding on this court unless

---

15.   As we noted above, Title VII incorporates a more relaxed standard of similarity between male and female-occupied jobs, thus plaintiff is not required to meet the exacting standard of substantial equality of positions set forth in the Equal Pay Act.

clearly erroneous. *Pullman–Standard v. Swint,* 456 U.S. 273, 287, 102 S.Ct. 1781, 1789, 72 L.Ed.2d 66 (1982).

We agree with the trial court's determination that the defendant's rationales for the disparity is "undercut by other evidence in the record and has been shown to be pretextual." The court noted that Miranda testified that she accepted the offer of the buyer's position at the stated pay of $400 (less than $25 a week more than her salary as a clerk) only because Bever, the President of B & B, promised to evaluate her within 30, 60, or 90 days because he was not familiar with her capabilities. However, no formal evaluation took place until nearly two years later. Further, Bever testified that although he knew within a matter of weeks that plaintiff could perform a buyer's job, he did not adjust her pay to the scale that the company had traditionally paid its buyers—a range of $625 to $650. This wage disparity was repeated in the year-end salary adjustments paid to the buyers: In 1987, the first full year that plaintiff, Kelley and Edenfield worked as buyers, each of the men received increases of $2500 but Miranda, the sole female buyer, received only a $160 increase. B & B contends that its policy of treating the move to buyer as a lateral transfer and its decision to pay Miranda less because of her lack of experience as a store manager constitute a "factor other than sex."

The trial court, however, took note of Bever's statement that "any third man would be astounded to have the title I'm giving you." This comment indicates that the company president did not view plaintiff in the same light as the other buyers, but only as comparable to a lower-level employee at the store level, at least in part because she had worked primarily in female-dominated positions.

In *Corning Glass,* the Supreme Court held that the fact that women will work for less than men is a "market force defense" and not a legitimate "factor other than sex." This court dealt with other such "market forces" defenses in *Glenn v. General Motors Corp.,* 841 F.2d 1567 (11th Cir.). In *Glenn,* the defendant had a policy against requiring an employee to take a cut in pay when transferring from hourly wage jobs into salaried positions. Because the men made more money at their positions than the women did, the men were paid more for doing the same job. This court rejected General Motors' argument that prior salary alone was a factor other than sex and affirmed the district court's ruling that the company had violated the Equal Pay Act.

The logic of *Glenn* is equally applicable here. Men are hired as "stock boys" and "bag boys," and can become fourth "man," third "man," assistant manager and, eventually, store manager. Buyers are generally required to have been store managers, and store managers have always come from the bagboy line of promotion. Women essentially have been excluded from the line of promotion that leads to management positions. Miranda was the only woman to have earned the title of "buyer" and when she reached that level, she was limited to the salary she had made as a clerical worker. B & B has demonstrated only its reliance on an illegitimate market force theory to justify its failure to pay Miranda the same salary as the male employees in her classification.

We are aware that other circuits view the relationship between Title VII and the Equal Pay Act differently. *See, e.g., Plemer v. Parsons–Gilbane,* 713 F.2d 1127, 1133 (5th Cir.1983); *E.E.O.C. v. Sears, Roebuck & Co.,* 839 F.2d 302, 343 (7th Cir.1988) (Without direct evidence of intentional sex-based wage discrimination, plaintiff "must meet the equal pay standard of the EPA to prove ... Title VII sex discrimination in wages claim"); *McKee v. Bi–State Development Agency,* 801 F.2d 1014, 1019 (8th Cir.1986) (The Eighth Circuit simply stated that "[w]here a claim is for unequal pay for equal work based upon sex, the standards of the Equal Pay Act apply whether the suit alleges a violation of the Equal Pay Act or of Title VII."). By applying Equal Pay Act standards whether the suit alleges an Equal Pay Act or a Title VII violation, these cases view *Gunther* and the anti-discrimination laws in an artificially constricted manner. As such, we decline to follow them.

For example, under *Plemer* when a plaintiff alleges "equal pay for equal work" based on sex, the Fifth Circuit would require evidence of a transparently sex-based wage discrimination system or *direct evidence* (other than that which the plaintiff offers in support of the EPA claim) of sex-based wage discrimination. Citing *Gunther*'s continual references to the uniqueness of the plaintiffs' claim and the strength of the evidence being offered (*i.e.* direct evidence) in *Gunther, Plemer* determined that the Supreme Court "was concerned with *blatant* cases of sex discrimination in which the only stumbling block to underpaid females' causes of action was the fact that the victimized women did not hold jobs similar to those held by men." We disagree.

We believe that the "direct evidence" standard, such as the one adopted by the Fifth Circuit, eviscerates the standards and burdens for a Title VII case as set out in *Burdine* and *McDonnell Douglas.* The argument that the Equal Pay Act and its standards and burdens are the *only* way to litigate an "equal pay for equal work" claim might be more persuasive if the Equal Pay Act had been passed after Title VII, as an effort to narrow the Civil Rights Act as it applies to gender-based discrimination. In fact, however, that was not the case. Incorporating the "direct evidence" standard would only help clever, but venal, employers who discriminate against women and are not compliant enough to admit it directly. Most importantly, it would shield employers who significantly underpay women but seek to avoid the requirements of the Equal Pay Act by changing the job description in a slight way that does not affect the substance of the responsibilities.

In sum, we agree with the trial court that Bever's statement "reveals an attitude on the part of the company president that plaintiff had no right to expect to be paid a buyer's wages for work which was at least similar to that performed by the other full buyers, all of whom were male." We therefore affirm the trial court's determination that B & B illegally discriminated against the plaintiff on the basis of her sex.

* * *

IV. *The Equal Pay Act Claim*

* * *

To establish a *prima facie* case under the Equal Pay Act of 1963, a complainant "must show that an employer pays different wages to employees of opposite sexes 'for equal work on jobs the performance of which requires equal skill, effort, and responsibility, and which are performed under similar working conditions.' " Once a plaintiff makes out a *prima facie* case, the burden shifts to the employer to prove that the difference in pay is justified by one of the four exceptions in the Equal Pay Act: "(i) a seniority system; (ii) a merit system; (iii) a system which measures earnings by quantity or quality of production; or (iv) a differential based on any other factor other than sex." The jobs held by the employees of opposite sexes need not be identical; rather, they need only be substantially equal.

The Equal Pay Act prescribes a form of strict liability: Once the disparity in pay between substantially similar jobs is demonstrated, the burden shifts to the defendant to prove that a "factor other than sex" is responsible for the differential. If the defendant fails, the plaintiff wins. The plaintiff is not required to prove discriminatory intent on the part of the defendant.

A plaintiff establishes a *prima facie* case by comparing the jobs held by the female and male employees, and by showing that those jobs are substantially equal, not by comparing the skills and qualifications of the individual employees holding those jobs. *Brock v. Georgia Southwestern College,* 765 F.2d 1026, 1032 (11th Cir.1985). Because at this stage the jobs and not the employees are compared, only the skills and qualifications actually needed to perform the jobs are considered. Therefore, Kelley's experience as a manager before he became a buyer is not relevant to whether or not his job and Miranda's are substantially similar.[18]

The prima facie case also focuses solely on the primary duties of each job, not duties that are incidental or insubstantial. Any extra duties that might be used to distinguish two jobs may not be tasks that are typically performed by other personnel at lower pay.

The plaintiff need not prove that the job held by her male comparator is identical to hers; she must demonstrate only that the skill, effort and responsibility required in the performance of the jobs are "substantially equal." Although job titles are entitled to some weight in this evaluation, "the controlling factor under the Equal Pay Act is job content"—the actual duties that the respective employees are called upon to perform.

---

18. Factors such as experience and education operate as a defense to liability rather than as part of a plaintiff's *prima facie* case under the Act. *See, e.g., Covington v. Southern Illinois University,* 816 F.2d 317 (7th Cir.1987).

Whether the buyer jobs held by Miranda and Kelley were substantially similar is a crucial issue in this case. The trial court determined that the plaintiff had not presented sufficient evidence to establish a *prima facie* case of substantial similarity. If, however, the evidence presented by Miranda, taken as true, would establish an Equal Pay Act violation and there was sufficient evidence such that a jury could find in Miranda's favor, then summary judgment is improper and a trial on the merits is necessary to resolve the factual disputes.

* * * Although both parties agree that Miranda and Kelley handled a different number of items to purchase, they disagree as to the significance of this fact, that is, whether the overall responsibility of her job was substantially the same as that of Kelley. Miranda argues that the number of products ordered is not determinative of the responsibility of the job. She points out that Harold Tidwell, the head buyer, considered her to be a "full-fledged" buyer, one with as many responsibilities as the other buyers and whose salary should have been adjusted upward. If reasonable minds could differ on the inferences arising from undisputed facts, then a court should deny summary judgment.

We also note that careful review of the affidavits attached to the Response to the Motion for Summary Judgment demonstrate that early in 1988 Miranda was given additional products to purchase, and was henceforth responsible for the same number of products as was Kelley. This fact was not specifically mentioned in the plaintiff's responsive pleading, however, and it is unclear whether the trial court considered it in weighing the motion for summary judgment.

After careful review of the facts presented to the trial court on the Partial Motion for Summary Judgment, we find that there exists a genuine issue of material fact as to the similarity of the jobs held by Karen Miranda and Don Kelley and that a reasonable jury could find that B & B violated the Equal Pay Act by failing to pay them equal wages. We therefore reverse the grant of summary judgment to B & B on this issue.

* * *

DUBINE, CIRCUIT JUDGE, concurring specially:

I concur with the majority's opinion. However, I write separately to note the uncertainty pervading the law as to Miranda's Title VII claim.

* * * [T]he majority's opinion confronts an issue about which there is much conflict. That is, what standards are to be applied to intentional sex-based wage discrimination claims brought under Title VII? The majority holds that traditional *McDonnell Douglas/Burdine* standards apply. I agree.

* * *

[A]ccording to the Fifth and Seventh Circuits, *Gunther* allows plaintiffs who cannot prove "equal work" under the EPA to proceed under Title VII, but only upon direct evidence of intentional wage discrimination based on sex. Absent such a showing, the Fifth and Seventh Circuits will not entertain suits based on a comparison of wages paid for dissimilar jobs.

The Ninth Circuit, on the other hand, accepts traditional *McDonnell Douglas/Burdine* proof of discriminatory intent. In *Spaulding v. University of Washington,* 740 F.2d 686 (9th Cir.), the Ninth Circuit declined to specify the minimum factors required for plaintiffs to establish a prima facie Title VII case of sex-based wage discrimination. However, noting *McDonnell Douglas'* flexibility, the court stated that a plaintiff's case rests "solely on evidence creating an inference that the wage disparity ... was more likely than not the result of intentional sex discrimination." Other courts have likewise adopted this standard.

* * * I am disturbed by a standard that requires direct evidence of sex-based wage discrimination in one case, but permits circumstantial evidence in an identical case brought upon a theory of race discrimination. Indeed, as I understand it, a black woman claiming wage discrimination based on *color* would need to proffer circumstantial evidence only; however, the same wage discrimination claim based this time on *sex* would then require direct evidence. This is not logical. It seems to me that plaintiffs who bring *Gunther*-based claims should be held to the same standards as any other Title VII disparate treatment plaintiff.

* * * This is a complex area of law, suffused with legislative and judicial uncertainty. Nonetheless, the majority's approach is correct. Miranda was discriminated against. Should she on remand fail to meet the equal work requirement of the EPA, the direct evidence standard advanced by the Fifth and Seventh Circuits would most likely strip her of legal recourse. *Gunther* teaches that Title VII is broader than the EPA. The majority's decision properly delineates the contours of its breadth.

---

c. Statistical Evidence of Motive

Elimination of chance as an hypothesis through the relatively simple binominal, standard deviation analysis has been endorsed by the Supreme Court for use in claims of hiring and promotion discrimination. However, this methodology has little usefulness in allegations of salary discrimination. This is because in setting salaries a wide variety of legitimate factors, or variables, regularly come into play: seniority, experience, education, past performance evaluations, and market pressures at a particular time. This does not, however, preclude the use of a more complex statistical device known as "multiple regression." See, *supra, p. 439.*

Coble v. Hot Springs School Dist. No. 6, 682 F.2d 721 (8th Cir. 1982):

* * * We have previously found statistics to speak loudly in employment discrimination cases. Statistics, however, must be used carefully." [G]ross statistical disparities alone may in a proper case consti-

tute prima facie proof of discrimination) "(T)he use of statistics 'is conditioned by the existence of proper supportive facts and the absence of variables which would undermine the reasonableness of the inference of discrimination which is drawn.'" The plaintiffs have the burden of establishing a prima facie case of sex discrimination; then the burden of production or going forward with the evidence "shifts to the employer to defeat the prima facie showing of a pattern or practice by demonstrating that the (plaintiffs') proof is either inaccurate or insignificant."

The burden is on the opposing party to clearly rebut statistical evidence; hypotheses or conjecture will not suffice. When a plaintiff submits accurate statistical data, and a defendant alleges that relevant variables are excluded, defendant may not rely on hypothesis to lessen the probative value of plaintiff's statistical proof. Rather, defendant, in his rebuttal presentation, must either rework plaintiff's statistics incorporating the omitted factors or present other proof undermining plaintiff's claims.

* * *

[A]t first glance, appellants' statistical data reveals pay and promotion disparities that are extremely suspect. However, upon further examination, we must conclude that the probative value of appellants' statistical data is undermined by the small sample size for promotions and the failure to consider the effect of education and experience together on salary. *See, Sainte Marie v. Eastern R.R. Ass'n,* 650 F.2d 395, 400–401 (2d Cir. 1981) (plaintiffs' statistical analysis produced standard deviations of 4 to 14.5, but statistical evidence underlying standard deviation analysis had little probative value);

It should be noted that the school district's rebuttal evidence with respect to the pay differences was speculative and hypothetical and thus would have been wholly inadequate to rebut a prima facie case. The school district challenged appellants' statistics on the basis that several relevant factors had been omitted from appellants' statistical analysis but failed to test its proffered hypotheses.

Kenny testified that he had prepared several analyses of the school district's salaries and that in his opinion the salary disparity expressed in the analyses was the product of sex discrimination. At first glance the salary analyses reveal consistent disparities in favor of male teachers. For example, Plaintiffs' Ex. 4 is an analysis of the average salary by sex, broken down into three professional groups (BA, MA, administrative), for four school years (1977–1978 through 1980–1981). In each year in every group the male teachers and administrators are paid more than the female teachers and administrators. Plaintiffs' Ex. 5 is an analysis of the average term of contract by sex, showing that the average term of male teachers' contracts is 10.1 months, the average term of female teachers' contracts is 9.4 months. Extended term contracts are apparently related to higher pay. Plaintiffs' Ex. 7 is a "test period approach" analysis; Kenny followed newly hired teachers as a group year by year from 1977–1978 to 1980–1981 to determine whether the salary disparity between male and female teachers was attributable to experience. Ex. 7 shows that in each year in each group of employees the male teachers on the average are paid more and that this salary disparity increased each year during the four year test period.

According to Kenny, Ex. 4 showed that the salary disparity between men and women with similar education or training is not attributable to education and Ex. 7 showed that this salary disparity is not attributable to experience or seniority. We must disagree. Kenny did not analyze the employment data using a method that considered the combined effect of education and experience on the salaries paid male and female teachers. Instead, Kenny analyzed education and experience separately, considering the effect of each factor in isolation. The key question is whether male and female teachers of comparable education and experience are paid the same salary. Appellants' statistical proof shows only that male teachers are paid more than female teachers with similar degrees on the average but without taking experience into consideration. Similarly, appellants' statistical proof showed that male teachers are paid more over time than female teachers on the average but without taking education into consideration. Appellants' statistical proof simply does not show that, after taking into account education and experience, female teachers received lower salaries than male teachers.

We think the deficiency lies in the method of statistical analysis used by appellants. Rather than approaching the variables of education and experience separately, appellants should have used multiple regression analysis.

Multiple regression is a statistical technique designed to estimate the effects of several independent variables on a single dependent variable. Properly used in a case such as this, the methodology provides the ability to determine how much influence factors such as sex, experience, and education each have had on determining the value of a variable such as salary level. The analysis also enables an observer to cumulate effects of the various factors so as to determine the degree to which explanation of the dependent variable can be attributed to the independent variables in combination. Regression analysis is well recognized by the literature and the courts in Title VII litigation.

As explained by Professor Fisher,

> (m)ultiple regression is well suited to answer (the question of sex discrimination in wages) fairly precisely. Moreover, without a multiple regression study it is difficult to see how it could be decided. The raw comparison of average wages for women and for men may make one suspicious, but it cannot tell one anything definite. Indeed, it can be misleading in either direction. For

example, it would be entirely possible in a different setting that women are paid on the average just as much as men but that a multiple regression analysis would show that there is indeed discrimination because women are more highly qualified in the measures that account for the variation in male pay.

Fisher, *Multiple Regression in Legal Proceedings*, 80 Colum.L.Rev. at 721. For example, in *Trout v. Hidalgo*, plaintiffs' expert first established the salary differentials for men and women and then sought to determine, using multiple regression analysis, whether the salary disparity was attributable to education and experience or more likely was attributable to sex discrimination. The district court in *Trout v. Hidalgo* found that plaintiffs had made a prima facie case of sex discrimination because multiple regression analysis showed that, when education and experience were taken into account, women were paid substantially lower salaries than men.

Assuming for the purpose of argument that appellants had established a prima facie case using multiple regression analysis, we think that the school district's rebuttal evidence would have been inadequate to undermine the accuracy or significance of appellants' statistical evidence. The school district did not counter appellants' expert analysis with comparable expert analysis but instead offered hypothetical variables unsupported by statistical analysis. In addition to education and experience, superintendent Meeks testified that postgraduate hours, the length of contract, extra responsibilities, and summer school teaching also affected teacher salaries. The effect of these variables on teacher salaries was not supported by any proof. The school district's failure to include these variables or more refined measurements of the education and experience variables in its own multiple regression analysis "must be interpreted as a concession that these refinements in the specification of the model (used by appellants) would not have affected the rejection of the hypothesis of no discrimination." * * *

Bazemore v. Friday, 478 U.S. 385, 106 S.Ct. 3000, 92 L.Ed.2d 315 (1986).

JUSTICE BRENNAN concurring with per curiam decision joined by unanimous Court.

       * * *

At trial, petitioners relied heavily on multiple regression analyses designed to demonstrate that blacks were paid less than similarly situated whites. The United States' expert prepared multiple regression analyses relating to salaries for the years 1974, 1975, and 1981. Certain of these regressions used four independent variables-race, education, tenure, and job title. Petitioners selected these variables based on discovery testimony by an Extension Service official that four factors were determinative of salary: education, tenure, job title, and job performance. In addition, regressions done by the Extension Service itself for 1971 included the variables race, sex, education, and experience; and another in 1974 used the variables race, education, and tenure to check for disparities between the salaries of blacks and whites.

The regressions purported to demonstrate that in 1974 the average black employee earned $331 less per year than a white employee with the same job title, education, and tenure, and that in 1975 the disparity was $395. The regression for 1981 showed a smaller disparity which lacked statistical significance.

The Court of Appeals stated:

> [The] district court refused to accept plaintiffs' expert testimony as proof of discrimination by a preponderance of the evidence because the plaintiffs' expert had not included a number of variable factors the court considered relevant, among them being the across the board and percentage pay increases which varied from county to county. The district court was, of course, correct in this analysis."

* * * The Court of Appeals erred in stating that petitioners' regression analyses were "unacceptable as evidence of discrimination," because they did not include "all measurable variables thought to have an effect on salary level." The court's view of the evidentiary value of the regression analyses was plainly incorrect. While the omission of variables from a regression analysis may render the analysis less probative than it otherwise might be, it can hardly be said, absent some other infirmity, that an analysis which accounts for the major factors "must be considered unacceptable as evidence of discrimination." Normally, failure to include variables will affect the analysis' probativeness, not its admissibility.[10]

Importantly, it is clear that a regression analysis that includes less than "all measurable variables" may serve to prove a plaintiff's case. A plaintiff in a Title VII suit need not prove discrimination with scientific certainty; rather, his or her burden is to prove discrimination by a preponderance of the evidence. Whether, in fact, such a regression analysis does carry the plaintiffs' ultimate burden will depend in a given case on the factual context of each case in light of all the evidence presented by both the plaintiff and the defendant. However, as long as the court may fairly conclude, in light of all the evidence, that it is more likely than not that impermissible discrimination exists, the plaintiff is entitled to prevail.

In this case the Court of Appeals failed utterly to examine the regression analyses in light of all the evidence in the record. Looked

---

10. There may, of course, be some regressions so incomplete as to be inadmissible as irrelevant; but such was clearly not the case here.

at in its entirety, petitioners offered an impressive array of evidence to support their contention that the Extension Service engaged in a pattern or practice of discrimination with respect to salaries. In addition to their own regression analyses described above, petitioners offered regressions done by the Extension Service for 1971 and 1974 that showed results similar to those revealed by petitioners' regressions. Petitioners also claim support from multiple regressions presented by respondents at trial for the year 1975. Using the same model that petitioners had used, and similar variables, respondents' expert obtained substantially the same result for 1975, a statistically significant racial effect of $384. Indeed, respondents also included in their analysis, "quartile rank" as an independent variable, and this *increased* the racial effect to $475.

C. "FRINGE BENEFITS"

1. TITLE VII

a. *Los Angeles Department of Water & Power v. Manhart*, reproduced *supra* p. 291. The employer's defined benefit pension program required female employees to make larger contributions into the fund than similarly situated male employees in order to secure similar monthly payments upon retirement. This, the Court held, was sex discrimination. The discrimination against individual women in the amount withheld was not justified by the fact that women as a class had a longer life expectancy and thus could be expected to draw a pension from the fund for more years than similarly situated men. Nor was the sex based actuarial table considered a "factor other than sex" allowing it to be utilized under the Equal Pay Act, and thus, via the "Bennett Amendment," serve as a defense to a Title VII claim.

b. *Arizona Governing Committee v. Norris,* noted *supra* p. 296 applied *Manhart* to a "defined contribution" fund provided by an employer, but underwritten by independent annuity companies. Here contributions by male and female employees would be determined by the employee and for similarly situated employees, contributions were equal. However, upon retirement female retirees received less of a monthly payment on a life annuity option than would similarly situated male retirees. The greater life expectancy of women as a class did not justify individual discrimination in pension payments.

c. Title VII does not require employers to provide health care benefits. When it does so, however, the Pregnancy Discrimination Amendments provide:

"Pregnancy, childbirth, or related medical conditions shall be treated the same for all employment-related purposes, including receipt of benefits under fringe benefit programs, as other persons not so affected but similar in their ability or inability to work." 42 U.S.C.A. s 2000e(k)

Newport News Shipbuilding & Dry Dock Co. v. EEOC, reproduced *supra, p. 93* held that while an employer had no obligation under the Pregnancy Discrimination Amendments to provide health care benefits to *dependents* of employees, when it did so, the benefit package for *dependents* had to cover pregnancy on par with other similar medical conditions. Failure of the plan to provide parity of protection for pregnancy of spouses of employee discriminated against male *employees* because of their sex in that female employees would have the pregnancy of their family unit covered while male employees would not.

Review Chapter 2 C 5, *supra* for materials on the benefits that must be included to comply with the PDA.

2. THE AGE DISCRIMINATION IN EMPLOYMENT ACT

a. Mandatory Retirement

By removing the upper age limit on protection Congress effectively prohibited most employers from imposing mandatory retirement based on age. In addition, the ADEA makes it clear that a retirement benefit program cannot impose mandatory retirement as part of that program. The three situations where mandatory retirement is permissible:

(i) Bona fide executives:

[An] employee who has attained 65 years of age, and who for the 2–year period immediately before retirement is employed in a bona fide executive or high policymaking position, if such employee is entitled to an immediate nonforfeitable annual retirement benefit * * * at least $44,000.

(ii) Firefighters and police officers: Congress has granted states and their subdivisions the authority to impose mandatory retirement ages if set pursuant to a "bona fide retirement plan that is not a subterfuge to evade the purposes of this Act."

(iii) BFOQ. If a younger age is a bona fide occupational qualification reasonably necessary for safe and effective job performance a person may be dismissed upon reaching a set age. See, *supra*, Chapter 3A.

b. "Voluntary" Retirement

29 U.S.C. § 623(f)(2)(B)(ii) provides that it is not unlawful for an employer to observe a bona fide "voluntary early retirement incentive plan * * *." The key word is "voluntary." A retirement is "voluntary" if the employer utilizes the "carrot" of inducement. Offers "too good to refuse" do not render their acceptance as involuntary. Typical, and permissible, inducements in return for retirement are lump sum payments, adding a set dollar amount multiplied by years of service to retirement, a flat dollar increase in the monthly retirement stipend, or additional years of service credit in calculating the retirement payments.

The early retirement incentive plan should accurately describe the benefits and the employee should be given adequate time to consider whether to accept or reject the benefits in return for retiring. Nonetheless, presenting employees with a reasonable time window in which to accept the offer in return for retirement does not render acceptance involuntary. *Henn v. National Geographic Society,* 819 F.2d 824 (7th Cir. 1987).

Even if it provides positive benefits, retirement will not be "voluntary" if it is secured by using the "stick," a threat, such as forcing the employee to choose between retirement and being laid off or reassigned with reduced pay and responsibility. *Vega v. Kodak Caribbean, Ltd.,* 3 F.3d 476 (1st Cir. 1993).

29 U.S.C. § 623 (*l*)(1)(A) provides: It shall not be a violation of * * * this section solely because—(i) an employee pension benefit plan * * * provides for the attainment of a minimum age as a condition of eligibility for normal or early retirement benefits." The plan and eligibility for participation in it may favor older over younger employees. See, *General Dynamics Land Systems v. Cline,* reproduced, *supra, p. 123.*

c. Benefit Packages

The basic rule is that compensation includes current and future fringe benefits such as life and health insurance, and age distinctions in allocating those benefits, is prohibited. However, **29 U.S.C. § 623(f)(2)** provides:

It shall not be unlawful for an employer, employment agency, or labor organization—* * *

(B) to observe the terms of a bona fide employee benefit plan—

(i) where, for each benefit or benefit package, the actual amount of payment made or cost incurred on behalf of an older worker is no less than that made or incurred on behalf of a younger worker * * *.

Notwithstanding clause (i) or (ii) of subparagraph (B), no such employee benefit plan or voluntary early retirement incentive plan shall excuse the failure to hire any individual, and no such employee benefit plan shall require or permit the involuntary retirement of any individual specified by section 631(a) of this title, because of the age of such individual. An [covered entity] * * * shall have the burden of proving that such actions are lawful in any civil enforcement proceeding brought under this chapter; or

---

EEOC Regulations, 29 C.F.R. § 1625.10

* * *

The legislative history of this provision indicates that its purpose is to permit age-based reductions in employee benefit plans where such reductions are justified by significant cost considerations. Accordingly, [the exemption] does not apply, for example, to paid vacations and uninsured paid sick leave, since reductions in these benefits would not be justified by significant cost considerations. Where employee benefit plans do meet the criteria of [the exemption] benefit levels for older workers may be reduced to the extent necessary to achieve approximate equivalency in cost for older and younger workers. A benefit plan will be considered in compliance with the statute where the actual amount of payment made, or cost incurred, in behalf of an older worker is equal to that made or incurred in behalf of a younger worker, even though the older worker may thereby receive a lesser amount of benefits or insurance coverage. Since [this] is an exception from the general non-discrimination provisions of the Act, the burden is on the one seeking to invoke the exception to show that every element has been clearly and unmistakably met. The exception must be narrowly construed.

* * *

(b) Bona fide employee benefit plan. * * *

A plan is considered "bona fide" if its terms (including cessation of contributions or accruals in the case of retirement income plans) have been accurately described in writing to all employees and if it actually provides the benefits in accordance with the terms of the plan. * * *. An "employee benefit plan" is a plan, such as a retirement, pension, or insurance plan, which provides employees with what are frequently referred to as "fringe benefits." The term does not refer to wages or salary in cash; neither [the exemption] nor any other section of the Act excuses the payment of lower wages or salary to older employees on account of age. * * *

* * *

(d)(1) Cost data—general. Cost data used in justification of a benefit plan which provides lower benefits to older employees on account of age must be valid and reasonable. This standard is met where an employer has cost data which show the actual cost to it of providing the particular benefit (or benefits) in question over a representative period of years. * * *

(2) Cost data—Individual benefit basis and "benefit package" basis. Cost comparisons and adjustments under section 4(f)(2) must be made on a benefit-by-benefit basis or on a "benefit package" basis * * *.

(ii) An older employee within the protected age group may be required as a condition of participation in a voluntary employee benefit plan to make a greater contribution than a younger employee only if the older employee is not thereby required to bear a greater proportion of the total premium cost (employer-paid and employee-paid) than the younger employee. * * *

(iii) An older employee may be given the option, as an individual, to make the additional contribution necessary to receive the same level of benefits as a younger employee (provided that the contemplated reduction in benefits is otherwise justified * * *.

---

29 U.S.C. § 623(i) provides:

(1) Except as otherwise provided * * * it shall be unlawful for [a covered entity] to establish or maintain an employee pension benefit plan which requires or permits—

(A) in the case of a defined benefit plan, the cessation of an employee's benefit accrual, or the reduction of the rate of an employee's benefit accrual, because of age, or

(B) in the case of a defined contribution plan, the cessation of allocations to an employee's account, or the reduction of the rate at which amounts are allocated to an employee's account, because of age.

(2) Nothing in this section shall be construed to prohibit a [covered entity] from observing any provision of an employee pension benefit plan to the extent that such provision imposes (without regard to age) a limitation on the amount of benefits that the plan provides or a limitation on the number of years of service or years of participation which are taken into account for purposes of determining benefit accrual under the plan.

NOTES

1. The above only sketches the outline of permissible distinctions. Technical and complex calculations mark the statute and EEOC guidance. The ADEA also allows employers to coordinate the benefits it provides with Social Security and Medicare benefits, such as reducing health care benefits to Medicare eligible retirees. The basis for this "coordination" also is complex.

2. ***KENTUCKY RETIREMENT SYSTEMS v. EEOC***, **554 U.S. 135, 128 S.Ct. 2361, 171 L.Ed.2d 322 (2008).** An employer's retirement system provided for both normal retirement based on reaching a certain age (55) and a minimum number of service years (5). These provisions were allowed by 29 U.S.C. § 623(*l*). The employer also provided a pension for employees forced to retire because of disabling injuries. An older employee eligible for normal retirement by virtue of age and years of service, retired because of a disability hindering his abilities. The employer's plan provided that younger employees who lacked the age or years in service to be eligible for normal retirement would receive a higher disability retirement than retirement pension-eligible employees. In effect, younger workers who became disabled received a "bonus" in their disability pension that was not available to workers entitled to

regular retirement because of their age and years of service. The Court held that this plan was not unlawful age discrimination, but a good faith attempt to address the economic consequences of younger workers who are forced to retire because of injury but were not eligible for a normal retirement pension.

3. THE AMERICANS WITH DISABILITIES ACT

The ADA imposes no obligation on employers to have insurance programs, even if the failure has an adverse impact on persons with disabilities. *Alexander v. Choate,* 469 U.S. 287, 105 S.Ct. 712, 83 L.Ed.2d 661 (1985). However, if the employer has an insurance program, the employer may not refuse to hire an individual with a disability because of the perceived economic impact on the benefit plan. 29 C.F.R. § 1630.16(f) App. Nor may the plan exclude persons with disabilities or who have a record of disabilities from the general coverage of the program because of their condition or record of disability. *Carparts Dist. Center, Inc. v. Automotive Wholesaler's Ass'n,* 37 F.3d 12 (1st Cir. 1994). Moreover, an employer may not discriminate against a person because of a relationship to an individual who has, is regarded as having, or has a record of having a disability, because of the anticipated impact on the employer's benefit program. *Trujillo v. Pacificorp,* 524 F.3d 1149 (10th Cir. 2008).

42 U.S.C. § 12201(c):

[T]his Act shall not be construed to prohibit or restrict—

(1) an insurer, hospital or medical service company, health maintenance organization or any agent or entity that administers benefit plans * * * from underwriting risks, classifying risks, or administering such risks that are based on or are not inconsistent with State law; or

(2) a person or organization covered by this Act from establishing, sponsoring, observing or administering the terms of a bona fide benefit plan that are based on underwriting risks classifying risks, or administering such risks that are based on or not inconsistent with State law; or

(3) a person or organization covered by this Act from establishing, sponsoring, observing or administering the terms of a bona fide benefit plan that is not subject to State laws that regulate insurance.

NOTES

1. *General precaution:* The history of the ADA indicates that it would not disrupt established insurance and similar benefit programs. However, the ADA prohibits health related distinctions in plans that facially discriminate on the basis of a disability. Individuals with disabilities are entitled to the same health care plan benefits as other employees and must be provided equal access to those programs.

2. *Conditions suffered by both disabled and non-disabled persons:* As a general proposition a plan may make distinctions for conditions that affect

both persons without disabilities and those with disabilities. For example, a plan may provide amounts for eye care that differ from physical rehabilitation in that both conditions include individuals who are disabled and not disabled. The plan may exclude certain kinds of physical impairments, such as dental needs, in that the exclusion affects both disabled and non-disabled persons. Co-payment obligations may vary by kind of condition, for example by requiring greater co-payment obligations on prescription drugs than on office visits to physicians. The Mental Health Parity Act of 1996, 42 U.S.C. § 300gg–5 generally requires, however, that when a health care plan allows for mental health benefits, those benefits must be on the same level as the plan provides for physical conditions.

3. *Conditions suffered only by persons with disabilities:* A plan is suspect and may lack bona fides if it excludes only persons with a particular disability or discriminates against a discrete disability or group of disabilities such as cancer, diabetes, or muscular dystrophy. However, see *Weyer v. Twentieth Century Fox Film Corp.,* 198 F.3d 1104 (9th Cir. 2000), which allowed a plan to limit benefits to particular disabilities when the exclusion was based upon accepted industry actuarial practices.

PART 4

ENFORCEMENT

■ ■ ■

CHAPTER 11

ENFORCEMENT PROCEDURES

■ ■ ■

Enforcement of the "big three" employment discrimination statutes is complicated and a potential trap for the unwary. An aggrieved individual may not simply file suit but must first exhaust administrative prerequisites which have complex and relatively short time limitations.

The ADA incorporates Title VII enforcement procedures by reference. The ADEA has its own procedures, but they are similar to Title VII's. Federal government executive department employees and applicants are required to exhaust a different and even more complex administrative process. The Equal Pay Act and the Reconstruction Era Civil Rights Act (42 U.S.C. §§ 1981 and 1983) have no administrative prerequisites to filing suit.

A. THE CHARGE FILING PROCESS

1. THE RELATIONSHIP BETWEEN THE EEOC AND STATE AND LOCAL AGENCIES

An aggrieved party, other than a federal employee or applicant, begins the Title VII, ADA and ADEA, enforcement process by filing a charge of discrimination, but how the complainant is required to proceed depends on whether the complained-of practice occurred in a jurisdiction that has a state or local law prohibiting the practice and a state or local authority empowered to grant or seek relief with respect to the practice. These are commonly referred to as "deferral states." (Most states now have such fair employment laws.)

Under Title VII and the ADA where the alleged discrimination occurs in a "deferral state" the aggrieved party first must file a charge with the relevant state or local authority and may not file a charge with the EEOC until 60 days thereafter, unless the state or local authority terminates proceedings earlier. If the alleged discrimination occurred in a deferral state, the EEOC charge must be deemed "filed" within 300 days of the alleged discriminatory act. In the few non-deferral jurisdictions the aggrieved party must file a charge with the EEOC within 180 days of the alleged discriminatory act. These complex requirements have spawned a considerable amount of litigation.

EEOC v. COMMERCIAL OFFICE PRODUCTS CO.

Supreme Court of the United States, 1988
486 U.S. 107, 108 S.Ct. 1666, 100 L.Ed.2d 96

JUSTICE MARSHALL announced the judgment of the Court and delivered the opinion of the Court with respect to Parts I, II–A, and III, and an opinion with respect to Parts II–B and II–C, in which JUSTICE BRENNAN, JUSTICE WHITE, and JUSTICE BLACKMUN joined.

This case raises two questions regarding the time limits for filing charges of employment discrimination with the Equal Employment Opportunity Commission (EEOC) under Title VII of the Civil Rights Act. The primary question presented is whether a state agency's decision to waive its exclusive 60–day period for initial processing of a discrimination charge, pursuant to a worksharing agreement with the EEOC, "terminates" the agency's proceedings within the meaning of § 706(c) of Title VII, 42 U.S.C. § 2000e–5(c), so that the EEOC immediately may deem the charge filed. In addition, we must decide whether a complainant who files a discrimination charge that is untimely under state law is nonetheless entitled to the extended 300–day federal filing period of § 706(e) of Title VII.

I

The time limit provisions of Title VII as interpreted by this Court establish the following procedures for filing discrimination charges with the EEOC. As a general rule, a complainant must file a discrimination charge with the EEOC within 180 days of the occurrence of the alleged unlawful employment practice. § 706(e). If a complainant initially institutes proceedings with a state or local agency with authority to grant or seek relief from the practice charged, the time limit for filing with the EEOC is extended to 300 days.

In order to give States and localities an opportunity to combat discrimination free from premature federal intervention, the Act provides that no charge may be filed with the EEOC until 60 days have elapsed from initial filing of the charge with an authorized state or local agency, unless that agency's proceedings "have been earlier terminated." § 706(c). The EEOC's referral of a charge initially filed with the EEOC to the appropriate state or local agency properly institutes the agency's proceedings within the meaning of the Act, and the EEOC may hold the charge in " 'suspended animation' " during the agency's 60–day period of exclusive jurisdiction. Love v. Pullman Co., 404 U.S. 522, 525–526, 92 S.Ct. 616, 618–619, 30 L.Ed.2d 679 (1972). In light of the 60–day deferral period, a complainant must file a charge with the appropriate state or local agency, or have the EEOC refer the charge to that agency, within 240 days of the alleged discriminatory event in order to ensure that it may be filed with the EEOC within the 300–day limit. See Mohasco Corp. v. Silver, 447 U.S. 807, 814, n. 16, 100 S.Ct. 2486, 2491, n. 16, 65 L.Ed.2d 532 (1980). If the complainant does not file within 240 days, the charge still may be timely filed with the EEOC if the state or local agency terminates its proceedings before 300 days.

The central question in this case is whether a state agency's waiver of the 60–day deferral period, pursuant to a worksharing agreement with the EEOC, constitutes a "termination" of its proceedings so as to permit the EEOC to deem a charge filed and to begin to process it immediately. This question is of substantial importance because the EEOC has used its statutory authority to enter into worksharing agreements with approximately three-quarters of the 109 state and local agencies authorized to enforce state and local employment discrimination laws. See § 709(b), 42 U.S.C. § 2000e–8(b) (authorizing the EEOC to "enter into written agreements" with state and local agencies to promote "effective enforcement" of the Act).

These worksharing agreements typically provide that the state or local agency will process certain categories of charges and that the EEOC will process others, with the state or local agency waiving the 60–day deferral period in the latter instance. In either instance, the nonprocessing party to the worksharing agreement generally reserves the right to review the initial processing party's resolution of the charge and to investigate the charge further after the initial processing party has completed its proceedings. Whether a waiver of the 60–day deferral period pursuant to a worksharing agreement constitutes a "termination" of a state or local agency's proceedings will determine not only when the EEOC may initiate its proceedings, but also whether an entire class of charges may be timely filed with the EEOC in the first instance.

The facts of the instant case concretely reflect what is at stake. On March 26, 1984, Suanne Leerssen filed a charge of discrimination with petitioner EEOC. She alleged that 290 days earlier, respondent Commercial Office Products Company had discharged her because of her sex in violation of Title VII. On March 30, the EEOC sent a copy of Leerssen's charge and a charge transmittal form to the Colorado Civil Rights Division (CCRD), which is authorized by the State to process charges of employment discrimination. The form stated that the EEOC would initially process the charge, pursuant to the worksharing agreement between the EEOC and the CCRD.

The CCRD returned the transmittal form to the EEOC, indicating on the form that the CCRD waived its right under Title VII to initially process the charge. On April 4, the CCRD sent a form letter to Leerssen explaining that it had waived its right to initial processing but stating that it still retained jurisdiction to act on the charge after the conclusion of the EEOC's proceedings. If the CCRD's waiver "terminated" its proceedings, then Leerssen's charge was filed with the EEOC just under the 300–day limit. If the waiver was not a "termination," however, then the charge was not timely filed with the EEOC because the 60–day deferral period did not expire until well after the 300–day limit.

The timeliness issue was raised in this case when the EEOC issued an administrative subpoena for information relevant to Leerssen's charge. Respondent refused to comply with the subpoena, maintaining that the EEOC lacked jurisdiction to investigate the charge because it was not timely filed. The EEOC commenced an action in the United States District Court for the District of Colorado seeking judicial enforcement of the subpoena. The District Court agreed with respondent and dismissed the EEOC's enforcement action, holding that the EEOC lacked jurisdiction over Leerssen's charge because it was not timely filed.

The Court of Appeals for the Tenth Circuit affirmed. As a threshold matter, the Court of Appeals rejected respondent's contention that the extended 300–day federal filing period was inapplicable because Leerssen had failed to file her charge with the CCRD within the State's own 180–day limitations period. The Court of Appeals agreed with the District Court, however, that Leerssen's charge was not filed within the 300–day period and that the EEOC therefore lacked jurisdiction over the charge. The Court of Appeals reasoned that a state agency "terminates" its proceedings within the meaning of § 706(c) only when it "completely surrenders its jurisdiction over a charge." Because the CCRD retained jurisdiction over Leerssen's charge, reserving the right to act at the conclusion of the EEOC's proceedings, it did not "finally and unequivocally terminate its authority" over the charge as the plain language of the statute required. * * *

We granted certiorari * * * and we now reverse.

II

A

First and foremost, respondent defends the judgment of the Court of Appeals on the ground that the language of the statute unambiguously precludes the conclusion that the CCRD's waiver of the deferral period "terminated" its proceedings. According to respondent, "terminated" means only "completed'" or "ended." * * * Because the CCRD retained authority to reactivate its proceedings after the EEOC's resolution of the charge, respondent maintains that the CCRD did not "terminate" its proceedings within the meaning of the Act.

We cannot agree * * * that "terminate" must mean "to end for all time." Rather, we find * * * that the definition of "termination" also includes "cessation in time." * * * Moreover, the * * * common usage of the words "terminate," "complete," or "end" often includes a time element, as in "ending negotiations despite the likely inevitability of their resumption" or "terminating work on the job-site knowing that it will resume the next day." These observations support the EEOC's contention that a state agency "terminates" its proceedings when it declares that it will not proceed, if it does so at all, for a specified interval of time.

To be sure, "terminate" also may bear the meaning proposed by respondent. Indeed, it may bear that meaning more naturally or more frequently in common usage. But it is axiomatic that the EEOC's interpretation of Title VII, for which it has primary enforcement responsibility, need not be the best one by grammatical or any other standards. Rather, the EEOC's interpretation of ambiguous language need only be reasonable to be entitled to deference. The reasonableness of the EEOC's interpretation of "terminate" in its statutory context is more than amply supported by the legislative history of the deferral provisions of Title VII, the purposes of those provisions, and the language of other sections of the Act, as described in detail below. Deference is therefore appropriate.

B

The legislative history of the deferral provisions of Title VII demonstrates that the EEOC's interpretation of § 706(c) is far more consistent with the purposes of the Act than respondent's contrary construction.

The deferral provisions of § 706 were enacted as part of a compromise forged during the course of one of the longest filibusters in the Senate's history. The bill that had passed the House provided for "deferral" to state and local enforcement efforts only in the sense that it directed the EEOC to enter into agreements with state agencies providing for the suspension of federal enforcement in certain circumstances. The House bill further directed the EEOC to rescind any agreement with a state agency if the EEOC determined that the agency was no longer effectively exercising its power to combat discrimination. In the Senate, this bill met with strenuous opposition on the ground that it placed the EEOC in the position of monitoring state enforcement efforts, granting States exclusive jurisdiction over local discrimination claims only upon the EEOC's determination that state efforts were effective. The bill's opponents voiced their concerns against the backdrop of the federal-state civil rights conflicts of the early 1960's, which no doubt intensified their fear of "the steady and deeper intrusion of the Federal power." These concerns were resolved by the "Dirksen–Mansfield substitute," which proposed the 60–day deferral period now in § 706(c) of the Act.

The proponents of the Dirksen–Mansfield substitute identified two goals of the deferral provisions, both of which fully support the EEOC's conclusion that States may, if they choose, waive the 60–day deferral period but retain jurisdiction over discrimination charges by entering into worksharing agreements with the EEOC. First, the proponents of the substitute deferral provisions explained that the 60–day deferral period was meant to give States a "reasonable opportunity to act under State law before the commencement of any Federal proceedings." Nothing in the waiver provisions of the worksharing agreements impinges on the opportunity of the States to have an exclusive 60–day period for processing a discrimination charge. The waiver of that opportunity in specified instances is a voluntary choice made through individually negotiated agreements, not an imposition by the Federal Government. * * *

In contrast, respondent's argument that States should not be permitted to waive the deferral period because its creation reflected a congressional preference for state as opposed to federal enforcement is entirely at odds with the voluntarism stressed by the proponents of deferral. Congress clearly foresaw the possibility that States might decline to take advantage of the opportunity for enforcement afforded them by the deferral provisions. It therefore gave the EEOC the authority and responsibility to act when a State is "unable or unwilling" to provide relief. This Court, too, has recognized that Congress envisioned federal intervention when "States decline, for whatever reason, to take advantage of [their] opportunities" to settle grievances in "a voluntary and localized manner." As counsel for the EEOC explained, deferral was meant to work as "a carrot, but not a stick," affording States an opportunity to act, but not penalizing their failure to do so other than by authorizing federal intervention. The waiver provisions of worksharing agreements are fully consistent with this goal.

In addition to providing States with an opportunity to forestall federal intervention, the deferral provisions were meant to promote "time economy and the expeditious handling of cases." Respondent's proposed interpretation of § 706(c), adopted by the Court of Appeals, is irreconcilable with this purpose because it would result in extraordinary inefficiency without furthering any other goal of the Act. The EEOC would be required to wait 60 days before processing its share of discrimination claims under a worksharing agreement, even though both the EEOC and the relevant state or local agency agree that the State or locality will take no action during that period. Or, in an effort to avoid this pointless 60–day delay, state and local agencies could abandon their worksharing agreements with the EEOC and attempt to initially process all charges during the 60–day deferral period, a solution suggested by respondent. Such a solution would create an enormous backlog of discrimination charges in States and localities, preventing them from securing for their citizens the quick attention to discrimination claims afforded under worksharing agreements. Or, in another scenario proposed by respondent, state or local agencies could rewrite their worksharing agreements with the EEOC to provide for "termination" of state or local proceedings in accordance with respondent's definition of that term—complete relinquishment of jurisdiction. This solution would prevent a pointless 60–day delay, but it would also preclude a State's reactivation of a discrimination charge upon the conclusion of federal proceedings. Requiring that States completely relinquish authority over claims in order to avoid needless delay turns on its head the dual purposes of the deferral provisions: deference to the States and efficient processing of claims. * * *

The most dramatic result of respondent's reading of the deferral provisions is the preclusion of any federal relief for an entire class of discrimination claims. All claims filed with the EEOC in worksharing States more than 240 but less than 300 days after the alleged discriminatory event, like Leerssen's claim in this case, will be rendered untimely because the 60–day deferral period will not expire within the 300–day filing limit. Respondent's interpretation thus requires the 60–day deferral period—

which was passed on behalf of state and local agencies—to render untimely a claim filed within the federal 300–day limit, despite the joint efforts of the EEOC and the state or local agency to avoid that result. As petitioner epigrammatically observes, a claim like Leerssen's that is filed with the EEOC within the last 60 days of the federal filing period is "too early until it is too late." This severe consequence, in conjunction with the pointless delay described above, demonstrates that respondent's interpretation of the language of § 706(c) leads to "absurd or futile results ... 'plainly at variance with the policy of the legislation as a whole,' " which this Court need not and should not countenance.

C

The EEOC's construction of § 706(c) also finds support in other, related sections of Title VII. These sections reinforce our reading of the legislative history that the 1964 Congress did not intend to preclude the operation of the waiver provisions of the worksharing agreements now widely in force.

Section 706(d) provides that when a member of the EEOC, rather than an individual complainant, files a discrimination charge in a State or locality with concurrent jurisdiction, "the Commission shall, before taking any action with respect to such charge, notify the appropriate State or local officials and, upon request, afford them a reasonable time, but not less than sixty days ... *unless a shorter period is requested,* to act." This language clearly permits state and local agencies to waive the 60–day deferral period and thus authorize the EEOC to take immediate action in cases arising under § 706(d). There is every reason to believe that Congress intended the same result in § 706(c), notwithstanding the variance in language. The legislative history of the deferral provisions reflects the legislators' understanding that the time limits of §§ 706(c) and (d) were the same. * * *

The EEOC's interpretation of § 706(c) also finds support in provisions of the Act calling for formal cooperation between the EEOC and state and local agencies. Section 705(g)(1) gives the EEOC the power "to cooperate with and, with their consent, utilize regional, State, local, and other agencies." Section 709(b) specifies that "[i]n furtherance of such cooperative efforts, the Commission may enter into written agreements with such State or local agencies." These sections clearly envision the establishment of some sort of worksharing agreements between the EEOC and state and local agencies, and they in no way preclude provisions designed to avoid unnecessary duplication of effort or waste of time. Because the EEOC's interpretation of the "termination" requirement of § 706(c) is necessary to give effect to such provisions in most of the existing worksharing agreements, we find that interpretation more consistent with the cooperative focus of the Act than respondent's contrary construction.

III

In the alternative, respondent argues in support of the result below that the extended 300–day federal filing period is inapplicable to this case because the complainant failed to file her discrimination charge with the CCRD within Colorado's 180–day limitations period. Respondent reasons that the extended 300–day filing period applies only when "the person aggrieved has initially instituted proceedings with a state or local agency with authority to grant or seek relief" from the practice charged, § 706(e), and that in the absence of a timely filing under state law, a state agency lacks the requisite "authority to grant or seek relief." * * *

[I]n *Oscar Mayer & Co. v. Evans,* 441 U.S. 750, 99 S.Ct. 2066, 60 L.Ed.2d 609 (1979), * * * we found in the Age Discrimination in Employment Act of 1967 (ADEA) context that a complainant's failure to file a claim within a state limitations period did not automatically render his federal claim untimely. We reasoned that the federal statute contained no express requirement of timely state filing, and we declined to create such a requirement in light of the remedial purpose of the ADEA and our recognition that it is a " 'statutory scheme in which laymen, unassisted by trained lawyers, initiate the process.' " In the instant case, we decide the separate question whether under Title VII, untimely filing under state law automatically precludes the application of the extended 300–day federal filing period, but the reasoning of *Oscar Mayer* is entirely apposite. As we noted in *Oscar Mayer* itself, the filing provisions of the ADEA and Title VII are "virtually *in haec verba,*" the former having been patterned after the latter. Title VII, like the ADEA, contains no express reference to timeliness under state law. In addition, the policy considerations that militate against importing such a hurdle into the federal ADEA scheme are identical in the Title VII context: Title VII also is a remedial scheme in which laypersons, rather than lawyers, are expected to initiate the process.

The importation of state limitations periods into § 706(e) not only would confuse lay complainants, but also would embroil the EEOC in complicated issues of state law. In order for the EEOC to determine the timeliness of a charge filed with it between 180 and 300 days, it first would have to determine whether the charge had been timely filed under state law, because the answer to the latter question would establish which of the two federal limitations periods should apply. This state-law determination is not a simple matter. The EEOC first would have to determine whether a state limitations period was jurisdictional or nonjurisdictional. And if the limitations period was nonjurisdictional, like Colorado's in this case, the EEOC would have to decide whether it was waived or equitably tolled. The EEOC has neither the time nor the expertise to make such determinations under the varying laws of the many deferral States and has accordingly construed the extended 300–day period to be available regardless of the state filing. In contrast to the difficulties presented by respondent's argument, our broadly worded statement in *Mohasco Corp. v. Silver,* 447 U.S. 807, 100 S.Ct. 2486, 65 L.Ed.2d 532 (1980), a case presenting a related issue regarding the application of the extended 300–day federal filing period, that a complainant "need only file his charge within 240 days of the alleged discriminatory employment practice in order to ensure that his federal rights will be preserved,"establishes a rule that is both easily understood by complainants and easily administered by the EEOC. We reaffirm that rule today.

Because we find that the extended 300–day federal limitations period is applicable to this case and that the CCRD's waiver of the 60–day deferral period "terminated" its proceedings within that 300–day limit, we conclude that Leerssen's claim was timely filed under Title VII. We therefore reverse the decision of the Court of Appeals and remand the case for further proceedings consistent with this opinion.

JUSTICE O'CONNOR concurring in part and concurring in the judgment.

I join Parts I and III of the Court's opinion. I also join Part II–A, in which the Court correctly concludes that in light of the statute's language, structure, and legislative history, sufficient ambiguity exists to warrant deference to the agency's construction of the word "terminated" in § 706(c). Indeed, deference is particularly appropriate on this type of technical issue of agency procedure. But while I agree with much of what the majority says in Parts II–B and II–C in indicating that the agency's construction is reasonable, in my view the majority goes too far by suggesting that the agency's position is the only one permissible. * * * Any such implication is incorrect. As the dissent concisely points out, the agency could quite reasonably conclude that the statutory language warrants giving the word "terminated" what the Court recognizes is its more natural reading.

In short, I believe the result in this case is correct solely due to the traditional deference accorded the EEOC in interpretation of this statute. Because Parts II–B and II–C could be read to go beyond this view, I join only Parts I, II–A, and III of the Court's opinion and in the judgment.

[The dissenting opinion of JUSTICE STEVENS, joined by CHIEF JUSTICE REHNQUIST and JUSTICE SCALIA, is omitted.]

NOTES

1. As originally enacted in 1964, Title VII required aggrieved parties to file charges with the EEOC within 90 days following the alleged discriminatory act. The 1972 amendments increased the time limits to 180 days in nondeferral states and 300 days in deferral states.

2. EEOC practice in deferral states is to refer charges that it receives to the relevant state or local agency. *Love v. Pullman*, cited in the principal case, approved of this referral process, and held that the EEOC could, in effect, hold the charge in suspended animation for sixty days or until the state agency terminated proceedings and consider the charge "filed" with the EEOC at that the termination of state processes. *Mohasco Corp. v. Silver*, also cited in the principal case, held that an aggrieved party could take advantage of the 300–day filing deadline even though the party did not file with the state agency within 180 days of the discriminatory action. The Court held, however, that the charge was not "filed" with the EEOC on the day that the charging party deposited the charge with the EEOC. The EEOC charge could be "filed"

only *after* the charge had been filed with the state agency. The Court indicated that charges filed with the EEOC within 240 days would be considered timely, as the EEOC would refer the charges to the state agency and sixty days later revive the charges from suspended animation and consider them filed at that point. However, charges filed between 240 and 300 days following the alleged discrimination would be timely only if the state agency terminated its proceedings before the 300 day period expired. In response to *Mohasco*, the EEOC entered into the work-sharing agreements described in the principal opinion.

3. In *Zipes v. Trans World Airlines, Inc.*, 455 U.S. 385, 102 S.Ct. 1127, 71 L.Ed.2d 234 (1982), the Court held that filing a timely charge is not a jurisdictional prerequisite to an individual's lawsuit and is subject to waiver, estoppel and equitable tolling.

4. The statutes delegate to the EEOC the authority to establish the necessary content of a charge. EEOC regulations implementing statutory directives specify that a charge must be in writing, name the charged and charging parties, identify the nature of the discrimination experienced, as well as the time and place of the challenged action. The EEOC receives hundreds of thousands of inquiries each year. Most of them are not charges. An individual who appears at an EEOC office may be asked to complete an informal "intake questionnaire" that seeks relevant information. *Federal Express Corp. v. Holowecki*, 552 U.S. 389, 128 S.Ct. 1147, 170 L.Ed.2d 10 (2008), held that to constitute a charge, a filing must identify allege discrimination and "be reasonably construed as a request for the agency to take remedial action to protect the employee's rights or otherwise settle a dispute between the employer and the employee." Consequently, an informal "intake questionnaire" can be considered a formal "charge" when it contains the critical information.

5. The statutes and EEOC rules also require that the charge be "in writing under oath or affirmation." *Edelman v. Lynchburg College*, 535 U.S. 106, 122 S.Ct. 1145, 152 L.Ed.2d 188 (2002), involved a situation where a party filed a charge that was not under oath within the 300–day period but verified the charge under oath *after* the expiration of the 300–day period. The Court approved the EEOC's regulation that allowed the verification (and other "technical" defects) to relate back to the date that the original charge was filed.

6. Complicated filing requirements remain a trap for the unwary. For example, in *Dezaio v. Port Authority of New York and New Jersey*, 205 F.3d 62 (2d Cir. 2000), plaintiff filed an ADEA charge against the Port Authority 286 days after his discharge. Unfortunately for plaintiff, the Port Authority is a bi-state authority not subject to the jurisdiction of state EEO agencies in New York or New Jersey. Consequently, the court held, plaintiff was subject to the 180–day time limit and his charge was untimely.

7. The ADEA does not specify, as do Title VII and the ADA, a sequential filing of state and then federal EEOC charges. While a charge of age discrimination must be filed with both the EEOC and any state enforcement agency, state charges may be filed prior to, simultaneously with, or even

subsequent to the EEOC charge. *Oscar Mayer & Co. v. Evans,* 441 U.S. 750, 99 S.Ct. 2066, 60 L.Ed.2d 609 (1979).

2. FEDERAL AGENCIES, FEDERAL EMPLOYEES

a. Introduction

Federal agencies are excluded from the statutory definition of "employer." (*See* Title VII, 42 U.S.C. § 2000e(b)). However, the core statutes proscribe discrimination that parallels the substantive prohibitions applicable to private and state and local government "employers." (*See,* 42 U.S.C. § 2000e–16(a)).[1] Federal employees and applicants are required to exhaust pre-requisites to filing a law suit that are markedly different from the procedures required of non-federal claimants. See, 29 C.F.R. Part 1615 and www.eeoc.gov.

b. Employing Agency

The exhaustion *required* is a formal complaint that allows review of the adverse action by the *employing agency*, not by the EEOC. Under Title VII and the Rehabilitation Act, the federal employee or applicant must first initiate a "pre-complaint contact" with the employing agency's Equal Employment Opportunity (EEO) Counselor. This pre-complaint contact must take place within 45 days of the discriminatory act. The agency's EEO counselor is expected to investigate the allegations and attempt an informal resolution. If no satisfactory resolution of the claim is accomplished, the claimant is notified by the EEO counselor of the right to file a formal complaint with the employing agency. The claimant must file this "formal complaint" with the employing agency within 15 days from receipt of the EEO counselor's notice that informal resolution has not been successful. Note the extremely short limitation periods for these two steps!

The employing agency may reject the formal complaint and issue a "final order" dismissing the complaint. Alternatively, the agency may accept the complaint and conduct an agency-organized investigation. Following the completion of the agency's investigation, the complainant may request an immediate "final decision" by the agency. Upon receipt of an adverse final decision (or allowing 60 days for the agency to issue such a decision) the complainant may file suit against the agency head in federal district court. There is no obligation under Title VII or the Rehabilitation Act to seek EEOC resolution.

The ADEA requires that the claimant file with the EEOC a "notice of intent to sue" the employing agency within 180 days of the discriminatory act, and wait 30 days after the filing of that notice. Thereafter, the claimant may file suit in federal court. Nonetheless, the ADEA claimant

---

1. Claims of disability discrimination against federal executive agencies are brought under the Rehabilitation Act of 1973, not the Americans With Disabilities Act. The substantive prohibitions of the two statutes are parallel. Claims of disability discrimination against federal executive department employers utilize the procedures prescribed for federal Title VII claims.

may elect to follow procedures established for Title VII and the Rehabilitation Act, set forth above, as well as the alternatives outlined below.

c. Alternative Pre–Suit Routes: Administrative Review by the EEOC

In addition to the mandatory requirement of seeking pre-complaint resolution and thereafter filing a formal complaint with the employing agency, regulations permit a complainant to secure EEOC review of the final agency action. The option of an EEOC review is commonly invoked by many, if not most, claimants. Claimants have a choice of EEOC pre-suit involvement:

1. EEOC Hearing: After the employing agency conducts its investigation of the complaint, rather than demand a final agency determination, the claimant may, at this juncture, request a hearing before an EEOC administrative judge. The result would be a formal adversarial proceeding after which the administrative judge makes findings of fact and conclusions of law. If the judge rules in favor of the claimant, the federal agency head (or designee) must implement or decline to implement the judge's decision. If it rejects the judge's decision, the agency must immediately appeal the judge's decision to the EEOC Office of Federal Operations (OFO). The OFO will review the judge's conclusions of law *de novo* and factual findings under a "substantial evidence" standard. If the OFO affirms the judge's decision against the agency, the agency is obligated to implement the EEOC/OFO determination.

If the EEOC administrative judge rules against the claimant, and in favor of the agency, the claimant may appeal the judge's decision to the OFO. The notice of appeal to the OFO must be filed within 30 days of the agency's final order based on the administrative judge's decision. If the OFO affirms the judge's ruling against the claimant, the claimant is free to file suit in federal district court. If the OFO reverses the judge's order, and rules for the claimant, the agency must implement the EEOC directive.

2. Appeal of the Agency Decision: If, after the agency investigation, the claimant demands a "final agency decision" (rather than an EEOC hearing), and the final agency decision rejects the claim of unlawful discrimination, the claimant may appeal the agency decision to the EEOC/OFO. If the OFO reverses the agency decision, the agency is obligated to implement the EEOC order. If the OFO affirms the final agency action, the claimant may file suit in federal court.

3. WHEN DOES THE FILING PERIOD START TO RUN?

DELAWARE STATE COLLEGE v. RICKS

Supreme Court of the United States, 1980
449 U.S. 250, 101 S.Ct. 498, 66 L.Ed.2d 431

JUSTICE POWELL delivered the opinion of the Court.

The question in this case is whether respondent, a college professor, timely complained under the civil rights laws that he had been denied academic tenure because of his national origin.

I

Columbus Ricks is a black Liberian. In 1970, Ricks joined the faculty at Delaware State College, a state institution attended predominantly by blacks. In February 1973, the Faculty Committee on Promotions and Tenure (the tenure committee) recommended that Ricks not receive a tenured position in the education department. The tenure committee, however, agreed to reconsider its decision the following year. Upon reconsideration, in February 1974, the committee adhered to its earlier recommendation. The following month, the Faculty Senate voted to support the tenure committee's negative recommendation. On March 13, 1974, the College Board of Trustees formally voted to deny tenure to Ricks.

Dissatisfied with the decision, Ricks immediately filed a grievance with the Board's Educational Policy Committee (the grievance committee), which in May 1974 held a hearing and took the matter under submission. During the pendency of the grievance, the College administration continued to plan for Ricks' eventual termination. Like many colleges and universities, Delaware State has a policy of not discharging immediately a junior faculty member who does not receive tenure. Rather, such a person is offered a "terminal" contract to teach one additional year. When that contract expires, the employment relationship ends. Adhering to this policy, the Trustees on June 26, 1974, told Ricks that he would be offered a 1–year "terminal" contract that would expire June 30, 1975. Ricks signed the contract without objection or reservation on September 4, 1974. Shortly thereafter, on September 12, 1974, the Board of Trustees notified Ricks that it had denied his grievance.

Ricks attempted to file an employment discrimination charge with the Equal Employment Opportunity Commission (EEOC) on April 4, 1975. Under Title VII of the Civil Rights Act of 1964, however, state fair employment practices agencies have primary jurisdiction over employment discrimination complaints. The EEOC therefore referred Ricks' charge to the appropriate Delaware agency. On April 28, 1975, the state agency waived its jurisdiction, and the EEOC accepted Ricks' complaint for filing. More than two years later, the EEOC issued a "right to sue" letter.

Ricks filed this lawsuit in the District Court on September 9, 1977. The complaint alleged, *inter alia*, that the College had discriminated against him on the basis of his national origin in violation of Title VII and 42 U.S.C. § 1981. The District Court sustained the College's motion to dismiss both claims as untimely. It concluded that the only unlawful employment practice alleged was the College's decision to deny Ricks' tenure, and that the limitations periods for both claims had commenced to run by June 26, 1974, when the President of the Board of Trustees officially notified Ricks that he would be offered a 1–year "terminal" contract. The Title VII claim was not timely because Ricks had not filed his charge with the EEOC within 180 days after that date. Similarly, the § 1981 claim was not timely because the lawsuit had not been filed in the District Court within the applicable 3–year statute of limitations.

The Court of Appeals for the Third Circuit reversed. It agreed with the District Court that Ricks' essential allegation was that he had been denied tenure illegally. According to the Court of Appeals, however, the Title VII filing requirement, and the statute of limitations for the § 1981 claim, did not commence to run until Ricks' "terminal" contract expired on June 30, 1975. The court reasoned:

" '[A] terminated employee who is still working should not be required to consult a lawyer or file charges of discrimination against his employer as long as he is still working, even though he has been told of the employer's present intention to terminate him in the future.' "

The Court of Appeals believed that the initial decision to terminate an employee sometimes might be reversed. The aggrieved employee therefore should not be expected to resort to litigation until termination actually has occurred. Prior resort to judicial or administrative remedies would be "likely to have the negative side effect of reducing that employee's effectiveness during the balance of his or her term. Working relationships will be injured, if not sundered, and the litigation process will divert attention from the proper fulfillment of job responsibilities." Finally, the Court of Appeals thought that a rule focusing on the last day of employment would provide a "bright line guide both for the courts and for the victims of discrimination." It therefore reversed and remanded the case to the District Court for trial on the merits of Ricks' discrimination claims. We granted certiorari.

For the reasons that follow, we think that the Court of Appeals erred in holding that the filing limitations periods did not commence to run until June 30, 1975. We agree instead with the District Court that both the Title VII and § 1981 claims were untimely. Accordingly, we reverse.

II

Title VII requires aggrieved persons to file a complaint with the EEOC "within one hundred and eighty days after the alleged unlawful employment practice occurred." 42 U.S.C. § 2000e–5(e). Similarly, § 1981 plaintiffs in Delaware must file suit within three years of the unfavorable employment decision. The limitations periods, while guaranteeing the protection of the civil rights laws to those who promptly assert their rights, also protect employers from the burden of defending claims arising from employment decisions that are long past.

Determining the timeliness of Ricks' EEOC complaint, and this ensuing lawsuit, requires us to identify precisely the "unlawful employment practice" of which he complains. Ricks now insists that discrimination motivated the College not only in denying him tenure, but also in terminating his employment on June 30, 1975. * * *

* * * It appears that termination of employment at Delaware State is a delayed, but inevitable, consequence of the denial of tenure. In order for the limitations periods to commence with the date of discharge, Ricks would have had to allege and prove that the manner in which his employment was terminated differed discriminatorily from the manner in which the College terminated other professors who also had been denied tenure. But no suggestion has been made that Ricks was treated differently from other unsuccessful tenure aspirants. Rather, in accord with the College's practice, Ricks was offered a 1–year "terminal" contract, with explicit notice that his employment would end upon its expiration.

In sum, the only alleged discrimination occurred—and the filing limitations periods therefore commenced—at the time the tenure decision was made and communicated to Ricks. That is so even though one of the *effects* of the denial of tenure-the eventual loss of a teaching position—did not occur until later. * * *

III

We conclude for the foregoing reasons that the limitations periods commenced to run when the tenure decision was made and Ricks was notified. The remaining inquiry is the identification of this date.

A

Three dates have been advanced and argued by the parties. As indicated above, Ricks contended for June 30, 1975, the final date of his "terminal" contract, relying on a continuing-violation theory. This contention fails, as we have shown, because of the absence of any allegations of facts to support it. The Court of Appeals agreed with Ricks that the relevant date was June 30, 1975, but it did so on a different theory. It found that the only alleged discriminatory act was the denial of tenure, but nevertheless adopted the "final date of employment" rule primarily for policy reasons. Although this view has the virtue of simplicity, the discussion in Part II of this opinion demonstrates its fallacy as a rule of general application. Congress has decided that time limitations periods commence with the date of the "alleged unlawful employment practice." Where, as here, the only challenged employment practice occurs before the termination date, the limitations periods necessarily commence to run before that date.[11] It

---

11. The Court of Appeals also thought it was significant that a final-date-of-employment rule would permit the teacher to conclude his affairs at a school without the acrimony engendered by

should not be forgotten that time-limitations provisions themselves promoted important interests; "the period allowed for instituting suit inevitably reflects a value judgment concerning the point at which the interests in favor of protecting valid claims are outweighed by the interests in prohibiting the prosecution of stale ones."

B

The EEOC, in its *amicus* brief, contends in the alternative for a different date. It was not until September 12, 1974, that the Board notified Ricks that his grievance had been denied. The EEOC therefore asserts that, for purposes of computing limitations periods, this was the date of the unfavorable tenure decision. Two possible lines of reasoning underlie this argument. First, it could be contended that the Trustees' initial decision was only an expression of intent that did not become final until the grievance was denied. In support of this argument, the EEOC notes that the June 26 letter explicitly held out to Ricks the possibility that he would receive tenure if the Board sustained his grievance. Second, even if the Board's first decision expressed its official position, it could be argued that the pendency of the grievance should toll the running of the limitations periods.

We do not find either argument to be persuasive. As to the former, we think that the Board of Trustees had made clear well before September 12 that it had formally rejected Ricks' tenure bid. The June 26 letter itself characterized that as the Board's "official position." It is apparent, of course, that the Board in the June 26 letter indicated a willingness to change its prior decision if Ricks' grievance were found to be meritorious. But entertaining a grievance complaining of the tenure decision does not suggest that the earlier decision was in any respect tentative. The grievance procedure, by its nature, is a *remedy* for a prior decision, not an opportunity to *influence* that decision before it is made.

As to the latter argument, we already have held that the pendency of a grievance, or some other method of collateral review of an employment decision, does not toll the running of the limitations periods. *Electrical Workers v. Robbins & Myers, Inc.*, 429 U.S. 229, 97 S.Ct. 441, 50 L.Ed.2d 427 (1976). The existence of careful procedures to assure fairness in the tenure decision should not obscure the principle that limitations periods normally commence when the employer's decision is made.

C

The District Court rejected both the June 30, 1975, date and the September 12, 1974, date, and concluded that the limitations periods had commenced to run by June 26, 1974, when the President of the Board notified Ricks that he would be offered a "terminal" contract for the 1974–1975

the filing of an administrative complaint or lawsuit. It is true that "the filing of a lawsuit might tend to deter efforts at conciliation." But this is the "natural effec[t] of the choice Congress has made," in explicitly requiring that the limitations period commence with the date of the "alleged unlawful employment practice".

school year. We cannot say that this decision was erroneous. By June 26, the tenure committee had twice recommended that Ricks not receive tenure; the Faculty Senate had voted to support the tenure committee's recommendation; and the Board of Trustees formally had voted to deny Ricks tenure. In light of this unbroken array of negative decisions, the District Court was justified in concluding that the College had established its official position—and made that position apparent to Ricks—no later than June 26, 1974.

We therefore reverse the decision of the Court of Appeals and remand to that court so that it may reinstate the District Court's order dismissing the complaint.

[The dissenting opinion of JUSTICE STEWART, joined by JUSTICES BRENNAN and MARSHALL, and the dissenting opinion of JUSTICE STEVENS are omitted.]

NOTES

1. ***Chardon v. Fernandez***, 454 U.S. 6, 102 S.Ct. 28 70 L.Ed.2d 6 (1981), applied *Ricks* to an action brought under 42 U.S.C. § 1983. The plaintiffs had been notified by letter that their employment would terminate on specified dates in the future. They sued claiming that their terminations were in retaliation for their exercise of their right of free speech, and thus violated the First Amendment. The Court held that their claims accrued on the dates they received the letters, not on the dates that their terminations were effective.

2. Evaluation of the date the time period starts running can be highly nuanced. For example in *Bailey v. United Airlines*, 279 F.3d 194 (3d Cir. 2002), plaintiff Bailey had been a pilot for Pam Am when United acquired some of Pan Am's routes upon Pan Am's bankruptcy. He began working for United as a first officer, a co-pilot position. Four months after completing United's first officer training, Bailey turned 60 years old. Under a Federal Aviation Administration regulation in effect at the time, no pilot or co-pilot could be 60 or older but second officers did not face that age limitation. Bailey sought to bid to a second officer, a flight engineer position. He entered United's training for second officers and received low evaluations. When he failed his simulator check ride, United convened a Board of Review to determine what action to take. On May 4, 1993, the Board of Review decided to terminate Bailey. On the same date, the new pilot supervisor called Bailey and, according to Bailey's deposition testimony, told him to report to the chief pilot's office to be terminated. He further testified that he contacted a number of people and asked them to contact the chief pilot on his behalf and that it was his understanding that the chief pilot was the final determiner of his fate. The new pilot supervisor stated in an affidavit that when he called Bailey on May 4, 1993, he told Bailey to report to the chief pilot where he would be removed from United's payroll and given the option to resign. Bailey met with the chief pilot on May 6, 1993, and the chief pilot gave him the option to resign or be terminated. Bailey filed a charge of age discrimination with the EEOC on March 2, 1994. He was within the 300–day filing period if the period began to run on May 6, but was untimely if the period began to run on May 4.

The district court granted United summary judgment, holding that the new pilot supervisor communicated the termination decision to Bailey on May 4, but the Third Circuit reversed, holding that there was a disputed issue of fact as to when Bailey received "unequivocal notice" of his termination.

3. Should the charge filing period begin to run from the date the plaintiff has notice of the adverse action or from the date that the plaintiff has notice that the adverse action may have resulted from discrimination? *See, e.g. Beamon v. Marshall & Ilsley Trust Co.*, 411 F.3d 854 (7th Cir. 2005) (holding that filing period may be tolled when "despite all due diligence, a plaintiff cannot obtain the information necessary to realize that he may possibly have a claim," but finding that in the case before it, the plaintiff was not entitled to toll the limitations period).

4. CONTINUING VIOLATIONS VERSUS CONTINUING EFFECTS OF PAST VIOLATIONS

UNITED AIR LINES, INC. v. EVANS

Supreme Court of the United States, 1977
431 U.S. 553, 97 S.Ct. 1885, 52 L.Ed.2d 571

JUSTICE STEVENS delivered the opinion of the Court.

Respondent was employed by United Air Lines as a flight attendant from November 1966 to February 1968. She was rehired in February 1972. Assuming, as she alleges, that her separation from employment in 1968 violated Title VII of the Civil Rights Act of 1964, the question now presented is whether the employer is committing a second violation of Title VII by refusing to credit her with seniority for any period prior to February 1972.

* * *

During respondent's initial period of employment, United maintained a policy of refusing to allow its female flight attendants to be married When she married in 1968, she was therefore forced to resign. Although it was subsequently decided that such a resignation violated Title VII, *Sprogis v. United Air Lines*, 444 F.2d 1194 (CA7 1971), respondent was not a party to that case and did not initiate any proceedings of her own in 1968 by filing a charge with the EEOC within 90 days of her separation. A claim based on that discriminatory act is therefore barred.

In November 1968, United entered into a new collective-bargaining agreement which ended the pre-existing "no marriage" rule and provided for the reinstatement of certain flight attendants who had been terminated pursuant to that rule. Respondent was not covered by that agreement. On several occasions she unsuccessfully sought reinstatement; on February 16, 1972, she was hired as a new employee. Although her personnel file carried the same number as it did in 1968, for seniority purposes she has been treated as though she had no prior service with United. * * *

Informal requests to credit her with pre–1972 seniority having been denied, respondent commenced this action. The District Court dismissed the complaint, holding that the failure to file a charge within 90 days of her separation in 1968 caused respondent's claim to be time barred and foreclosed any relief under Title VII.

A divided panel of the Court of Appeals initially affirmed; then, after our decision in *Franks v. Bowman Transportation Co.*, 424 U.S. 747, 96 S.Ct. 1251, 47 L.Ed.2d 444, the panel granted respondent's petition for rehearing and unanimously reversed. We granted certiorari, and now hold that the complaint was properly dismissed.

Respondent recognizes that it is now too late to obtain relief based on an unlawful employment practice which occurred in 1968. She contends, however, that United is guilty of a present, continuing violation of Title VII and therefore that her claim is timely. She advances two reasons for holding that United's seniority system illegally discriminates against her: First, she is treated less favorably than males who were hired after her termination in 1968 and prior to her re-employment in 1972; second, the seniority system gives present effect to the past illegal act and therefore perpetuates the consequences of forbidden discrimination. Neither argument persuades us that United is presently violating the statute.

It is true that some male employees with less total service than respondent have more seniority than she. But this disparity is not a consequence of their sex, or of her sex. For females hired between 1968 and 1972 also acquired the same preference over respondent as males hired during that period. Moreover, both male and female employees who had service prior to February 1968, who resigned or were terminated for a nondiscriminatory reason (or for an unchallenged discriminatory reason), and who were later re-employed, also were treated as new employees receiving no seniority credit for their prior service. Nothing alleged in the complaint indicates that United's seniority system treats existing female employees differently from existing male employees, or that the failure to credit prior service differentiates in any way between prior service by males and prior service by females. Respondent has failed to allege that United's seniority system differentiates between similarly situated males and females on the basis of sex.

Respondent is correct in pointing out that the seniority system gives present effect to a past act of discrimination. But United was entitled to treat that past act as lawful after respondent failed to file a charge of discrimination within the 90 days then allowed by § 706(d). A discriminatory act which is not made the basis for a timely charge is the legal equivalent of a discriminatory act which occurred before the statute was passed. It may constitute relevant background evidence in a proceeding in which the status of a current practice is at issue, but separately considered, it is merely an unfortunate event in history which has no present legal consequences.

Respondent emphasizes the fact that she has alleged a *continuing* violation. United's seniority system does indeed have a continuing impact on her pay and fringe benefits. But the emphasis should not be placed on mere continuity; the critical question is whether any present *violation* exists. She has not alleged that the system discriminates against former female employees or that it treats former employees who were discharged for a discriminatory reason any differently from former employees who resigned or were discharged for a non-discriminatory reason. In short, the system is neutral in its operation.

Our decision in *Franks v. Bowman Transportation Co.*, *supra*, does not control this case. In Franks we held that retroactive seniority was an appropriate remedy to be awarded under § 706(g) of Title VII, 42 U.S.C. § 2000e–5(g) an illegal discriminatory act or practice had been proved. When that case reached this Court, the issues relating to the timeliness of the charge and the violation of Title VII had already been decided; we dealt only with a question of remedy. In contrast, in the case now before us we do not reach any remedy issue because respondent did not file a timely charge based on her 1968 separation and she has not alleged facts establishing a violation since she was rehired in 1972.

* * *

The judgment of the Court of Appeals is reversed.

[The dissenting opinion of JUSTICE MARSHALL, joined by JUSTICE BRENNAN, is omitted.]

NATIONAL RAILROAD PASSENGER CORP. v. MORGAN

Supreme Court of the United States, 2002
536 U.S. 101, 122 S.Ct. 2061, 153 L.Ed.2d 106

JUSTICE THOMAS delivered the opinion of the Court.

Respondent Abner Morgan, Jr., sued petitioner National Railroad Passenger Corporation (Amtrak) under Title VII of the Civil Rights Act of 1964, alleging that he had been subjected to discrete discriminatory and retaliatory acts and had experienced a racially hostile work environment throughout his employment. Section 2000e–5(e)(1) requires that a Title VII plaintiff file a charge with the Equal Employment Opportunity Commission (EEOC) either 180 or 300 days "after the alleged unlawful employment practice occurred." We consider whether, and under what circumstances, a Title VII plaintiff may file suit on events that fall outside this statutory time period.

The United States Court of Appeals for the Ninth Circuit held that a plaintiff may sue on claims that would ordinarily be time barred so long as they either are "sufficiently related" to incidents that fall within the statutory period or are part of a systematic policy or practice of discrimination that took place, at least in part, within the limitations period. We reverse in part and affirm in part. We hold that the statute precludes recovery for discrete acts of discrimination or retaliation that occur outside the statutory time period. We also hold that consideration of the entire scope of a hostile work environment claim, including behavior alleged outside the statutory time period, is permissible for the purposes of assessing liability, so long as an act contributing to that hostile environment takes place within the statutory time period. The application of equitable doctrines, however, may either limit or toll the time period within which an employee must file a charge.

I

On February 27, 1995, Abner J. Morgan, Jr., a black male, filed a charge of discrimination and retaliation against Amtrak with the EEOC and cross-filed with the California Department of Fair Employment and Housing. Morgan alleged that during the time period that he worked for Amtrak he was "consistently harassed and disciplined more harshly than other employees on account of his race." The EEOC issued a "Notice of Right to Sue" on July 3, 1996, and Morgan filed this lawsuit on October 2, 1996. While some of the allegedly discriminatory acts about which Morgan complained occurred within 300 days of the time that he filed his charge with the EEOC, many took place prior to that time period. Amtrak filed a motion, arguing, among other things, that it was entitled to summary judgment on all incidents that occurred more than 300 days before the filing of Morgan's EEOC charge. The District Court granted summary judgment in part to Amtrak, holding that the company could not be liable for conduct occurring before May 3, 1994, because that conduct fell outside of the 300–day filing period. * * *

Morgan appealed. The United States Court of Appeals for the Ninth Circuit reversed, relying on its previous articulation of the continuing violation doctrine, which "allows courts to consider conduct that would ordinarily be time barred 'as long as the untimely incidents represent an ongoing unlawful employment practice.' " * * *

In the Ninth Circuit's view, a plaintiff can establish a continuing violation that allows recovery for claims filed outside of the statutory period in one of two ways. First, a plaintiff may show "a series of related acts one or more of which are within the limitations period. Such a "serial violation is established if the evidence indicates that the alleged acts of discrimination occurring prior to the limitations period are sufficiently related to those occurring within the limitations period." The alleged incidents, however, "cannot be isolated, sporadic, or discrete." Second, a plaintiff may establish a continuing violation if he shows "a systematic policy or practice of discrimination that operated, in part, within the limitations period—a systemic violation."

To survive summary judgment under this test, Morgan had to "raise a genuine issue of disputed fact as to (1) the existence of a continuing violation—be it serial or systemic," and (2) the continuation of the violation into the limitations period. Because Morgan alleged three types of Title VII claims, namely, discrimination, hostile environment, and retaliation, the Court of Appeals considered the allegations with respect to each category of claim separately and found that the prelimitations conduct was sufficiently related to the postlimitations conduct to invoke the continuing violation doctrine for all three. Therefore, "[i]n light of the relatedness of the incidents, [the Court of Appeals found] that Morgan ha[d] sufficiently presented a genuine issue of disputed fact as to whether a continuing violation existed." Because the District Court should have allowed events occurring in the prelimitations period to be "presented to the jury not merely as background information, but also for purposes of liability," the Court of Appeals reversed and remanded for a new trial.

We granted certiorari, and now reverse in part and affirm in part.

II

The Courts of Appeals have taken various approaches to the question whether acts that fall outside of the statutory time period for filing charges set forth in 42 U.S.C. § 2000e–5(e) are actionable under Title VII. While the lower courts have offered reasonable, albeit divergent, solutions, none are compelled by the text of the statute. In the context of a request to alter the timely filing requirements of Title VII, this Court has stated that "strict adherence to the procedural requirements specified by the legislature is the best guarantee of evenhanded administration of the law." *Mohasco Corp. v. Silver,* 447 U.S. 807, 826, 100 S.Ct. 2486, 65 L.Ed.2d 532 (1980). * * *

Title 42 U.S.C. § 2000e–5(e)(1) is a charge filing provision that "specifies with precision" the prerequisites that a plaintiff must satisfy before filing suit. * * *

For our purposes, the critical sentence of the charge filing provision is: "A charge under this section *shall be filed* within one hundred and eighty days *after the alleged unlawful employment practice occurred.*" § 2000e–5(e)(1). The operative terms are "shall," "after ... occurred," and "unlawful employment practice." "[S]hall" makes the act of filing a charge within the specified time period mandatory. ("[T]he mandatory 'shall,' ... normally creates an obligation impervious to judicial discretion"). "[O]ccurred" means that the practice took place or happened in the past. The requirement, therefore, that the charge be filed "after" the practice "occurred" tells us that a litigant has up to 180 or 300 days *after* the unlawful practice happened to file a charge with the EEOC.

The critical questions, then, are: What constitutes an "unlawful employment practice" and when has that practice "occurred"? Our task is to answer these questions for both discrete discriminatory acts and hostile work environment claims. The answer varies with the practice.

A

We take the easier question first. A discrete retaliatory or discriminatory act "occurred" on the day that it "happened." A party, therefore, must file a charge within either 180 or 300 days of the date of the act or lose the ability to recover for it.

Morgan argues that the statute does not require the filing of a charge within 180 or 300 days of each discrete act, but that the language requires the filing of a charge within the specified number of days after an "unlawful employment *practice*." "Practice," Morgan contends, connotes an ongoing violation that can endure or recur over a period of time. In Morgan's view, the term "practice" therefore provides a statutory basis for the Ninth Circuit's continuing violation doctrine. This argument is unavailing, however, given that 42 U.S.C. § 2000e–2 explains in great detail the sorts of actions that qualify as "[u]nlawful employment practices" and includes among such practices numerous discrete acts. See, *e.g.,* § 2000e–2(a) ("It shall be an unlawful employment practice for an employer—(1) to fail or refuse to hire or to discharge any individual, or otherwise to discriminate against any individual with respect to his compensation, terms, conditions, or privileges of employment, because of such individual's race, color, religion, sex, or national origin ...."). There is simply no indication that the term "practice" converts related discrete acts into a single unlawful practice for the purposes of timely filing.

* * *

[The Court discussed its prior decisions in *United Air Lines v. Evans* and *Delaware State College v. Ricks*.]

We derive several principles from these cases. First, discrete discriminatory acts are not actionable if time barred, even when they are related to acts alleged in timely filed charges. Each discrete discriminatory act starts a new clock for filing charges alleging that act. The charge, therefore, must be filed within the 180– or 300–day time period after the discrete discriminatory act occurred. The existence of past acts and the employee's prior knowledge of their occurrence, however, does not bar employees from filing charges about related discrete acts so long as the acts are independently discriminatory and charges addressing those acts are themselves timely filed. Nor does the statute bar an employee from using the prior acts as background evidence in support of a timely claim.

* * *

The Court of Appeals applied the continuing violations doctrine to what it termed "serial violations," holding that so long as one act falls within the charge filing period, discriminatory and retaliatory acts that are plausibly or sufficiently related to that act may also be considered for the purposes of liability. With respect to this holding, therefore, we reverse.

Discrete acts such as termination, failure to promote, denial of transfer, or refusal to hire are easy to identify. Each incident of discrimination and each retaliatory adverse employment decision constitutes a separate actionable "unlawful employment practice." Morgan can only file a charge to cover discrete acts that "occurred" within the appropriate time period. While Morgan alleged that he suffered from numerous discriminatory and retaliatory acts from the date that he was hired through March 3, 1995, the date that he was fired, only incidents that took place within the timely filing period are actionable. Because Morgan first filed his charge with an appropriate state agency, only those acts that occurred 300 days before February 27, 1995, the day that Morgan filed his charge, are actionable. During that time period, Morgan contends that he was wrongfully suspended and charged with a violation of Amtrak's "Rule L" for insubordination while failing to complete work assigned to him, denied training, and falsely accused of threatening a manager. All prior discrete discriminatory acts are untimely filed and no longer actionable.

B

Hostile environment claims are different in kind from discrete acts. Their very nature involves repeated conduct. * * *

* * *

In determining whether an actionable hostile work environment claim exists, we look to "all the circumstances," including "the frequency of the discriminatory conduct; its severity; whether it is physically threatening or humiliating, or a mere offensive utterance; and whether it unreasonably interferes with an employee's work performance." To assess whether a court may, for the purposes of determining liability, review all such conduct, including those acts that occur outside the filing period, we again look to the statute. It provides that a charge must be filed within 180 or 300 days "after the alleged unlawful employment practice occurred." A hostile work environment claim is composed of a series of separate acts that collectively constitute one "unlawful employment practice." The timely filing provision only requires that a Title VII plaintiff file a charge within a certain number of days after the unlawful practice happened. It does not matter, for purposes of the statute, that some of the component acts of the hostile work environment fall outside the statutory time period. Provided that an act contributing to the claim occurs within the filing period, the entire time period of the hostile environment may be considered by a court for the purposes of determining liability.

That act need not, however, be the last act. As long as the employer has engaged in enough activity to make out an actionable hostile environment claim, an unlawful employment practice has "occurred," even if it is still occurring. Subsequent events, however, may still be part of the one hostile work environment claim and a charge may be filed at a later date and still encompass the whole.

It is precisely because the entire hostile work environment encompasses a single unlawful employment practice that we do not hold, as have some of the Circuits, that the plaintiff may not base a suit on individual acts that occurred outside the statute of limitations unless it would have been unreasonable to expect the plaintiff to sue before the statute ran on such conduct. The statute does not separate individual acts that are part of the hostile environment claim from the whole for the purposes of timely filing and liability. And the statute does not contain a requirement that the employee file a charge prior to 180 or 300 days "after" the single unlawful practice "occurred." Given, therefore, that the incidents constituting a hostile work environment are part of one unlawful employment practice, the employer may be liable for all acts that are part of this single claim. In order for the charge to be timely, the employee need only file a charge within 180 or 300 days of any act that is part of the hostile work environment.

The following scenarios illustrate our point: (1) Acts on days 1–400 create a hostile work environment. The employee files the charge on day 401. Can the employee recover for that part of the hostile work environment that occurred in the first 100 days? (2) Acts contribute to a hostile environment on days 1–100 and on day 401, but there are no acts between days 101–400. Can the act occurring on day 401 pull the other acts in for the purposes of liability? In truth, all other things being equal, there is little difference between the two scenarios as a hostile environment constitutes one "unlawful employment practice" and it does not matter whether nothing occurred within the intervening 301 days so long as each act is part of the whole. Nor, if sufficient activity occurred by day 100 to make out a claim, does it matter that the employee knows on that day that an actionable claim happened; on day 401 all incidents are still part of the same claim. On the other hand, if an act on day 401 had no relation to the acts between days 1–100, or for some other reason, such as certain intervening action by the employer, was no longer part of the same hostile environment claim, then the employee cannot recover for the previous acts, at least not by reference to the day 401 act.

Our conclusion with respect to the incidents that may be considered for the purposes of liability is reinforced by the fact that the statute in no way bars a plaintiff from recovering damages for that portion of the hostile environment that falls outside the period for filing a timely charge. Morgan correctly notes that the timeliness requirement does not dictate the amount of recoverable damages. It is but one in a series of provisions requiring that the parties take action within specified time periods, none of which function as specific limitations on damages.

Explicit limitations on damages are found elsewhere in the statute. Section 1981a(b)(3), for example, details specific limitations on compensatory and punitive damages. Likewise, § 2000e–5(g)(1) allows for recovery of backpay liability for up to two years prior to the filing of the charge. If Congress intended to limit liability to conduct occurring in the period within which the party must file the charge, it seems unlikely that Congress would have allowed recovery for two years of backpay. And the fact that Congress expressly limited the amount of recoverable damages elsewhere to a particular time period indicates that the timely filing provision was not meant to serve as a specific limitation either on damages or the conduct that may be considered for the purposes of one actionable hostile work environment claim.

It also makes little sense to limit the assessment of liability in a hostile work environment claim to the conduct that falls within the 180– or 300–day period given that this time period varies based on whether the violation occurs in a State or political subdivision that has an agency with authority to grant or seek relief. It is important to remember that the statute requires that a Title VII plaintiff must wait 60 days after proceedings have commenced under state or local law to file a charge with the EEOC, unless such proceedings have earlier terminated. In such circumstances, however, the charge must still be filed within 300 days of the occurrence. The extended time period for parties who first file such charges in a State or locality ensures that employees are neither time barred from later filing their charges with the EEOC nor dissuaded from first filing with a state agency. ("The history identifies only one reason for treating workers in deferral States differently from workers in other States: to give state agencies an opportunity to redress the evil at which the federal legislation was aimed, and to avoid federal intervention unless its need was demonstrated"). Surely, therefore, we cannot import such a limiting principle into the provision where its effect would be to make the reviewable time period for liability dependent upon whether an employee lives in a State that has its own remedial scheme.

Simply put, § 2000e–5(e)(1) is a provision specifying when a charge is timely filed and only has the consequence of limiting liability because filing a timely charge is a prerequisite to having an actionable claim. A court's task is to determine whether the acts about which an employee complains are part of the same actionable hostile work environment practice, and if so, whether any act falls within the statutory time period.

With respect to Morgan's hostile environment claim, the Court of Appeals concluded that "the pre- and post-limitations period incidents involve[d] the same type of employment actions, occurred relatively frequently, and were perpetrated by the same managers." To support his claims of a hostile environment, Morgan presented evidence from a number of other employees that managers made racial jokes, performed racially derogatory acts, made negative comments regarding the capacity of blacks to be supervisors, and used various racial epithets. Although many of the acts upon which his claim depends occurred outside the 300 day filing period, we cannot say that they are not part of the same actionable hostile environment claim. On this point, we affirm.

* * *

[The opinion of JUSTICE O'CONOOR concurring in part and dissenting in part, joined by CHIEF JUSTICE REHNQUIST and joined in part by JUSTICES SCALIA, KENNEDY and BREYER, is omitted.]

NOTES

1. On what basis did the Ninth Circuit find a continuing violation? What portion of the Ninth Circuit's analysis did the Supreme Court reverse and what portion did it affirm? What does this mean for continuing violation analysis generally?

2. Has the Court set forth an analysis that applies only to hostile environment harassment claims? If so, what distinguishes such claims from all others?

3. Consider claims of constructive discharge. A constructive discharge arises where working conditions become so intolerable that a reasonable employee would feel compelled to quit. When should the filing period begin to run in a constructive discharge case: (1) on the date of the last act of discrimination that rendered working conditions so intolerable that a reasonable person would resign, (2) on the date the employee gives notice of resignation, or (3) on the employee's last day of work? *See Flaherty v. Metromail Corp.*, 235 F.3d 133 (2d Cir. 2000); *Draper v. Coeur Rochester, Inc.*, 147 F.3d 1104 (9th Cir. 1998).

5. THE LEDBETTER FAIR PAY ACT AND THE CONTINUING DIALOGUE BETWEEN THE COURT AND CONGRESS

In *Lorance v. AT&T Technologies, Inc.*, 490 U.S. 900, 109 S.Ct. 2261, 104 L.Ed.2d 961 (1989), AT&T's collective bargaining agreement had provided that employees accrued seniority for all time worked at the plant and retained that seniority when promoted to a new position. In 1979, AT&T and its union amended the collective bargaining agreement to provide that testers' seniority would be measured by the time worked as a tester. Plaintiffs were women promoted to tester between 1978 and 1980. In 1982, they were demoted because of an economic downturn. Had their seniority continued to be measured by the time worked in the plant, they would not have been demoted.

Plaintiffs alleged that the 1979 change in seniority computation was intended to discriminate against women who had recently been promoted to the previously male-dominated tester position. They filed their charges within 300 days of their demotions, but the Court held that their charges were time-barred. Relying on *United Air Lines v. Evans* and *Delaware State College v. Ricks*, the Court held that the alleged discriminatory act was the 1979 amendment to the seniority system and the filing period began to run at that time. The demotions were simply the present effects of a prior allegedly discriminatory act.

Congress reacted to *Lorance* in the Civil Rights Act of 1991. The act amended Title VII to provide:

> [A]n unlawful employment practice occurs, with respect to a seniority system that has been adopted for an intentionally discriminatory purpose in violation of this subchapter (whether or not that discriminatory purpose is apparent on the face of the seniority system), when the seniority system is adopted, when an individual becomes subject to the seniority system, or when a person aggrieved is injured by the application of the seniority system or provision of the system.

In *Ledbetter v. Goodyear Tire & Rubber Co.*, 550 U.S. 618, 127 S.Ct. 2162, 167 L.Ed.2d 982 (2007), the plaintiff, Lilly Ledbetter, had been a salaried employee at Goodyear's Gadsen, Alabama plant from 1979–1998. Salaried employees' pay increases were based on their performance evaluations. In March 1998, Ledbetter filed a charge with the EEOC claiming that her evaluations over the years were tainted by sex discrimination causing her salary to be considerably lower than her male colleagues. A jury agreed and returned a verdict for Ledbetter, but the Supreme Court held that Ledbetter's EEOC filing was untimely. According to the Court, each allegedly discriminatory performance evaluation and pay raise was a separate discriminatory act requiring that a charge be filed within 180 days of each act. Consequently, Ledbetter's claim could only relate to salary decisions made 180 days prior to March 1998 and there was no evidence that those decisions were discriminatory.

The Court distinguished ***Bazemore v. Friday***, 478 U.S. 385, 106 S.Ct. 3000, 92 L.Ed.2d 315 (1986). In *Bazemore*, the employer had deliberately segregated its employees by race prior to the effective date of Title VII, paying African–American employees less than whites. After Title VII took effect, the employer merged its classifications but continued to pay African–American employees less than whites. The *Bazemore* Court regarded each paycheck issued as a new violation which triggered a new charge-filing period. The *Ledbetter* Court read *Basemore* as being premised on each check continuing to be based on a facially discriminatory pay structure. Thus, with each new pay check, the employer engaged in a new act of discrimination. In contrast, the Court regarded each performance appraisal and resulting salary determination to be a separate act which, if discriminatory, merely had continuing effects. They did not establish a continuing violation.

Congress reacted by enacting the Lilly Ledbetter Fair Pay Act of 2009, Public Law No. 111–2, which amends Title VII, the ADA and the ADEA to provide that a discriminatory practice occurs "when a discriminatory compensation decision or other practice is adopted, when an individual becomes subject to a discriminatory compensation decision or other practice, or when an individual is affected by application of a discriminatory decision or other practice, including each time wages, benefits or other compensation is paid, resulting in whole or in part from such a decision or other practice."

NOEL v. THE BOEING CO.

United States Court of Appeals, Third Circuit, 2010
622 F.3d 266

FUENTES, CIRCUIT JUDGE

* * *

I.

A. Background

Noel is a black Haitian national, who began working for Boeing in 1990 as a sheet metal assembler at its Ridley Park, Pennsylvania facility. Noel was hired at Labor Grade 5 and repaired Chinook 47 aircraft. The terms of

Noel's employment were governed by a collective bargaining agreement ("CBA") between Boeing and the International Union of United Automobile Aerospace and Agricultural Implement Workers of America Local 1069, as well as internal Boeing policies.

Boeing employees were occasionally offered an opportunity to work at offsite locations. Because employees working offsite received greater pay, per diems and additional training, offsite positions were coveted and individuals volunteered for these assignments. Any promotions and corresponding raises were limited to the duration of the offsite assignment. According to the CBA that governed Noel's employment, seniority was not the only factor that Boeing considered when assigning workers offsite. Rather, skill and ability were the determining factors, and seniority was only considered when those factors were equal.

Noel took his first offsite assignment in 1991 at a Boeing facility in Shreveport, Louisiana; this lasted approximately six months. Although he sought an offsite assignment in May 2002, Noel was not assigned offsite again until November 2002, when he was designated an aircraft mechanic to work on modifications to the V–22 Osprey at the Bell Helicopter facility in Amarillo, Texas. That assignment resulted in Noel's labor grade rising from 7 to 8; he also received a $57 per diem. After two weeks of working in Amarillo, Noel's salary was increased from $26.11 per hour to $28.75 per hour.

Around the same time, Chris Carlin and Gary Newman, both white employees, were also assigned to Amarillo from the Ridley Park facility. They too were reclassified from Labor Grade 7 aircraft assemblers to offsite mechanics at Labor Grade 8. After working in Amarillo for seven months, Carlin and Newman were promoted to Offsite Mechanic General, Labor Grade 11, while Noel remained at the lower paying Grade 8. In September 2003, Noel complained about these promotions to a union representative and a Boeing labor relations representative. His complaints went unanswered. Noel filed a Title VII suit against Boeing and one of its managers alleging discrimination based on race and national origin. On March 25, 2005, Noel filed a formal grievance with the Equal Employment Opportunity Commission ("EEOC").

On June 20, 2006, Noel filed a four-count Title VII complaint against Boeing. * * * Relevant to this appeal, Noel complained: (1) that Boeing did not send him offsite to Amarillo in May 2002 when white, non-Haitian employees who held the same job as Noel but were junior to him were sent offsite; and (2) in 2003, while offsite at Amarillo, he was promoted to Labor Grade 8 while his junior, white, U.S.-born co-workers were promoted to Labor Grade 11.

B. The District Court's Ruling

Before trial, Boeing filed a motion for summary judgment. The District Court granted that motion as it related to Noel's claim that Boeing violated Title VII when it failed to send him offsite to Amarillo in May

2002 and when he was not promoted to offsite mechanic Labor Grade 11 in 2003, holding that this claim was time-barred since Noel did not file a charge of discrimination with the EEOC until March 2005, well outside the 300–day statutory time period. * * *

* * *

II.

The only aspect of the District Court's ruling that Noel challenges is its determination that he failed to administratively preserve his claim that, in 2003, Defendant failed to promote him to Offsite Mechanic General Labor Grade 11 in violation of Title VII. According to Noel, because of this discriminatory employment action, he received less pay than his white co-workers throughout his time at the Amarillo plant. Noel contends that the Lilly Ledbetter Fair Pay Act of 2009 ("FPA") makes clear that "in pay discrimination matters an unlawful employment practice occurs each time an individual is affected by application of a discriminatory compensation decision." Noel argues that the District Court erred as a matter of law when it granted summary judgment in Defendant's favor since Boeing's failure to promote him resulted in lower pay, and, therefore, each pay-check he received started the administrative clock anew.

* * * Before filing a claim in federal court, a Title VII plaintiff in Pennsylvania must file a charge of discrimination with the EEOC within 300 days of the alleged unlawful employment practice. * * *

Here, the adverse employment actions Noel complained of occurred between July and September 2003. Because Noel did not file his EEOC charge until March 25, 2005, well after the 300–day time period expired, the District Court ruled that any claims of discrimination stemming from the 2003 employment decisions were barred as a matter of law. Nevertheless, Noel argues that the FPA revives his claim since each paycheck he received during the requisite time period started the administrative clock ticking anew.

[The court recited the history of the FPA outlined in the text above]

Noel contends that the FPA revives his otherwise administratively time-barred claims because the "Court's assertion that [his] filing of his EEOC charge ... is outside of the filing period ... is based on the erroneous conclusion that the 300 day period started upon the act of failing to grant him a promotion/raise in Amarillo ... in the spring of 2003." According to Noel, "Boeing's discrimination in refusing to give [him] a raise to Labor Grade 11 while giving this grade to similarly situated white coworkers ... was perpetuated each time the resulting lower compensation was thereafter paid to" him, bringing his claim squarely within the FPA.

* * *

[W]e address an issue of first impression in this circuit: whether, under the FPA, a failure-to-promote claim constitutes "discrimination in compensation." Only one other circuit has addressed this issue.

The D.C. Circuit recently held that the FPA's terms do not cover failure-to-promote grievances. *See Schuler v. PricewaterhouseCoopers, LLP,* 595 F. 3d 370, 375 (D.C.Cir. 2010). In *Schuler,* the plaintiff brought an Age Discrimination in Employment Act ("ADEA") complaint against his employer for failure to promote him to partner. The district court dismissed it as administratively barred. Like Noel, Schuler on appeal argued that the FPA rendered his failure-to-promote claims timely. The D.C. Circuit rejected this argument, noting first that "[t]here can be no dispute that in order to benefit from the [FPA, plaintiff] must bring a claim involving 'discrimination in compensation' and point to a 'discriminatory compensation decision or other practice.' " The court next noted that in employment law, " 'discrimination in compensation' means paying different wages or providing different benefits to similarly situated employees, not promoting one employee but not another to a more remunerative position." In turn, the D.C. Circuit concluded that in "context, therefore, we do not understand 'compensation decision or other practice' to refer to the decision to promote one employee but not another to a more remunerative position."

We note, as did the D.C. Circuit, that the FPA was enacted with the specific intent to overrule the Supreme Court's *Ledbetter* decision, and the issue in that case was confined to pay discrimination. The FPA's focus on compensation decisions is evidenced by the "findings" section of the statute, which states:

The Supreme Court['s decision in *Ledbetter*] significantly impairs statutory protections against discrimination in compensation that Congress established and that have been bedrock principles of American law for decades. The *Ledbetter* decision undermines those statutory protections by unduly restricting the time period in which victims of discrimination can challenge and recover for discriminatory compensation decisions or other practices, contrary to the intent of Congress.... The limitation imposed by the Court on the filing of discriminatory compensation claims ignores the reality of wage discrimination....

In our view, Congress' motivation for enacting the FPA was to overturn the perceived harshness of *Ledbetter* and to provide greater protection against wage discrimination but not other types of employment discrimination. This intention is evidenced by Congress' use of the term "compensation," repeated five times throughout the Act, indicating that the driving force behind the FPA was remedying wage discrimination.[6]

---

6. This interpretation does not render the phrase "or other practice" superfluous. These words merely indicate that in order to fall within the ambit of the FPA, the discriminatory "other practice," while not actually setting a disparate remuneration level, must relate to pay disparity. *See Schuler,* 595 F. 3d at 375 (noting that "giving an employee a poor performance evaluation based upon her sex ... and then using the [unlawful] evaluation to determine her rate of pay" constitutes "an other practice" within the meaning of the FPA).

On the basis of a plain and natural reading, we conclude that the FPA does not apply to failure-to-promote claims. As noted above, the FPA states that "[f]or purposes of this section, an unlawful employment practice occurs, with respect to discrimination in compensation in violation of this subchapter, when a discriminatory compensation decision or other practice is adopted." This first clause of § 2000e–5(e)(3)(A) limits the scope of the Lilly Ledbetter Amendment by defining "unlawful employment practice" vis-a-vis "discrimination in compensation" violations. It then further confines its applicability to situations in which "a discriminatory compensation decision or other practice is adopted." Thus, the plain language of the FPA covers compensation decisions and not other discrete employment decisions.

* * *

Like the D.C. Circuit, we also note that our decision is consistent with Congress' intent when it passed the FPA. In her dissenting opinion in *Ledbetter,* Justice Ginsburg distinguished between compensation decisions and other employment decisions, noting that "[p]ay disparities are . . . significantly different from adverse actions such as termination, failure to promote, . . . or refusal to hire, all involving fully communicated discrete acts, easy to identify as discriminatory." Unlike the discrete employment acts identified by Justice Ginsburg, which are readily apparent since an individual will know when (s)he has been hired, fired, or promoted, compensation decisions are often cloaked in secrecy, and an employee may not know how much his or her co-workers earn. ("A worker knows immediately if she is denied a promotion. . . . And promotions . . . are generally public events, known to co-workers. When an employer makes a decision of such open and definitive character, an employee can immediately seek out an explanation and evaluate it for pretext. Compensation disparities, in contrast, are often hidden from sight."). Thus, the FPA was enacted to address a particular type of employment discrimination, compensation decisions, which are often concealed and not discovered until long after the 180– or 300–day administrative period expires. There is no indication, however, that Congress intended the FPA to apply to discrete employment decisions, like promotion decisions, and Noel cites no authority for that proposition.

* * *

In sum, because Noel filed his failure-to-promote discrimination charge with the EEOC outside of the 300–day period, and because a failure-to-promote claim is not a discrimination-in-compensation charge within the meaning of the FPA, we affirm the District Court's Order granting Boeing summary judgment.

* * *

NOTES

1. In reality how is a promotion denial different from a low performance evaluation? Noel alleged that two white employees were promoted while he was not. In other words, his claim arose out of the denial of a competitive promotion. What if an employer's policy is to promote employees to the next higher grade whenever the employee demonstrates the ability to perform at that grade level and there is sufficient work to be done at that grade level to occupy the employee? Would the denial of such a career ladder promotion be subject to the Ledbetter Fair Pay Act? *See Lipscomb v. Mabus,* 699 F.Supp.2d 171 (D.D.C. 2010). Should it apply to a demotion? *See Tryals v. Altairstrickland, LP,* 2010 WL 743917 (S.D.Tex. 2010). Should it apply to a position elimination followed by a transfer to lower paying position? *See Almond v. United School District No. 501,* 749 F.Supp.2d 1196 (D.Kan. 2010). Should it apply to a tenure denial in which a grant of tenure included a pay increase? *See Gentry v. Jackson State Univ.,* 610 F.Supp.2d 564 (S.D.Miss. 2009).

2. In *A T & T Corp. v. Hulteen,* 556 U.S. 701, 129 S.Ct. 1962, 173 L.Ed.2d 898 (2009), A T & T had, prior to the effective date of the Pregnancy Discrimination Act of 1979, not given employees on pregnancy leave the same credit toward pension accrual as it gave employees on other medical leaves of absence. After the PDA, A T & T ceased the disparate treatment but did not make any retroactive adjustments. As a result, female employees who took pregnancy leave before 1978 received lower pensions than they would have received had their leaves been treated the same as other medical leaves of absence. The Supreme Court held that the Ledbetter Fair Pay Act did not apply because the pre-PDA distinctions were lawful and, therefore, the plaintiffs were not affected by application of a discriminatory compensation decision or other practice.

3. Section 6 of the Ledbetter Act provides that the act applies to all claims pending on May 28, 2007 or later, a rather unusual retroactive application of a new law. *See Groesch v. City of Springfield,* 635 F.3d 1020 (7th Cir. 2011).

6. DISPARATE IMPACT CLAIMS

LEWIS v. CITY OF CHICAGO

Supreme Court of the United States, 2010
560 U.S. ___, 130 S.Ct. 2191, 176 L.Ed.2d 967

JUSTICE SCALIA delivered the opinion of the Court.

* * *

I

In July 1995, the City of Chicago administered a written examination to over 26,000 applicants seeking to serve in the Chicago Fire Department. After scoring the examinations, the City reported the results. It announced in a January 26, 1996, press release that it would begin drawing randomly from the top tier of scorers, *i.e.,* those who scored 89 or above (out of 100), whom the City called "well qualified." Those drawn from this group would proceed to the next phase—a physical-abilities test, background check, medical examination, and drug test—and if they cleared those hurdles would be hired as candidate firefighters. Those who scored below 65, on the other hand, learned by letters sent the same day that they had failed the test. Each was told he had not achieved a passing score, would no longer be considered for a firefighter position, and would not be contacted again about the examination.

The applicants in-between-those who scored between 65 and 88, whom the City called "qualified" were notified that they had passed the examination but that, based on the City's projected hiring needs and the number of "well-qualified" applicants, it was not likely they would be called for further processing. The individual notices added, however, that because it was not possible to predict how many applicants would be hired in the next few years, each "qualified" applicant's name would be kept on the eligibility list maintained by the Department of Personnel for as long as that list was used. Eleven days later, the City officially adopted an "Eligible List" reflecting the breakdown described above.

On May 16, 1996, the City selected its first class of applicants to advance to the next stage. It selected a second on October 1, 1996, and repeated the process nine more times over the next six years. As it had announced, in each round the City drew randomly from among those who scored in the "well-qualified" range on the 1995 test. In the last round it exhausted that pool, so it filled the remaining slots with "qualified" candidates instead.

On March 31, 1997, Crawford M. Smith, an African–American applicant who scored in the "qualified" range and had not been hired as a candidate firefighter, filed a charge of discrimination with the EEOC. Five others followed suit, and on July 28, 1998, the EEOC issued all six of them right-to-sue letters. Two months later, they filed this civil action against the City, alleging (as relevant here) that its practice of selecting for advancement only applicants who scored 89 or above caused a disparate impact on African–Americans in violation of Title VII. The District Court certified a class-petitioners here-consisting of the more than 6,000 African–Americans who scored in the "qualified" range on the 1995 examination but had not been hired.

The City sought summary judgment on the ground that petitioners had failed to file EEOC charges within 300 days after their claims accrued. See § 2000e–5(e)(1). The District Court denied the motion, concluding that the City's "ongoing reliance" on the 1995 test results constituted a "continuing violation" of Title VII. The City stipulated that the 89–point cutoff had a "severe disparate impact against African Americans," but argued that its cutoff score was justified by business necessity. After an 8–day bench trial, the District Court ruled for petitioners, rejecting the City's business-necessity defense. It ordered the City to hire 132 randomly selected members of the class (reflecting the number of African–Americans the Court found would have been hired but for the City's practices) and awarded backpay to be divided among the remaining class members.

The Seventh Circuit reversed. It held that petitioners' suit was untimely because the earliest EEOC charge was filed more than 300 days after the only discriminatory act: sorting the scores into the "well-qualified," "qualified," and "not-qualified" categories. The hiring decisions down the line were immaterial, it reasoned, because "[t]he hiring only of applicants classified 'well qualified' was the automatic consequence of the test scores rather than the product of a fresh act of discrimination." * * *

A

Before beginning a Title VII suit, a plaintiff must first file a timely EEOC charge. In this case, petitioners' charges were due within 300 days "after unlawful employment practice occurred." § 2000e–5(1). * * * Petitioners here challenge the City's practice of picking only those who had scored 89 or above on the 1995 examination when it later chose applicants to advance. Setting aside the first round of selection in May 1996, which all agree is beyond the cut-off, no one disputes that the conduct petitioners challenge occurred within the charging period. The real question, then, is not whether a claim predicated on that conduct is *timely,* but whether the practice thus defined can be the basis for a disparate-impact claim *at all.*

We conclude that it can. As originally enacted, Title VII did not expressly prohibit employment practices that cause a disparate impact. That enactment made it an "unlawful employment practice" for an employer "to fail or refuse to hire or to discharge any individual, or otherwise to discriminate against any individual with respect to his compensation, terms, conditions, or privileges of employment, because of such individual's race, color, religion, sex, or national origin," § 2000e–2(a)(1), or "to limit, segregate, or classify his employees or applicants for employment in any way which would deprive or tend to deprive any individual of employment opportunities or otherwise adversely affect his status as an employee, because of" any of the same reasons, § 2000e–2(a)(2). In *Griggs v. Duke Power Co.,* 401 U.S. 424, 431, 91 S.Ct. 849, 28 L.Ed.2d 158 (1971), we interpreted the latter provision to "proscrib[e] not only overt discrimination but also practices that are fair in form, but discriminatory in operation."

Two decades later, Congress codified the requirements of the "disparate impact" claims *Griggs* had recognized. 42 U.S.C. § 2000e–2(k). That provision states:

> "(1)(A) An unlawful employment practice based on disparate impact is established under this subchapter only if—
>
> > "(i) a complaining party demonstrates that a respondent uses a particular employment practice that causes a disparate impact on the basis of race, color, religion, sex, or national origin and the respondent fails to demonstrate that the challenged practice is job

related for the position in question and consistent with business necessity...."

Thus, a plaintiff establishes a prima facie disparate-impact claim by showing that the employer "*uses* a particular employment practice that causes a disparate impact" on one of the prohibited bases. See *Ricci v. DeStefano*, 557 U.S. 557, ___, 129 S.Ct. 2658, 2672–2673, 174 L.Ed.2d 490 (2009).

Petitioners' claim satisfies that requirement. Title VII does not define "employment practice," but we think it clear that the term encompasses the conduct of which petitioners complain: the exclusion of passing applicants who scored below 89 (until the supply of scores 89 or above was exhausted) when selecting those who would advance. The City "use[d]" that practice in each round of selection. Although the City had adopted the eligibility list (embodying the score cutoffs) earlier and announced its intention to draw from that list, it made use of the practice of excluding those who scored 88 or below each time it filled a new class of firefighters. Petitioners alleged that this exclusion caused a disparate impact. Whether they adequately proved that is not before us. What matters is that their allegations, based on the City's actual implementation of its policy, stated a cognizable claim.

The City argues that subsection (k) is inapposite because it does not address "accrual" of disparate-impact claims. Section 2000e–5(e)(1), it says, specifies when the time to file a charge starts running. That is true but irrelevant. Aside from the first round of selection in May 1996 (which all agree is beyond the 300–day charging period), the acts petitioners challenge—the City's use of its cutoff score in selecting candidates— occurred within the charging period. Accordingly, no one disputes that if petitioners could bring new claims based on those acts, their claims were timely. The issue, in other words, is not *when* petitioners' claims accrued, but *whether* they could accrue at all.

The City responds that subsection (k) does not answer *that* question either; that it speaks, as its title indicates, only to the plaintiff's "[b]urden of proof in disparate impact cases," not to the elements of disparate-impact claims, which the City says are be found in § 2000e–2(a)(2). That is incorrect. Subsection (k) does indeed address the burden of proof-not just who bears it, however, but also what it consists of. It *does* set forth the essential ingredients of a disparate-impact claim: It says that a claim "is established" if an employer "uses" an "employment practice" that "causes a disparate impact" on one of the enumerated bases. § 2000e– 2(k)(1)(A)(i). That it also sets forth a business-necessity defense employers may raise, § 2000e–2(k)(1)(A)(i), and explains how plaintiffs may prevail despite that defense, § 2000e–2(k)(1)(A)(ii), is irrelevant. Unless and until the defendant pleads and proves a business-necessity defense, the plaintiff wins simply by showing the stated elements.

B

Notwithstanding the text of § 2000e–2(k)(1)(A)(i) and petitioners' description of the practice they claim was unlawful, the City argues that the unlawful employment practice here was something else entirely. The only actionable discrimination, it argues, occurred in 1996 when it "used the examination results to create the hiring eligibility list, limited hiring to the 'well qualified' classification, and notified petitioners." That initial decision, it concedes, was unlawful. But because no timely charge challenged the decision, that cannot now be the basis for liability. And because, the City claims, the exclusion of petitioners when selecting classes of firefighters followed inevitably from the earlier decision to adopt the cutoff score, no new violations could have occurred. The Seventh Circuit adopted the same analysis.

The City's premise is sound, but its conclusion does not follow. It may be true that the City's January 1996 decision to adopt the cutoff score (and to create a list of the applicants above it) gave rise to a freestanding disparate-impact claim. If that is so, the City is correct that since no timely charge was filed attacking it, the City is now "entitled to treat that past act as lawful." *United Air Lines, Inc. v. Evans,* 431 U.S. 553, 558, 97 S.Ct. 1885, 52 L.Ed.2d 571 (1977). But it does not follow that no new violation occurred—and no new claims could arise—when the City implemented that decision down the road. If petitioners could prove that the City "use[d]" the "practice" that "causes a disparate impact," they could prevail.

The City, like the Seventh Circuit, insists that *Evans* and a line of cases following it require a different result. See also *Ledbetter v. Goodyear Tire & Rubber Co.,* 550 U.S. 618, 127 S.Ct. 2162, 167 L.Ed.2d 982 (2007); *Lorance v. AT & T Technologies, Inc.,* 490 U.S. 900, 109 S.Ct. 2261, 104 L.Ed.2d 961 (1989); *Ricks,* 449 U.S. 250, 101 S.Ct. 498, 66 L.Ed.2d 431. Those cases, we are told, stand for the proposition that present effects of prior actions cannot lead to Title VII liability.

We disagree. As relevant here, those cases establish only that a Title VII plaintiff must show a "present violation" within the limitations period. What that requires depends on the claim asserted. For disparate-treatment claims—and others for which discriminatory intent is required—that means the plaintiff must demonstrate deliberate discrimination within the limitations period. But for claims that do not require discriminatory intent, no such demonstration is needed. Our opinions, it is true, described the harms of which the unsuccessful plaintiffs in those cases complained as "present effect[s]" of past discrimination. But the reason they could not be the present effects of present discrimination was that the charged discrimination required proof of discriminatory intent, which had not even been alleged. That reasoning has no application when, as here, the charge is disparate impact, which does not require discriminatory intent.

The Seventh Circuit resisted this conclusion, reasoning that the difference between disparate-treatment and disparate-impact claims is only superficial. Both take aim at the same evil—discrimination on a prohibited basis—but simply seek to establish it by different means. Disparate-impact liability, the Court of Appeals explained, " 'is primarily intended to lighten the plaintiff's heavy burden of proving intentional discrimination after employers learned to cover their tracks.' " But even if the two theories were directed at the same evil, it would not follow that their reach is therefore coextensive. If the effect of applying Title VII's text is that some claims that would be doomed under one theory will survive under the other, that is the product of the law Congress has written. It is not for us to rewrite the statute so that it covers only what we think is necessary to achieve what we think Congress really intended.

* * *

The judgment of the Court of Appeals is reversed, and the case is remanded for further proceedings consistent with this opinion.

NOTES

1. On what basis did the Court distinguish its prior cases such as *Ricks, Evans, Lorrance,* and *Ledbetter*? Is it ironic that plaintiffs bringing disparate impact claims, which do not require a showing of intent to discriminate, receive a more favorable filing period than those bringing disparate treatment, i.e. intentional discrimination, claims?

2. In early 2005, an employer told all of its machine operators that their positions would be replaced by higher paid mechanic operator positions. Machine operators were given tests which, if they passed, qualified them for mechanic operator apprentice positions. Plaintiffs, African–American machine operators, failed the test. They were allowed to continue to work as machine operators but were required to attend weekend classes, while they trained newly hired mechanic operators. They failed the classes as well and by June 2006 they ceased trying to become mechanic operators. As additional mechanic operators were hired, plaintiffs saw their work hours reduced. They filed charges with the EEOC in June 2010 alleging that the test, the classes and the replacement of machine operators with mechanic operators had a disparate impact on African–Americans. Were their charges timely? *See Conley v. Nestle USA, Inc.,* 2011 WL 332525 (N.D.Ill. 2011).

3. What effect do statutes such as the Ledbetter Fair Pay Act and decisions such as *Lewis* have on an employer's need to retain records and other evidence?

B.   THE LAWSUIT

1.   PRE-REQUISITE: NOTICE OF RIGHT TO SUE

For Title VII and ADA actions, a claimant may not file a lawsuit until receiving a "Notice of Right to Sue" from the EEOC. The EEOC issues

Right to Sue Notices where it has decided not to sue after a failure of its attempt to conciliate the matter, where it has entered into a conciliation agreement but the party who filed the charge has not joined the agreement, where it has dismissed the charge, and where it has found no reasonable cause to believe that the charge has merit. A negative EEOC finding does not bar the charging party from filing suit. Indeed, if the EEOC has not issued a right to sue notice within 180 days from the filing of the charge, the charging party may demand that the EEOC issue a Notice of Right to Sue. Upon receipt of such demand the EEOC has a ministerial obligation to promptly issue the notice even if it has not completed its investigation of the charge or undertaken settlement discussions.

Parties who file charges under the ADEA do not have to await a "Right to Sue" notice from the EEOC. They may file suit after the EEOC and appropriate state agency (if any) have had the charge for 60 days. As neither the Equal Pay Act nor the Reconstruction Era Civil Rights Acts (42 U.S.C.A. § 1981) require exhaustion of pre-suit administrative procedures plaintiffs invoking these statutes will not have a "notice of right to sue."

2. THE SUIT

Under the core statutes the complaint must be filed within 90 days of the *receipt of the "notice of right to sue."*[2] The lapse of time between the unlawful action and the filing of the complaint is not material. Suits under the Equal Pay Act must be filed within two years of the receipt of the underpayment, or within three years if plaintiff can establish a willful violation of the Act. 29 U.S.C. § 255.

The Reconstruction Era Civil Rights Acts have no statute of limitations. In 1990 Congress enacted a general four year statute of limitation for claims arising under federal statutes enacted after December 1, 1990. Clearly, the original version of the statutes predates this enactment. However, major portions of the Acts were re-enacted, amended, or clarified, in the Civil Rights Act of 1991. As to those amendments the four year statute of limitations applies (hostile environment, termination and transfer). As to refusal to hire because of race, which was protected by the Nineteenth Century version of the statute, the precise limitation remains unclear. *See, **Jones v. R.R. Donnelley & Sons Co.**,* 541 U.S. 369, 124 S.Ct. 1836, 158 L.Ed.2d 645 (2004).

A complaint must satisfy the notice requirements of Rule 8(a)(2), Federal Rules of Civil Procedure. A mere request for appointment of attorney or the filing of the "Notice of Right to Sue" does not satisfy this requirement

---

2. Until "clarified" by the Civil Rights Act of 1991, ADEA suits could be brought within two years of the discriminatory act. The 1991 Amendments eliminated that provision and substituted a requirement that a suit must be brought within 90 days from the receipt of the Notice of Right to Sue, even though administrative procedures under the ADEA did not necessarily mandate the issuance of such a notice.

unless the document contains the elements required by the Rule. ***Baldwin County Welcome Center v. Brown,*** 466 U.S. 147, 104 S.Ct. 1723, 80 L.Ed.2d 196 (1984). ***Swierkiewicz v. Sorema, N.A.,*** 534 U.S. 506, 122 S.Ct. 992, 152 L.Ed.2d 1 (2002), held that local rules cannot require pleading of extensive factual detail. However, ***Ashcroft v. Iqbal,*** 556 U.S. 662, 129 S.Ct. 1937, 173 L.Ed.2d 868 (2009), a non-employment civil rights case, held:

> Under <u>Federal Rule of Civil Procedure 8(a)(2)</u>, a pleading must contain a "short and plain statement of the claim showing that the pleader is entitled to relief." * * * the pleading standard <u>Rule 8</u> announces does not require "detailed factual allegations," but it demands more than an unadorned, "the-defendant-unlawfully-harmed-me" accusation. A pleading that offers "labels and conclusions" or "a formulaic recitation of the elements of a cause of action will not do." Nor does a complaint suffice if it tenders "naked assertion[s]" devoid of "further factual enhancement."

Holmes v. Gates, 403 Fed.Appx. 670 (3d Cir. 2010), addressed a Title VII complaint that contained general allegations of race discrimination and retaliation through the defendant creating a hostile environment which included specific allegations of: (1) refusal of reimbursements granted similarly situated non-minority workers, (2) denial of leave granted others, (3) denial of promotion opportunities, (4) segregation of plaintiff to a "drafty hallway" to her physical detriment, and (5) repeated bogus suggestions of possible disciplinary action. Applying *Aschroft v. Iqual,* the Third Circuit affirmed the trial court's dismissal of the complaint as containing nothing more than naked conclusions.

Even a properly pleaded complaint can include only those incidents of discrimination set forth in the EEOC charge or such as might reasonably flow from a subsequent EEOC investigation of the charge. *Deravin v. Kerik,* 335 F.3d 195 (2d Cir. 2003). A charge alleging "age" discrimination, for example, may not authorize a plaintiff pleading that neutral, non-age factors had an adverse impact on plaintiff's age group. *Allen v. Highlands Hospital Corp.,* 545 F.3d 387 (6th Cir. 2008).

3. FEDERAL EMPLOYERS

The distinct administrative pre-requisites to suit outlined above, make no provision for federal employee complainants securing a "Notice of Right to Sue." A complainant need only secure an adverse final agency decision or, if the agency decision was appealed to the EEOC, an adverse EEOC determination. Thereupon, the claimant has 90 days from the "final order" in which to file suit in a federal district court. Notwithstanding the extensive administrative record and findings that may have been compiled before the EEOC, the trial in federal court is *de novo.* ***Chandler v. Roudebush,*** 425 U.S. 840, 96 S.Ct. 1949, 48 L.Ed.2d 416 (1976).

4. PUBLIC SUIT

The EEOC has authority to sue in its own name. When the EEOC decides to file suit, it does not issue a "Right to Sue" notice. An EEOC lawsuit cuts off the right of a private party to file suit. Charging parties are limited to "intervention." There is no expressed statutory time limit for the EEOC filing suit. Nor is such a limitation implied. *Occidental Life Ins. Co. of Cal. v. EEOC,* 432 U.S. 355, 97 S.Ct. 2447, 53 L.Ed.2d 402 (1977). Nonetheless, inordinate delay by the EEOC in bringing suit that prejudices the defendant may allow the defendant to assert the equitable defense of laches. *EEOC v. Great Atlantic & Pacific Tea Co.,* 735 F.2d 69 (3d Cir. 1984).

The statutes direct that the EEOC must undertake meaningful efforts at conciliation. Mere "take it or leave it" insistence upon full compliance with EEOC demands does not satisfy the requirement. The EEOC must engage in such meaningful conciliation efforts as a pre-condition to its initiating litigation. *EEOC v. Asplundh Tree Expert Co.,* 340 F.3d 1256 (11th Cir. 2003).

5. JURY TRIAL

Prior to 1991, Title VII and ADA parties had no right to a jury trial because all relief, including back pay, was considered equitable in nature. The Civil Rights Act of 1991 allowed for recovery of consequential and punitive damages and also recognized a right to jury trial over claims for these damages. Back pay remains an equitable remedy and a claim for equitable relief alone will not trigger a right to jury trial.

The ADEA originally adopted the enforcement scheme of the Fair Labor Standards Act under which back wages are considered damages and, thus, there has always been a right to jury trial under the ADEA.[3]

KREMER v. CHEMICAL CONSTRUCTION CORP.

Supreme Court of the United States, 1982
456 U.S. 461, 102 S.Ct. 1883, 72 L.Ed.2d 262

JUSTICE WHITE delivered the opinion of the Court.

* * *

I

Petitioner Rubin Kremer emigrated from Poland in 1970 and was hired in 1973 by respondent Chemical Construction Corp. (Chemico) as an engineer. Two years later he was laid off, along with a number of other employees. Some of these employees were later rehired, but Kremer was not although he made several applications. In May 1976, Kremer filed a

---

3. Federal employees have a right to a jury trial for complaints under Title VII and the Rehabilitation Act, but may not claim a jury trial for age discrimination claims.

discrimination charge with the Equal Employment Opportunity Commission (EEOC), asserting that his discharge and failure to be rehired were due to his national origin and Jewish faith. Because the EEOC may not consider a claim until a state agency having jurisdiction over employment discrimination complaints has had at least 60 days to resolve the matter, § 706(c), the Commission referred Kremer's charge to the New York State Division of Human Rights (NYHRD), the agency charged with enforcing the New York law prohibiting employment discrimination. N.Y.Exec.Law §§ 295(6), 296(1)(a).

After investigating Kremer's complaint, the NYHRD concluded that there was no probable cause to believe that Chemico had engaged in the discriminatory practices complained of. * * * The NYHRD's determination was upheld by its Appeal Board as "not arbitrary, capricious or an abuse of discretion." Kremer again brought his complaint to the attention of the EEOC and also filed, on December 6, 1977, a petition with the Appellate Division of the New York Supreme Court to set aside the adverse administrative determination. On February 27, 1978, five justices of the Appellate Division unanimously affirmed the Appeal Board's order. * * *.

Kremer then brought this Title VII action in District Court, claiming discrimination on the basis of national origin and religion. Chemico argued from the outset that Kremer's Title VII action was barred by the doctrine of res judicata. * * *

* * *

II

Section 1738 [28 U.S.C. § 1738] requires federal courts to give the same preclusive effect to state court judgments that those judgments would be given in the courts of the State from which the judgments emerged. Here the Appellate Division of the New York Supreme Court has issued a judgment affirming the decision of the NYHRD Appeals Board that the discharge and failure to rehire Kremer were not the product of the discrimination that he had alleged. There is no question that this judicial determination precludes Kremer from bringing "any other action, civil or criminal, based upon the same grievance" in the New York courts. By its terms, therefore, § 1738 would appear to preclude Kremer from relitigating the same question in federal court.

Kremer offers two principal reasons why § 1738 does not bar this action. First, he suggests that in Title VII cases Congress intended that federal courts be relieved of their usual obligation to grant finality to state court decisions. Second, he urges that the New York administrative and judicial proceedings in this case were so deficient that they are not entitled to preclusive effect in federal courts and, in any event, the rejection of a state employment discrimination claim cannot by definition bar a Title VII action. We consider this latter contention in Part III.

A

Allen v. McCurry, 449 U.S. 90, 99, 101 S.Ct. 411, 417, 66 L.Ed.2d 308 (1980), made clear that an exception to § 1738 will not be recognized unless a later statute contains an express or implied partial repeal. There is no claim here that Title VII expressly repealed § 1738; if there has been a partial repeal, it must be implied. "It is, of course, a cardinal principle of statutory construction that repeals by implication are not favored," and whenever possible, statutes should be read consistently. There are, however,

> " 'two well-settled categories of repeals by implication—(1) where provisions in the two acts are in irreconcilable conflict, the later act to the extent of the conflict constitutes an implied repeal of the earlier one; and (2) if the later act covers the whole subject of the earlier one and is clearly intended as a substitute, it will operate similarly as a repeal of the earlier act. But, in either case, the intention of the legislature to repeal must be clear and manifest. . . .' " *Radzanower v. Touche Ross & Co.*, 96 S.Ct., at 1993, quoting *Posadas v. National City Bank*, 296 U.S. 497, 503, 56 S.Ct. 349, 352, 80 L.Ed. 351 (1936).

The relationship of Title VII to § 1738 does not fall within either of these categories. * * *

No provision of Title VII requires claimants to pursue in state court an unfavorable state administrative action, nor does the Act specify the weight a federal court should afford a final judgment by a state court if such a remedy is sought. While we have interpreted the "civil action" authorized to follow consideration by federal and state administrative *agencies* to be a "trial *de novo*," *Chandler v. Roudebush*, 425 U.S. 840, 844–845, 96 S.Ct. 1949, 1951–52, 48 L.Ed.2d 416 (1976); *Alexander v. Gardner–Denver Co., supra*, at 38, 94 S.Ct., at 1015; *McDonnell Douglas Corp. v. Green, supra*, neither the statute nor our decisions indicate that the final judgment of a state *court* is subject to redetermination at such a trial. Similarly, the congressional directive that the EEOC should give "substantial weight" to findings made in state proceedings, § 706(b), 42 U.S.C. § 2000e–5(b), indicates only the minimum level of deference the EEOC must afford all state determinations; it does not bar affording the greater preclusive effect which may be required by § 1738 if judicial action is involved. To suggest otherwise, to say that either the opportunity to bring a "civil action" or the "substantial weight" requirement implicitly repeals § 1738, is to prove far too much. For if that is so, even a full trial on the merits in state court would not bar a trial *de novo* in federal court and would not be entitled to more than "substantial weight" before the EEOC. The state courts would be placed on a one-way street; the finality of their decisions would depend on which side prevailed in a given case.

Since an implied repeal must ordinarily be evident from the language or operation of a statute, the lack of such manifest incompatability between Title VII and § 1738 is enough to answer our inquiry. No different conclusion is suggested by the legislative history of Title VII. Although no inescapable conclusions can be drawn from the process of enactment, the legislative debates surrounding the initial passage of Title VII in 1964 and the substantial amendment adopted in 1972 plainly do not demonstrate that Congress intended to override the historic respect that federal courts accord state court judgments.

At the time Title VII was written, over half of the States had enacted some form of equal employment legislation. Members of Congress agreed that the States should play an important role in enforcing Title VII, but also felt the federal system should defer only to adequate state laws. Congress considered a number of possible ways of achieving these goals, ranging from limiting Title VII's jurisdiction to States without fair employment laws to having Congress or the President assess the adequacy of state laws. As Title VII emerged from the House, it empowered the EEOC to assess the adequacy of state laws and procedures. § 708(b), H.R. 7152, 88th Cong., 2d Sess. (1964). The Senate bill that was finally signed into law widened the state role by guaranteeing all States with fair employment practices laws an initial opportunity to resolve charges of discrimination. 42 U.S.C. § 2000e–5(c). * * *

* * *

Nothing in the legislative history of the 1964 Act suggests that Congress considered it necessary or desirable to provide an absolute right to relitigate in federal court an issue resolved by a state court. While striving to craft an optimal niche for the States in the overall enforcement scheme, the legislators did not envision full litigation of a single claim in both state and federal forums. Indeed, the requirement of a trial *de novo* in federal district court following EEOC proceedings was added primarily to protect employers from overzealous enforcement by the EEOC. A memorandum signed by seven Representatives accompanying the compromise measure ultimately adopted, concluded that "we believe the employer or labor union will have a fairer forum to establish innocence since a trial de novo is required in district court proceedings." Similar views were expressed in 1972 when Congress reconsidered whether to give the EEOC adjudicatory and enforcement powers. There is also reason to believe that Congress required that the EEOC give state findings "substantial weight" because the Commission had too freely ignored the determinations handed down by state agencies.

An important indication that Congress did not intend Title VII to repeal § 1738's requirement that federal courts give full faith and credit to state court judgments is found in an exchange between Senator Javits, a manager of the 1972 bill, and Senator Hruska. Senator Hruska, concerned with the potential for multiple independent proceedings on a single discrimination charge, had introduced an amendment which would have eliminated many of the duplicative remedies for employment discrimination. Senator Javits argued that the amendment was unnecessary because the doctrine of res judicata would prevent repetitive litigation against a single defendant:

"[T]here is the real capability in this situation of dealing with the question on the basis of res judicata. In other words once there is a litigation—a litigation started by the Commission, a litigation started by the Attorney General, or a litigation started by the individual—the remedy has been chosen and can be followed through and no relitigation of the same issues in a different forum would be permitted." 118 Cong.Rec. 3370 (1972).

Senator Williams, another proponent of the 1972 bill, echoed Senator Javits' remarks: "[I] do not believe that the individual claimant should be allowed to litigate his claim to completion in one forum, and then if dissatisfied, go to another forum to try again." *Id.*, at 3372. After Senator Javits and Senator Williams spoke, an evenly divided Senate refused to approve the Hruska amendment.

It is sufficiently clear that Congress, both in 1964 and 1972, though wary of assuming the adequacy of state employment discrimination remedies, did not intend to supplant such laws. We conclude that neither the statutory language nor the congressional debates suffice to repeal § 1738's long-standing directive to federal courts.

B

* * *

Finally, the comity and federalism interests embodied in § 1738 are not compromised by the application of res judicata and collateral estoppel in Title VII cases. Petitioner maintains that the decision of the Court of Appeals will deter claimants from seeking state court review of their claims ultimately leading to a deterioration in the quality of the state administrative process. On the contrary, stripping state court judgments of finality would be far more destructive to the quality of adjudication by lessening the incentive for full participation by the parties and for searching review by state officials. Depriving state judgments of finality not only would violate basic tenets of comity and federalism, but also would reduce the incentive for States to work towards effective and meaningful antidiscrimination systems.

III

The petitioner nevertheless contends that the judgment should not bar his Title VII action because the New York courts did not resolve the issue that the District Court must hear under Title VII—whether Kremer had suffered discriminatory treatment—and because the procedures provided were inadequate. Neither contention is persuasive. Although the claims presented to the NYHRD and subsequently reviewed by the Appellate Division were necessarily based on New York law, the alleged discriminatory acts are prohibited by both federal and state laws. The elements of a successful employment discrimination claim are virtually identical; petitioner could not succeed on a Title VII claim consistently with the judgment of the NYHRD that there is no reason to believe he was terminated or not rehired because of age or religion. The Appellate Division's affirmance of the NYHRD's dismissal necessarily decided that petitioner's claim under New York law was meritless, and thus it also decided that a Title VII claim arising from the same events would be equally meritless.

The more serious contention is that even though administrative proceedings and judicial review are legally sufficient to be given preclusive effect in New York, they should be deemed so fundamentally flawed as to be denied recognition under § 1738. We have previously recognized that the judicially created doctrine of collateral estoppel does not apply when the party against whom the earlier decision is asserted did not have a "full and fair opportunity" to litigate the claim or issue, "Redetermination of issues is warranted if there is reason to doubt the quality, extensiveness, or fairness of procedures followed in prior litigation." Montana v. United States, 99 S.Ct., at 979, n.11.

Our previous decisions have not specified the source or defined the content of the requirement that the first adjudication offer a full and fair opportunity to litigate. But for present purposes, where we are bound by the statutory directive of § 1738, state proceedings need do no more than satisfy the minimum procedural requirements of the Fourteenth Amendment's Due Process Clause in order to qualify for the full faith and credit guaranteed by federal law. It has long been established that § 1738 does not allow federal courts to employ their own rules of res judicata in determining the effect of state judgments. Rather, it goes beyond the common law and commands a federal court to accept the rules chosen by the State from which the judgment is taken. * * *

The State must, however, satisfy the applicable requirements of the Due Process Clause. A State may not grant preclusive effect in its own courts to a constitutionally infirm judgment, and other state and federal courts are not required to accord full faith and credit to such a judgment. Section 1738 does not suggest otherwise; other state and federal courts would still be providing a state court judgment with the "same" preclusive effect as the courts of the State from which the judgment emerged. In such a case, there could be no constitutionally recognizable preclusion at all.

We have little doubt that Kremer received all the process that was constitutionally required in rejecting his claim that he had been discriminatorily discharged contrary to the statute.* * Under New York law, a claim of employment discrimination requires the NYHRD to investigate whether there is "probable cause" to believe that the complaint is true. Before this determination of probable cause is made, the claimant is entitled to a "full opportunity to present on the record, though informally, his charges against his employer or other respondent, including the right to submit all exhibits which he wishes to present and testimony of witnesses in addition to his own testimony." The complainant also is entitled to an opportunity "to rebut evidence submitted by or obtained from the respondent." He may have an attorney assist him and may ask the division to issue subpoenas.

If the investigation discloses probable cause and efforts at conciliation fail, the NYHRD must conduct a public hearing to determine the merits of the complaint. A public hearing must also be held if the Human Rights Appeal Board finds "there has not been a full investigation and opportunity for the complainant to present his contentions and evidence, with a full record." Finally, judicial review in the Appellate Division is available to assure that a claimant is not denied any of the procedural rights to which he was entitled and that the NYHRD's determination was not arbitrary and capricious.

We have no hesitation in concluding that this panoply of procedures, complemented by administrative as well as judicial review, is sufficient under the Due Process Clause. Only where the evidence submitted by the claimant fails, as a matter of law, to reveal any merit to the complaint may the NYHRD make a determination of no probable cause without holding a hearing. And before that determination may be reached, New York requires the NYHRD to make a full investigation, wherein the complainant has full opportunity to present his evidence, under oath if he so requests. * * *

IV

* * * Because there is no "affirmative showing" of a "clear and manifest" legislative purpose in Title VII to deny res judicata or collateral estoppel effect to a state court judgment affirming that a claim of employment discrimination is unproved, and because the procedures provided in New York for the determination of such claims offer a full and fair opportunity to litigate the merits, the judgment of the Court of Appeals is

Affirmed.

JUSTICE BLACKMUN, with whom JUSTICE BRENNAN and JUSTICE MARSHALL join, dissenting.

Today the Court follows an isolated Second Circuit approach and holds that a discrimination complainant cannot bring a Title VII suit in federal court after unsuccessfully seeking state court "review" of a state antidiscrimination agency's unfavorable decision. * * * The Court reaches this result because it purports to find nothing in Title VII inconsistent with the application of the general preclusion rule of 28 U.S.C. § 1738 to the state court's affirmance of the state agency's decision. For a compelling array of reasons, the Court is wrong.

I

The Court, as it must, concedes that a state *agency* determination does not preclude a trial *de novo* in federal district court. Congress made it clear beyond doubt that state agency findings would not prevent the Title VII complainant from filing suit in federal court.

* * * By permitting a charge to be filed after termination of state proceedings, the statute expressly contemplates that a plaintiff may bring suit despite a state finding of no discrimination.

This fact is also made clear by § 706(b). In 1972 Congress amended that section by directing that the EEOC "accord substantial weight to final findings and orders made by State or local authorities in proceedings commenced under State or local law." If the original version of Title VII had given the outcomes of state "proceedings" preclusive effect, Congress would not have found it necessary to amend the statute in 1972 to direct that they be given "substantial weight." And if in 1972 Congress had intended final decisions in state "proceedings" to have preclusive effect, it certainly would not have instructed that they be given "substantial weight."

* * *

Yet the Court nevertheless finds that petitioner's Title VII suit is precluded by the termination of state "proceedings." In this case, the New York State Division of Human Rights (NYHRD) found no probable cause to believe that petitioner had been a victim of discrimination. Under the Court's own rule, that determination in itself does not bar petitioner from filing a Title VII suit in federal district court. According to the Court, however, petitioner lost his opportunity to bring a federal suit when he unsuccessfully sought review of the state agency's decision in the New York courts. As the Court applies preclusion principles to Title VII, the state court affirmance of the state agency decision—*not* the state agency decision itself—blocks any subsequent Title VII suit.

The Court reaches this result through a schizophrenic reading of § 706(b). According to the Court, when Congress amended § 706(b) so that state "proceedings" would be accorded "substantial weight," it meant two different things at the same time: it intended state agency "proceedings" to be accorded only "substantial weight," while, simultaneously, state judicial "proceedings" in review of those agency "proceedings" would be accorded "substantial weight and more"—that is, "preclusive effect." But the statutory language gives no hint of this hidden double meaning. Instead of reading an unexpressed intent into § 706(b), the Court should accept the plain language of the statute. All state "proceedings," whether agency proceedings or state judicial review proceedings, are entitled to "substantial weight," not "preclusive effect." As the Court implicitly concedes when it permits suit despite the conclusion of agency proceedings, "substantial weight" is a very different concept from "preclusive effect," and Congress thus did not intend for the termination of any state "proceeding" to foreclose a subsequent Title VII suit.

In addition, the Court must disregard the clear import of § 706(c). That section explicitly contemplates that a complainant can bring a Title VII suit despite the termination of state "proceedings." Once again, the statute contains no suggestion that any state "proceeding" has preclusive effect on a subsequent Title VII suit. Nonetheless, contrary to § 706(c), the Court bars petitioner's Title VII suit because of the termination of state "proceedings."

The Court's attempt to give § 706(b) a double meaning and to avoid the language of § 706(c) is made all the more awkward because the Court's decision artificially separates the proceedings before the reviewing state court from the state administrative process. Indeed, if Congress meant to permit a Title VII suit despite the termination of state agency proceedings, it is only natural to conclude that Congress also intended to permit a Title VII suit after the agency decision has been simply affirmed by a state court.

State court review is merely the last step in the administrative process, the final means of review of the state *agency's* decision. * * *

The Court purports to give preclusive effect to the New York court's decision. But the Appellate Division made no finding one way or the other concerning the *merits* of petitioner's discrimination claim. The NYHRD, not the New York court, dismissed petitioner's complaint for lack of probable cause. In affirming, the court merely found that the *agency's* decision was not arbitrary or capricious. Thus, although it claims to grant a state *court* decision preclusive effect, in fact the Court bars petitioner's suit based on the state *agency's* decision of no probable cause. The Court thereby disregards the express provisions of Title VII, for, as the Court acknowledges, Congress has decided that an adverse state agency decision will not prevent a complainant's subsequent Title VII suit.

Finally, if the Court is in fact giving preclusive effect only to the state *court* decision, the Court misapplies 28 U.S.C. § 1738 by barring petitioner's suit. The state reviewing court never considered the merits of petitioner's discrimination claim, the subject matter of a Title VII suit in federal court. It is a basic principle of preclusion doctrine that a decision in one judicial proceeding cannot bar a subsequent suit raising issues that were not relevant to the first decision. * * *

* * *

NOTES

1. What factors should counsel consider in deciding whether to seek review in state court of a state administrative agency decision over a discrimination claim?

2. Assume that an individual files a claim for Social Security Disability benefits and also files an ADA action. Does the claim for disability benefits estop the individual from claiming to be a qualified individual with a disability under the ADA? *See, **Cleveland v. Policy Mgmt Sys. Corp,** 526 U.S. 795, 119 S.Ct. 1597, 143 L.Ed.2d 966 (1999).

C. CLASS ACTIONS

Rule 23 of the Federal Rules of Civil Procedure governs class actions in federal court generally. Rule 23 applies to most employment discrimination statutes, but it does not apply to the ADEA or the Equal Pay Act. Those statutes adopt the class enforcement provisions of the Fair Labor Standards Act, 29 U.S.C. § 216(b). Unlike Rule 23 class actions where class members are included in the lawsuit unless they opt out, in ADEA and EPA actions, class members must affirmatively opt in to be included. They do so by filing a notice with the court. ***Hoffman–La Roche, Inc. v. Sperling,*** 493 U.S. 165, 110 S.Ct. 482, 107 L.Ed.2d 480 (1989), held that in an ADEA collective action, the trial judge has discretion to manage the process, including to order the defendant to provide the named plaintiffs with the names and addresses of all members of the putative class, to approve a form notice to be sent to members of the putative class and a consent form to be returned by class members, and to set cutoff dates for class members to opt into the case.

Under Rule 23, to proceed as a class action, an action must satisfy the four requirements of Rule 23(a) and one of the options under Rule 23(b). Rule 23(a)'s requirements are that the class is so numerous that joinder of individual members is not practicable ("numerosity"), there are questions of law or fact common to all class members ("commonality"), the claims of the named parties are typical of the claims of the class ("typicality") and the named parties will fairly and adequately protect the interests of the class. Rule 23(b)'s options are: (1) prosecution of separate individual actions would create a risk of inconsistent adjudications which would establish incompatible standards of conduct for the defendant, or of adjudications that, as a practical matter, would dispose of the interests of non-party members of the class or substantially impair their ability to protect their interests; (2) the defendant has acted or refused to act on grounds generally applicable to the class, making final injunctive or declarative relief for the class as a whole appropriate; *or* (3) questions of law or fact common to class members predominate over questions affecting individual members and a class action is superior to other available methods of adjudication.

By far, the largest Title VII class action ever filed was the sex discrimination class action filed against Wal–Mart Stores, Inc. The action alleged sex discrimination in pay and promotions and the trial court certified a class of "All women employed at any Wal–Mart domestic retail store at any time since December 26, 1998, who have been or may be subjected to Wal–Mart's challenged pay and management track promotions policies and practices." The class encompassed more than 1.5 million members. Although the Court of Appeals for the Ninth Circuit largely affirmed the class certification, the Supreme Court reversed. What follows is a discussion of strategy by the lead plaintiffs' attorney and the Supreme Court's opinion.

DISCRIMINATION REMEDIES: THE SHAPE OF LAWSUITS, THE SHAPE OF THE LAW: PROCEEDINGS OF THE 2008 ANNUAL MEETING ASSOCIATION OF AMERICAN LAW SCHOOLS SECTION ON EMPLOYMENT DISCRIMINATION LAW AND SECTION ON REMEDIES

12 Employee Rights & Employment Policy Journal 297 (2008)*

Brad Seligman. * * * [I]n 1964 and 1965 there was no developed class action jurisprudence so there wasn't any way to resolve that lack of compliance. At that time the EEOC had no remedial authority whatsoever. What was important was what happened in 1966, which was when Rule 23, the class action Federal Rule of Civil Procedure, was adopted. It's very interesting that the modern rule of class actions was developed right in the middle of the civil rights movement. The drafters * * * wanted to develop a streamlined and effective way for injunctive relief.

The center of that was the development of Rule 23(b)(2). * * * Rule 23(b)(2) covers cases where injunctive relief is the primary relief sought. In those cases, there is a very streamlined way to class certification. For example, you only have to show that there are common questions of law or fact. You don't have to show that those common issues predominate. You do not have to give class notice prior to trial. There is no right to opt out in injunctive relief class action. So it's the simplest way to certify a class, procedurally the quickest, because there's no notice requirement. You get your class certified, you go to trial, and away you go.

In contrast, because there might be damages claims out there, Rule 23(b)(3) was promulgated. In a 23(b)(3) class, the requirements for certification are much higher, but most importantly, instead of showing merely that common questions are present, we have to show that they predominate. We also have to show that class actions are superior to any other method to resolve the case, and we have to give notice. That is a significant factor, given that the Supreme Court later said that class notice costs will now be paid for by the plaintiffs. So if you, like me, had two million class members, you are talking about a lot of money.

The (b)(2)/(b)(3) battle was the critical question. If you were primarily seeking injunctive relief, the framers of Rule 23 said you should have a quick path to get class certification, and in the early years of Title VII, it was an incredibly quick path to get class certification. Courts were certifying damn near anything that came through the door that sought injunctive relief. They developed in those days what people call the "across the board theory." The across the board theory describes when you have one plaintiff who walks in the door complaining about one problem: "I was not promoted," or "I got a bad performance review."

---

* Reprinted by permission of Employee Rights & Employment Policy Journal.

That plaintiff claims race discrimination, and you bring in the case involving the whole spectrum of employment conduct—hiring, firing, demotion, pay, and performance reviews, everything in one case. With injunctive relief as the primary goal, you don't need to show any common question of fact; it was very easy to pursue those kinds of cases.

* * *

All that went fine for a number of years, but then several things happened. The first is that the Supreme Court said the across the board theory could not be used anymore in a case called *General Telephone v. Falcone* in 1982. That started diluting how easy it was to certify some of these cases, but it left intact the distinction between (b)(2) primary injunctive relief and (b)(3) cases. The jurisprudence that grew up in those days of Title VII provided that you could seek a (b)(2) certification as long as you sought injunctive relief, and still seek back pay as monetary relief because back pay was equitable and wasn't inconsistent with a (b)(2) certification. Virtually all class cases were certified under (b)(2).

* * *

The Civil Rights Act of 1991 for the first time created damages remedies under Title VII for emotional distress and punitive damages, and it also provided for a jury trial. That act was a big victory for plaintiffs, so we thought.

* * * Southern courts, particularly the Fifth Circuit, discovered that expanded Title VII was meant to destroy class action suits. In the mid–90s, the Fifth Circuit, in a case called *Allison v. Citgo Petroleum*, issued a truly astonishing interpretation. Comparing (b)(2) and (b)(3), while (b)(2) was fine in the good old days before there were damage remedies, the Fifth Circuit said that under the 1991 Act, people could seek damages, so we're going to create a new test. The test is, you can only certify a case under (b)(2) where you can show that injunctive relief predominates. You could only show that injunctive relief predominates when you receive a monetary remedy if the monetary relief "automatically flows from the judgment." I have been in practice for almost thirty years and I have never seen a case in any field of law where monetary relief automatically flowed from anything, particularly not in Title VII. Basically, the court was saying that if you say the word money along with the word injunction, it does not matter; you don't meet Rule 23(b)(2) criteria.

That was the bad news, and guess what—it gets worse. In Rule 23(b)(3) damages cases, common questions must predominate, so unless the monetary relief is automatic and it flows without any complicated proceedings, you'll never meet the (b)(3) standard either. Essentially, what the Fifth Circuit said is that if you are seeking monetary relief under Title VII, we don't care about your injunctive relief, you're just not going to get a class. That's what has happened. * * * [T]he Fourth Circuit and the Eleventh Circuit, largely followed. It is almost impossible to certify anything in the South these days.

The good news for my practice is that a split has emerged among the courts. The Second and the Ninth Circuits have rejected the *Allison* approach and said that if you seek monetary relief, they will look at each case and ask whether a reasonable plaintiff would have brought the case seeking solely injunctive relief. Is injunctive relief, in other words, important enough that it would justify litigation without damages? If you answer that yes, you certify the class.

* * *

Let me talk for a moment about the Wal–Mart cases. Allison came before we filed Wal–Mart and Wal–Mart actually was filed before the Ninth Circuit decision came out, but we knew injunctive relief was critical, so we did everything we could from day one to emphasize the primacy of injunctive relief. First, of course, it was the key to the case. This case was brought to change Wal–Mart; it was not brought solely to create a monetary remedy. * * *

* * *

The complaint makes it clear that what we are challenging is a largely standardless system, with no oversight, no objective criteria, no job analysis of any position, with no open promotion process, and with no bidding or application procedure or posting to get into management. Our complaint makes it very clear that we are seeking to set in place a transparent, objective system based on professionally developed standards, a posting process and an application process which is reviewed and which has accountable decision making, and affirmative action and by that I mean specific goals and timetables so we can make up the many, many, many years of lost ground at Wal–Mart. This was written right into our complaint at the start.

We had some other things though, in the beginning to emphasize the primacy of injunctive relief. We made one decision, which was a very difficult decision to make, especially after the 1991 Act. Theoretically, we had the right to seek back-pay, compensatory damages, punitive damages, and injunctive relief. We concluded that seeking compensatory damages in a class this large would undermine any attempt to certify the class. No one has yet explained, although they spend a lot of time thinking about it, how you try emotional distress damages in gross, because there is a subjective element to it. So we did not seek emotional distress damages. We limited the relief to back-pay, punitive damages, and injunctive relief in this case. We did one other thing, which is important, in setting these cases up. * * * We bit the expense bullet and proposed in our class that class notice and a right to opt out be offered, even in a (b)(2) class, because we did not want anyone to suggest that we would be undermining the due process rights of class members, going forward.

WAL–MART STORES, INC. v. DUKES

Supreme Court of the United States, 2011
564 U.S. ___, 131 S.Ct. 2541, 180 L.Ed.2d 374

JUSTICE SCALIA delivered the opinion of the Court.

We are presented with one of the most expansive class actions ever. The District Court and the Court of Appeals approved the certification of a class comprising about one and a half million plaintiffs, current and former female employees of petitioner Wal–Mart who allege that the discretion exercised by their local supervisors over pay and promotion matters violates Title VII by discriminating against women. In addition to injunctive and declaratory relief, the plaintiffs seek an award of backpay. We consider whether the certification of the plaintiff class was consistent with Federal Rules of Civil Procedure 23(a) and (b)(2).

I

A

Petitioner Wal–Mart is the Nation's largest private employer. It operates four types of retail stores throughout the country: Discount Stores, Supercenters, Neighborhood Markets, and Sam's Clubs. Those stores are divided into seven nationwide divisions, which in turn comprise 41 regions of 80 to 85 stores apiece. Each store has between 40 and 53 separate departments and 80 to 500 staff positions. In all, Wal–Mart operates approximately 3,400 stores and employs more than one million people.

Pay and promotion decisions at Wal–Mart are generally committed to local managers' broad discretion, which is exercised "in a largely subjective manner." Local store managers may increase the wages of hourly employees (within limits) with only limited corporate oversight. As for salaried employees, such as store managers and their deputies, higher corporate authorities have discretion to set their pay within preestablished ranges.

Promotions work in a similar fashion. Wal–Mart permits store managers to apply their own subjective criteria when selecting candidates as "support managers," which is the first step on the path to management. Admission to Wal–Mart's management training program, however, does require that a candidate meet certain objective criteria, including an above-average performance rating, at least one year's tenure in the applicant's current position, and a willingness to relocate. But except for those requirements, regional and district managers have discretion to use their own judgment when selecting candidates for management training. Promotion to higher office—e.g., assistant manager, co-manager, or store manager—is similarly at the discretion of the employee's superiors after prescribed objective factors are satisfied.

B

The named plaintiffs in this lawsuit, representing the 1.5 million members of the certified class, are three current or former Wal–Mart employees who allege that the company discriminated against them on the basis of their sex by denying them equal pay or promotions, in violation of Title VII of the Civil Rights Act of 1964.

* * *

These plaintiffs, respondents here, do not allege that Wal–Mart has any express corporate policy against the advancement of women. Rather, they claim that their local managers' discretion over pay and promotions is exercised disproportionately in favor of men, leading to an unlawful disparate impact on female employees. And, respondents say, because Wal–Mart is aware of this effect, its refusal to cabin its managers' authority amounts to disparate treatment. Their complaint seeks injunctive and declaratory relief, punitive damages, and backpay. It does not ask for compensatory damages.

Importantly for our purposes, respondents claim that the discrimination to which they have been subjected is common to *all* Wal–Mart's female employees. The basic theory of their case is that a strong and uniform "corporate culture" permits bias against women to infect, perhaps subconsciously, the discretionary decisionmaking of each one of Wal–Mart's thousands of managers—thereby making every woman at the company the victim of one common discriminatory practice. Respondents therefore wish to litigate the Title VII claims of all female employees at Wal–Mart's stores in a nationwide class action.

C

* * *

[R]espondents moved the District Court to certify a plaintiff class consisting of " '[a]ll women employed at any Wal–Mart domestic retail store at any time since December 26, 1998, who have been or may be subjected to Wal–Mart's challenged pay and management track promotions policies and practices' ". As evidence that there were indeed "questions of law or fact common to" all the women of Wal–Mart, as Rule 23(a)(2) requires, respondents relied chiefly on three forms of proof: statistical evidence about pay and promotion disparities between men and women at the company, anecdotal reports of discrimination from about 120 of Wal–Mart's female employees, and the testimony of a sociologist, Dr. William Bielby, who conducted a "social framework analysis" of Wal–Mart's "culture" and personnel practices, and concluded that the company was "vulnerable" to gender discrimination.

Wal–Mart unsuccessfully moved to strike much of this evidence. It also offered its own countervailing statistical and other proof in an effort to defeat Rule 23(a)'s requirements of commonality, typicality, and adequate representation. Wal–Mart further contended that respondents' monetary claims for backpay could not be certified under Rule 23(b)(2), first because that Rule refers only to injunctive and declaratory relief, and second because the backpay claims could not be manageably tried as a class without depriving Wal–Mart of its right to present certain statutory defenses. With one limitation not relevant here, the District Court granted respondents' motion and certified their proposed class.

D

A divided en banc Court of Appeals substantially affirmed the District Court's certification order. The majority concluded that respondents' evidence of commonality was sufficient to "raise the common question whether Wal–Mart's female employees nationwide were subjected to a single set of corporate policies (not merely a number of independent discriminatory acts) that may have worked to unlawfully discriminate against them in violation of Title VII." It also agreed with the District Court that the named plaintiffs' claims were sufficiently typical of the class as a whole to satisfy Rule 23(a)(3), and that they could serve as adequate class representatives, see Rule 23(a)(4). With respect to the Rule 23(b)(2) question, the Ninth Circuit held that respondents' backpay claims could be certified as part of a (b)(2) class because they did not "predominat[e]" over the requests for declaratory and injunctive relief, meaning they were not "superior in strength, influence, or authority" to the nonmonetary claims.

Finally, the Court of Appeals determined that the action could be manageably tried as a class action because the District Court could adopt the approach the Ninth Circuit approved in *Hilao v. Estate of Marcos,* 103 F.3d 767, 782–787 (1996). There compensatory damages for some 9,541 class members were calculated by selecting 137 claims at random, referring those claims to a special master for valuation, and then extrapolating the validity and value of the untested claims from the sample set. The Court of Appeals "s[aw] no reason why a similar procedure to that used in *Hilao* could not be employed in this case." It would allow Wal–Mart "to present individual defenses in the randomly selected 'sample cases,' thus revealing the approximate percentage of class members whose unequal pay or nonpromotion was due to something other than gender discrimination."

We granted certiorari.

II

The class action is "an exception to the usual rule that litigation is conducted by and on behalf of the individual named parties only." *Califano v. Yamasaki,* 442 U.S. 682, 700–701, 99 S.Ct. 2545, 61 L.Ed.2d 176 (1979). In order to justify a departure from that rule, "a class representative must be part of the class and 'possess the same interest and suffer the same injury' as the class members." *East Tex. Motor Freight System, Inc. v. Rodriguez,* 431 U.S. 395, 403, 97 S.Ct. 1891, 52 L.Ed.2d 453 (1977). Rule 23(a) ensures that the named plaintiffs are appropriate representatives of the class whose claims they wish to litigate. The Rule's four requirements—numerosity, commonality, typicality, and adequate representation—"effectively 'limit the class claims to those fairly encompassed by the named plaintiff's claims.' " *General Telephone Co. of Southwest v. Falcon,* 457 U.S. 147, 156, 102 S.Ct. 2364, 72 L.Ed.2d 740 (1982).

A

The crux of this case is commonality—the rule requiring a plaintiff to show that "there are questions of law or fact common to the class." Rule 23(a)(2). That language is easy to misread, since "[a]ny competently crafted class complaint literally raises common 'questions.' " Nagareda, Class Certification in the Age of Aggregate Proof, 84 N.Y.U.L.Rev. 97, 131–132 (2009). For example: Do all of us plaintiffs indeed work for Wal–Mart? Do our managers have discretion over pay? Is that an unlawful employment practice? What remedies should we get? Reciting these questions is not sufficient to obtain class certification. Commonality requires the plaintiff to demonstrate that the class members "have suffered the same injury," *Falcon, supra,* at 157, This does not mean merely that they have all suffered a violation of the same provision of law. Title VII, for example, can be violated in many ways—by intentional discrimination, or by hiring and promotion criteria that result in disparate impact, and by the use of these practices on the part of many different superiors in a single company. Quite obviously, the mere claim by employees of the same company that they have suffered a Title VII injury, or even a disparate-impact Title VII injury, gives no cause to believe that all their claims can productively be litigated at once. Their claims must depend upon a common contention—for example, the assertion of discriminatory bias on the part of the same supervisor. That common contention, moreover, must be of such a nature that it is capable of classwide resolution—which means that determination of its truth or falsity will resolve an issue that is central to the validity of each one of the claims in one stroke.

Rule 23 does not set forth a mere pleading standard. A party seeking class certification must affirmatively demonstrate his compliance with the Rule—that is, he must be prepared to prove that there are *in fact* sufficiently numerous parties, common questions of law or fact, etc. We recognized in *Falcon* that "sometimes it may be necessary for the court to probe behind the pleadings before coming to rest on the certification question," and that certification is proper only if "the trial court is satisfied, after a rigorous analysis, that the prerequisites of Rule 23(a) have been satisfied." * * *

In this case, proof of commonality necessarily overlaps with respondents' merits contention that Wal–Mart engages in a *pattern or practice* of discrimination. That is so because, in resolving an individual's Title VII claim, the crux of the inquiry is "the reason for a particular employment decision," *Cooper v. Federal Reserve Bank of Richmond,* 467 U.S. 867, 876, 104 S.Ct. 2794, 81 L.Ed.2d 718 (1984). Here respondents wish to sue about literally millions of employment decisions at once. Without some glue holding the alleged *reasons* for all those decisions together, it will be impossible to say that examination of all the class members' claims for relief will produce a common answer to the crucial question *why was I disfavored*.

B

This Court's opinion in *Falcon* describes how the commonality issue must be approached. There an employee who claimed that he was deliberately denied a promotion on account of race obtained certification of a class comprising all employees wrongfully denied promotions and all applicants wrongfully denied jobs. We rejected that composite class for lack of commonality and typicality, explaining:

> "Conceptually, there is a wide gap between (a) an individual's claim that he has been denied a promotion [or higher pay] on discriminatory grounds, and his otherwise unsupported allegation that the company has a policy of discrimination, and (b) the existence of a class of persons who have suffered the same injury as that individual, such that the individual's claim and the class claim will share common questions of law or fact and that the individual's claim will be typical of the class claims."

Falcon suggested two ways in which that conceptual gap might be bridged. First, if the employer "used a biased testing procedure to evaluate both applicants for employment and incumbent employees, a class action on behalf of every applicant or employee who might have been prejudiced by the test clearly would satisfy the commonality and typicality requirements of Rule 23(a)." Second, "[s]ignificant proof that an employer operated under a general policy of discrimination conceivably could justify a class of both applicants and employees if the discrimination manifested itself in hiring and promotion practices in the same general fashion, such as through entirely subjective decisionmaking processes." We think that statement precisely describes respondents' burden in this case. The first manner of bridging the gap obviously has no application here; Wal–Mart has no testing procedure or other companywide evaluation method that can be charged with bias. The whole point of permitting discretionary decisionmaking is to avoid evaluating employees under a common standard.

The second manner of bridging the gap requires "significant proof" that Wal–Mart "operated under a general policy of discrimination." That is entirely absent here. Wal–Mart's announced policy forbids sex discrimination, and as the District Court recognized the company imposes penalties for denials of equal employment opportunity. The only evidence of a "general policy of discrimination" respondents produced was the testimony of Dr. William Bielby, their sociological expert. Relying on "social framework" analysis, Bielby testified that Wal–Mart has a "strong corporate culture," that makes it " 'vulnerable' " to "gender bias." He could not, however, "determine with any specificity how regularly stereotypes play a meaningful role in employment decisions at Wal–Mart. At his deposition ... Dr. Bielby conceded that he could not calculate whether 0.5 percent or 95 percent of the employment decisions at Wal–Mart might be determined by stereotyped thinking." The parties dispute whether Bielby's testimony even met the standards for the admission of expert testimony under Federal Rule of Civil Procedure 702 and our *Daubert* case, see *Daubert v. Merrell Dow Pharmaceuticals, Inc.,* 509 U.S. 579, 113 S.Ct. 2786, 125 L.Ed.2d 469 (1993). The District Court concluded that *Daubert* did not apply to expert testimony at the certification stage of class-action proceedings. We doubt that is so, but even if properly considered, Bielby's testimony does nothing to advance respondents' case. "[W]hether 0.5 percent or 95 percent of the employment decisions at Wal–Mart might be determined by stereotyped thinking" is the essential question on which respondents' theory of commonality depends. If Bielby admittedly has no answer to that question, we can safely disregard what he has to say. It is worlds away from "significant proof" that Wal–Mart "operated under a general policy of discrimination."

C

The only corporate policy that the plaintiffs' evidence convincingly establishes is Wal–Mart's "policy" of *allowing discretion* by local supervisors over employment matters. On its face, of course, that is just the opposite of a uniform employment practice that would provide the commonality needed for a class action; it is a policy *against having* uniform employment practices. It is also a very common and presumptively reasonable way of doing business—one that we have said "should itself raise no inference of discriminatory conduct," *Watson v. Fort Worth Bank & Trust,* 487 U.S. 977, 990, 108 S.Ct. 2777, 101 L.Ed.2d 827 (1988).

To be sure, we have recognized that, "in appropriate cases," giving discretion to lower-level supervisors can be the basis of Title VII liability under a disparate-impact theory—since "an employer's undisciplined system of subjective decisionmaking [can have] precisely the same effects as a system pervaded by impermissible intentional discrimination." But the recognition that this type of Title VII claim "can" exist does not lead to the conclusion that every employee in a company using a system of discretion has such a claim in common. To the contrary, left to their own devices most managers in any corporation—and surely most managers in a corporation that forbids sex discrimination—would select sex-neutral, performance-based criteria for hiring and promotion that produce no actionable disparity at all. Others may choose to reward various attributes that produce disparate impact—such as scores on general aptitude tests or educational achievements. And still other managers may be guilty of intentional discrimination that produces a sex-based disparity. In such a company, demonstrating the invalidity of one manager's use of discretion will do nothing to demonstrate the invalidity of another's. A party seeking to certify a nationwide class will be unable to show that all the employees' Title VII claims will in fact depend on the answers to common questions.

Respondents have not identified a common mode of exercising discretion that pervades the entire company—aside from their reliance on Dr. Bielby's social frameworks analysis that we have rejected. In a company of

Wal–Mart's size and geographical scope, it is quite unbelievable that all managers would exercise their discretion in a common way without some common direction. Respondents attempt to make that showing by means of statistical and anecdotal evidence, but their evidence falls well short.

The statistical evidence consists primarily of regression analyses performed by Dr. Richard Drogin, a statistician, and Dr. Marc Bendick, a labor economist. Drogin conducted his analysis region-by-region, comparing the number of women promoted into management positions with the percentage of women in the available pool of hourly workers. After considering regional and national data, Drogin concluded that "there are statistically significant disparities between men and women at Wal–Mart ... [and] these disparities ... can be explained only by gender discrimination." Bendick compared work-force data from Wal–Mart and competitive retailers and concluded that Wal–Mart "promotes a lower percentage of women than its competitors."

Even if they are taken at face value, these studies are insufficient to establish that respondents' theory can be proved on a classwide basis. In *Falcon,* we held that one named plaintiff's experience of discrimination was insufficient to infer that "discriminatory treatment is typical of [the employer's employment] practices." A similar failure of inference arises here. As Judge Ikuta observed in her dissent, "[i]nformation about disparities at the regional and national level does not establish the existence of disparities at individual stores, let alone raise the inference that a company-wide policy of discrimination is implemented by discretionary decisions at the store and district level." A regional pay disparity, for example, may be attributable to only a small set of Wal–Mart stores, and cannot by itself establish the uniform, store-by-store disparity upon which the plaintiffs' theory of commonality depends.

There is another, more fundamental, respect in which respondents' statistical proof fails. Even if it established (as it does not) a pay or promotion pattern that differs from the nationwide figures or the regional figures in *all* of Wal–Mart's 3,400 stores, that would still not demonstrate that commonality of issue exists. Some managers will claim that the availability of women, or qualified women, or interested women, in their stores' area does not mirror the national or regional statistics. And almost all of them will claim to have been applying some sex-neutral, performance-based criteria—whose nature and effects will differ from store to store. In the landmark case of ours which held that giving discretion to lower-level supervisors can be the basis of Title VII liability under a disparate-impact theory, the plurality opinion *conditioned* that holding on the corollary that merely proving that the discretionary system has produced a racial or sexual disparity *is not enough*. "[T]he plaintiff must begin by identifying the specific employment practice that is challenged." *Watson,* 487 U.S., at 994, 108 S.Ct. 2777. That is all the more necessary when a class of plaintiffs is sought to be certified. Other than the bare existence of delegated discretion, respondents have identified no "specific employment practice"—much less one that ties all their 1.5 million claims together.

Merely showing that Wal–Mart's policy of discretion has produced an overall sex-based disparity does not suffice.

Respondents' anecdotal evidence suffers from the same defects, and in addition is too weak to raise any inference that all the individual, discretionary personnel decisions are discriminatory. * * * [R]espondents filed some 120 affidavits reporting experiences of discrimination—about 1 for every 12,500 class members—relating to only some 235 out of Wal–Mart's 3,400 stores. More than half of these reports are concentrated in only six States (Alabama, California, Florida, Missouri, Texas, and Wisconsin); half of all States have only one or two anecdotes; and 14 States have no anecdotes about Wal–Mart's operations at all. Even if every single one of these accounts is true, that would not demonstrate that the entire company "operate[s] under a general policy of discrimination," which is what respondents must show to certify a companywide class.

The dissent misunderstands the nature of the foregoing analysis. It criticizes our focus on the dissimilarities between the putative class members on the ground that we have "blend[ed]" Rule 23(a)(2)'s commonality requirement with Rule 23(b)(3)'s inquiry into whether common questions "predominate" over individual ones. That is not so. We quite agree that for purposes of Rule 23(a)(2) " '[e]ven a single [common] question' " will do. We have considered dissimilarities not in order to determine (as Rule 23(b)(3) requires) whether common questions *predominate,* but in order to determine (as Rule 23(a)(2) requires) whether there *is* "[e]ven a single [common] question." And there is not here. Because respondents provide no convincing proof of a companywide discriminatory pay and promotion policy, we have concluded that they have not established the existence of any common question.

In sum, we agree with Chief Judge Kozinski that the members of the class:

> "held a multitude of different jobs, at different levels of Wal–Mart's hierarchy, for variable lengths of time, in 3,400 stores, sprinkled across 50 states, with a kaleidoscope of supervisors (male and female), subject to a variety of regional policies that all differed.... Some thrived while others did poorly. They have little in common but their sex and this lawsuit." 603 F.3d, at 652 (dissenting opinion).

III

We also conclude that respondents' claims for backpay were improperly certified under Federal Rule of Civil Procedure 23(b)(2). Our opinion in *Ticor Title Ins. Co. v. Brown,* 511 U.S. 117, 121, 114 S.Ct. 1359, 128 L.Ed.2d 33 (1994) *(per curiam)* expressed serious doubt about whether claims for monetary relief may be certified under that provision. We now hold that they may not, at least where (as here) the monetary relief is not incidental to the injunctive or declaratory relief.

A

Rule 23(b)(2) allows class treatment when "the party opposing the class has acted or refused to act on grounds that apply generally to the class, so that final injunctive relief or corresponding declaratory relief is appropriate respecting the class as a whole." One possible reading of this provision is that it applies *only* to requests for such injunctive or declaratory relief and does not authorize the class certification of monetary claims at all. We need not reach that broader question in this case, because we think that, at a minimum, claims for *individualized* relief (like the backpay at issue here) do not satisfy the Rule. The key to the (b)(2) class is "the indivisible nature of the injunctive or declaratory remedy warranted—the notion that the conduct is such that it can be enjoined or declared unlawful only as to all of the class members or as to none of them." In other words, Rule 23(b)(2) applies only when a single injunction or declaratory judgment would provide relief to each member of the class. It does not authorize class certification when each individual class member would be entitled to a *different* injunction or declaratory judgment against the defendant. Similarly, it does not authorize class certification when each class member would be entitled to an individualized award of monetary damages.

* * *

Permitting the combination of individualized and classwide relief in a (b)(2) class is also inconsistent with the structure of Rule 23(b). Classes certified under (b)(1) and (b)(2) share the most traditional justifications for class treatment—that individual adjudications would be impossible or unworkable, as in a(b)(1) class, or that the relief sought must perforce affect the entire class at once, as in a (b)(2) class. For that reason these are also mandatory classes: The Rule provides no opportunity for (b)(1) or (b)(2) class members to opt out, and does not even oblige the District Court to afford them notice of the action. Rule 23(b)(3), by contrast, is an "adventuresome innovation" of the 1966 amendments, framed for situations "in which 'class-action treatment is not as clearly called for.'" It allows class certification in a much wider set of circumstances but with greater procedural protections. Its only prerequisites are that "the questions of law or fact common to class members predominate over any questions affecting only individual members, and that a class action is superior to other available methods for fairly and efficiently adjudicating the controversy." And unlike (b)(1) and (b)(2) classes, the (b)(3) class is not mandatory; class members are entitled to receive "the best notice that is practicable under the circumstances" and to withdraw from the class at their option. See Rule 23(c)(2)(B).

Given that structure, we think it clear that individualized monetary claims belong in Rule 23(b)(3). The procedural protections attending the (b)(3) class—predominance, superiority, mandatory notice, and the right to opt out—are missing from (b)(2) not because the Rule considers them unnecessary, but because it considers them unnecessary *to a (b)(2) class.* When a class seeks an indivisible injunction benefitting all its members at once, there is no reason to undertake a case-specific inquiry into whether class issues predominate or whether class action is a superior method of adjudicating the dispute. Predominance and superiority are self-evident. But with respect to each class member's individualized claim for money, that is not so—which is precisely why (b)(3) requires the judge to make findings about predominance and superiority before allowing the class. Similarly, (b)(2) does not require that class members be given notice and opt-out rights, presumably because it is thought (rightly or wrongly) that notice has no purpose when the class is mandatory, and that depriving people of their right to sue in this manner complies with the Due Process Clause. In the context of a class action predominantly for money damages we have held that absence of notice and opt-out violates due process. While we have never held that to be so where the monetary claims do not predominate, the serious possibility that it may be so provides an additional reason not to read Rule 23(b)(2) to include the monetary claims here.

B

Against that conclusion, respondents argue that their claims for backpay were appropriately certified as part of a class under Rule 23(b)(2) because those claims do not "predominate" over their requests for injunctive and declaratory relief. They rely upon the Advisory Committee's statement that Rule 23(b)(2) "does not extend to cases in which the appropriate final relief relates *exclusively or predominantly* to money damages." The negative implication, they argue, is that it *does* extend to cases in which the appropriate final relief relates only partially and nonpredominantly to money damages. Of course it is the Rule itself, not the Advisory Committee's description of it, that governs. And a mere negative inference does not in our view suffice to establish a disposition that has no basis in the Rule's text, and that does obvious violence to the Rule's structural features. The mere "predominance" of a proper (b)(2) injunctive claim does nothing to justify elimination of Rule 23(b)(3)'s procedural protections: It neither establishes the superiority of *class* adjudication over *individual* adjudication nor cures the notice and opt-out problems. We fail to see why the Rule should be read to nullify these protections whenever a plaintiff class, at its option, combines its monetary claims with a request—even a "predominating request"—for an injunction.

Respondents' predominance test, moreover, creates perverse incentives for class representatives to place at risk potentially valid claims for monetary relief. In this case, for example, the named plaintiffs declined to include employees' claims for compensatory damages in their complaint. That strategy of including only backpay claims made it more likely that monetary relief would not "predominate." But it also created the possibility (if the predominance test were correct) that individual class members' compensatory-damages claims would be *precluded* by litigation they had no power to hold themselves apart from. If it were determined, for example, that a particular class member is not entitled to backpay because her denial of increased pay or a promotion was *not* the product of discrimination, that employee might be collaterally estopped from independently seeking compensatory damages based on that same denial. That possibility underscores the need for plaintiffs with individual monetary claims to decide *for themselves* whether to tie their fates to the class representatives' or go it alone—a choice Rule 23(b)(2) does not ensure that they have.

The predominance test would also require the District Court to reevaluate the roster of class members continually. The Ninth Circuit recognized the necessity for this when it concluded that those plaintiffs no longer employed by Wal–Mart lack standing to seek injunctive or declaratory relief against its employment practices. The Court of Appeals' response to that difficulty, however, was not to eliminate *all* former employees from the certified class, but to eliminate only those who had left the company's employ by the date the complaint was filed. That solution has no logical connection to the problem, since those who have left their Wal–Mart jobs *since* the complaint was filed have no more need for prospective relief than those who left beforehand. As a consequence, even though the validity of a (b)(2) class depends on whether "final injunctive relief or corresponding declaratory relief is appropriate respecting the class *as a whole,*" Rule 23(b)(2) (emphasis added), about half the members of the class approved by the Ninth Circuit have no claim for injunctive or declaratory relief at all. Of course, the alternative (and logical) solution of excising plaintiffs from the class as they leave their employment may have struck the Court of Appeals as wasteful of the District Court's time. Which indeed it is, since if a backpay action were properly certified for class treatment under *(b)(3),* the ability to litigate a plaintiff's backpay claim as part of the class would not turn on the irrelevant question whether she is still employed at Wal–Mart. What follows from this, however, is not that some arbitrary limitation on class membership should be imposed but that the backpay claims should not be certified under Rule 23(b)(2) at all.

Finally, respondents argue that their backpay claims are appropriate for a (b)(2) class action because a backpay award is equitable in nature. The latter may be true, but it is irrelevant. The Rule does not speak of "equitable" remedies generally but of injunctions and declaratory judgments. As Title VII itself makes pellucidly clear, backpay is neither. See 42 U.S.C. § 2000e–5(g)(2)(B)(i) and (ii) (distinguishing between declaratory and injunctive relief and the payment of "backpay," see § 2000e–5(g)(2)(A)).

C

In *Allison v. Citgo Petroleum Corp.,* 151 F.3d 402, 415 (C.A.5 1998), the Fifth Circuit held that a (b)(2) class would permit the certification of monetary relief that is "incidental to requested injunctive or declaratory relief," which it defined as "damages that flow directly from liability to the class *as a whole* on the claims forming the basis of the injunctive or declaratory relief." In that court's view, such "incidental damage should not require additional hearings to resolve the disparate merits of each individual's case; it should neither introduce new substantial legal or factual issues, nor entail complex individualized determinations." We need not decide in this case whether there are any forms of "incidental" monetary relief that are consistent with the interpretation of Rule 23(b)(2) we have announced and that comply with the Due Process Clause. Respondents do not argue that they can satisfy this standard, and in any event they cannot.

Contrary to the Ninth Circuit's view, Wal–Mart is entitled to individualized determinations of each employee's eligibility for backpay. Title VII includes a detailed remedial scheme. If a plaintiff prevails in showing that an employer has discriminated against him in violation of the statute, the court "may enjoin the respondent from engaging in such unlawful employment practice, and order such affirmative action as may be appropriate, [including] reinstatement or hiring of employees, with or without backpay ... or any other equitable relief as the court deems appropriate." But if the employer can show that it took an adverse employment action against an employee for any reason other than discrimination, the court cannot order the "hiring, reinstatement, or promotion of an individual as an employee, or the payment to him of any backpay." § 2000e–5(g)(2)(A).

We have established a procedure for trying pattern-or-practice cases that gives effect to these statutory requirements. When the plaintiff seeks individual relief such as reinstatement or backpay after establishing a pattern or practice of discrimination, "a district court must usually conduct additional proceedings ... to determine the scope of individual relief." *Teamsters,* 431 U.S., at 361, 97 S.Ct. 1843. At this phase, the burden of proof will shift to the company, but it will have the right to raise any individual affirmative defenses it may have, and to "demonstrate that the individual applicant was denied an employment opportunity for lawful reasons."

The Court of Appeals believed that it was possible to replace such proceedings with Trial by Formula. A sample set of the class members would be selected, as to whom liability for sex discrimination and the backpay owing as a result would be determined in depositions supervised by a master. The percentage of claims determined to be valid would then be applied to the entire remaining class, and the number of (presumptively) valid claims thus derived would be multiplied by the average backpay award in the sample set to arrive at the entire class recovery—without further individualized proceedings. We disapprove that novel project. Because the Rules Enabling Act forbids interpreting Rule 23 to "abridge, enlarge or modify any substantive right," 28 U.S.C. § 2072(b); a class cannot be certified on the premise that Wal–Mart will not be entitled to litigate its statutory defenses to individual claims. And because the necessity of that litigation will prevent backpay from being "incidental" to the classwide injunction, respondents' class could not be certified even assuming, *arguendo,* that "incidental" monetary relief can be awarded to a 23(b)(2) class.

The judgment of the Court of Appeals is

Reversed.

JUSTICE GINSBURG, with whom JUSTICE BREYER, JUSTICE SOTOMAYOR, and JUSTICE KAGAN join, concurring in part and dissenting in part.

The class in this case, I agree with the Court, should not have been certified under Federal Rule of Civil Procedure 23(b)(2). The plaintiffs, alleging discrimination in violation of Title VII, seek monetary relief that is not merely incidental to any injunctive or declaratory relief that might be available. A putative class of this type may be certifiable under Rule 23(b)(3), if the plaintiffs show that common class questions "predominate" over issues affecting individuals—*e.g.*, qualification for, and the amount of, backpay or compensatory damages—and that a class action is "superior" to other modes of adjudication.

Whether the class the plaintiffs describe meets the specific requirements of Rule 23(b)(3) is not before the Court, and I would reserve that matter for consideration and decision on remand. The Court, however, disqualifies the class at the starting gate, holding that the plaintiffs cannot cross the "commonality" line set by Rule 23(a)(2). In so ruling, the Court imports into the Rule 23(a) determination concerns properly addressed in a Rule 23(b)(3) assessment.

I

A

Rule 23(a)(2) establishes a preliminary requirement for maintaining a class action: "[T]here are questions of law or fact common to the class." The Rule "does not require that all questions of law or fact raised in the litigation be common," 1 H. Newberg & A. Conte, Newberg on Class Actions § 3.10, pp. 3–48 to 3–49 (3d ed.1992); indeed, "[e]ven a single question of law or fact common to the members of the class will satisfy the commonality requirement," Nagareda, The Preexistence Principle and the Structure of the Class Action, 103 Colum. L.Rev. 149, 176, n. 110 (2003). See Advisory Committee's 1937 Notes on Fed. Rule Civ. Proc. 23, 28 U.S.C.App., p. 138 (citing with approval cases in which "there was only a question of law or fact common to" the class members).

A "question" is ordinarily understood to be "[a] subject or point open to controversy." American Heritage Dictionary 1483 (3d ed.1992). See also Black's Law Dictionary 1366 (9th ed.2009) (defining "question of fact" as "[a] disputed issue to be resolved . . . [at] trial" and "question of law" as "[a]n issue to be decided by the judge"). Thus, a "question" "common to the class" must be a dispute, either of fact or of law, the resolution of which will advance the determination of the class members' claims.

B

The District Court, recognizing that "one significant issue common to the class may be sufficient to warrant certification," found that the plaintiffs easily met that test. Absent an error of law or an abuse of discretion, an appellate tribunal has no warrant to upset the District Court's finding of commonality. See *Califano v. Yamasaki,* 442 U.S. 682, 703, 99 S.Ct. 2545, 61 L.Ed.2d 176 (1979) ("[M]ost issues arising under Rule 23 ... [are] committed in the first instance to the discretion of the district court.").

The District Court certified a class of "[a]ll women employed at any Wal–Mart domestic retail store at any time since December 26, 1998." The named plaintiffs, led by Betty Dukes, propose to litigate, on behalf of the class, allegations that Wal–Mart discriminates on the basis of gender in pay and promotions. They allege that the company "[r]eli[es] on gender stereotypes in making employment decisions such as ... promotion[s][and] pay." Wal–Mart permits those prejudices to infect personnel decisions, the plaintiffs contend, by leaving pay and promotions in the hands of "a nearly all male managerial workforce" using "arbitrary and subjective criteria." Further alleged barriers to the advancement of female employees include the company's requirement, "as a condition of promotion to management jobs, that employees be willing to relocate." Absent instruction otherwise, there is a risk that managers will act on the familiar assumption that women, because of their services to husband and children, are less mobile than men. See Dept. of Labor, Federal Glass Ceiling Commission, Good for Business: Making Full Use of the Nation's Human Capital 151 (1995).

Women fill 70 percent of the hourly jobs in the retailer's stores but make up only "33 percent of management employees." "[T]he higher one looks in the organization the lower the percentage of women." The plaintiffs' "largely uncontested descriptive statistics" also show that women working in the company's stores "are paid less than men in every region" and "that the salary gap widens over time even for men and women hired into the same jobs at the same time."

The District Court identified "systems for ... promoting in-store employees" that were "sufficiently similar across regions and stores" to conclude that "the manner in which these systems affect the class raises issues that are common to all class members." The selection of employees for promotion to in-store management "is fairly characterized as a 'tap on the shoulder' process," in which managers have discretion about whose shoulders to tap. Vacancies are not regularly posted; from among those employees satisfying minimum qualifications, managers choose whom to promote on the basis of their own subjective impressions.

Wal–Mart's compensation policies also operate uniformly across stores, the District Court found. The retailer leaves open a $2 band for every position's hourly pay rate. Wal–Mart provides no standards or criteria for setting wages within that band, and thus does nothing to counter unconscious bias on the part of supervisors.

Wal–Mart's supervisors do not make their discretionary decisions in a vacuum. The District Court reviewed means Wal–Mart used to maintain a "carefully constructed ... corporate culture," such as frequent meetings to reinforce the common way of thinking, regular transfers of managers between stores to ensure uniformity throughout the company, monitoring of stores "on a close and constant basis," and "Wal–Mart TV," "broadcas[t] . . . into all stores." The plaintiffs' evidence, including class members' tales of their own experiences, suggests that gender bias suffused Wal–Mart's company culture. Among illustrations, senior management often refer to female associates as "little Janie Qs." One manager told an employee that "[m]en are here to make a career and women aren't." A committee of female Wal–Mart executives concluded that "[s]tereotypes limit the opportunities offered to women."

Finally, the plaintiffs presented an expert's appraisal to show that the pay and promotions disparities at Wal–Mart "can be explained only by gender discrimination and not by . . . neutral variables." Using regression analyses, their expert, Richard Drogin, controlled for factors including, *inter alia,* job performance, length of time with the company, and the store where an employee worked. The results, the District Court found, were sufficient to raise an "inference of discrimination."

C

The District Court's identification of a common question, whether Wal–Mart's pay and promotions policies gave rise to unlawful discrimination, was hardly infirm. The practice of delegating to supervisors large discretion to make personnel decisions, uncontrolled by formal standards, has long been known to have the potential to produce disparate effects. Managers, like all humankind, may be prey to biases of which they are unaware. The risk of discrimination is heightened when those managers are predominantly of one sex, and are steeped in a corporate culture that perpetuates gender stereotypes.

The plaintiffs' allegations resemble those in one of the prototypical cases in this area, *Leisner v. New York Tel. Co.,* 358 F.Supp. 359, 364–365 (S.D.N.Y.1973). In deciding on promotions, supervisors in that case were to start with objective measures; but ultimately, they were to "look at the individual as a total individual." (internal quotation marks omitted). The final question they were to ask and answer: "Is this person going to be successful in our business?" It is hardly surprising that for many managers, the ideal candidate was someone with characteristics similar to their own.

We have held that "discretionary employment practices" can give rise to Title VII claims, not only when such practices are motivated by discriminatory intent but also when they produce discriminatory results. See *Watson v. Fort Worth Bank & Trust,* 487 U.S. 977, 988, 991, 108 S.Ct. 2777, 101 L.Ed.2d 827 (1988). * * * In *Watson,* as here, an employer had given its managers large authority over promotions. An employee sued the bank under Title VII, alleging that the "discretionary promotion system" caused a discriminatory effect based on race. Four different supervisors had declined, on separate occasions, to promote the employee. Their reasons were subjective and unknown. The employer, we noted "had not developed precise and formal criteria for evaluating candidates"; "[i]t relied instead on the subjective judgment of supervisors."

Aware of "the problem of subconscious stereotypes and prejudices," we held that the employer's "undisciplined system of subjective decisionmaking" was an "employment practic[e]" that "may be analyzed under the disparate impact approach."

The plaintiffs' allegations state claims of gender discrimination in the form of biased decisionmaking in both pay and promotions. The evidence reviewed by the District Court adequately demonstrated that resolving those claims would necessitate examination of particular policies and practices alleged to affect, adversely and globally, women employed at Wal–Mart's stores. Rule 23(a)(2), setting a necessary but not a sufficient criterion for class-action certification, demands nothing further.

II

A

The Court gives no credence to the key dispute common to the class: whether Wal–Mart's discretionary pay and promotion policies are discriminatory. ("Reciting" questions like "Is [giving managers discretion over pay] an unlawful employment practice?" "is not sufficient to obtain class certification."). "What matters," the Court asserts, "is not the raising of common 'questions,'" but whether there are "[d]issimilarities within the proposed class" that "have the potential to impede the generation of common answers."

The Court blends Rule 23(a)(2)'s threshold criterion with the more demanding criteria of Rule 23(b)(3), and thereby elevates the (a)(2) inquiry so that it is no longer "easily satisfied." Rule 23(b)(3) certification requires, in addition to the four 23(a) findings, determinations that "questions of law or fact common to class members predominate over any questions affecting only individual members" and that "a class action is superior to other available methods for . . . adjudicating the controversy."

The Court's emphasis on differences between class members mimics the Rule 23(b)(3) inquiry into whether common questions "predominate" over individual issues. And by asking whether the individual differences "impede" common adjudication, the Court duplicates 23(b)(3)'s question whether "a class action is superior" to other modes of adjudication. * * *

Because Rule 23(a) is also a prerequisite for Rule 23(b)(1) and Rule 23(b)(2) classes, the Court's "dissimilarities" position is far reaching. Individual differences should not bar a Rule 23(b)(1) or Rule 23(b)(2) class, so long as the Rule 23(a) threshold is met. * * * For example, in *Franks v. Bowman Transp. Co.,* 424 U.S. 747, 96 S.Ct. 1251, 47 L.Ed.2d 444 (1976), a Rule 23(b)(2) class of African–American truckdrivers complained that the defendant had discriminatorily refused to hire black applicants. We recognized that the "qualification[s] and performance" of individual class members might vary. "Generalizations concerning such individually applicable evidence," we cautioned, "cannot serve as a justification for the denial of [injunctive] relief to the entire class."

B

The "dissimilarities" approach leads the Court to train its attention on what distinguishes individual class members, rather than on what unites them. Given the lack of standards for pay and promotions, the majority says, "demonstrating the invalidity of one manager's use of discretion will do nothing to demonstrate the invalidity of another's."

Wal–Mart's delegation of discretion over pay and promotions is a policy uniform throughout all stores. The very nature of discretion is that people will exercise it in various ways. A system of delegated discretion, *Watson* held, is a practice actionable under Title VII when it produces discriminatory outcomes. 487 U.S., at 990–991, 108 S.Ct. 2777; A finding that Wal–Mart's pay and promotions practices in fact violate the law would be the first step in the usual order of proof for plaintiffs seeking individual remedies for company-wide discrimination. *Teamsters v. United States,* 431 U.S. 324, 359, 97 S.Ct. 1843, 52 L.Ed.2d 396 (1977). That each individual employee's unique circumstances will ultimately determine whether she is entitled to backpay or damages, should not factor into the Rule 23(a)(2) determination.

The Court errs in importing a "dissimilarities" notion suited to Rule 23(b)(3) into the Rule 23(a) commonality inquiry. I therefore cannot join Part II of the Court's opinion.

NOTES

1. The Court addressed two issues: whether the class action was properly certified under Rule 23(b)(2), even though the plaintiffs were seeking monetary relief in the form of back pay and punitive damages, in addition to injunctive relief; and whether the plaintiffs met the commonality requirement of Rule 23(a). On the Rule 23(b)(2) issue, the plaintiffs lost unanimously. Recall Mr. Seligman's discussion of the plaintiffs' strategy of not seeking compensatory damages in an effort to keep the action under Rule 23(b)(2). That strategy worked in the lower courts. Did it backfire in the Supreme Court?

2. With respect to the commonality requirement, has the Court effectively equated common issues of law or fact to identical issues of law or fact? Could plaintiffs likely meet the commonality requirement for a class of all current and former employees in a single division of Wal–Mart? In a single region? In a single store? Is it possible for plaintiffs in an employment discrimination case to meet the commonality requirement and still meet the numerosity requirement?

3. What effect does the Supreme Court's decision have on the ability of individual plaintiffs to sue Wal–Mart? In *Crown Cork & Seal Co. v. Parker,* 462 U.S. 345, 103 S.Ct. 2392, 76 L.Ed.2d 628 (1983), the Court held that the filing of a class action tolls the running of the 90–day period to file

suit after the issuance of a right to sue letter for all putative class members until the denial of a motion to certify the class. Putative class members who did not receive right to sue letters until after the class action was filed have a full 90 days from the denial of class certification to file their own individual actions or move to intervene in the original law suit.

4. ***General Telephone Co. v. EEOC,*** 446 U.S. 318, 100 S.Ct. 1698, 64 L.Ed.2d 319 (1980), held that the EEOC may bring an action under Title VII seeking class-wide relief without complying with Rule 23.

D. SETTLEMENTS AND RELEASES

OUBRE v. ENTERGY OPERATIONS, INC.

Supreme Court of the United States, 1998
522 U.S. 422, 118 S.Ct. 838, 139 L.Ed.2d 849

JUSTICE KENNEDY delivered the opinion of the Court.

* * *

I

Petitioner Dolores Oubre worked as a scheduler at a power plant in Killona, Louisiana, run by her employer, respondent Entergy Operations, Inc. In 1994, she received a poor performance rating. Oubre's supervisor met with her on January 17, 1995, and gave her the option of either improving her performance during the coming year or accepting a voluntary arrangement for her severance. She received a packet of information about the severance agreement and had 14 days to consider her options, during which she consulted with attorneys. On January 31, Oubre decided to accept. She signed a release, in which she "agree[d] to waive, settle, release, and discharge any and all claims, demands, damages, actions, or causes of action ... that I may have against Entergy ...." In exchange, she received six installment payments over the next four months, totaling $6,258.

The Older Workers Benefit Protection Act (OWBPA) imposes specific requirements for releases covering ADEA claims. OWBPA, § 201, 29 U.S.C. §§ 626(f)(1)(B), (F), (G). In procuring the release, Entergy did not comply with the OWBPA in at least three respects: (1) Entergy did not give Oubre enough time to consider her options. (2) Entergy did not give Oubre seven days after she signed the release to change her mind. And (3) the release made no specific reference to claims under the ADEA.

Oubre filed a charge of age discrimination with the Equal Employment Opportunity Commission, which dismissed her charge on the merits but issued a right-to-sue letter. She filed this suit against Entergy in the United States District Court for the Eastern District of Louisiana, alleging constructive discharge on the basis of her age in violation of the ADEA and state law. Oubre has not offered or tried to return the $6,258 to Entergy, nor is it clear she has the means to do so. Entergy moved for summary judgment, claiming Oubre had ratified the defective release by failing to return or offer to return the moneys she had received. The District Court agreed and entered summary judgment for Entergy. The Court of Appeals affirmed, and we granted certiorari.

II

The employer rests its case upon general principles of state contract jurisprudence. As the employer recites the rule, contracts tainted by mistake, duress, or even fraud are voidable at the option of the innocent party. See 1 Restatement (Second) of Contracts § 7. The employer maintains, however, that before the innocent party can elect avoidance, she must first tender back any benefits received under the contract. If she fails to do so within a reasonable time after learning of her rights, the employer contends, she ratifies the contract and so makes it binding. 1 Restatement (Second) of Contracts, *supra*, § 7, Comments. The employer also invokes the doctrine of equitable estoppel. As a rule, equitable estoppel bars a party from shirking the burdens of a voidable transaction for as long as she retains the benefits received under it. Applying these principles, the employer claims the employee ratified the ineffective release (or faces estoppel) by retaining all the sums paid in consideration of it. The employer, then, relies not upon the execution of the release but upon a later, distinct ratification of its terms.

These general rules may not be as unified as the employer asserts. Even if the employer's statement of the general rule requiring tender back before one files suit were correct, it would be unavailing. * * * The authorities cited do not consider the question raised by statutory standards for releases and a statutory declaration making nonconforming releases ineffective. It is the latter question we confront here.

In 1990, Congress amended the ADEA by passing the OWBPA. The OWBPA provides: "An individual may not waive any right or claim under [the ADEA] unless the waiver is knowing and voluntary.... [A] waiver may not be considered knowing and voluntary unless at a minimum" it satisfies certain enumerated requirements, including the three listed above. 29 U.S.C. § 626(f)(1).

The statutory command is clear: An employee "may not waive" an ADEA claim unless the waiver or release satisfies the OWBPA's requirements. The policy of the OWBPA is likewise clear from its title: It is designed to protect the rights and benefits of older workers. The OWBPA implements Congress' policy via a strict, unqualified statutory stricture on waivers, and we are bound to take Congress at its word. Congress imposed specific duties on employers who seek releases of certain claims created by statute. Congress delineated these duties with precision and without qualification: An employee "may not waive" an ADEA claim unless the employer complies with the statute. Courts cannot with ease presume ratification of that which Congress forbids.

The OWBPA sets up its own regime for assessing the effect of ADEA waivers, separate and apart from contract law. The statute creates a series of prerequisites for knowing and voluntary waivers and imposes affirmative duties of disclosure and waiting periods. The OWBPA governs the effect under federal law of waivers or releases on ADEA claims and incorporates no exceptions or qualifications. The text of the OWBPA forecloses the employer's defense, notwithstanding how general contract principles would apply to non-ADEA claims.

The rule proposed by the employer would frustrate the statute's practical operation as well as its formal command. In many instances a discharged employee likely will have spent the moneys received and will lack the means to tender their return. These realities might tempt employers to risk noncompliance with the OWBPA's waiver provisions, knowing it will be difficult to repay the moneys and relying on ratification. We ought not to open the door to an evasion of the statute by this device.

* * *

We reverse the judgment of the Court of Appeals and remand the case for further proceedings consistent with this opinion.

APPENDIX TO OPINION OF THE COURT

Older Workers Benefit Protection Act, § 201, 29 U.S.C. § 626(f):

(f) Waiver

(1) An individual may not waive any right or claim under this Act unless the waiver is knowing and voluntary. Except as provided in paragraph (2), a waiver may not be considered knowing and voluntary unless at a minimum—

(A) the waiver is part of an agreement between the individual and the employer that is written in a manner calculated to be understood by such individual, or by the average individual eligible to participate;

(B) the waiver specifically refers to rights or claims arising under this Act;

(C) the individual does not waive rights or claims that may arise after the date the waiver is executed;

(D) the individual waives rights or claims only in exchange for consideration in addition to anything of value to which the individual already is entitled;

(E) the individual is advised in writing to consult with an attorney prior to executing the agreement;

(F)(i) the individual is given a period of at least 21 days within which to consider the agreement; or

(ii) if a waiver is requested in connection with an exit incentive or other employment termination program offered to a group or class of employees, the individual is given a period of at least 45 days within which to consider the agreement;

(G) the agreement provides that for a period of at least 7 days following the execution of such agreement, the individual may revoke the agreement, and the agreement shall not become effective or enforceable until the revocation period has expired;

(H) if a waiver is requested in connection with an exit incentive or other employment termination program offered to a group or class of employees, the employer (at the commencement of the period specified in subparagraph (F)) informs the individual in writing in a manner calculated to be understood by the average individual eligible to participate, as to-

(i) any class, unit, or group of individuals covered by such program, any eligibility factors for such program, and any time limits applicable to such program; and

(ii) the job titles and ages of all individuals eligible or selected for the program, and the ages of all individuals in the same job classification or organizational unit who are not eligible or selected for the program.

2) A waiver in settlement of a charge filed with the Equal Employment Opportunity Commission, or an action filed in court by the individual or the individual's representative, alleging age discrimination of a kind prohibited under section 4 or 15 may not be considered knowing and voluntary unless at a minimum-

(A) subparagraphs (A) through (E) of paragraph (1) have been met; and

(B) the individual is given a reasonable period of time within which to consider the settlement agreement.

(3) In any dispute that may arise over whether any of the requirements, conditions, and circumstances set forth in subparagraph (A), (B), (C), (D), (E), (F), (G), or (H) of paragraph (1), or subparagraph (A) or (B) of paragraph (2), have been met, the party asserting the validity of a waiver shall have the burden of proving in a court of competent jurisdiction that a waiver was knowing and voluntary pursuant to paragraph (1) or (2).

(4) No waiver agreement may affect the Commission's rights and responsibilities to enforce this Act. No waiver may be used to justify interfering with the protected right of an employee to file a charge or participate in an investigation or proceeding conducted by the Commission.

[The concurring opinion of JUSTICE BREYER, joined by JUSTICE O'CONNOR; the dissenting opinion of JUSTICE SCALIA; and the dissenting opinion of JUSTICE THOMAS, joined by CHIEF JUSTICE REHNQUIST, are omitted.]

NOTES

1. In his concurring opinion, Justice Breyer opined that settlement agreements that fail to comply with the Older Workers Benefits Protection Act are not void, but rather are voidable, much like a contract made by a

minor or one induced by fraud or mistake. Consequently, for example, an employer is not free to cancel its obligations under the non-compliant agreement and an employer may seek restitution of payment made under the agreement or relief from any on-going obligations in the plaintiff's ADEA lawsuit. He further observed that five Justices took this view.

2. Following the Court's decision in *Oubre*, the EEOC issued regulations concerning non-compliant settlements and releases. The regulations provide that a plaintiff need not tender back consideration given under an invalid release as a condition of filing suit and a settlement agreement may not require tender back as a condition of filing suit. The regulations further provide that courts have discretion to award the employer restitution of payments made under the non-compliant settlement agreement but that such restitution may never exceed the amount the employee recovers on the ADEA claim or the amount received by the employee under the non-compliant settlement agreement. 29 C.F.R. § 1625.23.

3. The Older Worker Benefits Protection Act applies only to ADEA claims. Courts considering releases under other statutes, including Title VII and the ADA, have evaluated them either using basic principles of contract law or a totality of the circumstances test to determine whether they were made knowingly and voluntarily. *Compare e.g., Adams v. Philip Morris, Inc.,* 67 F.3d 580 (6th Cir. 1995) (ordinary contract principles) *with Myricks v. Federal Reserve Bank of Atlanta,* 480 F.3d 1036 (11th Cir. 2007).

E. ARBITRATION

In **_Alexander v. Gardner–Denver Co._**, 415 U.S. 36, 94 S.Ct. 1011, 39 L.Ed.2d 147 (1974), Alexander grieved his discharge and the union took the matter to arbitration where it lost. Alexander subsequently brought a Title VII lawsuit. The Court of Appeals for the Tenth Circuit held that the adverse arbitration award barred Alexander's lawsuit but the Supreme Court reversed. The Court held that the Title VII claim and the grievance were independent of each other. Consequently, Alexander could try his Title VII claim de novo even though his union had lost the grievance in arbitration. The Court applied *Gardner–Denver* to hold that an employee may bring an action under the Fair Labor Standards Act without first resorting to the collective bargaining agreement's grievance procedure in **_Barrentine v. Arkansas–Best Freight System, Inc._**, 450 U.S. 728, 101 S.Ct. 1437, 67 L.Ed.2d 641 (1981). **_McDonald v. City of West Branch,_** 466 U.S. 284, 104 S.Ct. 1799, 80 L.Ed.2d 302 (1984), extended these holdings to actions under 42 U.S.C. § 1983.

The Court in *Gardner–Denver* offered several rationales behind its holding. The Court observed that arbitration is intended to resolve claims under the collective bargaining agreement rather than claims under a statute that are independent of the contract. The Court also expressed concern that the union, rather than the individual employee, controlled the grievance process. The Court focused a good deal of its rationale, however, on the inappropriateness of arbitration for resolving statutory claims.

Particularly, after the Civil Rights Act of 1991 made available compensatory and punitive damages and jury trials in Title VII cases, some employers required employees as a condition of employment to agree to arbitrate any claims arising out of their employment, including claims for violation of anti-discrimination statutes, rather than sue in court. All federal circuit courts of appeals except for the Fourth Circuit, that considered the validity of such agreements relied on *Gardner–Denver* and held them unenforceable. The Fourth Circuit's decision to the contrary came before the Supreme Court in the following case.

GILMER v. INTERSTATE/JOHNSON LANE CORP.

Supreme Court of the United States, 1991
500 U.S. 20, 111 S.Ct. 1647, 114 L.Ed.2d 26

JUSTICE WHITE delivered the opinion of the Court.

* * *

I

Respondent Interstate/Johnson Lane Corporation (Interstate) hired petitioner Robert Gilmer as a Manager of Financial Services in May 1981. As required by his employment, Gilmer registered as a securities representative with several stock exchanges, including the New York Stock Exchange (NYSE). His registration application, entitled "Uniform Application for Securities Industry Registration or Transfer," provided, among other things, that Gilmer "agree[d] to arbitrate any dispute, claim or controversy" arising between him and Interstate "that is required to be arbitrated under the rules, constitutions or by-laws of the organizations with which I register." *Id.*, at 18. Of relevance to this case, NYSE Rule 347 provides for arbitration of "[a]ny controversy between a registered representative and any member or member organization arising out of the employment or termination of employment of such registered representative."

Interstate terminated Gilmer's employment in 1987, at which time Gilmer was 62 years of age. After first filing an age discrimination charge with the Equal Employment Opportunity Commission (EEOC), Gilmer subsequently brought suit in the United States District Court for the Western District of North Carolina, alleging that Interstate had discharged him because of his age, in violation of the ADEA. In response to Gilmer's complaint, Interstate filed in the District Court a motion to compel arbitration of the ADEA claim. In its motion, Interstate relied upon the arbitration agreement in Gilmer's registration application, as well as the Federal Arbitration Act (FAA), 9 U.S.C. § 1 *et seq.* The District Court denied Interstate's motion, based on this Court's decision in *Alexander v. Gardner–Denver Co.*, 415 U.S. 36, 94 S.Ct. 1011, 39 L.Ed.2d 147 (1974), and because it concluded that "Congress intended to protect ADEA claimants from the waiver of a judicial forum." The United States Court of Appeals for the Fourth Circuit reversed, finding "nothing in the text, legislative history, or underlying purposes of the ADEA indicating a congressional intent to preclude enforcement of arbitration agreements." We granted certiorari to resolve a conflict among the Courts of Appeals regarding the arbitrability of ADEA claims.

II

The FAA was originally enacted in 1925, 43 Stat. 883, and then reenacted and codified in 1947 as Title 9 of the United States Code. * * * Its primary substantive provision states that "[a] written provision in any maritime transaction or a contract evidencing a transaction involving commerce to settle by arbitration a controversy thereafter arising out of such contract or transaction ... shall be valid, irrevocable, and enforceable, save upon such grounds as exist at law or in equity for the revocation of any contract." 9 U.S.C. § 2. The FAA also provides for stays of proceedings in federal district courts when an issue in the proceeding is referable to arbitration, § 3, and for orders compelling arbitration when one party has failed, neglected, or refused to comply with an arbitration agreement, § 4. These provisions manifest a "liberal federal policy favoring arbitration agreements." *Moses H. Cone Memorial Hospital v. Mercury Construction Corp.*, 460 U.S. 1, 24, 103 S.Ct. 927, 941, 74 L.Ed.2d 765 (1983).

It is by now clear that statutory claims may be the subject of an arbitration agreement, enforceable pursuant to the FAA. Indeed, in recent years we have held enforceable arbitration agreements relating to claims arising under the Sherman Act, 15 U.S.C. §§ 1–7; § 10(b) of the Securities Exchange Act of 1934, 15 U.S.C. § 78j(b); the civil provisions of the Racketeer Influenced and Corrupt Organizations Act (RICO), 18 U.S.C. § 1961 *et seq.;* and § 12(2) of the Securities Act of 1933, 15 U.S.C. § 77*l*(2). See *Mitsubishi Motors Corp. v. Soler Chrysler–Plymouth, Inc.*, 473 U.S. 614, 105 S.Ct. 3346, 87 L.Ed.2d 444 (1985); *Shearson/American Express Inc. v. McMahon*, 482 U.S. 220, 107 S.Ct. 2332, 96 L.Ed.2d 185 (1987); *Rodriguez de Quijas v. Shearson/American Express, Inc.*, 490 U.S. 477, 109 S.Ct. 1917, 104 L.Ed.2d 526 (1989). In these cases we recognized that "[b]y agreeing to arbitrate a statutory claim, a party does not forgo the substantive rights afforded by the statute; it only submits to their resolution in an arbitral, rather than a judicial, forum." *Mitsubishi*, 473 U.S., at 628, 105 S.Ct., at 3354.

Although all statutory claims may not be appropriate for arbitration, "[h]aving made the bargain to arbitrate, the party should be held to it unless Congress itself has evinced an intention to preclude a waiver of judicial remedies for the statutory rights at issue." *Ibid.* In this regard, we note that the burden is on Gilmer to show that Congress intended to preclude a waiver of a judicial forum for ADEA claims. If such an intention exists, it will be discoverable in the text of the ADEA, its legislative history, or an "inherent conflict" between arbitration and the ADEA's underlying purposes. Throughout such an inquiry, it should be kept in mind that "questions of arbitrability must be addressed with a healthy regard for the federal policy favoring arbitration."

III

Gilmer concedes that nothing in the text of the ADEA or its legislative history explicitly precludes arbitration. He argues, however, that compulsory arbitration of ADEA claims pursuant to arbitration agreements would be inconsistent with the statutory framework and purposes of the ADEA. Like the Court of Appeals, we disagree.

A

Congress enacted the ADEA in 1967 "to promote employment of older persons based on their ability rather than age; to prohibit arbitrary age discrimination in employment; [and] to help employers and workers find ways of meeting problems arising from the impact of age on employment." 29 U.S.C. § 621(b). To achieve those goals, the ADEA, among other things, makes it unlawful for an employer "to fail or refuse to hire or to discharge any individual or otherwise discriminate against any individual with respect to his compensation, terms, conditions, or privileges of employment, because of such individual's age." § 623(a)(1). This proscription is enforced both by private suits and by the EEOC. In order for an aggrieved individual to bring suit under the ADEA, he or she must first file a charge with the EEOC and then wait at least 60 days. § 626(d). An individual's right to sue is extinguished, however, if the EEOC institutes an action against the employer. § 626(c)(1). Before the EEOC can bring such an action, though, it must "attempt to eliminate the discriminatory practice or practices alleged, and to effect voluntary compliance with the requirements of this chapter through informal methods of conciliation, conference, and persuasion." § 626(b).

As Gilmer contends, the ADEA is designed not only to address individual grievances, but also to further important social policies. We do not perceive any inherent inconsistency between those policies, however, and enforcing agreements to arbitrate age discrimination claims. It is true that arbitration focuses on specific disputes between the parties involved. The same can be said, however, of judicial resolution of claims. Both of these dispute resolution mechanisms nevertheless also can further broader social purposes. The Sherman Act, the Securities Exchange Act of 1934, RICO, and the Securities Act of 1933 all are designed to advance important public policies, but, as noted above, claims under those statutes are appropriate for arbitration. "[S]o long as the prospective litigant effectively may vindicate [his or her] statutory cause of action in the arbitral forum, the statute will continue to serve both its remedial and deterrent function."

We also are unpersuaded by the argument that arbitration will undermine the role of the EEOC in enforcing the ADEA. An individual ADEA claimant subject to an arbitration agreement will still be free to file a charge with the EEOC, even though the claimant is not able to institute a private judicial action. Indeed, Gilmer filed a charge with the EEOC in this case. In any event, the EEOC's role in combating age discrimination is not dependent on the filing of a charge; the agency may receive information concerning alleged violations of the ADEA "from any source," and it has independent authority to investigate age discrimination. * * *

Gilmer also argues that compulsory arbitration is improper because it deprives claimants of the judicial forum provided for by the ADEA. Congress, however, did not explicitly preclude arbitration or other nonjudicial resolution of claims, even in its recent amendments to the ADEA. "[I]f Congress intended the substantive protection afforded [by the ADEA] to include protection against waiver of the right to a judicial forum, that intention will be deducible from text or legislative history." Moreover, Gilmer's argument ignores the ADEA's flexible approach to resolution of claims. The EEOC, for example, is directed to pursue "informal methods of conciliation, conference, and persuasion," 29 U.S.C. § 626(b), which suggests that out-of-court dispute resolution, such as arbitration, is consistent with the statutory scheme established by Congress. In addition, arbitration is consistent with Congress' grant of concurrent jurisdiction over ADEA claims to state and federal courts, see 29 U.S.C. § 626(c)(1) (allowing suits to be brought "in any court of competent jurisdiction"), because arbitration agreements, "like the provision for concurrent jurisdiction, serve to advance the objective of allowing [claimants] a broader right to select the forum for resolving disputes, whether it be judicial or otherwise."

B

In arguing that arbitration is inconsistent with the ADEA, Gilmer also raises a host of challenges to the adequacy of arbitration procedures. Initially, we note that in our recent arbitration cases we have already rejected most of these arguments as insufficient to preclude arbitration of statutory claims. Such generalized attacks on arbitration "res[t] on suspicion of arbitration as a method of weakening the protections afforded in the substantive law to would-be complainants," and as such, they are "far out of step with our current strong endorsement of the federal statutes favoring this method of resolving disputes." Consequently, we address these arguments only briefly.

Gilmer first speculates that arbitration panels will be biased. However, "[w]e decline to indulge the presumption that the parties and arbitral body conducting a proceeding will be unable or unwilling to retain competent, conscientious and impartial arbitrators." In any event, we note that the NYSE arbitration rules, which are applicable to the dispute in this case, provide protections against biased panels. The rules require, for example, that the parties be informed of the employment histories of the arbitrators, and that they be allowed to make further inquiries into the arbitrators' backgrounds. In addition, each party is allowed one peremptory challenge and unlimited challenges for cause. Moreover, the arbitrators are required to disclose "any circumstances which might preclude [them] from rendering an objective and impartial determination." The FAA also protects against bias, by providing that courts may overturn arbitration decisions "[w]here there was evident partiality or corruption in the arbitrators." 9 U.S.C. § 10(b). There has been no showing in this case that those provisions are inadequate to guard against potential bias.

Gilmer also complains that the discovery allowed in arbitration is more limited than in the federal courts, which he contends will make it difficult to prove discrimination. It is unlikely, however, that age discrimination claims require more extensive discovery than other claims that we have found to be arbitrable, such as RICO and antitrust claims. Moreover, there has been no showing in this case that the NYSE discovery provisions, which allow for document production, information requests, depositions, and subpoenas, will prove insufficient to allow ADEA claimants such as Gilmer a fair opportunity to present their claims. Although those procedures might not be as extensive as in the federal courts, by agreeing to arbitrate, a party "trades the procedures and opportunity for review of the courtroom for the simplicity, informality, and expedition of arbitration." Indeed, an important counterweight to the reduced discovery in NYSE arbitration is that arbitrators are not bound by the rules of evidence.

A further alleged deficiency of arbitration is that arbitrators often will not issue written opinions, resulting, Gilmer contends, in a lack of public knowledge of employers' discriminatory policies, an inability to obtain effective appellate review, and a stifling of the development of the law. The NYSE rules, however, do require that all arbitration awards be in writing, and that the awards contain the names of the parties, a summary of the issues in controversy, and a description of the award issued. In addition, the award decisions are made available to the public. Furthermore, judicial decisions addressing ADEA claims will continue to be issued because it is unlikely that all or even most ADEA claimants will be subject to arbitration agreements. Finally, Gilmer's concerns apply equally to settlements of ADEA claims, which, as noted above, are clearly allowed.

It is also argued that arbitration procedures cannot adequately further the purposes of the ADEA because they do not provide for broad equitable relief and class actions. As the court below noted, however, arbitrators do have the power to fashion equitable relief. Indeed, the NYSE rules applicable here do not restrict the types of relief an arbitrator may award, but merely refer to "damages and/or other relief." The NYSE rules also provide for collective proceedings. But "even if the arbitration could not go forward as a class action or class relief could not be granted by the arbitrator, the fact that the [ADEA] provides for the possibility of bringing a collective action does not mean that individual attempts at conciliation were intended to be barred." Finally, it should be remembered that arbitration agreements will not preclude the *EEOC* from bringing actions seeking class-wide and equitable relief.

C

An additional reason advanced by Gilmer for refusing to enforce arbitration agreements relating to ADEA claims is his contention that there often will be unequal bargaining power between employers and employees. Mere inequality in bargaining power, however, is not a sufficient reason to hold that arbitration agreements are never enforceable in the employment context. * * * "Of course, courts should remain attuned to well-supported claims that the agreement to arbitrate resulted from the sort of fraud or overwhelming economic power that would provide grounds 'for the revocation of any contract.' " There is no indication in this case, however, that Gilmer, an experienced businessman, was coerced or defrauded into agreeing to the arbitration clause in his registration application. As with the claimed procedural inadequacies discussed above, this claim of unequal bargaining power is best left for resolution in specific cases.

IV

In addition to the arguments discussed above, Gilmer vigorously asserts that our decision in *Alexander v. Gardner–Denver Co.,* 415 U.S. 36, 94 S.Ct. 1011, 39 L.Ed.2d 147 (1974), and its progeny—*Barrentine v. Arkansas–Best Freight System, Inc.,* 450 U.S. 728, 101 S.Ct. 1437, 67 L.Ed.2d 641 (1981), and *McDonald v. West Branch,* 466 U.S. 284, 104 S.Ct. 1799, 80 L.Ed.2d 302 (1984)—preclude arbitration of employment discrimination claims. Gilmer's reliance on these cases, however, is misplaced.

In *Gardner–Denver,* the issue was whether a discharged employee whose grievance had been arbitrated pursuant to an arbitration clause in a collective-bargaining agreement was precluded from subsequently bringing a Title VII action based upon the conduct that was the subject of the grievance. In holding that the employee was not foreclosed from bringing the Title VII claim, we stressed that an employee's contractual rights under a collective-bargaining agreement are distinct from the employee's statutory Title VII rights:

> "In submitting his grievance to arbitration, an employee seeks to vindicate his contractual right under a collective-bargaining agreement. By contrast, in filing a lawsuit under Title VII, an employee asserts independent statutory rights accorded by Congress. The distinctly separate nature of these contractual and statutory rights is not vitiated merely because both were violated as a result of the same factual occurrence." 415 U.S., at 49–50, 94 S.Ct., at 1020.

We also noted that a labor arbitrator has authority only to resolve questions of contractual rights. The arbitrator's "task is to effectuate the intent of the parties" and he or she does not have the "general authority to invoke public laws that conflict with the bargain between the parties." By contrast, "in instituting an action under Title VII, the employee is not seeking review of the arbitrator's decision. Rather, he is asserting a statutory right independent of the arbitration process." We further expressed concern that in collective-bargaining arbitration "the interests of the individual employee may be subordinated to the collective interests of all employees in the bargaining unit."[5]

---

5. The Court in *Alexander v. Gardner–Denver Co.,* also expressed the view that arbitration was inferior to the judicial process for resolving statutory claims. That "mistrust of the arbitral process," however, has been undermined by our recent arbitration decisions. "[W]e are well past the time when judicial suspicion of the desirability of arbitration and of the competence of

* * *

There are several important distinctions between the *Gardner–Denver* line of cases and the case before us. First, those cases did not involve the issue of the enforceability of an agreement to arbitrate statutory claims. Rather, they involved the quite different issue whether arbitration of contract-based claims precluded subsequent judicial resolution of statutory claims. Since the employees there had not agreed to arbitrate their statutory claims, and the labor arbitrators were not authorized to resolve such claims, the arbitration in those cases understandably was held not to preclude subsequent statutory actions. Second, because the arbitration in those cases occurred in the context of a collective-bargaining agreement, the claimants there were represented by their unions in the arbitration proceedings. An important concern therefore was the tension between collective representation and individual statutory rights, a concern not applicable to the present case. Finally, those cases were not decided under the FAA, which, as discussed above, reflects a "liberal federal policy favoring arbitration agreements." Therefore, those cases provide no basis for refusing to enforce Gilmer's agreement to arbitrate his ADEA claim.

V

We conclude that Gilmer has not met his burden of showing that Congress, in enacting the ADEA, intended to preclude arbitration of claims under that Act. Accordingly, the judgment of the Court of Appeals is

Affirmed.

[The dissenting opinion of JUSTICE STEVENS, joined by JUSTICE MARSHALL, is omitted.]

NOTES

1. In his dissent, Justice Stevens maintained that section 1 of the FAA, 9 U.S.C. § 1, which provides that the act does not apply to "contracts of employment of seamen, railroad employees, or any other class of workers engaged in foreign or interstate commerce," precluded mandating arbitration of Gilmer's claim. However, ***Circuit City Stores, Inc. v. Adams,*** 532 U.S. 105, 121 S.Ct. 1302, 149 L.Ed.2d 234 (2001), interpreted this exclusion narrowly, holding that it applied only to employment contracts of workers in interstate transportation.

2. ***EEOC v. Waffle House, Inc.,*** 534 U.S. 279, 122 S.Ct. 754, 151 L.Ed.2d 755 (2002), held that an arbitration agreement to which the EEOC was not a party did not bind the EEOC and did not preclude the EEOC from seeking relief for alleged victims of discrimination in its own lawsuit, even though the alleged victims had agreed to arbitrate rather than litigate their claims. The Court reasoned that nothing in the ADA or Title VII reflected any congressional intent to allow private parties to restrict the EEOC's exercise of

arbitral tribunals inhibited the development of arbitration as an alternative means of dispute resolution."

its statutory authority to seek relief for individual victims of discrimination regardless of whether those victims had agreed to arbitrate their personal claims.

3. *Gilmer* indicated that, to be enforceable, the arbitration agreement must enable the employee to vindicate the statutory claims effectively. In *Hooters of America v. Phillips*, 173 F.3d 933 (4th Cir. 1999), the employer's arbitration rules required the employee to state the nature of her claim and the specific acts or omissions on which the claim was based and to provide a list of witnesses with a summary of the facts known to each, but imposed no similar requirements on the employer. The rules restricted the supposedly neutral arbitrator to those on a list completely controlled by Hooters. Furthermore, the rules allowed Hooters to seek summary judgment, to record the hearing and to sue to vacate the award if the arbitration panel exceeded its authority, but gave no similar rights to the employee. Lastly, the rules allowed the employer to amend them at any time without notice to the employee and allowed the company, but not the employee, to cancel the agreement to arbitrate by giving thirty days notice. The court refused to enforce the arbitration agreement, characterizing the system as "a sham system unworthy even of the name of arbitration."

4. In *Cole v. Burns International Security Services*, 105 F.3d 1465 (D.C. Cir. 1997), the court held that to provide a forum that allows employees to vindicate effectively their statutory claims, the arbitration procedure must "(1) provide[] for neutral arbitrators, (2) provide[] for more than minimal discovery, (3) require[] a written award, (4) provide[] for all of the types of relief that would otherwise be available in court, and (5) * * *not require employees to pay either unreasonable costs or any arbitrators' fees or expenses as a condition of access to the arbitration forum." However, in **Green Tree Financial Corp. v. Randolph,** 531 U.S. 79, 121 S.Ct. 513, 148 L.Ed.2d 373 (2000), a case involving the Truth in Lending Act, the Court, refused to deny enforcement to an agreement to arbitrate that required the claimant to pay half of the arbitrator's fee. The Court observed that the imposition of large arbitration costs on the claimant could preclude the claimant from being able to vindicate effectively the claim in the arbitral forum but held that the claimant resisting arbitration has the burden of proof on that issue.

5. A task force with representatives from the American Arbitration Association, the American Bar Association, the American Civil Liberties Union, the Federal Mediation and Conciliation Service, the National Academy of Arbitrators, the National Employment Lawyers Association and the Society of Professionals in Dispute Resolution developed A Due Process Protocol for Mediation and Arbitration of Statutory Disputes Arising out of the Employment Relationship, issued on May 9, 1995. The Protocol may be found at www.naarb.org/due_process/due_process.html. For a discussion of the development of the protocol by the individual who chaired the task force see Arnold M. Zack, *The Due Process Protocol: Getting There and Getting Over It*, 11 Employee Rights & Employment Policy J. 257 (2007).

6. The American Arbitration Association requires employer-imposed arbitration plans to comply with the Due Process Protocol. AAA Rules also require the employer to pay the full costs of the arbitration proceeding, except

for a modest filing fee paid by the employee and further provide that if there is a conflict between AAA Rules and the employer's plan, AAA Rules prevail. However, in *Brady v. Williams Capital Group, L.P.* 14 N.Y.3d 459, 928 N.E.2d 383 (2010), Williams imposed on its employees a requirement that they arbitrate their claims arising out of their employment in accordance with AAA rules "except as provided in this Agreement." The arbitration agreement further provided that the employee and Williams share equally the arbitrator's fee. Brady filed an arbitration demand with AAA over Williams' termination of her employment, alleging violations of Title VII and New York law. AAA determined that the demand was filed under an employer-promulgated plan and that Williams, the employer, was responsible for the entire arbitrator's fee. AAA invoiced Williams for a deposit of $42,300 to cover the arbitrator's anticipated fee. Williams refused to pay, insisting that Brady, the employee, pay half. AAA cancelled the arbitration. Brady sued to compel Williams, the employer, to pay or for the entry of a default judgment against Williams, but the court held that the provision in the arbitration agreement adopting AAA Rules except as otherwise provided in the Agreement required Brady, the employee, to pay half of the arbitrator's fee despite AAA rules to the contrary. Consequently, the court held, under *Green Tree Financial Corp. v. Randolph, supra* note 4, Brady had the burden to prove that the requirement that she pay half of the arbitrator's fee precluded her from arbitrating the case.

7. ***Circuit City Stores, Inc. v. Adams,*** 532 U.S. 105, 121 S.Ct. 1302, 149 L.Ed.2d 234 (2001), indicated that the validity of contractual waivers would be determined by state contract law. This has resulted in some lower courts refusing to enforce agreements to arbitrate to the exclusion of judicial enforcement on the grounds that no reasonable person would have perceived the "fine print" requiring arbitration to be a binding commitment that was "express, knowing, and voluntary," or, alternatively, that when arbitration provisions disproportionately disadvantage the employee they are "unconscionable." See, e.g., *Ingle v. Circuit City Stores,* 328 F.3d 1165 (9th Cir. 2003).

Some employers include in their arbitration agreements provisions mandating that claims be arbitrated on an individual basis only, precluding class or collective actions. Some courts held such class action waivers unenforceable under the common law doctrine of unconscionability. However, in ***AT & T Mobility, LLC v. Concepcion,*** 563 U.S. ___, 131 S.Ct. 1740, 179 L.Ed.2d 742 (2011), the Court held that the FAA preempted the application of California unconscionability doctrine to a provision in an arbitration mandate that prohibited class actions. The Concepcions brought a class action alleging false advertising and fraud when A T & T charged them sales tax on the retail value of phones that it had advertised as free. The arbitration agreement that A T & T imposed on all of its customers required arbitration on an individual basis. Under California law, such prohibitions on class actions were unconscionable contracts of adhesion particularly when involving predictably small amounts of damages. The Ninth Circuit held that the FAA did not preempt California law because the California rule applied to contracts generally, not just to contracts for arbitration. The Supreme Court reversed. The FAA permits holding arbitration agreements unenforceable on "such" grounds that exist at law or in equity for the revocation of any contract. The Court, however, declared that a primary purpose of the FAA is to enforce arbitration agreements in accordance with their own terms. If further maintained, "Requiring the availability of classwide arbitration interferes with fundamental attributes of arbitration and thus creates a scheme inconsistent with the FAA." What are the advantages and disadvantages to an employer of including a class action waiver in its arbitration agreements?

After *Gilmer*, most courts continued to apply *Gardner–Denver* to employees covered by collective bargaining agreements and held that those employees were not required to take their statutory discrimination claims through the contract's grievance and arbitration procedures but could sue in court. The Fourth Circuit, however, held to the contrary. In **Wright v. Universal Maritime Corp.**, 525 U.S. 70, 119 S.Ct. 391, 142 L.Ed.2d 361 (1998), the Court declined to resolve the conflict. Instead, it held that to bar an employee from litigating, a provision in a collective bargaining agreement mandating arbitration of statutory claims must be clear and unmistakable. The Court revisited the issue in the following case.

14 PENN PLAZA, LLC v. PYETT

Supreme Court of the United States, 2009
556 U.S. 247, 129 S.Ct. 1456, 173 L.Ed.2d 398

JUSTICE THOMAS delivered the opinion of the Court.

* * *

I

Respondents are members of the Service Employees International Union, Local 32BJ (Union). Under the National Labor Relations Act (NLRA), 49 Stat. 449, as amended, the Union is the exclusive bargaining representative of employees within the building-services industry in New York City, which includes building cleaners, porters, and doorpersons. In this role, the Union has exclusive authority to bargain on behalf of its members over their "rates of pay, wages, hours of employment, or other conditions of employment." Since the 1930's, the Union has engaged in industry-wide collective bargaining with the Realty Advisory Board on Labor Relations, Inc. (RAB), a multiemployer bargaining association for the New York City real-estate industry. The agreement between the Union and the RAB is embodied in their Collective Bargaining Agreement for Contractors and Building Owners (CBA). The CBA requires union members to submit all claims of employment discrimination to binding arbitration under the CBA's grievance and dispute resolution procedures:

> "§ 30 NO DISCRIMINATION. There shall be no discrimination against any present or future employee by reason of race, creed, color, age, disability, national origin, sex, union membership, or any other characteristic protected by law, including, but not limited to, claims

made pursuant to Title VII of the Civil Rights Act, the Americans with Disabilities Act, the Age Discrimination in Employment Act, the New York State Human Rights Law, the New York City Human Rights Code, . . . or any other similar laws, rules, or regulations. All such claims shall be subject to the grievance and arbitration procedures (Articles V and VI) as the sole and exclusive remedy for violations. Arbitrators shall apply appropriate law in rendering decisions based upon claims of discrimination.''

Petitioner 14 Penn Plaza LLC is a member of the RAB. It owns and operates the New York City office building where, prior to August 2003, respondents worked as night lobby watchmen and in other similar capacities. Respondents were directly employed by petitioner Temco Service Industries, Inc. (Temco), a maintenance service and cleaning contractor. In August 2003, with the Union's consent, 14 Penn Plaza engaged Spartan Security, a unionized security services contractor and affiliate of Temco, to provide licensed security guards to staff the lobby and entrances of its building. Because this rendered respondents' lobby services unnecessary, Temco reassigned them to jobs as night porters and light duty cleaners in other locations in the building. Respondents contend that these reassignments led to a loss in income, caused them emotional distress, and were otherwise less desirable than their former positions.

At respondents' request, the Union filed grievances challenging the reassignments. The grievances alleged that petitioners: (1) violated the CBA's ban on workplace discrimination by reassigning respondents on account of their age; (2) violated seniority rules by failing to promote one of the respondents to a handyman position; and (3) failed to equitably rotate overtime. After failing to obtain relief on any of these claims through the grievance process, the Union requested arbitration under the CBA.

After the initial arbitration hearing, the Union withdrew the first set of respondents' grievances—the age-discrimination claims—from arbitration. Because it had consented to the contract for new security personnel at 14 Penn Plaza, the Union believed that it could not legitimately object to respondents' reassignments as discriminatory. But the Union continued to arbitrate the seniority and overtime claims, and, after several hearings, the claims were denied.

In May 2004, while the arbitration was ongoing but after the Union withdrew the age discrimination claims, respondents filed a complaint with the Equal Employment Opportunity Commission (EEOC) alleging that petitioners had violated their rights under the ADEA. Approximately one month later, the EEOC issued a Dismissal and Notice of Rights * * *

Respondents thereafter filed suit against petitioners in the United States District Court for the Southern District of New York, alleging that their reassignment violated the ADEA and state and local laws prohibiting age discrimination. Petitioners filed a motion to compel arbitration of respondents' claims pursuant to § 3 and § 4 of the Federal Arbitration Act (FAA), 9 U.S.C. §§ 3, 4. The District Court denied the motion because under Second Circuit precedent, "even a clear and unmistakable union-negotiated waiver of a right to litigate certain federal and state statutory claims in a judicial forum is unenforceable." * * *

The Court of Appeals affirmed. According to the Court of Appeals, it could not compel arbitration of the dispute because *Gardner–Denver,* which "remains good law," held "that a collective bargaining agreement could not waive covered workers' rights to a judicial forum for causes of action created by Congress." (citing *Gardner–Denver*). * * *

II

A

The NLRA governs federal labor-relations law. As permitted by that statute, respondents designated the Union as their "exclusive representativ[e] . . . for the purposes of collective bargaining in respect to rates of pay, wages, hours of employment, or other conditions of employment." 29 U.S.C. § 159(a). As the employees' exclusive bargaining representative, the Union "enjoys broad authority . . . in the negotiation and administration of [the] collective bargaining contract." But this broad authority "is accompanied by a responsibility of equal scope, the responsibility and duty of fair representation." *Humphrey v. Moore,* 375 U.S. 335, 342, 84 S.Ct. 363, 11 L.Ed.2d 370 (1964). The employer has a corresponding duty under the NLRA to bargain in good faith "with the representatives of his employees" on wages, hours, and conditions of employment. 29 U.S.C. § 158(a)(5); see also § 158(d).

In this instance, the Union and the RAB, negotiating on behalf of 14 Penn Plaza, collectively bargained in good faith and agreed that employment-related discrimination claims, including claims brought under the ADEA, would be resolved in arbitration. This freely negotiated term between the Union and the RAB easily qualifies as a "conditio[n] of employment" that is subject to mandatory bargaining under § 159(a). * * *

Respondents, however, contend that the arbitration clause here is outside the permissible scope of the collective-bargaining process because it affects the "employees' individual, non-economic statutory rights." We disagree. Parties generally favor arbitration precisely because of the economics of dispute resolution. See *Circuit City Stores, Inc. v. Adams,* 532 U.S. 105, 123, 121 S.Ct. 1302, 149 L.Ed.2d 234 (2001) ("Arbitration agreements allow parties to avoid the costs of litigation, a benefit that may be of particular importance in employment litigation, which often involves smaller sums of money than disputes concerning commercial contracts"). As in any contractual negotiation, a union may agree to the inclusion of an arbitration provision in a collective-bargaining agreement in return for other concessions from the employer. Courts generally may not interfere in this bargained-for exchange. * * *

As a result, the CBA's arbitration provision must be honored unless the ADEA itself removes this particular class of grievances from the NLRA's broad sweep. It does not. This Court has squarely held that the ADEA does not preclude arbitration of claims brought under the statute.

* * *

The *Gilmer* Court's interpretation of the ADEA fully applies in the collective-bargaining context. Nothing in the law suggests a distinction between the status of arbitration agreements signed by an individual employee and those agreed to by a union representative. This Court has required only that an agreement to arbitrate statutory antidiscrimination claims be "explicitly stated" in the collective-bargaining agreement. *Wright*, 525 U.S., at 80, 119 S.Ct. 391. The CBA under review here meets that obligation. Respondents incorrectly counter that an individual employee must personally "waive" a "[substantive] right" to proceed in court for a waiver to be "knowing and voluntary" under the ADEA. As explained below, however, the agreement to arbitrate ADEA claims is not the waiver of a "substantive right" as that term is employed in the ADEA. Indeed, if the "right" referred to in § 626(f)(1) included the prospective waiver of the right to bring an ADEA claim in court, even a waiver signed by an individual employee would be invalid as the statute also prevents individuals from "waiv[ing] rights or claims that may arise after the date the waiver is executed."

Examination of the two federal statutes at issue in this case, therefore, yields a straightforward answer to the question presented: The NLRA provided the Union and the RAB with statutory authority to collectively bargain for arbitration of workplace discrimination claims, and Congress did not terminate that authority with respect to federal age-discrimination claims in the ADEA. Accordingly, there is no legal basis for the Court to strike down the arbitration clause in this CBA, which was freely negotiated by the Union and the RAB, and which clearly and unmistakably requires respondents to arbitrate the age-discrimination claims at issue in this appeal. Congress has chosen to allow arbitration of ADEA claims. The Judiciary must respect that choice.

B

The CBA's arbitration provision is also fully enforceable under the *Gardner–Denver* line of cases. Respondents interpret *Gardner–Denver* and its progeny to hold that "a union cannot waive an employee's right to a judicial forum under the federal antidiscrimination statutes" because "allowing the union to waive this right would substitute the union's interests for the employee's antidiscrimination rights." The "combination of union control over the process and inherent conflict of interest with respect to discrimination claims," they argue, "provided the foundation for the Court's holding [in *Gardner–Denver*] that arbitration under a collective-bargaining agreement could not preclude an individual employee's right to bring a lawsuit in court to vindicate a statutory discrimination claim." We disagree.

1

The holding of *Gardner–Denver* is not as broad as respondents suggest. The employee in that case was covered by a collective-bargaining agreement that prohibited "discrimination against any employee on account of race, color, religion, sex, national origin, or ancestry" and that guaranteed that "[n]o employee will be discharged ... except for just cause." The agreement also included a "multistep grievance procedure" that culminated in compulsory arbitration for any "differences aris[ing] between the Company and the Union as to the meaning and application of the provisions of this Agreement" and "any trouble aris[ing] in the plant."

The employee was discharged for allegedly producing too many defective parts while working for the respondent as a drill operator. He filed a grievance with his union claiming that he was " 'unjustly discharged' " in violation of the " 'just cause' " provision within the CBA. Then at the final prearbitration step of the grievance process, the employee added a claim that he was discharged because of his race.

The arbitrator ultimately ruled that the employee had been " 'discharged for just cause,' " but "made no reference to [the] claim of racial discrimination." After obtaining a right-to-sue letter from the EEOC, the employee filed a claim in Federal District Court, alleging racial discrimination in violation of Title VII of the Civil Rights Act of 1964. The District Court issued a decision, affirmed by the Court of Appeals, which granted summary judgment to the employer because it concluded that "the claim of racial discrimination had been submitted to the arbitrator and resolved adversely to [the employee]." In the District Court's view, "having voluntarily elected to pursue his grievance to final arbitration under the nondiscrimination clause of the collective-bargaining agreement," the employee was "bound by the arbitral decision" and precluded from suing his employer on any other grounds, such as a statutory claim under Title VII.

This Court reversed the judgment on the narrow ground that the arbitration was not preclusive because the collective-bargaining agreement did not cover statutory claims. As a result, the lower courts erred in relying on the "doctrine of election of remedies" to bar the employee's Title VII claim. "That doctrine, which refers to situations where an individual pursues remedies that are legally or factually inconsistent" with each other, did not apply to the employee's dual pursuit of arbitration and a Title VII discrimination claim in district court. The employee's collective-bargaining agreement did not mandate arbitration of statutory antidiscrimination claims. "As the proctor of the bargain, the arbitrator's task is to effectuate the intent of the parties." Because the collective-bargaining agreement gave the arbitrator "authority to resolve only questions of contractual rights," his decision could not prevent the employee from bringing the Title VII claim in federal court "regardless of whether certain contractual rights are similar to, or duplicative of, the substantive rights secured by Title VII."

The Court also explained that the employee had not waived his right to pursue his Title VII claim in federal court by participating in an arbitration that was premised on the same underlying facts as the Title VII claim. Thus, whether the legal theory of preclusion advanced by the employer rested on "the doctrines of election of remedies" or was recast "as resting instead on the doctrine of equitable estoppel and on themes of res judicata and collateral estoppel," it could not prevail in light of the collective-bargaining agreement's failure to address arbitration of Title VII claims. ("[W]e hold that the federal policy favoring arbitration does not establish that an arbitrator's resolution of a *contractual* claim is dispositive of a statutory claim under Title VII."

* * *

[I]n *Gilmer,* this Court made clear that the *Gardner–Denver* line of cases "did not involve the issue of the enforceability of an agreement to arbitrate statutory claims." Those decisions instead "involved the quite different issue whether arbitration of contract-based claims precluded subsequent judicial resolution of statutory claims. Since the employees there had not agreed to arbitrate their statutory claims, and the labor arbitrators were not authorized to resolve such claims, the arbitration in those cases understandably was held not to preclude subsequent statutory actions." *Gardner–Denver* and its progeny thus do not control the outcome where, as is the case here, the collective-bargaining agreement's arbitration provision expressly covers both statutory and contractual discrimination claims.[8]

2

We recognize that apart from their narrow holdings, the *Gardner–Denver* line of cases included broad dicta that was highly critical of the use of arbitration for the vindication of statutory antidiscrimination rights. That skepticism, however, rested on a misconceived view of arbitration that this Court has since abandoned.

First, the Court in *Gardner–Denver* erroneously assumed that an agreement to submit statutory discrimination claims to arbitration was tantamount to a waiver of those rights. * * *

The Court was correct in concluding that federal antidiscrimination rights may not be prospectively waived, but it confused an agreement to arbitrate those statutory claims with a prospective waiver of the substantive right. The decision to resolve ADEA claims by way of arbitration instead of litigation does not waive the statutory right to be free from workplace age discrimination; it waives only the right to seek relief from a court in the first instance. * * * The suggestion in *Gardner–Denver* that the decision to arbitrate statutory discrimination claims was tantamount to a substantive waiver of those rights, therefore, reveals a distorted under-

---

8. Because today's decision does not contradict the holding of *Gardner–Denver,* we need not resolve the *stare decisis* concerns raised by the dissenting opinions. But given the development of this Court's arbitration jurisprudence in the intervening years, *Gardner–Denver* would appear to be a strong candidate for overruling if the dissents' broad view of its holding * * * were correct. * * *

standing of the compromise made when an employee agrees to compulsory arbitration.

In this respect, *Gardner–Denver* is a direct descendant of the Court's decision in *Wilko v. Swan,* 346 U.S. 427, 74 S.Ct. 182, 98 L.Ed. 168 (1953), which held that an agreement to arbitrate claims under the Securities Act of 1933 was unenforceable. The Court subsequently overruled *Wilko* and, in so doing, characterized the decision as "pervaded by . . . 'the old judicial hostility to arbitration.'" *Rodriguez de Quijas v. Shearson/American Express, Inc.,* 490 U.S. 477, 480, 109 S.Ct. 1917, 104 L.Ed.2d 526 (1989). The Court added: "To the extent that *Wilko* rested on suspicion of arbitration as a method of weakening the protections afforded in the substantive law to would-be complainants, it has fallen far out of step with our current strong endorsement of the federal statutes favoring this method of resolving disputes." * * *

Second, *Gardner–Denver* mistakenly suggested that certain features of arbitration made it a forum "well suited to the resolution of contractual disputes," but "a comparatively inappropriate forum for the final resolution of rights created by Title VII." According to the Court, the "factfinding process in arbitration" is "not equivalent to judicial factfinding" and the "informality of arbitral procedure . . . makes arbitration a less appropriate forum for final resolution of Title VII issues than the federal courts." The Court also questioned the competence of arbitrators to decide federal statutory claims. ("[T]he specialized competence of arbitrators pertains primarily to the law of the shop, not the law of the land"); * * *

These misconceptions have been corrected. For example, the Court has "recognized that arbitral tribunals are readily capable of handling the factual and legal complexities of antitrust claims, notwithstanding the absence of judicial instruction and supervision" and that "there is no reason to assume at the outset that arbitrators will not follow the law." ("We decline to indulge the presumption that the parties and arbitral body conducting a proceeding will be unable or unwilling to retain competent, conscientious, and impartial arbitrators"). An arbitrator's capacity to resolve complex questions of fact and law extends with equal force to discrimination claims brought under the ADEA. Moreover, the recognition that arbitration procedures are more streamlined than federal litigation is not a basis for finding the forum somehow inadequate; the relative informality of arbitration is one of the chief reasons that parties select arbitration. Parties "trad[e] the procedures and opportunity for review of the courtroom for the simplicity, informality, and expedition of arbitration." * * *.

Third, the Court in *Gardner–Denver* raised in a footnote a "further concern" regarding "the union's exclusive control over the manner and extent to which an individual grievance is presented." The Court suggested that in arbitration, as in the collective-bargaining process, a union may subordinate the interests of an individual employee to the collective interests of all employees in the bargaining unit. * * *

We cannot rely on this judicial policy concern as a source of authority for introducing a qualification into the ADEA that is not found in its text. Absent a constitutional barrier, "it is not for us to substitute our view of . . . policy for the legislation which has been passed by Congress." * * * Until Congress amends the ADEA to meet the conflict-of-interest concern identified in the *Gardner–Denver* dicta, and seized on by respondents here, there is "no reason to color the lens through which the arbitration clause is read" simply because of an alleged conflict of interest between a union and its members. * * *

The conflict-of-interest argument also proves too much. Labor unions certainly balance the economic interests of some employees against the needs of the larger work force as they negotiate collective-bargain agreements and implement them on a daily basis. But this attribute of organized labor does not justify singling out an arbitration provision for disfavored treatment. * * * It was Congress' verdict that the benefits of organized labor outweigh the sacrifice of individual liberty that this system necessarily demands. Respondents' argument that they were deprived of the right to pursue their ADEA claims in federal court by a labor union with a conflict of interest is therefore unsustainable; it amounts to a collateral attack on the NLRA.

In any event, Congress has accounted for this conflict of interest in several ways. As indicated above, the NLRA has been interpreted to impose a "duty of fair representation" on labor unions, which a union breaches "when its conduct toward a member of the bargaining unit is arbitrary, discriminatory, or in bad faith." This duty extends to "challenges leveled not only at a union's contract administration and enforcement efforts but at its negotiation activities as well." Thus, a union is subject to liability under the NLRA if it illegally discriminates against older workers in either the formation or governance of the collective-bargaining agreement, such as by deciding not to pursue a grievance on behalf of one of its members for discriminatory reasons. * * *

In addition, a union is subject to liability under the ADEA if the union itself discriminates against its members on the basis of age. * * *

* * *

IV

We hold that a collective-bargaining agreement that clearly and unmistakably requires union members to arbitrate ADEA claims is enforceable as a matter of federal law. The judgment of the Court of Appeals is reversed, and the case is remanded for further proceedings consistent with this opinion.

JUSTICE SOUTER, with whom JUSTICE STEVENS, JUSTICE GINSBURG, and JUSTICE BREYER join, dissenting.

The issue here is whether employees subject to a collective-bargaining agreement (CBA) providing for conclusive arbitration of all grievances including claimed breaches of the Age Discrimination in Employment Act of 1967 (ADEA), lose their statutory right to bring an ADEA claim in court, § 626(c). Under the 35-year-old holding in *Alexander v. Gardner–Denver Co.,* they do not, and I would adhere to *stare decisis* and so hold today.

I

Like Title VII of the Civil Rights Act of 1964, the ADEA is aimed at " 'the elimination of discrimination in the workplace,' " and, again like Title VII, the ADEA "contains a vital element . . .: It grants an injured employee a right of action to obtain the authorized relief," "Any person aggrieved" under the Act "may bring a civil action in any court of competent jurisdiction for legal or equitable relief," 29 U.S.C. § 626(c), thereby "not only redress[ing] his own injury but also vindicat[ing] the important congressional policy against discriminatory employment practices."

Gardner–Denver considered the effect of a CBA's arbitration clause on an employee's right to sue under Title VII. One of the employer's arguments was that the CBA entered into by the union had waived individual employees' statutory cause of action subject to a judicial remedy for discrimination in violation of Title VII. Although Title VII, like the ADEA, "does not speak expressly to the relationship between federal courts and the grievance-arbitration machinery of collective-bargaining agreements," we unanimously held that "the rights conferred" by Title VII (with no exception for the right to a judicial forum) cannot be waived as "part of the collective bargaining process," We stressed the contrast between two categories of rights in labor and employment law. There were "statutory rights related to collective activity," which "are conferred on employees collectively to foster the processes of bargaining [, which] properly may be exercised or relinquished by the union as collective-bargaining agent to obtain economic benefits for union members." But "Title VII . . . stands on plainly different [categorical] ground; it concerns not majoritarian processes, but an individual's right to equal employment opportunities." Thus, as the Court previously realized, *Gardner–Denver* imposed a "seemingly absolute prohibition of union waiver of employees' federal forum rights."

We supported the judgment with several other lines of complementary reasoning. First, we explained that antidiscrimination statutes "have long evinced a general intent to accord parallel or overlapping remedies against discrimination," and Title VII's statutory scheme carried "no suggestion . . . that a prior arbitral decision either forecloses an individual's right to sue or divests federal courts of jurisdiction." We accordingly concluded that "an individual does not forfeit his private cause of action if he first pursues his grievance to final arbitration under the nondiscrimination clause of a collective-bargaining agreement."

Second, we rejected the District Court's view that simply participating in the arbitration amounted to electing the arbitration remedy and waiving the plaintiff's right to sue. We said that the arbitration agreement at issue covered only a contractual right under the CBA to be free from discrimination, not the "independent statutory rights accorded by Congress" in Title VII. Third, we rebuffed the employer's argument that federal courts should defer to arbitral rulings. We declined to make the "assumption that arbitral processes are commensurate with judicial processes," and described arbitration as "a less appropriate forum for final resolution of Title VII issues than the federal courts."

Finally, we took note that "[i]n arbitration, as in the collective bargaining process, the interests of the individual employee may be subordinated to the collective interests of all employees in the bargaining unit," a result we deemed unacceptable when it came to Title VII claims. In sum, _Gardner–Denver_ held that an individual's statutory right of freedom from discrimination and access to court for enforcement were beyond a union's power to waive.

* * *

II

The majority evades the precedent of _Gardner–Denver_ as long as it can simply by ignoring it. The Court never mentions the case before concluding that the ADEA and the National Labor Relations Act, "yiel[d] a straightforward answer to the question presented," that is, that unions can bargain away individual rights to a federal forum for antidiscrimination claims. If this were a case of first impression, it would at least be possible to consider that conclusion, but the issue is settled and the time is too late by 35 years to make the bald assertion that "[n]othing in the law suggests a distinction between the status of arbitration agreements signed by an individual employee and those agreed to by a union representative." In fact, we recently and unanimously said that the principle that "federal forum rights cannot be waived in union-negotiated CBAs even if they can be waived in individually executed contracts ... assuredly finds support in" our case law. * * *

Equally at odds with existing law is the majority's statement that "[t]he decision to fashion a CBA to require arbitration of employment-discrimination claims is no different from the many other decisions made by parties in designing grievance machinery." That is simply impossible to square with our conclusion in _Gardner–Denver_ that "Title VII ... stands on plainly different ground" from "statutory rights related to collective activity": "it concerns not majoritarian processes, but an individual's right to equal employment opportunities." * * *

When the majority does speak to _Gardner–Denver,_ it misreads the case in claiming that it turned solely "on the narrow ground that the arbitration was not preclusive because the collective-bargaining agreement did not cover statutory claims." That, however, was merely one of several reasons given in support of the decision, and we raised it to explain why the District Court made a mistake in thinking that the employee lost his Title VII rights by electing to pursue the contractual arbitration remedy. On need only read *Gardner–Denver* itself to know that it was not at all so narrowly reasoned, and we have noted already how later cases have made this abundantly clear. * * *

Nor, finally, does the majority have any better chance of being rid of another of *Gardner–Denver's* statements supporting its rule of decision, set out and repeated in previous quotations: "in arbitration, as in the collective-bargaining process, a union may subordinate the interests of an individual employee to the collective interests of all employees in the bargaining unit,"an unacceptable result when it comes to "an individual's right to equal employment opportunities." The majority tries to diminish this reasoning, and the previously stated holding it supported, by making the remarkable rejoinder that "[w]e cannot rely on this judicial policy concern as a source of authority for introducing a qualification into the ADEA that is not found in its text." It is enough to recall that respondents are not seeking to "introduc[e] a qualification into" the law; they are justifiably relying on statutory-interpretation precedent decades old, never overruled, and serially reaffirmed over the years. * * *

III

On one level, the majority opinion may have little effect, for it explicitly reserves the question whether a CBA's waiver of a judicial forum is enforceable when the union controls access to and presentation of employees' claims in arbitration, which "is usually the case," * * * But as a treatment of precedent in statutory interpretation, the majority's opinion cannot be reconciled with the *Gardner–Denver* Court's own view of its holding, repeated over the years and generally understood, and I respectfully dissent.

[The separate dissenting opinion of JUSTICE STEVENS is omitted.]

NOTES

1. In *Kravar v. Triangle Services, Inc.*, 2009 WL 1392595 (S.D.N.Y. 2009), the court faced the same SEIU Local 32BJ–RAB collective bargaining agreement. The court refused to compel the plaintiff to arbitrate her claim under the Americans with Disabilities Act. The court found that under the collective bargaining agreement, the union had the exclusive right to advance a grievance to arbitration and that the union refused to process the plaintiff's claim. The court concluded that the union's refusal to arbitrate the plaintiff's claim meant that if not allowed to proceed in court, she would not be able to bring her claim in any forum. Under the circumstances, the court opined, the collective bargaining agreement amounted to a waiver of plaintiff's substantive rights and was not enforceable. However, in *Duraku v. Tishman Speyer Properties, Inc.*, 714 F.Supp.2d 470 (S.D.N.Y. 2010), the court required plaintiffs to arbitrate their discrimination claims in light of a February 2010 supplemental agreement between RAB and Local 32BJ that expressly provides that an employee may proceed to arbitration if the union declines to do so.

2. In *Mathews v. Denver Newspaper Agency*, 2009 WL 1231776 (D. Colo. 2009), *rev'd*, 649 F.3d 1199 (10th Cir. 2011), the plaintiff grieved his demotion

on grounds that included allegations of national origin discrimination and retaliation for filing a prior discrimination complaint. The collective bargaining agreement contained a non-discrimination clause but did not obligate employees to bring their statutory claims through the grievance procedure. Plaintiff arbitrated, represented by his own attorney rather than a union advocate, and the arbitrator denied his grievance. The court interpreted *Pyett* as modifying *Gardner–Denver* and concluded, in light of the arbitration, that plaintiff's Title VII and 1981 actions were barred by the doctrine of *res judicata*. The Court of Appeals for the Tenth Circuit, however, reversed. The court held that *Gardner–Denver* controlled and that the arbitration concerned only the plaintiff's claims under the contract, reasoning and quoting *Pyett*:

> That Mathews' contractual rights and statutory rights were coterminous is of no moment: As the Supreme Court has recently reaffirmed, "[b]ecause the collective-bargaining agreement gave the arbitrator 'authority to resolve only questions of contractual rights,' his decision could not prevent the employee from bringing the Title VII claim in federal court *'regardless of whether certain contractual rights are similar to, or duplicative of, the substantive rights secured by Title VII.'*"

3. Most collective bargaining agreement grievance procedures contain very short time limits for filing claims. They also typically do not provide for extensive discovery and almost never provide for depositions. They frequently provide that each party agrees to bear its own costs and attorney fees and that the parties will share the arbitrator's fee and other common expenses, such as a court reporter. Some collective bargaining agreements provide that the party who loses the arbitration will pay all of the arbitrator's fee. Do any such provisions require modification for the collective bargaining agreement's arbitration procedure to allow aggrieved employees to vindicate effectively their statutory discrimination claims?

4. Even before *Pyett* and the suggestion in footnote 8 that *Gardner–Denver* may be ripe for overruling, litigants who had arbitrated their contractual claims and lost had a difficult time in the litigation. For example, in *Collins v. New York Transit Auth.*, 305 F.3d 113, 118 (2d Cir. 2002), in granting the defendant's motion for summary judgment on the Title VII claim of a plaintiff whose discharge had already been upheld in arbitration, the court opined: "[A] decision by an independent tribunal that is not itself subject to a claim of bias will attenuate a plaintiff's proof of the requisite causal link [between the adverse employment action and the allegedly illegal motive]. Where, as here, that decision follows an evidentiary hearing and is based on substantial evidence, the Title VII plaintiff, to survive a motion for summary judgment, must present strong evidence that the decision was wrong as a matter of fact—e.g. new evidence not before the tribunal—or that the impartiality of the proceeding was compromised." The Tenth Circuit, however, declined to follow *Collins* in *Mathews v. Denver Newspaper Agency LLP*, 649 F.3d 1199 (10th Cir. 2011), *supra* note 2.

CHAPTER 12

REMEDIES

■ ■ ■

A. INTRODUCTION

Section 706(g)(1) of Title VII provides:

> If the court finds that the respondent has intentionally engaged in or is intentionally engaging in an unlawful employment practice charged in the complaint, the court may enjoin the respondent from engaging in such unlawful employment practice and order such affirmative action as may be appropriate, which may include, but is not limited to, reinstatement or hiring of employees, with or without back pay (payable by the employer, employment agency, or labor organization, as the case may be, responsible for the unlawful employment practice), or any other equitable relief as the court deems appropriate. Back-pay liability shall not accrue from a date more than two years prior to the filing of a charge with the Commission. Interim earnings or amounts earnable with reasonable diligence by the person or persons discriminated against shall operate to reduce the back pay otherwise allowable.

Title VII's remedial provisions are incorporated into the ADA. The ADA and Equal Pay Act adopt the remedial provisions of the Fair Labor Standards Act, which authorizes reinstatement, back pay, declaratory and injunctive relief and attorney fees, as well as liquidated damages equal to the amount of back pay in the case of willful violations.

Prior to 1991, all relief available under Title VII and the ADA was equitable in nature. The Civil Rights Act of 1991, authorized compensatory and punitive damages subject to maxima based on the size of the employer.

At times, what might appear to be defenses to liability have been recast as limitations on remedies. In ***McKennon v. Nashville Banner Publishing Co.***, 513 U.S. 352, 115 S.Ct. 879, 130 L.Ed.2d 852 (1995), a case decided under the ADEA, McKennon sued Nashville Banner alleging that she was terminated because of her age. In her deposition, McKennon admitted that in her final year of employment she had copied and taken confidential financial documents as "insurance" and "protection" because she feared she was going to be discharged. The lower courts granted Nashville Banner summary judgment on the ground that even if McKennon had been terminated because of her age, her admitted misconduct was ground for discharge and barred her from any relief under the ADEA. The Supreme Court reversed. The Court reasoned that because Nashville Banner had not discovered McKennon's misconduct until after her discharge, the misconduct could not have motivated its decision to terminate her employment. Consequently, the after-acquired evidence of misconduct could not be a defense to liability. It was, however, relevant to the question of remedy.

The Court reasoned, "It would be both inequitable and pointless to order the reinstatement of someone the employer would have terminated, and will terminate, in any event and upon lawful grounds." Consequently, the Court held that where the evidence establishes that the employer would have discharged the employee on that basis alone had it known of it at the time of discharge, the employee may not be reinstated or awarded front pay. The plaintiff may still be entitled to back pay, but the after-acquired evidence limits the amount. The Court stated that as a starting point, back pay should be calculated from the date of the discharge to the date the employer learned of the information, which may be adjusted, "taking into further account extraordinary equitable circumstances that affect the legitimate interests of either party." The Court's reasoning indicated that its analysis would apply with equal force to Title VII.

Similarly, as discussed in Chapter 8, the Supreme Court held in **Price Waterhouse v. Hopkins,** 490 U.S. 228, 109 S.Ct. 1775, 104 L.Ed.2d 268 (1989), that where the plaintiff in a Title VII action proved that the plaintiff's protected class was a motivating factor in the adverse employment decision, the defendant could establish an affirmative defense by proving that it would have taken the same action if it had not considered the plaintiff's membership in the protected class. The Civil Rights Act of 1991, however, changed the mixed motive/same decision defense from a defense to liability to a defense to remedy. The 1991 Act added section 706(g)(2), which provides that where a defendant proves its defense, the court "shall not award damages or issue an order requiring any admission, reinstatement, hiring, promotion, or payment," but "may grant declaratory relief, injunctive relief (except as provided in clause (ii)), and attorney's fees and costs . . ."

B.   MAKE WHOLE RELIEF ("THE PRIME DIRECTIVE")

ALBERMARLE PAPER CO. v. MOODY

Supreme Court of the United States, 1975
422 U.S. 405, 95 S.Ct. 2362, 45 L.Ed.2d 280

JUSTICE STEWART delivered the opinion of the Court.

* * *

I

The respondents-plaintiffs in the District Court are a certified class of present and former Negro employees at a paper mill in Roanoke Rapids, N.C.; the petitioners-defendants in the District Court are the plant's owner, the Albemarle Paper Co., and the plant employees' labor union, Halifax Local No. 425. In August 1966, after filing a complaint with the Equal Employment Opportunity Commission (EEOC), and receiving notice of their right to sue, the respondents brought a class action in the United States District Court for the Eastern District of North Carolina, asking permanent injunctive relief against 'any policy, practice, custom or usage' at the plant that violated Title VII. The respondents assured the court that the suit involved no claim for any monetary awards on a class basis, but in June 1970, after several years of discovery, the respondents moved to add a class demand for backpay. The court ruled that this issue would be considered at trial.

At the trial, in July and August 1971, the major issues were the plant's seniority system, its program of employment testing, and the question of backpay. In its opinion of November 9, 1971, the court found that the petitioners had 'strictly segregated' the plant's departmental 'lines of progression' prior to January 1, 1964, reserving the higher paying and more skilled lines for whites. The 'racial identifiability' of whole lines of progression persisted until 1968, when the lines were reorganized under a new collective-bargaining agreement. The court found, however, that this reorganization left Negro employees "locked' in the lower paying job classifications.' The formerly 'Negro' lines of progression had been merely tacked on to the bottom of the formerly 'white' lines, and promotions, demotions, and layoffs continued to be governed—where skills were 'relatively equal'—by a system of 'job seniority.' Because of the plant's previous history of overt segregation, only whites had seniority in the higher job categories. Accordingly, the court ordered the petitioners to implement a system of 'plantwide' seniority.

The court refused, however, to award backpay to the plaintiff class for losses suffered under the 'job seniority' program. The court explained:

> 'In the instant case there was no evidence of bad faith non-compliance with the Act. It appears that the company as early as 1964 began active recruitment of blacks for its Maintenance Apprentice Program. Certain lines of progression were merged on its own initiative, and as judicial decisions expanded the then existing interpretations of the Act, the defendants took steps to correct the abuses without delay....
>
> 'In addition, an award of back pay is an equitable remedy.... The plaintiffs' claim for back pay was filed nearly five years after the institution of this action. It was not prayed for in the pleadings. Although neither party can be charged with deliberate dilatory tactics in bringing this cause to trial, it is apparent that the defendants would be substantially prejudiced by the granting of such affirmative relief. The defendants might have chosen to exercise unusual zeal in

having this court determine their rights at an earlier date had they known that back pay would be at issue.'

* * *

The petitioners did not seek review of the court's judgment, but the respondents appealed the denial of a backpay award * * *. A divided Court of Appeals for the Fourth Circuit reversed the judgment of the District Court, ruling that backpay should have been awarded * * * [T]he Court of Appeals held that an award could properly be requested after the complaint was filed and that an award could not be denied merely because the employer had not acted in 'bad faith,':

> Because of the compensatory nature of a back pay award and the strong congressional policy embodied in Title VII, a district court must exercise its discretion as to back pay in the same manner it must exercise discretion as to attorney fees under Title II of the Civil Rights Act. . . . Thus, a plaintiff or a complaining class who is successful in obtaining an injunction under Title VII of the Act should ordinarily be awarded back pay unless special circumstances would render such an award unjust.

* * *

II

Whether a particular member of the plaintiff class should have been awarded any backpay and, if so, how much, are questions not involved in this review. The equities of individual cases were never reached. Though at least some of the members of the plaintiff class obviously suffered a loss of wage opportunities on account of Albemarle's unlawfully discriminatory system of job seniority, the District Court decided that no backpay should be awarded to anyone in the class. The court declined to make such an award on two stated grounds: the lack of 'evidence of bad faith non-compliance with the Act,' and the fact that 'the defendants would be substantially prejudiced' by an award of backpay that was demanded contrary to an earlier representation and late in the progress of the litigation. * * * The petitioners argue that the Court of Appeals was in error—that a district court has virtually unfettered discretion to award or deny backpay, and that there was no abuse of that discretion here. * * *

The petitioners contend that the statutory scheme provides no guidance, beyond indicating that backpay awards are within the district court's discretion. We disagree. It is true that backpay is not an automatic or mandatory remedy; like all other remedies under the Act, it is one which the courts 'may' invoke. The scheme implicitly recognizes that there may be cases calling for one remedy but not another, and—owing to the structure of the federal judiciary—these choices are, of course, left in the first instance to the district courts. However, such discretionary choices are not left to a court's 'inclination, but to its judgment; and its judgment is to be guided by sound legal principles.' The power to award backpay was bestowed by Congress, as part of a complex legislative design directed at a historic evil of national proportions. A court must exercise this power 'in light of the large objectives of the Act,' That the court's discretion is equitable in nature, hardly means that it is unfettered by meaningful standards or shielded from thorough appellate review. * * *

It is true that '(e)quity eschews mechanical rules … (and) depends on flexibility.' But when Congress invokes the Chancellor's conscience to further transcendant legislative purposes, what is required is the principled application of standards consistent with those purposes and not 'equity (which) varies like the Chancellor's foot.' Important national goals would be frustrated by a regime of discretion that 'produce(d) different results for breaches of duty in situations that cannot be differentiated in policy.'

The District Court's decision must therefore be measured against the purposes which inform Title VII. As the Court observed in *Griggs v. Duke Power Co.*, the primary objective was a prophylactic one:

> 'It was to achieve equality of employment opportunities and remove barriers that have operated in the past to favor an identifiable group of white employees over other employees.'

Backpay has an obvious connection with this purpose. If employers faced only the prospect of an injunctive order, they would have little incentive to shun practices of dubious legality. It is the reasonably certain prospect of a backpay award that 'provide(s) the spur or catalyst which causes employers and unions to self-examine and to self-evaluate their employment practices and to endeavor to eliminate, so far as possible, the last vestiges of an unfortunate and ignominious page in this country's history.'

It is also the purpose of Title VII to make persons whole for injuries suffered on account of unlawful employment discrimination. This is shown by the very fact that Congress took care to arm the courts with full equitable powers. For it is the historic purpose of equity to 'secur(e) complete justice,' *Brown v. Swann*, 10 Pet. 497, 503, 9 L.Ed. 508 (1836); * * * Title VII deals with legal injuries of an economic character occasioned by racial or other antiminority discrimination. The terms 'complete justice' and 'necessary relief' have acquired a clear meaning in such circumstances. Where racial discrimination is concerned, 'the (district) court has not merely the power but the duty to render a decree which will so far as possible eliminate the discriminatory effects of the past as well as bar like discrimination in the future.' *Louisiana v. United States*, 380 U.S. 145, 154, 85 S.Ct. 817, 822, 13 L.Ed.2d 709 (1965). * * *

The 'make whole' purpose of Title VII is made evident by the legislative history. The backpay provision was expressly modeled on the backpay provision of the National Labor Relations Act. * * * We may assume that Congress was aware that the Board, since its inception, has awarded backpay as a matter of course—not randomly or in the exercise of a standardless discretion, and not merely where employer violations are peculiarly deliberate, egregious, or inexcusable. Furthermore, in passing the Equal Employment Opportunity Act of 1972, Congress considered several bills to limit the judicial power to award backpay. These limiting efforts were rejected, and the backpay provision was re-enacted substantially in its original form. A Section-by-Section Analysis introduced by Senator Williams to accompany the Conference Committee Report on the 1972 Act strongly reaffirmed the 'make whole' purpose of Title VII:

> 'The provisions of this subsection are intended to give the courts wide discretion exercising their equitable powers to fashion the most complete relief possible. In dealing with the present section 706(g) the courts have stressed that the scope of relief under that section of the Act is intended to make the victims of unlawful discrimination whole, and that the attainment of this objective rests not only upon the elimination of the particular unlawful employment practice complained of, but also requires that persons aggrieved by the consequences and effects of the unlawful employment practice be, so far as possible, restored to a position where they would have been were it not for the unlawful discrimination.' 118 Cong.Rec. 7168 (1972).

As this makes clear, Congress' purpose in vesting a variety of 'discretionary' powers in the courts was not to limit appellate review of trial courts, or to invite inconsistency and caprice, but rather to make possible the 'fashion(ing) (of) the most complete relief possible.'

It follows that, given a finding of unlawful discrimination, backpay should be denied only for reasons which, if applied generally, would not frustrate the central statutory purposes of eradicating discrimination throughout the economy and making persons whole for injuries suffered through past discrimination. The courts of appeals must maintain a consistent and principled application of the backpay provision, consonant with the twin statutory objectives, while at the same time recognizing that the trial court will often have the keener appreciation of those facts and circumstances peculiar to particular cases.

The District Court's stated grounds for denying backpay in this case must be tested against these standards. The first ground was that Albemarle's breach of Title VII had not been in 'bad faith.' This is not a sufficient reason for denying backpay. Where an employer has shown bad faith—by maintaining a practice which he knew to be illegal or of highly questionable legality—he can make no claims whatsoever on the Chancellor's conscience. But, under Title VII, the mere absence of bad faith simply opens the door to equity; it does not depress the scales in the employer's favor. If backpay were awardable only upon a showing of bad faith, the remedy would become a punishment for moral turpitude, rather than a compensation for workers' injuries. This would read the 'make whole' purpose right out of Title VII, for a worker's injury is no less real simply because his employer did not inflict it in 'bad faith.' Title VII is not concerned with the employer's 'good intent or absence of discriminatory intent' for 'Congress directed the thrust of the Act to the consequences of employment practices, not simply the motivation.' To condition the awarding of backpay on a showing of 'bad faith' would be to open an enormous chasm between injunctive and backpay relief under Title VII. There is nothing on the face of the statute or in its legislative history that justifies the creation of drastic and categorical distinctions between those two remedies.

The District Court also grounded its denial of backpay on the fact that the respondents initially disclaimed any interest in backpay, first asserting their claim five years after the complaint was filed. The court concluded that the petitioners had been 'prejudiced' by this conduct. The Court of Appeals reversed on the ground 'that the broad aims of Title VII require that the issue of back pay be fully developed and determined even though it was not raised until the post-trial stage of litigation'.

* * *

[A] party may not be 'entitled' to relief if its conduct of the cause has improperly and substantially prejudiced the other party. The respondents here were not merely tardy, but also inconsistent, in demanding backpay. To deny backpay because a particular cause has been prosecuted in an eccentric fashion, prejudicial to the other party, does not offend the broad purposes of Title VII. This is not to say, however, that the District Court's ruling was necessarily correct. Whether the petitioners were in fact prejudiced, and whether the respondents' trial conduct was excusable, are questions that will be open to review by the Court of Appeals, if the District Court, on remand, decides again to decline to make any award of backpay. But the standard of review will be the familiar one of whether the District Court was 'clearly erroneous' in its factual findings and whether it 'abused' its traditional discretion to locate 'a just result' in light of the circumstances peculiar to the case. On these issues of procedural regularity and prejudice, the 'broad aims of Title VII' provide no ready solution.

* * *

Accordingly, the judgment is vacated, and these cases are remanded to the District Court for proceedings consistent with this opinion.

NOTES

1. The basic make-whole award is an order of reinstatement or instatement and back pay. The award is designed to place the plaintiff in the position the plaintiff would have occupied had the discrimination not occurred. Consequently, courts do not limit awards to lost wages or salary but include such lost fringe benefits as vacation pay, retirement plan contributions, profit-sharing and bonuses. *See, e.g., Munoz v. Oceanside Resorts, Inc.*, 223 F.3d 1340 (11th Cir. 2000) (room service waiter terminated in violation of ADEA was entitled to back pay which included loss of vacation pay, reduced cost of meals and reduced health insurance). How should medical insurance be treated? Should a court award the value of the premiums the employer would have paid or the difference between what the plaintiff paid to obtain medical

coverage and what the plaintiff would have paid under the employer's plan, or the amount of out of pocket medical costs the plaintiff incurred that would have been covered under the employer's plan? The courts are divided on this question. *See, e.g. EEOC v. Dial Corp.*, 469 F.3d 735, 744 (8th Cir. 2006) (awarding amount of premiums employer would have paid and discussing approaches of other cases).

2. ***FRANKS v. BOWMAN TRANSPORTATION CO.***, 424 U.S. 747, 96 S.Ct. 1251, 47 L.Ed.2d 444 (1976), held that notwithstanding the discretionary language of § 706(g), the "make whole" obligation left trial courts little discretion to deny full retroactive remedial seniority to successful plaintiffs even though to do so would frustrate seniority expectations of some incumbent workers. The Court rejected defendant's argument that such an award was precluded by § 703(h)'s protection for bona fide seniority systems that are not the result of an intention to discriminate. The Court reasoned:

> [T]he thrust of the section is directed toward defining what is and what is not an illegal discriminatory practice in instances in which the post-Act operation of a seniority system is challenged as perpetuating the effects of discrimination occurring prior to the effective date of the Act. There is no indication in the legislative materials that § 703(h) was intended to modify or restrict relief otherwise appropriate once an illegal discriminatory practice occurring after the effective date of the Act is proved as in the instant case, a discriminatory refusal to hire.

3. It is often said that plaintiffs have a duty to mitigate damages. The statement is not quite accurate. There is no affirmative duty to mitigate, but a defendant can defeat a claim for back pay by proving that plaintiff, in the exercise of reasonable diligence, could have found substantially equivalent employment. This is an affirmative defense which the defendant waives by not raising and on which the defendant has the burden of proof. For example, in *Farfaras v. Citizens Bank & Trust Corp.*, 433 F.3d 558 (7th Cir. 2006), the plaintiff testified that although she could have started a new job in December 2000, she voluntarily waited to January 8, 2001 to begin. The court upheld the trial court's decision not to reduce plaintiff's back pay by the amount she would have earned had she started her new job earlier because defendant did not plead failure to mitigate or otherwise raise the issue at trial. The only possible reference to failure to mitigate at trial occurred when defendant cross-examined plaintiff on her decision not to delay beginning the new job, something the court considered to be ambiguous and insufficient to place plaintiff on notice that defendant was raising an alleged failure to mitigate.

FORD MOTOR CO. v. EEOC, 458 U.S. 219, 102 S.Ct. 3057, 73 L.Ed.2d 721 (1982), held that an employer who unlawfully refuses to hire a job applicant can cut off the running of back pay by offering unconditionally to hire the individual in the same or equivalent position even though the offer does not include retroactive seniority. The Court viewed the issue as one of mitigation of damages. It reasoned:

> An unemployed or underemployed claimant, like all other Title VII claimants, is subject to the statutory duty to minimize damages set out in § 706(g). This duty, rooted in an ancient principle of law, requires the claimant to use reasonable diligence in finding other suitable employ-

ment. Although the unemployed or underemployed claimant need not go into another line of work, accept a demotion, or take a demeaning position, he forfeits his right to backpay if he refuses a job substantially equivalent to the one he was denied. Consequently, an employer charged with unlawful discrimination often can toll the accrual of backpay liability by unconditionally offering the claimant the job he sought, and thereby providing him with an opportunity to minimize damages.

An employer's unconditional offer of the job originally sought to an unemployed or underemployed claimant, moreover, need not be supplemented by an offer of retroactive seniority to be effective, lest a defendant's offer be irrationally disfavored relative to other employers' offers of substantially similar jobs. The claimant, after all, plainly would be required to minimize his damages by accepting another employer's offer even though it failed to grant the benefits of seniority not yet earned. Of course, if the claimant fulfills the requirement that he minimize damages by accepting the defendant's unconditional offer, he remains entitled to full compensation if he wins his case. A court may grant him backpay accrued prior to the effective date of the offer, retroactive seniority, and compensation for any losses suffered as a result of his lesser seniority before the court's judgment.

4.   In ***HOFFMAN PLASTIC COMPOUNDS, INC. v. NLRB***, 535 U.S. 137, 122 S.Ct. 1275, 152 L.Ed.2d 271 (2002), the Court held that the Immigration Reform and Control Act's prohibition on employers hiring undocumented workers precluded the National Labor Relations Board from awarding back pay to undocumented workers terminated because of their union activities, even though the National Labor Relations Act prohibited such terminations. In *Rivera v. NIBCO, Inc.*, 364 F.3d 1057 (9th Cir. 2004), the court refused to overturn a district court's protective order precluding the defendant in a Title VII action from inquiring in discovery into the plaintiffs' immigration status. The court reasoned that such inquiry would deter employees from reporting Title VII violations:

> Granting employers the right to inquire into workers' immigration status in cases like this would allow them to raise implicitly the threat of deportation and criminal prosecution every time a worker, documented or undocumented, reports illegal practices or files a Title VII action. Indeed, were we to direct district courts to grant discovery requests for information related to immigration status in every case involving national origin discrimination under Title VII, countless acts of illegal and reprehensible conduct would go unreported.

The court further opined that is was unlikely that *Hoffman Plastic Compounds* applied to Title VII. The court observed three differences between the NLRA and Title VII. First, the NLRA relies on the NLRB to enforce the statute, whereas Title VII relies predominantly on private enforcement. Second, unlike the NLRA, Title VII provides for awards of compensatory and punitive damages to deter violations. Third, unlike the NLRB which presides in a case under the NLRA and has no authority to interpret the Immigration Reform and Control Act, a federal judge presides in a Title VII action and has full authority to interpret IRCA and balance its policies against the policies of

Title VII. The court stated, "The differences between the two statutes persuade us that *Hoffman* does not resolve the question whether federal courts may award backpay to undocumented workers who have been discharged in violation of Title VII. Resolving the conflicting statutory policies involved in determining whether IRCA bars such awards to employees discriminated against on the basis of their national origin necessitates a different analysis than the Court undertook in *Hoffman*."

C. FRONT PAY

POLLARD v. E.I. du PONT de NEMOURS & CO.

Supreme Court of the United States, 2001
532 U.S. 843, 121 S.Ct. 1946, 150 L.Ed.2d 62

JUSTICE THOMAS delivered the opinion of the Court.

This case presents the question whether a front pay award is an element of compensatory damages under the Civil Rights Act of 1991. We conclude that it is not.

I

Petitioner Sharon Pollard sued her former employer, E.I. du Pont de Nemours and Company (DuPont), alleging that she had been subjected to a hostile work environment based on her sex, in violation of Title VII of the Civil Rights Act of 1964. After a trial, the District Court found that Pollard was subjected to co-worker sexual harassment of which her supervisors were aware. The District Court further found that the harassment resulted in a medical leave of absence from her job for psychological assistance and her eventual dismissal for refusing to return to the same hostile work environment. The court awarded Pollard $107,364 in backpay and benefits, $252,997 in attorney's fees, and, as relevant here, $300,000 in compensatory damages—the maximum permitted under the statutory cap for such damages in 42 U.S.C. § 1981a(b)(3). The Court of Appeals affirmed, concluding that the record demonstrated that DuPont employees engaged in flagrant discrimination based on sex and that DuPont managers and supervisors did not take adequate steps to stop it.

* * * Although courts have defined "front pay" in numerous ways, front pay is simply money awarded for lost compensation during the period between judgment and reinstatement or in lieu of reinstatement. For instance, when an appropriate position for the plaintiff is not immediately available without displacing an incumbent employee, courts have ordered reinstatement upon the opening of such a position and have ordered front pay to be paid until reinstatement occurs. In cases in which reinstatement is not viable because of continuing hostility between the plaintiff and the employer or its workers, or because of psychological injuries suffered by the plaintiff as a result of the discrimination, courts have ordered front pay as a substitute for reinstatement. For the purposes of this opinion, it is not necessary for us to explain when front pay is an appropriate

remedy. The question before us is only whether front pay, if found to be appropriate, is an element of compensatory damages under the Civil Rights Act of 1991 and thus subject to the Act's statutory cap on such damages.

Here, the District Court observed that "the $300,000.00 award is, in fact, insufficient to compensate plaintiff," but it stated that it was bound by the Sixth Circuit's decision in *Hudson v. Reno,* 130 F.3d 1193 (1997), which held that front pay was subject to the cap. On appeal, Pollard argued that *Hudson* was wrongly decided because front pay is not an element of compensatory damages, but rather a replacement for the remedy of reinstatement in situations in which reinstatement would be inappropriate. She also argued that § 1981a, by its very terms, explicitly excludes from the statutory cap remedies that traditionally were available under Title VII, which she argued included front pay. The Court of Appeals agreed with Pollard's arguments but considered itself bound by *Hudson.* The Sixth Circuit declined to rehear the case en banc.

* * *

II

Plaintiffs who allege employment discrimination on the basis of sex traditionally have been entitled to such remedies as injunctions, reinstatement, backpay, lost benefits, and attorney's fees under § 706(g) of the Civil Rights Act of 1964. In the Civil Rights Act of 1991, Congress expanded the remedies available to these plaintiffs by permitting, for the first time, the recovery of compensatory and punitive damages. 42 U.S.C. § 1981a(a)(1) ("[T]he complaining party may recover compensatory and punitive damages as allowed in subsection (b) of this section, in addition to any relief authorized by section 706(g) of the Civil Rights Act of 1964"). The amount of compensatory damages awarded under § 1981a for "future pecuniary losses, emotional pain, suffering, inconvenience, mental anguish, loss of enjoyment of life, and other nonpecuniary losses," and the amount of punitive damages awarded under § 1981a, however, may not exceed the statutory cap set forth in § 1981a(b)(3). The statutory cap is based on the number of people employed by the respondent. In this case, the cap is $300,000 because DuPont has more than 500 employees.

The Sixth Circuit has concluded that front pay constitutes compensatory damages awarded for future pecuniary losses and thus is subject to the statutory cap of § 1981a(b)(3). For the reasons discussed below, we conclude that front pay is not an element of compensatory damages within the meaning of § 1981a, and, therefore, we hold that the statutory cap of § 1981a(b)(3) is inapplicable to front pay.

A

Under § 706(g) of the Civil Rights Act of 1964 as originally enacted, when a court found that an employer had intentionally engaged in an unlawful employment practice, the court was authorized to "enjoin the respondent from engaging in such unlawful employment practice, and order such affirmative action as may be appropriate, which may include, but is not limited to, reinstatement or hiring of employees, with or without back pay." 42 U.S.C. § 2000e–5(g)(1). This provision closely tracked the language of § 10(c) of the National Labor Relations Act (NLRA), 29 U.S.C. § 160(c), which similarly authorized orders requiring employers to take appropriate, remedial "affirmative action." (authorizing the National Labor Relations Board to issue an order "requiring such person to cease and desist from such unfair labor practice, and to take such affirmative action including reinstatement of employees with or without back pay, as will effectuate the policies of this subchapter"). The meaning of this provision of the NLRA prior to enactment of the Civil Rights Act of 1964, therefore, gives us guidance as to the proper meaning of the same language in § 706(g) of Title VII. In applying § 10(c) of the NLRA, the Board consistently had made awards of what it called "backpay" up to the date the employee was reinstated or returned to the position he should have been in had the violation of the NLRA not occurred, even if such event occurred after judgment. Consistent with the Board's interpretation of this provision of the NLRA, courts finding unlawful intentional discrimination in Title VII actions awarded this same type of backpay under § 706(g). In the Title VII context, this form of "backpay" occurring after the date of judgment is known today as "front pay."

In 1972, Congress expanded § 706(g) to specify that a court could, in addition to awarding those remedies previously listed in the provision, award "any other equitable relief as the court deems appropriate." After this amendment to § 706(g), courts endorsed a broad view of front pay. Courts recognized that reinstatement was not always a viable option, and that an award of front pay as a substitute for reinstatement in such cases was a necessary part of the "make whole" relief mandated by Congress and by this Court in *Albemarle*. See, *e.g., Shore v. Federal Express Corp.,* 777 F.2d 1155, 1158–1159 (C.A.6 1985) ("Front pay is … simply compensation for the post-judgment effects of past discrimination." It is awarded "to effectuate fully the 'make whole' purposes of Title VII"); *Brooks v. Woodline Motor Freight, Inc.,* 852 F.2d 1061, 1066 (C.A.8 1988) (stating that front pay was appropriate given substantial animosity between parties where "the parties' relationship was not likely to improve, and the nature of the business required a high degree of mutual trust and confidence"); *Fitzgerald v. Sirloin Stockade, Inc.,* 624 F.2d, at 957 (upholding award of front pay where continuing hostility existed between the parties); *Cassino v. Reichhold Chems., Inc.,* 817 F.2d 1338, 1347 (C.A.9 1987) (same). By 1991, virtually all of the courts of appeals had recognized that "front pay" was a remedy authorized under § 706(g). In fact, no court of appeals appears to have ever held to the contrary.

In 1991, without amending § 706(g), Congress further expanded the remedies available in cases of intentional employment discrimination to include compensatory and punitive damages. See 42 U.S.C. § 1981a(a)(1). At that time, Rev. Stat. § 1977, 42 U.S.C. § 1981, permitted the recovery of unlimited compensatory and punitive damages in cases of intentional race and ethnic discrimination, but no similar remedy existed in cases of intentional sex, religious, or disability discrimination. Thus, § 1981a brought all forms of intentional employment discrimination into alignment, at least with respect to the forms of relief available to successful plaintiffs. However, compensatory and punitive damages awarded under § 1981a may not exceed the statutory limitations set forth in § 1981a(b)(3), while such damages awarded under § 1981 are not limited by statute.

B

In the abstract, front pay could be considered compensation for "future pecuniary losses," in which case it would be subject to the statutory cap. § 1981a(b)(3). The term "compensatory damages . . . for future pecuniary losses" is not defined in the statute, and, out of context, its ordinary meaning could include all payments for monetary losses after the date of judgment. However, we must not analyze one term of § 1981a in isolation. See *Gade v. National Solid Wastes Management Assn.,* 505 U.S. 88, 99, 112 S.Ct. 2374, 120 L.Ed.2d 73 (1992) (" '[W]e must not be guided by a single sentence or member of a sentence, but look to the provisions of the whole law' "). When § 1981a is read as a whole, the better interpretation is that front pay is not within the meaning of compensatory damages in § 1981a(b)(3), and thus front pay is excluded from the statutory cap.

In the Civil Rights Act of 1991, Congress determined that victims of employment discrimination were entitled to *additional* remedies. Congress expressly found that "additional remedies under Federal law are needed to deter unlawful harassment and intentional discrimination in the workplace," without giving any indication that it wished to curtail previously available remedies. See Civil Rights Act of 1991, 105 Stat. 1071, § 2. Congress therefore made clear through the plain language of the statute that the remedies newly authorized under § 1981a were *in addition to* the relief authorized by § 706(g). Section 1981a(a)(1) provides that, in intentional discrimination cases brought under Title VII, "the complaining party may recover compensatory and punitive damages as allowed in subjection (b) of [§ 1981a], *in addition to any relief authorized by section 706(g) of the Civil Rights Act of 1964,* from the respondent." And § 1981a(b)(2) states that "[c]ompensatory damages awarded under [§ 1981a] shall not include backpay, interest on backpay, *or any other type of relief authorized under section 706(g) of the Civil Rights Act of 1964.*" (Emphasis added.) According to these statutory provisions, if front pay was a type of relief authorized under § 706(g), it is excluded from the meaning of compensatory damages under § 1981a.

As discussed above, the original language of § 706(g) authorizing backpay awards was modeled after the same language in the NLRA. This provision in the NLRA had been construed to allow awards of backpay up to the date of reinstatement, even if reinstatement occurred after judgment. Accordingly, backpay awards made for the period between the date of judgment and the date of reinstatement, which today are called front pay awards under Title VII, were authorized under § 706(g).

As to front pay awards that are made in lieu of reinstatement, we construe § 706(g) as authorizing these awards as well. We see no logical difference between front pay awards made when there eventually is reinstatement and those made when there is not. Moreover, to distinguish between the two cases would lead to the strange result that employees could receive front pay when reinstatement eventually is available but not when reinstatement is not an option—whether because of continuing hostility between the plaintiff and the employer or its workers, or because of psychological injuries that the discrimination has caused the plaintiff. Thus, the most egregious offenders could be subject to the least sanctions. Had Congress drawn such a line in the statute and foreclosed front pay awards in lieu of reinstatement, we certainly would honor that line. But, as written, the text of the statute does not lend itself to such a distinction, and we will not create one. The statute authorizes courts to "order such affirmative action as may be appropriate." 42 U.S.C. § 2000e–5(g)(1). We conclude that front pay awards in lieu of reinstatement fit within this statutory term.

Because front pay is a remedy authorized under § 706(g), Congress did not limit the availability of such awards in § 1981a. Instead, Congress sought to expand the available remedies by permitting the recovery of compensatory and punitive damages in addition to previously available remedies, such as front pay.

The judgment of the Court of Appeals is reversed, and the case is remanded for further proceedings consistent with this opinion.

NOTES

1. As the Court's opinion makes clear, front pay is an equitable remedy and a substitute for reinstatement, or instatement in the case of a failure to hire or failure to promote, where the equities weigh in favor of the monetary remedy. But reinstatement or instatement are the preferred remedies, and some courts of appeals have required district courts to articulate their reasons for finding that the preferred remedies are not appropriate. *See, e.g., Julian v. City of Houston*, 314 F.3d 721 (5th Cir. 2002); *Kucia v. Southeast Arkansas Community Action Corp.*, 284 F.3d 944 (8th Cir. 2002). Front pay has been awarded where reinstatement or instatement would have required that the plaintiff bump an innocent employee, where antagonism between the employer and the plaintiff make reinstatement or instatement infeasible, or other circumstances where reinstatement or instatement is not appropriate.

2. An award of front pay requires a prediction about the future. The Fifth Circuit has referred to its calculation as necessitating "intellectual guesswork." *Julian, supra*, 314 F.3d at 729. Nevertheless, "a plaintiff who seeks an award of front pay must provide the district court with the essential data necessary to calculate a reasonably certain front pay award. Such information includes the amount of the proposed award, the length of time

the plaintiff expects to work for the defendant, and the applicable discount rate. If the plaintiff fails to provide this information to the district court, the court will not abuse its discretion if it denies his request for front pay." *Bruso v. United Airlines, Inc.*, 239 F.3d 848, 862 (7th Cir. 2001).

3. Of course, just as a finding that a plaintiff's employment would have terminated subsequent to the actual termination but prior to the trial would cut off the running of back pay, it will also defeat a claim for front pay. The defendant bears the burden of proof which can be considerable. For example, in *Munoz v. Oceanside Resorts, Inc.*, 223 F.3d 1340 (11th Cir. 2000), the defendant terminated a room service waiter because of his age in violation of the ADEA. The court upheld an award of front pay to the plaintiff even though the evidence established that the defendant eliminated offering room service entirely. The court reasoned that the defendant failed to prove that the plaintiff was not qualified for another position or some other reason that reassignment following the elimination of room service was not feasible.

D. COMPENSATORY DAMAGES

Prior to the Civil Rights Act of 1991, compensatory damages were unavailable under Title VII and the ADA, but were available in cases of race discrimination under 42 U.S.C. § 1981. The 1991 Act sought to remedy this situation by adding 42 U.S.C. § 1981a which allows the award of compensatory damages against private entities, federal, state and local government agencies "provided the complaining party cannot recover under section 1981." Recovery of compensatory damages is capped at $50,000 against employers who employ 15 to 100 employees in each of 20 or more calendar weeks in the current or prior calendar year, $100,000 against employers with 101 to 200 employees, $200,000 against employers with 201 to 500 employees and $300,000 against employers with more than 500 employees. For private entities, the caps apply to the combination of compensatory and punitive damages. (Awards of punitive damages against governmental bodies are not authorized.)

Compensatory damages are available only for intentional discrimination. The Civil Rights Act of 1991 expressly provides that authorization of compensatory damages does not apply to disparate impact cases.

A key question that has arisen is whether plaintiffs may establish entitlement to compensatory damages for emotional distress through their testimony alone. Although it is clear that expert medical or psychological testimony is not required, whether the plaintiff's testimony alone will suffice depends on the facts of the individual case.

Kucia v. Southeast Arkansas Community Action Corp., 284 F.3d 944 (8th Cir. 2002), upheld an award of compensatory damages for a terminated Head Start teacher based solely on the teacher's testimony. The court described the testimony:

> Ms. Kucia's * * * stated, "It's hard for me to hold my head up, okay, not that I'm prouder than anybody else, but it has had an effect on me. Warren is a small community. I'm on edge, I can't be pleasant."

Ms. Kucia testified that since her termination she felt like she "couldn't be trusted with children anymore." She also referred to marital problems because her husband is a "military man" and "understands things differently than [she does]." On cross-examination, part of Ms. Kucia's deposition testimony was introduced in evidence. At her deposition, when asked whether she suffered any mental distress or anguish, Ms. Kucia replied "just personal insult, I guess." She also repeated at trial deposition testimony that she had lost sleep and felt anxious.

The court then compared the case to two prior decisions dealing with awards of compensatory damages based only on the plaintiff's testimony:

Two of our recent cases mark out the boundaries for our reviewing function. In *Forshee v. Waterloo Industries, Inc.,* [178 F.3d 527 (8th Cir. 1999)] a jury verdict of $9,631 for emotional distress was reversed for insufficiency of evidence. We noted that the verdict was based entirely upon the plaintiff's own testimony. "She testified that after being terminated she 'went home and sat and cried about the rest of the day,' and that she was forced to take a job at lower pay and work two jobs." Aside from the loss of the job itself, little else occurred. There was no medical treatment, and no corroborating evidence. The plaintiff found a new job almost immediately.

By contrast, in *Mathieu* [*v. Gopher News Co.,* 273 F.3d 769 (8th Cir. 2001)], the plaintiff's testimony was also the only evidence supporting an award for emotional distress. There was no testimony by a medical professional. However, the plaintiff had lost a job of 34 years, was forced to reduce his standard of living, and had become depressed. A judgment declining to set aside a jury award of $165,000 for emotional distress was affirmed.

We think the evidence was sufficient in this case. It is not exactly like *Forshee* or *Mathieu.* Each case must be considered on its own facts, with a healthy regard for the prerogatives of the trier of fact and the presiding judge. The plaintiff's period of employment was much shorter than that of the plaintiff in *Mathieu,* but her testimony of mental distress and disruption of life was, we think, stronger than that presented in *Mathieu,* at least as reflected in our published opinion. In these circumstances, though the question perhaps is close, we cannot say that the jury award was wholly lacking in reason, or so excessive as to shock the judicial conscience. The District Court's action in declining to set the award aside will be affirmed.

E. PUNITIVE DAMAGES
KOLSTAD v. AMERICAN DENTAL ASSOCIATION
Supreme Court of the United States, 1999
527 U.S. 526, 119 S.Ct. 2118, 144 L.Ed.2d 494

JUSTICE O'CONNOR delivered the opinion of the Court.

Under the terms of the Civil Rights Act of 1991 (1991 Act), punitive damages are available in claims under Title VII of the Civil Rights Act of 1964, and the Americans with Disabilities Act of 1990(ADA). Punitive damages are limited, however, to cases in which the employer has engaged in intentional discrimination and has done so "with malice or with reckless indifference to the federally protected rights of an aggrieved individual." Rev. Stat. § 1977, as amended, 42 U.S.C. § 1981a(b)(1). We here consider the circumstances under which punitive damages may be awarded in an action under Title VII.

I

A

In September 1992, Jack O'Donnell announced that he would be retiring as the Director of Legislation and Legislative Policy and Director of the Council on Government Affairs and Federal Dental Services for respondent, American Dental Association (respondent or Association). Petitioner, Carole Kolstad, was employed with O'Donnell in respondent's Washington, D.C., office, where she was serving as respondent's Director of Federal Agency Relations. When she learned of O'Donnell's retirement, she expressed an interest in filling his position. Also interested in replacing O'Donnell was Tom Spangler, another employee in respondent's Washington office. At this time, Spangler was serving as the Association's Legislative Counsel, a position that involved him in respondent's legislative lobbying efforts. Both petitioner and Spangler had worked directly with O'Donnell, and both had received "distinguished" performance ratings by the acting head of the Washington office, Leonard Wheat.

Both petitioner and Spangler formally applied for O'Donnell's position, and Wheat requested that Dr. William Allen, then serving as respondent's Executive Director in the Association's Chicago office, make the ultimate promotion decision. After interviewing both petitioner and Spangler, Wheat recommended that Allen select Spangler for O'Donnell's post. Allen notified petitioner in December 1992 that he had, in fact, selected Spangler to serve as O'Donnell's replacement. Petitioner's challenge to this employment decision forms the basis of the instant action.

B

After first exhausting her avenues for relief before the Equal Employment Opportunity Commission, petitioner filed suit against the Association in Federal District Court, alleging that respondent's decision to promote Spangler was an act of employment discrimination proscribed under Title VII. In petitioner's view, the entire selection process was a sham. Counsel for petitioner urged the jury to conclude that Allen's stated reasons for selecting Spangler were pretext for gender discrimination, and that Spangler had been chosen for the position before the formal selection process began. Among the evidence offered in support of this view, there was testimony to the effect that Allen modified the description of O'Donnell's post to track aspects of the job description used to hire Spangler. In petitioner's view, this "preselection" procedure suggested an intent by the Association to discriminate on the basis of sex. Petitioner also introduced testimony at trial that Wheat told sexually offensive jokes and that he had referred to certain prominent professional women in derogatory terms. Moreover, Wheat allegedly refused to meet with petitioner for several weeks regarding her interest in O'Donnell's position. Petitioner testified, in fact, that she had historically experienced difficulty gaining access to meet with Wheat. Allen, for his part, testified that he conducted informal meetings regarding O'Donnell's position with both petitioner and Spangler, although petitioner stated that Allen did not discuss the position with her.

The District Court denied petitioner's request for a jury instruction on punitive damages. The jury concluded that respondent had discriminated against petitioner on the basis of sex and awarded her backpay totaling $52,718. Although the District Court subsequently denied respondent's motion for judgment as a matter of law on the issue of liability, the court made clear that it had not been persuaded that respondent had selected Spangler over petitioner on the basis of sex, and the court denied petitioner's requests for reinstatement and for attorney's fees.

Petitioner appealed from the District Court's decisions denying her requested jury instruction on punitive damages and her request for reinstatement and attorney's fees. Respondent cross-appealed from the denial of its motion for judgment as a matter of law. In a split decision, a panel of the Court of Appeals for the District of Columbia reversed the District Court's decision denying petitioner's request for an instruction on punitive damages. In so doing, the court rejected respondent's claim that punitive damages are available under Title VII only in " 'extraordinarily egregious cases.' " The panel reasoned that, "because 'the state of mind necessary to trigger liability for the wrong is at least as culpable as that required to make punitive damages applicable,' " the fact that the jury could reasonably have found intentional discrimination meant that the jury should have been permitted to consider punitive damages. The court noted, however, that not all cases involving intentional discrimination would support a punitive damages award. Such an award might be improper, the panel reasoned, in instances where the employer justifiably believes that intentional discrimination is permitted or where an employee engages in discrimination outside the scope of that employee's authority. Here, the court concluded, respondent "neither attempted to justify the use of sex in its promotion decision nor disavowed the actions of its agents."

The Court of Appeals subsequently agreed to rehear the case en banc, limited to the punitive damages question. In a divided opinion, the court affirmed the decision of the District Court. The en banc majority concluded that, "before the question of punitive damages can go to the jury, the evidence of the defendant's culpability must exceed what is needed to show intentional discrimination." Based on the 1991 Act's structure and legislative history, the court determined, specifically, that a defendant must be shown to have engaged in some "egregious" misconduct before the jury is permitted to consider a request for punitive damages. Although the court declined to set out the "egregiousness" requirement in any detail, it concluded that petitioner failed to make the requisite showing in the instant case. Judge Randolph concurred, relying chiefly on § 1981a's structure as evidence of a congressional intent to "limi[t] punitive damages to exceptional cases." Judge Tatel wrote in dissent for five judges, who agreed generally with the panel majority.

* * *

II

A

Prior to 1991, only equitable relief, primarily backpay, was available to prevailing Title VII plaintiffs; the statute provided no authority for an award of punitive or compensatory damages. With the passage of the 1991 Act, Congress provided for additional remedies, including punitive damages, for certain classes of Title VII and ADA violations.

The 1991 Act limits compensatory and punitive damages awards, however, to cases of "intentional discrimination"—that is, cases that do not rely on the "disparate impact" theory of discrimination. 42 U.S.C. § 1981a(a)(1). Section 1981a(b)(1) further qualifies the availability of punitive awards:

> "A complaining party may recover punitive damages under this section against a respondent (other than a government, government agency or political subdivision) if the complaining party demonstrates that the respondent engaged in a discriminatory practice or discriminatory practices *with malice or with reckless indifference to the federally protected rights of an aggrieved individual.*" (Emphasis added.)

The very structure of § 1981a suggests a congressional intent to authorize punitive awards in only a subset of cases involving intentional discrimination. Section 1981a(a)(1) limits compensatory and punitive awards to instances of intentional discrimination, while § 1981a(b)(1) requires plaintiffs to make an additional "demonstrat[ion]" of their eligibility for punitive damages. Congress plainly sought to impose two standards of liability-one for establishing a right to compensatory damages and another, higher standard that a plaintiff must satisfy to qualify for a punitive award.

The Court of Appeals sought to give life to this two-tiered structure by limiting punitive awards to cases involving intentional discrimination of an "egregious" nature. We credit the en banc majority's effort to effectuate congressional intent, but, in the end, we reject its conclusion that eligibility for punitive damages can only be described in terms of an employer's "egregious" misconduct. The terms "malice" and "reckless" ultimately focus on the actor's state of mind. See, *e.g.,* Black's Law Dictionary 956–957, 1270 (6th ed.1990); see also W. Keeton, D. Dobbs, R. Keeton, & D. Owen, Prosser and Keeton, Law of Torts 212–214 (5th ed.1984) (defining "willful," "wanton," and "reckless"). While egregious misconduct is evidence of the requisite mental state, Keeton, *supra,* at 213–214, § 1981a does not limit plaintiffs to this form of evidence, and the section does not require a showing of egregious or outrageous discrimination independent of the employer's state of mind. Nor does the statute's structure imply an independent role for "egregiousness" in the face of congressional silence. On the contrary, the view that § 1981a provides for punitive awards based solely on an employer's state of mind is consistent with the 1991 Act's distinction between equitable and compensatory relief. Intent determines which remedies are open to a plaintiff here as well; compensatory awards are available only where the employer has engaged in "*intentional* discrimination." § 1981a(a)(1).

Moreover, § 1981a's focus on the employer's state of mind gives some effect to Congress' apparent intent to narrow the class of cases for which punitive awards are available to a subset of those involving intentional discrimination. The employer must act with "malice or with reckless indifference *to the [plaintiff's] federally protected rights.*" § 1981a(b)(1). The terms "malice" or "reckless indifference" pertain to the employer's knowledge that it may be acting in violation of federal law, not its awareness that it is engaging in discrimination.

We gain an understanding of the meaning of the terms "malice" and "reckless indifference," as used in § 1981a, from this Court's decision in *Smith* v. *Wade,* 461 U.S. 30, 103 S.Ct. 1625, 75 L.Ed.2d 632 (1983). The parties, as well as both the en banc majority and dissent, recognize that Congress looked to the Court's decision in *Smith* in adopting this language in § 1981a. Employing language similar to what later appeared in § 1981a, the Court concluded in *Smith* that "a jury may be permitted to assess punitive damages in an action under § 1983 when the defendant's conduct is shown to be motivated by evil motive or intent, or when it involves reckless or callous indifference to the federally protected rights of others." While the *Smith* Court determined that it was unnecessary to show actual malice to qualify for a punitive award, its intent standard, at a minimum, required recklessness in its subjective form. The Court referred to a "subjective consciousness" of a risk of injury or illegality and a " 'criminal indifference to civil obligations.' " (quoting *Philadelphia, W. & B.R. Co.* v. *Quigley,* 21 How. 202, 214, 16 L.Ed. 73 (1858)); see also *Farmer* v. *Brennan,* 511 U.S. 825, 837, 114 S.Ct. 1970, 128 L.Ed.2d 811 (1994) (explaining that criminal law employs a subjective form of recklessness, requiring a finding that the defendant "disregards a risk of harm of which he is aware"); see generally 1 T. Sedgwick, Measure of Damages §§ 366, 368, pp. 528, 529 (8th ed. 1891) (describing "wantonness" in punitive damages context in terms of "criminal indifference" and "gross negligence" in terms of a "conscious indifference to consequences"). The Court thus compared the recklessness standard to the requirement that defendants act with " 'knowledge of falsity or reckless disregard for the truth' " before punitive awards are available in defamation actions, *Smith, supra,* at 50, 103 S.Ct. 1625 (quoting *Gertz* v. *Robert Welch, Inc.,* 418 U.S.

323, 349, 94 S.Ct. 2997, 41 L.Ed.2d 789 (1974)), a subjective standard, *Harte–Hanks Communications, Inc. v. Connaughton,* 491 U.S. 657, 688, 109 S.Ct. 2678, 105 L.Ed.2d 562 (1989). Applying this standard in the context of § 1981a, an employer must at least discriminate in the face of a perceived risk that its actions will violate federal law to be liable in punitive damages.

There will be circumstances where intentional discrimination does not give rise to punitive damages liability under this standard. In some instances, the employer may simply be unaware of the relevant federal prohibition. There will be cases, moreover, in which the employer discriminates with the distinct belief that its discrimination is lawful. The underlying theory of discrimination may be novel or otherwise poorly recognized, or an employer may reasonably believe that its discrimination satisfies a bona fide occupational qualification defense or other statutory exception to liability. See, *e.g.,* 42 U.S.C. § 2000e–2(e)(1) (setting out Title VII defense "where religion, sex, or national origin is a bona fide occupational qualification"); see also § 12113 (setting out defenses under ADA). In *Hazen Paper Co. v. Biggins,* 507 U.S. 604, 616, 113 S.Ct. 1701, 123 L.Ed.2d 338 (1993), we thus observed that, in light of statutory defenses and other exceptions permitting age-based decisionmaking, an employer may knowingly rely on age to make employment decisions without recklessly violating the Age Discrimination in Employment Act of 1967 (ADEA). Accordingly, we determined that limiting liquidated damages under the ADEA to cases where the employer "knew or showed reckless disregard for the matter of whether its conduct was prohibited by the statute," without an additional showing of outrageous conduct, was sufficient to give effect to the ADEA's two-tiered liability scheme.

* * *

Egregious misconduct is often associated with the award of punitive damages, but the reprehensible character of the conduct is not generally considered apart from the requisite state of mind. Conduct warranting punitive awards has been characterized as "egregious," for example, *because* of the defendant's mental state. * * *

To be sure, egregious or outrageous acts may serve as evidence supporting an inference of the requisite "evil motive." "The allowance of exemplary damages depends upon the bad motive of the wrong-doer *as exhibited by his acts."* * * * Again, however, respondent has not shown that the terms "reckless indifference" and "malice," in the punitive damages context, have taken on a consistent definition including an independent, "egregiousness" requirement. Cf. *Morissette v. United States,* 342 U.S. 246, 263, 72 S.Ct. 240, 96 L.Ed. 288 (1952) ("[W]here Congress borrows terms of art in which are accumulated the legal tradition and meaning of centuries of practice, it presumably knows and adopts the cluster of ideas that were attached to each borrowed word in the body of learning from which it was taken and the meaning its use will convey to the judicial mind unless otherwise instructed").

B

The inquiry does not end with a showing of the requisite "malice or ... reckless indifference" on the part of certain individuals, however. 42 U.S.C. § 1981a(b)(1). The plaintiff must impute liability for punitive damages to respondent. * * *

* * *.

The common law has long recognized that agency principles limit vicarious liability for punitive awards. This is a principle, moreover, that this Court historically has endorsed. * * *

* * * The Restatement of Agency places strict limits on the extent to which an agent's misconduct may be imputed to the principal for purposes of awarding punitive damages:

"Punitive damages can properly be awarded against a master or other principal because of an act by an agent if, but only if:

"(a) the principal authorized the doing and the manner of the act, or

"(b) the agent was unfit and the principal was reckless in employing him, or

"(c) the agent was employed in a managerial capacity and was acting in the scope of employment, or

"(d) the principal or a managerial agent of the principal ratified or approved the act." Restatement (Second) of Agency, *supra,* § 217C.

The Restatement, for example, provides that the principal may be liable for punitive damages if it authorizes or ratifies the agent's tortious act, or if it acts recklessly in employing the malfeasing agent. The Restatement also contemplates liability for punitive awards where an employee serving in a "managerial capacity" committed the wrong while "acting in the scope of employment." Restatement (Second) of Agency, *supra,* § 217C; see also Restatement (Second) of Torts, *supra,* § 909 (same). "Unfortunately, no good definition of what constitutes a 'managerial capacity' has been found," and determining whether an employee meets this description requires a fact-intensive inquiry * * *

Additional questions arise from the meaning of the "scope of employment" requirement. The Restatement of Agency provides that even intentional torts are within the scope of an agent's employment if the conduct is "the kind [the employee] is employed to perform," "occurs substantially within the authorized time and space limits," and "is actuated, at least in part, by a purpose to serve the" employer. Restatement (Second) of Agency, § 228(1), at 504. According to the Restatement, so long as these rules are satisfied, an employee may be said to act within the scope of employment even if the employee engages in acts "specifically forbidden" by the employer and uses "forbidden means of accomplishing results." *Id.,* § 230, at 511, Comment *b*. On this view, even an employer who makes every effort to comply with Title VII would be held liable for the discriminatory acts of agents acting in a "managerial capacity."

Holding employers liable for punitive damages when they engage in good faith efforts to comply with Title VII, however, is in some tension with the very principles underlying common law limitations on vicarious liability for punitive damages-that it is "improper ordinarily to award punitive damages against one who himself is personally innocent and therefore liable only vicariously." Restatement (Second) of Torts, *supra,* § 909, at 468, Comment *b*. Where an employer has undertaken such good faith efforts at Title VII compliance, it "demonstrat[es] that it never acted in reckless disregard of federally protected rights." 139 F.3d, at 974 (Tatel, J., dissenting); see also *Harris,* 132 F.3d, at 983, 984 (observing that, "[i]n some cases, the existence of a written policy instituted in good faith has operated as a total bar to employer liability for punitive damages" and concluding that "the institution of a written sexual harassment policy goes a long way towards dispelling any claim about the employer's 'reckless' or 'malicious' state of mind").

Applying the Restatement of Agency's "scope of employment" rule in the Title VII punitive damages context, moreover, would reduce the incentive for employers to implement antidiscrimination programs. In fact, such a rule would likely exacerbate concerns among employers that § 1981a's "malice" and "reckless indifference" standard penalizes those employers who educate themselves and their employees on Title VII's prohibitions. Dissuading employers from implementing programs or policies to prevent discrimination in the workplace is directly contrary to the purposes underlying Title VII. The statute's "primary objective" is "a prophylactic one"; it aims, chiefly, "not to provide redress but to avoid harm." With regard to sexual harassment, "[f]or example, Title VII is designed to encourage the creation of antiharassment policies and effective grievance mechanisms." *Burlington Industries, Inc.,* 524 U.S., at 764, 118 S.Ct. 2257. The purposes underlying Title VII are similarly advanced where employers are encouraged to adopt antidiscrimination policies and to educate their personnel on Title VII's prohibitions.

In light of the perverse incentives that the Restatement's "scope of employment" rules create, we are compelled to modify these principles to avoid undermining the objectives underlying Title VII. *Meritor Savings Bank, FSB,* 477 U.S., at 72, 106 S.Ct. 2399 ("[C]ommon-law principles may not be transferable in all their particulars to Title VII"). Recognizing Title VII as an effort to promote prevention as well as remediation, and observing the very principles underlying the Restatements' strict limits on vicarious liability for punitive damages, we agree that, in the punitive damages context, an employer may not be vicariously liable for the discriminatory employment decisions of managerial agents where these decisions are contrary to the employer's "good-faith efforts to comply with Title VII." 139 F.3d, at 974 (Tatel, J., dissenting). As the dissent recognized, "[g]iving punitive damages protection to employers who make good-faith efforts to prevent discrimination in the workplace accomplishes"

Title VII's objective of "motivat[ing] employers to detect and deter Title VII violations.

We have concluded that an employer's conduct need not be independently "egregious" to satisfy § 1981a's requirements for a punitive damages award, although evidence of egregious misconduct may be used to meet the plaintiff's burden of proof. We leave for remand the question whether petitioner can identify facts sufficient to support an inference that the requisite mental state can be imputed to respondent. The parties have not yet had an opportunity to marshal the record evidence in support of their views on the application of agency principles in the instant case, and the en banc majority had no reason to resolve the issue because it concluded that petitioner had failed to demonstrate the requisite "egregious" misconduct. Although trial testimony established that Allen made the ultimate decision to promote Spangler while serving as petitioner's interim executive director, respondent's highest position, it remains to be seen whether petitioner can make a sufficient showing that Allen acted with malice or reckless indifference to petitioner's Title VII rights. Even if it could be established that Wheat effectively selected O'Donnell's replacement, moreover, several questions would remain, *e.g.,* whether Wheat was serving in a "managerial capacity" and whether he behaved with malice or reckless indifference to petitioner's rights. It may also be necessary to determine whether the Association had been making good faith efforts to enforce an antidiscrimination policy. We leave these issues for resolution on remand.

For the foregoing reasons, the judgment of the Court of Appeals is vacated, and the case is remanded for proceedings consistent with this opinion.

[The opinion of CHIEF JUSTICE REHNQUIST, joined by JUSTICE THOMAS, concurring in part and dissenting in part, and the opinion of JUSTICE STEVENS, joined by JUSTICES SOUTER, GINSBURG and BREYER, concurring in part and dissenting in part are omitted.]

NOTES

1. The Civil Rights Act of 1991 authorizes claims of punitive damages, subject to the statutory caps, against private entities and only for violations of Title VII, the ADA and the Rehabilitation Act. The ADEA and EPA adopt the remedies available under the Fair Labor Standards Act which provides for liquidated damages equal to the amount of back pay in cases of willful violations.

2. The Court identified three elements to a punitive damage claim. First, the plaintiff must prove that the defendant acted with malice or reckless indifference toward the plaintiff's federal statutory rights. Second, the plaintiff must prove that the actor acted within the scope of the agency, i.e., in a managerial capacity. Third, the employer may escape liability for punitive damages where the manager's decisions are contrary to the employer's good faith efforts to comply with Title VII. Are the first and third

elements consistent? Are there circumstances where an employer might act through its agent with malice or reckless disregard for the plaintiff's statutory rights but still escape liability because the manager's actions were contrary to the employer's good faith efforts to comply with the law?

3. The mere existence of a non-discrimination policy alone may not insulate an employer from liability for punitive damages. For example, *Bruso v. United Airlines, Inc.*, 239 F.3d 848, 862 (7th Cir. 2001), held that the plaintiff was entitled to a jury instruction on punitive damages even though the defendant had a zero tolerance policy for discrimination. The court observed that there was evidence that the investigation conducted under the policy was a sham designed to protect upper level managers who should have taken action to correct the sexual harassment sooner.

F. AFFIRMATIVE RELIEF

In addition to the specific remedies already discussed, courts have broad discretion to order such affirmative relief as necessary to effectuate the purposes of the employment discrimination laws. Thus, courts commonly enjoin unlawful employment practices and issue other orders such as orders for the removal of discrimination-tainted materials from employee personnel files. By far, the most controversy has surrounded orders of race-conscious affirmative relief that benefits members of the protected class who are not themselves identified victims of discrimination.

In *Firefighters Local 1784 v. Stotts,* 467 U.S. 561, 104 S.Ct. 2576, 81 L.Ed.2d 483 (1984), the City of Memphis settled a class action race discrimination case by agreeing, among other things, to a plan to increase the percentage of African Americans in all ranks within its fire department until the percentage reached the percentage of African Americans in the county. The settlement was embodied in a consent decree. Subsequently, budget cuts required the layoff of firefighters. The lower courts enjoined the city from laying off firefighters strictly by seniority on the grounds that such action would impede the purposes of the consent decree. The Supreme Court reversed.

The Court found the injunction inconsistent with section 703(h)'s protection for bona fide seniority systems. It regarded the injunction as effectively awarding retroactive competitive seniority to newly hired minority firefighters who were not themselves victims of discrimination, something that the Court opined section 703(h) prohibited.

LOCAL 28 SHEET METAL WORKERS INTERNATIONAL ASSOCIATION v. EEOC
Supreme Court of the United States, 1986
478 U.S. 421, 106 S.Ct. 3019, 92 L.Ed.2d 344 (1986)

JUSTICE BRENNAN announced the judgment of the Court and delivered the opinion of the Court with respect to Parts I, II, III, and VI, and an opinion with respect to Parts IV, V, and VII in which JUSTICE MARSHALL, JUSTICE BLACKMUN, and JUSTICE STEVENS join.

In 1975, petitioners were found guilty of engaging in a pattern and practice of discrimination against black and Hispanic individuals (nonwhites) in violation of Title VII of the Civil Rights Act of 1964, 42 U.S.C. § 2000e *et seq.,* and ordered to end their discriminatory practices, and to admit a certain percentage of nonwhites to union membership by July 1981. In 1982 and again in 1983, petitioners were found guilty of civil contempt for disobeying the District Court's earlier orders. They now challenge the District Court's contempt finding, and also the remedies the court ordered both for the Title VII violation and for contempt. Principally, the issue presented is whether the remedial provision of Title VII, see 42 U.S.C. § 2000e–5(g), empowers a district court to order race-conscious relief that may benefit individuals who are not identified victims of unlawful discrimination.

I

Petitioner Local 28 of the Sheet Metal Workers' International Association (Local 28) represents sheet metal workers employed by contractors in the New York City metropolitan area. Petitioner Local 28 Joint Apprenticeship Committee (JAC) is a management-labor committee which operates a 4–year apprenticeship training program designed to teach sheet metal skills. Apprentices enrolled in the program receive training both from classes and from on-the-job work experience. Upon completing the program, apprentices become journeyman members of Local 28. Successful completion of the program is the principal means of attaining union membership.

In 1964, the New York State Commission for Human Rights determined that petitioners had excluded blacks from the union and the apprenticeship program in violation of state law. The State Commission found, among other things, that Local 28 had never had any black members or apprentices, and that "admission to apprenticeship is conducted largely on a nepot[is]tic basis involving sponsorship by incumbent union members," creating an impenetrable barrier for nonwhite applicants. Petitioners were ordered to "cease and desist" their racially discriminatory practices. The New York State Supreme Court affirmed the State Commission's findings, and directed petitioners to implement objective standards for selecting apprentices. *State Comm'n for Human Rights v. Farrell,* 43 Misc.2d 958, 252 N.Y.S.2d 649 (1964).

When the court's orders proved ineffective, the State Commission commenced other state-court proceedings in an effort to end petitioners' discriminatory practices. Petitioners had originally agreed to indenture two successive classes of apprentices using nondiscriminatory selection procedures, but stopped processing applications for the second apprentice class, thus requiring that the State Commission seek a court order requiring petitioners to indenture the apprentices. *State Comm'n for Human Rights v. Farrell,* 47 Misc.2d 244, 262 N.Y.S.2d 526, aff'd, 24 App.Div.2d 128, 264 N.Y.S.2d 489 (1st Dept.1965). The court subsequently denied the union's request to reduce the size of the second apprentice class, and chastised the union for refusing "except for token gestures, to further the integration process." *State Comm'n for Human Rights v. Farrell*, 47 Misc.2d 799, 800, 263 N.Y.S.2d 250, 252 (1965). Petitioners proceeded to disregard the results of the selection test for a third apprentice class on the ground that nonwhites had received "unfair tutoring" and had passed in unreasonably high numbers. The state court ordered petitioners to indenture the apprentices based on the examination results. *State Comm'n for Human Rights v. Farrell*, 52 Misc.2d 936, 277 N.Y.S.2d 287, aff'd, 27 App.Div.2d 327, 278 N.Y.S.2d 982 (1st Dept.), aff'd 19 N.Y.2d 974, 281 N.Y.S.2d 521, 228 N.E.2d 691 (1967).

In 1971, the United States initiated this action under Title VII and Executive Order No. 11246, 3 CFR 339 (1964–1965 Comp.) to enjoin petitioners from engaging in a pattern and practice of discrimination against black and Hispanic individuals (nonwhites). The New York City Commission on Human Rights (City) intervened as plaintiff to press claims that petitioners had violated municipal fair employment laws, and had frustrated the City's efforts to increase job opportunities for minorities in the construction industry. *United States v. Local 638, Enterprise Assn. of Steam, Hot Water, Hydraulic Sprinkler, Pneumatic Tube, Compressed Air, Ice Machine, Air Conditioning, and General Pipefitters*, 347 F.Supp. 164 (SDNY 1972). In 1970, the City had adopted a plan requiring contractors on its projects to employ one minority trainee for every four journeyman union members. Local 28 was the only construction local which refused to comply voluntarily with the plan. In early 1974, the City attempted to assign six minority trainees to sheet metal contractors working on municipal construction projects. After Local 28 members stopped work on the projects, the District Court directed the JAC to admit the six trainees into the apprenticeship program, and enjoined Local 28 from causing any work stoppage at the affected job sites. The parties subsequently agreed to a consent order that required the JAC to admit up to 40 minorities into the apprenticeship program by September 1974. The JAC stalled compliance with the consent order, and only completed the indenture process under threat of contempt.

Following a trial in 1975, the District Court concluded that petitioners had violated both Title VII and New York law by discriminating against nonwhite workers in recruitment, selection, training, and admission to the union. Noting that as of July 1, 1974, only 3.19% of the union's total membership, including apprentices and journeymen, was nonwhite, the court found that petitioners had denied qualified nonwhites access to union membership through a variety of discriminatory practices. First, the court found that petitioners had adopted discriminatory procedures and standards for admission into the apprenticeship program. The court examined some of the factors used to select apprentices, including the entrance examination and high-school diploma requirement, and determined that these criteria had an adverse discriminatory impact on nonwhites, and were not related to job performance. The court also observed that petitioners had used union funds to subsidize special training sessions for friends and relatives of union taking the apprenticeship exam.

Second, the court determined that Local 28 had restricted the size of its membership in order to deny access to nonwhites. The court found that Local 28 had refused to administer yearly journeyman examinations despite a growing demand for members' services. Rather, to meet this increase in demand, Local 28 recalled pensioners who obtained doctors' certificates that they were able to work, and issued hundreds of temporary work permits to nonmembers; only one of these permits was issued to a nonwhite. Moreover, the court found that "despite the fact that Local 28 saw fit to request [temporary workers] from sister locals all across the country, as well as from allied New York construction unions such as plumbers, carpenters, and iron workers, it never once sought them from Sheet Metal Local 400," a New York City union comprised almost entirely of nonwhites. The court concluded that by using the temporary permit system rather than continuing to administer journeyman tests, Local 28 successfully restricted the size of its membership with the "illegal effect, if not the intention, of denying nonwhites access to employment opportunities in the industry."

Third, the District Court determined that Local 28 had selectively organized nonunion sheet metal shops with few, if any, minority employees, and admitted to membership only white employees from those shops. The court found that "[p]rior to 1973 no non-white ever became a member of Local 28 through the organization of a non-union shop." The court also found that, despite insistent pressure from both the International Union and local contractors, Local 28 had stubbornly refused to organize sheet metal workers in the local blowpipe industry because a large percentage of such workers were nonwhite.

Finally, the court found that Local 28 had discriminated in favor of white applicants seeking to transfer from sister locals. The court noted that from 1967 through 1972, Local 28 had accepted 57 transfers from sister locals, all of them white, and that it was only after this litigation had commenced that Local 28 accepted its first nonwhite transfers, two journeymen from Local 400. The court also found that on one occasion, the union's president had incorrectly told nonwhite Local 400 members that they were not eligible for transfer.

The District Court entered an order and judgment (O & J) enjoining petitioners from discriminating against nonwhites, and enjoining the specific practices the court had found to be discriminatory. Recognizing that "the record in both state and federal court against these defendants is replete with instances of ... bad faith attempts to prevent or delay affirmative action," the court concluded that "the imposition of a remedial racial goal in conjunction with an admission preference in favor of nonwhites is essential to place the defendants in a position of compliance with [Title VII]." The court established a 29% nonwhite membership goal, based on the percentage of nonwhites in the relevant labor pool in New

York City, for the union to achieve by July 1, 1981. The parties were ordered to devise and to implement recruitment and admission procedures designed to achieve this goal under the supervision of a court-appointed administrator.

The administrator proposed, and the court adopted, an Affirmative Action Program which, among other things, required petitioners to offer annual, nondiscriminatory journeyman and apprentice examinations, select members according to a white-nonwhite ratio to be negotiated by the parties, conduct extensive recruitment and publicity campaigns aimed at minorities, secure the administrator's consent before issuing temporary work permits, and maintain detailed membership records, including separate records for whites and nonwhites. Local 28 was permitted to extend any of the benefits of the program to whites and other minorities, provided that this did not interfere with the programs' operation.

The Court of Appeals for the Second Circuit affirmed the District Court's determination of liability, finding that petitioners had "consistently and egregiously violated Title VII." The court upheld the 29% nonwhite membership goal as a temporary remedy, justified by a "long and persistent pattern of discrimination," and concluded that the appointment of an administrator with broad powers was clearly appropriate, given petitioners' refusal to change their membership practices in the face of prior state and federal court orders. However, the court modified the District Court's order to permit the use of a white-nonwhite ratio for the apprenticeship program only pending implementation of valid, job-related entrance tests. Local 28 did not seek certiorari in this Court to review the Court of Appeals' judgment.

On remand, the District Court adopted a Revised Affirmative Action Program and Order (RAAPO) to incorporate the Court of Appeals' mandate. RAAPO also modified the original Affirmative Action Program to accommodate petitioners' claim that economic problems facing the construction industry had made it difficult for them to comply with the court's orders. Petitioners were given an additional year to meet the 29% membership goal. RAAPO also established interim membership goals designed to "afford the parties and the Administrator with some device to measure progress so that, if warranted, other provisions of the program could be modified to reflect change [sic] circumstances." The JAC was directed to indenture at least 36 apprentices by February 1977, and to determine the size of future apprenticeship classes subject to review by the administrator. A divided panel of the Court of Appeals affirmed RAAPO in its entirety, including the 29% nonwhite membership goal. Petitioners again chose not to seek certiorari from this Court to review the Court of Appeals' judgment.

In April 1982, the City and State moved in the District Court for an order holding petitioners in contempt. They alleged that petitioners had not achieved RAAPO's 29% nonwhite membership goal, and that this failure was due to petitioners' numerous violations of the O & J, RAAPO, and orders of the administrator. The District Court, after receiving detailed evidence of how the O & J and RAAPO had operated over the previous six years, held petitioners in civil contempt. The court did not rest its contempt finding on petitioners' failure to meet the 29% membership goal, although nonwhite membership in Local 28 was only 10.8% at the time of the hearing. Instead, the court found that petitioners had "failed to comply with RAAPO ... almost from its date of entry," identifying six "separate actions or omissions on the part of the defendants [that] have impeded the entry of non-whites into Local 28 in contravention of the prior orders of this court." Specifically, the court determined that petitioners had (1) adopted a policy of underutilizing the apprenticeship program in order to limit nonwhite membership and employment opportunities; (2) refused to conduct the general publicity campaign required by the O & J and RAAPO to inform nonwhites of membership opportunities; (3) added a job protection provision to the union's collective-bargaining agreement that favored older workers and discriminated against nonwhites (older workers provision); (4) issued unauthorized work permits to white workers from sister locals; and (5) failed to maintain and submit records and reports required by RAAPO, the O & J, and the administrator, thus making it difficult to monitor petitioners' compliance with the court's orders.

To remedy petitioners' contempt, the court imposed a $150,000 fine to be placed in a fund designed to increase nonwhite membership in the apprenticeship program and the union. The administrator was directed to propose a plan for utilizing the fund. The court deferred imposition of further coercive fines pending receipt of the administrator's recommendations for modifications to RAAPO.

In 1983, the City brought a second contempt proceeding before the administrator, charging petitioners with additional violations of the O & J, RAAPO, and various administrative orders. The administrator found that the JAC had violated RAAPO by failing to submit accurate reports of hours worked by apprentices, thus preventing the court from evaluating whether nonwhite apprentices had shared in available employment opportunities, and that Local 28 had: (1) failed, in a timely manner, to provide the racial and ethnic data required by the O & J and RAAPO with respect to new members entering the union as a result of its merger with five predominantly white sheet metal locals, (2) failed to serve copies of the O & J and RAAPO on contractors employing Local 28 members, as ordered by the administrator, and (3) submitted inaccurate racial membership records.

The District Court adopted the administrator's findings and once again adjudicated petitioners guilty of civil contempt. The court ordered petitioners to pay for a computerized recordkeeping system to be maintained by outside consultants, but deferred ruling on additional contempt fines pending submission of the administrator's fund proposal. The court subsequently adopted the administrator's proposed Employment, Training, Education, and Recruitment Fund (Fund) to "be used for the purpose of remedying discrimination." The Fund was used for a variety of purposes. In order to increase the pool of qualified nonwhite applicants for the apprenticeship program, the Fund paid for nonwhite union members to serve as liaisons to vocational and technical schools with sheet metal programs, created part-time and summer sheet metal jobs for qualified nonwhite youths, and extended financial assistance to needy apprentices. The Fund also extended counseling and tutorial services to nonwhite apprentices, giving them the benefits that had traditionally been available to white apprentices from family and friends. Finally, in an effort to maximize employment opportunities for all apprentices, the Fund provided financial support to employers otherwise unable to hire a sufficient number of apprentices, as well as matching funds to attract additional funding for job training programs.

The District Court also entered an Amended Affirmative Action Plan and Order (AAAPO) which modified RAAPO in several respects. AAAPO established a 29.23% minority membership goal to be met by August 31, 1987. The new goal was based on the labor pool in the area covered by the newly expanded union. The court abolished the apprenticeship examination, concluding that "the violations that have occurred in the past have been so egregious that a new approach must be taken to solve the apprentice selection problem." Apprentices were to be selected by a three-member Board, which would select one minority apprentice for each white apprentice indentured. Finally, to prevent petitioners from underutilizing the apprenticeship program, the JAC was required to assign to Local 28 contractors one apprentice for every four journeymen, unless the contractor obtained a written waiver from respondents.

Petitioners appealed the District Court's contempt orders, the Fund order, and the order adopting AAAPO. A divided panel of the Court of Appeals affirmed the District Court's contempt findings, except the finding based on adoption of the older workers' provision. The court concluded that "[p]articularly in light of the determined resistance by Local 28 to all efforts to integrate its membership, ... the combination of violations found by [the District Court] amply demonstrates the union's foot-dragging egregious noncompliance ... and adequately supports [its] findings of civil contempt against both Local 28 and the JAC." The court also affirmed the District Court's contempt remedies, including the Fund order, and affirmed AAAPO with two modifications: it set aside the requirement that one minority apprentice be indentured for every white apprentice, and clarified the District Court's orders to allow petitioners to implement objective, nondiscriminatory apprentice selection procedures. The court found the 29.23% nonwhite membership goal to be proper in light of Local 28's "long continued and egregious racial discrimination," and because it "will not unnecessarily trammel the rights of any readily ascertainable group of non-minority individuals." The court rejected petitioners' argument that the goal violated Title VII or the Constitution. The court also distinguished AAAPO from the race-conscious order invalidated by this Court in *Firefighters v. Stotts,* 467 U.S. 561, 104 S.Ct. 2576, 81

L.Ed.2d 483 (1984), on three grounds: (1) unlike the order in *Stotts,* AAAPO did not conflict with a bona fide seniority plan; (2) the *Stotts* discussion of § 706(g) of Title VII applied only to "make whole" relief and did not address the prospective relief contained in AAAPO and the Fund order; and (3) this case, unlike *Stotts,* involved intentional discrimination.

Local 28 and the JAC filed a petition for a writ of certiorari. They present several claims for review: (1) that the District Court relied on incorrect statistical data; (2) that the contempt remedies ordered by the District Court were criminal in nature and were imposed without due process; (3) that the appointment of an administrator to supervise membership practices interferes with their right to self-governance; and (4) that the membership goal and Fund are unconstitutional. Principally, however, petitioners, supported by the Solicitor General, maintain that the membership goal and Fund exceed the scope of remedies available under Title VII because they extend race-conscious preferences to individuals who are not the identified victims of petitioners' unlawful discrimination. We granted the petition, and now affirm the Court of Appeals.

II

[The Court rejected the argument that the District Court relied on incorrect statistical evidence in violation of Title VII and of petitioners' right to due process.]

* * *

III

[The Court rejected the argument that the District Court had imposed penalties for criminal contempt without following the procedures required for criminal contempt proceedings and held that the District Court held petitioners in civil contempt.]

* * *

IV

Petitioners, joined by the EEOC, argue that the membership goal, the Fund order, and other orders which require petitioners to grant membership preferences to nonwhites are expressly prohibited by § 706(g), 42 U.S.C. § 2000e–5(g), which defines the remedies available under Title VII. Petitioners and the EEOC maintain that § 706(g) authorizes a district court to award preferential relief only to the actual victims of unlawful discrimination. They maintain that the membership goal and the Fund violate this provision, since they require petitioners to admit to membership, and otherwise to extend benefits to, black and Hispanic individuals who are not the identified victims of unlawful discrimination. We reject this argument, and hold that § 706(g) does not prohibit a court from ordering, in appropriate circumstances, affirmative race-conscious relief as a remedy for past discrimination. Specifically, we hold that such relief may be appropriate where an employer or a labor union has engaged in persistent or egregious discrimination, or where necessary to dissipate the lingering effects of pervasive discrimination.

A

* * *

The language of § 706(g) plainly expresses Congress' intent to vest district courts with broad discretion to award "appropriate" equitable relief to remedy unlawful discrimination. Nevertheless, petitioners and the EEOC argue that the last sentence of § 706(g) prohibits a court from ordering an employer or labor union to take affirmative steps to eliminate discrimination which might incidentally benefit individuals who are not the actual victims of discrimination. This reading twists the plain language of the statute.

The last sentence of § 706(g) prohibits a court from ordering a union to admit an individual who was "refused admission ... for any reason other than discrimination." It does not, as petitioners and the EEOC suggest, say that a court may order relief only for the actual victims of past discrimination. The sentence on its face addresses only the situation where a plaintiff demonstrates that a union (or an employer) has engaged in unlawful discrimination, but the union can show that a particular individual would have been refused admission even in the absence of discrimination, for example, because that individual was unqualified. In these circumstances, § 706(g) confirms that a court could not order the union to admit the unqualified individual. In this case, neither the membership goal nor the Fund order required petitioners to admit to membership individuals who had been refused admission for reasons unrelated to discrimination. Thus, we do not read § 706(g) to prohibit a court from ordering the kind of affirmative relief the District Court awarded in this case.

B

The availability of race-conscious affirmative relief under § 706(g) as a remedy for a violation of Title VII also furthers the broad purposes underlying the statute. * * *.

In most cases, the court need only order the employer or union to cease engaging in discriminatory practices, and award make-whole relief to the individuals victimized by those practices. In some instances, however, it may be necessary to require the employer or union to take affirmative steps to end discrimination effectively to enforce Title VII. Where an employer or union has engaged in particularly longstanding or egregious discrimination, an injunction simply reiterating Title VII's prohibition against discrimination will often prove useless and will only result in endless enforcement litigation. In such cases, requiring recalcitrant employers or unions to hire and to admit qualified minorities roughly in proportion to the number of qualified minorities in the work force may be the only effective way to ensure the full enjoyment of the rights protected by Title VII.

Further, even where the employer or union formally ceases to engage in discrimination, informal mechanisms may obstruct equal employment opportunities. An employer's reputation for discrimination may discourage minorities from seeking available employment. In these circumstances, affirmative race-conscious relief may be the only means available "to assure equality of employment opportunities and to eliminate those discriminatory practices and devices which have fostered racially stratified job environments to the disadvantage of minority citizens." Affirmative action "promptly operates to change the outward and visible signs of yesterday's racial distinctions and thus, to provide an impetus to the process of dismantling the barriers, psychological or otherwise, erected by past practices."

Finally, a district court may find it necessary to order interim hiring or promotional goals pending the development of nondiscriminatory hiring or promotion procedures. In these cases, the use of numerical goals provides a compromise between two unacceptable alternatives: an outright ban on hiring or promotions, or continued use of a discriminatory selection procedure.

* * *

C

Despite the fact that the plain language of § 706(g) and the purposes of Title VII suggest the opposite, petitioners and the EEOC maintain that the legislative history indicates that Congress intended that affirmative relief under § 706(g) benefit only the identified victims of past discrimination. To support this contention, petitioners and the EEOC rely principally on statements made throughout the House and Senate debates to the effect that Title VII would not require employers or labor unions to adopt quotas or preferences that would benefit racial minorities.

Our examination of the legislative history of Title VII convinces us that, when examined in context, the statements relied upon by petitioners and the EEOC do not indicate that Congress intended to limit relief under § 706(g) to that which benefits only the actual victims of unlawful discrimination. Rather, these statements were intended largely to reassure opponents of the bill that it would not require employers or labor unions to use racial quotas or to grant preferential treatment to racial minorities in order to avoid being charged with unlawful discrimination. The bill's supporters insisted that this would not be the intent and effect of the legislation, and eventually agreed to state this expressly in § 703(j). Contrary to the arguments made by petitioners and the EEOC, these statements do not suggest that a court may not order preferential relief under § 706(g) when appropriate to remedy past discrimination. Rather, it is clear that the bill's supporters only wished to emphasize that an employer would not violate the statute merely by having a racially imbalanced work force, and, consequently, that a court could not order an employer to adopt racial preferences merely to correct such an imbalance.

* * *

[M]any opponents of Title VII argued that an employer could be found guilty of discrimination under the statute simply because of a racial imbalance in his work force, and would be compelled to implement racial "quotas" to avoid being charged with liability. At the same time, supporters of the bill insisted that employers would not violate Title VII simply because of racial imbalance, and emphasized that neither the Commission nor the courts could compel employers to adopt quotas solely to facilitate racial balancing. The debate concerning what Title VII did and did not require culminated in the adoption of § 703(j), which stated expressly that the statute did not require an employer or labor union to adopt quotas or preferences simply because of a racial imbalance. However, while Congress strongly opposed the use of quotas or preferences merely to maintain racial balance, it gave no intimation as to whether such measures would be acceptable as *remedies* for Title VII violations.

Congress' failure to consider this issue is not surprising, since there was relatively little civil rights litigation prior to the adoption of the 1964 Civil Rights Act. More importantly, the cases that had been litigated had not resulted in the sort of affirmative-action remedies that, as later became apparent, would sometimes be necessary to eliminate effectively the effects of past discrimination. Thus, the use of racial preferences as a *remedy* for past discrimination simply was not an issue at the time Title VII was being considered. Our task then is to determine whether Congress intended to preclude a district court from ordering affirmative action in appropriate circumstances as a remedy for past discrimination. Our examination of the legislative policy behind Title VII leads us to conclude that Congress did not intend to prohibit a court from exercising its remedial authority in that way. Congress deliberately gave the district courts broad authority under Title VII to fashion the most complete relief possible to eliminate "the last vestiges of an unfortunate and ignominious page in this country's history," As we noted above, affirmative race-conscious relief may in some instances be necessary to accomplish this task. In the absence of any indication that Congress intended to limit a district court's remedial authority in a way which would frustrate the court's ability to enforce Title VII's mandate, we decline to fashion such a limitation ourselves.

Our reading of the scope of the district court's remedial powers under § 706(g) is confirmed by the contemporaneous interpretations of the EEOC and the Justice Department. Following the enactment of the Civil Rights Act of 1964, both the Justice Department and the EEOC, the two federal agencies charged with enforcing Title VII, steadfastly maintained that race-conscious remedies for unlawful discrimination are available under the statute. Both agencies have, in appropriate cases, sought court orders and consent decrees containing such provisions. The agencies' contemporaneous reading of the statute lends strong support to our interpretation.

Finally, our interpretation of § 706(g) is confirmed by the legislative history of the Equal Employment Opportunity Act of 1972, which amended Title VII in several respects. One such change modified the language of § 706(g) to empower a court to order "such affirmative action as may be appropriate, which may include, *but is not limited to* reinstatement or hiring of employees ... *or any other equitable relief as the court deems appropriate.*" (emphasized language added in 1972). This language was intended "to give the courts wide discretion exercising their equitable powers to fashion the most complete relief possible." 118 Cong.Rec. 7168 (1972). While the section-by-section analysis undertaken in the Conference Committee Report stressed the need for "make-whole" relief for the "victims of unlawful discrimination," *id.,* at 7168, 7565, nowhere did Congress suggest that a court lacked the power to award preferential remedies that might benefit nonvictims. Indeed, the Senate's rejection of two other amendments supports a contrary conclusion.

During the 1972 debates, Senator Ervin introduced an amendment to counteract the effects of the Department of Labor's so-called Philadelphia Plan. The Philadelphia Plan was established pursuant to Executive Order No. 11246, and required prospective federal contractors to submit affirmative-action programs including "specific goals of minority manpower utilization." *Contractors Assn. of Eastern Pa. v. Secretary of Labor,* 442 F.2d 159, 163 (CA3), cert. denied, 404 U.S. 854, 92 S.Ct. 98, 30 L.Ed.2d 95 (1971). Attacking the Plan as "[t]he most notorious example of discrimination in reverse," Senator Ervin proposed an amendment to Title VII that read, in relevant part: "No department, agency, or officer of the United States shall require an employer to practice discrimination in reverse by employing persons of a particular race ... in either fixed or variable numbers, proportions, percentages, quotas, goals, or ranges." Senator Ervin complained that the amendment was needed because both the Department of Labor and the EEOC were ignoring § 703(j)'s prohibition against requiring employers to engage in preferential hiring for racial minorities.

Senator Javits vigorously opposed Senator Ervin's proposal. First, he recognized that the amendment, while targeted at the Philadelphia Plan, would also jettison "the whole concept of 'affirmative action' as it has been developed under Executive Order 11246 *and as a remedial concept under Title VII.*" (emphasis added). He explained that the amendment would "deprive the courts of the opportunity to order affirmative action under title VII of the type which they have sustained in order to correct a history of unjust and illegal discrimination in employment." * * *

Senator Ervin proposed a second amendment that would have extended § 703(j)'s prohibition against racial preferences to "Executive Order Numbered 11246, or any other law or Executive Order,"; this amendment was also defeated resoundingly. Thus, the legislative history of the 1972 amendments to Title VII confirms the availability of race-conscious affirmative action as a remedy under the statute. Congress was aware that both the Executive and Judicial Branches had used such measures to remedy past discrimination, and rejected amendments that would have barred such remedies. Instead, Congress reaffirmed the breadth of the court's remedial powers under § 706(g) by adding language authorizing courts to order "any other equitable relief as the court deems appropriate." * * *

D

Finally, petitioners and the EEOC find support for their reading of § 706(g) in several of our decisions applying that provision. Petitioners refer to several cases for the proposition that court-ordered remedies under § 706(g) are limited to make-whole relief benefiting actual victims of past discrimination. See *Ford Motor Co. v. EEOC,* 458 U.S. 219, 102 S.Ct. 3057, 73 L.Ed.2d 721 (1982); *Connecticut v. Teal,* 457 U.S. 440, 102 S.Ct. 2525, 73 L.Ed.2d 130 (1982); *Teamsters v. United States,* 431 U.S. 324, 97 S.Ct. 1843, 52 L.Ed.2d 396 (1977); *Franks v. Bowman Transportation Co.,* 424 U.S. 747, 96 S.Ct. 1251, 47 L.Ed.2d 444 (1976); *Albemarle Paper Co. v. Moody,* 422 U.S. 405, 95 S.Ct. 2362, 45 L.Ed.2d 280 (1975). This reliance is misguided. The cases cited hold only that a court may order relief designed to make individual victims of racial discrimination whole. None of these decisions suggested that individual "make-whole" relief was the *only* kind of remedy available under the statute; on the contrary, several cases emphasized that the district court's remedial powers should be exercised both to eradicate the effects of unlawful discrimination as well as to make the victims of past discrimination whole. Neither do these cases suggest that § 706(g) prohibits a court from ordering relief which might benefit nonvictims; indeed several cases acknowledged that the district court has broad authority to "devise prospective relief designed to assure that employers found to be in violation of [Title VII] eliminate their discriminatory practices and the effects therefrom."

Petitioners claim to find their strongest support in *Firefighters v. Stotts,* 467 U.S. 561, 104 S.Ct. 2576, 81 L.Ed.2d 483 (1984). In *Stotts,* the city of Memphis, Tennessee, had entered into a consent decree requiring affirmative steps to increase the proportion of minority employees in its Fire Department. Budgetary cuts subsequently forced the city to lay off employees; under the city's last-hired, first-fired seniority system, many of the black employees who had been hired pursuant to the consent decree would have been laid off first. These employees sought relief, and the District Court, concluding that the proposed layoffs would have a racially discriminatory effect, enjoined the city from applying its seniority policy "insofar as it will decrease the percentage of black[s] that are presently employed." We held that the District Court exceeded its authority.

First, we rejected the claim that the District Court was merely enforcing the terms of the consent decree since the parties had expressed no intention to depart from the existing seniority system in the event of layoffs. Second, we concluded that the District Court's order conflicted with § 703(h) of Title VII, which "permits the routine application of a seniority system absent proof of an intention to discriminate." Since the District Court had found that the proposed layoffs were not motivated by a discriminatory purpose, we held that the court erred in enjoining the city from applying its seniority system in making the layoffs.

We also rejected the Court of Appeals' suggestion that the District Court's order was justified by the fact that, had plaintiffs prevailed at trial, the court could have entered an order overriding the city's seniority system. Relying on *Teamsters, supra,* we observed that a court may abridge a bona fide seniority system in fashioning a Title VII remedy only to make victims of intentional discrimination whole, that is, a court may award competitive seniority to individuals who show that they had been discriminated against. However, because none of the firefighters protected by the court's order was a proven victim of illegal discrimination, we reasoned that at trial the District Court would have been without authority to override the city's seniority system, and therefore the court could not enter such an order merely to effectuate the purposes of the consent decree.

While not strictly necessary to the result, we went on to comment that "[o]ur ruling in *Teamsters* that a court can award competitive seniority only when the beneficiary of the award has actually been a victim of illegal discrimination is consistent with the policy behind § 706(g)" which, we noted, "is to provide 'make-whole' relief only to those who have been actual victims of illegal discrimination." Relying on this language, petitioners, joined by the EEOC, argue that both the membership goal and the Fund order contravene the policy behind § 706(g) since they extend preferential relief to individuals who were not the actual victims of illegal discrimination. We think this argument both reads *Stotts* too broadly and ignores the important differences between *Stotts* and this case.

Stotts discussed the "policy" behind § 706(g) in order to supplement the holding that the District Court could not have interfered with the city's seniority system in fashioning a Title VII remedy. This "policy" was read to prohibit a court from awarding make-whole relief, such as competitive seniority, backpay, or promotion, to individuals who were denied employment opportunities for reasons unrelated to discrimination. The District Court's injunction was considered to be inconsistent with this "policy" because it was tantamount to an award of make-whole relief (in the form of competitive seniority) to individual black firefighters who had not shown that the proposed layoffs were motivated by racial discrimination. However, this limitation on *individual* make-whole relief does not affect a court's authority to order race-conscious affirmative action. The purpose of affirmative action is not to make identified victims whole, but rather to dismantle prior patterns of employment discrimination and to prevent discrimination in the future. Such relief is provided to the class as a whole rather than to individual members; no individual is entitled to relief, and beneficiaries need not show that they were themselves victims of discrimination. In this case, neither the membership goal nor the Fund order required petitioners to indenture or train particular individuals, and neither required them to admit to membership individuals who were refused admission for reasons unrelated to discrimination. We decline petitioners' invitation to read *Stotts* to prohibit a court from ordering any kind of race-conscious affirmative relief that might benefit nonvictims. This reading would distort the language of § 706(g), and would deprive the courts of an important means of enforcing Title VII's guarantee of equal employment opportunity.

E

Although we conclude that § 706(g) does not foreclose a district court from instituting some sorts of racial preferences where necessary to remedy past discrimination, we do not mean to suggest that such relief is always proper. While the fashioning of "appropriate" remedies for a particular Title VII violation invokes the "equitable discretion of the district courts," we emphasize that a court's judgment should be guided by sound legal principles. In particular, the court should exercise its discretion with an eye towards Congress' concern that race-conscious affirmative measures not be invoked simply to create a racially balanced work force. In the majority of Title VII cases, the court will not have to impose affirmative action as a remedy for past discrimination, but need only order the employer or union to cease engaging in discriminatory practices and award make-whole relief to the individuals victimized by those practices. However, in some cases, affirmative action may be necessary in order effectively to enforce Title VII. As we noted before, a court may have to resort to race-conscious affirmative action when confronted with an employer or labor union that has engaged in persistent or egregious discrimination. Or such relief may be necessary to dissipate the lingering effects of pervasive discrimination. Whether there might be other circumstances that justify the use of court-ordered affirmative action is a matter that we need not decide here. We note only that a court should consider whether affirmative action is necessary to remedy past discrimination in a particular case before imposing such measures, and that the court should also take care to tailor its orders to fit the nature of the violation it seeks to correct. In this case, several factors lead us to conclude that the relief ordered by the District Court was proper.

First, both the District Court and the Court of Appeals agreed that the membership goal and Fund order were necessary to remedy petitioners' pervasive and egregious discrimination. The District Court set the original 29% membership goal upon observing that "[t]he record in both state and federal courts against [petitioners] is replete with instances of their bad faith attempts to prevent or delay affirmative action." The court extended the goal after finding petitioners in contempt for refusing to end their discriminatory practices and failing to comply with various provisions of RAAPO. In affirming the revised membership goal, the Court of Appeals observed that "[t]his court has twice recognized Local 28's long continued and egregious racial discrimination ... and Local 28 has presented no facts to indicate that our earlier observations are no longer apposite." In light of petitioners' long history of "foot-dragging resistance" to court orders, simply enjoining them from once again engaging in discriminatory practices would clearly have been futile. Rather, the District Court properly determined that affirmative race-conscious measures were necessary to put an end to petitioners' discriminatory ways.

Both the membership goal and Fund order were similarly necessary to combat the lingering effects of past discrimination. In light of the District Court's determination that the union's reputation for discrimination operated to discourage nonwhites from even applying for membership, it is unlikely that an injunction would have been sufficient to extend to nonwhites equal opportunities for employment. Rather, because access to admission, membership, training, and employment in the industry had traditionally been obtained through informal contacts with union members, it was necessary for a substantial number of nonwhite workers to become members of the union in order for the effects of discrimination to cease. The Fund, in particular, was designed to insure that nonwhites would receive the kind of assistance that white apprentices and applicants had traditionally received through informal sources. On the facts of this case, the District Court properly determined that affirmative, race-conscious measures were necessary to assure the equal employment opportunities guaranteed by Title VII.

Second, the District Court's flexible application of the membership goal gives strong indication that it is not being used simply to achieve and maintain racial balance, but rather as a benchmark against which the court could gauge petitioners' efforts to remedy past discrimination. The court has twice adjusted the deadline for achieving the goal, and has continually approved of changes in the size of the apprenticeship classes to account for the fact that economic conditions prevented petitioners from meeting their membership targets; there is every reason to believe that both the court and the administrator will continue to accommodate *legitimate* explanations for petitioners' failure to comply with the court's orders. Moreover, the District Court expressly disavowed any reliance on petitioners' failure to meet the goal as a basis for the contempt finding, but instead viewed this failure as symptomatic of petitioners' refusal to comply with various subsidiary provisions of RAAPO. In sum, the District Court has implemented the membership goal as a means by which it can measure petitioners' compliance with its orders, rather than as a strict racial quota.

Third, both the membership goal and the Fund order are temporary measures. Under AAAPO "[p]referential selection of [union members] will end as soon as the percentage of [minority union members] approximates the percentage of [minorities] in the local labor force." Similarly, the Fund is scheduled to terminate when petitioners achieve the membership goal, and the court determines that it is no longer needed to remedy past discrimination. The District Court's orders thus operate "as a temporary tool for remedying past discrimination without attempting to 'maintain' a previously achieved balance."

Finally, we think it significant that neither the membership goal nor the Fund order "unnecessarily trammel[s] the interests of white employees." Petitioners concede that the District Court's orders did not require any member of the union to be laid off, and did not discriminate against *existing* union members. While whites seeking admission into the union may be denied benefits extended to their nonwhite counterparts, the court's orders do not stand as an absolute bar to such individuals; indeed, a majority of new union members have been white. Many provisions of the court's orders are race-neutral (for example, the requirement that the JAC assign one apprentice for every four journeyman workers), and petitioners remain free to adopt the provisions of AAAPO and the Fund order for the benefit of white members and applicants.

V

Petitioners also allege that the membership goal and Fund order contravene the equal protection component of the Due Process Clause of the Fifth Amendment because they deny benefits to white individuals based on race. We have consistently recognized that government bodies constitutionally may adopt racial classifications as a remedy for past discrimination. We have not agreed, however, on the proper test to be applied in analyzing the constitutionality of race-conscious remedial measures. We need not resolve this dispute here, since we conclude that the relief ordered in this case passes even the most rigorous test-it is narrowly tailored to further the Government's compelling interest in remedying past discrimination.

In this case, there is no problem * * * with a proper showing of prior discrimination that would justify the use of remedial racial classifications. Both the District Court and Court of Appeals have repeatedly found petitioners guilty of egregious violations of Title VII, and have determined that affirmative measures were necessary to remedy their racially discriminatory practices. More importantly, the District Court's orders were properly tailored to accomplish this objective. First, the District Court considered the efficacy of alternative remedies, and concluded that, in light of petitioners' long record of resistance to official efforts to end their discriminatory practices, stronger measures were necessary. The court devised the temporary membership goal and the Fund as tools for remedying past discrimination. More importantly, the District Court's orders will have only a marginal impact on the interests of white workers. Again, petitioners concede that the District Court's orders did not disadvantage *existing* union members. While white applicants for union membership may be denied certain benefits available to their nonwhite counterparts, the court's orders do not stand as an absolute bar to the admission of such individuals; again, a majority of those entering the union after entry of the court's orders have been white. We therefore conclude that the District Court's orders do not violate the equal protection safeguards of the Constitution.

VI

[The Court rejected Local 28's argument that the District Court's appointment of an administrator with broad powers to supervise its compliance with the court's orders unjustifiable interference with the statutory right of a labor organization to self-governance.]

* * *

VII

To summarize our holding today, six members of the Court agree that a district court may, in appropriate circumstances, order preferential relief benefitting individuals who are not the actual victims of discrimination as a remedy for violations of Title VII, see Parts IV–A through IV–D, opinion of BRENNAN, J., joined by MARSHALL, J., BLACKMUN, J., and STEVENS, J.; POWELL, J., concurring in part and concurring in the judgment; WHITE, J., dissenting; that the District Court did not use incorrect statistical evidence in establishing petitioners' nonwhite membership goal, see Part II–A, that the contempt fines and Fund order were proper remedies for civil contempt, see Part III, *supra,* and that the District Court properly appointed an administrator to supervise petitioners' compliance with the court's orders, see Part VI, *supra.* Five members of the Court agree that in this case, the District Court did not err in evaluating petitioners' utilization of the apprenticeship program, see Part II–B, and that the membership goal and the Fund order are not violative of either Title VII or the Constitution, see Parts IV–E, V, opinion of Brennan of BRENNAN, J., joined by MARSHALL, J., BLACKMUN, J., and STEVENS, J.; POWELL, J., concurring in part and concurring in the judgment. The judgment of the Court of Appeals is hereby affirmed.

JUSTICE POWELL, concurring in part and concurring in the judgment.

I join Parts I, II, III, and VI of JUSTICE BRENNAN'S opinion. I further agree that § 706(g) does not limit a court in all cases to granting relief only to actual victims of discrimination. I write separately with respect to the issues raised in Parts IV and V to explain why I think the remedy ordered under the circumstances of this case violated neither Title VII nor the Constitution.

I

Petitioners contend that the Fund order and the membership goal imposed by the District Court and upheld by the Court of Appeals are forbidden by § 706(g) because that provision authorizes an award of preferential relief only to the actual victims of unlawful discrimination. The plain language of Title VII does not clearly support a view that all remedies must be limited to benefiting victims. And although the matter is not entirely free from doubt, I am unpersuaded by petitioners' reliance on the legislative history of Title VII. Rather, in cases involving particularly egregious conduct a district court may fairly conclude that an injunction alone is insufficient to remedy a proven violation of Title VII. This is such a case.

The history of petitioners' contemptuous racial discrimination and their successive attempts to evade all efforts to end that discrimination is well stated in Part I of the Court's opinion. Under these circumstances the District Court acted within the remedial authority granted by § 706(g) in establishing the Fund order and numerical goal at issue in this case. This Court's decision in *Firefighters v. Stotts,* 467 U.S. 561, 104 S.Ct. 2576, 81 L.Ed.2d 483 (1984), is not to the contrary. There, the question whether Title VII might *ever* authorize a remedy that benefits those who were not victims of discrimination was not before us, although there is language in the opinion suggesting an answer to that question.

II

There remains for consideration the question whether the Fund order and membership goal contravene the equal protection component of the Due Process Clause of the Fifth Amendment because they may deny benefits to white individuals based on race. I have recently reiterated what I believe to be the standard for assessing a constitutional challenge to a racial classification:

> " 'Any preference based on racial or ethnic criteria must necessarily receive a most searching examination to make sure that it does not conflict with constitutional guarantees.' *Fullilove v. Klutznick,* 448 U.S. 448, 491 [100 S.Ct. 2758, 2781, 65 L.Ed.2d 902] (1980) (opinion of BURGER, C.J.). There are two prongs to this examination. First, any racial classification 'must be justified by a compelling governmental interest' Second, the means chosen by the State to effectuate its purpose must be 'narrowly tailored to the achievement of that goal.' *Fullilove, supra,* 448 U.S., at 480 [100 S.Ct., at 2776]." *Wygant v. Jackson Board of Education,* 476 U.S. 267, 273–274, 106 S.Ct. 1842, 1847, 90 L.Ed.2d 260 (1986).

The finding by the District Court and the Court of Appeals that petitioners have engaged in egregious violations of Title VII establishes, without doubt, a compelling governmental interest sufficient to justify the imposition of a racially classified remedy. It would be difficult to find defendants more determined to discriminate against minorities. My inquiry, therefore, focuses on whether the District Court's remedy is "narrowly tailored," to the goal of eradicating the discrimination engaged in by petitioners. I believe it is.

The Fund order is supported not only by the governmental interest in eradicating petitioners' discriminatory practices, it also is supported by the societal interest in compliance with the judgments of federal courts.

The Fund order was not imposed until *after* petitioners were held in contempt. In requiring the Union to create the Fund, the District Court expressly considered " 'the consequent seriousness of the burden' to the defendants." Moreover, the focus of the Fund order was to give minorities opportunities that for years had been available informally only to nonminorities. The burden this imposes on nonminorities is slight. Under these circumstances, I have little difficulty concluding that the Fund order was carefully structured to vindicate the compelling governmental interests present in this case.

The percentage goal raises a different question. In *Fullilove v. Klutznick,* 448 U.S. 448, 100 S.Ct. 2758, 65 L.Ed.2d 902 (1980), this Court upheld the constitutionality of the "minority business enterprise" provision of the Public Works Employment Act of 1977, which required, absent administrative waiver, that at least 10% of federal funds granted for local public works projects be used by grantees to procure services or supplies from businesses owned by minority group members. In my concurring opinion, I relied on four factors that had been applied by Courts of Appeals when considering the proper scope of race-conscious hiring remedies. Those factors were: (i) the efficacy of alternative remedies; (ii) the planned duration of the remedy; (iii) the relationship between the percentage of minority workers to be employed and the percentage of minority group members in the relevant population or work force; and (iv) the availability of waiver provisions if the hiring plan could not be met. A final factor of primary importance that I considered in *Fullilove,* * * * was "the effect of the [remedy] upon innocent third parties." Application of those factors demonstrates that the goal in this case comports with constitutional requirements.

First, it is doubtful, given petitioners' history in this litigation, that the District Court had available to it any other effective remedy. That court, having had the parties before it over a period of time, was in the best position to judge whether an alternative remedy, such as a simple injunction, would have been effective in ending petitioners' discriminatory practices. Here, the court imposed the 29% goal in 1975 only after declaring that "[i]n light of Local 28's and JAC's failure to 'clean house' this court concludes that the imposition of a remedial racial goal ... is essential to place the defendants in a position of compliance with the 1964 Civil Rights Act." *EEOC v. Local 638,* 401 F.Supp. 467, 488 (SDNY 1975). On these facts, it is fair to conclude that absent authority to set a goal as a benchmark against which it could measure progress in eliminating discriminatory practices, the District Court may have been powerless to provide an effective remedy. Second, the goal was not imposed as a permanent requirement, but is of limited duration. Third, the goal is directly related to the percentage of nonwhites in the relevant work force.

As a fourth factor, my concurring opinion in *Fullilove* considered whether waiver provisions were available in the event that the hiring goal could not be met. The requirement of a waiver provision or, more generally, of flexibility with respect to the imposition of a numerical goal reflects a recognition that neither the Constitution nor Title VII requires a particular racial balance in the workplace. Indeed, the Constitution forbids such a requirement if imposed for its own sake. "We have recognized, however, that in order to remedy the effects of prior discrimination, it may be necessary to take race into account." Thus, a court may not choose a remedy for the purpose of attaining a particular racial balance; rather, remedies properly are confined to the elimination of proven discrimination. A goal is a means, useful in limited circumstances, to assist a court in determining whether discrimination has been eradicated.

The flexible application of the goal requirement in this case demonstrates that it is not a means to achieve racial balance. The contempt order was not imposed for the Union's failure to achieve the goal, but for its failure to take the prescribed steps that would facilitate achieving the goal. Additional flexibility is evidenced by the fact that this goal, originally set to be achieved by 1981, has been twice delayed and is now set for 1987.

It is also important to emphasize that on the record before us, it does not appear that nonminorities will be burdened directly, if at all. Petitioners' counsel conceded at oral argument that imposition of the goal would not require the layoff of nonminority union workers, and that therefore the District Court's order did not disadvantage existing union members. * * *

My view that the imposition of flexible goals as a remedy for past discrimination may be permissible under the Constitution is not an endorsement of their indiscriminate use. Nor do I imply that the adoption of such a goal will always pass constitutional muster.

JUSTICE O'CONNOR, concurring in part and dissenting in part.

I join Parts II–A, III, and VI of the Court's opinion. I would reverse the judgment of the Court of Appeals on statutory grounds insofar as the membership "goal" and the Fund order are concerned, and I would not reach petitioners' constitutional claims. I agree with JUSTICE WHITE, however, that the membership "goal" in this case operates as a rigid racial quota that cannot feasibly be met through good-faith efforts by Local 28. In my view, § 703(j), 42 U.S.C. § 2000e–2(j), and § 706(g), 42 U.S.C. § 2000e–5(g), read together, preclude courts from ordering racial quotas such as this. I therefore dissent from the Court's judgment insofar as it affirms the use of these mandatory quotas.

In *Firefighters v. Stotts, [supra]* the Court interpreted § 706(g) as embodying a policy against court-ordered remedies under Title VII that award racial preferences in employment to individuals who have not been subjected to unlawful discrimination. The dissenting opinion in *Stotts* urged precisely the position advanced by Justice BRENNAN's plurality opinion today—that any such policy extends only to awarding make-whole relief to particular nonvictims of discrimination, and does not bar class-wide racial preferences in certain cases. The Court unquestionably rejected that view in *Stotts*. Although technically dicta, the discussion of § 706(g) in *Stotts* was an important part of the Court's rationale for the result it reached, and accordingly is entitled to greater weight than the Court gives it today.

It is now clear, however, that a majority of the Court believes that the last sentence of § 706(g) does not in all circumstances prohibit a court in a Title VII employment discrimination case from ordering relief that may confer some racial preferences with regard to employment in favor of non-victims of discrimination. Even assuming that some forms of race-conscious affirmative relief, such as racial hiring goals, are permissible as remedies for egregious and pervasive violations of Title VII, in my view the membership "goal" and Fund order in this case were impermissible because they operate not as goals but as racial quotas. Such quotas run counter to § 703(j) of Title VII, and are thus impermissible under § 706(g) when that section is read in light of § 703(j), as I believe it should be.

The plurality asserts that § 703(j) in no way "qualifies or proscribes a court's authority to order relief otherwise appropriate under § 706(g) in circumstances where an illegal discriminatory act or practice is established." According to the plurality, § 703(j) merely provides that an employer or union does not engage in unlawful discrimination simply on account of a racial imbalance in its work force or membership, and thus is not required to institute preferential quotas to avoid Title VII liability. Thus, the plurality concedes that § 703(j) is aimed at racial quotas, but interprets it as limiting only the substantive liability of employers and unions, not the remedial powers of courts.

This interpretation of § 703(j) is unduly narrow. * * *

In *Steelworkers v. Weber,* 443 U.S. 193, 205, n. 5, 99 S.Ct. 2721, 2728, n. 5, 61 L.Ed.2d 480 (1979), the Court stated that "Section 703(j) speaks to substantive liability under Title VII." While this is *one* purpose of § 703(j), the Court in *Weber* had no occasion to consider whether it was the *exclusive* purpose. In my view, the words "Nothing contained in this title shall be interpreted to require" plainly make § 703(j) applicable to the interpretation of *any* provision of Title VII, including § 706(g). Therefore, when a court interprets § 706(g) as authorizing it to require an employer to adopt a racial quota, that court contravenes § 703(j) to the extent that the relief imposed as a purported remedy for a violation of Title VII's substantive provisions in fact operates to require racial preferences "on account of [a racial] imbalance." In addition, since § 703(j) by its terms limits the circumstances in which an employer or union may be required to extend "preferential treatment to any individual *or to any group* because of ... race," the plurality's distinction between make-whole and classwide relief is plainly ruled out insofar as § 703(j) is concerned.

The plurality's restrictive reading of § 703(j) rests largely on its view of the legislative history, which the plurality claims establishes that Congress simply did not consider the use of racial preferences to remedy past discrimination when it enacted Title VII. According to the plurality, the sole focus of concern over racial quotas involved the scope of substantive liability under Title VII: the fear was that employers or unions would be found liable for violating Title VII merely on account of a racial imbalance.

This reading of the legislative history ignores authoritative statements—relied on by the Court in *Stotts,*—addressing the relief courts could order, and making plain that racial *quotas,* at least, were not among the permissible remedies for past discrimination. * * *

The plurality's reading of the legislative history also defies common sense. Legislators who objected to racial quotas obviously did so because of the harm that such quotas would impose on innocent nonminority workers as well as because of the restriction on employer freedom that would follow from an across-the-board requirement of racial balance in every workplace. Racial quotas would inflict such harms on nonminority workers whether such quotas were imposed directly by federal law in the form of a requirement that every work force be racially balanced, or imposed as part of a court-ordered remedy for an employer's violations of Title VII. The legislative history, fairly read, indicates that such racial quotas are impermissible as a means of enforcing Title VII, and that even racial preferences short of quotas should be used only where clearly necessary if these preferences would benefit nonvictims at the expense of innocent nonminority workers.

* * *

The plurality correctly indicates that, as to any racial goal ordered by a court as a remedy for past discrimination, the employer *always* has a potential defense by virtue of § 706(g) against a claim that it was required to hire a particular employee, to wit, that the employee was not hired for "reasons unrelated to discrimination." Although the plurality gives no clues as to the scope of this defense, it is clear that an employer would remain free to refuse to hire unqualified minority applicants, even if as a result the employer failed to meet a racial hiring goal. Thus, an employer's undoubted freedom to refuse to hire unqualified minority applicants, even in the face of a court-ordered racial hiring goal, operates as one important limitation on the extent of any racially preferential treatment that can result from such a goal.

The plurality offers little guidance as to what separates an impermissible quota from a permissible goal. Reference to benchmarks such as the percentage of minority workers in the relevant labor pool will often be entirely proper in order to *estimate* how an employer's work force would be composed absent past discrimination. But it is completely unrealistic to assume that individuals of each race will gravitate with mathematical exactitude to each employer or union absent unlawful discrimination. That, of course, is why there must be a substantial statistical disparity between the composition of an employer's work force and the relevant labor pool, or the general population, before an intent to discriminate may be inferred from such a disparity. Thus, the use of a rigid quota turns a sensible rule of thumb into an unjustified conclusion about the precise extent to which past discrimination has lingering effects, or into an unjustified prediction about what would happen in the future in the absence of continuing discrimination. The imposition of a quota is therefore not truly remedial, but rather amounts to a requirement of racial balance, in contravention of § 703(j)'s clear policy against such requirements.

To be consistent with § 703(j), a racial hiring or membership goal must be intended to serve merely as a benchmark for measuring compliance with Title VII and eliminating the lingering effects of past discrimination, rather than as a rigid numerical requirement that must unconditionally be met on pain of sanctions. To hold an employer or union to achievement of a particular percentage of minority employment or membership, and to do so regardless of circumstances such as economic conditions or the number of available qualified minority applicants, is to impose an impermissible quota. By contrast, a permissible goal should require only a good-faith effort on the employer's or union's part to come within a range demarcated by the goal itself.

* * *

If, as the Court holds, Title VII sometimes allows district courts to employ race-conscious remedies that may result in racially preferential treatment for nonvictims, it does so only where such remedies are truly necessary. In fashioning any such remedy, including racial hiring goals, the court should exercise caution and "take care to tailor its orders to fit the nature of the violation it seeks to correct." As the plurality suggests, goals should generally be temporary measures rather than efforts to maintain a previously achieved racial balance, and should not unnecessarily trammel the interests of nonminority employees. Furthermore, the use of goals is least likely to be consistent with § 703(j) where the adverse effects of any racially preferential treatment attributable to the goals will be "concentrated upon a relatively small, ascertainable group of non-minority persons." _EEOC v. Local 638,_ 753 F.2d 1172, 1186 (CA2 1985). In sum, the creation of racial preferences by courts, even in the more limited form of goals rather than quotas, must be done sparingly and only where manifestly necessary to remedy violations of Title VII if the policy underlying § 703(j) and § 706(g) is to be honored.

In this case, I agree with JUSTICE WHITE that the membership "goal" established by the District Court's successive orders in this case has been administered and will continue to operate "not just [as] a minority membership goal but also [as] a strict racial quota that the union was required to attain." It is important to realize that the membership "goal" ordered by the District Court goes well beyond a requirement, such as the ones the plurality discusses approvingly, that a union "admit qualified minorities roughly in proportion to the number of qualified minorities in the work force." The "goal" here requires that the racial composition of Local 28's entire membership mirror that of the relevant labor pool by August 31, 1987, without regard to variables such as the number of qualified minority applicants available or the number of new apprentices needed. The District Court plainly stated that "[i]f the goal is not attained by that date, defendants will face fines that will threaten their very existence."

I see no reason not to take the District Court's mandatory language at face value, and certainly none is supplied by the plurality's conclusory assertion that "the District Court has been willing to accommodate *legitimate* reasons for petitioners' failure to comply with court orders." As Judge Winter persuasively argued in dissent below, the District Court was clearly *not* willing to take due account of the economic conditions that led to a sharp decline in the demand for the union skills involved in this case. Indeed, notwithstanding that petitioners have "voluntarily indentured 45% nonwhites in the apprenticeship classes since January 1981," the District Court ordered the JAC to indenture one nonwhite apprentice for every white apprentice. The Court of Appeals set this portion of the District Court's order aside as an abuse of discretion, but the District Court's willingness to impose such a rigid hiring quota certainly suggests that the District Court intended the membership "goal" to be equally absolute.

It is no answer to these observations that the District Court on two previous occasions postponed the final date for full compliance with the membership goal. At the time of the Court of Appeals' decision, Local 28's membership was approximately 10.8% nonwhite, and at oral argument counsel for petitioners represented that Local 28's membership of about 3,100 workers is now approximately 15.5% nonwhite. Absent an enormous expansion in the size of the apprentice program—which would be feasible only if the demand for the services of Local 28's members were dramatically to increase—it is beyond cavil that neither the "voluntary" 45% minority ratio now employed for apprenticeship classes nor the District Court's 1-to-1 order could achieve the 29.23% membership goal by Aug. 31, 1987. Indeed, at oral argument counsel for respondents conceded as much.

I do not question that petitioners' past violations of Title VII were egregious, or that in some respects they exhibited inexcusable recalcitrance in the face of the District Court's earlier remedial orders. But the timetable with which petitioners were ordered to comply was quite unrealistic and clearly could not be met by good-faith efforts on petitioners' part. In sum, the membership goal operates as a rigid membership quota, which will in turn spawn a sharp curtailment in the opportunities of nonminorities to be admitted to the apprenticeship program. Indeed, in order for the District Court's timetable to be met, this fixed quota would appear to require "the replacement of journeymen by apprentices on a strictly racial basis."

Whether the unequivocal rejection of racial quotas by the Congress that enacted Title VII is said to be expressed in § 706(g), in § 703(j), or in both, a "remedy" such as this membership quota cannot stand. For similar reasons, I believe that the Fund order, which created benefits for minority apprentices that nonminority apprentices were precluded from enjoying, operated as a form of racial quota. Accordingly, I would reverse the judgment of the Court of Appeals on statutory grounds insofar as the membership "goal" and Fund order are concerned, without reaching petitioners' constitutional claims.

JUSTICE WHITE, dissenting.

As the Court observes, the general policy under Title VII is to limit relief for racial discrimination in employment practices to actual victims of the discrimination. But I agree that § 706(g) does not bar relief for nonvictims in all circumstances. Hence, I generally agree with Parts I through III of the Court's opinion and with Parts IV–A through IV–D of the plurality opinion. It may also be that this is one of those unusual cases where nonvictims of discrimination were entitled to a measure of the relief ordered by the District Court and affirmed by the Court of Appeals. But Judge Winter, in dissent below, was correct in concluding that critical parts of the remedy ordered in this case were excessive under § 706(g), absent findings that those benefiting from the relief had been victims of discriminatory practices by the union. As Judge Winter explained and contrary to the Court's views, the cumulative effect of the revised affirmative-action plan and the contempt judgments against the union established not just a minority membership goal but also a strict racial quota that the union was required to attain. We have not heretofore approved this kind of racially discriminatory hiring practice, and I would not do so now. Beyond this, I am convinced, as Judge Winter was, that holding the union in contempt for failing to attain the membership quota during a time of economic doldrums in the construction industry and a declining demand for the union skills involved in this case was for all practical purposes equivalent to a judicial insistence that the union comply even if it required the displacement of nonminority workers by members of the plaintiff class. The remedy is inequitable in my view, and for this reason I dissent from the judgment affirming the Court of Appeals.

[The dissent of JUSTICE REHNQUIST, joined by CHIEF JUSTICE BURGER, is omitted.]

NOTE

In **United States v. Paradise**, 480 U.S. 149, 107 S.Ct. 1053, 94 L.Ed.2d 203 (1987), the Court upheld against constitutional attack an order that the Alabama Department of Public Safety promote one qualified African–American state trooper for every white promoted until the Department's ranks were 25% African–American or until the Department developed a promotion plan that did not have a disparate impact against black candidates. The order allowed the Department to deviate from the one-for-one requirement when there were no qualified African–American candidates.

A four justice plurality held that the order was narrowly tailored to achieve a compelling state interest of eradicating racial discrimination in the Department. The order followed findings that the Department had blatantly discriminated against blacks to the point that in its 37–year history it had never had an African–American trooper. Those findings produced an order that the Department hire one black at the entry level for every white hired until its troopers were 25% black. It also led to orders that the Department develop non-discriminatory promotion plans. The one-for-one promotion order came only after the Department continuously failed to develop non-discriminatory promotion plans. The plurality relied on this history to find that remedies short of race-conscious promotions would not be adequate. The plurality further found that the remedy imposed was flexible, allowing exceptions where qualified black candidates were not available and applying only until the Department developed promotion plans that did not have a disparate impact on blacks. Justice Stevens concurred, opining that he would employ a test that was more liberal than the "narrowly tailored to promote a compelling state interest" test employed by the plurality.

G. ATTORNEY FEES

Section 706(k) of Title VII provides:

> In any action or proceeding under this Title the court, in its discretion, may allow the prevailing party, other than the Commission or the United States, a reasonable attorney's fee (including expert fees) as part of the costs * * *

Thus, under Title VII and the ADA, which incorporates Title VII's enforcement and remedies, the trial court has discretion to award the prevailing party attorney fees. The Civil Rights Attorney Fees Awards Act of 1976, 42 U.S.C. § 1988, uses essentially the same language for cases under 42 U.S.C. §§ 1981, 1981a, 1982, 1983, 1985 and 1986. In contrast, the ADEA and EPA adopt the remedy provisions of the Fair Labor Standards Act, which provide that "the court * * * shall, in addition to any judgment awarded to the plaintiff or plaintiffs, allow a reasonable attorney's fee to be paid by the defendant and costs of the action." 29 U.S.C. § 216. Thus, in ADEA and EPA cases, the award of attorney fees to prevailing plaintiffs is mandatory.

HENSLEY v. ECKERHART

Supreme Court of the United States, 1983
461 U.S. 424, 103 S.Ct. 1933, 76 L.Ed.2d 40

JUSTICE POWELL delivered the opinion of the Court.

Title 42 U.S.C. § 1988 provides that in federal civil rights actions "the court, in its discretion, may allow the prevailing party, other than the United States, a reasonable attorney's fee as part of the costs." The issue in this case is whether a partially prevailing plaintiff may recover an attorney's fee for legal services on unsuccessful claims.

I

A

Respondents brought this lawsuit on behalf of all persons involuntarily confined at the Forensic Unit of the Fulton State Hospital in Fulton, Missouri. The Forensic Unit consists of two residential buildings for housing patients who are dangerous to themselves or others. Maximum-security patients are housed in the Marion O. Biggs Building for the Criminally Insane. The rest of the patients reside in the less restrictive Rehabilitation Unit.

In 1972 respondents filed a three-count complaint in the District Court for the Western District of Missouri against petitioners, who are officials at the Forensic Unit and members of the Missouri Mental Health Commission. Count I challenged the constitutionality of treatment and conditions at the Forensic Unit. Count II challenged the placement of patients in the Biggs Building without procedural due process. Count III sought compensation for patients who performed institution-maintaining labor.

Count II was resolved by a consent decree in December 1973. Count III largely was mooted in August 1974 when petitioners began compensating patients for labor pursuant to the Fair Labor Standards Act, 29 U.S.C. § 201 *et seq.* In April 1975 respondents voluntarily dismissed the lawsuit and filed a new two-count complaint. Count I again related to the constitutionality of treatment and conditions at the Forensic Unit. Count II sought damages, based on the Thirteenth Amendment, for the value of past patient labor. In July 1976 respondents voluntarily dismissed this back-pay count. Finally, in August 1977 respondents filed an amended one-count complaint specifying the conditions that allegedly violated their constitutional right to treatment.

In August 1979, following a three-week trial, the District Court held that an involuntarily committed patient has a constitutional right to minimally adequate treatment. The court then found constitutional violations in five of six general areas: physical environment; individual treatment plans; least restrictive environment; visitation, telephone, and mail privileges; and seclusion and restraint. With respect to staffing, the sixth general area, the District Court found that the Forensic Unit's staffing levels, which had increased during the litigation, were minimally adequate. Petitioners did not appeal the District Court's decision on the merits.

B

In February 1980 respondents filed a request for attorney's fees for the period from January 1975 through the end of the litigation. Their four attorneys claimed 2,985 hours worked and sought payment at rates varying from $40 to $65 per hour. This amounted to approximately $150,000. Respondents also requested that the fee be enhanced by thirty to fifty percent, for a total award of somewhere between $195,000 and $225,000. Petitioners opposed the request on numerous grounds, including inclusion of hours spent in pursuit of unsuccessful claims.

The District Court first determined that respondents were prevailing parties under 42 U.S.C. § 1988 even though they had not succeeded on every claim. It then refused to eliminate from the award hours spent on unsuccessful claims:

> "[Petitioners'] suggested method of calculating fees is based strictly on a mathematical approach comparing the total number of issues in the case with those actually prevailed upon. Under this method no consideration is given for the relative importance of various issues, the interrelation of the issues, the difficulty in identifying issues, or the extent to which a party may prevail on various issues."

Finding that respondents "have obtained relief of significant import," the District Court awarded a fee of $133,332.25. This award differed from the fee request in two respects. First, the court reduced the number of hours claimed by one attorney by thirty percent to account for his inexperience and failure to keep contemporaneous records. Second, the court declined to adopt an enhancement factor to increase the award.

The Court of Appeals for the Eighth Circuit affirmed on the basis of the District Court's memorandum opinion and order. We granted certiorari, and now vacate and remand for further proceedings.

II

In *Alyeska Pipeline Service Co. v. Wilderness Society*, 421 U.S. 240, 95 S.Ct. 1612, 44 L.Ed.2d 141 (1975), this Court reaffirmed the "American Rule" that each party in a lawsuit ordinarily shall bear its own attorney's fees unless there is express statutory authorization to the contrary. In response Congress enacted the Civil Rights Attorney's Fees Awards Act of 1976, 42 U.S.C. § 1988, authorizing the district courts to award a reasonable attorney's fee to prevailing parties in civil rights litigation. The purpose of § 1988 is to ensure "effective access to the judicial process" for persons with civil rights grievances. H.R.Rep. No. 94–1558, p. 1 (1976). Accordingly, a prevailing plaintiff " 'should ordinarily recover an attorney's fee unless special circumstances would render such an award unjust.' " S.Rep. No. 94–1011, p. 4 (1976), U.S.Code Cong. & Admin.News 1976, p. 5912 (quoting *Newman v. Piggie Park Enterprises*, 390 U.S. 400, 402, 88 S.Ct. 964, 966, 19 L.Ed.2d 1263 (1968)).

The amount of the fee, of course, must be determined on the facts of each case. On this issue the House Report simply refers to twelve factors set forth in *Johnson v. Georgia Highway Express, Inc.*, 488 F.2d 714 (CA5 1974). The Senate Report cites to *Johnson* as well and also refers to three district court decisions that "correctly applied" the twelve factors. One of the factors in *Johnson*, "the amount involved and the results obtained," indicates that the level of a plaintiff's success is relevant to the amount of fees to be awarded. * * *

* * *

In this case petitioners contend that "an award of attorney's fees must be proportioned to be consistent with the extent to which a plaintiff has prevailed, and only time reasonably expended in support of successful claims should be compensated." Respondents agree that a plaintiff's success is relevant, but propose a less stringent standard focusing on "whether the time spent prosecuting [an unsuccessful] claim in any way contributed to the results achieved." Both parties acknowledge the discretion of the district court in this area. We take this opportunity to clarify the proper relationship of the results obtained to an award of attorney's fees.

III

A

A plaintiff must be a "prevailing party" to recover an attorney's fee under § 1988. The standard for making this threshold determination has been framed in various ways. A typical formulation is that "plaintiffs may be considered 'prevailing parties' for attorney's fees purposes if they succeed on any significant issue in litigation which achieves some of the benefit the parties sought in bringing suit." *Nadeau v. Helgemoe*, 581 F.2d 275, 278–279 (CA1 1978). This is a generous formulation that brings the plaintiff only across the statutory threshold. It remains for the district court to determine what fee is "reasonable."

The most useful starting point for determining the amount of a reasonable fee is the number of hours reasonably expended on the litigation multiplied by a reasonable hourly rate. This calculation provides an objective basis on which to make an initial estimate of the value of a lawyer's services. The party seeking an award of fees should submit evidence supporting the hours worked and rates claimed. Where the documentation of hours is inadequate, the district court may reduce the award accordingly.

The district court also should exclude from this initial fee calculation hours that were not "reasonably expended." S.Rep. No. 94–1011, p. 6 (1976). Cases may be overstaffed, and the skill and experience of lawyers vary widely. Counsel for the prevailing party should make a good faith effort to exclude from a fee request hours that are excessive, redundant, or otherwise unnecessary, just as a lawyer in private practice ethically is obligated to exclude such hours from his fee submission. * * *

B

The product of reasonable hours times a reasonable rate does not end the inquiry. There remain other considerations that may lead the district court to adjust the fee upward or downward, including the important factor of the "results obtained." This factor is particularly crucial where a plaintiff is deemed "prevailing" even though he succeeded on only some of his claims for relief. In this situation two questions must be addressed. First, did the plaintiff fail to prevail on claims that were unrelated to the claims on which he succeeded? Second, did the plaintiff achieve a level of success that makes the hours reasonably expended a satisfactory basis for making a fee award?

In some cases a plaintiff may present in one lawsuit distinctly different claims for relief that are based on different facts and legal theories. In such a suit, even where the claims are brought against the same defendants—often an institution and its officers, as in this case—counsel's work on one claim will be unrelated to his work on another claim. Accordingly, work on an unsuccessful claim cannot be deemed to have been "expended in pursuit of the ultimate result achieved." The congressional intent to limit awards to prevailing parties requires that these unrelated claims be treated as if they had been raised in separate lawsuits, and therefore no fee may be awarded for services on the unsuccessful claim.

It may well be that cases involving such unrelated claims are unlikely to arise with great frequency. Many civil rights cases will present only a single claim. In other cases the plaintiff's claims for relief will involve a common core of facts or will be based on related legal theories. Much of counsel's time will be devoted generally to the litigation as a whole, making it difficult to divide the hours expended on a claim-by-claim basis. Such a lawsuit cannot be viewed as a series of discrete claims. Instead the district court should focus on the significance of the overall relief obtained by the plaintiff in relation to the hours reasonably expended on the litigation.

Where a plaintiff has obtained excellent results, his attorney should recover a fully compensatory fee. Normally this will encompass all hours reasonably expended on the litigation, and indeed in some cases of exceptional success an enhanced award may be justified. In these circumstances the fee award should not be reduced simply because the plaintiff failed to prevail on every contention raised in the lawsuit. Litigants in good faith may raise alternative legal grounds for a desired outcome, and the court's rejection of or failure to reach certain grounds is not a sufficient reason for reducing a fee. The result is what matters.

If, on the other hand, a plaintiff has achieved only partial or limited success, the product of hours reasonably expended on the litigation as a whole times a reasonable hourly rate may be an excessive amount. This will be true even where the plaintiff's claims were interrelated, nonfrivolous, and raised in good faith. Congress has not authorized an award of fees whenever it was reasonable for a plaintiff to bring a lawsuit or whenever conscientious counsel tried the case with devotion and skill. Again, the most critical factor is the degree of success obtained.

Application of this principle is particularly important in complex civil rights litigation involving numerous challenges to institutional practices or conditions. This type of litigation is lengthy and demands many hours of lawyers' services. Although the plaintiff often may succeed in identifying some unlawful practices or conditions, the range of possible success is vast. That the plaintiff is a "prevailing party" therefore may say little about whether the expenditure of counsel's time was reasonable in relation to the success achieved. In this case, for example, the District Court's award of fees based on 2,557 hours worked may have been reasonable in light of the substantial relief obtained. But had respondents prevailed on only one of their six general claims, * * * a fee award based on the claimed hours clearly would have been excessive.

There is no precise rule or formula for making these determinations. The district court may attempt to identify specific hours that should be eliminated, or it may simply reduce the award to account for the limited success. The court necessarily has discretion in making this equitable judgment. This discretion, however, must be exercised in light of the considerations we have identified.

C

A request for attorney's fees should not result in a second major litigation. Ideally, of course, litigants will settle the amount of a fee. Where settlement is not possible, the fee applicant bears the burden of establishing entitlement to an award and documenting the appropriate hours expended and hourly rates. The applicant should exercise "billing judgment" with respect to hours worked, and should maintain billing time records in a manner that will enable a reviewing court to identify distinct claims.

* * * It remains important, however, for the district court to provide a concise but clear explanation of its reasons for the fee award. When an adjustment is requested on the basis of either the exceptional or limited nature of the relief obtained by the plaintiff, the district court should make clear that it has considered the relationship between the amount of the fee awarded and the results obtained.

IV

In this case the District Court began by finding that "[t]he relief [respondents] obtained at trial was substantial and certainly entitles them to be considered prevailing...., without the need of examining those issues disposed of prior to trial in order to determine which went in [respondents'] favor." It then declined to divide the hours worked between winning and losing claims, stating that this fails to consider "the relative importance of various issues, the interrelation of the issues, the difficulty in identifying issues, or the extent to which a party prevails on various issues." Finally, the court assessed the "amount involved/results obtained" and declared: "Not only should [respondents] be considered prevailing parties, they are parties who have obtained relief of significant import. [Respondents'] relief affects not only them, but also numerous other institutionalized patients similarly situated. The extent of this relief clearly justifies the award of a reasonable attorney's fee."

These findings represent a commendable effort to explain the fee award. Given the interrelated nature of the facts and legal theories in this case, the District Court did not err in refusing to apportion the fee award mechanically on the basis of respondents' success or failure on particular issues. And given the findings with respect to the level of respondents' success, the District Court's award may be consistent with our holding today.

We are unable to affirm the decisions below, however, because the District Court's opinion did not properly consider the relationship between the extent of success and the amount of the fee award. The court's finding that "the [significant] extent of the relief clearly justifies the award of a reasonable attorney's fee" does not answer the question of what is "reasonable" in light of that level of success. We emphasize that the inquiry does not end with a finding that the plaintiff obtained significant relief. A reduced fee award is appropriate if the relief, however significant, is limited in comparison to the scope of the litigation as a whole.

V

We hold that the extent of a plaintiff's success is a crucial factor in determining the proper amount of an award of attorney's fees under 42 U.S.C. § 1988. Where the plaintiff has failed to prevail on a claim that is distinct in all respects from his successful claims, the hours spent on the unsuccessful claim should be excluded in considering the amount of a reasonable fee. Where a lawsuit consists of related claims, a plaintiff who has won substantial relief should not have his attorney's fee reduced simply because the district court did not adopt each contention raised. But where the plaintiff achieved only limited success, the district court should award only that amount of fees that is reasonable in relation to the results obtained. On remand the District Court should determine the proper amount of the attorney's fee award in light of these standards.

The judgment of the Court of Appeals is vacated, and the case is remanded for further proceedings consistent with this opinion.

[The concurring opinion of CHIEF JUSTICE BURGER and the opinion of JUSTICE BRENNAN, joined by JUSTICE MARSHALL, BLACKMUN and STEVENS concurring in part and dissenting in part are omitted.]

NOTES

1. The Court made clear that the threshold issue is whether the plaintiffs are prevailing parties. The Court quoted one formulation defining who is a prevailing party. "[P]laintiffs may be considered 'prevailing parties' for attorney's fees purposes if they succeed on any significant issue in litigation which achieves some of the benefit the parties sought in bringing suit." The Court elaborated on the standards for determining who is a prevailing party in *Texas State Teachers Ass'n v. Garland Independent School Dist.*, 489 U.S. 782, 109 S.Ct. 1486, 103 L.Ed.2d 866 (1989), a § 1983 case in which the plaintiffs lost on their claim that the school district violated the First Amendment by denying union representatives access to school property during school hours, but won on their claims that the school district's prohibition of teacher-to-teacher communications about unions during school hours violated their First Amendment rights. The lower courts denied the

plaintiffs attorney fees on the ground that they failed to prevail on the central issue in their lawsuit. The Supreme Court reversed, opining that to be a prevailing party, a plaintiff must have succeeded on "any significant issue in litigation which achieved some of the benefit the parties sought in bringing suit" and "changes the legal relationship" between the parties. The degree of success is a factor in determining the amount of a reasonable award but is not relevant to determining the threshold question of whether the plaintiff is a prevailing party. Thus, in **Farrar v. Hobby,** 506 U.S. 103, 113 S.Ct. 566, 121 L.Ed.2d 494 (1992), the Court held that a plaintiff who is awarded only nominal damages is a prevailing party. However, the Court affirmed the lower court's denial of attorney fees on the ground that where a plaintiff fails to prove any tangible injury and consequently secures only nominal damages, "the only reasonable fee is usually no fee at all . . ."

2. To be a prevailing party, the plaintiff's victory must not be fleeting. **Sole v. Wyner,** 551 U.S. 74, 127 S.Ct. 2188, 167 L.Ed.2d 1069 (2007), held that a plaintiff who secures preliminary injunctive relief but ultimately loses on the merits in the final judgment is not a prevailing party entitled to attorney fees.

3. As the Court indicated in *Hensley*, calculation of the fee is based on a "loadstar" approach. The prevailing plaintiff submits a fee petition supported by detailed time records reflecting the number of hours and a claim of an hourly rate typically supported by affidavits from other attorneys who are established in the field averring to what reasonable and customary billing rates are. On several occasions, the Supreme Court has rejected arguments by prevailing parties to enhance the loadstar amount. The most recent case was **Perdue v. Kenny A.,** 559 U.S. ___, 130 S.Ct. 1662, 176 L.Ed.2d 494 (2010). The Court reversed the lower courts' enhancement of the loadstar amount for superior attorney performance. The Court summarized its enhancement jurisprudence:

> We have stated in previous cases that such an increase is permitted in extraordinary circumstances, and we reaffirm that rule. But as we have also said in prior cases, there is a strong presumption that the lodestar is sufficient; factors subsumed in the lodestar calculation cannot be used as a ground for increasing an award above the lodestar; and a party seeking fees has the burden of identifying a factor that the lodestar does not adequately take into account and proving with specificity that an enhanced fee is justified.

4. Some district courts have adopted local rules to encourage settlement of attorney fee petitions. For example, the U.S. District Court for the Northern District of Illinois' Local Rule 54.3 requires the parties to confer in good faith and attempt to agree on the amount of fees before the prevailing party files a motion for fees. The moving party must provide the respondent with detailed time records and an indication of all time for which fees will be sought, and the hourly rates sought and evidence supporting those hourly rates. If the parties do not reach agreement on the amount of fees after this information is provided, the respondent must provide the moving party with the amount of fees it incurred in the litigation, its attorneys' work records, its attorneys' billable rates and all evidence to be relied on in opposing the fee

petition. If the parties remain unable to reach agreement, they must develop a joint statement detailing the fees that are not in dispute and those that are in dispute and a brief description of the remaining disputes. The prevailing party must attach the joint statement to the fee petition.

5. Title VII and § 1988 allow awards of attorney fees to prevailing parties, a term not limited to prevailing plaintiffs. In **Christiansburg Garment Co. v. EEOC**, 434 U.S. 412, 98 S.Ct. 694, 54 L.Ed.2d 648 (1978), the Supreme Court rejected the argument that the same standard for awarding attorney fees to prevailing plaintiffs should apply to prevailing defendants. The court opined:

> That § 706(k) allows fee awards only to *prevailing* private plaintiffs should assure that this statutory provision will not in itself operate as an incentive to the bringing of claims that have little chance of success. To take the further step of assessing attorney's fees against plaintiffs simply because they do not finally prevail would substantially add to the risks inhering in most litigation and would undercut the efforts of Congress to promote the vigorous enforcement of the provisions of Title VII. Hence, a plaintiff should not be assessed his opponent's attorney's fees unless a court finds that his claim was frivolous, unreasonable, or groundless, or that the plaintiff continued to litigate after it clearly became so. And, needless to say, if a plaintiff is found to have brought or continued such a claim in *bad faith*, there will be an even stronger basis for charging him with the attorney's fees incurred by the defense.

In *Fox v. Vice*, ___ U.S. ___, 131 S.Ct. 2205, 180 L.Ed.2d 45 (2011), the Court held that where a case combines frivolous and non-frivolous claims, the prevailing defendant may receive an award of attorney fees but the award must be limited to "the portion of his fees that he would not have paid but for the frivolous claim." Thus a prevailing defendant is not entitled to an award of attorney fees for work performed on the frivolous claims if the attorney would have performed the same work had the frivolous claims not been included in the law suit.

INDEX

References are to Pages

†